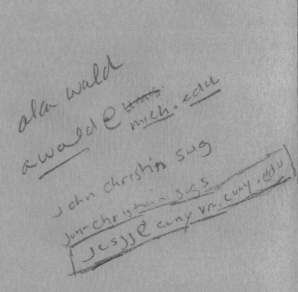

alan wald
awald@umich.edu

john christian sug
jon-christian sgs
jesjj@cuny vn.cuny.edu

RADICAL REPRESENTATIONS

POST-CONTEMPORARY INTERVENTIONS

Series Editors:

Stanley Fish and Fredric Jameson

RADICAL REPRESENTATIONS

➢

Politics and Form

in U.S. Proletarian

Fiction, 1929–1941

BARBARA FOLEY

DUKE UNIVERSITY PRESS   DURHAM AND LONDON   1993

© 1993 Duke University Press
Printed in the United States of America on acid-free paper ∞
Designed by Cherie Holma Westmoreland   Typeset in Melior
with Eurostile bold face display by Tseng Information Systems
Library of Congress Cataloging-in-Publication Data appear
on the last printed page of this book.

CONTENTS

[v]

PREFACE

>

As I use it in this study, the term "U.S. proletarian fiction" refers to novels written in the ambience of the Communist-led cultural movement that arose and developed in the United States in the context of the Great Depression. One could, if one wanted, extend the temporal rubric of the term: arguably Rebecca Harding Davis's *Life in the Iron Mills* (1861), Jack London's *The Iron Heel* (1908), John Oliver Killens's *Youngblood* (1954), and Thomas McGrath's *This Coffin Has No Handles* (1984) are, in one sense or another, all "proletarian" novels. But none of the authors of these texts (except possibly McGrath, who had roots in 1930s literary radicalism) would have called himself or herself a "proletarian" writer. The great majority of the writers and critics I treat in *Radical Representations*, however, were conscious participants in a literary movement that named itself "proletarian." Some of them debated at length—and without resolution—whether proletarian novels were by, for, about, or "written from the perspective of" the working class. But to different degrees the literary proletarians all adhered to left-wing politics and viewed their work as contributing to the arousal of class consciousness. Proletarian writers constitute a distinct school in American literary and cultural history.

The year 1993 may seem like an odd time to come out with a book about writers committed to depicting class conflict. The years during which this book was written witnessed the unraveling of "actually existing socialism" in Eastern Europe; the USSR, seemingly a stable entity when I began to write, is now "former." If what we have witnessed is indeed the death of Communism—or what the neo-Hegelian State Department theorist Francis Fukuyama still more apocalyptically calls the "end of history"—then proletarian fiction is little more than an antiquarian curiosity, deserving the neglect that has for the most part been its lot over the past fifty years. Moreover, the novels' routine depiction of proletarians as workers in heavy industry may seem out of joint with a U.S. economy moving increasingly away from the productive and toward the service sector. If class struggle is a thing of the past, and if classes themselves need to be radically redefined, why seek to revise critical estimates of, and renew popular interest in, a literary school that took class as its premise and heightened class struggle as its goal?

Contentiously, however, I seek such revision and renewal. I do not deny that proletarian novels are irrevocably dated in some ways. Reading them puts us in a time warp. The ritual invocation of the Soviet Union as an embodiment of egalitarian promise now seems a cruel irony; the frequent references to machines echo emptily over steel and auto plants with silent furnaces and assembly lines. Moreover, many proletarian novels employ archaic representational strategies. Some pursue a transparent realism that seems aesthetically and philosophically naive in an age of postmodernist self-consciousness. Others use experimental techniques that in hindsight represent the dead ends rather than the forward directions of modernism. If we look to these novels for models of oppositional discourses, we recognize an epistemological gap between their era and ours.

Nonetheless, proletarian novels have enduring interest and value, as well as—I hate to use the word but know none better—"relevance" to our present situation. Even if the configuration of the working class has changed since the 1930s, the United States still has a massive proletariat, native- as well as foreign-born. Situated in both manufacturing and service industries, these workers fit Marx's definition of proletarians as those who, owning no means of production, have to sell their labor power in order to live. There is every indication that these workers' situations will continue to deteriorate in the foreseeable future. If we look beyond national boundaries, moreover, we witness the steady proletarianization—and impoverishment—of the globe. Inequalities, indeed, polarities, of class have if anything deepened over the past decade or two. A literature focusing centrally on exploitation and class conflict has much to say about—and to—the contemporary proletariat.

Furthermore, *pace* Fukuyama, the emancipatory "message" of 1930s literary radicalism retains much of its force. As long as inequality exists, egalitarian social movements will exist. Depression-era proletarian literature, arising as it did in a moment when many felt the great day was coming soon, offers sustenance and inspiration—another troublesome but irreplaceable word—to those who still hope and work for the great day to come (if, it must be conceded, after many years' delay, and along a far more circuitous path than any of the 1930s leftists realized). But proletarian novels are valuable not only for giving nostalgic glimpses of the "red" movement before the socialist fall but also for reflecting and portending various aspects of that fall. If people sympathetic with left-wing values and goals reject the notion that intrinsic human selfishness is the original sin dooming attempts to construct egalitarian societies, it is incumbent upon them to analyze the historical course by which twentieth-century movements for such societies have been arrested and, eventually, reversed. Proletarian novels—as well as the contemporaneous debates about politics and art influencing their production—give crucial insight into the limits within which 1930s Marxism was working. If Marxism is to arise like a phoenix from the ashes of state capitalism, it is useful to study texts inspired by this phoenix in an earlier incarnation—for their cautionary lessons as well as their testaments to possibility.

One does not need to be a left-wing millenarian, however, to find continuing interest and value in the productions of Depression-era literary radicalism. Some of the most important work currently being done in literary theory and literary history centers on the discursive strategies by which marginalized subjects articulate selfhood and challenge dominant cultures. The study of proletarian fiction, which is replete with images and voices of the dispossessed seeking possession, makes an important contribution to this inquiry. Several of the most important writers were women; black writers, while few in number, wrote some of the most compelling proletarian novels. In fact, many proletarian writers focused on the formation of working-class experience and consciousness (or false consciousness) in relation to race and gender. The line and practice of the left with regard to the "woman question" and the "Negro question" were, to varying degrees, problematic; moreover, workerist and revolutionary tendencies commingled in the left's construction of class. Nonetheless, the political discourse in proletarian fiction centrally addresses the intersection of class with gender and race and thus bears directly on many key issues in contemporary cultural studies.

Indeed, proletarian fiction can help to sharpen the terms of analysis in this scholarship. For class, routinely treated as one subject position among three in what Terry Eagleton calls the "contemporary Holy Trinity" of gender, race, and class, is often shunted to one side. The arguments for doing so are at times explicitly anti-Marxist: class needs to be kept in its place lest it overwhelm the particularities of other subject positions. Proletarian novels, in which class consciousness is central to both rhetoric and representation, illuminate why Marxism constructs class as both a subject position and a moment in the historical dialectic. Race and gender are also socially constructed categories enabling hierarchy and exploitation. But they signal experiential realities: there is a limited sense in which they can be abolished. Class, however, is nothing but a social relationship: it is, indeed, the quintessential social relationship. Proletarians are people whose ultimate interest lies in their self-abolition as proletarians—that is, as inhabitants of a subject position—and in their becoming, in the words of the "Internationale," the "human race." Yet their immediate interest lies in acquiring class consciousness: somewhat paradoxically, in order eventually to supersede their class position, they must first acknowledge and understand it. In representing selfhood through narrative, proletarian novels address many concerns about marginalization and hegemony also preoccupying writers who focus on gender and race. But the goal of achieved self-consciousness in proletarian texts is quite different—for readers as well as for characters. Proletarian novels can be illuminated by contemporary theory about gender, race, and class; they can also help to advance that theory.

Radical Representations is divided into two parts. The first examines issues of politics, history, and aesthetics. Since this discussion involves virtually a complete rewriting of the standard narrative about writers and the left, it opens with an examination of the anti-Communist paradigms that have shaped, and continue to shape, most analysis of 1930s literary radicalism. Chapters 2 through 4 address the influence of the USSR on U.S. literary proletarianism and analyze the movement's key debates—over modernism and experimentation, over the definition of proletarian literature, and over the relation of art to propaganda. Chapters 5 and 6 explore the Communist line on the "woman question" and the "Negro question" and examine the principal themes—and political tensions—that emerge in novels treating issues of sexuality, gender, race, and racism.

My premise throughout these discussions is that awareness of what was said in the New Masses and Partisan Review—that is, of the debates over "line" influencing the practice of left-wing culture in the 1930s—is crucial. I reject the frequently argued thesis that authors were urged to write in a heavily didactic fashion or that they undertook to follow "formulas" set forth by Marxist critics. If anything, I suggest, the critics were wedded to a cognitivist and antididactic aesthetic. But literary proletarianism was called into being as a purposive political strategy; absent Communist party politics and organization, it would have existed on a less ambitious scale and would have looked very different. Discussions about politics and aesthetics within the Communist-led left, I argue, had a significant influence on many proletarian novels—not because these discussions disciplined and constrained writers but because they established certain parameters of the discourse in which these writers were engaged.

Part II begins with a discussion of the politics of novelistic realism and sets forth a narratological framework for analyzing rhetorical strategies in politically didactic fiction. The principal concern of this section is the four major genres of proletarian fiction—the fictional autobiography, the bildungsroman, the social novel, and the collective novel. To what extent, I ask, did writers succeed in using inherited forms to embody their chosen themes of class consciousness and class struggle? To what extent did the generic conventions of novelistic realism hamper the articulation of left-wing conceptions of selfhood and social conflict? Did the use of experimental novelistic modes—the testimonial fictional autobiography, the collective novel—enable writers more effectively to embody a class-conscious doctrinal politics? I shall consider the major criticisms of proletarian fiction—by both 1930s Marxists and subsequent critics. If "conversion" tales smack of "wish-fulfillment," to what can this utopianism be attributed? If some texts are "formulaic," is this quality a function of generic politics, doctrinal politics, or their intersection and mutual reinforcement?

As these summary comments indicate, my principal interest is in the larger claims one can make about politics and representational strategy in proletarian fiction. While I do not shun "interpretive" criticism as such, undertaking detailed readings of individual texts is not my goal in *Radical Representations*. Instead, I shall offer omnibus analyses generalizing about the relation of generic to doctrinal politics in a broad range of novels. Recognizing that politics is a plural as well as a singular term, I continually point out specific points of political "line" in particular novels. Doctrinal politics do not furnish a raw material on which form is put to work; they operate as the premise of various formal choices an author makes. The question to which I continually revert, however, is whether certain novelistic genres have proved better suited to the articulation of left-wing politics than others.

As a rehabilitative project, *Radical Representations* aims to encourage general readers to read, and academics to teach, proletarian novels, of which a number have recently been reissued in paperback. I am hopeful that, if we clear away the detritus of several decades of distorting critical commentary, more of these texts will receive the attention they deserve. Nonetheless, I try to avoid the note of hushed reverence sometimes accompanying revisionary readings of "oppositional" or "subversive" schools of writing. I am just as interested in what prevented proletarian fiction from being more revolutionary as I am in what enabled it to be as revolutionary as it was.

➢   ➢   ➢   ➢   ➢

A number of people have contributed significantly to this project. Neil Larson, Greg Meyerson, Grover Furr, Fran Bartkowski, Art Casciato, Paul Sporn, Peter Rabinowitz, and Jim Phelan offered incisive criticisms of various segments of the manuscript. Walter Rideout, as reader for the Duke University Press, gave very useful comments on the whole. Cary Nelson, also a reader for Duke, wrote a helpful report and offered invaluable aid in locating and reproducing the illustrations and book cover. Alan Wald, Douglas Wixson, Constance Coiner, Sandra Adickes, Lawrence Schwartz, Russell Reising, Geraldine Murphy, and Judy Kutulas have generously shared their work on literary radicalism. Paula Rabinowitz gave an early formulation of my thesis a spirited critique at a Midwest MLA meeting. As copanelists at MLA conventions, Faith Berry, Jim Miller, Cary Nelson, Bram Dijkstra, and Paul Lauter have sharpened my appreciation of what is at stake in doing good work on the 1930s. Ben Green and Elizabeth and Ed Huberman shared valuable materials from their libraries. Susan Hirsch and Rima Schwartz, coresearchers at the Newberry Library, gave useful research leads. A. B. Magil, Lloyd Brown, and S. Carl Hirsch, veterans of 1930s radicalism, consented to be interviewed and provided me with detailed, highly colored, and informative accounts of the 1930s left, literary and otherwise. H. Bruce Franklin provided lively political discussion and useful practical advice. For helpful correspondence, I wish to thank Daniel Aaron, Mary Battenfield, Jim Bloom, Robin Kelley, Deborah Rosenfelt, Anna Shannon-Elfenbein, Christian Suggs, Bob Wess, and Richard Yarborough. Heyward Ehrlich, David Soyka, and Louie Crew have rescued me from periodic computer crises. The graduate students in my 1988 seminar on Proletarian Writers and my 1990 seminar on Urban Literature helped me develop insights into various texts, as did Mary Beth Iannaccone, Marvin Carnes, Peggy McGlone, and Susan Lancellotti in independent study classes. Participants in the NEH/Newberry Library seminar of 1987–88 helped shape my ideas about literary radicalism.

The staffs at the Newberry Library, the Arents Library of Syracuse University, the Labor History Archives at Wayne State University, the Tamiment Library of New York University, Butler Library of Columbia University, the Labadie Library at the University of Michigan, the Special Collections room at Northwestern University Library, the University of Oregon Library, the New York Public Library, and the Hoover Institute were very helpful in locating valuable archival materials.

I wish to thank the Newberry Library and the National Endowment for the Humanities for the 1987–1988 grant that enabled me to commence the research for this project, as well as Rutgers University for the 1990 semester's FASP grant that enabled me to do some of the writing.

Reynolds Smith of the Duke University Press arranged very helpful reader's reports and has given unerring editorial advice.

Lorriane Elias and Felicia Polito of the English Department at Rutgers— Newark were generous with the use of their equipment when they were very busy.

My husband, Houston Stevens, and my children, Adam and Margaret Stevens, did what needed to be done on the domestic front and sustained me in the larger political commitments involved in undertaking this project; my gratitude to them cannot be measured.

I dedicate this book to my mother and stepfather, Margaret and Russell Ames, who have taught me much of what I know about values and commitments, albeit in a context somewhat different from that of 1930s literary radicalism.

PART ONE

CHAPTER 1

>

The Legacy of Anti-Communism

In the last decade, the canon-busting movement in American literary study has brought into view texts and traditions of several previously marginalized groupings of writers. Feminist criticism has required that critics reconstitute not only the lineup of "standard" authors but also the traditional rubrics for demarcating literary historical periods. Commentary on African American, Hispanic, Asian American, and Native American literatures has prompted reconsideration of the domain of the "literary," as well as of the politics embedded in conventions and genres. Recent challenges to the notion of "great books" have called into question the presumably timeless and apolitical aesthetic values sustaining a sexist, racist, and elitist literary canon. As Jane Tompkins observes, "Great literature does not exert its force over and against time, but changes with the changing currents of social and political life." Amidst all this revisionary activity, a sound drubbing has been given to the New Critics, whose privileging of qualities such as opacity, paradox, and ambiguity is routinely seen as an ideological maneuver rationalizing a conservative and exclusionary conception of literary value.[1]

When the New Critics proclaimed the superiority of showing over telling or the heroism of holding opposed ideas in balance without committing oneself to a single point of view, they were announcing their departure from philological, biographical, and history-of-ideas modes of literary study. But they were also articulating a mandarin distaste for the unabashedly leftist social commitments guiding much literature and criticism produced and read in the 1930s. In 1933 Allen Tate, commenting on the incompatibility between Communist politics and poetry, argued that "[t]he task of poetry is the constant rediscovery of the permanent nature of man.

1. Jane Tompkins, *Sensational Designs: The Cultural Work of American Fiction 1790–1860* (New York: Oxford UP, 1985), p. 192.

[3]

Propagandist art exhibits that side of his nature in which he is most interested at the moment; it is a temporary oversimplification of the human predicament . . . an escape from reality." When revolutionary poets issue their call, Tate concluded, "We get neither art nor politics; we get heresy." In 1936 Robert Penn Warren claimed that proletarian literature failed because it "politicalized literature." Even if the writer was sincere, Warren stated, "[h]is very sincerity, the very fact of the depth and mass of his concern, may not do more than imperil his achievement unless his sensibility is so attuned and his critical intelligence so developed that he can effect the true marriage of his convictions, his ideas, that is, his theme, with the concrete projection in experience, that is, his subject." In 1950 Robert Gorham Davis, who in the 1930s had written for the *New Masses* and *Partisan Review* under the pen name "Obed Brooks," sardonically commented on how the Agrarians had triumphed in the realm of literary theory. According to the emerging New Critical evaluative standards, Davis noted, "holding liberal-democratic-progressive views with any conviction made one incapable of appreciating imaginative literature at all."[2]

In the postwar years the New Critics for the most part put into storage the explicitly conservative political agenda that had guided their Agrarian manifesto *I'll Take My Stand* (1930), for which Tate and Warren had considered the catchy subtitle, "A Tract against Communism." But, Alexander Karanikas argues, Tate, Warren, and their colleagues "succeeded . . . as New Critics . . . in doing what they failed to do as Agrarians: to denigrate the democratic content in American literature, to smother its traditional note of social protest, and to elevate in its stead new literary gods and canons more acceptable to the rightist tradition." Moreover, as Lawrence Schwartz has recently demonstrated in his study of the process by which William Faulkner became "great," the potential political uses of New Critical doctrine were not lost on the government and business groupings providing New Critical journals and graduate programs with the funds and

---

2. Allen Tate, "Poetry and Politics," *New Republic* 75 (August 2, 1933): 310; Robert Penn Warren, cited in Alexander Karanikas, *Tillers of a Myth: Southern Agarians as Social and Literary Critics* (Madison, Milwaukee, London: U of Wisconsin P, 1966), p. 119; Robert Gorham Davis, "The New Criticism and the Democratic Tradition," *American Scholar* 19 (Winter 1950–51): 10. See also Cleanth Brooks, "Irony as a Principle of Structure," in *Literary Opinion in America*, rev. ed., ed. Morton D. Zabel (New York: Harper, 1951), p. 731; and Tate, *The Man of Letters in the Modern World* (New York: Meridian, 1955), p. 335.

support necessary to ensure their rapid ascent to cultural hegemony in the postwar period. Anti-Marxism, in short, provided much of the political motivation for the formalistic critical program currently under assault by canon-busting critics.[3]

Texts by women and people of color have thus far been the principal beneficiaries of the demise of New Criticism and the gate-crashing democ-ratization in U.S. cultural studies. In recent years, however, there has also been a significant renewal of interest in the Depression-era literary radi-cals whose influence the New Critics set out to combat. Over a dozen 1930s left-wing novels have been reprinted; there is a major new anthology of women's writings; several significant articles and four book-length studies have been published, with more currently in manuscript. It would ap-pear that the inquisitors have been vanquished and the heretics now have the field.[4]

3. Karanikas, p. viii; Lawrence Schwartz, *Creating Faulkner's Reputation: The Poli-tics of Modern Literary Criticism* (Knoxville: U of Tennessee P, 1988).

4. In addition to the works of John Steinbeck, John Dos Passos, and James T. Farrell that have been continuously in print since the 1930s, the following proletarian novels are currently in paperback, most of them brought out in the past decade: Nelson Algren, *Somebody in Boots* (New York: Thunder's Mouth P, 1987); William Attaway, *Blood on the Forge*, Foreword by John Oliver Killens, Afterword by Richard Yarborough (New York: Monthly Review, 1987); Arna Bontemps, *Black Thunder*, Introduction by Arnold Rampersad (Boston: Beacon, 1992); Fielding Burke, *Call Home the Heart*, Afterwords by Sylvia J. Cook and Anna W. Shannon (Old Westbury: Feminist P, 1983); Jack Conroy, *The Disinherited*, Introduction by Douglas C. Wixson (Columbia, MO: U of Missouri P, 1991); Guy Endore, *Babouk*, Afterword by David Barry Gaspar and Michel-Ralph Trouil-lot (New York: Monthly Review, 1991); Mike Gold, *Jews Without Money* (New York: Carroll and Graf, 1984); Albert Halper, *Union Square*, Introduction by Marcus Klein (Detroit: Omnigraphics, 1990); Josephine Herbst, *Rope of Gold*, Afterword by Elinor Langer (Old Westbury: Feminist P, 1984); Tom Kromer, *Waiting for Nothing and Other Writings*, Introduction by Arthur D. Casciato and James L. West III (Athens and Lon-don: U of Georgia P, 1986); Meridel Le Sueur, *The Girl*, rev. ed. (Albuquerque: West End P, 1990); Ruth McKenney, *Industrial Valley*, Introduction by Daniel Nelson (Ithaca: ILRP, 1990); Tillie Olsen, *Yonnondio: From the Thirties* (New York: Dell, 1974); Myra Page, *Daughter of the Hills*, Introduction by Deborah Rosenfelt (New York: Feminist P, 1986); Agnes Smedley, *Daughter of Earth*, Introduction by Paul Lauter (Old Westbury: Feminist P, 1973); Clara Weatherwax, *Marching! Marching!*, Introduction by Christian Suggs (Detroit: Omnigraphics, 1990). The University of Illinois Press will soon begin issuing a series of paperback reprints of twentieth-century left-wing fiction, with Alan Wald as series editor. The most recent anthology is *Writing Red: An Anthology of Ameri-can Women Writers, 1930–1940*, ed. Paula Rabinowitz and Charlotte Nekola (New York:

But it is premature to assume that the ground is clear for fruitful reconsideration of the texts now being exhumed. For, even though the New Critics' aesthetic program has been—at least for the moment—relegated to the
antiquarian wing of the critical museum, the anti-Communism that.sup-
plied much of its animus has not. In part the presence of anti-Communism
in work on the 1930s is attributable to the continuing influence of the New
York Intellectuals, with whom the New Critics formed what Maxwell Geismar called an "interlocking directorate" in the postwar years. Several of
them former Trotskyists or Trotskyist sympathizers, a few of them former
Communists, the New York Intellectuals developed a narrative about the
role of the Communist party (CP) in Depression-era cultural movements
that shapes much analysis of U.S. literary radicalism to this day. But anti-
Communism also retains its force because of its covert incorporation into
various premises guiding postmodernist theory. In writings on cultural
leftism in general or the 1930s in particular, references to Stalinism and

---

Feminist P, 1987). Recent book-length studies are: James D. Bloom, *Left Letters: The
Culture Wars of Mike Gold and Joseph Freeman* (New York: Columbia UP, 1992); James
Murphy, *The Proletarian Moment: The Controversy over Leftism in Literature* (Urbana
and Chicago: U of Illinois P, 1991); Cary Nelson, *Repression and Recovery: Modern
American Poetry and the Politics of Cultural Memory, 1910–1945* (Madison: U of Wisconsin P, 1989); and Paul Rabinowitz, *Labor and Desire: Women's Revolutionary Fiction
in Depression America* (Chapel Hill and London: U of North Carolina P, 1992). Critical
books by Wald (on twentieth-century literary radicalism) and Douglas Wixson, *Worker-
Writer in America* (New York: Columbia UP, 1993) are forthcoming. Recent works of
revisionary scholarship on the CPUSA include Mark Naison, *Communists in Harlem
during the Depression* (New York: Grove, 1983); Robin D. G. Kelley, *Hammer and Hoe:
Alabama Communists during the Depression* (Chapel Hill: U of North Carolina P, 1991);
Gerald Horne, *Communist Front?: The Civil Rights Congress, 1946–1956* (Teaneck, NJ:
Fairleigh Dickinson UP, 1988); Fraser M. Ottanelli, *The Communist Party of the United
States: From the Depression to World War II* (New Brunswick and London: Rutgers UP,
1991); and Robbie Lieberman, *"My Song Is My Weapon": People's Songs, American Com-
munism, and the Politics of Culture, 1930–1950* (Urbana and Chicago: U of Illinois P,
1989). For instances of recent scholarship continuing in the tradition of Theodore Draper,
Irving Howe, and Lewis Coser, see Harvey Klehr, *The Heyday of American Commu-
nism: The Depression Decade* (New York: Basic Books, 1984); Harvey Klehr and John
Earl Haynes, *The American Communist Movement: Storming Heaven Itself* (New York:
Twayne, 1992); Guenter Levy, *The Cause That Failed: Communism in American Political
Life* (New York: Oxford UP, 1990); and Stephen J. Whitfield, *The Culture of the Cold War*
(Baltimore and London: Johns Hopkins UP, 1991).

[6]

party orthodoxies can often be found unproblematically intertwined with analyses of logocentricity, patriarchy, and textual monologism. We cannot understand the politics and history of literary proletarianism until we hack this Gordian knot or—to use a metaphor less liable to the charge of "Stalinism"—disentangle this ideological skein.[5]

In this chapter I shall delineate how anti-Communism, taking different forms over the past five decades, has shaped, and continues to shape, much of the discourse about 1930s literary radicalism. First, I shall sample contemporaneous responses to proletarian literature to demonstrate that, rather than being intrinsically "bad," it garnered significant respect from mainstream critics and reviewers. An examination of this generally hospitable reception suggests that the subsequent denigration and dismissal of this literature have been prompted by something other than purely literary considerations. Next, I shall describe the hostile assessment of proletarian literature that was offered by the first generation of anti-Stalinist critics, codified in various influential statements of *Partisan Review* editor Philip Rahv. I shall then describe the process by which commentary on the 1930s increasingly relied upon a priori assumptions about Communism and its relation to literature that attained the status of unquestioned dogma. I shall close with some comments on recent work in the field, noting how continuing Cold War assumptions detract from a scholarship that is otherwise expanding and deepening our understanding of the 1930s cultural left.

At various points in this discussion I shall treat the terms "anti-Communist," "anti-Marxist," and "anti-Stalinist" as interchangeable. This practice may trouble readers who consider it important to maintain distinctions between Marxism, Communism, and, especially, Stalinism. I recognize that these terms signify different theoretical and historical phe-

---

5. Maxwell Geismar, "The Higher and Higher Criticism," *Nation* 183 (November 10, 1956): 407. For more on the New York Intellectuals, see Geraldine Murphy, "Romancing the Center: Cold War Politics and Classic American Literature," *Poetics Today* 9 (1988): 737–47; Alan Wald, *The New York Intellectuals: The Rise and Fall of the Anti-Stalinist Left from the 1930s to the 1980s* (Chapel Hill: U of North Carolina P, 1986); William O'Neill, *A Better World: The Great Schism: Stalinism and the American Intellectuals* (New York: Simon and Schuster, 1982); James B. Gilbert, *Writers and Partisans: A History of Literary Radicalism in America* (New York, London, and Sydney: John Wiley, 1968); and Terry A. Cooney, *The Rise of the New York Intellectuals: Partisan Review and Its Circle, 1934–1945* (Madison: U of Wisconsin P, 1986).

nomena and that "Stalinism" in particular carries a powerful political charge. But I persist in this practice precisely because, in my view, the majority of commentators who use the term "anti-Stalinist" hide behind it. They rarely define it, let alone question its theoretical or historical legitimacy. "Stalinism" has become a virtually undeconstructable term, presumably attesting to the user's political acumen ("Communism" would be too crude), but retaining all the standard stereotypical significations— cynical manipulation, subordination of means to ends, cold rationality— routinely associated with the "C-word." As Robbie Lieberman has noted in a recent study of the People's Song movement, "[T]he terms 'Stalinism' and 'Communist front' [are] . . . used too often as abusive terms and as excuses to dismiss the work of the Communist movement as totalitarian, conspiratorial, and duplicitous. Such labels do not contribute to a balanced analysis of left-wing thought and activity, nor do they reflect how cultural workers . . . viewed themselves." If we are to achieve a "balanced analysis of left-wing thought and activity" in the literary sphere, we need to understand how the literary leftists "viewed themselves"—not to approach their project with the a prioristic notion that, because it was "Stalinist," it was doomed.[6]

In pronouncing the illegitimacy of the discursive construction of "Stalinism," I am not perversely giving my stamp of approval to all things "Stalinist." I do not have the opportunity in this study to address the many serious issues raised in criticisms of the Stalin era—for example, the forced collectivization of the peasantry, the proclamation of an end to the class struggle in the USSR in the mid-1930s, the abolition of abortion in 1936, the stress upon Great Russian chauvinism in the Patriotic War, the resurgence of anti-Semitism in the postwar period, the mass incarcerations and executions. The movement toward an egalitarian society in the USSR was reversed during the Stalin period—though not for the reasons routinely offered in the anti-Stalinist scholarship. But the denigrating use of the term "Stalinist" to describe all events in the world revolutionary movement between the death of Lenin and the ascent of Khrushchev enables commentators to dismiss out of hand tremendous achievements that also occurred in this period: the involvement of millions of workers in socialist construction, the emancipation of women from feudalistic practices, the struggle against racism and anti-Semitism, the fostering of previously sup-

6. Lieberman, p. xx.

[8]

pressed minority cultures, the Soviet role in the defeat of the Nazis, as well as—our principal concern here—the creation of a revolutionary proletarian culture, in both the USSR and other countries. Enough is heard from all sides about the failures of the 1930s left-wing movement. Scholarship on the 1930s literary left needs to take into account the other side of the balance sheet.[7]

The Contemporaneous Reception of Proletarian Fiction

In an anthology of essays on the 1930s published about a decade ago, the editors proclaim that "the best writers and most thoughtful critics refused to follow the party line." The lesson taught by those who did follow the party line, the editors conclude, is that artists who "allow . . . their art to be shaped by a party line or other nonartistic considerations rather than their own creative judgments . . . court disaster."[8] It is assumed in advance here that literature committed to a political program associated with a specific political formation is condemned to a barren instrumentalism and that artists' "creative judgments" necessarily conflict with the "party line" they endorse. Students currently approaching proletarian literature with a knowledge only of the postwar critical reputation contained in statements like these may be somewhat surprised to learn that quite a few proletarian novels—often explicitly Communist ones—were read sympathetically and evaluated positively when they first appeared.

As might be expected, proletarian writers received generally favorable

7. For sharply opposed assessments of the Stalin era in the USSR, see, on the one hand, John Arch Getty, *Origins of the Great Purges: The Soviet Communist Party Reconsidered, 1933–1938* (Cambridge: Cambridge UP, 1985), and Roberta T. Manning, *Government in the Soviet Countryside in the Stalinist Thirties: The Case of Belyi Raion in 1937* (Pittsburgh: Center of Russian and East European Studies, University of Pittsburgh, 1984); and, on the other hand, Robert Conquest, *The Great Terror: Stalin's Purge of the Thirties*, rev. ed. (London: Macmillan, 1973), and Roy Medvedev, *Let History Judge: The Origins and Consequences of Stalinism*, rev. ed. (New York: Columbia UP, 1989). For left-wing critiques of the decline of Soviet socialism, see Charles Bettelheim, *Class Struggles in the USSR*, trans. Brian Pearce, 2 vols. (London: Monthly Review, 1976–78), and Ira Gollobin, *Dialectical Materialism: Its Laws, Categories and Practice* (New York: Petras, 1986), pp. 457–506.

8. Ralph Bogardus and Fred Hobson, eds., *Literature at the Barricades: The American Writer in the 1930s* (University, AL: U of Alabama P, 1982), pp. 6, 8.

treatment in the pages of left-liberal periodicals such as *The New Republic* and *The Nation*. A 1930 *New Republic* review of Mary Heaton Vorse's *Strike!* even evaluated the text in accordance with the definition of proletarian literature that Marxist critic Mike Gold had offered three months previously in the *New Masses*, the main literary organ of the Communist left. Equally predictably, radical writers were consistently dragged over the coals in the conservative *New York Times Book Review*, whose principal contributors detested the emerging genre of proletarian literature. *NYTBR* literary editor J. Donald Adams, proclaiming individualism to be "the life blood of art," decried the "young left-wing novelists" who were "merging the individual in the mass, or in the class." The *NYTBR* rarely missed an opportunity to attack writers from the new literary school.[9]

The *Saturday Review* also published its fair share of dismissive reviews. H. L. Mencken, criticizing the unabashed political partisanship of the *New Masses*, declared that the iconoclastic, witty radicals of the old *Masses* group had been replaced by political hacks. "The old-timers, if there had been any Moscow then, would have bidden it be damned," he proclaimed. "But the newcomers appear to sing whatever hymn is lined out, though always a couple of measures behind the beat, and in a faltering

9. Murray Godwin, review of Mary Heaton Vorse, *Strike!*, cited in Howard Hertz, "Writer and Revolutionary: The Life and Works of Michael Gold, Father of Proletarian Literature in the United States," 2 vols., Ph.D. Thesis, U of Texas at Austin, vol. 2, pp. 578–79; J. Donald Adams, "Literature and Individualism," *Saturday Review of Literature* (hereinafter *SRL*) 10 (February 3, 1934): 446. Gold's criteria for defining proletarian literature were articulated in "Proletarian Realism," *New Masses* (hereinafter *NM*) 6 (September 1930): 5. For examples of dismissive *New York Times Book Review* (hereinafter *NYTBR*) reviews, see John Cournos's review of Myra Page's *Moscow Yankee*, "Americans in Russia," *NYTBR* (April 28, 1935), 7; Fred T. Marsh's review of Jack Conroy's *A World to Win*, "Class-Conscious," *NYTBR* (May 5, 1935), 7, 18; Harold Strauss's review of William Cunningham's *The Green Corn Rebellion*, *NYTBR* (September 1, 1935), 6–7. For more on the right-wing politics of the *NYTBR*, see Granville Hicks, "White Guards on Parade: Reviewing the New York Times' Red-Baiting Book Review Section," *NM* 13 (October 2, 1934): 17–22. Eugene Lyons, one of the earliest anti-Communist polemicists, was largely unjustified in his complaint that the book review sections of all the major bourgeois organs had gone Communist in 1930s: "[F]or many years the New York *Times*, the *Herald Tribune*, *Current History*, the *New Yorker*, and many of the so-called class magazines used largely 'proletarian' standards in measuring literature" (*The Red Decade: The Stalinist Penetration of America* [Indianapolis and New York: Bobbs-Merrill, 1941], p. 133).

key." Elmer Davis, striking a similar note in a review of Fielding Burke's *Call Home the Heart* entitled "The Red Peril," noted, "The Red infiltration into present-day literature is a nuisance because it imports alien and irrelevant values. It is like a conversation in two languages between people who do not understand each other. The Communist standard of truth and beauty is incommensurable with all other standards, past and present." Noting a disjunction in the novel's shift into explicitly leftist political rhetoric in its second half, Davis proclaimed, "A work of art aims at producing what may be called an illusion, in default of a better word; if the propaganda (or anything else) shatters that illusion, the novel has been spoiled by bourgeois standards of taste and the propaganda—also by bourgeois standards—becomes unconvincing."[10]

Yet the *Saturday Review* grudgingly noted in the "Books of This Fall" column in October 1934 that "the proletarian novel, which has been usurping more and more interest for some time past, still waxes strong." A number of *Saturday Review* commentators expressed admiration for the new literary school. N. L. Rothman adjudged Isidor Schneider's *From the Kingdom of Necessity* "exceptional and brilliant" for its "fus[ing of] the naked ugliness of the tenement jungle life" with a "ponder[ing] . . . upon the social forces that had of necessity to produce that jungle." William Rollins's *The Shadow Before*, B. Traven's *The Death Ship*, Robert Cantwell's *The Land of Plenty*, Josephine Herbst's *The Executioner Waits*, Ralph Bates's *Lean Men*, and Jack Conroy's *A World to Win*—works all motivated by a Marxist analysis of exploitation, alienation, and class struggle—received warm praise. Henry Seidel Canby, the magazine's editor, proclaimed that Clara Weatherwax's *Marching! Marching!* conveyed "a workers' world seething about a revolutionary idea, spitting it down, yielding to it, frightened and exultant:—workers, unite." "[N]ot a tract," the novel is "humanitarian," he declared, the "first story of the American proletariat that succeeds in conveying its passion to the reader without benefit of previous conversion

10. H. L. Mencken, "Illuminations of the Abyss," *SRL* 11 (October 6, 1934): 156; Elmer Davis, "The Red Peril," *SRL* 8 (April 16, 1932): 662. Gold called the *SRL* a "pillar of the capitalist status quo" in his statement for the *SRL* 1934 symposium, "Twenty-Six Estimates of Our First Ten Years" (*SRL* 11 [October 16, 1934]: 182). "Thanks for the few friendly gestures you make now and then toward your proletarian enemy," he remarked. "There are at least a hundred first-class young writers in the proletarian camp today, and it is possible that they will soon be writing most of the good books that appear."

to the cause." Canby's swipe at other proletarian novels as "tract[s]" pre-supposing "previous conversion" indicates a less than sympathetic judg-ment of the genre. Interestingly, however, he reacted warmly to *Marching! Marching!*, one of the most didactic proletarian novels in its detailed illus-tration of the party line. For the *Saturday Review*'s editor-in-chief, the novel's adherence to party politics was not in and of itself cause for dis-missal, so long as the text portrayed contemporaneous reality in a creative and compelling—"humanitarian"—manner.[11]

In its divided response to literary radicalism, the *Saturday Review* was not alone among mainstream periodicals. The *Herald-Tribune* Sunday book supplement published its share of openly anti-Communist commentaries, such as Babette Deutsch's approving assessment of Max Eastman's attack on Soviet cultural policy in *Artists in Uniform: A Study in Literature and Bureaucratism*. Generally, however, NYHTB published sympathetic com-mentaries on literary radicalism. Horace Gregory wrote a series of lauda-tory reviews of new radical novels, proclaiming of *The Shadow Before* author William Rollins that "there is no young novelist in America who has a better sense of dramatic form"; calling *The Land of Plenty* author Robert Cantwell "a prose stylist of extraordinary subtlety and power"; noting that Langston Hughes's short stories *The Ways of White Folks* had the mark of "genius" and rendered moot any controversy about "art and propaganda." Other reviewers added their positive judgments, showering praise upon Myra Page's *Moscow Yankee*, Anna Louise Strong's *I Change Worlds*, Tom Tippett's *Horse Shoe Bottoms*, and Grace Lumpkin's *A Sign for Cain*—texts containing patently left-wing perspectives on revolution-ary militancy, Soviet socialist construction, the CP line on the "Negro Question," and unionization.[12]

11. Anonymous, "Books of the Fall," *SRL* 11 (October 6, 1934): 194; N. L. Rothman, "From the East Side," *SRL* 13 (November 2, 1935): 6; Seldon Rodman, "Thump—Throb—Thump—Throb," review of William Rollins, *The Shadow Before*, *SRL* 10 (March 17, 1934): 558; William Doerflinger, review of B. Traven, *The Death Ship*, *SRL* 10 (May 5, 1934): 677; H. S. Canby, "Plenty of Trouble," review of Robert Cantwell, *The Land of Plenty*, *SRL* 19 (May 5, 1934): 677; Seldon Rodman, review of Josephine Herbst, *The Exe-cutioner Waits*, *SRL* 11 (November 10, 1934): 273; W. H. Hale, review of Ralph Bates, *Lean Men*, *SRL* 11 (February 19, 1935): 471; Louis Adamic, "Nothing to Lose," review of Jack Conroy, *A World to Win*, *SRL* 12 (May 11, 1935): 14; H. S. Canby, "Workers, Unite!" *SRL* 13 (January 14, 1936): 12.

12. Babette Deutsch, "Dictatorship and the Artist," *NYHTB* (June 3, 1934), 10; Horace

Some *NYHTB* critics even presumed to criticize literary proletarianism for not being left enough. Horace Gregory commented that Joseph Freeman's introduction to the CP-sponsored anthology *Proletarian Literature in the United States*, although "perhaps the best definition of a Marxian point of view that I have ever read," was "less deadly than it should have been" in its treatment of Eastman. Bernard Smith faulted John Steinbeck's *In Dubious Battle* for its unsympathetic—and, Smith averred, inaccurate—portrayal of Communist organizers as cold-blooded and manipulative. In a review of Fielding Burke's *A Stone Came Rolling*, Smith chided the novelist for expressing too much love and too little "coldness and bitterness" in her compassionate portrait of the liberal industrialist Bly Emberson. Gregory—an independent radical poet—and Smith—an editor at Knopf with an interest in Marxism but no close party ties—maintained a careful distance from the CP; other members of the *NYHTB* reviewing staff were even less closely affiliated. Nonetheless, it would seem that reviewers for this mainstream literary organ took seriously the phenomenon of literary radicalism, routinely—and respectfully—including proletarian novelists in their coverage of significant arrivals on the literary scene. Smith was hardly speaking for himself alone when he remarked, "It is a curious and perhaps significant fact that the leading writers of the Left are among our most sophisticated artists." [13]

When in January 1935 Granville Hicks, literary editor of the *New Masses*, reviewed the 1934 roll call of proletarian fiction and boasted that proletarian literature was occupying a secure position in the cultural mainstream, he was not as far off the mark as subsequent assessments of 1930s literary production would have us think. In 1935 the *Year Book Review Digest* recognized proletarian literature as a distinct category. In 1936

Gregory, "The Simple, Truthful Story of a Strike," *NYHTB* (March 11, 1934), 7; "The World Within a Factory," *NYHTB* (April 9, 1934), 6; review of *The Ways of White Folks*, *NYHTB* (July 1, 1934), 4; Fred T. Marsh, review of *Moscow Yankee*, *NYHTB* (April 7, 1935), 20; Rose C. Field, "A Pioneer Woman Emigrates to Russia," *NYHTB* (April 21, 1935), 1–2; Erskine Caldwell, review of Grace Lumpkin, *A Sign for Cain*, *NYHTB* (October 27, 1935), 4.

13. Gregory, "Criticism from the Left," review of *Proletarian Literature in the United States*, *NYHTB* (October 13, 1935), 16; Bernard Smith, "John Steinbeck Comes of Age," *NYHTB* (February 2, 1935), 6; Smith, "Life in a Carolina Town," *NYHTB* (December 8, 1935), 4.

the *New Masses* reprinted a front-page article from the *London Times* in which the reviewer, reflecting upon both the proceedings of the 1935 American Writers Congress and the contents of *Proletarian Writers in the United States*, congratulated the American proletarians for their rejection of dogmatism. It is perhaps curious that the *New Masses* editors should have been pleased to receive the approbation of so thoroughly bourgeois a cultural organ. Clearly, however, even before the full turn into the Popular Front, left-wing literature—much of it articulating a distinctly Third-Period class consciousness and militancy—was receiving a hospitable hearing. As Charles and Mary Beard observed in 1936,

> When the great metropolitian reviews . . . devoted space and considerable cordiality of treatment to members of the newest school of revolt, this was proof of a stronger kind that some of the protestants represented a force of theme and a manner of manipulation meaningful in and for America . . .
>
> No editors in fact clung so tenaciously to the genteel tradition as to reject completely the tales of life and struggle at the lowest levels of economic subsistence. Literary militancy 'made' the front pages of reviews and drew serious consideration from the leading critics of the country.[14]

My purpose in detailing the largely favorable reception afforded proletarian literature in the first half of the Depression decade is not simply to prove that literary critics of the day were receptive to literary radicalism. This point is readily conceded by the detractors of proletarian literature, who frequently bemoan the gullibility of the naively liberal intellectual establishment to the blandishments of the left. Rather, I am noting that mainstream reviewers testified to a positive *aesthetic* response to proletarian literature. Liberal literary intellectuals may not have agreed with the politics of their radical peers, but they were generally unaffected by strong prejudices against political doctrines in literature. Notions of aesthetic au-

14. Granville Hicks, "Revolutionary Literature of 1934," *NM* 14 (January 1, 1935): 36–38; "American Writers Look Left," reprint from the *London Times*, *NM* 19 (June 6, 1936): 24–25; Charles and Mary Beard, *America in Midpassage* (New York: Macmillan, 1936), p. 690. Archibald MacLeish, addressing the National Association of Book Publishers in 1935, noted that "the current literary fashion is the Revolution." Publishers, he added, "have accepted it not only with enthusiasm but with a scientific objectivity which borders on the naive" ("The Writer and Revolution, *SRL* 11 [January 6, 1935]: 441). For more on the relations of liberals to the C P, see Frank A. Warren, III, *Liberals and Communism: The 'Red Decade' Revisited* (Bloomington and London: Indiana UP, 1966).

tonomy were largely irrelevant to their evaluative standards. These critics' stance was a kind of progressive Jamesianism: so long as writers did not unduly subordinate showing to telling, they should be granted their données and, indeed, applauded for portraying urgent social issues of the day.

Even conservative commentators qualified their negativity. Despite his ironic dismissal of the *New Masses* pundits, Mencken, as editor of the *American Mercury*, encouraged Jack Conroy, the young worker-author of *The Disinherited*, as well as other proletarian talents.[15] Adams openly granted that his antipathy to the proletarians' aesthetics was premised on philosophical individualism. Elmer Davis admitted that his aesthetic standards were "bourgeois"; he made no pretension to their universality. In other words, the critical establishment's debates over literary value exhibited considerable awareness of the interrelations between political and aesthetic criteria. Mainstream critics did not conclude that the writer who subscribed to a party line "court[ed] disaster" or suffered from an impairment of "creative judgment." Indeed, *pace* Tate, Warren, and other critics setting the postwar national aesthetic agenda, there was widespread belief that "liberal-democratic-progressive views" were entirely compatible with both the production and the reception of imaginative literature.

The Formation of an Anti-Stalinist Aesthetic

With the exception of Max Eastman's early Trotskyist polemic against Soviet literary policy, *Artists in Uniform* (1934), until about 1937 the attack upon proletarian literature was confined to the more or less ad hoc statements of conservative reviewers having no particular political axes to grind. By the end of the 1930s, however, significant numbers of formerly sympathetic writers and intellectuals had broken with the CP, and the self-proclaimed "anti-Stalinist left" had begun to outline the basic tenets of its

15. Conroy noted to Hicks, "[Mencken] prefers the attitude of the cynical philosopher sitting aloft and sneering at the antics of comically earnest insects, but he has been very kind to me and encouraging, and I appreciate it. However, I think this [sic] social views are antipodal to my own" (Conroy to Hicks, n.d., Box 14, Hicks Papers, Arents Library, Syracuse U.). For more on the Conroy-Mencken relationship, as well as on Mencken's support of other writers treating proletarian themes, see Douglas Wixson's Introduction to the recent reissue of *The Disinherited* (U of Missouri P, 1991).

[15]

critique of proletarian literature. Although, as James Murphy points out, James T. Farrell's *A Note on Literary Criticism* (1936) adumbrated the key features of the anti-Stalinist critique, the most influential spokesman for this emerging position was Philip Rahv. In the early 1930s, Rahv was a party member and, with William Phillips (then known as Wallace Phelps), coedited *Partisan Review*, then the official organ of the New York John Reed Club. Rahv participated actively in Third-Period discussions about revolutionary literature and criticism. After the *Partisan Review* disaffiliated with the party in 1937, however—around the Popular Front strategy adopted in 1935–36 and then the Moscow trials—Rahv published sharply critical retrospective articles on the failings of proletarian literature. Rahv's arguments, which have exerted significant influence upon subsequent discussions of proletarian literature, warrant a brief recapitulation.[16]

Rahv's principal criticism of proletarian literature was that—in a phrase that would be often repeated in subsequent commentary—it was "the literature of a party disguised as the literature of a class." Although Rahv himself had written positive reviews of certain proletarian novels—for example, of Arnold Armstrong's *Parched Earth* and Rollins's *The Shadow Before*—and was briefly a left firebrand, by 1937 he was concluding that proletarian literature had been from the outset an impossible proposition. Rahv based his new argument substantially upon the work of Leon Trotsky, who had maintained in *Literature and Revolution* (1924, trans. 1926) that proletarian culture was a contradiction in terms. The proletariat would create a culture genuinely reflective of its outlook, Trotsky declared, only when, after decades of socialist construction, it had abolished its self-identity as a class. Until then, the task of Communists was "the systematic, painful and, of course, critical imparting to the backward masses of the culture which already exists." The attempt to foster "proletarian" culture—even in the Soviet workers' state, let alone in prerevolutionary situations elsewhere—

---

16. James Murphy argues for the broad influence of Farrell's *A Note on Literary Criticism* (New York: Vanguard, 1936) in constructing the anti-Stalinist narrative shaping subsequent commentary on the 1930s (pp. 165–172). Farrell's book certainly played a role, but, in my view, the writings of Rahv, Phelps, and the group around the reorganized *Partisan Review* were of much greater importance. Although Farrell in fact became a Trotskyist and developed more clearly formulated political commitments than did the *Partisan Review* group, he never became part of their "school" and argued his critical points in a somewhat quirky and individualistic manner. See Wald, *James T. Farrell: The Revolutionary Socialist Years* (New York: New York UP, 1978).

was, Trotsky argued, doomed, since the proletariat, as a dispossessed class, had no culture of its own. The effort to create such a culture ex nihilo was an invitation to bureaucratism and authoritarian control of the arts.[17]

Rahv, building upon Trotsky's theory, charged that the CP's attempt to foster the growth of revolutionary culture in the early 1930s had been founded upon the error of "leftism." "Leftism," he argued, meant the dogmatic imposition upon literature of a political doctrine identified with the external tactical imperatives of a party program. This error was compounded during the Popular Front, when the CP abandoned its commitment to revolutionary art and instead required writers to follow every twist and turn in its increasingly opportunist line. The CP during the Popular Front phase, he sardonically remarked, became interested "primarily . . . not in literature but in *authors*." Whether left-wing writers were urged to arouse revolutionary fervor against the capitalists or to foster antifascist unity, the essential problem was the same. Literature, which follows its own laws and requires freedom and autonomy as preconditions of its production, had been subordinated to the exigencies of a repressive political doctrine and practice. Because proletarian literature was, as Rahv concluded, "the literature of a party disguised as the literature of a class," in his mind "this fact explains both the speed of its development and the speed of its disintegration."[18]

Rahv was justifiably skeptical about the party's Popular Front-era de-

17. Philip Rahv, "The Novelist as Partisan," *Partisan Review* (hereinafter PR) 1 (April–May 1934): 50–52; Leon Trotsky, *Literature and Revolution*, trans. Rose Strunsky (Ann Arbor: U of Michigan P, 1960), pp. 184–214, quoted p. 193. Trotsky's position was widely criticized in *International Literature* in the early 1930s and became the object of increasingly inflamed polemics as the decade went on. Trotsky was accused of promoting an un-Marxist view of bourgeois culture as universal and classless and of adopting an elitist attitude toward the culture of the proletariat. As one American commentator on the debate noted in 1937, "If there can be bourgeois culture, as the expression of *the interests and aspirations* of the middle class, then proletarian culture, articulating the will and hope of the workers, is also possible" (Harry Slochower, *Three Ways of Modern Man*, with a Foreword by Kenneth Burke [New York: International P, 1937], pp. 177–78). Phelps denied that he or Rahv ever had any close political affiliation with Trotsky. For Phelps's narrative of himself and Rahv as champions of art versus Stalinist bureaucratism, see William Phillips, *A Partisan View: Five Decades of Literary Life* (New York: Stein and Day, 1983), pp. 33–46.

18. Rahv, "Proletarian Literature: A Political Autopsy," *Southern Review* 4 (Winter 1939): 616–28, quoted 625, 623.

cision to abandon its commitment to the John Reed Clubs and instead to cultivate liberal and fellow-traveling writers with substantial reputations. But his formulation offered a distorted description of the actual relations between writers and the Communist left. His often-to-be-quoted statement about the literature of a party being passed off as the literature of a class conflated rejection of particular aspects of the CP's line and practice with rejection of "party" as such. In essays written after the 1937 *Partisan Review/New Masses* split, Rahv conveniently omitted mention of his own membership in the CP during the early 1930s, as well as his former approval of the party's cultivation of literary proletarianism.

Moreover, Rahv's argument was self-contradictory. He charged that Third-Period literature suffered from "leftism" and, specifically, from requiring that texts contain a "conversion" ending preaching revolutionary doctrine. Yet he complained that literature influenced by the Popular Front CP abandoned its earlier revolutionary commitment. By such logic, Third-Period literary proletarianism had been at once insufficiently leftist and ultraleftist—a judgment that leaves writers suspended in a peculiar political space. As Judy Kutulas has noted of Rahv and Phelps, "The Communist Party could not win; either [they] found [the Party] unrealistically revolutionary or not revolutionary at all." Moreover, Rahv's portraiture of CP policy was inconsistent. For his contention that the party exerted a repressive control in aesthetic matters was undermined by his admission that the proletarian writer was free to "choose his own subjects, deal with any characters, and work in any style he chose." The only thing asked by the Communist-led literary left in the early 1930s, Rahv admitted, was that "[t]he writer should ally himself with the working class and recognize the class struggle as the central fact of modern life"—a doctrine offering few barriers to writers drawn to literary proletarianism precisely for these reasons. Rahv thus largely refuted his own portrait of a bureaucratic party suppressing artistic freedom.[19]

19. Kutulas, " 'Toward the Beautiful Tomorrow': American Intellectuals on the Left and Stalin's Russia, 1930–1940," Ph.D. Thesis, UCLA, 1986, p. 108; Rahv, "Political Autopsy," 618–19. Marcus Klein notes that Rahv and Phelps put writers in a political box, since according to their prescriptions "the revolutionary writer could not go left, right, or down the middle" (*Foreigners: The Making of American Literature 1900–1940* [Chicago and London: U of Chicago P, 1981], p. 136). For more on Rahv's late-1930s stance, see, in addition to "Political Autopsy," Rahv, "The Years of Progress—From Waldo Frank to

Further, Rahv proposed conflicting theoretical formulations of the relation of art to politics. He charged that left-wing critics had failed in their
primary task of articulating the basic principles of a revolutionary aesthetic. But this claim counters his Trotskyist credo that such an aesthetic
was irrelevant, indeed injurious, since the literary proletarians were attempting to call into being a literature whose time had not yet come. Rahv
also offered a contradictory analysis of the epistemology of CP-influenced
writers. He accused proletarian novelists of wrenching narratives to ac-
commodate the dictates of the "formula of conversion" and imposing an
externally derived doctrine upon the irreducibility and complexity of lived
experience. (Apparently he forgot his own earlier praise of Rollins and
Armstrong for their lack of "preaching and finger-pointing" and for their
creation of an "inevitable logic of social necessity materializing in highly
articulate images of existing life.") But—uncritically invoking a racist iconography—Rahv also accused the 1930s literary radicals of being "red-
skins" committed to an anti-intellectual empiricism privileging fact over
concept, undigested experience over theory. "The effect of the popular
political creeds of our time," he concluded, "has been to increase [the]
habitual hostility to ideas, sanctioning the relaxation of standards and jus-
tifying the urge to come to terms with semiliterate audiences." As we shall
see in future chapters, Rahv quite correctly directed attention to the positivist epistemology motivating some proletarian writers. He blurred his
critique, however, by simultaneously insisting that these writers relied
upon undigested lumps of political commentary to make their points clear.
Rahv's retrospective diatribe against literary proletarianism showed more
animus than logic. Indeed, the only consistent thread running though his
commentary was his now-inalterable opposition to the influence of the CP,

---

Donald Ogden Stewart," PR 4 (February 1938): 22–30; Rahv, "Twilight of the Thirties,"
PR 6 (Summer 1939): 3–15; Rahv, "The Cult of Experience in American Writing" (1940),
rpt. in Essays on Literature and Politics 1932–1972, ed. Arabel J. Porter and Andrew J.
Drosin (Boston: Houghton Mifflin, 1978), pp. 8–27; and Rahv, "Paleface and Redskin,"
in Essays, pp. 3–7. The argument in these essays differs markedly from that set forth in
his and Phelps's "Problems and Perspectives in Revolutionary Literature," PR 1 (June–
July 1934): 3–10. This early essay, while critical, had an insider's viewpoint and was
included, in slightly abbreviated form, as "Recent Problems of Revolutionary Literature"
in Proletarian Literature in the United States, ed. Hicks et al. (New York: International,
1935), pp. 367–73.

which he charged with destroying the artistic potential of a generation of politically progressive American writers.[20]

Despite their flaws, Rahv's arguments were to set the terms for much of the anti-Communist commentary on proletarian literature in subsequent decades. Alfred Kazin, whose *On Native Grounds: An Interpretation of Modern American Prose Literature* (1942) contained a bitterly satirical diatribe against 1930s literary radicalism, cited Rahv as an authority: the party, Kazin averred, was ultimately "interested, as Philip Rahv has said, in authors rather than in books." But where Rahv grudgingly respected the project of Third-Period writers, Kazin offered the broadside generalization that all 1930s radical writers—except, of course, those like Dos Passos and Farrell whom he happened to admire—had "fallen under the influence of a country that had never known democracy," thereby producing "dozens of cheaply tendentious political novels." For the party, Kazin concluded, "Proletarian literature was important, but political correctness was more important still. In the Stalinist cosmogony writers, like people, were notoriously cheap." To Kazin—who cited not a single proletarian novel for "cheap tendentious[ness]"—it was apparently unnecessary to offer grounds for such generalizations. References to a "Stalinist cosmogony" obviated the necessity for textual analysis.[21]

Dixon Wecter, whose *The Age of the Great Depression 1929–1941* was published in 1948 as part of Arthur Schlesinger's revisionary Cold War publishing project, the History of American Life Series, also adopted a tone of cavalier dismissal toward proletarian literature. Wecter's method of denigrating 1930s literary radicalism was twofold: either he completely overlooked radical writers or he claimed that they had never been radi-

20. Rahv, "The Novelist as Partisan," 50; Rahv, "Paleface and Redskin," 5. As the remark on "semiliterate audiences" suggests, Rahv was something of an elitist. Herbst, who knew the *Partisan Review* group well, noted that Calmer, Rahv, and Phillips "have no faith in the workers. They don't understand them and have no living contact with them" (Herbst to Hicks, September 21, 1937, Box 27, Hicks Papers). Neil Jumonville, in his recent book on the New York intellectuals, argues that "even in the 1930s the intellectuals had clear tendencies toward what later became neoconservatism. . . . [T]heir elevated, theoretical, intellectual socialism . . . was interlaced with a fear of the masses" (*Critical Crossings*, (Berkeley: U of Calif. Press, 1991).

21. Alfred Kazin, *On Native Grounds: An Interpretation of Modern American Prose Literature* (New York: Reynal and Hitchcock, 1942), pp. 375, 376.

cal to begin with. Devoting a mere two pages to proletarian writers in a lengthy chapter on Depression-era literature, Wecter performed a curious sleight of hand, pronouncing that certain palatable novels—Cantwell's *The Land of Plenty*, Leane Zugsmith's *A Time to Remember*, Thomas Bell's *All Brides Are Beautiful*, as well as works by Caldwell, Wright, Farrell, and Dos Passos—had somehow managed to escape the scourge of left-wing commitment. Other texts reflected the inevitably ruinous effect of Communism upon literature. "Today the novels of Albert Halper, Meyer Levin, Michael Gold, Grace Lumpkin and Albert Maltz are almost unreadable," he opined. "Doctrinaire communism, in particular, seemed curiously at odds with good writing, as if Marx's own ineptitude were inherited by his cult." No doubt it would have greatly surprised Albert Halper—whose *Union Square* caricatured Communists as clumsy and doctrinaire, and whose *The Foundry* widely skirted revolutionary politics—to learn that he was more of a Marxist than Cantwell, who openly proclaimed himself a writer of leftist "propaganda," or than Bell, whose *All Brides Are Beautiful* features a Communist hero and ends with an explicit prophecy of impending class warfare. But Wecter's analytical strategy typified a course that would become increasingly popular in commentary on the American 1930s. Writers to be salvaged from the decade's ruins were humanists or ironists, while those to be rejected were hopelessly mired in Marxist commitments.[22]

The early years of the Cold War witnessed the appearance of influential works of cultural criticism effectively driving the nail into proletarian literature's coffin. Arthur Schlesinger's *The Vital Center: The Politics of Freedom* (1949) assaulted the "dough-faced progressivism" based on a "sentimental belief in progress" and on the denial that aggression is a "core" human characteristic. Seeking to split off from the left those liberals still motivated by Popular Front loyalties, Schlesinger argued that the appeal of progressivism was totalitarian. "The totalitarian man denies the testimony of his private nerves and conscience until they wither away before the authority of the Party and history," he declared. "He is the man persuaded by the absolute infallibility of the Party's will and judgment, the agent who knows no misgivings and no scruples, the activist who

22. Dixon Wecter, *The Age of the Great Depression 1929–1941*, History of American Life, vol. 13, ed. Arthur M. Schlesinger and Dixon Ryan Fox (New York: Macmillan, 1948), p. 253.

has no hesitation in sacrificing life to history." Against such "totalitarian certitude," Schlesinger intoned, "free society can only offer modern man devoured by alienation and fallibility." Such being the modern human condition, the only genuine art was that which acknowledged this truth and took "anxious man" as its hero. Proletarian literature, an escape from freedom, had been both an artistic travesty and a philosophical lie—simply a "cult" by which, Schlesinger charged, the CP had attempted "to establish firm control over the literary scene." By defining genuine art as art preoccupied with existential *angst*, Schlesinger ruled out of court all art characterized by unambiguous—much less deeply felt—political commitments. It was not necessary to refer to any specific texts: the very term "proletarian literature" was an oxymoron.[23]

Lionel Trilling also berated the liberal intelligentsia for its residual support for the left, noting that "Stalinism becomes endemic to the American middle class as soon as that class begins to think." Commenting on the "shallowness" of the "liberal-democratic" world outlook, he chastised its adherents for their "middlebrow" anti-intellectualism—their "habit of conceiving of ideas to be pellets of intellection, a crystallization of thought, precise and completed, and defined by their coherence and their procedural recommendations." "The dogged tendency of our time," he complained, is "to ideologize all things into grayness." "Ideology"—meaning, of course, Communist or pro-Communist doctrine, not Trilling's own set of premises—"is not the product of thought," he proclaimed. "[I]t is the habit or the ritual of showing respect for certain formulas to which, for various reasons having to do with emotional safety, we have very strong ties of whose meaning and consequences in activity we have no clear understanding." Proletarian literature, he asserted, had been produced by "dull unreverberant minds" marked by "dreary limitation." Interestingly, however, Trilling took as his target not so much the 1930s literary left—which was, in his eyes, beneath contempt—as the entire tradition of literary progressivism that had engendered Depression-era literary radicalism and provided it with a receptive audience. In Trilling's critical discourse, Russell Reising has argued, "Mr. Stalin," "Mr. Dreiser," and "Mr. Parrington" are equally the antagonists of "the liberal mind."[24]

23. Arthur M. Schlesinger, *The Vital Center: The Politics of Freedom* (1949; rpt. Boston: Houghton Mifflin, 1962), pp. 56–57, 122.

24. Lionel Trilling, *The Liberal Imagination: Essays on Literature and Society* (New York: Viking, 1951), pp. 302, 286; *The Last Decade: Essays and Reviews, 1965–75*

Anti-Stalinist commentators from Kazin to Trilling increasingly took for granted the incommensurability of Communism and literature. But it was Irving Howe and Louis Coser, who, in their *The American Communist Party: A Critical History* (1957), elaborated the first full-fledged formulation of the devastating effects of the CPUSA upon the artists and intellectuals in its orbit. Stalinism, Howe and Coser theorized, was a cultural phenomenon comprised of the following features: fetishism of the party, the absorption of the individual in "the politics of the counterfeit collective," submission to the "systematized intellectual reassurance afforded by hierarchy and bureaucracy," the elimination of free discussion and the blind worship of centralism, and the subordination of theory and serious intellectual activity to a specious pragmatism. The writers who surrendered themselves to Stalinist influences during the Depression, Howe and Coser argued—quoting Rahv's by now well-worn phrase—were led "not merely to literary failures but, far worse, to the moral deceit of passing off 'the literature of a party disguised as the literature of a class.'" Moreover, the proletarian writers were engaged in an act of "political masochism":

> The belief in some Ultimate Reality that Communists alone had been able to penetrate; the implicit assumption that by adopting the pose of ruthlessness the party was proving its claim to a deeper seriousness; the impulse to self-abasement ('down with us') that so many intellectuals felt in the presence of the working class or, more frequently, a caricature of the working class in the person of a party functionary—all these are central to the experience of the thirties.

Taking it as a premise that proletarian literature was an unequivocal failure —even a grudging admiration of selected writers was no longer possible— Howe and Coser argued that the "barely fulfilled qualities" of writers such as Herbst, Cantwell, and Rollins "suggest how much talent was betrayed in the thirties, how high a price such writers paid for surrendering their

---

(New York and London: Harcourt Brace and Jovanovich, 1979), pp. 4, 21; Russell J. Reising, "Lionel Trilling, the Liberal Imagination and the Cultural Discourse of Anti-Communism," forthcoming in *boundary 2*. For more on Trilling's anti-Stalinism, see Mark Krupnick, *Lionel Trilling and the Fate of Cultural Criticism* (Evanston: Northwestern UP, 1986), and William Chace, *Lionel Trilling: Criticism and Politics* (Stanford: Stanford UP, 1980). Chace argues that anti-Stalinism was so integral to Trilling's entire critique of American culture that Trilling was seriously derailed for several years by the waning of the Cold War in the 1960s.

gifts to the wardens of the party." Any formal options exercised in proletarian fiction were direct reflections of party dominance: the proletarian
novel was to be written in accordance with a strictly defined "formula," in
which the "conversion ending" was "the tithe the writer paid the party."
Endorsement of Communist party politics, Howe and Coser concluded, entailed "a vast and programmatic oversimplification of the nature of human
experience and a contempt for those aspects of life that could not be contained by a narrow political utilitarianism." With the publication of The
Communist Party: A Critical History, critics bent upon demonstrating the
failings of proletarian literature could now invoke a fully articulated theory
of "Stalinism" to buttress their arguments.[25]

Studies of 1930s American literary radicalism undertaken during the
first phases of the Cold War inevitably reflected the dominant political
ethos. Walter B. Rideout's The Radical Novel in the United States 1900–
1954 (1956), up to now the definitive account of the proletarian novel, is
noteworthy for its avoidance of the Manichaean political rhetoric characterizing most contemporaneous commentaries on the left. Rideout's study
has weathered the decades remarkably well; the recently reissued text
will continue to be useful to students of proletarian literature. In a clear
swipe against governmental repression, Rideout defended the "Marxist
novel" against "the critic or the Congressman" who would "proscribe" it
on political grounds. Rideout, often generous in his assessment of particular texts, offered important insights into the rhetorical challenges faced
by the consciously didactic left-wing novelist. His anatomy of the principal themes and representational strategies adopted in proletarian fiction
remains a valuable guide to students of the genre. Yet even Rideout's relatively benign perspective partook of a certain repressive tolerance. For he
concluded that the novel is, qua artistic form, "essentially a humanizing
force" and that the future of the radical novel rests not with Communist
novelists, who work in a self-imposed regime of "intellectual terrorism,"
but with "the independent radical." Commenting upon Granville Hicks's
resignation from the CPUSA upon the signing of the 1939 Nonaggression
Pact, Rideout remarked, "It was Hicks who pronounced, as though it were
an epitaph for the decade, one of the soundest lessons to be learned by a

25. Irving Howe and Lewis Coser, The American Communist Party: A Critical History
(1919–1957) (Boston: Beacon, 1957), pp. 507, 519, 520, 305, 280–81, 306, 304, 305.

literary man in the thirties: 'Politics is no game for a person whose attention is mostly directed elsewhere.'" For Rideout the novel espousing an
organized leftist politics may not pose a threat to the body politic, but it
"robs" literature of its "special" and "high" function: "to inquire relentlessly and unceasingly and on its own terms into the human condition."
Despite Rideout's generally fair-minded treatment of the politics of 1930s
literary proletarianism, his adherence to New Critical aesthetic doctrine
and a conception of the "human condition" carrying strong "vital center"
overtones limited his ability to grasp the revolutionary commitments of
proletarian novelists.[26]

Daniel Aaron's *Writers on the Left: Odysseys in American Literary Communism* (1961)—also recently reissued—is often taken as the definitive
work on 1930s literary leftism. But it has thrust up further barriers to a
critical reconsideration of proletarian fiction. Focusing exclusively upon
the relation of critics (and a very few writers) to the party, Aaron's study
makes no pretension to analyzing literary texts—most of which, he remarked, "violated almost every literary canon and . . . positively reeked of
the Depression." *Writers on the Left* deals principally with the biographical
front in what Edmund Wilson called "the literary class war."[27]

To his credit Aaron uncovered previously unexplored archival materials and called attention to some relatively unknown figures. But his adjudication of who were the significant writers of literary proletarianism has had
the unfortunate effect of focusing attention on the New York-based critics
and away from the more diverse grouping of literary figures who actually
constituted the movement—including many more rural-based, working-
class, female, and black writers than Aaron's lineup suggests. Moreover,
Aaron's study—part of Clinton Rossiter's anti-Communist Fund for the

26. Walter B. Rideout, *The Radical Novel in the United States 1900–1954: Some Interrelations of Literature and Society* (New York: Hill and Wang, 1956), pp. 290, 291, 254.
The 1992 reissue is from Columbia UP.

27. Daniel Aaron, *Writers on the Left: Odysseys in American Literary Communism*
(1961; rpt. New York: Avon, 1964), p. 169. It was actually Rahv who coined the term
"literary class war" in a 1932 *New Masses* article of that title (8 [August 1932]: 7–10),
but Edmund Wilson gave it widespread currency in his early 1930s essay, "The Literary
Class War," rpt. in *The Shores of Light: A Literary Chronicle of the Twenties and Thirties*
(New York: Farrar, Straus and Young, 1952), pp. 534–39. The 1992 reissue is also from
Columbia, with an introduction by Alan Wald.

Republic series, which includes Theodore Draper's *The Roots of Ameri-can Communism* and Schlesinger's *The Vital Center*—was founded on the familiar premise that involvement with the CPUSA had to have disastrous effects upon progressive American intellectuals. Even when Aaron offered particular assertions negating this proposition, his heavily sarcastic tone reinforced anti-Communist assumptions. Consider, for example, his de-scription of the relation of writers to the party in the early 1930s. "The majority, the talented and the untalented alike, never goose-stepped to party orders, but in the next decade a good many accepted uncritically and emotionally the party's diagnosis of society and world politics and were led, if not driven, by the party gods into red pastures." By a curious turn of the metaphorical wheel, Aaron turned the manifest content of his as-sertion—writers willingly accepted the CPUSA's analysis of the capitalist crisis—into its opposite: party leaders *were* in fact authoritarian mythogra-phers tempting innocent writers with false promises of emancipation and social purpose. Cold War liberals like Aaron themselves developed some adeptness at double-think.[28]

The theses set by Rahv, Rideout, Howe and Coser, and Aaron have set the political agenda for most subsequent articles and critical anthologies. In David Madden's 1968 anthology of criticism, *Proletarian Writers of the*

28. Aaron, p. 136. Aaron had ready access to letters and other archival materials in part because he was a personal friend of Hicks, Davis, and Cowley. The recantatory posture of these three former literary radicals had a significant influence on Aaron's per-spective in *Writers on the Left*. The anti-Communist stance taken in a number of the memoirs left by the literary leftists has significantly influenced the secondary scholar-ship on the subject of literary proletarianism. See, for example: Phillips, *A Partisan View*; Hicks, *Where We Came Out* (New York, Viking, 1954); Albert Halper, *Good-Bye, Union Square: A Writer's Memoir of the Thirties* (Chicago: Quadrangle, 1970); Cowley, *The Dream of the Golden Mountains* (New York: Viking, 1980); Richard Wright, *Ameri-can Hunger* (New York: Harper and Row, 1974); and Edward Dahlberg, *Do These Bones Live* (New York: Harcourt, Brace, 1941). Less jaundiced memoirs are not cited nearly so often—e.g., Joseph North, *No Men Are Strangers* (New York: International, 1958); Matthew Josephson, *Infidel in the Temple: A Memoir of the Nineteen-Thirties* (New York: Knopf, 1967); and Cowley's own earlier *Think Back on Us: A Contemporary Chronicle of the 1930s*, ed. Henry Dan Piper (Carbondale and Edwardsville: Southern Illinois UP, 1967). David Peck discusses the influence of recantatory memoirs on 1930s scholarship, as well as changes that the memoirists worked on their own versions of events, in his " 'The Cry of Apology': The Recent Revaluation of Literature of the Thirties," *Science and Society* 32 (Fall 1968): 37–82.

Thirties, there is almost uniform agreement on two central theses: proletarian literature largely failed and it did so because of the CP's nefarious
influence. Chester Eisinger argues that the Marxist-influenced writers of
the 1930s were wedded to an "emphasis upon the generalized and the
typical" that was "destructive of any writer's intention or desire to portray an individual character in all his idiosyncratic complexity." Central
to this weakness, he declares, is the Marxist failure to appreciate "ambivalence": "Without ambivalence between society and self, between objective
and subjective reality, the novel written in the Marxian ambience . . . fails
to give the imaginative satisfactions we can legitimately expect from fiction." Frederick J. Hoffman interprets the proletarian novel along the lines
of Rahv's redskin/paleface argument, finding that "there was as much resistance to an 'imported ideology' as there was attention paid to it. The
American proletarian novel was often a strange mixture of native realism
and sudden dips into ideological editorial or melodrama." Marxist politics
negated aesthetic effect. Most proletarian novels, according to Hoffman,
engaged in "leftist histrionics" and "now mainly exist as period pieces,
to which one refers from time to time, but almost unbelievingly." David
Madden, in his introductory essay to the volume, assumes the antipathy of
literary value to leftist politics. The works of proletarian literature possessing abiding value, he determines, are those in which "intense subjectivity"
is "untutored" by the "ideological angling" resulting from the imposition
of "an external, abstract doctrine." Putting the seal on the achievement
of the proletarian writers, Madden concludes that, to be tolerated, their
works should be read as "journalism uplifted": judging them primarily by
aesthetic standards," he states, is "an easy task, resulting in dismissal." For
Madden and most of the essayists included in his volume, it is a canonical assumption, barely worth acknowledging, let alone contesting, that the
great majority of proletarian novelists constitute at best a historical oddity
and deserve at most a patronizing glance.[29]

29. Chester Eisinger, "Character and Self in Fiction on the Left," in David Madden,
ed., *Proletarian Writers of the Thirties* (Carbondale and Edwardsville: Southern Illinois
UP, 1968), pp. 160, 173–74; Frederick J. Hoffman, "Aesthetics of the Proletarian Novel,"
in Madden, pp. 186, 193; Madden, Introduction, pp. xxix–xxx. The main strategy by
which most of Madden's critics recuperate literary proletarianism is to reduce its political leftism and read texts as expressions of a pragmatic native radicalism alien to Soviet-
exported dogma. This strategy is also pursued by Marcus Klein in *Foreigners*; William

A more recent critical anthology on 1930s literary radicalism, Ralph Bogardus's and Fred Hobson's *Literature at the Barricades: The American Writer in the 1930s* (1982), reinforces many now-familiar assumptions about the relation of 1930s writers to the organized left. Bogardus and Hobson, relatively up-to-date in their anti-Stalinism, posit a critical distance between themselves and the New York Intellectuals who, they say, "lamented" the "presumed hiatus of modernism" in the 1930s and "decried the artists' supposed willingness to march vacant-eyed to the tune of the Stalinist drummer." Bogardus and Hobson propose that the left-wing writers of the Depression years were more closely aligned with the modernist movement than the New York Intellectuals have been willing to grant. Much of this literary radicalism, the editors claim, can be rehabilitated if we acknowledge its modernist pedigree. Bogardus's and Hobson's rehabilitative effort is, however, modest. For they still view politics as a "subject matter" external to processes of aesthetic formalization and conclude that "[s]o long as artists have the gifts—the imaginative intelligence and the sense of craft—to make art, they can use politics just as they are able to use any other subject: to probe the human condition, to get at what it is to be human, and to unfold truths and beauties that reside in these things." Including in their anthology almost exclusively writers and critics harshly critical of the CPUSA's literary program, Bogardus and Hobson only superficially distance themselves from the tradition of literary anti-Stalinism that they claim to view critically. If proletarian writers are to be salvaged as exploratory modernists, this recovery occurs in spite of rather than because of their specific political commitments.[30]

Stott in *Documentary Expression and Thirties America* (New York: Oxford UP, 1973); and Richard Pells, *Radical Visions and American Dreams: Culture and Social Thought in the Depression Years* (New York: Harper and Row, 1973). See, for example, Pells's contention that *The Land of Plenty* and *The Disinherited* explore "the classic theme of the solitary hero who responds to a crisis on the basis of his own inner strength and conviction" (p. 205).

30. Bogardus and Hobson, p. 3. The major anthologies of proletarian literature appearing since the 1930s have reproduced the anti-Stalinist bias of the literary criticism. Louis Filler's *The Anxious Years: America in the Nineteen Thirties: A Collection of Contemporary Writings* (New York: G. P. Putnam's Sons, 1963) contains not a single text by a left-wing writer who remained loyal to the CP; the entire volume is given over to anti-Communist diatribe. Harvey Swados's *The American Writer and the Great Depression*

Until quite recently, it has been almost uncontested in U.S. critical circles that left-wing partisanship—to many writers and critics of the 1930s a sine qua non of meaningful representation—is a guarantor of moral dishonesty and aesthetic failure. Standards of literary judgment and historical scholarship have been abysmally low. All that has been routinely necessary to clinch a judgment is the ritual incantation of some highly loaded binary opposition—for example, "creative judgment" versus "party line." In the atmosphere of chilled intellectual discourse created by this pervasive anti-Stalinism, it has become difficult to inquire into the relation between the organized left and the literary proletarians, much less into the value of the texts these writers generated.

Cold War Ideology and the New Scholarship

One might suppose that critics influenced by recent developments in poststructuralism, feminism, New Historicism, and neo-Marxism would be able to break the hold of anti-Communist paradigms upon scholarship of the 1930s. The criteria for literary evaluation developed by the New Critics and the New York Intellectuals offer classic instances of logocentric discourse, positing an unproblematic origin from which all aesthetic judgments presumably flow and construing one position in political debate as irremediably "other." Since contemporary criticism has developed theoretical tools enabling it to be especially alert to loaded binary oppositions, we might hope that recent scholarship would put these tools to use in a critical analysis of 1930s literary radicalism.

Some important steps have in fact been taken to redress the errors of

---

(Indianapolis and New York: Bobbs-Merrill, 1966) is prefaced by the ritual attack on the CP for its "perversion and betrayal of the idealistic dreams of a generation of writers and intellectuals, who had confided their aspirations to the keeping of a clique of second-rate politicians." Swados concludes, "At their best [proletarian writers] transcended politics" (pp. xviii, xxxiii). Peck concludes that "the canon of Thirties literature which we have established in the last ten years has been carefully constructed to suggest that social, political and economic questions played no major role in the literature of the period and that Marxism was not a major intellectual force or an influential literary orientation, but an insignificant and 'shallow' idea which the more important writers of the decade either ignored or attacked" (" 'The Cry of Apology,' " 377).

past scholarship; these have opened the field to exciting new approaches and concerns. A few studies have squarely confronted the historical narrative inherited from the New York Intellectuals and have insisted on new criteria for describing and assessing left-wing literature. Too often, however, the view of the CP as monolithic, authoritarian, and philistine is still accepted in its essentials: too few studies grant, let alone explore, nuanced conceptions of the 1930s cultural left that touch on its zones of inconsistency and debate. As a result, complex textual tensions and ambiguities are often read not as expressing contradictions *internal to* the left, but as articulating conflicts *between* writers *and* the left, whether it is construed as "orthodox," "masculinist," or—still—"Stalinist."

While my primary concern here is with new scholarship specifically focusing on the 1930s U.S. literary left, I shall first comment briefly on the postmodernist textual radicalism that supplies the context in which this scholarship is being written and read. Jonathan Arac's recent *Postmodernism and Politics* (1987) offers an instance of the limitations imposed on postmodernist leftism when it fails fully to interrogate its intellectual origins. Arac, a self-proclaimed proponent of "postmodern Marxist intellectual activity," laudably dissociates his project from the knee-jerk anti-Stalinism of Lionel Trilling and other New York Intellectuals. Arac observes that Trilling's valorization of " 'contingency, vigilance, and effort' " as "the substance of real politics"—a politics to which the Stalinists presumably reacted with " 'disgust' "—was yoked "in a quite remarkable idealization" with " 'such energies of the human spirit as are marked by spontaneity, complexity, and variety.' " Quoting neo-Marxist theorist Stanley Aronowitz's critique of the New York Intellectuals, Arac notes that Trilling became to younger generations " 'the mirror image of Zhdanov,' . . . independent only in relation to his chosen opponent." "The great impasse against which Trilling's generation and their inheritors struggled" was that their "reject[ion of] the false experience of Stalinism in the thirties seemed only to yield the false experience of conformity in the fifties. In certain respects we are better positioned," Arac concludes. "Let us grant that they eradicated from American culture the dangers of Stalinism; now that it is gone, we are again free to explore possibilities on the left." [31]

31. Jonathan Arac, *Postmodernism and Politics*, Theory and History of Literature, vol. 28 (Minneapolis: U of Minnesota P, 1986), p. xxxiii. Andrei Zhdanov, an active par-

Arac's sense of emancipation from the stultifying terms of Cold War controversy is shared by many on the cultural left. But Arac feels "free" to transcend the New York Intellectuals' debate with 1930s and 1940s Marxism not because he has deconstructed these critics' reductive formulations of Stalinism, but simply because he is confident that Stalinism has been vanquished from the scene by the superior discursive politics of postmodernism. Arac successfully queries the false binary oppositions of Trilling's dogmatic humanism. But he incorrectly attributes his emancipated stance to the defeat of the "dangers" embodied in "Zhdanov"—a signifier here taken to refer not to a "signified," always already textualized through discourse, but to a prelinguistic presence, endowed with almost terroristic referential power. The use of "Zhdanov" as a metonym for "the experience of Stalinism in the thirties" makes it impossible to ask what exactly that experience might have been. (Did it, for example, include all of literary proletarianism? all of socialist construction?) While Arac astutely notes that Trilling's generation simply substituted a "false experience of conformity" for what they were rejecting, the "postmodern intellectual activity" he embraces would seem to share the dismissive assessment of 1930s culture formulated by the New York Intellectuals. Anti-Stalinism is not exorcized but reincorporated on a subliminal level of discourse.

In postmodernist discussions of leftist cultural politics, Stalinism often lurks in the background but is rarely called by its name; the kind of party-bashing engaged in by Howe and Coser is out of vogue. But the antipathy formerly attached to the party as such is transferred to "orthodox" Marxism's class-based analytical paradigm, which becomes invested with a malign authoritarian power. Paul Bové's "The Ineluctability of Difference: Scientific Pluralism and the Critical Intelligence" exemplifies the anti-Stalinist underpinnings of a good deal of poststructuralist Marxism. Drawing, like Arac, on the work of Aronowitz, Bové argues that the only possibility for a genuinely oppositional theory and practice resides in a pluralism rejecting as "scientific" all "master discourses" for historical change and relinquishing "the Leninist model of the vanguard party" in favor of "an alliance of autonomous, sometimes competing groups."

---

ticipant in debates about politics and culture during the 1930s and the USSR's cultural commissar in the postwar period, is widely held among Western critics to represent the most authoritarian aspects of Soviet socialist realist policy for the arts.

This alliance would consist of "interest groups" rather than classes, since classes have no material reality, being constituted only "as a result of a struggle 'about class.' " Not merely is it "fictional" to posit class struggle as the primary determinant of historical motion: because of its "implicit commitment to [a] mode[l] of single causality and progress," class analysis "fails to comprehend historically specific conditions that call for alternative discourses to describe multiple causations" and in fact ends up being "as coercive as the hegemony [it] oppose[s]."[32]

Furthermore, Bové argues, the dangers of this "leftist totalization" are not confined to explicitly political discourse. Textual critics play key roles in "this movement of forces opposed to tyrannical totalization and representation." Bové mentions "Stalinism" only in passing: Adorno, he claims, "offers a critique both of Western liberalism and of Stalinism" (presumably comparable entities). But Bové's attack upon "leftist totalization" presupposes a reading of Marxism as authoritarian and repressive, recapitulating the principal features of the anti-Stalinist argument. As the specific political issues prompting the first wave of anti-Stalinism—the Popular Front, the Moscow trials, the Hitler-Stalin Pact—recede in memory, the critique of Stalinism is elided into the critique of logocentricity as the ground of "leftist totalization." Now Stalinism and Cold War liberalism, in their common commitment to "realism" and common postulation of a unified and coherent subject, emerge as two sides of the same epistemological coin. Emancipation is therefore to be sought not in any globally conceived—or "scientistic"—alternative political program, but in a micropolitics committed to dispersion and difference and alert to language's role in empowering repressed and marginalized subjectivities. Postmodern textual radicalism, while apparently alert to repressive logic, routinely presupposes a crudely totalizing—indeed, "totalitarian"—equation of "Stalinism" with Leninism with "orthodox" Marxism with positivism.[33]

Arac and Bové make little mention of 1930s cultural leftism in their comments on textual politics. But Aronowitz, whom both cite authorita-

32. Paul Bové, "The Ineluctability of Difference: Scientific Pluralism and the Critical Intelligence," in Arac, pp. 5, 9, 11.

33. Ibid., pp. 14, 1, 22. I develop this critique of post- and neo-Marxism in "Marxism in the Poststructuralist Moment: Some Notes on the Problem of Revising Marx," *Cultural Critique* 15 (Spring 1990): 5–38, and "Class," *Rethinking Marxism* 5 (Summer 1992): 117–28.

tively, quite unabashedly resurrects the old stereotypes. Discussing the U.S. literary left, Aronowitz remarks,

> A new genre of execrable "proletarian" novels was born in the early 1930s fostered to a large extent by Gold and the Communist party. This was the novel of struggle, in which friends and enemies were clearly defined, where the outcome was predictable if the reader understood the formula, and resembled the Communist version of pulp fiction. The workers would strike, their divisions would be overcome, the union would make them strong, thanks to the tireless efforts of the Communist organizer who selflessly gave himself to the struggle. Although the final resolution of the class struggle was never more than indicated, its inevitability was always assured.[34]

Ignoring the actual diversity of proletarian fiction—many novels do not deal with strikes, and rarely are strike leaders identified as Communists—Aronowitz perpetuates the inaccurate view that the CP imposed a series of ultraleft prescriptions upon party and fellow-traveler writers. Moreover, he cites not a single novel or critical text in support of his argument. Perhaps, opposition to logocentricity does not commit the postmodern Marxist to examining the archive or to relinquishing binary oppositions when the relation of writers to the Communist left is at issue. The postmodernist critique of class reductionism can itself be based on a reductionist and empirically unsubstantiated set of claims.

Among the recent studies of 1930s U.S. literary proletarianism, two are distinguished for breaking decisively with inherited anti-Communist paradigms. In *Repression and Recovery: Modern American Poetry and the Politics of Cultural Memory*, Cary Nelson defends proletarian poetry as "one of the real treasures of our literary heritage" and points out that the New Critical literary standards invoked to depreciate its value are political to the core: "[I]t is ideology—not transcendent criteria for excellence—that has led critics to find religious self-abnegation, as in Eliot's *Four Quartets*, so appealing, and a revolutionary commitment so unacceptably unpoetic." But Nelson also contests the legacy of the New York Intellectuals:

> The myth, set in motion by statements like Philip Rahv's polemical 1939 *Southern Review* essay, "Proletarian Literature: A Political Autopsy," is that to recognize the party's influence is to recognize that nothing more need be

---

34. Stanley Aronowitz, *The Crisis in Historical Materialism: Class, Politics and Culture in Marxist Theory* (New York: Praeger, 1981), p. 235.

said about much of the political poetry of the 1930s. . . . [T]he poetry is too diverse to fit any simple model of party influence. Indeed, even if the CPUSA had never been founded, the Great Depression would have intensified existing American traditions of labor poetry and poetry about class conflict. The party helped to rearticulate these traditions partly to its own interests and it helped give these traditions counter-hegemonic force for a period of time. But it could not in the end control the varied poems its cultural influence helped produce. Neither then nor now do party politics even begin to exhaust the semiotic effects these poems can have.

Reacting against the thesis that the CP imposed an authoritarian regime on writers, Nelson if anything underplays the importance—and influence—of aesthetic debates on the left. But his study eloquently defends the political commitments of proletarian poetry, asserting that "[d]ismissals of proletarian poetry based on the fact that predicted revolutions did not come to pass have . . . been effective in achieving ideological closure for us within literary history [and] . . . have blocked us from asking what the poetic vision of a revolutionary working class might still contribute to our culture."[35]

In *The Proletarian Moment: The Controversy over Leftism in Literature,* James Murphy exorcizes Rahv's ghost by returning to the archive and proposing an alternative narrative of the 1930s literary left. Rejecting the canonical opposition of Stalinist philistines and proto-Trotskyist defenders of modernism and literary value, Murphy demonstrates that, in the early 1930s, Rahv and Phelps attacked the conservative high modernists as frequently as the *New Masses* group defended them and that both groups were, moreover, opposed to "leftism." Murphy argues that only after splitting with the Stalinists over nonliterary issues and reversing their earlier sponsorship of proletarian literature did the *Partisan Review* group devise the narrative that has subsequently become so influential:

> The problem that . . . confronted the editors of the new magazine [the post-1937 independent *Partisan Review*] was how to reconcile [their] wholesale repudiation of the proletarian literature movement and the aesthetic theory that had developed around it, with the fact that the original *Partisan Review*

35. Cary Nelson, *Repression and Recovery,* pp. 102, 152, 163–64. See also Nelson and Jefferson Hendricks, *Edwin Rolfe: A Biographical Essay and Guide to the Rolfe Archives at the University of Illinois at Urbana - Champaign* (Urbana: University of Illinois P, 1990).

had been one of the principal organs of the same movement. The solution was to construct a straw man—the orthodox, doctrinaire, Stalinist leftist *New Masses* approach to literature and aesthetics—and to portray their own role as a dissident one from the beginning.

Murphy proves his thesis through exhaustive documentation from the magazines of the literary left as well as the *Daily Worker,* a source rarely consulted in commentaries on 1930s cultural politics. I differ with Murphy somewhat over how to judge the outcome of 1930s critical debates: as will become clear in future chapters, I am less sanguine than he that the defeat of "leftism" was such a good thing for the literary proletarians. I support wholeheartedly, however, his assessment that the pervasive scholarly acceptance of the narrative of the decade provided by the New York Intellectuals offers "a classic example of how politics affects the writing of history." Murphy concludes, "The distortion and misrepresentation that have resulted can only be described as an indictment of much of the American scholarship in this area." *The Proletarian Moment* sets a new standard in the field, preventing future scholars from blithely repeating the inherited litanies about Stalinist antimodernism.[36]

Alan Wald's work on 1930s literary radicalism exemplifies various contradictions in the recent scholarship in the field. Much of Wald's work is rich and exciting. Wald treats a wide range of left-wing writers and argues for a view of the twentieth-century U.S. revolutionary tradition extending significantly before and beyond the 1930s. He notes, too, that " 'radical' or even 'Communist' writers for the most part . . . had to produce the kind of literature that could be sold: pulp, romance, children's, science fiction, detective, horror, Westerns, and so forth." Wald's investigation thus contests the notion that left-wing writers necessarily write in the "proletarian" mode. Moreover, Wald evinces an admirable openness in assessing writers whose politics he finds problematic. Despite uneasiness with Edwin Rolfe's Stalinist loyalties, Wald affirms Rolfe's "essential decency as a human being and . . . devotion to literary craft," noting that "we may be able to learn far more [from him] than from many of his antagonists who

36. Murphy, pp. 187, 5. While I am indebted to Murphy's meticulous research, I had independently arrived at several of the points he argues prior to reading his book. A careful examination of the available archive *requires* that scholars abandon the reductive and distorting narrative of 1930s literary radicalism inherited from the anti-Stalinists.

might have been more 'politically correct' about a certain international question or more subtle in critical exegesis."[37]

Furthermore, Wald's antipathy to the Third International does not prevent him from offering acute judgments of various figures in the tradition of literary anti-Stalinism. In their worshipful attitude toward modernism in the postwar period, Wald remarks, most of the New York Intellectuals "came to embrace the very supraclass theories they had once rejected." Rahv's "critical preoccupation with the ironies and tensions in modernist literature," for example, "makes him a strange cousin to the school of New Criticism." Critically reassessing Alfred Kazin's dismissal of 1930s literary leftism, Wald comments on Kazin's "thin documentation" and observes that Kazin's "oversimplification" is "tantamount to the creation of a 'straw Marxism' against which he can easily counterpose a more sophisticated world view." In this context Wald specifically refutes Kazin's "wholesale endorsement of Philip Rahv's notoriously exaggerated statement that 'Proletarian literature was the literature of a party disguised as the literature of a class.'" The invocation of Rahv reveals, Wald argues, Kazin's "succumbing" to the "pursui[t] [of] prejudice to the point of absurdity" with which Kazin himself charged other critics. Wald points out that Kazin evades confronting "the left-wing literary tendency on the actual terrain of the debates of the 1930s," thus "trivializ[ing] . . . as escapist compulsions" the "ambitious . . . if at times botched" critical concerns of Marxists like Joseph Freeman and Granville Hicks.[38]

Despite his subtle rereadings of literary and critical traditions, however, Wald promulgates certain misconceptions about the 1930s literary left. First, he perpetuates the notion that, against the "Stalinist shibboleths" promoted by Gold and other critics belonging to the CP, Rahv and Phelps evinced "willingness to openly blend Marxism with an aggressive sympathy for the modernist themes and techniques of the 1920." CP-connected critics may have "privately held views similar to those of Phillips and Rahv," but, according to official party doctrine, "symbolic form" was "judged criminal." As Murphy argues—and as we shall see in

37. Wald, review of Nelson and Hendricks, *Edwin Rolfe*, *Journal of English and Germanic Philology* 91 (July 1992): 465, 467.

38. Wald, *The New York Intellectuals*, pp. 217, 219; Wald, "In Retrospect: On Native Grounds," *Reviews in American History* 20 (1992): 285, 284, 286.

future chapters—this is simply not the case: up to 1937 all the literary leftists, around both the *Partisan Review* and the *New Masses*, publicly exhibited contradictory views toward modernism. Moreover, Wald argues that the "subordination of art to politics" was "characteristic of many Communist Party critics"—that " 'Art is a weapon' " was a "Stalinist homily." Contesting this view is a major thesis of *Radical Representations:* I shall demonstrate that most CP critics, while not guided by anything resembling a party "line" on aesthetic matters, were in fact uneasy with the view of literature as weaponry and repudiated the notion that proletarian literature should be written as "propaganda." Finally, Wald mentions "the constraints of the Communist institutions through which the left writers tried to function" without saying what these constraints actually were. Wald remarks that it is "appropriate to demystify the notion of a homogeneous lockstep Communist literary movement" and that "young as well as leading writers around the Communist movement behaved as subjectively, egocentrically, and in as a [sic] refractory manner as most other writers." Yet he warns, "[T]he main difference, however, is that all of this happened within the general conventions, structures, and tropes of Stalinism." Wald is of course entitled to his view that the tradition of "revolutionary Trotskyism" offers a more positive cultural and political program than did that historically embodied in the Stalinist left. But his work has not demonstrated that Stalinism in fact operated as a repressive force among 1930s literary radicals. Indeed, Wald's nuanced readings of individual proletarian writers and critics suggest quite the opposite conclusion.[39]

Because of the very freshness of its insights and judgments, James Bloom's *Left Letters: The Culture Wars of Mike Gold and Joseph Freeman*

39. Wald, "Revolutionary Intellectuals: *Partisan Review* in the 1930s," in Bogardus and Hobson, p. 190; Wald, *The New York Intellectuals*, pp. 94, 95; Wald, "In Retrospect," 283; Wald, review of *Edwin Rolfe*, 467. Wald, who starting writing on 1930s literary radicalism over a decade ago, bridges the older and more recent schools of scholarship. In 1983 he wrote that the CP's espoused interest in aesthetic matters was "primarily a vehicle by which the party officialdom could police the writers on the left" and that proletarian literature was "a short-lived and unsuccessful hothouse experiment fostered by the Communist party for political reasons after 1928–29 and abandoned in 1935." While Wald may still espouse the former judgment, his more recent work on left-wing literature suggests that he has probably altered the latter. See, for example, his penetrating comments on Endore's *Babouk* in "The Subaltern Speaks," *Monthly Review* 43 (April 1, 1992): 17–29.

underlines all the more the need for a completely revised narrative of the relation of literary proletarianism to the organized left. Bloom undertakes a spirited defense of Gold and Freeman, remarking that the "thirties-inspired view of literature, especially of criticism," was "inevitably embattled." Noting that Gold in particular has been unjustly dismissed as a "bully and a vulgarian," Bloom argues that both Freeman and Gold attempted to "reconcile left politics and modernist poetics, a traditionally schooled literary sensibility and an egalitarian commitment to the masses." Moreover, Bloom's interest in Freeman and Gold is not antiquarian, for he maintains that their texts, rather than illustrating crude Marxist reductionism, in various ways anticipate postmodernist inscriptions of the politics of textuality. Remarking on the critical fortunes of Freeman's autobiography, Bloom offers the important insight that "[t]he intellectual McCarthyism that has obscured *An American Testament* may still be in force today. It takes the form, ironically, of academic Marxism. Out of a fear of seeming 'vulgar,' such Marxists evade the problem of Stalin and, out of an anxiety not to appear influenced by such naive base-superstructure paleo-Marxism, produce instead an 'elistist deformation of Marxism.' " [40]

Bloom's own hesitancies in coming to terms with the " 'problem of Stalin,' " however, in various ways detract from his otherwise boldly revisionary study. Bloom notes that, with the defusing of Cold War tensions, Stalinism should "become a troubling, fascinating historical problem, no longer a demonizing name for mass murder or a reproach to the integrity of nonviolent leftisms." By continually referring to the "party-line view of 'art as a weapon' " and party "orthodoxy," however, Bloom to a degree reinforces the very thinking he wishes to discourage. While conceding that Gold himself was in some ways "orthodox," Bloom refers to not a single other critic articulating this presumably official line. Besides perpetuating without evidence the inherited view of a shadowy, anonymous party issuing authoritarian mandates, this proposition has two important consequences. [41]

First, the invocation of an unnamed and unspecific "orthodoxy" diminishes the importance of both Gold's and Freeman's Communist commitments, portraying them as complicated and interesting primarily for

40. Bloom, pp. 9, 14, 113, 94.
41. Ibid., pp. 6, 9.

their departures from the party "line." Gold is read as denying privileged authority to the revolutionary narratorial voice in *Jews Without Money:* the text's contention "is not simply partisan animus and ideological assertion but rather dialogic contestation." Freeman—who, as the CP critic closest to being an "official" theorist, authored the important introduction to *Proletarian Literature in the United States*—is praised for his "antinomian Marxism" and "antidoctrinal proletarian aesthetic." Contradictions that were in fact *internal* to the Communist-led literary left are thus displaced onto contradictions *within* individual consciousness or *between* writers and the left. Bloom justly observes that Gold's and Freeman's "complexity" refutes "received views of them as crude, reductive, partisan, and sentimental." He associates this quality, however, not with the political complexity of literary proletarianism, but with "the limitations and contradictions of high modernism," into which Gold and Freeman need to be placed.[42]

Second, Bloom's uneasiness with treating Gold and Freeman as synecdochic of the literary left leads him to view them as historically significant largely for anticipating the concerns of contemporary textual radicalism. Gold is seen to articulate a "proto-New Left cultural politics" through his practice of "intertextual subversion and revisionist appropriation." Gold's "self-consciously oral style and the overall dialogic movement of his narrative," Bloom argues, place *Jews Without Money* in what Salman Rushdie calls "the arena of discourse, the place where the struggle of languages can be acted out." Not Marxist dialectics but Bakhtinian dialogics provide the paradigm for Gold's juxtaposition of opposing tendencies in the world of his East Side youth. Freeman is applauded for "anticipat[ing] and illuminat[ing] the now familiar, diversely construed conflict between intrinsic and extrinsic critical approaches, formalism and historicism, aesthetic 'disinterestedness' and partisan engagement" at a time when "literati, on both sides of these divides, were near unanimous in assuming that such divisions were clear-cut." "[T]roubled and sustained by this tension between aestheticism and social consciousness," Bloom concludes, Freeman was "like many literary Marxists today." Bloom's establishment of multiple links between Depression-era and contemporary Marxism makes an extremely important contribution to the study of 1930s literary radical-

42. Ibid., pp. 29, 79, 118.

ism, rescuing it from a pigeonhole in cultural history. But his reluctance to grant the full contradictoriness and depth of the project of the entire Depression-era literary left—their *lack* of unanimity over urgent critical issues—will have to be addressed by future work drawing such crucial historical connections.[43]

Paula Rabinowitz's recent work on feminist radicals of the 1930s combines paradigm-shattering new insights with an insufficiently scrutinized adherence to certain features of the received narrative of the 1930s. Rabinowitz argues that both a new typology for proletarian fiction and a new literary history result when one starts from the concerns and strategies given priority in women's texts: "Most critics present the history of 1930s literary radicalism as a corollary to the history of the Communist movements of the decade. I argue that the absent presence of gender in these two fields alters the shape of both the political and the literary history of the Left and recasts their relationships to one another." The model of literary history placing causal primacy upon the line of the CP, she charges, "reads literary (and critical) writings as epiphenomena of political doctrine": critics from Rahv through Rideout, Aaron and beyond adhere to a model that is both male-centered and mechanistic. Moreover, when scholarship focuses not just on "labor" but on "desire" as constitutive of radical and proletarian women's consciousness, Rabinowitz argues, not only do the inherited categories for classifying proletarian fiction need to be jettisoned, but the entire narrative of the decade needs to be recast: "[W]omen's novels challenge the critical convention that links literary radicalism, through a narrow reading of the narrative of history, to the Party's political shifts from the Third Period to the Popular Front."[44]

Rabinowitz argues, furthermore, that women's texts reveal complex relations between gender and class often occluded in both male-authored narratives and the critical paradigms based on these narratives. Class was often symptomatically gendered in 1930s discourse—not only in the routine inscription of the proletariat as male but also in the representation of the bourgeoisie as effete and impotent. But "[g]ender and sexuality served as metaphors rather than as historically determined and determining structures of oppression. . . . They were not recognized as sites for the con-

43. Ibid., pp. 21, 29, 81.
44. Rabinowitz, *Labor and Desire*, pp. 18, 19, 62.

struction of the political subject." At the same time, in women's texts gender was classed. Albeit through genres—proletarian realism, traditional women's fiction—necessitating narrative "gaps," women's revolutionary novels construct a "class-conscious female subjectivity as both hungry and desiring, as both a member of the body politic and a sexual body." These women's texts incorporate but move beyond the class-based narrative of the hunger accompanying "labor," intertwining a narrative of subjective and sexual "desire."[45]

Rabinowitz's book poses an exciting challenge to many of the categories through which 1930s U.S. literary radicalism has thus far been read. Paradoxically, however, it retains features of the inherited methodology for examining proletarianism that simplify its critique of that very methodology. First, in charging that Rahv's attribution of primacy to the party in shaping literary proletarianism "reproduce[s] . . . the hierarchically organized system of democratic centralism," Rabinowitz conflates democratic centralism (a method of political organization) with mechanistic materialism (a method of historical analysis) with Rahv's own antipathy to the specific line and practice of the CP. The relations among these three categories are much more complex and mediated than this line of argument allows—particularly when we consider that Rideout and Aaron, presumably adherents of the same analytical model as Rahv, can hardly be viewed as exponents of democratic centralism. When we remember, too, that the Rahv who penned his early influential critiques of Stalinist proletarianism was, as then a disciple of Trotsky, himself inalterably opposed to democratic centralism, Rabinowitz's charge tars Rahv with the brush of his own anti-Stalinism but explains little. The critique of a masculinist literary history excluding the contributions of women to literary proletarianism is simply conflated, through the rhetoric of a residual anti-Stalinism, with the mechanistic and repressive practices of an authoritarian party. Rabinowitz may be right that studies of 1930s literary radicalism that stress debates among the male Marxists in the *New Masses* and the *Partisan Review* do fail to illuminate the writings of women. But she would more persuasively argue her point if she did not drag in the old bogeys.[46]

Second, Rabinowitz's subtle and interesting argument about the gender-

45. Ibid., pp. 60, 63.
46. Ibid., p. 20.

ing of class and the classing of gender loses some of its force through its portraiture of an unremittingly sexist party. As we shall see in chapter 6, there are many grains of truth to the critique of the CP posed by Rabinowitz and other feminist critics. But it is one-sided to claim that, for the 1930s left, gender and sexuality were seen as simply "metaphors rather than . . . historically determined and determining structures of oppression" or that—as Rabinowitz states elsewhere—"women, and the representation of woman, were used in different ways quite cynically." Such statements not only distort the uneven but by no means insignificant achievements of the 1930s CP in relation to the "woman question"; in addition, they treat as distinct the categories of "the Party" and "women," when female party members—for better or worse—played key roles in formulating its line and practice on this issue. As important, the implied binary opposition informing Rabinowitz's study—authoritarian male party leaders confined to discourse of labor versus subversive female radicals capable of merging labor with desire—has the effect of closing all male-authored discourses out of the zone of desire. Rabinowitz is indeed right that women's novels in general confront sexuality—and subjectivity—with more depth and honesty than do many novels by men. But this statement is hardly valid across the board. The shadowy invocation of a Stalinist, male-dominated party throughout *Labor and Desire* needlessly confines to women a concern with sexual and personal emancipation that is—if only partially articulated— also a component of the "hunger" for fuller selfhood inscribed in many proletarian novels by men.[47]

➢   ➢   ➢   ➢   ➢

I am hopeful that the preceding critique of other scholars currently working on 1930s literary radicalism will not appear mean-spirited. My own work is indebted to the important discoveries being made by the critics cited here—not only Nelson and Murphy, with whom I substantially agree, but also Wald, Bloom, and Rabinowitz, whose work I clearly contest on various points but regard nonetheless as sophisticated and ground-breaking.

47. Rabinowitz, "Introduction" to *Writing Red*, p. 7. For a critique of this earlier essay's anti-Stalinism—which is moderated in *Labor and Desire*—see my "Women and the Left in the 1930s," *American Literary History* 2 (Spring 1990): 150–69.

I have offered these comments on the scholarship in process in order to clarify those areas where I see the necessity for further work.

In particular, I have been arguing that the relationship between the CP and writers in its orbit needs to be completely rethought if scholarship is to make the next crucial strides. In criticizing the dominant anti-Stalinist paradigm, I do not wish to put in its place a hagiography of virtuous and maligned literary Communists—although I do believe that this paradigm prevents full appreciation of these writers' achievements. As I shall point out, the literary left—both critics and writers—were restricted and limited in a number of ways. But these constraints did not come from the quarter to which they are usually attributed. More ground-clearing is needed if we are fully to reassess U.S. Depression-era left-wing literature. The rest of *Radical Representations* will be devoted to such ground-clearing and reassessment.

CHAPTER 2

>

Influences on American Proletarian Literature

As we have seen, the charge most frequently leveled at proletarian literature is Rahv's often-repeated accusation that it was the literature of a party passing itself off as the literature of a class. Through writers' formations and critical organs where their influence dominated, the argument goes, the party critics who were based in the *New Masses* issued directives about matters ranging from politics to subject matter to style. Even though some talented writers were attracted to the proletarian movement, their creativity was straitjacketed by the requirement that their work conform to a formulaic set of guidelines, often imported wholesale from Moscow. Proletarian literature was crippled at the outset by the prescriptiveness of Marxist criticism.

These are serious charges; even if only partially true, they do much to discredit the project of proletarian literature. Moreover, they cannot be dismissed out of hand, for proletarian literature *was* to a significant extent the brainchild of the American left and was from its beginnings involved in a discourse about itself. It did not come into being as most literary schools do, through a gradual, indirect and highly mediated response to changes in social relationships and the discourses surrounding these relationships. Absent the Communist movement, no doubt some kind of left-wing literature would have sprung up in the U.S. as a response to Soviet socialist construction on the one hand and the 1930s economic crisis on the other. Nonetheless, the critical judgments offered by Marxist commentators were clearly intended to serve an advisory, even a prophetic, function. While other manifestoes in the history of poetics can be considered more stringent—"The Marxists [sic] dogmas are much less limiting and confining than those of Aristotle," the proletarian novelist Robert Cantwell opined—the generalized statements of literary purpose associated with various literary schools and trends have historically tended to be offered a posteriori, based on extensive acquaintance with existing models.[1] By contrast, many definitions of proletarian literature's principles and purposes were focused as much on what this writing *ought* to be as on what it actually *was*. American proletarian literature was to a considerable degree born out of an a priori conception of itself.

To concede that there was a direct link between the Communist-led movement and American proletarian literature is not to concede to Philip Rahv's argument about the literature of a party engaging in textual sub-stitutionalism. But it is to point out that analysis of the proletarian novel cannot proceed without examination of the relation of the organized left to the literary movement that it both generated and cultivated. It could of course be objected that, in laying stress upon the critical discourse about proletarian literature, I am compounding the a priorism of which the 1930s Marxist critics were presumably guilty. Perhaps I am unduly deemphasiz-ing the creative writers' role in defining the proletarian novel through their own practice—a practice that may have had relatively little to do with any guidelines laid down by the critics.

Nowhere in *Radical Representations* shall I make the argument that pro-letarian novelists composed their texts in response to guidelines laid out in the *New Masses* or other leftist organs or that any such guidelines by them-selves account for any text or group of texts. Particularly after proletarian novels began appearing in significant numbers, any schemes concocted by critics were as much reactions to existing production as they were pre-scriptions for future production. But proletarian novelists for the most part had some sort of sympathetic relationship with the CP; especially during the Third Period, many considered themselves revolutionaries. Moreover, in spite of a certain amount of fussing and fuming, the novelists generally assumed that the Communist movement was their "left"—that is, a politi-cal force that would urge them toward revolutionary, as opposed to liberal or reformist, practice. Certain writers, we shall see, did in fact stake out positions on some issues that were more left than the line of the party. But on the whole the CP *did* function as the writers' ideological leadership, both inspiring them with a sense of revolutionary possibility and setting the limits within which they could imagine this possibility. Our examina-

1. Robert Cantwell to James T. Farrell, June 1, 1934, Cantwell Papers, U of Oregon Library.

tion of literary proletarianism should therefore assign an important role to what the Communist movement said and did about both politics and literature. It is only when we understand the precise nature of the prescriptions said to have been imposed upon proletarian writers, after all, that we may begin to estimate the extent to which these prescriptions shaped or did not shape literary practice.

In chapters 3 and 4 I shall examine in detail two closely related debates that preoccupied the literary proletarians—that over the definition of proletarian literature and that over the issue of propaganda or "leftism." The focus of both chapters will be the *substance* of various positions set forth by Marxist critics regarding questions of content and form in proletarian fiction. But since until very recently the model of a philistine, coercive, and antimodernist party has routinely been invoked in treatments of the relationship between writers and the organized left, it is necessary first to address in a more general way the question of influences on American proletarian writers. Accordingly, I shall begin by characterizing the dynamics of the interactions between American critics and novelists. I shall then analyze the usable past that the literary proletarians devised for themselves in American and Anglo-European literary traditions, both Marxist and non-Marxist. Finally, I shall set forth certain features of the relationship of U.S. literary radicalism to the Soviet experience. The "literature of a class/literature of a party" argument assumes that the imperatives of Soviet policy dictated the development of American literary proletarianism and that the Americans pretty much followed lockstep in the tracks of the Russians. In the final part of this chapter I shall offer a broad assessment of the outlines of the U.S./USSR relationship that differs from the standard narrative on some important points.

Marxist Critics and Proletarian Novelists

The relationship between actual proletarian novels and the body of contemporaneous theorizing about proletarian literature is complex and variegated; no summary of writers' attitudes toward critics can purport to account for features of proletarian fiction in general, much less of specific texts. Nonetheless, a sampling of various proletarian writers' comments about Marxist critics and Marxist criticism, as well as of the critics' remarks about their own enterprise, can serve as a starting point for an investigation into the political and historical context out of which proletarian literature emerged.

On the one hand, it is clear that quite a few writers experienced a degree of alienation from the official arbiters of Marxist theory, who as a group possessed a cultural style often quite different from their own. The most influential Third-Period Marxist critics who were clustered around the *New Masses* and the *Partisan Review*—Michael Gold, Joseph Freeman, Joshua Kunitz, Alan Calmer, Edwin Seaver, Edwin Berry Burgum, Granville Hicks, Philip Rahv, Wallace Phelps, Walt Carmon, Obed Brooks, Isidor Schneider—hardly represented a cross-section of the participants in 1930s literary radicalism. Preponderantly Jewish and from middle-class or at least educated backgrounds, these critics constituted a much more homogeneous grouping than did the creative writers, who not only came from all parts of the United States but also included in their ranks more worker-writers, women, and blacks. Moreover, most of the New York critics were primarily that—critics. Schneider and Freeman, it is true, had garnered substantial reputations for themselves as poets in the 1920s and continued to write poetry, fiction, and autobiography throughout the 1930s; Seaver wrote two novels; Gold authored the landmark proletarian novel *Jews Without Money* and a variety of poems and "mass-chants" in addition to his many journalistic and critical pieces for the *Daily Worker* and the *New Masses*. But several of the most influential New York critics had little direct experience with the actual production of proletarian literature. The writers could therefore with some justification view the critics as urban intellectuals engaged in weaving theoretical webs possessing limited relevance to literary practice.

Practicing proletarian novelists thus tended to view either individual Marxist critics or the group as a whole with a certain degree of skepticism. Conroy, who was to work briefly—and disastrously—with Rahv and Phelps as coeditors of the short-lived merger of *Partisan Review and Anvil* in 1936, expressed considerable hostility to what he saw as the arrogance and elitism of the *Partisan Review;* he sarcastically referred to its sharp-tongued young editors as the "irrepressible Bobbsey twins of leftist literature." In a 1934 *New Masses* symposium on novelists' reactions to Marxist critics, Erskine Caldwell, whose *Kneel to the Rising Sun* had attracted favorable reviews in the left press, dismissed the commentary he had received from Marxist critics as "90 percent soap suds." Edward Dahlberg, author of *Bottom Dogs*, complained that Granville Hicks, then the literary editor of the *New Masses*, "dislikes good writing" and that "the nuances and pigments of prose are, if not offensive to him, altogether baroque." Josephine Herbst, whose feelings seem to have been bruised by Hicks's reaction to her *The Executioner Waits*, in return lambasted the discussion of historical fiction in his "Revolution and the Novel" *New Masses* series. Farrell too lashed out at Hicks in resentment at the "grades" that, he charged, Hicks handed out to proletarian writers. Claiming that he himself had received a B+, Farrell in 1936 circulated a bitterly satiric set of "strike demands" to Cantwell and other literary leftists in which he lampooned "Professor" Hicks as the "Holy Ghost of Contemporary Literature" and demanded "public penance by Mr. Hicks for his literary sins." The literary editor of the *New Masses*, it seems, aroused the hackles of quite a few practicing writers.[2]

On the other hand, as a group proletarian writers were neither hostile nor indifferent to the opinions of Marxist critics. Nor can it be argued that the writers embraced substantially different views of the goals of proletar-

---

2. Jack Conroy, "The Literary Underworld of the Thirties," in Jack Salzman and David Ray, eds., *The Jack Conroy Reader* (New York: Burt Franklin, 1979), p. 163; Caldwell, Dahlberg, and Herbst, "Author's Field Day," *NM* 12 (July 3, 1934): 27–32 (all "Author's Field Day" reference from this issue); Farrell to Cantwell, January 29, 1936, "An Open Letter to Whom It May Concern," "Strike Bulletin," Cantwell Papers. Conroy refers to the "ideological tempests raging in the New York coffee pots" (p. 153) and details the *Partisan Review and Anvil* relationship (pp. 151–64). Phelps disliked Conroy as much as Conroy disliked him, referring to Conroy as "too populist and anti-intellectual" to be an effective coeditor (*A Partisan View: Five Decades of Literary Life* [New York: Stein and Day, 1983], p. 38). Herbst wrote to Hicks about what she felt was his hypercritical attitude toward the efforts of fledgling proletarian writers. See Herbst to Hicks, July 14 (n.d.), Box 27, Hicks Papers, Arents Library, Syracuse U. Herbst's reaction to Hicks's review of *The Executioner Waits* is somewhat unaccountable, since the review was preponderantly favorable. The Farrell document is signed "Jonathan Titelson Fogarty, Chairman," and "Abraham Lefkowitz O'Halloran, Secy." Farrell had used the O'Halloran pseudonym in a letter of November 27, 1934, circulated to Joshua Kunitz and other *New Masses* editors. See Farrell to Kunitz, Kunitz Papers, Butler Library, Columbia U. Farrell's correspondence with Cantwell reveals his growing alienation from the CP. See Farrell to Cantwell, February 7, 1934, April 30, 1934, June 20, 1934, and January 29, 1936, Cantwell Papers. For a clear definition of the position he had arrived at by the midthirties, see Farrell's *A Note on Literary Criticism* (New York: Vanguard, 1936).

ian literature. Farrell, to be sure, remained largely hostile to the CP critics and, as we have seen, by the mid-thirties had become a confirmed anti-Stalinist, extremely critical of the entire project of proletarian literature. But Herbst, despite a general prickliness of personality as well as a legitimate anger at her exclusion from the political and literary conferences of the "head-boys," offered acerbic criticisms that, as Elinor Langer puts it, "emerged from and were directed toward the inside" of the CP-led movement. Conroy was for the most part friendly to the leftist critics and made careful distinctions among them, praising Gold for "re-affirming that faith in proletarian writers which he held steadfastly when proletarian literature was a laughing stock for all the Olympian critics who have at least been forced to recognize its existence." Caldwell wrote to Freeman about his difficulties in conveying the "revolution" taking place among "whites and blacks in Georgia" and commented self-critically, "I may never reach the status of a revolutionary writer. If that is the case, the fault is mine." Dahlberg conceded that his dislike of Hicks did not extend to all Marxist critics; Kunitz, the *New Masses'* principal commentator on Soviet literature, had, in Dahlberg's view, "genuine warmth and sympathy with the problems of the revolutionary writer."[3]

Indeed, some of the writers asked the critics to be still more rigorous in their political criticisms. Cantwell defended Marxist criticism against its detractors. When Malcolm Cowley wrote a piece in the *New Republic* denigrating Marxist criticism for what he saw as its banal reductiveness, Cantwell angrily responded, "As a characterization of a known body of Marxian criticism, your Note is partial, marginal, incorrect, and misleading. Misleading above all, since you make the method so uninspiring." Yet Cantwell had criticisms of his own, complaining that Hicks and other left-wing reviewers of *The Land of Plenty* had not evaluated the ending of his

---

3. Herbst cited in David Madden, "Introduction" to *Proletarian Writers of the Thirties* (Carbondale and Edwardsville: Southern Illinois UP, 1968), p. xxi; Elinor Langer, *Josephine Herbst* (Boston and Toronto: Little, Brown, 1983), p. 204; Conroy, "Author's Field Day," 27; Caldwell to Freeman, April 11, 1933, Freeman Papers, Butler Library, Columbia U; Dahlberg, "Author's Field Day," 28. In 1937 Herbst wrote to Hicks that the *Partisan Review* group "glorify what they call 'intellectual leadership.' We on the other hand as manifested by our papers, are inclined to be too anti-intellectual" (Herbst to Hicks, September 21, 1937, Box 27, Hicks Papers). Herbst was critical of the *New Masses* group, but her identification with them at this point is apparent.

novel in accordance with sufficiently stringent political standards. He had written the novel as "a work of propaganda," he declared; he expected it to be assessed as such. Myra Page, whose *Gathering Storm: A Story of Life in the Black Belt* had been given short shrift in the *Daily Worker* and virtually ignored in other leftist organs, called upon Marxist critics to deepen their commitment to politicized criticism. "Many of our critics have freed themselves only in part from the old bourgeois methods and approach in which they've been schooled," she remarked. "'Art is a Weapon,' they repeat, but in practice, forget." The poet Robert Gessner complained that Marxist critics reviewing his work had made "aesthetic" comments concerned "solely with image and diction." He asked, "What kind of criticism should a revolutionary writer expect from a revolutionary magazine? His work should be given the closest scrutiny from the point of view of Marxism-Leninism as to its value for the proletariat in formulating and intensifying their movement toward revolution." Left-wing writers might cavil about the practice of particular critics, but this did not mean that they felt out of sympathy with the broader goal of establishing a political framework for guiding and assessing proletarian literature. Indeed, some of them sought a sharper definition of this framework.[4]

Moreover, the critics themselves were acutely aware that the Marxist literary commentary they were practicing was exploratory. Particularly in their correspondence with one another, they admitted to considerable insecurity and lamented the theoretical void in which they felt themselves to be working. For example, in 1930 Walt Carmon, then literary editor of

4. Cantwell, "Author's Field Day," 27; Cantwell to Cowley, n.d., Cowley Papers, Newberry Library; Page, "Author's Field Day," 31–32; Gessner, "Author's Field Day," 29–30. Page never complained in public of her treatment by critics, but she wrote Hicks that "[f]or writers . . . to be held up repeatedly as horrible examples of what they *didn't* do, is rather tough going. Not that we don't have to learn to take it, and profit thereby. But some positive criticism also has its value. As you no doubt know, it seems a peculiarly strong trait in writers and artists . . . that they require some sort of appreciative help." Page's suggestion, in a letter of April 27, 1934, that Hicks organize a discussion on " 'What Revolutionary Writers Expect from Marxist Criticism,' or some such title" may have been the inspiration of the "Author's Field Day" symposium published two months later. See Page to Hicks, Box 48, Hicks Papers. Meridel Le Sueur also testified to the positive influence of the party on her artistic production, noting that without the CP she "wouldn't have developed as a writer" (cited in Linda Ray Pratt, "Woman Writer in the CP: The Case of Meridel Le Sueur," *Women's Studies* 14, no. 3 [1988]: 255).

the *New Masses*, wrote to Kunitz in Moscow urgently requesting an essay on Marxist criticism. "If anything is necessary that type of thing is," he declared. "Much more important than anything we can think of." He soon followed this request with a call for an article "summarizing Plekhanov's views on literature from a Marxian viewpoint to give us a sort of guiding line for our own work. You must recall that there isn't a single word of it in the English language as yet and this would have a decided value." Hicks, who signaled his assumption of the literary editorship of the *New Masses* in January 1934 with an essay entitled "The Crisis in American Criticism," wrote to Kunitz the preceding fall about his sense of the task confronting him. "I believe that Marxist critics have been a little too timid," he stated. "They have been so afraid of making mistakes that they have kept their silence on fundamental issues. For myself, though I should like to avoid the ordeal of heresy-mongering, I prefer to be wrong rather than to be timid." Clearly even the "Professor Hicks" who was to receive so thorough a drubbing—from writers of his own time as well as subsequent commentators on the 1930s—recognized that his aggressive attempts to outline the rudiments of leftist literary commentary would at times result in flawed or erroneous judgments. Burgum—an NYU English professor who was to retain his commitment to Marxist criticism and the CPUSA long after Hicks, Cowley, Brooks, and others had left the movement—re-flected to Kenneth Burke on the sketchy achievements of Marxist criticism midway through the decade. "[I doubt whether the Marxist critic], writing in America in the year 1936," Burgum mused, "is really capable of turn-ing out valid Marxian criticism, free from the adulteration of absolutist or of pragmatic survivals." Although the "commissars" of leftist criticism have been criticized for dogmatism and arrogance, they were in fact quite ready to acknowledge that not merely proletarian literature but American Marxist criticism was in its infancy.[5]

Finally, the core group of New York-based critics, while influential, hardly exercised a monopoly over Marxist literary criticism in the 1930s. As David Peck has remarked in his study of the influence of the *New Masses* upon 1930s Marxist criticism, at least half of the novelists publish-

---

5. Carmon to Kunitz, October 3, 1930, and November 5, 1930, Kunitz Papers; Hicks to Kunitz, October 31, 1933, Kunitz Papers; Burgum to Kenneth Burke, February 20, 1936, Schneider Papers, Butler Library, Columbia U.

ing works of proletarian fiction before 1935 were affiliated with the *New Masses* in some way or another, usually as book reviewers. Since much of the theorizing about proletarian literature in effect took place in the ad hoc arena of the book review, quite a few proletarian novelists actually had—and took—the opportunity to join the debate over their craft. Moreover, almost all the participants in the various John Reed Clubs that sprang up around the country between 1932 and 1934 were aspiring writers. The manifestoes about proletarian literature issued in literary organs like *Left Front* (Chicago), *Left* (Davenport, Iowa), *Leftward* (Boston), *Partisan* (West Coast), and *New Force* (Detroit) thus articulated the sentiments of practicing (if not widely published) writers, and not just of self-appointed critical arbiters in the Northeast. Even writers who did not participate in Reed Club activity because of either geography or gender—the clubs were preponderantly located in large cities and consisted almost exclusively of men—maintained some sort of tie with the literary organs of the movement. Fielding Burke never contributed to the *New Masses*, but she wrote to *International Literature* describing her conscious intentions as a revolutionary writer, remarking that she envisioned her novel *Call Home the Heart* as contributing to "breaking down intolerance . . . to Communism." The Minnesota papermill worker and poet Joseph Kalar wrote to his friend and fellow-writer Warren Huddlestone of the eagerness with which he waited every month for his issues of the *Anvil*, the *Partisan Review*, *International Literature*, and of course the *New Masses*. Kalar registered strong reactions to various debates contained in these organs and even ventured to write a couple of short critical pieces about proletarian literature for the *New Masses*.[6]

Even if some radical writers maintained a certain ironic distance from

6. David Peck, "The Development of an American Marxist Literary Criticism: The Monthly *New Masses*," Ph.D. Thesis, Temple U, 1968, p. 111; Fielding Burke, "Letters from Writers," *International Literature* (hereinafter *IL*) 2 (1933): 129; Joseph Kalar, *Joseph A. Kalar, Poet of Protest: An Anthology*, ed. Richard G. Kalar (Minneapolis: RGK Publications, 1985), pp. 147–232 (letters 1932–36). See also Peck's " 'The Tradition of Revolutionary American Literature': The Monthly *New Masses*, 1926–1933" (*Science and Society* 42 [Winter 1978–79]: 385–409), where he argues that the pre-1930 editorial policies of the *New Masses* played a key role in directing "both the creative and critical forms" of 1930s American literature. One student of the John Reed Clubs estimates that "[p]erhaps only 25% of the JRC members were simultaneously CP members" (Laurie Ann Alexandre, "The John Reed Clubs: A Historical Reclamation of the Role of Revolutionary Writers in the Depression," M.A. Thesis, California State U—Northridge, 1977, p. 106).

the debates of the literary left, and others made only infrequent and fragmentary contributions, most were acquainted with the central issues being discussed and can be said to have participated in a common political and literary culture. While the secondary scholarship on the 1930s routinely portrays Marxist critics as overbearing and authoritarian, the actual comments of writers at the time indicate that very few of them dismissed out of hand the leftist critics' attempt to formulate theoretical categories for analyzing and evaluating proletarian literature. A number of writers participated on some level in this activity; according to Peck, even those who did not "were obviously influenced by the campaign for proletarian literature conducted within the magazine."[7]

As we attend to the often hortatory statements about proletarian literature issued through the various organs of the Communist-led cultural movement, we should bear in mind the political situation in which these statements occurred. When Hicks extended a general invitation to writers to participate in book reviewing, he offered a telling characterization of what he considered to be their points of unity. "We constitute a diverse group," he declared. "And yet any one of us can speak with confidence of the group's point of view. Every one of us believes that the capitalist system must be destroyed by the power of the proletariat, in alliance with the exploited farmers, the ruined middle class and the aroused intellectual and professional class. . . . These convictions and this determination are fundamental, the very basis of the attitudes and judgments that our reviews will express."[8] Few contemporary scholars share the premises that united leftist writers and critics of the Depression years. It is difficult for many of us to envision a situation in which large numbers of critics and writers would be of one mind about the politics of the larger "ought" governing their common enterprise; to some present-day critics, Hicks's stipulation may sound authoritarian and repressive. But all critical pronouncements contain an "ought" of some kind or another. As we attempt to reconstruct the context within which proletarian literature was produced, we should remember that critics could assume a fairly high level of political agreement with the writers whose texts they were evaluating.

The question is, finally, not whether the critics were attempting to influ-

---

7. Peck, "The Development of an American Marxist Criticism," p. 111.

8. Hicks, "An Open Letter to *New Masses* Reviewers," rpt. in *Granville Hicks in the New Masses*, ed. Jack Allan Robbins (Port Washington, NY: Kennikat P, 1974), p. 15.

ence what the novelists were writing; clearly this was true. The question is whether on the whole this influence can be said to have been a good thing. The Rahv of 1939 who bemoaned the literature of a party masquerading as the literature of a class gives us the answer that has shaped almost all discussion of this issue. But we should recall that the Rahv of 1934 remarked of the emerging literary scene, "The new . . . novels coming off the press month after month, the new literary magazines springing up all over the country—all these are signs of a promise fulfilled. They prove the fusion of theory and practice in American revolutionary literature." There is no reason to assume in advance that this "fusion of theory and practice" was harmful rather than beneficial. Indeed, as Hicks proposed, the continual evaluation of proletarian literature according to the yardstick of Marxist criticism may have "exert[ed] a positive, dynamic influence on the creation of an informed, sensitive body of readers."[9]

American Literary Proletarianism and Modernism

Commentators adhering to the position that the 1930s Marxist critics set forth formulaic prescriptions often make the claim that these critics—particularly those grouped around the New Masses—were scornful of inherited literary traditions and, in particular, suspicious of contemporaneous modernism. These critics were presumably adherents of a crude Proletkult doctrine which held that politics was all, technique nothing: revolutionary literature would emerge from the crucible of the factory, and lessons from the bourgeois masters would simply taint the articulation of pure proletarian consciousness. In particular, it is charged, writers were cut off from the most exciting and productive developments in contemporary literature and consigned to a sterile, banal, and—ironically—conservative realism.

As we shall see in Part II, the binary opposition implied here—bad realism versus good experimentalism—is, to say the least, politically loaded. Whether or not realism can be successfully harnessed to left-wing poli-

9. Rahv, "The Novelist as Partisan," PR 1 (April–May 1934): 50; Hicks, "The Development of Marxist Criticism," American Writers Congress, ed. Henry Hart (New York: International, 1935) (hereinafter AWC), p. 90.

tics is not an issue that can be resolved by resort to a priori assumptions about politics and form. What I want to note here, however, is that the 1930s literary radicals' own views on this question were far from simple or predictable. The proletarians did often express sympathy with representational strategies that they described as "realistic." Moreover, they frequently evinced considerable distaste for the figures who have subsequently come to be associated with high modernism. At times this preference for a straightforward and easily communicated realism entailed an explicit repudiation of literary experimentalism in all its forms. Ralph Cheney, a proponent of the simple styles of Wobbly poetry, condemned "crude free verse" on the grounds that "workers like rhyme and rhythm, emotional appeal, and drama." Conroy, in his address to the 1935 Writers Congress, denigrated the notion that the proletarian writer should "evolve some new and distinctive technique. . . . The effect of this desperate striving for novelty of phrase and imagery is often that of achieving a semi-private terminology almost unintelligible to the masses, and a lamentable dullness in the narrative the innovator has set out to enliven and enrich." Particularly among commentators committed to reaching working-class audiences with proletarian literature, there was voiced at times a marked skepticism about the importance—indeed, the desirability—of voicing a radical political outlook by means of unfamiliar or formally challenging literary techniques.[10]

As proletarian literature started to come into its own, or at least to be talked about as a real possibility, literary leftists frequently stressed its affinities with early twentieth-century writers who could loosely be grouped as realistic or naturalistic rather than with writers associated with symbolism or stream-of-consciousness narrative. In 1925 V. F. Calverton, an enthusiast for proletarian literature in the days before his deeply hostile split with the Communist left, declared that proletarianism and contemporary realism were virtually identical: the works of Masters, O'Neill, Dreiser, Lewis, and Cather, he argued, signaled the "birth of a literature which represents the proletarian concept." Martin Russak, a worker-writer from the Paterson, New Jersey, textile mills, stated that Jack London's radical naturalistic novel The Iron Heel was "the first great classic of America's

10. Ralph Cheney, "Letter," NM 5 (February 1930): 2; Conroy, "The Worker as Writer," AWC, p. 83.

proletarian literature." Gold, who in a famous phrase denounced Proust as the "master masturbator of the middle class," proclaimed, "I am through . . . with the form-searchers. . . . [T]o hold its own, literature will have to become simple again, realistic and socially valuable. . . . New forms without a new content seem as worthless to me as walnut shells whose meat the little bugs have gnawed away." In the pages of the *New Masses*, Upton Sinclair and Theodore Dreiser were spoken of with respect, even though the prewar socialist writers were generally seen as genteel and lacking in revolutionary verve.[11]

The proletarians thus saw no contradiction between coupling the terms "realistic" and "socially valuable" and declaring that the project in which they were engaged constituted a revolutionary new direction in American letters. The manifestoes of the John Reed Clubs stressed formal inventiveness as a necessary companion to revolutionary politics. *The Left* carried on its masthead the description "A Quarterly Review of Radical and Experimental Art"; its first issue proclaimed that "*The Left* believes that new forms and techniques must be hammered out to express the fresh substance, the faster tempos and rhythms of the new world order and encourage that experimentation." Dos Passos's innovative novels *The Forty-Second Parallel* and *Nineteen Nineteen* received more fervent commendation than any other novels of the Third Period. Hicks, in *The Great Tradition*, considered Dos Passos to have "shown the way" for proletarian literature in the future. The experimental technique of William Rollins's *The Shadow Before*—which included huge typography to convey the thump of factory machinery, excerpts from newspaper accounts of the Gastonia trial, and other unconventional novelistic devices—was enthusiastically greeted by leftist commentators. Clara Weatherwax's prize-winning *Marching! Marching!*, a novel notable for its admixture of formal experimental-

---

11. V. F. Calverton, *The Newer Spirit: A Sociological Criticism of Literature* (New York: Boni and Liveright, 1925), p. 142; Martin Russak, "Jack London: America's First Proletarian Writer," *NM* 4 (January 1929): 13; Gold, "Proletarian Realism," *NM* 6 (September 1930): 5. In November 1928 the *New Masses* featured Sinclair on its cover and contained laudatory appreciations by Gold, Scott Nearing, and Floyd Dell. For more on the aura of gentility surrounding earlier socialist fiction, see Fay M. Blake, *The Strike in the American Novel* (Metuchen, NJ: Scarecrow P, 1972), pp. 91–93. For more on Gold's relation to Dreiser, see Kenneth William Payne, "Naturalism and the Proletarians: The Case of Michael Gold," *Anglo-American Studies* 3 (April 1983): 21–37.

ism with party politics—Newton Arvin caustically described it as "compounded of a little unadulterated Virginia Woolf with a good deal of early Upton Sinclair and large doses of the old *Daily Worker*"—was praised in the *New Masses* by Emjo Basshe for its revolutionary emergy and its daring formal innovations. "The workers won't have any trouble understanding it," opined Basshe. "And if they do stumble here and there, they won't mind learning because this is of them and for them." Weatherwax thematized her enthusiasm for artistic experimentation by presenting as a character in the novel a composer/pianist who enraptures his working-class audience with discordant chords played by the elbows. As in Albert Halper's *The Foundry*—which also features a modernist composer exciting a proletarian audience—the impulse to rebel against the social order is aligned with the impulse to transgress inherited forms. The charge that the majority of American literary proletarians repudiated literary innovation simply does not stand up under the evidence. The concept of "realism" guiding most literary radicals' sense of their enterprise may not have been rigorously defined. But it seems not to have precluded, but instead to have fostered, experimentation of various kinds.[12]

Nor does the charge hold up that during the Third Period the *New Masses* critics and those around the *Partisan Review* were divided into two camps, the former issuing crude slogans about literature as weaponry in the class war while the latter struggled to adhere to standards of literary excellence and to direct attention to the stylistic achievements of bourgeois writers. This dichotomy has become a staple of much critical commentary on the decade. Phelps argued for such a division as early as 1934: anticipating arguments he was to make in a more hostile vein many

12. "Editorial: Left!" *Left* 1 (Spring 1931): 3; Hicks, *The Great Tradition: An Interpretation of American Literature since the Civil War* (New York: Macmillan, 1933), p. 292; Mary Heaton Vorse, review of *The Shadow Before*, NM 11 (April 17, 1934): 6; Newton Arvin to Robert Gorham Davis, March 1, 1936, Davis Papers, Butler Library, Columbia U; Emjo Basshe, "Singing Workers," NM 18 (January 7, 1936): 24. Writers routinely associated with "Stalinist" politics were often closely in touch with contemporaneous developments in the arts: Weatherwax's husband was a modernist composer, while Freeman was married to Charmion Von Wiegand, an abstract expressionist painter. Louis Aragon, the Surrealist poet turned Communist, was frequently cited as a model for the new revolutionary literature and was an honored speaker at the 1935 Writers Congress. See Aragon, "From Dada to Red Front," *AWC*, pp. 33–38.

years later as William Phillips, he declared that the "strain and exigencies of pioneering" had kept the older generation of *New Masses* critics from "assimilating the literary spirit of the twenties." By contrast, he noted, the younger writers around the Reed Clubs were heirs to a dual legacy and felt obliged to "tie these threads, to use whatever heritage is at our disposal for our revolutionary tasks." James Gilbert, following Phelps's cue, argues that the *New Masses* group actively discouraged the debates over cultural radicalism that the *Partisan Review* group wished to foster. Alan Wald concludes that Rahv and Phelps engaged in a "search for a truly Marxist aesthetic . . . throughout the 1930s," whereas the Communist International— and its American adherents—treated "slogans" and "Stalinist shibboleths" as "sufficient guides for revolutionary writers and critics." Harvey Teres claims that Phelps's and Rahv's receptivity to T. S. Eliot's conception of sensibility enabled them to formulate a "subtle critique of the orthodox Marxist criticism" proposed by the Stalinists.[13]

As we shall see in chapter 4, the most consistent attack on "leftism"— which was routinely associated with a heavy-handed documentary realism, among other things—did indeed emanate principally from the *Partisan Review* group. But critics did not align themselves neatly in actual debates. In the first place, up to 1936 the *Partisan Review* group were not so unequivocally wedded to the view that any literary style could be taken over and used for radical purposes as they later claimed to have been. Phelps charged that in *Ulysses* Joyce had "detached his characters from significant social patterns." Joyce's method, Phelps concluded, was limited by its subjectivism and "could hardly be used to present social conflict or human conflict against a background of class struggle." Rahv argued that writers should be open to learning from the techniques developed by nonradical contemporaries such as Hemingway, from whom, he claimed, "the danger of ideological inoculation . . . is very small . . . and the bene-

13. Wallace Phelps, "Three Generations," PR 1, 4 (Sept.–Oct. 1934): 51. James Burkhart Gilbert, *Writers and Partisans: A History of Literary Radicalism in America* (New York, London, Sydney: John Wiley and Sons, 1968), pp. 110–17; Alan Wald, *The New York Intellectuals: The Rise and Decline of the Anti-Stalinist Left from the 1930s to the 1980s* (Chapel Hill and London: U of North Carolina P, 1987), p. 79; Harvey Teres, "Remaking Marxist Criticism: *Partisan Review*'s Eliotic Leftism, 1934–1936," *American Literature* 64 (March 1992): 129. See also Giordano De Biasio, *La frontiera proletaria: Marxismo, intellettuali e letteratura in America (1926–1936)* (Longo, 1982).

fits many." Yet he was frequently guilty of exactly the intolerance toward modernist decadence of which he was later to accuse the "Stalinists." For example, he invoked an epistemology that was if anything reductively materialist when he dismissed Faulkner's style: "The language becomes a function of the author's metaphysics, of spiritual relations and of reverie . . . . [I]t no longer sticks to the object, but to the author's idea of the object." He concluded that Eliot, who had fallen into the "swamp of mysticism and scholasticism," must be "discounted as a positive force in literature. His place is definitely with the retarders of the revolutionary urge towards the creation of a new *human* humanity." In a formulation one might be more tempted to attribute to Gold, Rahv asserted that the technical innovations in contemporaneous bourgeois writing amounted to "[e]ndless, ideologically barren experimentation and superficial cleverness, esthetic and intellectual dandyism without a breath of life." The Rahv who was to emerge as the apostle of alienated modernism in the reorganized *Partisan Review* was, during the era of literary proletarianism, hardly its unequivocal advocate.[14]

Conversely, the principal *New Masses* critics were nowhere near as antagonistic to contemporaneous modernism as has often been supposed. Gold, who clearly detested what he saw as the inaccessibility and mandarin elitism of much contemporary writing, nonetheless agreed with Rahv that proletarian writers had lessons to learn from modernists like Hemingway. Gold valued William Carlos Williams for "reflect[ing] as in a faithful mirror the raw powerful force of the unorganized American worker, and the horrors of the slum life he leads." Moreover, he held that "proletarian realism" was an effect, not a form. "Within this living world of proletarian literature there are many living forms," he declared. "It is dogmatic to seize upon any single literary form, and erect it into a pattern for all proletarian literature." James Bloom argues that Gold was in fact "an early advocate of allying Marxism and modernism." Freeman—who along with Gold has been dismissed as a "party hatchetm[an]"—considered *Ulysses* "a marvelous mirror of the decay of capitalist civilization." He observed,

14. Wallace Phelps, "The Methods of Joyce," *NM* 10 (February 20, 1934): 26; Rahv, review of Ernest Hemingway, *Winner Take Nothing*, *PR* 1 (February–March 1934): 59; Rahv, review of William Faulkner, *Absalom, Absalom!*, *NM* 21 (November 4, 1936): 20; Rahv, "T. S. Eliot," *Fantasy* (Winter 1932), 19; Rahv, "Marxist Criticism and Henry Hazlitt," *IL* (June 1934), 115.

"[It] is a great book, and the man who wrote it is a genius." Hicks too—upon close examination of what he actually wrote, as opposed to what is *said* about what he wrote—emerges as something other than an antimodernist dogmatist. In his 1934 "Revolution and the Novel" series for the *New Masses*, Hicks praised Proust for the depth of his characterizations and the "extraordinarily full and detailed picture of a certain society." Moreover, adopting the position that form is essentially free of ideological implication, he urged the proletarian novelist to feel free to experiment with all available novelistic forms. "I have no desire to urge upon authors one method as opposed to others," he declared. "All I want is to indicate the variety of methods in order that novelists may be more acutely conscious of the possibilities offered to them." [15]

Indeed, as James Murphy points out, the organs most closely identified with the Communist party—the *New Masses* and, especially, the *Daily Worker*—were quite hospitable to literary innovations of various kinds. The *Daily Worker* reviewer of Rollins's highly experimental *The Shadow Before*, for example, observed that

> Rollins has drawn upon the works of Dos Passos and Joyce for his form. In doing so, . . . he has answered for all revolutionary writers the problem that has concerned them so, what can we take and what must we leave untouched in decadent literature. . . . He has taken those positive elements from decadence that allow him to disclose the tensions, complexities, rhythms and neuroses of modern life.

When Brecht's *The Mother* was staged by the Theatre Union, some Communist critics evinced quite a sophisticated understanding of Brecht's technique. Moissaye Olgin—a founding member of the CPUSA and editor of the Yiddish daily *Freiheit*—noted that the production had in fact been too conventionally realistic: "The realism of the Theatre Union often violated the special realism required by Brecht's conception and this jeop-

15. Gold, "American Intellectuals and Communism," *Daily Worker* (hereinafter *DW*) (October 12, 1923), 5; Gold, "Proletarian Realism," 5; James D. Bloom, *Left Letters: The Culture Wars of Mike Gold and Joseph Freeman* (New York: Columbia UP, 1992), p. 113; Jonathan Wilson, "On Radical Writing in the 1930s," *Literary Review* 7 (Fall 1983): 41; Freeman, *An American Testament: A Narrative of Rebels and Romantics* (New York: Farrar and Rinehart, 1936), p. 636; Hicks, "The Crisis in American Criticism," in Robbins, p. 13; "Revolution and the Novel," in Robbins, p. 52.

ardized artistic unity." Stanley Burnshaw, in his *New Masses* review of the play, concluded that both the "realistic play" and the "agit-prop play" can be "powerful revolutionary drama. One form does not exclude the other." Murphy concludes, "At no time in the thirties was there a campaign against 'decadence' or 'formalism' in the American movement, and some of the most highly praised proletarian [writers] employed modernist technique." [16]

It would seem that, at least up to 1936, whatever differences over literary matters distinguished the *Partisan Review* group from the *New Masses* group were not so definitive as to drive them into separate camps. Allegiances were in fact mixed and various. Obed Brooks described himself as influenced by Trotskyists and close to the *Partisan Review* group before he finally joined the party in 1937. He was an advocate of modernism, favorably comparing Proust and Joyce with Huxley and Dreiser and declaring that the former had "given [him] new emphases, new connections in experience, new sensitivity." Yet during these years Brooks was also writing frequent reviews for the *New Masses* and cementing what would be a lifelong friendship with Hicks, with whom he planned a treatise on proletarian literature. Alan Calmer, former president of the National John Reed Clubs, in 1936 issued in the *Saturday Review* a vituperative attack on proletarian literature, "Portrait of the Artist as a Proletarian," in which he echoed Phelps's earlier claim that there was a generational divide between Gold and Freeman and the younger proletarian writers. But Calmer also wrote to Hicks disavowing any association with what he called the "anti-Party position" of Rahv and Phelps. Even though Calmer was an editor of the *Partisan Review*, he published most of his polemical criticisms of "leftism" in the *New Masses* and continued to edit and publish for International Publishers

16. Robert Adler, " 'The Shadow Before' Is Stirring Novel of Textile Mill Workers," *DW* (April 21, 1934), 7; Moissaye Olgin, "Mother: The Theatre Union's New Play," *DW* (November 22, 1935), 5; Stanley Burnshaw, review of Bertolt Brecht and Hans Eissler, *The Mother*, NM 17 (December 3, 1935): 28; James Murphy, *The Proletarian Moment: The Controversy over Leftism in Literature* (Urbana and Chicago: U of Illinois P, 1991), p. 139. I am indebted to Murphy for pointing out the two *DW* reviews cited here. For the view that an American variant on the Brecht-Lukács debate was embodied in the controversy between the *New Masses* and James T. Farrell over *A Note on Literary Criticism*, see Alan M. Wald, *The Revolutionary Imagination: The Poetry and Politics of John Wheelwright and Sherry Mangan* (Chapel Hill and London: U of North Carolina P, 1983), p. 14.

up to the end of the decade. It is thus a mistake to read the split between Stalinists and Trotskyists back into Third-Period theoretical debates or to argue that the Trotskyists-to-be were all along engaged in running battles with Stalinist philistinism. It was primarily debates over the direction of the revolutionary movement and the nature of the Soviet Union, and only secondarily debates over matters of aesthetics, that produced the decisive divisions in the literary left.[17]

In short, much Depression-era literary radicalism was intimately involved in the project of "mak[ing] it new." The conflation of "modernism" with the high modernism of Eliot, Joyce, and Pound—a definition of literary-historical categories that occurred only under the postwar hegemony of Trilling, Rahv, and other anti-Stalinists—can be argued only at the risk of fundamentally distorting the intentions and perspectives of those who were actually engaged in literary production during the proletarian period. The literary proletarians were *part* of modernism. This does not mean that, as Marcus Klein has suggested, proletarianism was simply "a literary rebellion within a literary revolution, to which it was loyal." The political differences dividing the proletarians from their bourgeois experimentalist contemporaries were too strong to admit such an assimilationist maneuver. But it does mean that the literary proletarians, creative writers and critics alike, saw themselves as "exploit[ing] a new and vivifying experiential basis for art." As Eva Goldbeck wrote in 1935, "The class-struggle opens up a new world, factually and psychologically: that is why it is a great literary theme. The bourgeois writer has to criticize and conserve;

17. Brooks to Hicks, April 9, 1934, Box 16, Hicks Papers; Calmer, "Portrait of the Artist as a Proletarian," SRL 16 (July 31, 1937): 3–4, 14; Calmer to Hicks, n.d., Box 11, Hicks Papers. In his youth Calmer was a student of V. F. Calverton in the Baltimore public schools; he served on the editorial board of the Modern Monthly in 1927–28 (Leonard Wilcox, V. F. Calverton: Radical in the American Grain [Philadelphia: Temple UP, 1992], p. 150). Calmer apparently severed his ties with both the New Masses and the Partisan Review in the latter part of the decade. In the letter cited—which, because it makes reference to his SRL piece, as well as to the PR split with the CP, must be dated in 1937 or later—Calmer noted that even though political loyalties prevented him from joining the Trotskyists, he refused henceforth to write for the New Masses. He had, he declared, "nothing but the greatest contempt for the kind of thinking, and often writing, that appears in the New Masses." Calmer kept some relation with the party, however, for in 1939 he edited the International Publishers pamphlet, Get Organized: Stories and Poems about Trade Union People: A Literary Pamphlet (New York: International, 1939).

the proletarian writer must destroy and construct. He is a pioneer, with a pioneer's necessity to be creative." The view that the literary proletarians were hostile to modernism can be argued only if one accepts the New York Intellectuals' rewriting of the debates in the 1930s left and their subsequent redefinition of modernism itself.[18]

Soviet Influences on American Literary Radicalism

The overwhelming majority of American proletarian writers could not read Russian and never visited the Soviet Union. Nonetheless, Soviet cultural developments exerted significant influences upon Depression-era literary radicalism. Indeed, 1930s literary radicalism would not have existed at all—or would have existed in dramatically different form—if the Bolshevik Revolution had not set in motion the vast changes, including cultural changes, that altered permanently the face of twentieth-century life. At the same time, a close examination of the precise nature of the Soviet influence upon American literary radicalism calls into question the thesis that the American Marxists simply attempted to clone themselves off the Soviet example.

From its beginnings American cultural proletarianism was explicitly linked with the Proletkult (1918–20) movement that sprang up in the Soviet Union in the wake of the Bolshevik Revolution. Indeed, the very terms "proletarian art" and "proletarian literature" were derived from the Soviet model. Even though, according to Joseph Freeman, the term "proletarian poet" had appeared in a 1901 issue of *The Comrade*, a publication of the Socialist party, the term routinely used to refer to radical literature in prewar leftist magazines (in succession, *The Comrade*, the *International Socialist Review*, and the *Masses*) was "socialist literature." It was only after 1917 that the term "proletarian literature" came into common coinage to describe literature about the class struggle written from a left-wing perspective. In 1919, Freeman notes, the Bohemian radical critic Floyd

18. Marcus Klein, "The Roots of Radicals: Experience in the Thirties," in Madden, p. 137; Klein, *Foreigners: The Making of American Literature 1900–1940* (Chicago and London: U of Chicago P, 1981), p. 140; Eva Goldbeck, review of Thomas Bell's *The Second Prince* and Nelson Algren's *Somebody in Boots* (Box 10, Blitzstein Papers, Wisconsin State Historical Society).

Dell began using the term "proletarian literature" to describe literature that "stirred the worker's . . . desire to win the fight for a new society." In 1921 the young Gold gave the term widespread currency when he spoke of the possibilities for a revolutionary art in the United States. Gold drew a direct connection between what he saw as the American workers' hunger for an "earth-built proletarian culture" and the "proletarian culture" that "in Russia . . . has begun forming its grand outlines against the sky." The term "proletarian culture," which gained popularity among American leftists over the decade, continued to be openly associated with the heritage of the 1917 revolution. In 1926 the Marxist-feminist historian Emmanuel Kanter envisioned his *The Amazons* as "add[ing] its mite to the nascent proletarian culture, which is to reap its aureate fruits in the future." Other scholars, he urged, should take the side of the workers in the cultural battle: "If the proletarians are to defeat the Bourgeoisie they must do so not only on the economic, political and military fields, but also on the cultural." While the idealistic tropes used by Kanter and the young Gold reveal the abiding influence of the old socialist movement's high-flown rhetorical style, the two writers' commitment to the project of a revolutionary workers' culture is evident. Proletarian art and cultural criticism were to play a vital role in the worldwide cause of workers' emancipation.[19]

As the interest in fostering and discussing proletarian literature in-

19. See Joseph Freeman, "Introduction," *Proletarian Literature in the United States: An Anthology*, ed. Hicks et al. (New York: International, 1935), pp. 24–25; Gold, "Toward Proletarian Art," rpt. in *Mike Gold: A Literary Anthology*, ed. Michael Folsom (New York: International, 1972), p. 69; Emmanuel Kanter, *The Amazons* (Chicago: Charles Kerr, 1926), pp. 5–6; Kanter, letter to Kerr, February 1, 1926, Kerr Papers, Newberry Library. The Newberry Library has recently acquired the archives of the Charles Kerr Publishing Company, the premier publisher of left-wing literature in the United States in the prewar period. Although for the most part the materials in these archives predate the scope of this study, I recommend them highly to scholars interested in earlier periods of U.S. literary radicalism. Walter Rideout argues that the CP-led literary radicals of the 1920s ignored the fact that "a sizable number of novelists with a conscious orientation toward Marxism had published books during the century's first two decades. Doubtless the decline of the Socialist Party as a political force and the fierce antagonism of the Communists toward the non-Communist radicals helped the critics and reviewers to forget or overlook most of the native pioneers in the art of which they wrote" (*The Radical Novel in the United States, 1900–1954: Some Interrelations of Literature and Society* [New York: Hill and Wang, 1956], p. 130).

creasingly dominated the pages of the *New Masses*—which, as the principal organ of the American cultural left from 1926 onward, superseded the now defunct *Liberator* (1920–23), itself the successor to the original *Masses*—the Soviet example continued to influence the magazine's principal projects. From 1918 to 1932, when sharp debates about the direction of cultural policy were carried on among various Soviet tendencies and groupings—including Proletkult, the Smithy, October, VAPP, RAPP, Litfront, and LEF—there was divergence over many questions but overall agreement that workers must be involved actively in cultural production. As Freeman enthusiastically reported in the 1930 volume *Voices of October: Art and Literature in the Soviet Union*, by the end of the 1920s the average Soviet paper had 122 worker-correspondents and 190 peasant-correspondents; in all there were 250,000 workers and peasants actively involved in writing for Soviet press. Between 1924 and 1926, *Moskovskaya Krestyanskaya Gazetta*, a prominent Moscow newspaper, received in all 470,000 communications from worker- and peasant-correspondents. The early *New Masses*' fervent call upon workers to contribute stories, sketches, and poems relating their own experiences cannot be understood apart from the Soviet campaign for mass cultural participation on the part of an increasingly literate proletariat.[20]

Moreover, the American critics' recommendations for writers of middle-class origin were shaped by the cultural revolution taking place in the Soviet Union in the late 1920s and early 1930s. In 1930 the New York John Reed Club recommended that each writer "attach himself to one of the industries . . . so that when he writes of it he will write like an insider, not like a bourgeois intellectual observer." During the first Five-Year Plan, as Katerina Clark reports, significant numbers of Soviet writers, many non-Communist, sought to bring themselves into closer contact with the laboring masses and give their literary labors the authenticity derived from close observation of work processes. "Large sections of the literary community wanted to find a way of participating in the experience of socialist construction," Clark remarks. "They set out to *remake* the institution of literature, and even to *remake* themselves." This development was perhaps epitomized by the example of Marietta Shaginian, who spent four years as

20. Joseph Freeman, Joshua Kunitz, and Louis Lozowick, *Voices of October: Art and Literature in the Soviet Union* (New York: Vanguard, 1930), p. 26.

a laborer on a construction site and subsequently wrote the popular novel *Hydro-Central*.[21]

Furthermore, American debates over the forms and techniques appropriate for proletarian fiction were significantly influenced by contemporaneous Soviet developments. The early *New Masses'* enthusiasm for a literature of fact paralleled the proliferation of documentary texts, particularly texts authored by workers, in the era of the Soviet cultural revolution. Gold's declaration that "facts are the new poetry" echoed the contention of the Russian writer Serge Tretiakov that writers "must write facts, facts. . . . [N]othing must be made up out of the writer's head." Indeed, among Soviet critics at this time there appeared a new literary category, the "sketch," to denote the brief, first-person, usually nonfictional text in which the beginning worker-writer could attempt to put his/her experiences into literary form. Conroy's oft-quoted statement of preference for a literature of fact— "to me a strike bulletin or an impassioned leaflet are of more moment than three hundred prettily and faultlessly written pages about the private woes of a society gigolo"—had precedent in the enthusiasm for texts documenting the "biography of objects" that, at least until 1932, prevailed in Soviet literary circles.[22]

Finally, the Americans' interest in various forms of literary collectivism—whether texts collectively authored or the genre of the "collective novel"—also had historical precedent in Soviet experience. The text composed by large numbers of workers became a popular literary mode in the USSR. In 1932 *International Literature* printed a piece of reportage jointly written by a group of "shock-workers" who detailed their trip to the capitalist West. The next year it mentioned a book-length account of socialist construction written by 200 railway workers; apparently the volume sold well, reaching an audience of 7,000,000. In the United States the practice of collective authorship hardly took hold on this scale. The short story "Stockyard Stella—Serial Love Story," published in *Working Woman*

21. "A Program for Workers," *NM* 5 (January 1930): 21; Katerina Clark, "Little Heroes, Big Deeds: Literature Responds to the Five-Year Plan," in Sheila Fitzpatrick, ed., *Cultural Revolution in Russia, 1928–1931* (Bloomington: Indiana UP, 1978), pp. 194, 198–99.

22. Gold, "Notes of the Month," *NM* 5 (January 1930): 7; Serge Tretiakov, cited in Matthew Josephson, "The Role of the Writer in the Soviet Union," *AWC*, p. 41; Conroy, "The Worker as Writer," *AWC*, p. 83; Tretiakov, cited in Regine Robin, *Socialist Realism: An Impossible Aesthetic*, trans. Catherine Porter (Stanford: Stanford UP, 1992), p. 31.

in 1935 and described as "written by a group of workers and Jane Benton"—was one of very few forays into group authorship by the American
left. But the genre of the collective novel itself was, arguably, significantly
influenced by Soviet experiments with literary form. Especially between
1928 and 1931, there transpired in the Soviet Union sharp debates between
the leading aestheticians in RAPP, who favored the representation of the
"living man" in the inherited form of the "Tolstoyan" novel, and the members of LEF, who were hostile to texts that "psychologized" and "heroized"
their characters and declared that "our epic is the newspaper." A novel
such as Valentin Kataev's Time, Forward!, which recounts the developing
dynamics among a group of cement makers intent upon setting new production standards to hasten socialist construction, exemplified the type
of text advocated by the latter group. Hicks, in his discussion of the collective novel in "Revolution and the Novel," cited Time, Forward!, along
with Fadeyev's The Nineteen and Newkrantz's Barricades in Berlin, as a
model of the important emerging form that he was calling to the attention of
American writers. The key formal innovations associated with American
literary proletarianism thus had precedents in the revolutionary literary
experiments being carried on in the USSR, as well as in Germany and other
countries with developed proletarian cultural movements.[23]

There was a good deal of mutual curiosity among Soviet and Ameri-

23. Shock workers, "The First Cruise," IL 1 (1932): 3–15; Tretiakov, "Words become
Deeds: The Press and Books in the Soviet Union," IL 3 (1933): 56; "Stockyard Stella—
Serial Love Story—by a Group of Workers and Jane Benton," Working Woman 6 (Janu-
ary 1935): 4–5; 6 (February 1935): 4–5; 6 (March 1935): 5–6; and 6 (April 1935): 4–5;
Robin, p. 208; Hicks, "Revolution and the Novel," p. 27. The debate between LEF and
other tendencies within RAPP is treated in Clark, "Little Heroes and Big Deeds"; Herman
Ermolaev, Soviet Literary Theories 1917–1934: The Genesis of Socialist Realism, U of
California Publications in Modern Philosophy, vol. 69 (Berkeley and Los Angeles: U of
California P, 1963), pp. 7–80; and Edward Brown, The Proletarian Episode in Russian
Literature 1928–1932 (1953; rpt. New York: Farrar, Straus and Giroux, 1971), pp. 132–
49. Contributions to International Literature indicate that there were proletarian literary
movements throughout Western, Central, and Eastern Europe, as well as in China, India,
and Japan; Germany was considered to have the most advanced revolutionary literary
movement outside of the USSR. For more on Japanese literary proletarianism, see G. T.
Shea, Leftwing Literature in Japan: A Brief History of the Proletarian Literary Movemnt
(Tokyo: Hosei UP, 1964); for more on the French movement, see Rosemary Chapman,
Henry Poulaille and Proletarian Literature 1920–1939 (Amsterdam: Rodopi, 1992).

can literary radicals. Americans interested in contemporaneous literary developments among their Soviet counterparts—as well as among proletarian writers in Germany, Italy, Hungary, England, France, Japan, and China, the major sites of revolutionary cultural production—could after 1931 read of these matters in *International Literature*, the organ of the International Union of Revolutionary Writers (IURW), a Comintern-sponsored organization founded at the Kharkov Conference of 1930. Kalar wrote from his outpost in Minnesota, "Living as I do in a comparatively backwards county, where books by Soviet writers are difficult to obtain, I have read but little of Soviet literature. Therefore am I so enthusiastically grateful for *International Literature*." The poet Herman Spector declared in 1934 that *International Literature* was "the most stimulating and advanced magazine we see in America." In the same year Rahv reported that

> *International Literature* is rapidly acquiring in this country the esteem and popularity which is its due as the central organ of revolutionary literature. Time and again the writer has observed workers discussing the contents of this magazine. He has seen them coming into bookshops inquiring whether a new number of the magazine has arrived. The magazine is also read by writers and artists in search of theoretical guidance.

As we shall see in chapter 4, *International Literature*'s 1933 publication of some important translations of writings by Marx and Engels on art and literature proved highly influential in the U.S. debate over literary "leftism."[24]

Moreover, a number of American presses took a growing interest in translating and publishing books from and about the Soviet Union. An editor for Jonathan Cape wrote to Kunitz in 1931 urging him to finish his current "book on Russian literature," noting that "there are going to be so many Russian novels published here this Fall that, I think, your book will be of real importance." The *New Masses* published reviews of recently translated works by Soviet authors—for example, Gladkov, Kollontai, Pilniak, Babel, Sholokhov, Ehrenbourg, Fadeyev, and Kataev. That Americans were inspired by the accounts of socialist construction conveyed in some of the Soviet texts is suggested by Conroy's remarks to the 1935 Writers Congress. Warmly praising the documentary *Those Who Built Stalingrad*,

---

24. Kalar, "Where We Stand: A Symposium," *IL* 3 (1934): 92; Spector and Rahv, both cited in Murphy, p. 109.

which recorded the achievements of a group of shock workers, Conroy remarked, "The men and women who built Stalingrad are the stuff we proletarian writers of America must be looking for." If American literary radicals wished to be acquainted with contemporaneous Soviet literary developments and knew where to go for information, a representative (if limited and slightly outdated) fund of material was available to them.[25]

At the same time, American proletarian writers sparked considerable interest and commentary among Soviet critics and readers. In 1932 the *Daily Worker* reported that both Soviet and German publishers were planning anthologies of American proletarian literature in translation. The cultural historian and biographer Matthew Josephson wrote to Kunitz in 1933 that members of the Soviet Union of Revolutionary Writers took a strong interest in the *New Masses* and were "keen to have any books—new American—that are worth reading." Josephson sent a special message to Dos Passos: "If you see Dos Passos tell him that the two most discussed foreign writers are Dos Passos and Shakespeare." Agnes Smedley's *Daughter of Earth* gained instant international recognition after it was published in a Russian first edition of one million copies; subsequently it was translated into fourteen different languages. Myra Page's *The Gathering Storm* and James Steele's (Robert Cruden's) *Conveyor* were also first published in the USSR. John Steinbeck's *The Grapes of Wrath*, published in the United States in 1939, was rapidly translated into Russian and sold 300,000 copies in 1941 alone. Short stories and poems by a number of American writers—Joseph Kalar, Langston Hughes, Jack Conroy, Ed Falkowski, Sterling Brown, as well as Cruden and Smedley—appeared in *International Literature*.[26]

25. Harrison Smith to Kunitz, April 7, 1931, Kunitz Papers; Conroy, "The Worker as Writer," *AWC*, p. 85. Malcolm Cowley noted that there was a significant delay between a text's appearance in the Soviet Union and its translation and publication in the United States. On the average, he declared, Soviet works published in the United States were about five years out of date ("Where We Stand: A Symposium," *IL* 3 [1934]: 8). Jon Christian Suggs concludes that "with only a few exceptions, there were gaps of at least three and as many as twelve years between publishing dates of works published first in the Soviet Union and subsequently in this country by International Publishers. The usual delay was four to five years" ("The Influence of Marxist Aesthetics on American Fiction: 1929–1940," Ph.D. Thesis, U of Kansas, 1978, p. 108). Rideout concurs that Soviet novels had little influence on their American counterparts (*The Radical Novel*, p. 207).

26. *DW* (January 4, 1932), 3; Josephson to Kunitz, December 30, 1933, Kunitz papers; Smedley to Cowley, n.d., Cowley Papers; Page, Tape no. 1, Oral History of the Ameri-

As the American proletarians evinced increasing interest in questions of aesthetic theory, various statements from Soviet critics found their way into the organs of the U.S. literary left. As we shall see in chapter 4, these statements, appearing in both the *New Masses* and the *Partisan Review*, generally served as artillery in the fight against "leftism." The *New Masses* in 1932 published a piece by Anatoli Lunacharski entitled "Marxism and Art" that urged writers to adopt an inclusive view of the literary heritage and to engage in the representation of three-dimensional human beings. In what was clearly a swipe at the hortatory and documentarist Proletkult program advocated by LEF, Lunacharski declared that revolutionary writers were abrogating their task if they "avoid[ed] all living content and re-sort[ed] to the empty play of intellectual or vaporous dreams." Humanism, he urged—"man's faith in his own powers, of aspiration for knowledge and a just life"—must be at the center of proletarian literature. Nicolai Bukharin's "Poetry and Socialist Realism," published in the *Partisan Review* in 1935, argued that poetry is concrete, implicit, and imagistic; didactic intrusions, Bukharin argued, were not properly part of the poet's enterprise. The *Partisan Review* in the same year published an important piece by Georg Lukács, "Partisanship or Propaganda?" in which the Hungarian critic set forth a critique of "tendentiousness" that would exercise significant influence upon the anti-"leftist" arguments of Calmer and Rahv.[27]

---

can Left, Tamiment Library, NYU; Deming Brown, *Soviet Attitudes Toward American Writing* (Princeton: Princeton UP, 1962), p. 74. Presses in the USSR also aided struggling writers who were seeking publication in other capitalist countries: the British proletarian writer Harold Heslop, for example, was first published in the USSR. See H. Gustav Klaus, "Harold Heslop, Miner Novelist," *The Literature of Labour: Two Hundred Years of Working-Class Writing* (New York: St. Martin's P, 1985), pp. 89–105.

27. Anatoli Lunacharski, "Marxism in Art," trans. Joseph Freeman, NM 8 (November 1932): 13; N. Bukharin, "Poetry and Socialist Realism," PR 1 (November–December 1934): 11–15; Georg Lukács, "Propaganda or Partisanship?" trans. Leonard F. Mins, PR 1 (April–May 1934): 36–46. The *New Masses* also published a piece by Maxim Gorki entitled "Proletarian Literature Today," NM 13 (October 2, 1934): 9–33. As Murphy notes, Lunacharski's article was to be cited in what would be "the first major confrontation in [the *New Masses*] over leftism" (p. 75). While Rahv was to pose himself as the leader of the attack on "leftism," in his 1932 article entitled "The Literary Class War" he dismissed Joyce and Faulkner as decadent nihilists and declared that only writers who had made a commitment to Communism could write literature of value (Rahv, "The Literary Class War," NM 8 [August 1932]: 7–10). Rahv was sharply upbraided by A. B. Magil for failing

Finally, American commentators who knew Russian attempted to keep readers abreast of the principal developments and debates on the Soviet literary scene. In a *New Masses* series entitled "Literary Wars in the USSR," Kunitz analyzed the principal theoretical and political debates being waged in Soviet literary circles and refuted Eastman's charge that writers at the 1930 Kharkov Conference had been "put into uniform." Especially since 1932, Kunitz argued, fellow-traveling writers were being provided with unprecedented support by the CPSU. In 1935 Edwin Seaver contributed to the *New Masses* a review of the proceedings of the 1934 Soviet All-Union Writers Congress in which he summarized the principal tenets of the emerging doctrine of socialist realism. The 1935 volume *American Writers Congress*, which covered the proceedings of the first convention of the League of American Writers, included three accounts—by Josephson, Olgin, and the left-wing editor and publisher Henry Hart—about literature in the USSR. Covering a variety of topics such as author/audience relations, the abolition of RAPP, the formation of the new Soviet Writers Union, and the definition of socialist realism, these pieces indicate that the American literary left attempted to keep up with what was going on in the Soviet Union and considered themselves to be involved in a common cultural project.[28]

Soviet cultural developments clearly shaped the outlook and goals of American literary radicals. The nature and extent of this influence, however, need to be defined with greater precision than is usually the case in

---

to grasp Lunacharski's point that "even in the period of its decline the art of a dying class is still capable of making significant contributions in the field of form, . . . that the innovations of individual bourgeois writers . . . can . . . serve to enrich the arsenal of proletarian art and make possible a fuller and truer picture of objective reality" ("Pity and Terror," *NM* 8 [December 1932]: 18). Lunacharski was cited by Myra Page in her "Author's Field Day" contribution (*NM* 12 [July 3, 1934]: 31). Parts of Andrei Zhdanov's remarks to the 1934 Soviet Writers Congress were reported in Olgin's article on the Soviet Writers Congress ("A Pageant of Soviet Life: The All-Union Writers' Congress in Moscow," *NM* 13 [October 16, 1934]: 16–20).

28. Kunitz, "Literary Wars in the USSR," *NM* 11 (June 12, 1934): 13–15; 11 (June 19, 1934): 20–23; 11 (June 26, 1934): 18–20; 12 (July 10, 1934): 22–24; 12 (July 17, 1934): 18–20; Edwin Seaver, "Socialist Realism," *NM* 17 (October 22, 1935): 23–25; Josephson, "The Role of the Writer in the Soviet Union," *AWC*, pp. 38–45; Olgin, "The First All-Union Congress of Soviet Writers," *AWC*, pp. 45–51; Hart, "Contemporary Publishing and the Revolutionary Writer," *AWC*, pp. 159–62.

scholarship on the 1930s literary left. Many commentators on the Soviet-American relationship assert that Soviet cultural commissars handed out directives to American party critics, who then scrambled to do the Soviets' bidding by issuing in their turn a series of prescriptions for U.S. proletarian writers. Eric Homberger sums up the prevailing view:

> From 1921, when Mike Gold issued his call for a proletarian literature, until 1930, when the "correct" line was established at Kharkov, the example of the Proletcult was the dominant influence on the American literary left. In this period Gold, at first almost single-handedly and then in *The New Masses*, sought to create an American proletarian literature. Between 1930 and 1934 the IURW, following the left turn of the Comintern, emphasized a policy which wholly integrated literature within the class struggle. The John Reed Clubs were created for this purpose, but the literary dimension of JRC activities progressively withered under party and IURW pressure. From 1935 the party's attempt to create a people's front was accompanied by a substantial move to the right. Leftist and sectarian attitudes were to be avoided. . . . At each stage of its brief career, proletarian literature followed as closely as possible the current Soviet line. This attempt is so obvious that the experience of the left in American literature is scarcely comprehensible without a firm grasp of the ways Soviet literary policy was emulated.[29]

The Communist-led cultural movement in the United States certainly looked to the Soviet Union for leadership. The career of American proletarian literature cannot be understood without reference to the "left turn" beginning in 1928 and ending with the endorsement of the Popular Front and the dissolution of the Reed Clubs in 1935—strategies shaped by the Comintern's analysis of the principal imperatives facing the world Communist movement. Nonetheless, within this general framework there are many protracted time lags between Soviet and American developments, as well as many particularities in the American literary left's formulation of its goals, which indicate anything but a slavish desire on the Americans' part to "follo[w] as closely as possible the current Soviet line."

Since Kharkov is often cited as a key indicator of the Americans' dominance by Moscow, it is useful to begin with a consideration of its actual

---

29. Eric Homberger, *American Writers and Radical Politics, 1900–1939: Equivocal Commitments* (New York: St. Martin's P, 1986), pp. 139–40.

significance. Held in the Ukraine in 1930, the Kharkov Conference was the first serious attempt by the international cultural left to formulate a unified program for revolutionary artists and writers. Delegates attended from around the world, but the Soviets played the major role in articulating policy and formulating criticisms of the revolutionary cultural movements in various capitalist countries. (Germany and the United States were the two non-Soviet countries singled out for special attention at Kharkov.) Max Eastman set the paradigm for subsequent commentary on Kharkov when, in his 1935 *Artists in Uniform*, he portrayed the leaders of the International Bureau of Revolutionary Writers (the predecessor of the IURW) as authoritarian dogmatists compelling the delegates' acquiescence to the empty slogan, "The method of creative art is the method of dialectic materialism." At Kharkov, Eastman argued, the Americans were subjected to "such a dressing down as might flatten a worm into the mud, but would certainly produce a recoil in any creature possessing the rudimentary lime-deposits of a vertebrate organization." Kharkov began a pattern of Soviet hegemony that extended, Eastman charged, to the mid-thirties when he was writing, since after 1932 "the dialectic method was revoked, rescinded, and annulled" as an "erroneous formula" that had been supplanted by the "new and more accurately proletarian recipe of Socialist Realism." In short, Eastman asserted, Soviet cultural policy of the past ten years had to be understood as "a systematic effort of the bureaucratic political machine set up in Soviet Russia after Lenin died to whip all forms of human expression into line behind its organizational plans and its dictatorship." [30]

Subsequent commentary on Kharkov has built upon Eastman's description. Howe and Coser ignore the fact that at Kharkov the Americans were reprimanded for their sectarian attitude toward fellow travelers and mention only the recommendation that the Americans "draw in new proletarian elements." The Ukraine conference, Howe and Coser conclude, expunged the last traces of free-wheeling radicalism from the American cultural left and "imposed . . . a harsh, self-defeating line." Although he offers no evidence of coercion, Harvey Klehr too claims that the Americans "had to acquiesce" to the ten-point program developed for them at Kharkov and subsequently refers to the Kharkov proposals as "directives."

30. Max Eastman, *Writers in Uniform: A Study of Literature and Bureaucratism* (New York: Knopf, 1934), pp. 22, 18–19, 3.

Interestingly, even when critics concede that Eastman misrepresented important aspects of the Kharkov conference, they conclude that his thesis about Soviet control over the Americans is accurate. Daniel Aaron, for instance, admits that Eastman distorted a number of events that transpired at Kharkov and concludes that Kunitz's account is "probably more correct in its details than Eastman's." Nonetheless, he determines that Kunitz "did not make a convincing case against Eastman's charges of the subsequent subservience of the American revolutionary writers to Soviet directives." Homberger compares Eastman's account of Kharkov with the transcription appearing in *International Literature* and concludes that Eastman's "leftist caricature" is "cruder than the original, but . . . a great deal more useful for his anti-Stalinist polemics." Nonetheless, like Aaron, Homberger supports Eastman in his larger point: greatly to the detriment of proletarian literature, the Americans followed the Kharkov principles for five years in slavish "emulation" of Soviet cultural policy.[31]

At least up to 1932, the IURW did continue to offer criticisms of what they saw as the Americans' tendencies toward reformism and workerism. Anne Elistratova, in a 1932 *International Literature* article assessing the political performance of the *New Masses* for 1931, scolded the American Marxists for their insufficient "politicalization." *New Masses*, in Elistratova's estimate, was not Leninist enough in its appreciation of the role played by the party. Moreover, she noted, in its graphics and fiction the *New Masses* too often conveyed a passive and defeatist view of the working class; it was weak in attracting worker-correspondents but also sectar-

---

31. Howe and Coser, *The American Communist Party: A Critical History (1919–1957)* (Boston: Beacon, 1957), pp. 278–79; Harvey Klehr, *The Heyday of American Communism: The Depression Decade* (New York: Basic Books, 1984), pp. 73, 75; Daniel Aaron, *Writers on the Left: Odysseys in American Literary Communism* (1961; rpt. New York: Avon, 1964), p. 240; Homberger, p. 135. Homberger, comparing Eastman's account with the account of the conference in the 1931 Special Number of *Literature of the World Revolution*, notes that the former produced "serious distortions . . . by removing a phrase from its context." For example, "Eastman prints 'Art is a class weapon' (in fact, the slogan of the John Reed Clubs), where the printed resolution reads, 'Proletarian literature is nothing more than a weapon in the class struggle'; what was appropriately qualified at Kharkov is a universal in Eastman." Similarly, "The Kharkov resolution reads 'every proletarian artist must be a dialectic materialist. The creative method of proletarian literature is the method of dialectic materialism.' Eastman dropped the qualifying 'proletarian' in the second sentence, so it reads 'The method of creative art is the method of dialectical materialism'" (Homberger, p. 135).

ian in its attitude toward fellow travelers; it contained spotty coverage of international developments in proletarian culture.[32]

In addition to the piece by Elistratova, *International Literature* published some other reviews and essays sharply critical of the American proletarians. *Linkskurve* editor Otto Biha dismissed the Reed Club recommendation that middle-class writers "gain a mandate as cultural representatives of the working class" by themselves taking jobs in factories. This proposal was, Biha asserted, a "Proletkult delusion" reflecting "the assumption that it is possible to create a proletarian culture by some social organizations and little circles that are secretly paving the way for a new culture." The Americans' abiding tendency to define the proletarian novel according to criteria other than revolutionary perspective was continually criticized. The British Marxist Maurice Helfand criticized the American critic Bernard Smith for suggesting that proletarian authorship might serve as the basis for determining whether or not a text should be considered proletarian. Leon Dennen was rebuked by an anonymous *International Literature* reviewer for adopting a "noncritical attitude toward Plekhanov's system of ideology as a whole." Dennen had failed to recognize, the reviewer charged, that Plekhanov's ideas entailed "a Menshevik elimination of the revolutionary essence of Marxism." All in all, IURW commentators concluded, the American Marxists adhered to a theory and practice strongly influenced by mechanism, empiricism, pragmatism, and reformism.[33]

32. Anne Elistratova, *"New Masses," IL* 1 (1932): 107–14. In a rather cruel historical irony, Elistratova noted that an American writer exceptional for his dynamic portrayal of Communist characters was Whittaker Chambers—the former Communist who testified for the U.S. government against Alger Hiss in the famous McCarthy-era espionage trial. Chambers, in his recantatory autobiography *Witness*, remarked that the short stories Elistratova had praised for their forthright presentation of the CP were in fact not really about Communism at all, but about the "spirit of man"; Communism, he claimed, merely provided the "context" for his exploration of this theme. See *Witness* (New York: H. Wolff, 1952), pp. 61–64.

33. Otto Biha, "On the Question of Proletarian Revolutionary Literature in Germany," *Literature of the World Revolution* (hereinafter *LWR*) 4 (1931): 91; Helfand, review of *Left, LWR* 3 (1931): 139–43; Anonymous, *"Left No. 2," IL* 2–3 (1932): 148. The attack on Dennen was somewhat unfair, since in 1931 *Literature of the World Revolution* (the predecessor to *International Literature*) had itself reprinted large segments of Plekhanov's *Art and Social Life*, accompanied by only the briefest of negative critical commentaries. See *LWR* 2 (1931) and 3 (1931).

The principles enunciated at Kharkov had a profound impact on the editorial policies of the *New Masses* and the founding principles of the John Reed Clubs. In their report on the Kharkov Conference in the *New Masses* of August 1931, the editors detailed the conference resolutions and pledged themselves to following more revolutionary and less bohemian political principles in the future. Moreover, the statement of goals for the John Reed Clubs that was endorsed at the 1932 convention of federation, and subsequently reprinted in the first issue of various JRC magazines, was pure Kharkov:

> —To make the club a functioning center of proletarian culture; to clarify and elaborate the point of view of proletarian as opposed to bourgeois culture; to extend the influence of the club and the revolutionary working class movement;
>
> —To create and publish art and literature of a proletarian character; to make familiar in this country the art and literature of the world proletariat, and particularly that of the Soviet Union; to develop the critique of bourgeois and working class culture; to develop organizational techniques for establishing and consolidating contacts of the Clubs with potentially sympathetic elements; to assist in developing . . . worker-writers and worker-artists; to engage in and give publicity to working class struggles; to render technical assistance to the organized revolutionary movement.[34]

The principles adopted at Kharkov guided discussion of the goals of proletarian literature in the United States throughout the Third Period. Indeed, the call to the 1935 American Writers Congress reiterated most of the 1930 program. The course of American literary proletarianism up to 1935 was definitively shaped by a desire to adhere to the resolutions adopted at Kharkov.

The leadership of the IURW directed some sharp criticisms at their U.S. colleagues; the American literary radicals took seriously their commitment to act upon the Kharkov principles. But it is questionable that these phenomena are unambiguous indicators of the American cultural movement's subservience to the CPSU. For one thing, *International Literature* published its harshest comments on the American proletarians when the IURW was being guided by the policies of RAPP, the leading Soviet

---

34. John Reed Clubs Program, Box 153, Joseph Freeman Papers, Hoover Institute.

writers' organization of the years 1928–32. Although Eastman characterized Leopold Auerbach, the RAPP chairman, as a minion of Stalin and
lampooned the leaders of the IBRW as "under-probationary lay-writers of
the Holy See of the Russian revelation," RAPP never received any official
endorsement from the CPSU and in fact often clashed with it. According
to Edward Brown, Auerbach and other RAPP leaders continually resisted
the efforts on the part of the CPSU to enlist writers in the production of
"utilitarian" literature. Sheila Fitzpatrick disputes the inherited wisdom
that RAPP exercised "a repressive . . . dictatorship over literary publication
and criticism." RAPP was, she maintains, "in fact not under effective Central Committee control." Katerina Clark argues that, during the 1928–31
Soviet cultural revolution, writers "were not, whatever else was the case,
following a central 'Party line' on literature, since the Party never gave
any explicit instructions for the writers to follow." James Murphy points
out that writers such as Boris Pilniak and Maxim Gorki, when attacked
by various figures within RAPP, were defended by the CPSU; indeed, the
Central Committee stepped into the Gorki dispute and characterized the
RAPP accusations against the writer as "grossly mistaken and bordering on
hooliganism." [35]

While Sovietologists offer differing evaluations of the roles played by
RAPP and the CPSU in literary matters, most agree that RAPP was anything
but omnipotent. *International Literature's* criticisms of the American literary radicals were hardly coercive. Elistratova, the somewhat overbearing
and arrogant author of the extended critique of the *New Masses*, was a mere
twenty years old; it is difficult to imagine that the CPSU would have entrusted a 'Party line' criticism of the entire American cultural left to such
a callow critic. Otto Biha, who faulted the Americans for their adherence
to the "Proletkult delusion," did so in the context of a self-criticism of
German proletarian writing; there is no evidence that his remarks had the
status of an order to the Americans. Maurice Helfand may have criticized
Smith and other Americans for standing by authorship as the basis for defining proletarian literature. The British, however, were dressed down even
more harshly in *International Literature* than were the Americans; Hel-

35. Eastman, p. 18; Edward Brown, pp. 87–105; Sheila Fitzpatrick, "Cultural Revolution as Class War," in Fitzpatrick, ed., *Cultural Revolution in Russia, 1928–1931*, p. 29;
Clark, "Little Heroes and Big Deeds," p. 193; Murphy, *Proletarian Moment*, pp. 86–87.

fand hardly wrote from a position of invincibility. Commentators on the U.S./USSR relationship routinely posit that the IURW was trying to bully the Americans into conformity. It makes more sense, however, to see the IURW's criticisms as just that—criticisms—rather than as "directives."

Furthermore, the Americans' responses to the IURW assessments of their work hardly indicate that they felt themselves obliged to knuckle under. In 1932 Hicks, who was not yet a *New Masses* editor, was invited to comment on the draft of the IURW criticisms before it was printed in the *New Masses*. He agreed with some points, disagreed with others, and sent back a long cover letter detailing his responses—hardly the reaction of a slavish emulator. A. B. Magil, a party member who attended the Kharkov Conference and took part in the *New Masses* discussion of the IURW criticisms, recalls that the literary radicals clustered around the magazine debated the document at length. The *New Masses* finally printed the document, Magil maintains, because most of the participants in the debate were won over to the IURW's criticisms of the magazine's work and felt that these criticisms ought to be printed. Unless one is predisposed to disbelieve the *New Masses* editors, there is no reason not to accept the statement accompanying the magazine's reprinting of the IURW criticisms. "A general discussion was held in which the Contributing Editors, the members of the John Reed Club of New York City, worker-writers, representatives of the foreign-language press, and fellow-travellers participated," the statement read. "The Resolution was enthusiastically approved. . . . The Editorial Board accepts the analysis of the IURW."[36]

Indeed, as Lawrence Schwartz has pointed out, what the American left's passionate adherence to the Kharkov principles demonstrates is not so much the Americans' subservience to Moscow as their relative independence from cultural policies being developed in the USSR. The dominant position of commentators on U.S./USSR literary relations is that the Americans adopted the Kharkov program in keeping with the hard line of the RAPP ascendancy and then softened their position with the abolition of RAPP. The dissolution of the John Reed Clubs and the call for the April

36. "Resolution on the Work of the New Masses in 1931," Box 44, Hicks Papers; Hicks to Komorowski, n.d., Box 44, Hicks Papers; Interview of author with Magil, March 1990; Preface, "Resolution on the Work of the New Masses for 1931," NM 8 (September 1932): 20.

1935 American Writers Congress, with the subsequent formation of the League of American Writers, are routinely interpreted as attempts to ape the formation of the 1934 Soviet Writers Union and to pave the way for the adoption of the Popular Front, which became official policy in September 1935. But in fact the 1935 Writers Congress can only with difficulty be seen as an attempt on the Americans' part to clone themselves off the Soviet example. Not once in the entire proceedings was any mention made of any parallel between the Soviet Writers Union and the League of American Writers. Moreover, the call for the Congress was a virtually unadulterated reprise of the Kharkov program.[37]

Nor can the 1935 American Congress be convincingly interpreted as an attempt on the part of the party to introduce through the back door a Soviet-inspired anticipation of the Popular Front. The American Writers Congress took place in April 1935, whereas Georgi Dimitrov announced the Comintern's Popular Front position only in September of that year. The critical approaches taken by various speakers at the 1935 American Congress reveal a certain rhetorical mellowing on the part of the American cultural left: five years' practice of proletarian literature meant that discussions could reflect actual production rather than simply offer goal-setting prescriptions. By mid-1935, moreover, many left-leaning liberal writers were gravitating toward the left, where they were treated with friendliness and respect. But the principles explicitly or implicitly endorsed by the great majority of the speakers at the 1935 Congress do not depart in their fundamentals from those articulated at Kharkov some five years before. The conference billed itself as a call to "revolutionary writers" who "do not need to be convinced of the decay of capitalism or the inevitability of revolution." It extended a welcome to "those writers not yet so convinced," but asserted that the Congress would "seek to influence [them] and win [them] to our side." Moreover, the barrage of attacks leveled against Kenneth Burke for proposing that the Communist movement substitute the term "people" for "workers" in its propaganda indicates that the tenor of the Congress was anything but Popular Frontist. The spirit of Kharkov was alive and well in the U.S. literary left up to the formation of the Popular Front.[38]

37. Lawrence Schwartz, *Marxism and Culture: The CPUSA and Aesthetics in the 1930s* (Port Washington, NY: Kennikat, 1980), pp. 41–47.

38. Hart, "Introduction," *AWC*, p. 10; "Discussion and Proceedings," *AWC*, pp. 165–

There is no question that, in its broad outlines, the project of the American proletarians was based largely on Soviet influences. But if we view the Americans as pursuing their goals in a relatively independent fashion, some otherwise anomalous features of the U.S./USSR relationship make more sense. Certain variations in the terms of the debate over proletarian literature lose their ambiguity and simply emerge as indices to the different understandings of their enterprise held by critics of different nations. For example, the Soviets characteristically used the term "revolutionary literature" to denote texts written more or less in sympathy with socialist values. "Proletarian literature," by contrast, meant literature written from a party perspective. As Serafina Gopner put it, "[R]evolutionary literature cannot but evolutionize toward proletarian literature." Karl Radek noted in his address to the 1934 Soviet Writers Congress that "revolutionary" writers were essentially bourgeois fellow travelers, while "proletarian" writers were distinguished by their commitment to building socialism. In the United States, the terms were used quite differently. "Revolutionary" writers were those who, as Newton Arvin stipulated, "adhere to the party line" or, as Henry Hart noted, "do not need to be convinced of the decay of capitalism, or the inevitability of revolution." By contrast, "proletarian" literature was a contested term, taken variously to signify authorship, audience, subject matter, or political perspective. Never, however, was the term "proletarian literature" taken in the United States to denote writing that was doctrinally further to the left than "revolutionary" literature. E. A. Schachner argued that " 'revolutionary literature' . . . consciously supports

---

72. Burke's sharpest critic at the Congress was Freeman, who stated that Burke's invocation of "the people" was at best opportunist and at worst protofascist. Anti-Communist commentary on the 1930s has treated Burke's reception at the Congress as an exemplary instance of Stalinist dogmatism. Burke himself maintained a humorous distance on the episode, however, and after the Congress praised the CP as the only organization that could have "assembled and carried through a congress of this sort" (*Nation* 140 [May 15, 1935]: 571). Although he was never fully committed to the Communist program, Burke maintained respect for the revolutionary left throughout the decade and beyond. In a 1966 symposium on the 1930s at which coparticipants such as Cowley and Hicks outdid one another in backpedaling, Burke recalled that Freeman's behavior at the 1935 Congress had been hostile and intimidating. But he also kept asking, "Does there have to be a [scape]goat?" See Symposium, "Thirty Years Later: Memories of the First American Writers Congress," *American Scholar* 35 (Summer 1966): 495–516.

the movement for the revolutionary overthrow of capitalism," whereas " 'proletarian literature' " . . . reflects the life of any typical cross section of the proletariat and need not be more revolutionary than the proletariat itself is at the time the novel is written." The terms were not necessarily seen as separate, of course. Schachner noted, as did Edwin Berry Burgum, that distinctions between revolutionary and proletarian fiction would tend to disappear in situations of revolutionary crisis where the working class undergoes intense politicization. Nonetheless, the relation of terms is essentially reversed in the two critical discourses. For the Soviets, it was the revolutionary novel that metamorphosed into the proletarian novel; for the Americans, the opposite was the case. If the Americans were taking orders from Moscow, they were clearly getting their signals crossed on some fairly basic matters.[39]

Similarly, the debate over "leftism" took a significantly different form in the United States than in the USSR. While we shall treat this subject in greater detail in chapter 4, we may note here that the American literary leftists were grinding some distinctive axes of their own in the way they framed the debate. In the USSR, according to IURW critic Franc Schiller, "leftism" signified primarily three things: a "left"-sectarian attitude toward non-Communist writers, a "Proletkult" enshrinement of worker-writers, and a contemptuous attitude toward precedent literary traditions ("the 'left' idea of throwing the classics overboard the modern ship"). The Soviet and IURW theorists developed a forceful critique of what they termed "utilitarianism" and "tendentiousness" in literature, but they never included these faults under the rubric of "leftism." As Murphy points out, however, the Americans from the outset grouped their criticisms of didactic and agitational literature with their criticisms of what they considered to be contemptuous attitudes toward bourgeois literary tradition and ex-

39. S. Gopner, "Speech of the Representative of the ECCI," LWR special number (1931): 1; Karl Radek, "Contemporary World Literature and the Tasks of Proletarian Art," in Zhdanov et al., pp. 136–37; Newton Arvin to Hicks, December 26, 1934, Box 3, Hicks Papers; E. A. Schachner, "Revolutionary Literature in the U. S. Today," Windsor Quarterly 2 (Spring 1934): 59; Edwin Berry Burgum, "Discussion," Writers Congress Issue, PR 2 (April–May 1935): 9. Magil affirms that for the Soviets "proletarian literature" meant literature that "projects a socialist future," while "revolutionary literature" meant literature that is "in some limited way critical of capitalism." These meanings, Magil notes, did not carry over into the U.S. context (Interview with author, March 1990).

cessive cultivation of writers from the working class. Indeed, the attack on didacticism became the key aspect of the U.S. radicals' war against "leftism." What was for the Soviets a term signifying attitudes that would keep fellow-traveling writers away from the Communist movement was to become for the Americans—particularly for the *Partisan Review* critics—the basis for a criticism of the entire political project of proletarian literature.[40]

Other features of Soviet cultural policy or terms in Soviet cultural debate appeared only after a considerable time lag; still others never gained currency at all. Although, as we shall see in the next chapter, the Americans increasingly came to favor Marxist perspective, as opposed to authorship or subject matter, as the principal basis for defining proletarian literature, up to 1935 significant numbers of writers and critics argued that the encouragement and training of worker-writers was the top priority of the left-wing cultural movement. At the 1935 Congress, Gold, Hart, and the worker-writer Martin Russak raised serious questions about the proposal that left-leaning middle-class writers could be seen as "proletarian" writers. Yet the key theoreticians in RAPP had argued as early as 1928 that the perspective of dialectical materialism, and not proletarian authorship, was the distinguishing feature of proletarian literature. Moreover, the various definitions of socialist realism that began to be formulated in the USSR in 1932 were essentially silent on the question of proletarian authorship. If the Americans were bent on "emulating" the Soviets, as Homberger charges, it is odd that they should have been so recalcitrant on this issue.[41]

Indeed, it is noteworthy that socialist realism, which was discussed among U.S. critics starting in 1934, seems not to have sparked any particular zeal for imitation. Seaver's *New Masses* review of the translation of the proceedings at the 1934 Soviet Writers Congress cited Radek approvingly on the point that "socialist realism demands the ability to generalize, to 'seek out the main phenomena in the totality of phenomena.'" Yet Seaver

---

40. F. Schiller, "Friedrich Engels on Literature," *IL* 2 (1933): 128; Murphy, *Proletarian Moment*, p. 6 and passim. Olgin, in his address to the 1935 American Writers Congress, noted that in the USSR the terms "right" and "left" had an exclusively political signification. The "rightist" position on literary questions, associated with Bukharin, had to do with minimizing the representation of the party; the "leftist" position involved "a certain mistrust towards those [fellow-traveler] writers who had 'come over'" (*AWC*, p. 50).

41. Hart, "Proceedings and Discussion," *AWC*, pp. 165–67; Katerina Clark, *The Soviet Novel: History as Ritual* (Chicago and London: U of Chicago P, 1981), pp. 32–34.

did not propose that Americans practicing such an epistemology view themselves as socialist realists. Moissaye Olgin was one of very few critics to equate the projects of the Soviets and the Americans when he noted in his review of *Proletarian Literature in the United States* that "[i]f socialist realism consists in truthfully depicting reality by showing the essential, not some accidental or illusory, traits of reality, by revealing the historical tendencies inherent in that reality and by making clear the inevitability of the victory of the new over the old social forces, then the bulk of this volume is socialist realism." Yet in his extended description of the 1934 Soviet Congress at the 1935 American Congress, Olgin never once suggested that U.S. writers envision their project as a socialist realist one. Socialist realism—the emerging focus of Soviet cultural policy after 1932 and official doctrine after 1934—never acquired any real importance for the American literary radicals.[42]

All in all, the attitude of the Americans toward the critical debates being carried forward in the Soviet Union can be seen as essentially eclectic, evidencing little control from a monolithic (or monologic) center. Leading party theorists, for example, seem to have felt no obligation to voice a party line on such an important development as the dissolution of RAPP. At the 1932 Reed Clubs Convention, Gold and Freeman—the two most prominent party spokesmen present—offered conflicting views on this issue.

---

42. Seaver, "Socialist Realism," *NM* 17 (October 22, 1935): 23–4; Olgin, "First Choice of New Book Union Is a Comprehensive Anthology of Proletarian Literature of High Order," *DW* (October 10, 1935), 5. Whether or not socialist realism should be seen as continuous or disjunctive with earlier Soviet aesthetic theories is disputed. Proponents of the view that socialist realism entailed a qualitative change include Schwartz (pp. 20–44), Edward Brown (pp. 200–218), and Ermolaev (pp. 122–23). Scholars endorsing the opposite view include Murphy (pp. 85–104), Robin (pp. 77–160), and C. Vaughan James (*Soviet Socialist Realism: Origins and Theory* [New York: St. Martin's P, 1973], pp. 83–86 and passim). According to Michael Scriven, the French literary radicals also operated relatively autonomously: in 1934, he argues, they embarked on a protoPopular Frontist program without any interference from Moscow one way or the other. Both Robin and Scriven argue that the literary controversies occurring in the USSR itself were at this point largely free of any central control. At the 1934 All-Union Soviet Writers Congress, the debate between Zhdanov and Bukharin—and multiple other tendencies—was a genuine debate—indeed, according to Robin, a "cacophony." Both Robin and Scriven also assert that Stalin exercised no particular control over the Congress (Robin, pp. 9–36; Scriven, *Paul Nizan: Communist Novelist* [London: Macmillan, 1988], pp. 78–93).

Gold proposed that RAPP had been dissolved because of the "dominance of petty bureaucrats." Freeman, correcting him, argued that the Soviet writers' organization "was liquidated because Soviet intellectuals were so convinced by the subsequent success of the Five Year Plan that they whole-heartedly accepted the Soviet regime." Similarly, in their responses to Eastman's charges in *Artists in Uniform*, *New Masses* critics took quite different lines of defense. Leon Dennen focused on Eastman's demonization of the "'sinister' and 'all-powerful' figure of Stalin" and argued that Stalin had in fact had very little to do with the dissolution of RAPP. Olgin, by contrast, stated at the 1935 Writers Congress that Stalin had coined the term "socialist realism" and that RAPP had been dissolved through his initiative. What is significant here is not so much the substance as the *fact* of these disagreements. If the American party closely "emulated" the Soviets and felt obliged to explain and defend their every move, it is odd that the CPUSA's leading literary lights did not have a unified position on questions so vital to the legitimation of cultural policy in the USSR.[43]

The American literary proletarians drew inspiration from the Soviet model; at the same time, they had a distinctive sense of their own mission. The many differences between Soviet and American creative and critical practices are, accordingly, understood far better according to a model of influence than according to one of coercion. It is clear that the American literary radicals sought to learn from Soviet writers and critics and that, in particular, the 1930 Kharkov Conference left a lasting impression on the development of literary proletarianism in the United States. But recommendations, criticisms, and programs developed by the Americans' Soviet colleagues possessed the status of examples, suggestions, and possible guideposts rather than of directives. The American radicals' literary efforts, while shaped in their broad outlines by Communist cultural policy, were thus in their particularities largely determined by political discourses and decisions having little direct connection with what was being written or done in the USSR. American Marxist criticism—and, to an even greater degree, American proletarian fiction—developed to a significant degree along markedly American lines.

---

43. "The John Reed Club Convention," Box 153, Freeman Papers; Dennen, "Bunk by a Bohemian," PR 1 (June–July 1934): 22–26; Olgin, "First All-Union Congress of Soviet Writers," AWC, p. 49. Robin notes that at the 1934 Soviet Congress Stalin held a minority position in favor of the term "communist realism" (p. 38).

➤   ➤   ➤   ➤   ➤

The standard view of 1930s literary radicalism would have it that the literary proletarians were "influenced" to death. Proletarian literature originated in the imperatives of a harsh and instrumentalist party line; it was isolated from the most progressive developments in contemporaneous modernism; above all, it was obliged to follow lockstep in the tracks of Soviet cultural policy. I hope here to have demonstrated the fallacy of this view.

To assert that the literary proletarians were not forced to accept party doctrine does not, however, prove that the formulation of the relation between literature and politics enjoying currency among the 1930s U.S. left was necessarily a revolutionary one. We may now consider the literary left's debates over aesthetic doctrine.

CHAPTER 3

>

Defining Proletarian Literature

In *A Note on Literary Criticism* (1936), James T. Farrell somewhat sardonically set forth the principal criteria by which one might conclude that a novel could be considered "proletarian":

> It seems to me that there are the following possible definitions of proletarian literature: it can be defined as creative literature written by a member of the industrial proletariat, regardless of the author's political orientation; as creative literature that reveals some phase of the experience of the industrial proletariat, regardless of the political orientation of the author; as creative literature written by a member of the industrial proletariat who is class-conscious in the Marxian sense, and a member of the proletarian vanguard; as creative literature written by a class-conscious member of the proletariat and treating solely (or principally) of some phase of the life of that group; as creative literature written about that group within the proletariat regardless of the author's class status or his group status within his class; as creative literature written in order to enforce, through its conclusions and implications, the view of the proletarian vanguard; as creative literature read by the proletariat; as creative literature read by the proletarian vanguard; or as creative literature combining these features in differing combinations.[1]

Farrell's deliberately long-winded taxonomy reveals his satiric attitude. At the time of writing *A Note on Literary Criticism*, Farrell was moving from his position of sparring animosity toward Hicks and Gold to one of outright and formulated opposition; within a short time he would be a self-professed Trotskyist. Despite—or perhaps because of—the hostility of Farrell's summary, however, it provides a useful starting point for a discussion of the debates over the definition of proletarian literature that preoccupied large numbers of leftist commentators in the early 1930s. First,

1. James T. Farrell, *A Note on Literary Criticism* (New York: Vanguard, 1936), pp. 86–87.

Farrell's categories outline the four main grounds upon which definitions were routinely formulated—namely, authorship, audience, subject matter, and political perspective. Second, through the frequent interposition of the term "vanguard," the taxonomy suggests an abiding tension between the three categories that might be termed "empirical"—authorship, audience, and subject matter—and the more obviously "ideological" category of political perspective. Third, through its parody of scholastic hair-splitting, Farrell's description of different possible definitions focuses attention on the important issue of prescriptiveness. Did the debate over the definition of proletarian literature result in the marginalization of some definitions and the privileging of others? Did the party have a "line" on this question? Did the debate have an actual effect on the texts that were produced by left-wing writers? Can the debate—in the way it was either conducted or concluded—be seen as in any way coercive?

In this chapter I shall analyze the different grounds for defining proletarian literature that were advanced between the late 1920s and the mid-1930s. I shall attempt to explain the ways in which various definitions competed with one another at any given moment. But I shall also outline broad shifts that took place over this period, shifts that by 1935 resulted in a downplaying of authorship and an increased stress upon perspective as the key distinguishing feature of proletarian literature. Throughout this discussion I shall indicate how positions on the definition of proletarian literature related to larger debates over the goals of revolutionary culture. I shall reserve for chapter 4 a full analysis of the "art versus propaganda" controversy and the related attack on "leftism."

The Criterion of Authorship

When the clarion call for proletarian literature began to issue from the monthly *New Masses* in 1926, the criterion for considering a text "proletarian" that was heard most frequently was that the text should exhibit proletarian authorship. A 1928 appeal by Gold is representative of the magazine's early approach to its readers: "Everyone has a great tragic-comic story to tell. Almost every one in America feels oppressed and wants to speak out somewhere. Tell us your story. It is sure to be significant. Tell it simply and sincerely, in the form of a letter. Don't worry about style, grammar or syntax. Write as you talk. Write. Let America know the heart and mind of the workers." In 1928 the magazine's masthead read, "A Magazine of Workers' Life and Literature." By June 1928 the magazine had begun to run a regular column entitled "Poems by Workers," and over the next few years it published a considerable amount of poetry and reportage by workers who had apparently never—or rarely—set pen to paper before. The "Poems by Workers" column of August 1928 contained pieces by Ed Falkowski, a miner, Raymond Kresenski and T. E. Bogardus, both steel workers, Samuel Becker, a lumber worker, and H. S. Ross, an oil driller. A year later the magazine featured a narrative entitled "We Are Mill Workers" by Ella Ford, a textile worker involved in the CP-led strike in Gastonia, N.C. The December 1931 issue contained several poems by striking miners from Harlan, Kentucky. Especially while it was a monthly (1926–33), the *New Masses* published a substantial number of poems, short stories, journalistic pieces, and quasi-autobiographical "sketches" by beginning working-class writers who would gain stature as proletarian poets or novelists: Falkowski, Richard Wright, Louis Colman, Jack Conroy, Joseph Kalar, Martin Russak, Robert Cruden, and Agnes Smedley. The *New Masses* editors—like those of the *Daily Worker*, which, in the early 1930s, also prominently featured worker-correspondents in its pages—were doing their best to make the "worker-writer" a reality in the American radical press.[2]

When full-length novels by worker-writers began to appear, the excitement among critics and reviewers was palpable. Walt Carmon warmly

2. Gold, "A Letter to Workers' Art Groups," NM 5 (September 1929): 16; "Poems By Workers," NM 4 (August 1928): 4; Ella Ford, "We Are Mill Workers," NM 5 (August 1929): 3–5; "The Harlan Miners Speak," NM 7 (December 1931): 5–6. The Minnesota paper mill worker Joseph Kalar, writing to his friend and fellow worker-writer Warren Huddlestone, noted that the *New Masses*, which had greatly encouraged him by publishing a number of his poems in the early 1930s, had brought him into contact with the left-wing literary movement and given him an identity as a proletarian writer. "I am a real proletarian writer," he declared, "writing in odd moments when I just have to write. . . . I write because I have to and because I'm entirely proletarian-minded and because I am perfectly willing to throw my destiny, and merge it, with the destiny of the proletariat" (Kalar to Huddlestone, September 4, 1932, in *Joseph A. Kalar: Poet of Protest*, ed. Richard G. Kalar [Minneapolis: RGK Publications, 1985], p. 147). In 1930 the young worker-writer Fred R. Miller noted that, given the mind-numbing fatigue resulting from long hours of manual labor, "the great wonder . . . is that workers write at all" ("Letter," NM 6 [September 1930]: 22).

greeted the 1929 edition of Agnes Smedley's *Daughter of Earth*. "The broad healthy stride of this novel is that of a woman, a proletarian to her marrow," he declared. "She is a fellow-worker. She is one of us." Conroy's *The Disinherited* was hailed throughout the left press as an instance of authentic proletarian writing from a genuine literary talent. Lawrence A. Harper, reviewing Conroy's novel for the *New Masses*, noted that with its publication "the masses are not only finding their place in literature but they are making a literature as strong and husky as the shoulders of any worker." Gold, who at the 1932 John Reed Clubs conference bemoaned the slow rate at which writers were emerging from the ranks of the proletariat, played Emerson to Conroy's Whitman, congratulating the young author on his novel: "You are a proletarian shock-trooper whose weapon is literature." A review in *Red Pen* noted that in *The Disinherited* "the hitherto mute American worker has become articulate." An advertisement for the novel in *Pollen* took up the same theme, proclaiming, "The Young American Worker Becomes Articulate." *The Disinherited* was prized above all for its enfranchisement of the worker as speaker and revolutionist.[3]

Conroy himself, reviewing William Cunningham's *The Green Corn Rebellion*, a novel about antiwar activity among Oklahoma farmers during World War I, noted that the story was valuable for its presentation of an "overalled, bare-footed, dust-and-sandstorm-covered" point of view. Robert Forsythe remarked that *S.S. Utah*, worker-writer Mike Pell's account of U.S. sailors' enthusiastic responses to the Five-Year Plan, "may not be literature, but it reads like Dashiell Hammett and I'm crazy about it." He concluded, "If this is worker's correspondence, maybe what America needs is more worker's correspondence." Even Hicks, who is generally known for supplanting Gold's roll-up-the-sleeves radicalism with a more academic Marxism when he took over the *New Masses* literary editorship in 1934, placed a high value on what he saw as unhewn but genuine workers' writing. As he remarked of B. Traven's *The Death Ship*, "Traven is unspoiled; he is a worker first and only incidentally a writer." Passing over Traven's patently anarchist—and, in *The Death Ship*, markedly anti-Bolshevik—politics, Hicks concluded, "His book does not hew to the Party line, but

3. Walt Carmon, review of Agnes Smedley, *Daughter of Earth*, NM 5 (August 1929): 17; Lawrence A. Harper, review of Jack Conroy, *The Disinherited*, *Partisan* 1 (January 1934): 7; Gold, "A Letter to the Author of a First Book," NM 10 (January 9, 1934): 26; review of *The Disinherited*, *Red Pen* 1 (1934): 11; *Pollen* 1 (March–April 1934): 16.

he knows what the class struggle is because he has fought in it." For many Third-Period critics and reviewers, working-class authorship constituted a key basis for determining not merely the *proletarianism* of a text, but also its value.[4]

The sense that radical worker-writers were constituting an important new school was epitomized in Gold's frequently quoted remarks of 1929:

> A new writer has been appearing; a wild youth of about twenty-two, the son of working-class parents, who himself works in the lumber camps, coal mines, steel mills, harvest fields and mountain camps of America. He is sensitive and impatient. He writes in jets of exasperated feeling and has no time to polish his work. He is violent and sentimental by turns. He lacks self-confidence but writes because he must.
>
> He is a Red but has few theories. It is all instinct with him. His writing is not a conscious strain after proletarian art, but the natural flower of his environment. He writes that way because it is the only way for him. His 'spiritual' attitudes are all mixed up with tenements, factories, lumber camps and steel mills, because that is his life.[5]

In an enthusiastic blend of description and advocacy, Gold signaled his excitement that the "proletarian art" for which he had been issuing a call since 1921 was no longer a purely prophetic category: it was beginning to be written.

Throughout the Third Period, a welcoming hand was increasingly extended to radical writers of petty bourgeois origin. In line with the strong Proletkult influence on U.S. literary radicalism, however, there remained in place a strong "affirmative action" policy of fostering writers from working-class backgrounds. The 1932 national draft manifesto of the John Reed Clubs read, "Allies from the disillusioned middle-class intellectuals are to be welcomed. But of primary importance at this stage is the development of the revolutionary culture of the working class itself." A year later *Left*

---

4. Conroy, review of William Cunningham, *The Green Corn Rebellion*, *Windsor Quarterly* 3 (Fall 1935): 77; Robert Forsythe, "What America Needs," *NM* 10 (February 13, 1934): 2; Hicks, "Revolutionary Literature of 1934," *NM* 14 (January 1, 1935): 38. Josephine Herbst, registering her dissatisfaction with Gold's *New Masses* review of Conroy's *The Disinherited* in a letter to Hicks, noted that "Mike's review is pretty bad because his praise is patronizing. . . . I doubt if [Conroy] really cares about being a Symbol" (Herbst to Hicks, January 8 [1934?], Box 27, Hicks Papers, Arents Library, Syracuse U).

5. Gold, "Go Left, Young Writers!" *NM* 4 (January 1929): 3–4.

Front, describing the program of the Chicago John Reed Club, included among its various functions the goal of "assist[ing] in developing (through cooperation with the Workers Cultural Federation and other revolutionary organizations) worker-writers and worker-artists." The *New Masses/John Day* Publishing Company novel contest of 1935 stipulated that submissions by all writers were welcome, but that workers, who were more likely to achieve superior "authenticity," were especially urged to send in their work. In 1934 *Pollen* issued an invitation for submissions from poets with the "dung not yet dry on their shoes." Conroy unequivocally stated that, as editor of the *Anvil*, he preferred "crude vigor to polished banality." The literary left actively solicited literature from worker-writers. At times their calls for such texts were couched in somewhat patronizing—and, as we shall note at greater length in chapter 5, sexist—terms. Bernard Smith, for example, characterized working-class writing as "blunt, direct, masculine, rough, a little crude, a little naive." Nonetheless, such formulations were not so much left-wing prescriptions for crudeness as they were invitations to ignore bourgeois prescriptions for gentility and polish. As James Murphy has noted, Gold's often-quoted remark that "[t]echnique makes cowards of us all" did not mean that craft was unimportant, but that beginning writers should not feel obliged to emulate bourgeois stylistic models. The class war extended to considerations of literary style, and in assigning value to texts by authors with limited literary education, the leftists can be seen as making a statement against elitism.[6]

Some middle-class writers responded to this call for texts by proletarian authors by claiming for themselves credentials that were, if not

6. John Reed Clubs Convention, Box 153, Freeman Papers, Hoover Institute; "The John Reed Clubs: Editorial," *Left Front* 1 (June 1933): 3; *NM* 11 (June 5, 1934): 7–8; *Pollen* 2 (1934): 10; Conroy, quoted in *The Jack Conroy Reader*, ed. Jack Salzman and David Ray (New York: Burt Franklin, 1979), p. 131; Bernard Smith, "A Footnote for 'Proletarian Literature,'" *Left* 1 (1934): 12; James Murphy, *The Proletarian Moment: The Controversy over Leftism in Literature* (Urbana and Chicago: U of Illinois P, 1991), pp. 122–23. Alan Calmer's description of the manuscripts submitted to the *New Masses*/John Day contest indicates that most of the writers who entered the competition were previously unpublished and that many appeared to be workers. "Most of [the manuscripts] must have been written by people who lived through the events they tried to describe," he wrote. "[T]hey did not have to go outside of their own background for the proletarian subject-matter of their books" ("Reader's Report," *NM* 16 [September 10, 1935]: 23). See also "Proletarian Novelist Prize Contest," *New Masses* File, Box 44, Hicks Papers.

precisely proletarian, at least indicative of close acquaintance with proletarian experience. Clara Weatherwax prefaced her *Marching! Marching!*,
which focuses upon a strike in a Pacific Northwest lumber mill, with a brief
authorial sketch in which she assured her readers that she "was born and
schooled in Aberdeen, with the sound of sawmills in her ears. Her earliest
days were spent in a papoose basket which her mother got from Indians at
the Auinault Indian Reservation." Moreover, Weatherwax claimed to have
worked at "a variety of jobs—both white-collar and proletarian, mostly for
fifty dollars a month or less, and the kinds of work mentioned or described
in this book she knows through experience or close contact. She has participated in the labor movement on the Coast." Even Erskine Caldwell, who
articulated a much less openly leftist political platform in his work than
did Weatherwax, attested to his own reliability as an observer of Southern
whites. As he remarked in his prefatory note to *God's Little Acre*, when
he was young, "the folkways of the South penetrated his spirit"; between
the ages of sixteen and twenty, he "worked at various jobs, ranging from
manufacturing screwdriver handles to reporting city news for *The Atlanta
Journal* and carrying a time-clock in a cotton-seed mill." For Weatherwax
and Caldwell, petty-bourgeois class privilege was presumably leavened by
close acquaintance with the lives of the working class.[7]

Indeed, the often profound ambivalence expressed by middle-class
writers toward their origins reveals the extent to which the criterion of proletarian authorship exercised a potent influence upon Third-Period American literary radicals. Dos Passos, who spoke disparagingly in *U.S.A.* of his

---

7. Clara Weatherwax, *Marching! Marching!* (New York: John Day, 1935), p. 2; Erskine
Caldwell, *God's Little Acre* (New York: Modern Library, 1934), p. vi. In Weatherwax's
case, it is difficult to determine whether the author was speciously laying claim to proletarian credentials. Cantwell stated that Weatherwax's "people founded the place [Aber-
deen]" ("A Town and Its Novels," *NR* 86 [February 19, 1936]: 51). In his introduction to
the recent reissue of *Marching! Marching!*, however, Christian Suggs states that Weatherwax's father died when she was a child and that she worked to help support the family.
See "Introduction," *Marching! Marching!* (1935; rpt. Detroit: Omnigraphics, Proletarian
Literature Series, 1990), p. iv. Caldwell, although not from a working-class background,
experienced declassing and poverty. Matthew Josephson's biographer reports that, in
the summer of 1931, "Josephson took the lanky Southern writer out to lunch and was
shocked to discover that the impecunious Caldwell had spent the previous night sleep-
ing on a sofa in the lobby of a fashionable Fifth Avenue apartment building" (David E.
Shi, *Matthew Josephson, Bourgeois Bohemian* [New Haven and London: Yale UP, 1981],
p. 137).

own years under the "ethercone" at Harvard, noted with considerable envy
that Gold was "lucky to have been born on a real garbage-heap, instead of
on the garbage dumps of dead ideas the colleges are, to have started life as
a worker instead of as an unclassed bourgeois." The poet Genevieve Taggard—whose attacks on the shallowness of middle-class life reflect an insider's knowledge of her subject—declared that writers of petty-bourgeois
origin were potentially a liability to any revolutionary movement. "There
is nothing more irritating," she wrote, "than a person with a long, vague
look in his eye to have around, when you're trying to bang an army into
shape, or put over an N. E. P. . . . If I were in charge of a revolution, I'd
get rid of every single artist immediately and trust to luck that the fecun-
dity of the earth would produce another crop when I had got some of the
hard work done." In 1932 no less a revolutionary firebrand than Rahv—
uncannily anticipating the contemptuous political obituary that Gold was
to write of him at the end of the decade—expressed doubt about the stay-
ing power of the middle-class writers who were gravitating toward Communism and predicted that they would soon return to their class origins.
"The emotional, romantic approach to Communism is a paper bridge to
anyone who wants to cross over into the camp of revolution," he concluded. Hicks, making his debut as literary editor of the New Masses, noted
of the revolutionary writer that "inasmuch as literature grows out of the
author's entire personality, his identification with the proletariat should
be as complete as possible. He should not merely believe in the cause of
the proletariat; he should be, or should try to make himself, a member of
the proletariat." Rollins, defending the legitimacy of the proletarian novel
from Louis Adamic and other attackers, nonetheless expressed uneasiness
with calling himself a "proletarian novelist" because of his middle-class
origins.[8]

8. John Dos Passos, "The Making of a Writer," NM 4 (March 1929): 23; Genevieve
Taggard, "Are Artists People?: Some Answers to the New Masses Questionnaire," NM 2
(January 1927): 6; Rahv, "The Literary Class War," NM 8 (August 1932): 10; Hicks, "The
Crisis in American Criticism," in Jack Allen Robbins, ed., Granville Hicks in the New
Masses (Port Washington, NY, and London: Kennikat, 1974), p. 1; William Rollins, "What
Is a Proletarian Writer?" NM 14 (January 7, 1935): 22–23. Taggard's poems frequently
feature the states of mind of alienated middle-class women caught in a dynamic of attrac-
tion and repulsion toward the revolutionary movement. See, for example, "Interior" and
"A Middle-Aged, Middle-Class Woman at Midnight," in Jack Salzman and Leo Zanderer,
eds., Social Poetry of the 1930s (New York: Burt Franklin, 1978), pp. 293, 297–98.

Howe and Coser, we will recall, interpreted such expressions of regret at being born into the middle class as evidence of the destructive influence of "Stalinism," which demanded that intellectuals undergo rituals of "self-abasement ('down with us')" when confronted with "the working class or, more frequently, a caricature of the working class in the person of a party functionary." Jonathan Wilson argues that, for most proletarian novelists, "to be any kind of creative writer was inevitably to betray the working class." There may have been a degree of self-flagellation in some of the middle-class writers' apologies for their origins. But the writers' testimonies indicate the seriousness with which Third-Period literary radicals viewed the criterion of subject position in defining the project of proletarian literature. Middle-class American radicals did not as a rule follow the dramatic example of *Hydro-Central* author Marietta Shaginian. Nor did they act widely on the John Reed Club proposal—even though it was enthusiastically seconded and promoted in the *New Masses* by Gold—that they immerse themselves in the workings of a specific industry. But their eagerness to lay claim to personal knowledge of working-class life, as well as their self-critical scrutiny of their class's shortcomings, indicate that, like their Soviet colleagues, many American writers of middle-class origin felt themselves part of a cultural revolution. Katerina Clark's description of the Soviet writers who participated in the 1928–31 "revolution from below" in Russian letters applies to the Americans as well: "They set out to *remake* the institution of literature and even to *remake* themselves." One's status as a member of an elite did not make one an asset to the revolutionary movement, but if anything functioned as a potential barrier to full participation in the revolutionary process. Bent upon avoiding the example of early twentieth-century socialist literature, which they viewed as irretrievably genteel, middle-class, and reformist, the 1930s literary radicals sought out—and sought to identify with—the real thing.[9]

Pace Howe and Coser, the definition of proletarian literature as literature written by proletarians did not primarily signal neurotic self-abnegation on the part of the middle-class writer or critic, but rather a

9. Howe and Coser, *The American Communist Party: A Critical History* (1919–1957) (Boston: Beacon, 1957), pp. 280–81; Jonathan Wilson, "On Radical Writing in the 1930s," *Literary Review* 7 (Fall 1983): 43; Katerina Clark, " 'Little Heroes and Big Deeds': Literature Responds to the First Five-Year Plan," in Sheila Fitzpatrick, ed., *Cultural Revolution in Russia, 1928–1931* (Bloomington: Indiana UP, 1978), p. 194.

recognition of the centrality of class to discursive subject position. At times, however, the critics' eagerness to promote "genuine" worker-writers did blur the articulation of the political goals of proletarian literature. For in discussions of proletarian authorship it was often not clear, as Farrell points out, whether the term "proletarian author" denoted a "radical" or "revolutionary" proletarian author or simply one "from the proletariat." In fact, the terms of analysis routinely shifted back and forth between a somewhat reductionist empiricism ("this book is by a genuine worker and that is enough") and a voluntarist idealism ("this book is by a genuine worker and that makes it revolutionary"). Hicks lauded Traven for his genuineness and passed over his anti-Communist politics. Yet he complained that Conroy insufficiently subordinated the novel's "pictures of proletarian life" to the text's overarching political "theme." Although Conroy's Larry became "militant," Hicks remarked, the novel did not strongly enough "recommend militancy as a general solution for the workers' problems." Even Gold, who celebrated the proletarian writer as having "few theories" and hailed Conroy as "a proletarian shock-trooper whose weapon is literature," also noted that Conroy would have produced a more effective novel if he had "known more about Marxism." Frequently Gold wrote of "revolutionary spirit" and "revolutionary élan" as necessary components of proletarian literature. Obviously Hicks and Gold envisioned Marxist politics as playing a crucial role in works of proletarian literature. Because this role remained for the most part unspecified, however, the critics' grounds for judgment appear to have shifted from text to text, and their critical standards give the impression of being somewhat ad hoc and inconsistent.[10]

An inevitable effect of the critics' failure to theorize rigorously the relation of politics to authorship was the occasional promotion of an essentialist and romantic conception of the working class—what is known as

10. Hicks, "Revolutionary Literature of 1934," NM 14 (January 1, 1935): 38; Hicks, review of Conroy, The Disinherited, PR 1 (February–March 1934): 57; Gold, "A Letter to the Author of a First Book," NM 10 (January 9, 1934): 4; Gold, "Notes of the Month," NM 6 (September 1930): 5. Hicks, as a reader of The Disinherited for Macmillan, was quite sharp in his criticisms of the book's politics and did not recommend it for publication. Conroy wrote to him, "Max Lieber [Conroy's editor] told me that Macmillan rejected Edwin Seaver's last book because it was too revolutionary, now the reader objects to mine because it isn't revolutionary enough!" Possibly echoing Gold's original name for his "Change the World!" Daily Worker column, Conroy concluded, "What a world!" (Conroy to Hicks, n.d., Box 14, Hicks Papers).

"ouvrierism" or "workerism." In Hicks's comments on *The Death Ship*, for example, Traven's elemental experience as a worker presumably compensates for his deviation from the party line. But there are several troublesome implications to this formulation. To begin with, it significantly underrates the sophistication of Traven's rhetorical strategy, which relies on articulating the viewpoint of a worker-narrator who is, rather than naive and spontaneous, in fact shrewd and acerbic in his political judgments. Furthermore, Hicks sloughs over the issue of anti-Bolshevism in his suggestion that the deviant ideas expressed by Traven's worker-narrator are not ideas at all, but simply aspects of his experience, conceived as an "unspoiled" store of raw material that in some way, despite itself, affirms the "line" to which the text does not "hew." By such a logic, it would be virtually impossible for any author of proletarian heritage—who must be, after all, "only incidentally a writer"—to reproduce bourgeois ideology or be in political error. Ironically, Hicks ends up signaling a somewhat patronizing attitude toward the very working-class discourse that he sets out to elevate. Finally, Hicks's formulation offers a problematic description of the relation between the "line" and its basis in both practice and theory. For Communist policy was in fact devised not only as a response to workers' experiences of oppression but also as a consequence of debates with alternative political strategies—anarchist, socialist, liberal—for addressing and interpreting those experiences. Hicks's comments on Traven distort the theoretical importance of the party line, leaving the reader with the impression that the line exists in isolation from competing political paradigms.

This tendency to essentialize working-class consciousness as intrinsically anticapitalist is even more marked in Gold's description of the "wild youth" who "writes in jets." In postulating that this young worker-writer is a "Red" but has "few theories," Gold suggests that the proletarian author's consciousness is elemental and undifferentiated, almost wholly guided by "instinct." Presumably Marxism is the truth that the wild youth's experience at the point of production unconsciously affirms; his intuitive grasp of this theory is what makes him a "Red." But the youth's relation to discourse is a simple consequence of his subject position—"a natural flower of his environment"—virtually unmediated by ideological constructs of any kind. Correct revolutionary understanding is thus corroborated by the wild youth's writing without being integral to it; a text can be "Red" in essence without explicitly endorsing revolutionary politics. The description's sexual essentialism underscores its economism. For the obviously sexualized "jets of feeling" emanating from the "wild youth" furnish further evidence that his revolutionary essence is virtually a biological feature—"it is all instinct with him"—rather than the product of conscious experience. Indeed, the strongly gendered language of several of the descriptions of proletarian authorship cited above—language that, in Carmon's review, essentially turns Smedley into a man—reveals a marked tendency to associate leftness with broad strides and muscled shoulders—as if physical strength were not simply a metaphor for, but an actual carrier of, revolutionary politics. The egalitarian impulse to value the articulations of authentic proletarian subjects could converge with patronizing and sexist assumptions about who those subjects in fact were.

Hicks, Gold, and other Marxist critics were obviously eager to extend a welcoming hand to writers of working-class origin. In one sense, the critics' enthusiastic celebration of worker-writers could be said to carry a prescriptive ring: the critics were declaring that, as much as possible, proletarian literature *ought* to be authored by proletarians and that middle-class writers should identify themselves with the proletariat as fully as possible. But prescriptions for authorship seem to have halted here, for Marxist critics quite cautiously refrained from further stipulating that worker-writers conform to specific features of party politics. Contrary to the inherited wisdom about Third-Period literary radicalism, which posits that critics imposed stringent criteria of *partinost*—that is, loyalty to the party line— on proletarian writers, it would appear that *narodnost*—that is, truth to "popular" currents of thought—was, at least some of the time, given primacy by the American Marxists. Elistratova and other I U R W commentators on the U.S. literary scene complained with some justice of the Americans' "undue spontaneity" and "empirical social portraiture." American Marxist critics' prescriptions about proletarian authorship tended to essentialize the authenticity of actual worker-writers, even to the point of positing that genuine expressions of working-class consciousness could be simply conflated with the party line. If the line lost some of its Leninist clarity in the process of this conflation, apparently this was a risk the theorists were willing to take.[11]

11. For a discussion of these terms—as well as of the related term *klassvost*, or class consciousness—in relation to the project of Soviet literature, see C. Vaughan James,

The Criterion of Audience

While Third-Period discussions of proletarian authorship were biased toward an empirical conception of the proletariat, the same cannot necessarily be said of debates over the question of the audience of proletarian literature. This is not to say that Marxist commentators denied the importance or desirability of proletarian literature's reaching a mass working-class readership. But they hesitated to make proletarian literature's success in attracting a certain type or size of audience a defining criterion of this writing or an index to its legitimacy.

In the early discussions of proletarian art and literature in the *New Masses*, considerable attention was devoted to the ways in which revolutionary culture would both articulate the present life of the masses and inspire them to higher levels of consciousness and activity. Lenin was cited on the necessity for creating an art that would be meant not for the hundreds and the thousands, but for the millions. "Art must organize the feeling, thought, and will of the masses," Lenin declared. "Let us always have the workers and peasants in mind." Lenin was frequently quoted as saying that literature was a "cog in [the] vast social mechanism." In 1929 the revolutionary European dramatist Erwin Piscator wrote in the *New Masses* of the necessity for the leftist theater to be "in living touch with the masses." He concluded, "A revolutionary theatre without its most living element, the revolutionary public, is a contradiction which has no meaning." Russak, in his 1929 testimonial to Jack London as "America's first proletarian novelist," noted that London deserved this designation largely because "he was the most popular writer of the American working class." Hicks, along similar lines, considered much of Traven's significance as

---

Soviet Socialist Realism: Origins and Theory (New York: St. Martin's, 1973), passim. James Weinstein articulates the standard New Left critique of CP workerism when he remarks that "Party culture, the glorification of the worker as worker, the development of 'proletarian' literature, the vision of the factory as the center of future social life, were parts of [a] syndicalist tendency, at once being strengthened by it and reinforcing it" (*Ambiguous Legacy: The Left in American Politics* [New York: New Viewpoints, Franklin Watts, 1975], p. 49). Weinstein is correct on this point but wrong in his larger assertion that this workerism reflected American subservience to Soviet directives. The IURW critics, as we have seen, were quite consistent in their chastisement of the American radicals for their lack of *partinost*.

a proletarian novelist to consist in the fact that "hundreds of thousands of European workers read his novels." If proletarian literature was to be a weapon aiding the proletariat in the class struggle, these critics were saying, this weapon must be wielded by actually existing workers.[12]

From the late 1920s to the mid-1930s, the *New Masses* aggressively fostered and publicized the growth of participatory cultural activities in which workers were both creators and audience. In 1928 Gold, contrasting the meager beginnings of proletarian culture in the United States with more advanced developments abroad, dolefully remarked that "there is no Communist audience for art in America." Soon, however, Gold was reporting enthusiastically on the proliferation of workers' cultural collectives in the United States, ranging from the 500-member Japanese Workers Camera Club to the Labor Sports Union to the New York Dramatic Council, with its membership of 1,000 drawn from twenty-one different language groups. In a September 1929 "Letter to Workers' Art Groups," Gold estimated that there had sprung up in the United States fifty small workers' theater groups, one hundred cinema groups, "dozens" of nature study groups, and twenty schools for studying economics, literature, and history. "My conservative conclusion is that 50,000 revolutionary workers in America are connected with some local group for the discovery and practice of Workers' Art," he stated. Two years later he expanded this estimate, noting that in New York City alone there were about 230 workers' cultural formations, with an area membership of 6,000. In the nation as a whole he speculated that up to 100,000 workers were now involved in some form of organized cultural activity—whether it be dance or photography, theater or music—and that this activity often conveyed left-wing or class-conscious politics. Throughout the discussions of "workers' art" in the early *New Masses*, production

12. "Lenin on Working Class Literature," trans. Anna Rochester, NM 5 (October 1929): 7; Joshua Kunitz, "Max Eastman's Unnecessary Tears," NM 9 (September 1933): 13; Erwin Piscator, "The Social Theatre," NM 5 (October 1929): 14; Russak, "Jack London: America's First Proletarian Writer," NM 4 (January 1929): 13; Hicks, "Revolutionary Literature of 1934," 38. Some scholars have claimed that Lenin's view of literature as "a cog in [the] vast social mechanism" referred merely to agitational, as opposed to imaginative, literature. This interpretation is too narrow. While Lenin did in various ways subscribe to distinctly bourgeois ideas about beauty in art, he also made a number of statements suggesting an unabashedly instrumentalist view of art's role in the service of revolution. See *Lenin on Culture and Cultural Revolution* (Moscow: Progress, 1966).

and consumption were treated as virtually inseparable phenomena; proletarian art could be defined as art *by* workers because it was, in an operative sense, *for* workers as well. Indeed, the success of the *New Masses* itself was a gauge of growing workers' interest in revolutionary culture. *New Masses* editors boasted of the magazine's sizable circulation among workers and declared it was the expanded audience for proletarian literature that required the changeover from monthly to a weekly format.[13]

The growth of participatory workers' cultural groups and the expanded circulation of the *New Masses* were not the only indicators of the left's increasing success in reaching a mass working-class audience with revolutionary culture. According to the critic E. A. Schachner in 1934, "Symposiums on revolutionary poetry and recitals of revolutionary poetry at which none too well-fed workmen in tattered clothing are conspicuously present, are being held regularly in all the large cities under the direction of the CP." More crucially, the theater was proving a highly effective artistic means of bringing radical ideas to the proletariat. George Sklar's and Albert Maltz's *Peace on Earth* had by 1932 been attended by over 100,000 people, most of them workers. In 1934 Gold reported that "upward of seventy farmers' revolutionary theatre groups" were touring the rural United States, putting on performances in barns. Gold informed the 1935 American Writers Congress that Theatre Union plays had reached audiences totaling 500,000, 75 percent of whom were workers. The Negro People's Theatre production of Odets's *Waiting for Lefty*—in which the

13. Gold, "Three Schools of U. S. Writing," *NM* 4 (September 1928): 14; Gold, "Workers' Art," *NM* 5 (March 1930): 20–21; Gold, "Letter to Workers' Art Groups," *NM* 5 (September 1929): 16; Gold *NM* 7 (June 1931): 23. When the *New Masses* editors decided to change over from a monthly to a weekly format, they declared that "the weekly *New Masses* will positively NOT be edited for a limited audience of intellectuals. It will reach for the broadest possible circulation among all strata of workers and professionals" ("An Editorial Announcement," *NM* 9 [September 1933]: 2). Bernard Smith remarked that from 1928 to 1930 or 1931 the *New Masses* "had several thousand readers in labor circles, but reached very few in the literary community and by those few was naively regarded as a sort of politicized *transition*" (*Forces in American Criticism: A Study in the History of American Literary Thought* [New York: Harper, Brace, 1939], p. 369). *New Masses* reached a circulation of 25,000 per week by January 1935. According to Harvey Klehr, it "outsold the *New Republic* and was within 9,000 of the *Nation*; its newsstand sales were higher than those of both its liberal competitors combined" (*The Heyday of American Communism: The Depression Decade* [New York: Basic Books, 1984], pp. 350–51).

word "Negro" had been substituted for the word "Jewish" throughout the text—attracted an audience of 5,000, "by far the largest group of people ever . . . to see a play in Harlem," according to one Harlem activist. Plays on working-class themes were popular throughout the decade: Erskine Caldwell's *Tobacco Road*, Marc Blitzstein's *The Cradle Will Rock*, Langston Hughes's *Don't You Want to Be Free?*, and the trade union musical *Pins and Needles* drew substantial audiences, some over a period of many years. Commentators on the American Depression-era theater differ in their assessments of such works but agree that leftist drama emerged as a major art form in the United States and enjoyed substantial popularity.[14]

Even though hostile commentators have argued that the CP's cultural offensive never reached significant numbers of workers, there is little justification for the claim. At least in the arenas of participatory workers' organizations and the theater, significant numbers of workers came into contact with the left through cultural activity. But the readership of proletarian novels was another matter. It was a source of continual distress to the literary left that sales of proletarian novels were never high, and indeed frequently embarrassingly low. Gold, who always tried to give the most positive possible construction to the left's cultural activities, conceded in the *Daily Worker* in 1934 that "even radical workers do not buy [proletarian

14. E. A. Schachner, "Revolutionary Literature in the U. S. Today," *Windsor Quarterly* 2 (Spring 1934): 53, 44; Gold, "Change the World!" *DW* (January 25, 1934), 5; Henry Hart, "Discussion," *American Writers Congress (AWC)* (New York: International, 1935), p. 181; Mark Naison, *Communists in Harlem during the Depression* (New York: Grove, 1983), pp. 152–53. One student of the U.S. left-wing theater estimates that twelve million theatergoers were exposed to progressive ideas in the Federal Theatres alone before 1939. See Rudolf Suhnell, "The Marxist Trend in Literary Criticism in the U.S.A. in the Thirties," *Jahrbuch für Amerikastudien* 7 (Winter 1962), 60. For assessments of 1930s left-wing drama, see Morgan T. Himelstein, *Drama Was a Weapon: The Left-Wing Theatre in New York, 1929–1941* (New Brunswick: Rutgers UP, 1963); Sam Smiley, *The Drama of Attack: Didactic Plays of the American Depression* (Columbia: U of Missouri P, 1972); Malcolm Goldstein, *The Political Stage: American Drama and Theatre of the Great Depression* (New York: Oxford UP, 1974), especially "Proletarian Theatre in the Early Thirties," pp. 27–57; R. C. Reynolds, *Stage Left: The Development of the American Social Drama in the Thirties* (Troy, NY: Whitson, 1986); and Wendy Smith, *Real Life Drama: The Group Theatre and America, 1931–1940* (New York: Alfred Knopf, 1990). For a discussion of left-wing documentary films of the period, see William Alexander, *Film on the Left: American Documentary Film from 1931 to 1942* (Princeton: Princeton UP, 1981), especially "The Workers Film and Photo League, 1930–1938," pp. 3–64.

novels]." When Hicks observed that Traven's novels were read by "hundreds of thousands of European workers," or Matthew Josephson remarked upon the audiences of millions available to Soviet novelists, they sounded a note of envy, for the American situation was different indeed. As Henry Hart reported to the 1935 Congress, the data that had been gathered by Knopf editor Bernard Smith indicated that even well-reviewed proletarian novels met with little popular success: Cantwell's *Land of Plenty* sold 3,000 copies, Conroy's *The Disinherited* 2,700 (1,000 of these at discount), and Rollins's *The Shadow Before* fewer than 1,200. "Sales such as these mean that the bourgeois publishers are going to begin to refuse to publish our novels," he sadly observed. Hart's grimness was largely justified, for International Publishers, the party press, could publish only very few works of fiction, and alternative presses such as Hart's own Equinox Press simply could not afford to have its books remaindered. Proletarian writers had to rely primarily on mainstream publishers if they wished their work to appear in print.[15]

Hart's address to the American Writers Congress came in the midst of a controversy over the readership of proletarian fiction that had been sparked in December 1934 by Louis Adamic's *Saturday Review of Literature* article, "What the Proletariat Reads: Conclusions Based on a Year's Study among Hundreds of Workers in the United States." In this vituperative attack, Adamic maintained that the only plausible rationale for the use of the term "proletarian literature" was to signify a body of work directed at—and consumed by—the working class. Yet, citing Trotsky sympathetically on the point that proletarian literature was an impossibility, Adamic claimed that, according to his findings, the proletarian novel was seen as essentially irrelevant by the workers it hoped to reach. "The overwhelming majority of the American working class does not read books and serious, purposeful magazines," Adamic asserted. "In fact, the American working class hardly reads anything apart from the local daily and Sunday newspapers and an occasional copy of *Liberty*, *True Stories*, *Wild*

15. Gold, "Change the World!" *DW* (December 14, 1934), 5; Matthew Josephson, "The Role of the Writer in the Soviet Union," *AWC*, p. 45; Hart, "Contemporary Publishing and the Revolutionary Writer," *AWC*, p. 161. See also Hart's *A Relevant Memoir: Story of the Equinox Cooperative Press* (New York: Three Mountains, 1977). Hart noted to Hicks that the Book Union had close to 1,000 members but that novels were among the least popular texts distributed (Hart to Hicks, n.d., Box 26, Hicks Papers).

West Tales, or Screen Romances." At best, he claimed, one-half of one percent of American workers read proletarian fiction—"most of them, if I may
venture, are among the exceptionally intelligent and avid-minded Jewish
garment workers in Manhattan." Adamic claimed that, according to his
survey—which included workers' responses to Lumpkin's *To Make My
Bread*, Catherine Brody's *Nobody Starves*, Rollins's *The Shadow Before*,
Conroy's *The Disinherited*, and Dos Passos's *Nineteen Nineteen*—nonradical workers were displeased by what they took as an insulting representation of the poverty of their lives, while radical workers were repelled
by the artistic mannerisms used in many of the books. The solution, he
argued, was for radical writers to abandon experimentalism, make a less
stridently class-conscious appeal, and compose novels "with no villains"
that would appeal to a reader's sense of "shame and indignation . . . regardless of class." The logic of Adamic's position was that, given the lack of
immediate widespread enthusiasm among working-class readers, novelists
should cease attempting to write proletarian fiction altogether.[16]

Adamic's polemic fueled the fires of critics hostile to literary proletarianism. V. F. Calverton, by 1937 firmly established as a pro-Trotskyist and
"renegade," proclaimed in a *Saturday Review of Literature* piece entitled
"Proletarianitis" that "the American proletariat is the last class to identify itself as proletarian." The proletarian novel, he lamented, had been
"gobble[d] up" by "middle-class romantics." Until the American working
class becomes "proletarian-conscious," he declared, "we shall not be able
to develop a proletarian literature of any scope or power." In the same year
Alan Calmer, previously a proponent of proletarian literature, followed up
on Adamic's and Calverton's attack, declaring that the proletarian novel
had been destroyed by its "blind worship of a hypothetical reader, endowed
with the cheapest cultural traits of the American layman." Antagonists of
literary proletarianism routinely argued that the new left-wing literature
was a hothouse creation; the *real* proletarian literature consisted of the
Westerns and romances read in large numbers by the working class.[17]

16. Louis Adamic, "What the Proletariat Reads: Conclusions Based on a Year's Study
Among Hundreds of Workers in the United States," *SRL* 11 (December 1, 1934): 321, 322.

17. V. F. Calverton, "Proletarianitis," *SRL* 15 (January 9, 1937): 14, 16; Alan Calmer,
"Portrait of the Artist as a Proletarian," *SRL* 16 (July 31, 1937): 14. Calverton had earlier
been a strong advocate of literary proletarianism. "The proletarian spirit," he noted in

But Adamic's article also inflamed the defenders of literary proletarianism. One *Saturday Review* reader from Montana complained that Adamic's methodology was suspect, since his study claimed to be based upon "hundreds" of workers' responses but quoted only a selected few and offered no "hard" data. Moreover, Adamic based his findings about workers' tastes on book sales alone and completely ignored the role of public libraries in workers' lives. The library in Butte, the reader maintained, "is used almost exclusively by workers. . . . It is a rare event to see anyone coming in who looks like a business man." Robert Cantwell, taking up the point about library use, commented that recent research showed businessmen and their wives to be the most frequent borrowers of romances and detective stories; most borrowers of serious bourgeois literature—for example, Hardy, Twain, Shaw—were workers, many of them blue-collar workers. Even though this group of readers might not immediately have been translated into an audience for proletarian literature, Cantwell noted, it constituted a "growing and grasping and eager audience acquainted with the higher achievements of bourgeois culture," one that was "actually straining the resources of the library system in its search for intellectually adequate

---

1934, "is now no longer the property of a few hardy enthusiasts but is in the main stream of American letters. . . . Few writers, especially of the younger generation, have escaped the impact of this movement" ("Literature Goes Left," *Current History* [December 1934], 6). Calverton, who was referred to as an "arch enemy of the working class" at the 1932 Reed Clubs conference, became pro-Trotskyist in the mid-1930s and was the object of polemics matched in fury only by those against Max Eastman (Leonard Wilcox, *Victor Francis Calverton: Radical in the American Grain* [Philadelphia: Temple UP, 1992], pp. 98–176, quoted p. 149). Calmer seems to have been rather erratic. In spite of his elitist comments in 1937 about the "hypothetical reader . . . endowed with the cheapest traits of the American layman," in 1939 his editorial comments accompanying a CP-sponsored anthology of proletarian poems and stories praised the book's contributors for "trying hard to find [their] way back to the common people, to get close to the heart-throb and pulse-beat of those who must lead humanity onward" (*Get Organized: Stories and Poems About Trade Union People: A Literary Pamphlet* [New York: International, 1939], p. 45). For the argument that proletarian literature is the type of literature that is popular with readers in the working class, see Merle Curti, "Dime Novels and the American Tradition," *Yale Review* 26 (Summer 1937): 761–68. For a discussion of working-class readership of dime novels in the nineteenth century, see Michael Denning, *Mechanic Accents: Dime Novels and Working-Class Culture in America* (London and New York: Verso, 1987), especially " 'The Unknown Public': Dime Novels and Working-Class Readers," pp. 27–46.

reading." Citing *Publishers Weekly,* Cantwell remarked that the production of inexpensive editions would bring about a qualitative change in American reading habits: "If someone ever solves the problem of how to put good new books on the market cheaply, an entirely new audience will be available." [18]

Cantwell was backed up by other literary radicals who examined the demographics of the proletarian novel's reception. Conroy, carrying out an ad hoc survey of his own, showed his copy of *The Land of Plenty* to some workers and middle-class intellectuals and found the former far more inclined to enjoy it. The poet Norman MacLeod pointed out that the publishing industry as a whole was in a crisis in the early to mid-1930s, and that a sale of 3,000—such as Hart estimated for *The Land of Plenty*—was actually quite respectable for any novel, proletarian or otherwise. Malcolm Cowley, who as literary editor for the *New Republic* had a professional interest in the book trade, disagreed somewhat with Hart's low estimates of the sales of proletarian fiction, venturing that the sales were probably 50 percent higher than Hart allowed. Nonetheless, attempting to account for sales that were still disastrously low, he calculated the real cost of books relative to workers' incomes and demonstrated that the average hardcover text constituted a real luxury item in the straitened budget of the average working-class family. According to both Cowley and the poet Ruth Lechlitner, the League of American Writers recognized that book prices were

18. Waino Nyland, "Proletarian Readers in Libraries," *SRL* 11 (December 2, 1934): 384; Cantwell, "What the Working Class Reads," *NR* 83 (July 17, 1935): 275–76. The Book Union, which distributed left-wing literature at reduced prices, boasted that "a large proportion of the membership is drawn from the ranks of workers; i.e., manual workers and brain workers—farmers, mechanics, teachers, nurses, doctors, architects, white collar workers. It is obvious that books are an important commodity in the intellectual life of the class-conscious worker and that he is eager to get books which speak of the things he senses are true" (Book Union pamphlet, n.d., Box 8, Hicks Papers). Included among the fictional offerings of the Book Union were *Uncle Tom's Children, A Stone Came Rolling, Marching! Marching!,* and *A Time to Remember.* A study of the personal library of John Edwin Peterson, a rank-and-file IWW militant, indicates that Peterson owned a higher percentage of fiction and poetry (28.5 percent) than of any other category of reading material. See Larry Peterson, "The Intellectual World of the IWW: An American Worker's Library in the First Half of the 20th Century," *History Workshop Journal* 2 (Autumn 1986): 164.

prohibitive for most workers and tried to interest publishers in bringing out proletarian novels in paperback editions, but failed. John Scott Bowman, a radical young academic, in 1939 completed a dissertation on proletarian literature that made use of still-extant data about library borrowing in the years 1935–36. Bowman concluded that proletarian novels had been three to four times as popular as other works of fiction. He demonstrated that 40 percent of his targeted titles were in virtually continuous circulation and that "labor reads the proletarian novels in more than twice the degree to which it reads the best-sellers."[19]

Hostile critics such as Adamic and Calverton, who insisted that the definition of proletarian literature hinge upon the issue of audience, were thus somewhat hasty in their conclusion that proletarian fiction attracted no significant interest among workers. It would probably have been more accurate to say that by 1936 a small but growing group of working-class

19. Conroy, cited in *Jack Conroy Reader*, p. 67; Norman MacLeod, "Letters from Writers," *IL* 3 (1933): 129; Cowley, "The Audience," Work Folder, Cowley Papers, Newberry Library; Cowley, "Cheaper and Better Books," *Forum and Century* 84 (September 1930): 167–70; Cowley, "Manifesto to the Trade," *NR* 69 (February 3, 1932): 326–27; Ruth Lechlitner, "The 1930s: A Symposium," *Carleton Miscellany* 6 (Winter 1965): 81; John Scott Bowman, "The Proletarian Novel in America," Ph.D. Thesis, Pennsylvania State College, 1939, pp. 167–78. Bowman was an early partisan of proletarian literature in the academy; he wrote to Hicks in 1935 marveling at the "revolutionary fact" that he had "managed to get such a contemporary and significant dissertation topic past my dissertation committee" (October 23, 1935, Box 9, Hicks Papers). One contemporaneous researcher noted that "[d]emand for library books doubled between 1926, when 226,142,926 volumes were in circulation, and 1934, when 449,998,845 books were borrowed. By 1936, one out of five people in the U. S. had a library card" (Louis R. Wilson, *The Geography of Reading: A Study of the Distribution and Status of Libraries in the United States* [Chicago: American Library Association and U of Chicago P, 1938], pp. 96–98, quoted 106). But libraries suffered from severe budget cutbacks during the Depression. "The income of public libraries decreased considerably from 1931 to 1934, while the demand for their services during the same period greatly increased" (Wilson, *The Geography of Reading*, p. 94). Another scholar notes, "The same year *The Disinherited* came out, the New York Public Library announced that it would be purchasing 50,000 books that year—instead of their usual 250,000" (Paul Garon, "American Labor Fiction in the 20th Century," *A. B. Bookman's Weekly* [February 19, 1990], 744). With regard to paperback publishing, Hellmut Lehmann-Haupt remarked that in 1929 Liveright had tried to publish fifty cent paperbacks, and in 1930 Simon and Schuster tried to bring out dollar paperbacks; both enterprises failed (*The Book in America: A History of Books in the United States* [New York: R. R. Bowker, 1939], pp. 225–27).

and middle-class readers had begun to be attracted by the emerging school of writing. Had the revolution in paperback publishing occurred a decade earlier in the United States, we may speculate that significantly more proletarian novels might have made their way to interested working-class readers. Still, even if we take into account the prohibitive prices for hardcover novels and the likelihood that library copies of proletarian novels routinely reached sizeable numbers of working-class readers, the fact remains that the proletarian novel can hardly be said to have attracted a mass audience. If proponents of the proletarian novel adhered to the criterion of audience as central to their definition of proletarian fiction, clearly they would encounter some problems.

Literary leftists were unhappy that proletarian fiction did not reach a larger working-class audience. But their discomfiture did not generally affect their conception of the goal and function of the proletarian novel. In a 1934 *New Quarterly* symposium entitled "For Whom Do You Write?" a clear majority of the leftist writers who responded evinced a willingness to address an audience defined in fairly broad sociological and political terms. Some—including the playwright John Howard Lawson, Conroy, Caldwell, and the midwest writer W. D. Trowbridge—saw themselves as speaking to the traditional proletariat; their conception of audience was explicitly empirical and made no stipulations about prior levels of political development or agreement. Lawson remarked that the writer "can no longer appeal to the decayed bourgeoisie which has furnished the audience for books and plays in the period of capitalism. He must write in a new way, for an entirely new audience—the workers!" Caldwell was quoted as saying that he wrote for "workers, laborers, farmers, simple, inarticulate people." Trowbridge described his audience as "the American section of that great productive class [the world proletariat]." Conroy declared, "I should like to think that I am writing for the proletariat; I know that I am writing at them." Even though "the comparatively small sale of the few proletarian novels as yet published may cause discouragement," workers' tastes were changing:

> Workers are tiring of the a-shot-rang-out, on-the-sweet-scented-hay-beneath-the-wise-old-harvest-moon-I-gave-all-a-girl-has-to-give pulp and confession fodder. . . . The publication and increasing distribution of such books as Robert Cantwell's "The Land of Plenty," William Rollins' "The Shadow Be-

fore," and Arnold Armstrong's "Parched Earth" is significant of a trend that is sure to gather momentum.[20]

Some of the respondents held out for the actual proletariat as the audience of their work. A significantly larger number, however—including Rahv, Hicks, Freeman, Schneider, Dahlberg, Farrell, Seaver, Calmer, and John Reed Clubs Secretary Oakley Johnson—envisioned their audience as a mixture of workers and intellectuals that was defined by a combination of objective class position and political stance. Schneider praised this diverse "revolutionary" audience as "the clearest-headed, most alert, most responsive of any I have written for." Johnson described his audience as consisting of farmers, students, teachers, workers ("those who actually and potentially are the revolutionary vanguard"), Negroes, the foreign-born, and the "professional men and women" who are "potential allies of the revolutionary proletariat." Hicks expressed the desire that literary radicalism reach "intellectuals who have moved or are moving to the left," "intellectuals who are only beginning to question the existing order," and "class-conscious proletarians." Freeman declared that he was writing for "all who are oppressed and exploited by capitalism, and to those intellectuals who, when the truth dawns upon them, loathe this oppression and exploitation."[21]

The New Quarterly symposium has only limited value as an index to the ideas about audience held by most practicing proletarian novelists, for it was clearly slanted toward the urban intellectual wing of the movement. This bias is interesting, however, for it shows that even the commentators generally charged with having been the "commissars" of the literary left were the least inclined to limit the audience of literary proletarianism in accordance with any strict stipulations. The more theoretically inclined commentators were not demanding that proletarian texts should address an audience assumed in advance to be either proletarian or pro-Communist. And even those respondents who claimed to be writing for a working-class audience cannot be charged with having constructed in fan-

20. "For Whom Do You Write?: Replies from Forty American Writers," New Quarterly 1 (Summer 1934): 8, 13. Conroy stressed that workers would for financial reasons have limited access to his work. As he wrote to Hicks, "[M]y book will be a cry de profundis to horrify the bourgeois who can afford to buy novels. But maybe a few workers will read it, too" (Conroy to Hicks, May 28, 1932, Box 14, Hicks Papers).
21. Ibid., 7, 11, 12.

tasy a mass audience of workers, class-conscious or not. Conroy, we will recall, conceded that the audience "at" which he was aiming might not necessarily be the one he was actually writing "for."

In short, the literary leftists manifested a fairly clear-eyed understanding of the relation between actual and potential audiences, and they seem to have taken in stride the proletarian novel's slowness in attracting substantial numbers of working-class readers. As Cantwell put it in his riposte to Adamic, the proletarian novel could not be said to be "addressed" to the working class in the same way that a romance or Wild West tale was. The proletarian novel's goal was to "advance the heritage of human culture," he declared. "It is a cultural product and its value cannot be determined in any important way by the size of its immediate audience." Gold, also responding to Adamic, remarked, "One cannot say with the assumed air of finality of Mr. Adamic that because workers do not read our writings today, they never will." For Adamic, Calverton, and other adherents to the Trotskyist position, the empirical criterion of audience played a central role in discrediting the genre's claim to legitimacy. For Cantwell, Gold, and other Third-Period Marxists, however, empirical findings regarding the size and composition of actual audiences functioned as a spur for heightened activity. They did not call into question the project of proletarian fiction.[22]

The Criterion of Subject Matter

The definition of proletarian literature as literature treating the subject matter of working-class experience was perhaps the most commonly invoked criterion for determining whether or not a text should be defined as "proletarian." The judges of the New Masses proletarian novel contest, for example, were unequivocal in their requirement that submitted manuscripts "deal with the American proletariat."[23] It was not sufficient that the text be written "from the point of view of the proletariat," they warned. Throughout the Third Period—and even to some degree into the Popular Front, despite the increasing substitution of "the people" for "the workers" in Communist rhetoric—there was general agreement among writers and

22. Cantwell, "What the Working Class Reads," 274; Gold, "Change the World!" *DW* (December 14, 1934): 5.

23. NM 11 (June 5, 1934): 7.

critics alike that proletarian literature should represent primarily if not exclusively the life of the proletariat.

The Marxist critics' emphasis upon the importance of working-class subject matter manifested itself in a number of the evaluative criteria they adopted in their reviews and commentaries. One such criterion was an open preference for novels treating working-class characters and settings and a corollary skepticism about novels focusing largely upon the dilemmas of middle-class characters. Some texts were exempted from such judgments. Herbst's *The Executioner Waits* received near-universal praise, as did the different volumes of Dos Passos's *U.S.A.* trilogy, even though both texts treat many characters from the middle class. Few hackles were raised by fielding Burke's warmly sympathetic depiction in *A Stone Came Rolling* of Bly Emberson, the mill owner alienated from his class. But these texts, as Hicks pointed out, were all complex or collective novels in which "representative proletarian characters" could be "set over against representative bourgeois characters." When confronted with novels focusing more narrowly upon the consciousness of bourgeois or petty bourgeois characters, however, critics were likely to come out with more strongly negative judgments. Edwin Seaver noted that Waldo Frank's *The Death and Birth of David Markand*, a novel detailing the alienation and eventual political awakening of a petty bourgeois, "shows a purely religious quest that has very little to do with the acceptance of the class struggle and the proletarian philosophy." Lauren Gilfillan's *I Went to Pit College*, an autobiographical narration of a young middle-class reporter's jaunt of living among striking coal miners, was dismissed in the left press as an elitist distortion of working-class reality. André Malraux's *Man's Fate*, while widely respected for its acute psychological portraiture, was criticized for its focus upon revolutionary intellectuals and exclusion of workers and coolies. "There is hardly a glimpse of all this and without it the relationships between Malraux's characters are only psychological ones, arbitrarily concerned and unrelated to the real causes of the Chinese revolutionary awakening," noted the *New Masses* reviewer. "The world of this book is not above the revolution, but it is apart from it." [24]

24. Hicks, "Revolution and the Novel," in Robbins, p. 33; "Change the World!" *DW* (October 2, 1934), 5. Edwin Seaver, "Waldo Frank's Unceasing Quest," *NM* 13 (November 13, 1934): 24; Ben Field, "From Smith College to Pit College," *PR* 1 (April–May 1934): 54–56; review of *I Went to Pit College*, *Partisan* 1 (April 1934): 7; Alfred Hirsch,

Often accompanying this stress upon the importance of representing the life of the proletariat was an emphasis upon doing so with strict verisimilitude: subject matter comprised not only "raw material" but fidelity to detail, especially with regard to work processes. Gold's 1929 proposal that writers associate themselves with a major industry was intended to enable the novelist to write about work processes "like an insider, not like a bourgeois intellectual observer." A 1930 *New Masses* reader, sharing Gold's rigorous standards for accuracy in the representation of work, sent in a detailed critique of a picture of a lumberjack that had appeared in a previous issue. The artist had portrayed the worker standing so close to the wood he was cutting, noted this partisan of authenticity, that the lumberjack would have been in danger of lopping off his foot. Hicks also held up verisimilitude as a criterion for excellence in proletarian literature. Comparing *A Stone Came Rolling* with the earlier *Call Home the Heart*, he congratulated Burke for overcoming her own lack of direct acquaintance with the experience of mill workers. Her success, he declared, was a "challenge to the revolutionary novelists who have allowed themselves to be beaten by ignorance." Mary Heaton Vorse noted Rollins's use of actual trial transcripts in his Gastonia novel *The Shadow Before* and praised the novel for its truth to life. Comparing *The Shadow Before* with her own earlier Gastonia novel *Strike!*, Vorse commented on "how much closer to the truth the author has gone than have any of his predecessors, how much more of the reality of a labor conflict he has managed to pack into his pages than the rest of us did." [25]

"The Sympathies of Malraux," *NM* 12 (July 3, 1934): 43–44. Edwin Berry Burgum also reviewed Frank's novel somewhat unsympathetically, remarking that Frank "became a novelist too early and a communist too late" ("Six Authors in Search of Their Future," *PR* 1 [November–December 1934]: 47. After the publication of Hirsch's review there ensued in the *New Masses* a debate over his evaluation of Malraux's novel. Haakon Chevalier, the novel's translator, defended Malraux's represented cross-section of society (*NM* 12 [September 4, 1934]: 27–28). Hicks responded by supporting the political critique in Hirsch's original review (*NM* 12 [September 4, 1934]: 28–30).

25. Gold, "A Program for Writers," *NM* 5 (January 1930): 1; Harold Roland Johnson, "Letter," *NM* 5 (February 1930): 32; Hicks, "Better Than 'Call Home the Heart,'" *NM* 17 (December 3, 1935): 23; Mary Heaton Vorse, "The Feeling of a Strike," *NM* 11 (April 17, 1934): 26. If Vorse valued verisimilitude so highly, it is somewhat odd that she made no mention in her review of Rollins's decision to transpose the Gastonia events to a New England mill town inhabited by an international work force containing substantial num-

Marxist critics could be rigorous in their demand for accuracy in writers' representations of locales and work processes. Their stipulations regarding subject matter rarely extended, however, to requests that writers construct certain types of plots or portray specific political subjects. As Freeman sought to reassure Anderson, "There are no formulas. The range is unlimited; the only thing which revolutionary writers have in common is an opposition to capitalism and adherence to socialism." Although Aronowitz would have it that the "formula" for proletarian fiction entailed a key role for a Communist organizer, the CP—*as* the CP—actually appeared quite infrequently in proletarian fiction. The leftist "mentor" characters who routinely peopled proletarian novels were as likely to be associated with the IWW, or some vaguely defined socialist movement, as with the CP itself. Soviet critics, as Deming Brown points out, routinely chastised American writers for giving short shrift to the Communist party in their novels. But American critics rarely treated the representation of the party as a key criterion for assessing a novel's political effectiveness. Rahv and Phelps—in their short-lived Bolshevik phase—declared that the "new types of characters appearing in the Communist Party" called out for representation in proletarian literature. V. J. Jerome expressed regret that the "Northern organizer" in *Call Home the Heart* did not play a more central role. But the great majority of commentators upon proletarian fiction neither praised novels for successfully portraying actual card-carrying Communists nor faulted them for failing to do so. The reviewers of *Parched Earth* did not focus on Armstrong's representation of the Communist organizer Dave Washburne; commentators on *The Land of Plenty* did not query Cantwell's choice to assign the only left-wing discourse in *The Land of Plenty* to the Wobbly Vin Garl. Dos Passos's *The Big Money* and Steinbeck's *In Dubious Battle*—both of which contained highly denigrating portraits of Communist organizers—received light if any chastisement in the left press for their negative representations of the party.[26]

---

bers of Portuguese workers—that is, very like New Bedford, the site of a militant 1932 textile strike in which the CP was also deeply involved. Hicks, who liked *The Shadow Before*, felt that the novel's key weakness was that the switch of locales made the novel "too synthetic" in its representation of class struggle ("Revolutionary Literature of 1934," *WM* 14 [January 1, 1935], 37).

26. Freeman to Anderson, October 30, 1934, Freeman Papers, Butler Library, Columbia U; Rahv and Phelps, "Problems and Perspectives of Revolutionary Literature," *PR* 1 (June–July 1934): 4; Jerome, "Toward a Proletarian Novel," *NM* 8 (August 1932): 14–15.

Nor did writers for the *New Masses* or other journals of the literary left routinely object to fictional representations that curtailed the expression of revolutionary ideas. Individual reviewers at times complained of an overall lack of political clarity. In his review of *To Make My Bread*, Moishe Nadir faulted Lumpkin for writing "for the most part not from her present point of view as a revolutionist, but from the point of view of the backward workers she is describing." While noting that the novel's "revolutionary section is the weakest artistically," he offered no specific criticism of Lumpkin's timid representation of the party in the revolutionary organizer John Stevens, who takes aside John McClure at the end of the novel and imparts to him the "message" that has presumably emancipated workers in "another country"—a "message" of which the reader overhears only fragments. In reviews of *To Make My Bread* and other novels purporting to treat Communism as an explicit issue, left-wing critics were notably silent on the party as an issue in literary representation. Indeed, they often reserved their warmest praise for novels—*The Land of Plenty*, *The Disinherited*—in which the party is in fact not explicitly present at all. Hostile critics have routinely denigrated literary proletarianism for its Leninist dogmatism. Ironically, however, a careful scrutiny of both proletarian novels and what was said about them reveals that reformism and spontaneism were widely articulated and tolerated—even to a degree promoted—by the 1930s literary left.[27]

Isidor Schneider gently demurred with Dos Passos's stereotypical portraiture of Communists in Ben Compton and Don Stevens but declared that *The Big Money* was "great," containing some of the "finest realized individuals in our literature" ("Greatness," *NM* 20 [August 11, 1936]: 40, 41). Walter Ralston, in his *New Masses* review of *In Dubious Battle*, specifically defended Steinbeck's depiction of Mac and Jim ("California Battleground," *NM* 18 [February 18, 1936]: 22–23). Bernard Smith, by contrast, was highly critical of Steinbeck's treatment of Mac, noting that "Mr. Steinbeck makes that man say things for which he could be expelled in disgrace from his party twenty times over. Specifically, this man displays a recklessness and a cold-blooded manipulation of violence which are romantic fictions of the author's imagination." Curiously, Smith's review appeared not in the left press but in the *New York Herald-Tribune Books* (February 2, 1936, p. 6). One of the sharper critiques of Rollins's depiction of the role played by the Communist leader Marvin in *The Shadow Before* was given by Rahv. The strike is "too spontaneous," Rahv remarked. "The conscious element in the leadership is not sufficiently stressed" ("The Novelist as Partisan," *PR* 1 [April–May 1934]: 52).

27. Moishe Nadir, "To Make My Bread," *NM* 8 (February 1933): 19, 20; Grace Lumpkin, *To Make My Bread* (New York: Macaulay, 1932), pp. 324–28. Clearly a discussion

Marxist critics did not specifically urge proletarian novelists to incorporate the Communist party into their narratives' subject matter. But Marxist politics still crept through the back door of discussions of the subject matter of proletarian fiction. For when it came to deciding what was essential to or representative of working-class experience, there was considerable debate: what the writer felt to be representative or typical could be, in the eyes of the critic, distorted or idiosyncratic. The editors of the *New Masses* appended to Meridel Le Sueur's description of the unemployed women, "Women on the Breadlines," the comment that "[t]his representation of the plight of the unemployed, able as it is, and informative, is defeatist in attitude, lacking in the revolutionary spirit and direction which characterizes the usual contribution to *New Masses*. We feel it our duty to add, that there is a place for the unemployed women, as well as men, in the ranks of the unemployed councils and in all branches of the organized revolutionary movement." Joseph North, in a review of Halper's *The Foundry*, a novel set among unionized Chicago print-shop workers in the months leading up to

---

of the extent to which the Third-Period CPUSA was or was not a Leninist organization is beyond the scope of this study. While it would be foolish to argue that the party which took as its manifesto William Z. Foster's 1932 *Toward Soviet America* was simply a reformist organization, recent scholarship on the CPUSA suggests that the organization may not deserve its Draper-school reputation for steeled and sectarian Leninism. See, in particular, Roger Keeran, *The Communist Party and the Auto Workers Unions* (Bloomington and London: Indiana UP, 1980); James Weinstein, *Ambiguous Legacy: The Left in American Politics* (New York: New Viewpoints, Franklin Watts, 1975); Mark Naison, *Communists in Harlem during the Depression* (New York: Grove P, 1983); James R. Prickett, "Anti-Communism and Labor History," *Industrial Relations* 13 (October 1974): 219–27; and Fraser M. Ottanelli, *The Communist Party of the United States: From the Depression to World War II* (New Brunswick and London: Rutgers UP, 1991). A random glance through the *Communist* and the *Daily Worker* yields ample evidence of rank-and-file dissatisfaction with the CP leadership's hesitancy about keeping revolutionary politics in the foreground. See, for example, Gertrude Haessler, "How Not to Apply the Open Letter," *Communist* 13 (March 1934): 261–71, and Max Salzman, "Do Not Permit 'Leftist' Errors to Liquidate the Results of the Hunger March," *DW* (January 9, 1932), 6. Mauritz Hallgren, a liberal journalist who observed the mounting class struggles in the early 1930s with excitement, referred to the CP's "timid Communism" and noted, "[I]t is evident that at no time were the Communists actively preparing for insurrection. All that they aspired to, apparently, was to awaken the class consciousness of the more advanced proletarians. They believed that an 'objective situation' had to arise before they could even think of striking" (*Seeds of Revolt: A Study of American Life and the Temper of the American People during the Depression* [New York: Alfred Knopf, 1933], p. 338.

the stock market crash, chided Halper for not having depicted the workers' revolutionary potential. Halper's apolitical, passive foundry workers are not "typical" proletarians, North complained: "One must not be left with the impression that *these* workers are the proletariat." Leon Dennen commented adversely upon Hughes's option not to depict militancy among black proletarians in *The Ways of White Folks*. "Truth in our days is revolutionary," he opined. "The drama of the rising revolutionary consciousness of the Negro masses in America has altogether escaped [Hughes]." Two reviews of Zora Neale Hurston's work claimed that Hurston had evaded the central issues of concern to impoverished Southern blacks. The folk depicted in *Mules and Men*, Sterling Brown declared, were too "meek" and "socially unconscious"; the text "should be more bitter; it would be nearer the total truth." In *Their Eyes Were Watching God*, Richard Wright asserted, Hurston dwelt too exclusively upon her heroine's personal development: as a result, the novel had "no theme, no message, no thought." [28]

It was not necessarily inappropriate for left-wing reviewers to judge texts for the adequacy of their representations of reality. Typicality is a political, and not merely an aesthetic, category of analysis; politics *is* (*are*) implicated in reference. Marxist commentators were bent upon fostering cultural representations that revealed the emergent revolutionary tendencies in the proletariat. But the critics erred when they assumed that left-wing class consciousness was in some way intrinsic to subject matter. In essence, they were arguing that reality, the realm of the objective, supplies the terms of its own transcription without the mediation of perception, analysis, interpretation. The realm of the subjective—whence comes, presumably, the conclusion that revolution is on the agenda—is simply a reflex of that reality. The problem of adequate reflection is, for the commentators cited here, little more than a problem of recording the self-evident; revolutionary optimism hinges upon the representation of an intrinsically optimistic reality—the much-touted "way out." [29]

28. "Note," *NM* 7 (January 1932): 7; Joseph North, "Still on the Fence," *NM* 12 (September 25, 1934): 24–25; Leon Dennen, "Negroes and Whites," review of *The Ways of White Folks*, *PR* 1 (November–December 1934): 51; Sterling Brown, "Old Time Tales," *NM* 18 (February 25, 1936): 24–25; Richard Wright, "Between Laughter and Tears," *NM* 25 (October 5, 1937): 22, 25.

29. Joseph North, in an account of his feelings after having addressed a black congregation in Red Bank, New Jersey, about the Scottsboro case—and then having been escorted to the train station by the entire congregation, who anticipated a right-wing backlash—

It was simply not sufficient, however, to say that Halper's workers are not *the* proletariat, or that Le Sueur's unemployed women do not display an appropriate spirit of resistance, or that Hurston's rural blacks are oblivious to the viciousness of Southern racism. For in fact each of these authors depicts phenomena that are empirically "true," in the sense of actually existing. The problem is that the authors do not find ways to let the reader know that the reality being represented is in fact contradictory. The appearance of passivity does not necessarily signal a corresponding univocal essence; it does not tell the whole story. In order for a text to suggest a "way out," in other words, it does not need to depict the insurgent proletariat as an empirical fact, but only to signal that, while the consciousness of the proletariat is an admixture of bourgeois and revolutionary tendencies, aspects of this consciousness which are currently secondary will in time become primary and essence-determining. Instead of calling upon writers to come up with depictions of the working class reflecting its internal contradictions, however, some commentators substituted the part for the whole, concluding that the text does not represent reality at all if it does not share the Marxist critic's estimate of which aspects of that reality are essence-determining. A pragmatist conception of the "total truth" supplanted the dialectical conception of totality.[30]

The types of prescriptions accompanying Third-Period discussions of the subject matter of proletarian literature partake of an odd blend of open-

---

gives a concrete formulation of what the dialectical category of the "emergent" (or, as he puts it here, the "nascent") meant to 1930s Communist organizers:

> The episode served to dispel the doubts assailing me, for here in Red Bank I believed I had seen that which is "nascent"—the new that was being born—displacing that which is "moribund"—the old that was dying—an expression from my Marxist readings which impressed me indelibly. It seemed to me the epitome of the Marxist attitude toward reality. . . .
>
> I had no illusions about my adventure in the small Jersey town. It was the exceptional, even though it represented the new. (*No Men Are Strangers* [New York: International, 1958], pp. 93–94)

30. The terms "primary" and "secondary" contradiction, "primary aspect" and "secondary aspect" of a contradiction, and "essence-determining" are drawn from Mao Zedong's important development of dialectical theory, "On Contradiction" (*Selected Readings from the Works of Mao Tsetung* [Peking: Foreign Languages P, 1971], pp. 432–79).

ness and dogmatism. Contrary to the received wisdom, critics actually made few stipulations about the topics that writers should or should not represent. They offered no "formulas" about conversion plots, triumphant workers, or heroic party members: so long as writers addressed some aspect of working-class experience and indicated its relation to the class struggle, they should follow the bidding of their own imaginations. Criticisms of the adequacy of a text's representation of reality were offered a posteriori: no a priori guidelines were set forth for proletarian writers. Yet Marxist critics frequently muddied the theoretical waters by conflating subject matter with perspective. Rather than directly criticizing writers for the analytical paradigms shaping their appropriation of given segments of social reality, the critics directed attention to the issue of typicality. Rather than chastising writers for failing to represent the emergent as a contradiction between "is" and "will be," the critics more commonly faulted texts for being "not true" to reality. The critics were bending over backward to avoid the posture of dogmatism: Freeman spoke sincerely when he promised Anderson that "the range is unlimited." But by collapsing "will be" into "is," the commentators at times treated "ought" as a category of reality itself, rather than of the praxis needed to shape and change reality. Like the debates over authorship, discussions of the subject matter of proletarian literature betrayed an empiricist and reformist bent. Dogmatism crept in the back door not because the critics were handing down Leninist mandates, but because they were conflating experience with theory.

The Criterion of Perspective

Third-Period discussions about proletarian literature were founded on a paradox. Marxist critics were eager to foster a literature solidly based in working-class life. They wished to cultivate writers of working-class origins, to address working-class audiences, and to represent working-class existence. Yet they sought a literature saturated in proletarian experience not because they viewed the working class as either colorful or pitiable, but because they saw it as the class uniquely positioned to bring about revolutionary change. The great majority of literary leftists were exactly that—leftists. They sought not merely a general heightening of consciousness about exploitation and suffering but the establishment of a socialist system more or less in consonance with the Soviet example. Most envisioned revolution as the necessary path for achieving workers' power and saw literature as a means of arousing and preparing the proletariat and its allies for their historical tasks. As a result, the Marxists' critical pronouncements often signaled the strong—if theoretically unspecified—conviction that proletarian literature, as a "weapon," should be revolutionary rather than reformist in its implications. Freeman wrote to Anderson that, even if there were "no formulas" and the "range" of proletarian literature was "unlimited," revolutionary writers all shared "an opposition to capitalism and adherence to socialism." Hicks, speaking to the "diverse" potential contributors to the New Masses, noted that "every one of us believes that the capitalist system must be destroyed by the power of the proletariat, in alliance with the exploited farmers, the ruined middle class and the aroused intellectual and professional class." Gold wrote of the "revolutionary spirit" uniting all writers engaged in creating proletarian literature. According to the leading Marxist critics, proletarian texts should convey ideas and attitudes that would impel their readers to take action against existing social conditions—that is, move them leftward.

Curiously, however, the notion that writers should adhere to an unambiguously Marxist conceptual framework was in fact raised quite infrequently in critical discussions of the late 1920s and early 1930s, when in other respects the line of the party was as far left as it would ever be. Commentators like Nadir, who advocated that texts be written from the "point of view of . . . a revolutionist," were in fact in a distinct minority. The Third Period is routinely viewed as an ultraleftist phase when Communist critics advocated that proletarian literature be openly propagandistic on behalf of revolution. But, somewhat ironically, it was only in the months immediately preceding the endorsement of the Popular Front that Marxist perspective came to be widely discussed as the basis for defining proletarian literature. Moreover, it was only at this time that explicit avowal of adherence to the party became an issue on the literary left.

In an issue of Partisan Review devoted exclusively to the upcoming 1935 Writers Congress, considerable space was given over to an analysis of the proletarian novel. The main paper under discussion was Edwin Seaver's "What Is a Proletarian Novel? Notes Toward a Definition," which would be the main paper on proletarian fiction at the Congress. "The proletarian novel," Seaver declared, "is not necessarily a novel written by a worker about workers or for workers. . . . It is possible for an author of middleclass origin to write a novel about petty-bourgeois characters which will appeal primarily to readers of the same class, and yet such a work can come within the classification, Proletarian Novel." The key to any determination of whether an author had written a novel that should be considered proletarian, Seaver decided, resided exclusively in its political orientation:

> It is not the class origin of the novelist that matters but his present class alignment, not the period of history in which he sets his story, or the kind of characters he writes about, but his ideological approach to his story and characters, which approach is entirely conditioned by his acceptance of the Marxian interpretation of history. And not only the acceptance, but the use of this interpretation as a compelling factor in his work.

On the basis of this criterion, Seaver noted, Herbst's *The Executioner Waits*, while written by a middle-class writer primarily about middle-class people, qualified as a proletarian novel more than did Halper's *The Foundry*, even though Halper's origins were closer to the working class and he was writing about workers on a shop floor. The criterion of perspective, Seaver concluded, enabled literary proletarianism to "eliminate the sorry confusion that has prevailed and still does prevail in so many discussions of proletarian literature."[31]

Seaver's paper sparked considerable discussion, both in the *Partisan Review* pre-Congress issue and at the Congress itself. Edwin Berry Burgum seconded Seaver's thesis, positing that "the proletarian novel is a novel written under the influence of dialectical materialism from the point of view of the class-conscious proletariat." Moreover, he noted, "at the present time, the proletarian novel is usually not read by the proletariat, whether class-conscious or not, and it is seldom written by a proletarian." Indeed, Burgum went so far as to state—and in so doing to contradict the clearly pro-worker-writer policy of *New Masses* to date—that workers tended not to write good proletarian literature at all, since their novels tended to be "reportage, the diary, the sketch"—"true to experience," but lacking "that selective ordering of experience under the control of a dominating social point of view which is the primary condition of form in lit-

---

31. Seaver, "What Is a Proletarian Novel?: Notes Toward a Definition," *PR* 2 (April–May 1935): 5, 7; Seaver, "The Proletarian Novel," in Hart, ed., *AWC*, p. 100.

erature." For Seaver and Burgum, the "point of view of the proletariat" was equivalent to Marxism; proletarian authorship, audience, or subject matter were not necessary so long as a novel espoused "the Marxian interpretation of history."[32]

It would appear that the invocation of Marxist perspective as the key criterion for defining proletarian literature gained adherents in the months preceding and following the 1935 Congress. In his introduction to *Proletarian Literature in the United States*, which was published soon after the Congress, Freeman stated unequivocally that proletarian literature was literature usually written by the middle class, but from the viewpoint of the revolutionary proletariat. He set forth a new criterion for adjudicating how this "viewpoint" was to be defined: the revolutionary writer, he declared, was now faced with confronting the connection between "poetry, politics, and party." Seaver, along similar lines, upbraided the fellow-traveling poet Horace Gregory for his reluctance to commit himself to the party. In February 1935, Seaver declared, "The literary honeymoon is over, and I believe the time is fast approaching when we will no longer classify authors as proletarian writers and fellow-travelers, but as Party writers and non-Party writers." Discussions about what constituted a work of proletarian literature had changed substantially from Gold's early appeal that workers "write. . . . Tell us your story. It is sure to be significant."[33]

The Seaver/Burgum/Freeman position by no means went uncontested by other convention participants. The worker-writer Martin Russak complained that Seaver's position came close to a non-class-conscious humanism: "If we understand the nature of class division," he warned, "we would not say that all people are the same." In the working class, Russak argued, there is "a distinct kind of human being" which it is the duty of the proletarian novel to represent. Gold attempted to mediate between Seaver and Russak. Expressing concern that "our literary movement is in danger of becoming a petty bourgeois movement," Gold declared, "We must stand equally against the idea that proletarian literature has a place only for novels about the working class . . . as well as against the idea that novels about workers are not important." Moreover, Gold maintained, "One of

32. Edwin Berry Burgum, "Discussion," *PR* 2 (April–May 1935): 8, 9, 10.

33. Freeman, "Introduction," *Proletarian Literature in the United States*, pp. 13, 20–21; Seaver, "Another Writer's Position," *NM* 14 (February 19, 1935): 22.

the basic tasks of every writer is to stimulate and encourage and help the growth of proletarian literature which is written by workers." Nonetheless, it was clear, both at the Congress and in various commentaries that followed it, that some of the younger writers—of whom a substantial proportion were worker-writers—were concerned that the new interest in "perspective" might simply serve as a pretext for bypassing writers of proletarian origin in favor of middle-class progressives who could not write about the proletariat because they had no direct experience with it. Fred Miller, editor of *Blast* and author of several "red" short stories, sharply attacked the new interest in middle-class writers that was emerging from the Congress, declaring that not merely *Partisan Review* but the *New Masses* as well had been printing "the soggy stuff of 'revolutionary' dabblers and opportunists." He stated his preference for the smaller and less prestigious "mushroom mags" of the left, which published the work of "the young jobless men from the proletariat and the lower middle-class coming to literary maturity in this the last depression, young men hard as nails, nobody's fools, knowing the class war from experience, the men fitted to give you the real stuff of proletarian literature." [34]

How are we to understand the politics involved in the dramatic alteration in the grounds for defining proletarian fiction that occurred around the time of the 1935 Writers Congress? The standard view is that the new stress upon perspective, along with the downplaying of proletarian authorship, were part of the party's overall shift in strategy around the time of the Popular Front. At this time, the argument goes, the John Reed Clubs were disbanded and the party, bent upon centralizing its power base in the cultural realm, began to cultivate connections with the liberal antifascist writers drawn together under the umbrella of the party-led League of American Writers. In this context the advocacy of political perspective as the determinant of whether or not a text could be adjudged "proletarian" can be seen as an essentially opportunist move, designed not to urge writers to become more Marxist but to foster a literary program less

34. Hart, "Discussion and Proceedings," *AWC*, pp. 166–67; Fred R. Miller, quoted in Daniel Aaron, *Writers on the Left: Odysseys in American Literary Communism* (1961; rpt. New York: Avon, 1964), p. 312. The politics of the debate were complicated. Miller here sounds workerist. Conroy, however, observed that Miller was "a member of the Rahv faction in the New York chapter of the Rebel Poets" (Curt Johnson and Conroy, *Writers in Revolt: The Anvil Anthology* [New York and Westport: Lawrence Hill, 1973], p. xv).

geared toward specifically working-class concerns and participation and more palatable to the inclinations of the progressive middle-class writers the party was attempting to woo. Burgum's denigration of worker-writers' "sketches" could thus be seen not just as the articulation of one critic's idiosyncratic elitism, but as an expression of a party-sanctioned shift in attitudes and preferences. As we noted in chapter 2, it is generally concluded that, with the formation of the League of American Writers out of the Congress, the Americans demonstrated their subservience to the latest line from Moscow, since they were aping the 1934 formation of the All-Russian Soviet Writers Union. According to this line of argument, the decline of interest in the quasi-journalistic offerings of worker-writers and the newfound stress upon fictional forms that would enable writers to address the interactions among classes are evidence of the American party's relinquishment of its "Proletkult delusions" and its acceptance of an Americanized variant on socialist realism. Seaver's and Freeman's explicit calls for connecting the Marxist politics of proletarian literature with the specific program of the Communist party are read not as part of an attempt to bolshevize creative writers, but instead as an effort to garner broad-based support for a party that had become, in Rahv's words, more interested in writers than in writing. At issue in the debate with Gregory was not left politics, but party loyalty.[35]

Some important changes had indeed been occurring within the American literary left in the months preceding the Congress. John Chamberlain, hardly one of the Congress's more sympathetic observers, reported, "I had gone expecting a lot of dismal and empty talk about 'art as a class weapon,' with the cliché Marxism beating a rat-tat-tat upon the tympani, but it was apparent from the start that the RAPP period in American literary communism has been liquidated." Remarking upon the dominance of positions represented by Herbst and Seaver over "those who urged on all proletarian writers the example of Zola who went out to investigate the lot of the coal miners in France," Chamberlain congratulated the literary left on the "right-about-face in the communist ranks." Chamberlain explicitly cor-

---

35. The standard version of this position is put forward by Aaron, pp. 297–324. See also Cowley, *The Dream of the Golden Mountains* (New York: Viking, 1980), and Harvey Klehr, *The Heyday of American Communism: The Depression Years* (New York: Basic Books, 1984), pp. 69–84, 167–85.

related this shift away from the "art as a class weapon" thesis with the abandonment of authorship and subject matter as criteria for defining proletarian literature; he specifically cited Seaver's advocacy of "perspective" when he applauded the Congress for its sensible reformulation of proletarian literature. By Seaver's criterion, Chamberlain argued, many a work of modern bourgeois literature could now be welcomed into the fold of the left: "If Proust or Joyce, for instance, serve to make a reader thoroughly dissatisfied with our civilization and willing to explore the communist or socialist proposals for a way out, Proust or Joyce is functioning on a 'revolutionary' level to a certain extent." For Chamberlain the left's adoption of perspective as the main criterion for defining proletarian literature released literary proletarianism from the obligation to train working-class writers, address a working-class audience, or treat working-class experience—all enterprises with which he apparently had little sympathy. Indeed, in Chamberlain's view the perspective criterion required of writers little more than a stance of protest against some aspect of modern life. In Chamberlain's eyes the Congress gave its stamp of approval to the liberal middle-class values with which he felt comfortable.[36]

That perspective could indeed become coterminous with a vaguely oppositional progressiveness was to be amply illustrated by much of the distinctly nonrevolutionary literature subsequently produced under the influence of Popular Front antifascism and patriotism. But it is too simplistic to view the increasing interest in perspective as a party-engineered response to the changing imperatives of the Communist International. As I argued in the preceding chapter, the 1935 Congress must be seen not only in the context of the impending Popular Front but also in that of Kharkov. The Congress's assertion that writers should align themselves with

36. John Chamberlain, "The Literary Left Grows Up," *SRL* 12 (May 11, 1933): 3–4, 17–18; "The First American Writers' Congress," *SRL* 12 (May 4, 1935): 4. For more on Chamberlain's attitude toward the literary radicals, see Alfred Kazin's memoir of the decade, *Starting Out in the Thirties* (Boston, Toronto: Little, Brown, 1965). In 1934 Hicks argued that Chamberlain's criticisms of the literary left's supposed sectarianism masked a contempt for literary radicalism as such: "Why should he pretend to be opposing only the excesses of what he pleasantly calls 'an American RAPP' when what he really objects to are the basic assumptions of Marxist criticism?" (*NM* 13 [October 9, 1934]: 22). Chamberlain articulated his version of anti-Communist liberalism in *Farewell to Reform: The Rise, Life and Decay of the Progressive Mind in America* (Chicago: Quadrangle, 1932).

the revolutionary movement; the frank advocacy of Soviet-style social-ism; the sharp confrontation with Burke over substituting the term "the people" for "the workers"—these and other features of the Congress sug-gest that the American literary left saw itself as adhering to the platform to which it had pledged itself at Kharkov several years before. Even posi-tions that anticipate the Popular Front, such as the broadened appeal to middle-class writers, had also been part of the Kharkov program. Rather than representing, as Chamberlain suggests, the "liquida[tion] . . . of the RAPP period in American literary communism," the adoption of Marxist perspective as the distinguishing feature of proletarian literature signaled if anything the Americans' endorsement of "dialectical materialism" and "the living man"—slogans epitomizing the RAPP program. To the extent that it indicated any change in the cultural line of the American left, the 1935 Congress demonstrates not primarily a turn toward liberal Popular Frontism, but the articulation and consolidation of a literary and epistemo-logical program that had been guiding much of U.S. literary proletarianism for several years.

Besides, there is no evidence that the position developed by Seaver and Burgum at the 1935 Congress enjoyed the particular blessing of the party leadership. Neither Seaver nor Burgum was at this point a particu-larly important figure in party cultural circles. Calmer remarked to Hicks in January 1935, four months before the Congress, that Seaver wrote as an "'outsider,' a bourgeois writer who admits there is something good about Marxism." Burgum came to assume significant stature as a party intellec-tual toward the end of the decade, but in 1935 he was not a key player. It is unlikely that, had the party wanted to put forward a distinct "line" on aesthetic matters at the Congress, it would not have entrusted the task to Hicks, Freeman, or Gold. More importantly, there is simply no evidence that the party *did* have any such line. Extant documents recording party-level discussions about mid-1930s cultural work indicate that mundane organizational questions almost completely preoccupied important party figures. In 1934 Calmer—then head of the national John Reed Clubs and a close party ally—complained to "Comrade" Trachtenberg, the party's cul-tural "commissar," about the "almost completely planless development" of the literary movement. As item no. 14 on a long list of suggestions for increased party activity, Calmer noted the need for a "Program of Study of Marxism for ideological development of writers (to include also Marxian approach to literature)." Calmer did not specify what this "Marxian approach" might be. It is difficult to believe that a Communist-affiliated leadership viewing itself as so out of control of the cultural movement could have formulated—much less organized to put over—a particular line on questions of literary representation.[37]

Moreover, CPUSA Chairman Earl Browder, in his address to the Congress, stated that "the first demand of the Party upon its writer-members is that they shall be good writers, constantly better writers." His only comment on what being a "good" writer meant was vague: "[F]ine literature must arise directly out of expressing not only [the] problems, but, at the same time, all the richness and complexity of detail of life itself." Browder denied that the party wanted to "politicalize" fellow-traveling writers by "imposing upon them its pre-conceived ideas of subject matter, treatment and form." The party hoped to play "a leading role in the field of fine literature," but this could not be done "by means of Party resolutions giving judgment upon artistic, aesthetic questions." He concluded, "There is no fixed 'Party line' by which works of art can be automatically separated into sheep and goats." Anti-Communist commentators routinely construe Browder's pluralism as evidence of the party's plan to entice unwitting liberals into its web. Browder was no doubt eager to reassure the liberal writers gravitating toward the left that the party was not going to browbeat them into writing propaganda. But Browder did not need to lie in order to produce such reassurance. He was simply articulating the party line—which was that, as regards literary matters, it really had no line at all.[38]

Finally, and most crucially, there is no reason to assume that the abandonment of the more "empirical" grounds for defining proletarian literature—authorship, audience, subject matter—and the adoption of the criterion of perspective should lead in a conservative direction. Indeed, quite the opposite case could be argued: the proposal that Marxist politics should guide the creation of proletarian literature could be seen as evidence that the U.S. literary left was finally freeing itself from the workerist and empiricist tendencies that had frequently muddied its analysis of authorship

37. Calmer to Hicks, January 15, 1935, Box 11, Hicks Papers; Calmer to Trachtenberg, July 29, 1934, and "Draft Plan for Reorganization of Cultural Movement," both in Box 2, Trachtenberg Papers, Wisconsin State Historical Society.

38. Earl Browder, "Communism and Literature," in AWC, pp. 69, 68.

and subject matter. Burgum's judgment that most workers could not write effective proletarian fiction bespeaks an undeniable elitism. But not all advocates of the perspective criterion envisioned it as a way of superseding specifically working-class voices or concerns. Freeman, in his introduction to *Proletarian Literature in the United States*, urged that proletarian writers—whether artists who come from the ranks of the working class or those who go over to it from other class sectors—"must produce a class art which is revolutionary." Proletarian art, he declared, is art which "illumines the whole of the contemporary world from the only viewpoint from which it is possible to see it steadily and see it whole." There is nothing in Freeman's advocacy of perspective to suggest a retreat from revolutionary politics. Indeed, he is suggesting that what is distinctive to the proletarian perspective is its capacity to grasp social totality—a formulation that, we shall see, precisely echoes Lenin's description of the role of the revolutionary party in *What Is To Be Done?* In Freeman's discussion the designation of perspective as the defining trait of proletarian literature carries distinctly revolutionary implications: "poetry, politics, and party" must be connected not because party politics dictate the exploitation of poets, but because only the politics of the party can guide poetry in the representation of emancipatory truths.[39]

➣   ➣   ➣   ➣   ➣

To assert that the CPUSA did not control the specific contents or outcomes of debates over aesthetic questions is not to deny its definitive sponsorship and guidance of the movement as a whole. There is no question that, with the adoption of the Popular Front, the party used all its influence to temper the revolutionism of the Third Period. As Arthur Casciato has pointed out, even before the 1935 Congress the party was proposing the dissolution of the Reed Clubs—of which there were approximately thirty, with a membership of around 1200—and the establishment of a more inclusive

39. Freeman, "Introduction" to *Proletarian Literature in the United States*, p. 18. Seaver coupled perspective with explicitly revolutionary politics: the writer should, he remarked, "take a conscious part in leading the reader through the maze of history toward Socialism and the classless society" ("Socialist Realism," *NM* 17 [October 22, 1935]: 23–24).

League of American Writers. By the end of 1935 almost all of the Reed Clubs had folded; by the end of 1936 the term "proletarian literature" was infrequently encountered in the pages of the *New Masses*. At the Second American Writers Congress in 1937, virtually no worker-writers were in attendance and little was said about reaching a working-class readership or even portraying working-class life. The Freeman who had charged Burke with social fascism in 1935 now proclaimed that the first task facing the writers in attendance was "to fight for a great American culture." Furthermore, he posited an almost completely depoliticized basis for literary production: "If [the writer] is a writer at all, he deals with experience, and in our time, simply to record experience is to record aspects of a universal conflict and the most profound transformation in the history of mankind." Not only had proletarian authorship, audience, and subject matter gone by the boards in the aesthetic program of the left. Perspective—in the sense of Marxist perspective—had also disappeared and been supplanted by a positivist reflectionism in which "experience" needs simply to be "recorded" in order to display the "profound transformation" of contemporaneous history.[40]

Literary proletarianism failed to move ahead and develop because the priorities of the left-wing movement—including the priorities of most of the writers who attached themselves to that movement—altered dramatically with the Popular Front, not because the prescriptions issued by Marxist critics brought it to a dead end. The adoption of perspective as the principal defining feature of proletarian literature did not cause this change, nor was it necessarily symptomatic of a rightward drift. From the outset the literary radicals advocated a somewhat contradictory formulation of what proletarian literature should be and do. It should be written by workers, for workers, about workers; yet it should also convey "revolution-

40. Arthur Domenic Casciato, "Citizen Writers: A History of the League of American Writers, 1935–1942," Ph.D. Thesis, U of Virginia, 1986; Freeman, "Toward the Forties," in Hart, ed., *The Writer in a Changing World* (New York: Equinox, 1937), pp. 32, 15. Two latter-day defenses of the term "proletarian literature" stand out in the *New Masses* of the late 1930s for their exceptionality: Joshua Kunitz's "In Defense of a Term," *NM* 28 (July 12, 1938), section 2: 145–47, and Samuel Sillen's "The Funeral is Off Again," *NM* 29 (November 8, 1938): 23–24. For more on the shift from the Third Period to the Popular Front, see Walter Rideout, *The Radical Novel in the United States, 1900–1954: Some Interrelations of Literature and Society* (New York: Hill and Wang, 1956), pp. 241–54.

ary élan" and contribute to the overthrow of capitalism. As the left-wing literary movement reached the first stages of maturity in the mid-1930s, the growing consensus around perspective as the key criterion for defining proletarian literature represented in many ways an advance beyond the pragmatist epistemology dominant in earlier phases. Rather than strait-jacketing literary radicals, Third-Period Marxist critics in fact played an increasingly positive and constructive role in setting forth the overall aims of proletarian literature. On the verge of the Popular Front, these critics were clarifying the issues at stake in left-wing literature, responding to the growing body of proletarian texts, and extending the domain of works that might be considered "proletarian" without compromising the larger revolutionary goals of the movement.

There is little basis to the common charge that Third-Period Marxist critics imposed a narrow, sectarian, or ultraleft definition of proletarian literature upon writers in the orbit of the left. There were some serious problems with the critical assumptions that guided the recommendations of the 1930s Marxists. These problems are best understood, however, not as manifestations of the strictures of party politics, but as expressions of the literary leftists' largely uncritical acceptance of an aesthetic theory that was essentially bourgeois rather than revolutionary. The flaws in the project of proletarian literature need to be subjected to critique not from the right, but from the left.

1929

1930

JEWS WITHOUT MONEY

BY

MICHAEL GOLD

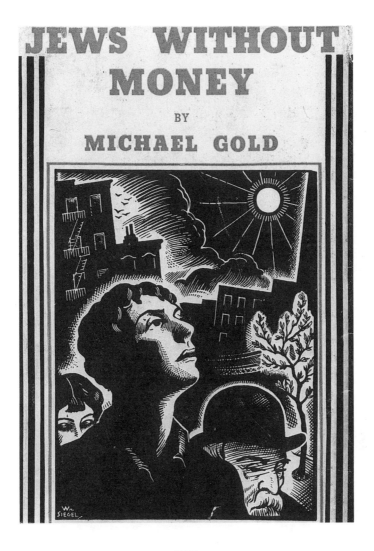

1930

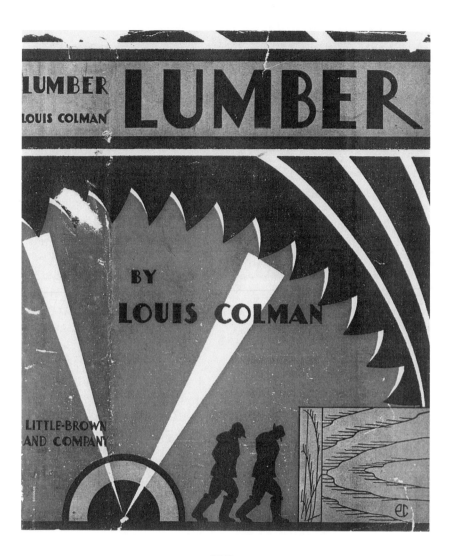

LUMBER

LOUIS COLMAN

BY

LOUIS COLMAN

LITTLE-BROWN
AND COMPANY

1931

➤

CHAPTER 4

Art or Propaganda?

The 1930s literary radicals, I have demonstrated, brought various considerations to bear in their definitions of proletarian literature. There was, however, no party line on the subject. As Jack Conroy remarked retrospectively
about the debates over what proletarian literature was, "We used to talk
about it endlessly and never arrived at any definite conclusion." Commentators hostile to 1930s literary radicalism might concede that there was
open debate over defining proletarian literature but still insist that proletarian writers felt pressured by what Fraser Ottanelli calls the "heavy
ideological limitations imposed by the third-period analysis on artistic and
aesthetic considerations." Howe and Coser charge that proletarian authors
wrote in accordance with "formulas" and that the "conversion ending"
was "the tithe the writer paid the party." Alfred Kazin characterizes proletarian novels as " 'conversion' epics which always ended with the hero
raising his fist amidst a sea of red flags." Murray Kempton asserts that the
"formula" of the proletarian novel was: "[B]oy sees vision of exploitation,
boy goes on strike, boy finds vision of freedom. . . . The proletarian novel's
hero was an Alger boy who had learned that the road upward is blocked
and that the future is with him who looks to his own class." Even if writers
did not feel bound to one or another definition of proletarian literature,
these critics argue, they felt obliged to conform to a rigid didacticism involving stock characters, formulaic plots, and a programmatic optimism.
Art had to be a weapon and, as such, an instrument of propaganda. But
since art and propaganda are antagonistically opposed, left-wing didactic
literature was condemned to mouthing slogans and preaching conversion
to the cause.[1]

1. Robert Thompson, "An Interview with Jack Conroy," *Missouri Review* 7 (Fall 1983):
159; Fraser M. Ottanelli, *The Communist Party of the United States: From the Depression to World War II* (New Brunswick and London: Rutgers UP, 1991), pp. 63–64; Irving

In future chapters we will have the opportunity to determine whether proletarian novels were in fact as formulaic and predictable as their detractors charge. What I shall argue in this chapter is that there is very limited validity to the charge that routinely accompanies accusations of political straitjacketing—namely, that Third-Period Marxist critics, as mouthpieces for the party line, sought to impose a specifically propagandistic view of literature upon the writers in the party orbit. I shall show that left-wing literary commentators only rarely promoted the notion that literary works should impart or promote specific tenets of party doctrine; insofar as the critics had a coherent aesthetic theory, this theory was almost exclusively cognitive and reflectionist rather than agitational and hortatory. Indeed, I shall argue that in certain important ways the American approach to questions of representation and ideology was committed—as was the dominant tendency in all Marxist criticism of this period, Soviet and European—to a number of premises about literary form that were bourgeois rather than revolutionary. Literary radicals might applaud proletarian novelists whose works encouraged revolutionary class partisanship. Gold hailed Conroy as "a proletarian shock-trooper whose weapon is literature"; the novelist Ruth McKenney wrote Isidor Schneider that his *From the Kingdom of Necessity* was "a more powerful weapon than any tear gas the other side can manufacture." In general, however, commentators, critics and novelists alike, held back from theorizing—let alone legislating—any of the representational maneuvers specific to this literary weaponry. Their espoused commitment to the notion that all literature is propaganda for one side or another in the class struggle was countered by a deep antipathy to viewing proletarian literature as propagandistic in any of its distinctive rhetorical strategies. The 1930s literary radicals never fully repudiated the bourgeois counterposition of art to propaganda: to them, proletarian literature con-

---

Howe and Lewis Coser, *The American Communist Party: A Critical History (1919–1957)* (Boston: Beacon, 1957), p. 304; Alfred Kazin, *On Native Grounds: An Interpretation of Modern American Prose Literature* (1942; rpt. New York: Harcourt, Brace, Jovanovich, 1970), p. 380; Murray Kempton, *Part of Our Time: Some Ruins and Monuments of the Thirties* (New York: Simon and Schuster, 1955), p. 136. According to Paul Buhle, the party leadership, aided by the "megalomaniac sectarianism of literary czar Gold," drove "the more inventive and heterodox contributors (i.e., the more true to life) from the Party ranks or into subject matter and treatment where they could not succeed" (*Marxism in the United States: Remapping the History of the American Left* [London: Verso, 1987], p. 177).

tained very different values and assumptions, but as literature, it was just like any other kind of writing. Ironically, to the extent that they were pre-scriptive in advocating any given set of aesthetic principles, the Marxist critics urged a largely depoliticized conception of mimetic practice that coexisted only uneasily with many of the values and ideas that they con-gratulated writers for articulating in their texts.[2]

The American Debate over Propaganda

When it was a matter of exposing the formalist and elitist premises of con-temporaneous bourgeois critics, the Marxists had no trouble subscribing to the notion that all literature is propaganda for one side or another in the class war. Gold, in his famous 1929 polemic against Thornton Wilder, threw down the gauntlet, declaring that Wilder's "air of good breeding, . . . decorum, priestliness, glossy high finish . . . , conspicuous inutility, caste feeling, [and] love of the archaic" provided the "parvenu class" with a humanistic fantasy that "disguises the barbaric sources of their income, the billions wrung from American workers and foreign peasants and coolies." Oakley Johnson declared the superiority of Communist literature over bourgeois literature on the grounds that it is simply better propaganda: "Novels containing propaganda which derives from intense personal con-viction, or even sacrifice, are likely to have far more power . . . than those in which the propaganda springs from a decayed patriotism or from con-formity to a fashionable prejudice." Freeman asserted that the experience upon which bourgeois art is based is "the experience of personal sensation, emotion, and conduct, the experience of the parasitic classes." The liberal "Man in White" considers proletarian literature 'propaganda' because

> it seems that only a decree from Moscow could force people to write about factories, strikes, political discussions. He knows that only force would com-pel *him* to write about such things; he would never do it of his own free will, since the themes of proletarian literature are outside his life. But the worker writes about the very experiences which the bourgeois labels "propaganda," those experiences which reveal the exploitation upon which the prevailing society is based.

2. Mike Gold, "A Letter to the Author of a First Book," *NM* 10 (January 1934): 26; Ruth McKenney to Isidor Schneider, n.d., Schneider Papers, Butler Library, Columbia U.

There was no such thing as apolitical art or literature, the Marxist critics argued. Proletariat and bourgeoisie had opposing systems of value that were of necessity reflected in the discourses by which the different social classes articulated their views of the world.[3]

While Marxist critics felt at ease in using the term "propaganda" to describe any text's class affiliation, they had more difficulty reconciling themselves to the view that the term might denote literature characterized by specific types of didactic maneuvers. On this issue, it becomes difficult to distinguish the statements of the Marxists from those of many of the liberals and fellow travelers who gravitated toward the left but remained uncomfortable with the idea that art or literature should be hortatory. For example, in the first issue of Hub—a magazine whose stated editorial policy was to welcome "all sincere work"—the painter Thomas Hart Benton proclaimed the positive impact that he saw Communism having upon artistic production. "International Communism," he declared, is a "revolt against the emptiness which is characteristic of the art coming out of this [bourgeois] background . . . a recognition of the fact that art cannot live healthily upon itself alone." For all its rebelliousness, "International Communism" preserved art's high social function, for it entailed a "return to the classic attitude which saw the form of art as the servant of meaning." William Carlos Williams, in a 1933 issue of Contact, expressed a comparably fervent appreciation of the compatibility of left-wing ideas with artistic truth. "I cannot swallow the half-alive poetry which knows nothing of totality," he stated. "It is one of the reasons to welcome communism. Never, may it be said, has there ever been great Poetry that was not born out of a com-

3. Gold, "Thornton Wilder: Prophet of the Genteel Christ," rpt. in Michael Folsom, ed., Mike Gold: A Literary Anthology (New York: International, 1972), p. 202; Oakley Johnson, "Pure Propaganda and Impure Art," Left 1 (Summer–Fall 1934): 33; Joseph Freeman, "Introduction" to Proletarian Literature in the United States (New York: International, 1935), pp. 12–13. Gold's polemic against Wilder prompted many excited responses, positive and negative. See New Republic 65 (December 17, 1930): 141; and Freeman, "On the Literary Front," NM 6 (January 1931): 4–6. See also Edmund Wilson's discussion of the uproar following the appearance of Gold's piece in "The Literary Class War," rpt. in The Shores of Light: A Literary Chronicle of the Twenties and Thirties (New York: Farrar, Straus and Young, 1952), pp. 534–39. Wilson remarked in some delight, "It has now become plain that the economic crisis is to be accompanied by a literary one" (p. 539).

munist intelligence." Indeed, he asserted, Dante and Shakespeare could be cited as instances of "communist intelligence." For Benton and Williams, Communism took on broadly humanistic meaning, becoming essentially coterminous with artistic propositionality and even artistic genius.[4]

Although Benton and Williams welcomed Communism, their enthusiasm in no way supplanted their prior commitment to a view of art as being divorced from propaganda. For they insisted that pro-Communist art and literature perform their roles in an entirely implicit manner. Benton stipulated that "Art does not teach its meanings, it reveals them. . . . Art reveals itself like the human personality through acquaintance, not through overt declaration. . . . Propaganda subsequently may accompany [art] but it cannot accord it substantial meaning or lead to the establishment of those new relations which mark vital form." Williams even more emphatically rejected any association between literature and didactic purpose. "Writing . . . has nothing to do with truth but is true," he declared. "A writer has no use for theories or propaganda, he has use for but one thing, the word that is possessing him at the moment he writes." For Benton and Williams, sympathy with Communism clearly did not entail acceptance of an instrumentalist view of art or literature, which they saw as by their nature antithetical to political programs or doctrines.[5]

Benton's and Williams's grafting of left-wing partisanship onto inherited notions of aesthetic autonomy was a prevalent stance among most of the progressive artists and writers who were associated with the cultural left in the early 1930s. Articles and reviews in various left-leaning little magazines routinely interlaced positive responses to the political propositions embedded in individual works of proletarian literature with cautionary remarks about the danger of politicizing art. Frederick W. Maxham, in *Kosmos*, noted that in *The Disinherited* Conroy "has written propaganda, but he has developed his narrative with such astuteness that the 'point' is almost entirely implicit." Conroy's novel illustrates "*the limit to which propaganda can be carried*; it gives the reader an accurate emotional (and to a lesser extent) intellectual realization of his faith in the proletariat, with-

4. Editorial, *Hub* 1, no. 1 (1934): 2; Thomas Hart Benton, "American Art," *Hub* 1, no. 1 (1934): 31; William Carlos Williams, "Comment," *Contact* 1, no. 3 (February 1934): 131, 132.

5. Benton, 32–33; Williams, "Comment," *Contact* 1, no. 1 (February 1932): 8.

out in any wise detracting from the work as a novel." Editorials in *Kosmos* took a similar tack, expressing "aversion" to stories which were "nothing but desire projections" and declaring that propaganda had to be "skilfully enmeshed" in a story. *Kosmos* published a "literature of sincerity," the editors announced. "Praiseworthy is the fact that writers feel no Messianic call to preachment; their writings are solid enough not to need moral direction." A contributor to *Blast* chided *Dynamo* for rejecting a story by Williams because the point of view of its doctor-narrator was not adequately "proletarian": "The mirror to industrialism must be kept clear of paint, and this magazine exclusively of proletarian 'stories' is continuing the work of Flaubert and the Goncourts. It does a work vastly more solid than the organs of propagandist ergoteurs." Most non-Communist critics and readers drawn toward the literary left were skeptical of literature that too openly declared its propagandistic intentions, even if they were not averse to leftist writers making their views known by implication.[6]

One might anticipate that writers and critics in or close to the Communist party would express a more unabashed sympathy with texts overtly expressing revolutionary attitudes and ideas. To a degree this was true. Some Third-Period literary radicals argued that revolutionary optimism was a vital ingredient in proletarian fiction and urged writers to designate, or at least suggest, the revolutionary "way out" from the miseries produced by capitalism. The editors of the John Reed Club publication *Partisan* informed potential participants in a proletarian fiction contest that the submissions "will be judged by their ability to picture the incidents in the class struggle, and in making them into a powerful appeal for the revolutionary movement. Stories confined to depicting the misery under capitalism will not be acceptable, they must, above all, be an inspiration to building the revolutionary movement." Hicks, in his generally laudatory review of *The Land of Plenty*, chided Cantwell for leaving young Johnny Hagen in the rain, mourning his murdered father and uncertain about the outcome of the strike. "Cantwell relies too much on obliqueness, and the heroism of the embattled workers is a little obscured," Hicks remarked.

6. Frederick W. Maxham, review of *The Disinherited*, *Kosmos* 2 (January–February 1934): 31; Editorial, "In Defense of Preciousness," *Kosmos* 3 (August–September 1934): 23; Jay Harrison, "Editorial," *Kosmos* 2 (February–March 1935): 16; letter from the *New English Weekly*, *Blast* 1 (October–November 1934): 1.

"As a result *The Land of Plenty* fails to sweep the reader along, as William Rollins' *The Shadow Before* does, to high resolve and a sense of ultimate triumph." *New Masses* critic Emjo Basshe praised *Marching! Marching!* for portraying a "singing army" that "can never be conquered," a "chorus which has kept the air filled with its challenge through strike and lock-out, in the face of vigilantes, police and militia guns, against starvation, tar and feathers." To represent reality truly, these critics urged, the writer should depict the growing insurgence of the proletariat and leave readers with increased determination to involve themselves in the class struggle.[7]

Moreover, occasionally Marxist commentators voiced the view that pro-letarian literature should be forthrightly propagandistic. Cantwell averred that his *The Land of Plenty* had been written as a work of "propaganda" and chided Marxist critics for giving him a political critique that was "distinguished by its vagueness." E. A. Schachner faulted Conroy's *The Disinherited* for the very quality that Maxham admired, complaining of the novel's "studied carelessness and primitivism" and declaring that it "eschews interpretation as if it were a bourgeois plague. . . . [It is] more averse to direct statement than any Philadelphia lawyer." Moishe Nadir, we will recall, admired the Marxist lessons implicit in *To Make My Bread* but criticized Grace Lumpkin for telling the story from the vantage point of "backward workers" rather than from that of her own vanguard conscious-ness. Eugene Gordon, in his *New Masses* review of Guy Endore's *Babouk*, praised the novelist for his frequent excursions into the history of colo-nialism, noting that the narrative "loses nothing by the author's frequent stepping out of character to chat amiably or satirically with the reader." While faulting the novel for black nationalism, Gordon commended its hortatory narrative voice, which several mainstream reviewers had found jarring. Explicit in such critical judgments, both negative and positive, was the notion that proletarian fiction, to be politically effective, should wear its politics upon its sleeve.[8]

7. "Stories of Struggle," *Partisan* 1 (April 1934): 1; Hicks, review of *The Land of Plenty*, NM 11 (May 8, 1934): 25–26; Emjo Basshe, "Singing Workers," *NM* 18 (January 7, 1936): 23.

8. Robert Cantwell, "Author's Field Day," *NM* 12 (July 3,1934): 27; E. A. Schach-ner, "Revolutionary Literature in the U. S. Today," *Windsor Quarterly* 2 (Spring 1934): 61; Moishe Nadir, "To Make My Bread," *NM* 8 (February 1933): 19, 20; Eugene Gordon,

But critical expressions of approval for revolutionary didacticism were relatively few and far between. Marxist critics were frequently uneasy with texts that displayed their partisanship through the direct articulation of revolutionary doctrine. Obed Brooks wrote in the *New Masses* that Herbst's *The Executioner Waits* was praiseworthy for its "complete freedom from lumpy ideology." Conversely, he disliked Isidor Schneider's reliance upon authorial editorializing in *From the Kingdom of Necessity* and considered the novel successful only where it relied upon narrative alone to convey its political analysis. Leon Dennen, while criticizing Langston Hughes for not having portrayed the black proletariat as sufficiently class-conscious in *The Ways of White Folks,* castigated left-wing writers who "indulg[e] in 'revolutionary' hysterics." Hicks asserted that *The Treasure of the Sierra Madre* was "so thoroughly revolutionary in all its implications that slogans are unnecessary." By contrast, Hicks argued, Upton Sinclair interferes with his "imaginative recreation" in *The Jungle* by introducing "long passages of straight exposition." Hicks concluded, "[E]very such interruption is destructive." In his largely negative assessment of the majority of the submissions to the *New Masses* novel contest, Calmer concluded that "the worst scourge of proletarian literature" was "the tendency to sloganize, editorialize, rather than let the propositions emerge from the narrative." Moissaye Olgin, praising the contributions to *Proletarian Literature in the United States,* observed that "[t]here is a happy avoidance of sermonizing in the volume, and wherever there appears a revolutionary action, it seems to grow out of the very soil of the workers' lives." The Communist poet Edwin Rolfe remarked in his review of Caldwell's *American Earth* that "[i]n [Caldwell's] hands propaganda is so expertly woven into the texture of his stories that they by far outdo in effectiveness the slogans of his more conscious but less gifted fellow-writers." A. B. Magil, also invoking

---

"Black and White, Unite and Fight," *NM* 13 (October 23, 1934): 24–25. Cantwell did not remain so eager to receive criticism of his work from Marxist critics. In 1936 he wrote to Farrell, "I simply cannot read Hicks, Gold or Kunitz. They have only influenced me in a negative fashion." But Cantwell still endorsed Marxism as a theoretical ground for criticism: "The Marxian point of view, even if imperfectly grasped and crudely applied supplies a superior method of criticism than any that our reactionary colleagues can possible achieve. Bad as Granny is now, he would be a thousand times worse if he did not have the rudimentary understanding of Marx that he has picked up" (Cantwell to Farrell, February 3, 1936, Cantwell Papers, U of Oregon).

the loom metaphor that frequently appears in discussions of fiction and propaganda, faulted Lumpkin for relying too heavily on speech-making in the final portion of *To Make My Bread*. Revolutionary ideas should be conveyed not in "formal declarations," he remarked, but "as part of the creative process," woven "in the warp and woof of a story."[9]

Most 1930s critics and reviewers were, moreover, hesitant to prescribe optimistic closure as a necessary ingredient of the proletarian novel; they disliked novels that represented the "way out" in a forced or obligatory fashion. In the *New Masses* Alice Withrow Field faulted Myra Page for ending *Moscow Yankee* with a "pink sunset." Calmer directed his ire against the "*subjective tendentiousness* of the conversion ending" in proletarian fiction, which he saw as the "revolutionary equivalent of the Cinderella formula." Edward Newhouse, himself the author of two pro-Communist novels (*You Can't Sleep Here* and *This Is Your Day*), praised Tom Kromer's bleak *Waiting for Nothing* for its gritty realism, concluding, "I hope no one starts beefing about the fact that this novel doesn't show 'the way out.'"[10]

Even critics who believed that the proletarian novel should leave its reader in an optimistic frame of mind treated the issue of narrative closure as a problem, not a prescription. Gold remarked, "Anybody can write the first two acts of a revolutionary play. It is the last act, the act that resolves the conflicts, that has baffled almost every revolutionary playwright and novelist in the country. For you can't truthfully say in your last act or last chapter that there has been a victorious Communist revolution in this country." Conroy was vulnerable to the charge of projecting

9. Obed Brooks, "In the Great Tradition," *NM* 13 (November 27, 1934): 23; Brooks, "In the Mold of Poverty," *Partisan Review and Anvil* 3 (February 1936): 28, 29; Leon Dennen, "Negroes and Whites," *PR* 1 (November–December 1934): 50; Hicks, "Proletarian Mastery," *NM* 16 (July 16, 1935): 23; Hicks, "Revolution and the Novel," in Jack A. Robbins, ed., *Granville Hicks in the New Masses* (Port Washington, NY: Kennikat, 1974), p. 57; Calmer, "Reader's Report," *NM* 16 (September 10, 1935): 23; Moissaye Olgin, "First Choice of New Book Union is a Comprehensive Anthology of Proletarian Literature of High Order," *DW* (October 10, 1935), 5, quoted in James Murphy, *The Proletarian Moment: The Controversy over Leftism in Literature* (Urbana and Chicago: U of Illinois P, 1991), p. 126; Edwin Rolfe, review of Erskine Caldwell, ed., *American Earth*, *Left* 1 (Summer–Autumn 1931): 84; A. B. Magil, cited in Murphy, p. 127.

10. Alice Withrow Field, "Soviet Tempo in an American Novel," *NM* 15 (June 11, 1934): 26; [Alan Calmer, "The Proletarian Short Story," *NM* 16 (July 7, 1935): 17;] Edward Newhouse, "Why Wait?," *NM* 14 (March 12, 1935): 25.

"wish-fulfillment," for both *The Disinherited* and *A World to Win* could be said to end with the protagonists' "conversion" to revolutionary activism. Yet when he spoke about problems in proletarian fiction before the 1935 Writers Congress, he elaborated on Gold's metaphor:

> In the [final] act, the action must be resolved into some sort of climax—the strike is lost but the workers, undaunted, pledge themselves to continue the struggle; the central character awakens to social consciousness; or the strike is won and gives the workers fresh courage for the ultimate battle. And how is the proletarian novelist or dramatist to accomplish this naturally, imparting to the reader or audience a sense of reality and inevitability? That is one of his major concerns.

Hicks, defending himself against the accusations of the recently alienated *Partisan Review* group in 1936, argued that "the essential hopefulness of Communism is a fact, not mere theory. The understanding of events that Communism gives does inspire a confidence that is capable of changing human lives." There is, he maintained, "a dramatic reality in conversion and a powerful story in a strike." But he took care to disclaim any responsibility for encouraging writers to produce rote texts, noting, "I have hoped that some day the formulas would be transcended." Thus even the critic who is often singled out for fostering a crudely propagandistic and instrumentalist view of literature disavowed any intention to promote a specifically didactic program. If novelists produced works with formulaic plots, Hicks protested, this was in spite of, rather than because of, his urging.[11]

There was in fact widespread agreement among 1930s Marxists that explicit didacticism was undesirable. Gold wrote in 1929 that "the function of a revolutionary writer is not to suggest political platforms and theses, but to portray the life of the workers and to inspire them with solidarity and revolt." Hicks, in his response to the IURW criticisms of the *New Masses* work in 1931, noted that "schematism and abstractness" constituted "one of the principal dangers of proletarian writing, and must be guarded against." V. J. Jerome criticized the "beatific expounding of social

---

11. Gold, "Change the World!" *DW* (February 9, 1934), 5; Conroy, "The Worker as Writer," *American Writers Congress*, ed. Henry Hart (New York: International, 1935), hereinafter *AWC*, p. 84; Hicks, review of Horace Gregory, *New Letters in America*, rpt. in Robbins, pp. 382, 383.

ultimates" in the "implausible oratory" of the Northern organizer who, in Fielding Burke's Gastonia novel *Call Home the Heart*, gives a lengthy speech about Communism from the back of a train to striking mill workers. Freeman, in his introduction to *Proletarian Literature in the United States*, argued that "[a]rt at its best does not deal with abstract anger. When it does it becomes abstract and didactic. The best art deals with specific experience which arouses specific emotion in specific people at a specific moment in a specific locale, in such a way that other people who have had similar experiences in other places and times recognize it as their own." Accordingly, "[the artist] does not repeat party theses; he communicates the experience out of which the theses arose." The most influential Marxist critics were committed to the view that literary texts should make their politics felt through implicit, concrete, and nondidactic means.[12]

Commentators unfavorable to 1930s literary radicalism have routinely posited that the campaign against "leftism" waged by the "dissident" group clustered around *Partisan Review* should be credited with defeating the crudely didactic aesthetic put forward by the *New Masses* group. As Rahv and Phelps themselves claimed after their 1937 split with the Stalinists, they and other "younger critics" had "stigmatized as 'leftism' the passion for uniformity, the pious utilitarianism, and the contempt for tradition that, despite all protestations to the contrary, determined the mentality of the sectarian Marxists." Beginning with the publication of their 1934 essay, "Problems and Perspectives in Revolutionary Literature," Rahv and Phelps did condemn "sloganized and inorganic writing" that "drains literature of its specific qualities" and "distorts and vulgarizes the complexity of human nature, the motives of action and their expression in thought and feeling." This criticism resonated through practically everything Rahv and Phelps wrote during their tenure in the proletarian movement. They also stipulated the superiority of a cognitive to an instrumentalist conception of literature. "Success cannot be gauged by immediate, agitational significance," they declared, "but by [the writer's] recreation of social forces in their entirety. . . . Literature is a medium steeped in sensory experience, and does not lend itself to the conceptual forms that the socio-political

12. Gold, "Notes of the Month," *NM* 15 (December 1929): 23; Hicks to Conrad Komorowski, *New Masses* folder, August 11, 1932, Box 44, Hicks Papers; V. J. Jerome, "Toward a Proletarian Novel," *NM* 8 (August 1932): 14; Freeman, "Introduction," pp. 13, 11.

content of the class struggle takes most easily. Hence the translation of this content into images of *physical life* determines—in the esthetic sense—the extent of the writer's achievement." [13]

It was, moreover, Rahv and Phelps who coined the term "leftism" to denote the critical tendency to deny the bourgeois heritage, promote a propagandist conception of literature, and encourage overt didacticism. As James Murphy has noted, Rahv and Phelps adapted "leftism" to their own polemical ends: where RAPP theorists used the term mainly to denote a "Proletkult" contempt for the classics and a sectarian attitude toward fellow travelers, Rahv and Phelps expanded the term's meaning to include "disregard for aesthetic values, the limitation of literary criticism to sociological analysis, and the demand that proletarian literature be narrowly agitational in character." Soviet critics often used the term "tendencious" in a value-free or even a positive way. Lunacharski signified by "tendencious" the process by which the writer "seeks to organize his material toward a definite end." Zhdanov claimed that "Soviet literature is tendencious, for in an epoch of class struggle there is not and cannot be a literature which is not class literature, not tendencious, allegedly non-political." Rahv and Phelps, however, equated "tendentiousness" with "leftism," which they took to mean "the stereotyped portrayal of workers and capitalists as heroes and villains, the insertion of abstract propaganda into fiction, poetry, and drama, and the general distortion or coloring of reality for political ends." [14]

Rahv and Phelps may have spearheaded the attack on overt didacticism and given currency to the term "leftism" to denote a multitude of didactic sins. But the *Partisan Review* group did not wage a solitary campaign against Stalinist propagandism. When Rahv and Phelps launched their assault against "leftism" in 1934, they were in fact repeating arguments that

13. William Phillips and Philip Rahv, "Literature in a Political Decade," in *New Letters in America*, ed. Horace Gregory (New York: W. W. Norton, 1937), p. 172; Rahv and Phelps, "Problems and Perspectives in Revolutionary Literature," *Partisan Review* 1 (June–July 1934): 5, 9.

14. Murphy, p. 1; Anatoli Lunacharski, "Marxism and Art," trans. Joseph Freeman, NM 8 (November 1932): 12; A. Zhdanov, "Soviet Literature—The Richest in Ideas, the Most Advanced Literature," in Zhdanov, et al., *Problems of Soviet Literature: Reports and Speeches of the First Soviet Writers' Congress*, ed. H. G. Scott (1935; rpt. Westport, CT: Greenwood, 1979), p. 21. The term "tendentious" was usually spelled "tendencious" in 1930s English translations from German and Russian.

had been made previously in the pages of the *New Masses* by party stalwarts such as Gold, Freeman, Olgin, and Hicks, who had already been taking writers to task for didacticism, abstraction, and schematism. In fact, the key figures whom Calmer cited approvingly in his 1934 obituary on "leftism," "All Quiet on the Literary Front," included not just Rahv and Phelps but also Hicks, Freeman, and Seaver. Even Gold, who has been stigmatized as "leftist" more than any other 1930s literary radical, himself noted in 1935 that "for years the health of our proletarian literary movement was enfeebled by the injection of a whole mass of wrong, leftist theory." Rahv's and Phelps's only original contribution to the attack on "leftism," Murphy argues, was to focus the meaning of the term primarily on questions of didacticism and literary form.[15]

Through 1936 the *New Masses* group and the *Partisan Review* group were in fact far less easy to distinguish from one another than subsequent commentary on the 1930s literary left would have us believe. Calmer and Brooks, who considered themselves philosophically aligned with Rahv and Phelps on aesthetic issues, were skeptical of the politics of the *Partisan Review* core group and decided to publish most of their own critiques of "leftism" in the pages of the *New Masses*. Moreover, the relations between the *New Masses* and the *Partisan Review* were mostly affable. It was in the *New Masses* that Rahv published his negative assessment of Faulkner's modernist style as late as 1936. In the same year Alexander Trachtenberg, the head of International Publishers, congratulated the *Partisan Review* for having "from the very beginning . . . fought against all attempts to reduce literature to sloganized, lifeless writing." The *Partisan Review* was asked to be the official organ of the League of American Writers (LAW).[16]

15. Calmer, "All Quiet on the Literary Front," PR & A 3 (March 1936): 13; Gold, DW (May 6, 1935), 5; Murphy, p. 1.

16. Rahv, review of William Faulkner, *Absalom, Absalom!*, NM 21 (November 24, 1936): 20–21; Alexander Trachtenberg, "Revolutionary Literature," DW (July 1, 1935), 5, quoted in Murphy, p. 176. Calmer was never a party member, and his criticisms of Hicks, Gold, and Freeman were scathing. He wrote to Hicks sometime in 1937, "[Y]ou could have changed the prevailing literary codes set up by Mike and company. Instead of ending his stupid reign, you succumbed to his general point of view. . . . I could have forgiven many of your errors ordinarily but, considering the commanding position you had and the power you had to change things, I was and am very angry at the road you took which, as long as it is maintained in the movement, can serve only to drive away the most gifted literary writers who are interested primarily in literature; and to keep only cripples like

It is only hindsight knowledge of the 1937 split between the two journals, coupled with the determining role played by anti-Stalinists in constructing the canonical narrative of the decade, that makes it possible to construe the battle over "leftism" as indicative of deep and abiding political and philosophical differences. "Leftism" went down to official defeat at the 1934 convention of the JRCs, where, Calmer happily reported, there was unanimity in the belief that the abstract and sloganeering approach to proletarian literature was a dead end. This was, however, something of a hollow victory, since "leftism" had never been staunchly defended in the first place.[17]

The Ideological Roots of the Attack on "Leftism"

The attack on "leftism" did not come out of nowhere. The U.S. literary radicals' antipathy to overt didacticism had its roots in a number of sources, both non-Marxist and Marxist. Soviet critics of U.S. literary radicalism frequently made the point that the Americans manifested a distinctly pragmatic and antitheoretical streak. The IURW critic Anne Elistratova, we will recall, chastised the Americans for insufficient "politicalization." The

[Henry] Hart and [Harry] Slochower who, because they have no literary ability, do not object to sacrificing what they haven't got to suit the immediate political aims of Joe Freeman and Mike too (who, I hardly need to tell you, always manage somehow to drive away practically every talented writer that comes anywhere near the movement, leaving them with the uncontested leadership)." Interestingly, however, Calmer noted that when he had been invited to join the "new Partisan Review crowd," "Of course I wouldn't because of their anti-party position." For another expression of Calmer's growing negativism toward proletarian literature, see his "Portrait of the Artist as a Proletarian," SRL 16 (July 31, 1937): 3–4, 14. Brooks remarked retrospectively that "very early [I was] associated with the people who edited Partisan Review. . . . Between 1934 and 1937 I had some very strong criticisms of the Party, being influenced by Trotskyists and other ideas, but in 1937, with my eyes fairly open, I decided that the moment had come and you have to commit yourself" (cited in Ellen W. Schrecker, No Ivory Tower: McCarthyism and the Universities [New York and Oxford: Oxford UP, 1986], p. 33).

17. Calmer, "A New Phase in American Proletarian Literature," IL 7 (1935): 73–75. Orrick Johns's account of the 1934 John Reed Clubs convention differs in emphasis from Calmer's. Johns notes in passing the conference's condemnation of "narrowness" and "leftism" but stresses the clubs' successful cultivation of working-class writers and their commitment to "win[ning] writers and artists to the revolution" ("The John Reed Clubs Meet," NM 13 [October 30, 1934]: 25, 26).

Americans' cult of authenticity, she argued, was based on the assumption that working-class authorship would in itself guarantee truthful representation. This doctrine, she urged, was in turn based on the empiricist notion that truth is signaled through immediacy and verisimilitude, rather than through a genuinely dialectical grasp of concreteness. The anonymous *International Literature* reviewer of the John Reed Club publication *Left* asserted that the lack of dialectical thinking among American Marxists was traceable largely to their intellectual roots. "The relative youth of [the movement in the United States] . . . [and] . . . the disdainful attitude towards theory that is characteristic of American bourgeois culture as a whole—having evolved its 'creeping empiricism' into a system in the shape of pragmatism, with William James at the head—an attitude which was bound to prove contagious to some extent also for our revolutionary movement in its early stages—all this has conditioned a quantitative shortage of theoretical cadres for the revolutionary cultural movement, as well as a generally inadequate theoretical level of preparation." [18]

Various U.S. critics have also argued that there is something distinctly American in the U.S. radicals' pragmatist and empiricist bent. Rahv, in a 1940 polemic against what he called the "cult of experience" in American writing, argued that the literary proletarians' preoccupation with authenticity was an extreme version of the anti-intellectualism endemic to almost all American literature. The American pragmatism that constituted the philosophical basis of literary proletarianism, he charged, "exhibits a singular pattern consisting, on the one hand, of a disinclination to thought and, on the other, of an intense predilection for the real; and the real appears in it as a vast phenomenology swept by waves of sensation and feeling." Subsequent critics have also concluded that American literary proletarianism was empiricist and antitheoretical, though they generally view these qualities as virtues, not defects. Frederick Hoffman, we will recall, argues that the American proletarians were largely resistant to "imported ideology." Marcus Klein applauds the literary proletarians for being less committed to articulating Communist doctrine than to portraying an authentic new—and American—subject matter. [19]

18. Anne Elistratova, "*New Masses*," *IL* 1 (1932): 107–14; Anonymous, "*Left* No. 2," *IL* 2–3 (1932): 147.

19. Rahv, "The Cult of Experience in American Writing," rpt. in *Essays on Literature and Politics 1932–1972*, ed. Anabel J. Porter and Andrew J. Drosin (Boston: Houghton

The U.S. literary radicals' comments on the goals of proletarian literature do frequently reveal a distinct pragmatism and distrust of theory. Gold
argued that the literary artist has no need to "present theses" because "facts
are the new poetry. The proletarian writer will work with facts. Facts are
his strength. Facts are his passion." He declared to the 1935 Congress, "A
great body of proletarian literature will show the concrete facts . . . [and]
will be the greatest argument we can present to those people who struggle
with the theories of Communism and fascism. . . . We must use this [picture
of real life] as . . . the final answer to . . . the intellectual abstractions of the
bourgeoisie." Hicks, too, asserted that there was no need for the proletarian writer to engage in open declarations about the need for revolutionary
change because reality would reveal its own meanings: "If [the writer] is
wise he will find in facts his all-sufficient bulwark." Freeman accepted a
fundamental dualism between theory and experience as the basis of his
aesthetic program. His chastisement of texts that are "abstract and didactic" was based on the premise that the province of literary discourse is the
immediate and the concrete: we will recall his proclamation that literature
"deals with specific experience which arouses specific emotion in specific
people at a specific moment, in a specific locale." Even Rahv and Phelps,
who sought to distance themselves from the epistemology of the "leftists,"
were, as Klein notes, also absorbed in the cult of authenticity. Their recommendation that writers represent " 'images of *physical life*' . . . in effect
was . . . advice to writers to experience ever more profoundly the discrete
actualities of lower-class life." For the major American Marxist critics, a
largely positivist conception of "fact" and "experience" constituted the
epistemological basis of literary representation. Theory was abstract, an intrusion into the realm of the real; any literary work that aspired to represent
the real had to stress at all points the primacy of the concrete.[20]

Moreover, the American literary radicals never engaged in a critical

---

Mifflin, 1978), p. 11; Frederick J. Hoffman, "Aesthetics of the Proletarian Novel," in David
Madden, ed., *Proletarian Writers of the Thirties* (Carbondale and Edwardsville: South-
ern Illinois UP, 1968), pp. 185–186; Marcus Klein, *Foreigners: The Making of American
Literature 1900–1940* (Chicago and London: U of Chicago P, 1981), pp. 134–54.

20. Gold, "Notes of the Month," NM 5 (January 1930): 7; Hicks, *The Great Tradition*
(New York: Macmillan, 1935), p. 305; Freeman, "Introduction," p. 13; Klein, *Foreigners*,
p. 136.

encounter with bourgeois aesthetic theory and, as a consequence, relied upon an eclectic theoretical model drawn from non-Marxist as well as Marxist sources. A name that is cited approvingly with surprising frequency in the writings of American left-wing critics is that of I. A. Richards. Richards, perhaps the most influential Anglo-American critic of the 1920s and 1930s—and an important influence upon the New Critics—was an unabashed empiricist and formalist. He developed a theory of literature that stressed physical sensation as the basis of aesthetic response; he collapsed ideas and doctrines into attitudes and emotions. Moreover, he espoused a militantly antipropositional conception of literary discourse and sharply distinguished between language's "scientific" use, which aims at questions of truth and falsity, and its "emotive" use, which is presumably nonreferential. "The bulk of the beliefs involved in the arts are . . . provisional acceptances," he declared, "holding only in special circumstances (in the state of mind which is the poem or work of art) acceptances made for the sake of the 'imaginative experience' which they make possible." Creators of artistic works, Richards maintained, are concerned above all with aesthetic effect: "[T]he artist is not as a rule consciously concerned with communication, but with getting the work, the poem or play or statue or painting or whatever it is, 'right', apparently regardless of its communicative efficacy." [21]

One might think that Marxist critics concerned with making art into a weapon would have repudiated Richards's doctrine. Curiously, however, Richards was frequently invoked by literary radicals attempting to devise theories of proletarian literature. Freeman somewhat anomalously coupled Richards with Voronski, a prominent Soviet theorist of the pre-RAPP period, in the pantheon of socially conscious critics: "[T]he best literary minds of all times have agreed on some kind of social sanction for art, from Plato and Aristotle to Wordsworth and Shelley, to Voronsky and I. A. Richards." Hicks chastised Richards for ignoring the "limits of class morality" in literary evaluation. But he applauded Richards's "account of the psychological effect of art" as "the soundest yet proposed." Moreover, in drafting their projected (though never published) pamphlet on proletarian literature, Hicks and Brooks referred to Richards in their correspon-

21. I. A. Richards, *Principles of Literary Criticism*, 4th ed. (New York: Harcourt, Brace, 1930), pp. 278, 26.

dence and drew heavily upon his sensationalist model of the imagination. In an eight-point outline describing "the writer's creative process," for example, they inserted "the role of ideas in creation; relation to didacticism" as point six, preceded by a series of Richardsian categories describing various features of literary form and the imaginative process. Hicks and Brooks clearly cared about a text's political content. But they seem not to have achieved much theoretical synthesis of "content" and "form." "Ideas" and "didacticism" were for them, as for Richards, categories largely marginal to the "creative process" itself.[22]

Clearly U.S. Marxist critics were influenced by Anglo-American empiricism; their antipathy to the presence of "abstract" ideas in literature reflected a characteristically American tendency to privilege fact and experience over theory. But it would be incorrect to exaggerate the Americanness of the U.S. literary radicals' cult of authenticity. Even though, as I argued in chapter 2, the Americans were under no mandate to imitate the Soviet example, it strongly influenced U.S. literary radicalism in all its phases. The Americans' interest in a literature based on factuality and verisimilitude reflected in large part their continuing loyalty to the Proletkult concept— the "fact, facts, facts" of which Serge Tretiakov had written with such enthusiasm. The promotion of worker-correspondents in the *Daily Worker* and the *New Masses*, the encouragement given to middle-class writers to acquaint themselves with the intimate details of work-processes, even the carryover of the Soviet term "sketch" to describe brief worker-authored factual accounts—these and related features of U.S. literary proletarianism were directly borrowed from the Soviet experience. The Americans' lively interest in the "real thing" was not, as Hoffman suggests, a sign of

22. Freeman, "Introduction," p. 14; Hicks, "Revolution and the Novel," in Robbins, pp. 60–61; Brooks to Hicks, March 8, 1934, Box 16, Hicks papers; "Outline" for Proletarian Literature pamphlet, Box 105, Hicks Papers. Hicks also grouped Richards with a prominent Soviet commentator on aesthetics. Responding to Eastman's diatribe in *Artists in Uniform*, Hicks observed that Eastman disliked Richards's account of literary response "partly, it appears, because it bears some resemblance to Bukharin's." Hicks noted that Bukharin and Richards "naturally differ on what is desirable" with regards to the changes that literary texts work in their readers. But he praised the American and the Soviet for their common commitment to an emotion- and sensation-based theory of poetry. See Hicks, "The Vigorous Abandon of Max Eastman's Mind," *NM* 13 (November 6, 1934): 22.

"resistance to an imported ideology," but part of the documentary legacy of Proletkult.

Furthermore, the U.S. critics' antipathy to overt didacticism was not simply a manifestation of a characteristically American resistance to theory. For from 1928 onward the dominant tendency in Soviet and European Marxist aesthetics stressed the incommensurability of literature with overt expressions of political doctrine. Georgi Plekhanov, the key Marxist philosopher invoked in RAPP-era discussions of aesthetics, held that science and journalism deployed wholly different methods of analysis and representation than did art and literature. The former, he argued, described reality through abstractions, the latter through concrete images. "[W]hen the writer operates with logical arguments instead of with images or when the images are invented in order to prove a certain thesis," Plekhanov warned, "he is not an artist but a journalist." The principles of dialectical materialism and the "living man" that undergirded the RAPP program were drawn primarily from Plekhanov's anti-instrumentalist view of literature, which was itself, Régine Robin argues, derived from nineteenth-century Russian theories of realism. As the U.S. literary radicals had increasing commerce with literary theorists in the international Communist movement through the medium of *International Literature*, the doctrines that they encountered called not for more didacticism, but less. Contrary to the widespread view that the Soviets continually pushed the Americans toward a more propagandistic conception of proletarian literature, the Soviets in fact routinely criticized the Americans for "abstraction" and "schematism."[23]

The writings of Plekhanov—and to a lesser degree of Franz Mehring—furnished Soviet Marxists with arguments in support of the doctrine of literary concreteness. But it was the writings of Marx and Engels that provided the epistemological foundation upon which full-fledged criticisms of

23. Plekhanov, quoted in Murphy, pp. 28–29; Regine Robin, *Socialist Realism: An Impossible Aesthetic*, trans. Catherine Porter (Stanford: Stanford UP, 1992), pp. 91–110, 151–54. See Deming Brown, *Soviet Attitudes toward American Writing* (Princeton: Princeton UP, 1962), pp. 56–82, for an overview of the criticism of "schematism" and "empiricism" in American proletarian literature. For more on Plekhanov's changing fortunes with the Soviet literary left, see Herman Ermolaev, *Soviet Literary Theories: The Genesis of Socialist Realism*, U of California Publications in Modern Philology, vol. 69 (Berkeley and Los Angeles: U of California P, 1963), pp. 79–88.

"leftism" would be built. In particular, the 1933 translations into both Russian and English of letters written by Marx and Engels to left-wing writers of their time—Marx's and Engels's to Ferdinand Lassalle and Engels's to Margaret Harkness and Minna Kautsky—came to be frequently cited in discussions of "tendentiousness" and "propaganda" in proletarian literature.

In the *Eighteenth Brumaire* Marx issued a call for a literature that would "draw its poetry . . . from the future." Both he and Engels applauded and encouraged writers—Heine, Freilegath, Herwegh, as well as Lassalle, Harkness, and Kautsky—who articulated and supported the workers' cause. But both Marx and Engels unequivocally advocated a cognitive as opposed to an instrumentalist conception of literature, and they continually counseled left-wing writers against wearing their politics on their sleeve. Thus Marx chided Lassalle for writing "à la Schiller"—that is, "transform[ing] individuals into mere mouthpieces of the spirit of the time." Engels, also addressing Lassalle, remarked that effective dramatic characters conveyed the essential forces of history not through dialogue but through action: they must be "alive, active, so to speak rooted in nature." Moreover, Engels warned the prosocialist writers Kautsky and Harkness of the dangers of *tendenz*. He praised the realism of Kautsky's characters: "[E]ach one is a type, but at the same time a definite individual person, a '*Dieser*,' as old Hegel expressed it." But he criticized the novelist's tendency to point a moral. "I think that the purpose must become manifest from the situation and the action themselves without being expressly pointed out," he remarked. "[T]he author does not have to serve on a platter the future historical resolution of the social conflicts he describes." Engels criticized Harkness for her representation of the working class in her novel *City Girl* on the grounds that "the working class figures as a passive mass, unable to help itself and not even showing (making) any attempt at striving to help itself. All attempts to drag it out of its torpid misery come from without, from above." Yet, Engels went on to say, "I am far from finding fault with your not having written a point-blank socialist novel, a *Tendenzroman*, as we Germans call it, to glorify the social and political views of the authors. That is not at all what I mean. The more the opinions of the author remain hidden, the better for the work of art." [24]

24. Marx, *The Eighteenth Brumaire of Louis Bonaparte*, in *Selected Writings of Marx and Engels* (New York: International, 1968), p. 99; Marx to Ferdinand Lassalle, in *Marx*

In advocating that procedures of literary evaluation take into account a text's adequacy in depicting as "typical" the emergent revolutionary forces of any era, Marx and Engels were departing from the mainstream of the German classical philosophy in which they had been trained. But, as Peter Demetz has pointed out, the greater part of Marx's and Engels's aesthetic was drawn directly from Hegel and shared the epistemological premises guiding the mimetic theories of contemporaneous bourgeois disciples of Hegel such as Taine. Marx's and Engels's criticisms of Lassalle were based on the notion that the dramatist had failed to view his characters as the embodiment of the "concrete universal," a central concept of Hegel's philosophy. Marx's and Engels's antipathy to the direct expression of ideas in literature reflected their agreement with Hegel's tenet that the fundamental unit of representation in literature was the "image," which distilled in its complex particularities the dialectical relations among larger general meanings. The invocation of Schiller as the epitome of undialectical polemicism was also drawn directly from Hegel, who declared that Schiller had "given way to a stormy violence that expanded outward without a real core." Moreover, Engels's postulation of the centrality of the "type" to realistic representation paralleled the formulation of Taine, who, Demetz notes, "demands of the writer that he create representative figures (*caractères*) who unfold their spiritual essence to the reader in sensory form." By the 1860s, Demetz notes, this conception of the "type" had become a "literary cliché," blending the scientifically defined type (the "representative example of what is already existent") with the literarily defined type (the "character") and with the theological type (the "prophetic or normative," bearing within itself "what the future world order ought to be"). In the advice they offered authors about strategies of representation appropriate to realistic texts, Marx and Engels were recapitulating key tenets of bourgeois aesthetic theory of the day.[25]

To point out that Marx and Engels based their aesthetic theory—or, more properly, their prolegomenon toward such a theory—on bourgeois

---

and Engels on Literature and Art (Moscow: Progress Publishers, 1976), p. 100; Engels to Lassalle, ibid., p. 103; Engels to Minna Kautsky, ibid., pp. 87, 88; Engels to Margaret Harkness, ibid., pp. 90, 91.

25. Peter Demetz, *Marx, Engels, and the Poets: Origins of Marxist Literary Criticism* (Chicago and London: U of Chicago P, 1967), pp. 107–38. The quoted passages are from pp. 111, 134, 135, 136.

sources, particularly Hegel, is not in itself an especially damning observa-tion. Without Hegel's dialectical idealism, as Marx and Engels were them-selves the first to point out, there would have been no historical material-ism. But where Marx and Engels stood Hegel's dialectic "on its head" in their writings on history and political economy, they undertook no such critical exercise when they wrote about aesthetic matters. Indeed, they seem to have accepted without question Hegel's premises that literature is cognitive rather than hortatory and that its basic unit of cognition is the concrete universal. Marx had declared elsewhere that "[t]he Communists disdain to conceal their views and aims. They openly declare that their ends can be attained only by the forcible overthrow of all existing social conditions." But apparently Communists who were writing novels were to adopt a different rhetorical strategy. Moreover, despite their support of writers who sought to aid the working-class cause, Marx and Engels—especially Marx—remained classicist in their literary preferences and con-sidered much aesthetic experience to be beyond politics. In short, in their ideas about art and literature, the founders of scientific socialism were mainstream nineteenth-century philosophers rather than "Marxists." As James Scully has remarked, Engels's objections to didacticism are "based on narrow formalist concerns" and proceed from "a metaphysical rather than a materialist distinction between form and content." Raymond Wil-liams, putting the point more bluntly, observes that in his letters to Kautsky and Harkness the later Engels moved "towards a slightly grumpy bourgeois position rather than necessarily a Marxist one."[26]

If Marx and Engels were uncritical in their absorption of Hegel, the 1930s Communist critics who interpreted Marx's and Engels's writings on aesthetics to the left literary community were more uncritical still. The letters to Lassalle, Harkness, and Kautsky, which had never before been translated or widely disseminated, rapidly assumed the status of holy texts. Mikhail Lifschitz welcomed Marx's attack on Friedrich Schiller as an at-tack on "the Idealist method of converting the living character into an automaton to prove the abstract concept of the author." Marx, he argued, advocated not didacticism but partisanship in art, conveyed through the

---

26. Marx, *The Communist Manifesto, Selected Writings*, p. 63; James Scully, *Line-Break: Poetry as Social Practice* (Seattle: Bay Press, 1988), pp. 68, 69; Raymond Williams, "The Writer: Commitment and Alignment," *Marxism Today* (June 1980), 23.

"self-development of a sensually-concrete reality." In commentaries accompanying the texts of the letters to Kautsky and Harkness, the critic Franc Schiller (not to be confused with Friedrich Schiller) noted that the recently translated texts had "present meaning for our times." The letter to Harkness, he opined, demonstrated Engels's antipathy to abstract ideology and revealed the necessity for literature to represent reality implicitly, through concrete characters and incidents. The letter to Kautsky, he commented, had even more relevance to the present day:

> The clear statements of Engels in his letter to Kautsky on the individual and the type, on purpose and its expression in literature, show once again the error of the creative slogans of the theoreticians of the proletcult, left and literary front groups on contrasting abstract personality with the group, the dissolving of individuality with a drop drowning in the current (the group), of a schematic depiction of good and bad. . . . [L]ikewise the statements of Engels in this and other letters are incompatible with the "left" idea of "throwing the classics overboard from the modern ship" or a one-sided attitude to the great realists (Tolstoy) or a publicist sharpening of views.

The literary-critical writings of Marx and Engels were greeted with enthusiasm not just because, as Franc Schiller put it, they "fil[l] a considerable gap in the hitherto little explored subject of the attitude of Marx and Engels to questions of literature and criticism," but because they furnished artillery in the battle against "tendentiousness" and "leftism."[27]

Schiller and Lifschitz provided influential commentaries on Marx's and Engels's writings on literature. It was up to Georg Lukács, however, to develop the aesthetic embedded in these writings into a full-blown theory of literary mimesis. Lukács, Schiller, and Lifschitz collaborated in the USSR on a project of publishing and interpreting an anthology of Marx's and Engels's writings on literature and art. Lukács's theories of realism and typicality drew upon this collective project and articulated what was becoming the dominant position in Soviet debates. In 1931, in fact, Lukács traveled from the Soviet Union to Germany at the behest of the IURW in order to help guide the debates over politics and form that were being waged in the German literary movement. For a period of two

27. Mikhail Lifschitz, "Marx on Esthetics," trans. G. D. Kogan, IL 2 (1933): 84; F. Schiller, "Marx and Engels on Balzac," trans. Jessie Lloyd, IL 3 (1933): 113, 119; F. Schiller, "Friedrich Engels on Literature," trans. Jessie Lloyd, IL 2 (1933): 122, 128.

years Lukács polemicized against tendentiousness and "leftism," aligning himself with Linkskurve editor Otto Biha, a strong opponent of "Prolet-kult delusion[ism]." In a series of articles on proletarian literature, Lukács criticized propagandistic tendencies in proletarian fiction and argued for a realism based on concreteness and typicality, which he viewed as the correct literary embodiment of dialectical materialism. Lukács was in fact one of the leading figures—and consciously so—in the assault on "leftism." [28]

Lukács's essay "Propaganda or Partisanship?" which was published in the Partisan Review, played a significant role in the battle against "leftism" that was being waged in the United States in 1934. Lukács invoked Engels as he sharply criticized the rhetorical strategy of including overtly hortatory statements in proletarian fiction. Such a practice, he warned, implicates the text in "subjective idealism" because the writer's revolutionary stance becomes "a demand, a summons, an ideal, which the writer contrasts with reality." Instead, Lukács maintained, "[t]here is no room for an 'ideal,' either moral or esthetic," for the revolutionary work must be "a portrayal of objective reality, its actual motive forces and its actual trends of development." To portray this reality truthfully did not entail assuming a pseudo-neutral stance, Lukács argued. "Correct dialectical portrayal and literary re-creation of reality presuppose partisanship on the writer's part." A successful demonstration of the relationship between "is" and "ought" thus requires the writer not to impose his/her own desires upon reality, but to reveal how the dialectic of reality embodies insurgent and oppositional forces. Too often, however, the proletarian writer's legitimate motivation to "re-create . . . the subjective factor in revolutionary development . . . is replaced by a merely subjective (because uncreated) 'wish' on the author's part: 'propaganda.' And when the author portrays this wish as objective and fulfilled, instead of truly (i.e., dialectically) recreating the subjective factor with its desires and its behavior, the portrayal becomes 'propagandistic.' " [29]

28. Murphy, pp. 45–49. Otto Biha's "On the Question of Proletarian Revolutionary Literature in Germany" (IL 1, no. 4 [1931]: 88–105) provides a classic statement of the anti-"leftist" position, revealing that the arguments developed in 1934 in the United States were anticipated by a good three years in Germany.

29. Georg Lukács, "Propaganda or Partisanship?" trans. Leonard F. Mins, PR 1 (April–May 1934): 40, 43, 44, 46. The title of this essay was translated in a somewhat misleading fashion, since the term "propaganda" is never used in the essay, only the term

Both the recently translated writings of Marx and Engels and the work of Lukács were cited by the prominent U.S. literary Marxists. Although it is sometimes asserted that the U.S. Marxists operated in virtual ignorance of Marx's and Engels's statements about literature and art, this is not the case. In 1932 the *New Masses* reprinted Engels's comments on Goethe. Calmer praised Schiller's pieces in *International Literature*, as did Hicks, who wrote of the journal that "[p]erhaps the most interesting and valuable critical material . . . may be found in the various letters on literary questions by Marx and Engels with comments by F. Schiller." Rahv thanked *International Literature* for "present[ing] the long-awaited Marx and Engels correspondence with La Salle [sic]. . . . The concrete and profound insights of Marx and Engels into the problems of tragedy and the revolutionary viewpoint in literature will undoubtedly illumine many dark corners in our young proletarian criticism." Lukács's essay also influenced the U.S. literary radicals' critique of "leftism." In a clear echo of the Hungarian critic, Calmer castigated the writer of the proletarian short story for "forcing [his] desires down the throats of his characters (or, to express the same thing in esthetic terminology, . . . *subjective tendentiousness*)." Rahv praised Lukács as a "foremost European critic" whose "critical operations" had delivered a "blow both to 'pure' art and to the 'leftists' in the proletarian camp." In sum, the opponents of "leftism" in the United States were aware of the relevance of Marx's and Engels's writings to their cause and were conversant with the terms of the debate in the USSR.[30]

"tendency." David Fernbach's 1980 translation is entitled " 'Tendency' or Partisanship?" (Georg Lukács, *Essays on Realism,* ed. Rodney Livingstone [Cambridge, Mass.: MIT P, 1980] pp. 33–44). It is tempting to speculate about the reasons for the altered title in the *Partisan Review* version. Rahv expressed great admiration for the piece but admitted to having some reservations about Lukács's "definition of the term [propaganda]," insofar as "people do not always *mean his meaning* when they use the word" (Rahv, "Valedictory on the Propaganda Issue," *Little Magazine* [September–October 1934], 2). This statement is somewhat confusing, since Lukács did not use the term "propaganda" at all. The conflation of "tendency" with "propaganda" in fact coincided neatly with Rahv's campaign to convert the struggle against "leftism" into one against didacticism.

30. "Engels on Goethe," *NM* 8 (September 1932): 13–14; Calmer, *IL* (July 1934): 159; Hicks, "Of the World Revolution," *NM* 10 (January 9, 1934): 26; and Rahv, " 'International Literature' Grows in Popularity among American Workers," *DW* (January 22, 1934), 5 (all cited in Murphy, pp. 109–10); Calmer, "The Proletarian Short Story," *NM* 16 (July 2, 1935): 17; Rahv, "Valedictory," 2. For the argument that the American Marxists were ignorant

The Attack on "Leftism" and the Program for Proletarian Writers

Critics committed to fostering the growth of proletarian literature could find useful guidelines sketched in the works of Marx and Engels and developed in those of Schiller, Lifschitz, and especially Lukács. The dialectical conception of the type as a concrete embodiment of general historical processes and contradictions; the stipulation that in proletarian texts the category of the typical should encompass an emergent class-conscious proletariat; the notion that revolutionary theory should not be imposed from without, but portrayed as flowing from reality—these and other tenets of the Hegelian-Marxist-Lukácsian theory of realism provide useful tools for analyzing both strengths and deficiencies in proletarian fiction. Yet this theory of realism also displays some severe shortcomings, not only as a standard for evaluation but also as a guide for practice. For the attack on "leftism," which was premised upon this theory of realism, sent out ambiguous signals to left-wing writers, not only about the techniques by which revolutionary ideas might be communicated but also about the desirability of expressing these ideas at all.

The antipathy to overt didacticism shared by most 1930s Marxists— Soviet, German, and American alike—was based upon the doctrine that lit-

---

of Marx's and Engels's writings on art and literature, see Mary E. Papke, "An Analysis of Selected American Marxist Criticism, 1920–1941: From Dogma to Dynamic Strategies," *minnesota review* 13 (Fall 1979): 41–69. Commentators on 1930s literary proletarianism who see in the *Partisan Review/New Masses* split an American playing out of the Brecht/ Lukács debate should note that the presumed "Brechtians" (i.e., the anti-Stalinists) drew upon Lukács for their conceptual artillery. It is noteworthy that the LEF/Litfront group never had a defender among the few American critics who knew Russian and acted as interpreters of the Soviet debates. Kunitz, for example, harshly put down Tretiakov and his colleagues:

> They were characteristic expressions of the NEP, of the bourgeois elements in the NEP. The groveled before American *business*, American efficiency, American technology. They attempted to transfer these concepts to art. Unable to fully orient themselves in the complex and everchanging Soviet reality, they attempted to simplify that reality for themselves by reducing to mechanics, technology, craft, mass production, in the arts. To these scions of the bourgeoisie, psychology was worse than poison; for psychological writing would reveal their utter hollowness and lack of inner comprehension of the proletarian world about them. Both the *Lefs* and the *Constructivists*, though loudly proclaiming their revolutionism, had not a Communist among them, not a worker among them. ("Max Eastman's Unnecessary Tears," *NM* 9 [September 1933]: 13)

erature is an essentially cognitive rather than agitational type of discourse. Although proletarian texts were supposed to influence their readers' beliefs and attitudes—art was, after all, a weapon—audience response was, as a theoretical category, virtually irrelevant. A text's partisanship was manifested not through appeals or arguments addressed to the reader, but through its dialectical grasp of the text's historical referent. Truth to the object, rather than arousal of the reader, constituted the principal determinant of value in a proletarian text—although it was assumed that arousal might well result from the reader's encounter with truth.

The insistence upon reflection as the basis of mimesis had the undoubted merit of cautioning writers that revolutionary ideas should not be tacked onto the story, thereby fashioning, as Lukács warned, "a *demand*, a *summons*, an *ideal*, which the writer *contrasts* with reality." But the doctrine that art entailed exclusively cognitive activity was in some ways problematic. First, it meant that writers of proletarian novels were not to look upon their enterprise as entailing any distinctive rhetorical procedures. As Hicks put it, proletarian literature is "not propaganda in any sense that bourgeois literature is not. The aim of the proletarian author is the aim of any author: he wants to write about representative persons and significant events in such a way as to bring out what he believes to be the truth about them." In effect, then, Marxist critics had no specific advice to offer writers about *how* most effectively to bring revolutionary ideas to the attention of their readers. "Content" might differ, but the fictional strategies adopted in proletarian fiction were for all practical purposes identical to those found in all fiction. In answer to Cantwell's complaint that Marxist critics had failed to treat his novel as a "work of propaganda" and had offered only "vagu[e]" comments about its politics, Hicks replied, "I do not know what he means and I doubt he does."[31]

Second, the stipulation that literature is qualitatively distinct from science and journalism—and that this distinctiveness consists in literature's use of implicit and concrete modes of representation—perpetuated a formalist conception of the aesthetic sphere. The opponents of "leftism" maintained, of course, that their view of the aesthetic was dialectical materialist

31. Hicks, quoted in John Scott Bowman, "The Proletarian Novel in America," Ph.D. Thesis, Pennsylvania State College, 1939, p. 111; Hicks, "Author's Field Day," NM 12 (July 3, 1934): 32.

and that a text written in accordance with its specifications was peculiarly privileged to render cognition of social reality. But their premise that ideas should not be directly expressed in literature, and that fiction in particular should present a seamless and transparent analogy to real life, a sensuous concreteness, meant that texts which violated this stipulation were not merely not politically effective, but not literary. Raymond Williams, specifically contesting this intrusion of formalist theory into the critical consideration of left-wing fiction, has written, "The author, or a decisive character, offers a socialist interpretation of what is happening, what happened, what might have happened, what could yet happen. Heavily warned off by the dominant culture. No preaching in novels. No ideas in novels. To hell. Do it." [32] To the extent that the 1930s Marxists engaged in precisely such "heav[y] warn[ing] off," they were ruled by the "dominant culture."

Third, the wholesale dismissal of overt didacticism meant that Marxist critics tended to lump together all the literary sins that they considered "leftist" without considering how different types of rhetorical effects produce different didactic strategies. The admixture of journalism into fiction, the construction of "conversion" plots conveying "wish-fulfillment," the inclusion of long political speeches by fictional characters, the interventions of intrusive narrators—these and other techniques for highlighting political ideas were generally treated as virtually identical. In fact, as we shall see in Part II, such devices position—and "teach"—a text's audience in quite different ways. Some of them presuppose a high level of readerly agreement and in effect instruct through co-optation. Others presuppose a relatively low level of political education on the part of readers and take them by the hand. Had Marxist critics of the 1930s developed an audience-centered approach to questions of literary representation, they might have been able to help writers distinguish among different types of rhetorical approaches to different audiences. Obed Brooks, recognizing this inadequacy in left-wing criticism, proposed to Hicks that their proposed pamphlet on proletarian literature was weakened by its privileging of the "*reflective* aspects of literature" over the "*functional*." He and Hicks should focus more,

---

32. Raymond Williams, "Working-Class, Proletarian, Socialist: Problems in Some Welsh Novels," in H. Gustav Klaus, ed., *The Socialist Novel in Britain: Towards the Recovery of a Tradition* (New York: St. Martin's Press, 1982), p. 120.

Brooks suggested, on "what [literature] does for a class or for individuals, rather than the way in which it is influenced by, or characteristic of, class or individual traits."[33] This proposal was never pursued by Brooks and Hicks themselves or any other 1930s radical critic, with the exception of Kenneth Burke.

Burke was perhaps the quirkiest of the CP's literary allies in the 1930s. His relationship with the party is generally thought to be epitomized in the dispute that broke out at the 1935 Writers Congress over Burke's suggestion that the party use the term "the people" in place of "the workers" in its "propaganda." Of more real substance, however, is the dispute between Burke and Hicks over the issue of "propaganda" itself. In his *New Masses* review of Burke's *Counter-Statement*, Hicks criticized Burke as one of a few "sympathizers, . . . fortunately in a minority, [who] argue somewhat in this fashion: if the class struggle is the central fact in life, and if the proletariat not only ought to win but is, historically speaking, certain to win, that literature is best which so affects its readers that they struggle better in behalf of the proletariat." Burke was "simplistic"; his "underlying error," Hicks charged, was "the conception of literary effect. . . . It implies that the effect of reading a book is such that the reader goes out and does some specific thing."[34]

Burke never published a reply to Hicks's review, but he privately sent to the *New Masses* literary editor an infuriated response in the form of a news release: "Extree! Extree! NEW MASSES GOES REVISIONIST." Burke lashed out in a statement that is worth quoting at length:

> How can a magazine, devoted to propaganda, as the New Masses presumably is, attack a 'theory of effect' which makes provision for aiming at specific effects? For what is propaganda literature, by very definition, but literature aimed at specific effects?
>
> It so happens that Hicks has completely mis-stated my theory . . . [which], it so happens, makes no selection between propaganda literature and 'pure'

33. Brooks to Hicks, September 13, 1933, Box 16, Hicks Papers. For more on the Marxist critics' shortcomings in developing a rhetorically based aesthetic theory, see Robert William Glenn, "Rhetoric and Poetics: The Case of Leftist Fiction and Criticism During the Thirties," Ph.D. Thesis, Northwestern U, 1971.

34. "Proceedings," in *AWC*, pp. 165–71; Hicks, review of Burke, *Counter-Statement*, cited in Burke to Hicks, "Copy," n.d., Box 10, Hicks Papers. Hicks reiterated his criticism of *Counter-Statement* in "The Crisis in American Criticism," in Robbins, pp. 9–10.

literature. It says that some books may aim at very specific effects, and some may aim at much broader effects. The New Masses might reasonably have attacked it for admitting the 'broader' aspect—*but to print an attack upon the 'narrower' aspect (upon its recognition of the fact that there is a usable literary machinery for aiming at specific effects) is simply to involve the editors in an implied attack upon the very raison d'etre of the New Masses itself.* (italics added)

Burke ended with a swipe at the New Masses editors in general and at Hicks in particular:

> My respect for the editors of the New Masses is not such as to cause surprise in me at this failure to understand the implications of their own contributions.
>
> But what the devil! What can one expect, if the Communists are to get their Communist theory from an ex-divinity student, a former Unitarian, a seeker after "revealed values," and at present a teacher in one of those typical survivals from feudalistic stratification, a 'better' New England college? [35]

Burke signed his letter "yours for muddle-headed liberalism." It was true that Burke was nowhere near as committed to revolutionary politics as were fellow travelers such as his good friend Malcolm Cowley. "Marxism does provide some necessary admonition as to our faulty institutions," he wrote to Matthew Josephson, "but as I understand it it is exactly 180 degrees short of being a completely rounded philosophy of human motivation." Throughout his writings during the 1930s, however, Burke evinced considerable sympathy with the project of proletarian literature. In particular, he outlined various elements of a rhetorical approach to literature—a description of the "usable literary machinery for aiming at specific effects"—potentially of great value to the literary left. The view of literature as the "dancing of an attitude"; the unabashed advocacy that writers adopt a "propagandistic attitude"; the attachment of legitimacy to the "hortatory" and "forensic" features of literature; the distinction between a symbolism that integrates readers into dominant values and one that promotes questioning of dominant ideology; the persistent attention to literary texts as constituted by contractual bonds between authors and readers—these and other tenets of Burke's rhetorical program could have clarified and ad-

---

35. Burke to Hicks, "Copy," n.d., Box 10, Hicks Papers.

vanced the project of 1930s literary radicalism. That Hicks chose to dismiss *Counter-Statement* as "simplistic" testifies not to his own petty-bourgeois pedigree (a low cut on Burke's part) but to a fundamental contradiction underlying the entire critical project of the 1930s literary left. Even though they called for a literature that would arouse the working class to action, the Marxist critics chastised literature outrightly attempting to do this. The leading figures of the literary left were indeed, as Burke sardonically put it, "involve[d] . . . in an implied attack upon the very raison d'etre of the New Masses itself."[36]

The strongly antididactic aesthetic theory espoused by the 1930s Marxists gave a contradictory message to proletarian writers: their texts were to be used as weaponry in the class struggle but should not too closely resemble weapons. As the frankly revolutionary—indeed, "leftist"—novelist Myra Page complained in 1934, "Many of our critics . . . have freed themselves only in part from the old bourgeois method and approach in which they've been schooled. 'Art is a weapon', they repeat, but in prac-

36. Burke, cited in David E. Shi, *Matthew Josephson: Bourgeois Bohemian* (New Haven and London: Yale UP, 1981), p. 174. Burke noted to Isidor Schneider that too many Marxist critics weakened their own case by conflating Marxist with sociological criticism. There is an opposition between sociological and aesthetic criticism, Burke argued, but not between aesthetic and Marxist criticism, which has no need to "handle 'form' and 'content' by different coordinates." Burke concluded, "A genuine political approach to art can never exist so long as critics, as they sometimes do in the *New Masses* itself, are forced to say that a book is 'wrong' but 'well done' " (Burke to Schneider, October 3, 1932, Schneider Papers, Butler Library, Columbia University). For Burke's elaboration on his rhetorical theory in relation to proletarian literature, see, in addition to *Counter-Statement* (New York: Harcourt, Brace, 1931), *The Philosophy of Literary Form: Studies in Symbolic Action* (Baton Rouge: Louisiana State UP, 1941), pp. 1–137; "Symbolic War," *Southern Review* 2 (Summer 1936): 134–47; *Attitudes toward History*, vol. 2 (New York: New Republic, 1937), pp. 6–9, 50; "Revolutionary Symbolism in America," *AWC*, pp. 87–94; and "The Relation Between Literature and Science," *The Writer in a Changing World*, ed. Henry Hart (New York: Equinox, 1937), pp. 158–71. In relation to his specific views on Communism and capitalism, Burke once observed that his principal objection to capitalism was that its "great instability interferes with the firm establishment of the moral-esthetic superstructure which the artist draws upon" ("My Approach to Communism," *NM* 10 [March 20, 1934]: 20). Burke occasionally participated in activist politics: Josephson describes Burke's getting arrested on a CP-led picket line in support of a writers' union (*Infidel in the Temple: A Memoir of the Nineteen-Thirties* [New York: Knopf, 1967], pp. 356–57).

tice, forget. That they're not in the classroom or salon, but speaking for and to a class fighting to destroy and rebuild the world. A class for whom books are necessarily a weapon." [37] The ambiguity of the Marxist critics' message was compounded by the term used to describe what was undesirable in left-wing literature—namely, "leftism." For the invariably pejorative use of this term carried an unmistakable political implication: if "leftist" literature was bad, then good writing must be "centrist" or even (within the context of left politics) "rightist." Particularly since the "leftist" errors with which writers were most frequently charged—that is, "editorializing" in narration, "sloganeering" in dialogue, and "wish-fulfillment" in plot— usually involved moments in texts when explicitly revolutionary politics were being raised, the message the critics were sending was politically troubling: to write a good novel one could not try to teach too much, one could not be too "left."

"Leftism," Murphy reminds us, meant different things in the contexts of the USSR and the United States. In the former, it signified sectarian attitudes toward nonparty writers and contempt for inherited literary tradition. In the latter, the term incorporated this meaning but came to encompass those issues of form and politics that were for the Soviets grouped under "tendenciousness." Even if the U.S. Marxists were largely on their own in the way they defined and deployed the term, however, their use of it inevitably carried over a cluster of meanings gathered in the Soviet context. It is necessary to understand why the USSR critics dubbed their opponents "leftists" if we wish to grasp the full political import of the term, even in its etiolated American form.

"Leftism" was not, in the Soviet context, exclusively a literary term. It was directed against forces in the cultural revolution of 1928–31 that were on the "left," and it was deployed by forces that were of the "center" and the "right." During the RAPP period, the charge of "leftism" was directed against LEF and its successor Litfront, which took issue with the RAPP leadership's stress upon psychological portraiture of the "living man." The "leftists" abjured the heroization of single protagonists, called for multiple-authored texts to counter the individualism of the bourgeois concept of authorship, and crammed their narratives full of facts and statistics about technological achievements. "The theory of the 'harmonious man' and the emphasis upon 'psychologism' were condemned as idealis-

37. Page, "Authors' Field Day," 32.

tic soul-searching, diverting writers from social themes and the depiction of the working class," observes Herman Ermolaev. "The slogan 'Study the classics' was brushed aside as a manifestation of formalism which hindered the social education of proletarian writers." Indeed, fictionalization itself was seen as politically suspect, since "[i]n works of fiction the materials of life were subordinate to, and 'neutralized' by, the laws of plot construction. Hence fiction was incapable of an exact portrayal of realities. The true 'living man' could be presented only in documentary genres, where he was allowed to live his natural life." [38]

LEF and Litfront were stigmatized as "empiricist" and "naturalist" by the "dialectical materialists" in the leadership of RAPP, who adhered to the cognitive approach to literature laid out by Plekhanov. As Katerina Clark has observed, LEF's and Litfront's strong documentarist tendency did "reflec[t] the cultural values of what was a starkly 'proletarian' and positivist age." But this positivism was also associated, she points out, with the cultural revolution's impetus to use the machine to eradicate distinctions between mental and manual labor: documentarism was inextricably bound up with "utopian enthusiasm" for "socialist egalitarianism." In keeping with the first Five-Year Plan's "militant antielitism," the Soviet literature of fact posited "a democratic, undifferentiated way of knowing: no fact was manifestly superior to any other, the only ground of value being verifiability." Positivism was thus linked with the representation of the "new Soviet man." But the LEF/Litfront program was not exclusively documentarist. As Edward Brown points out, the "leftist" opposition to the RAPP leadership also laid stress on the "subjective element" in representation. The cognitive aesthetic of psychological realism was beset by "objectivist errors," claimed the Litfrontists. Writers needed to register their emotional reactions to socialist construction. Somewhat paradoxically, the "leftist" opposition conjoined documentarism and romanticism in advocating that literature be simultaneously instrumentalist and agitational. [39]

During the RAPP period, all literary controversy occurred toward the left wing of the political spectrum. The defenders of "dialectical materi-

38. Ermolaev, pp. 78, 74. For the futuristic LEF manifesto, see William G. Rosenberg, ed., *Bolshevik Visions: First Phase of the Cultural Revolution in Soviet Russia* (Ann Arbor: Ardis, 1984), pp. 408–9.

39. Katerina Clark, *The Soviet Novel: History as Ritual* (Chicago and London: U of Chicago P, 1981), pp. 34, 95; Edward Brown, *The Proletarian Episode in Russian Literature 1928–1932* (1953; rpt. New York: Farrar, Straus and Giroux, 1971), pp. 154–56.

alism" and the "living man" envisioned their cognitive aesthetic as the basis of a proletarian literature that would "tear off the masks." The First Congress of Proletarian Writers urged representing the "complex human psyche, with all its contradictions, elements of the past and seeds of the future, both conscious and unconscious" not because they wanted to promote bourgeois individualism, but because they felt that this aesthetic program would best embody dialectical materialist principles and advance the cause of the proletariat. Although Leopold Auerbach and other elements in the RAPP leadership resisted the documentarism of the "leftists," they also strongly advocated that middle-class writers go to the factories; moreover, they recruited shock workers into the field of literature. Brown concludes that RAPP for the most part adopted a "compromise position between the 'extreme right,' which tended to regard art as pure cognition of life, and the 'extreme left,' which minimized its cognitive function in favor of a view of art as a class instrument."[40]

As calls for socialist realism increasingly supplanted the advocacy of proletarian literature, however, the tenor of the debate shifted. For socialist realism took as its premise the notion that class struggle in the USSR had ceased and that the nation was now seamlessly united in the project of socialist construction. The formulation of socialist realism, which took place over the two-year period between 1932 and 1934, coincided, Clark notes, with a new "policy of 'encouragement and concern' toward the old intelligentsia," which was itself premised on a rejection of what Stalin called " 'vulgar egalitarianism.' " "Proletarian" literature—with its implication that the "proletariat" still existed, as an identifiable class with distinct class interests to articulate and defend—was to be superseded by a literary project that aimed to reflect a classless reality presumed already in existence. This new reality was, the theorists of socialist realism urged, still riddled with contradictions; it was the task of the writer to grasp these contradictions from a dialectical standpoint. As Karl Radek put it in his address to the 1934 Soviet Writers Congress, "Realism does not mean the embellishment or arbitrary selection of revolutionary phenomena; it means reflecting reality as it is, in all its complexity, in all its contrariety, and not only capitalist reality, but also that other, new reality—the reality of socialism."[41]

40. Quoted in Edward Brown, p. 78; Edward Brown, p. 59.
41. Clark, "Little Heroes and Big Deeds: Literature Responds to the First Five-Year Plan," in Sheila Fitzpatrick, ed., Cultural Revolution in Russia, 1928–1931 (Bloomington:

The shift toward socialist realism had three consequences of particular significance to our inquiry here. First, there was no necessity for the authors of socialist realist texts to come from the ranks of the proletariat. Professional middle-class writers who were sympathetic fellow travelers were as well equipped—indeed, in technical terms, usually better equipped—to represent the emergent national reality. Second, texts need not abjure psychological portraiture or, for that matter, heroization of great individuals. Just as Stakhanovism would hold up for public acclaim—and reward with material incentives—those "shock workers" who epitomized the spirit of dedication to the nation's industrial development, socialist realist texts—which should be full-fledged fictions, not documentaries—would feature, as Maxim Gorki proposed, "individuals in [whom] the miraculous energy of the masses is concentrated." Finally, the task of writers was now unequivocally to be seen as mimetic rather than hortatory: the creation of concrete "images" embodying and distilling the complex but nonantagonistic contradictions of socialist construction. Writers should not engage in agitational polemics that would disrupt realism's illusion of seamless transparency: the objective portrayal of existing realities was adequate testimony to socialist partisanship.[42]

The establishment of cognitive aesthetics as the principal position in twentieth-century Marxist theories of literature was not the result of a preordained logic, but itself the product of class struggle. In their call for a documentary literature defined and conceived in agitational and instru-

Indiana UP, 1978), p. 203; Karl Radek, "Contemporary World Literature and the Tasks of Proletarian Art," in Zhdanov, et al., pp. 156–57. The post-1932 attitude of the CPSU toward "equalitarianism" is summarized in Stalin's comment: "The roots of equalitarianism lie in the mentality of the peasant, in the psychology of share and share alike, the psychology of primitive peasant 'communism'" ("Interview with Emil Ludwig," IL 2–3 [1933]: 107). Lest this attack on egalitarianism seem to be exclusive to Stalin, we should note that the notion of "socialist inequality" is a staple of Marxist doctrine first articulated by Marx himself in "The Critique of the Gotha Program," where he argued against the applicability of the slogan "From each according to his ability, to each according to his need" to the period of socialism, as opposed to Communism. See Selected Writings, pp. 315–35.

42. Maxim Gorki, Culture and the People (New York: International, 1939), p. 197. For more on the difference between agitational propaganda, which seeks to overturn an old regime, and integrative propaganda, which seeks to secure allegiance for an established regime, see A. P. Foulkes, Literature and Propaganda (New York and London: Methuen, 1983).

mentalist terms, the figures associated with LEF and Litfront were espousing a radical egalitarianism and, moreover, calling for a continuation of the class struggle in the realm of culture. The cognitivists who enlisted Marx and Engels in support of their arguments, by contrast, were participants in a larger ideological assault upon "leftism," as both a literary and a more broadly political program. Franc Schiller, we will recall, referred to "the theoreticians of the proletcult, left, and literary front groups" that wanted to "throw the classics overboard from the modern ship" as the forces that ought to be dislodged by Engels's letter to Kautsky. Ermolaev, pointing out that the criticisms of the left within RAPP were eventually directed against RAPP in its entirety, remarks that Engels's letter to Harkness "became one of the main weapons used in attacking RAPP for having overplayed the importance of ideological influences on the aesthetic aspects of literature." After 1932, advocates of cognitivist positions who had been sharply attacked as rightists during the previous four years—Lunacharski, Bukharin, even Lenin's great favorite Gorki—became prominent advocates of the distinct socialist realist blend of "dialectical materialism" and "revolutionary romanticism." By the time of the 1934 All-Union Soviet Writers Congress, there appears to have developed virtual unanimity on the proposition that literature should render "objectively partisan" portraits of socialist construction and that, in these portraits, the fundamental unit of literary representation was the "image." [43]

43. Ermolaev, pp. 115–16. The Hegelian notion that the "image" constitutes the key unit of literary representation was highly influential in Soviet aesthetic theory from Plekhanov forward. The pre-RAPP cognitive theorist Bogdanov theorized the "image" as the principal mode of literary communication. Victor Stanislavski (who, while a non-Marxist, was cited more frequently by Soviet aestheticians in *International Literature* than was his antagonist Brecht) noted that "the theatre should not act as a 'tutor,' but should draw the spectator by means of images, leading him on through the images to the idea of the play" ("Two Letters," *IL* 1 [1933], 125). Radek, in his address to the 1934 Soviet Writers Congress, praised the Japanese writer Kobayashi Takiji for showing that "Japan is approaching a democratic revolution, which will evolve into a socialist revolution . . . by means of images—not asserting it, not proving it by arguments" (Zhdanov et al., p. 169). Bukharin was perhaps the foremost champion of the view that the "image" is the fundamental unit for articulating a dialectical materialist standpoint ("Poetry, Politics, and the Problems of Poetry in the USSR," in Zhdanov et al., pp. 183–258). Robin, who details how the polarization of aesthetic from scientific language was attacked from various quarters at the 1934 Congress, remarks that the legacy of this concept was a continuing "difficulty in conceptualizing the relation between ideas and artistic qualities" (p. 151).

We should bear in mind that, in the USSR during the late 1920s and early 1930s, the terms "left" and "right" denoted complex political realities. LEF had its roots in futurism, which, branching in another direction, became implicated in the culture of fascism: there was nothing intrinsically "proletarian" about it. Moreover, the "leftists" in the USSR, who embraced the machine as the harbinger of socialist equality, were in their way as committed to productive-forces determinism as were their opponents who announced that rapid industrialization was precluding the necessity for continuing class struggle. It would therefore be simplistic to equate the documentarism urged by the "leftists" with an intrinsically "left" politics or the concrete and imagistic fictionality urged by their opponents with an intrinsically "right" politics. It would also be erroneous to dub the cognitivist aesthetic "Stalinist"—since Stalin played no significant role in its formulation—or to associate the "leftists" with Trotsky, since Trotsky, a confirmed Plekhanovite, was a conservative on literary questions. In the "cacophony" of the 1934 Soviet Writers Congress, Robin observes, "where [Zhdanov's] discourse, . . . however prescriptive, is not fundamentally different from Gor'kii's or Radek's," positions on literary matters bore no self-evident relation to other political issues.[44]

If we take all these complications into account, however, it remains significant that the triumph of the cognitivist position in the USSR was historically associated with the abandonment of large-scale recruitment of worker-writers, the reconciliation of the party with previously alienated middle-class intellectuals, the pronouncement that class war had come to an end, and, increasingly, the substitution of nationalist ideology and material wage incentives for the movement toward egalitarianism and the abolition of wages. The adoption of a cognitive aesthetics based on reflection theory thus coincided with a number of developments that, viewed retrospectively, contributed to the ultimate reversal of socialism in the USSR. The debate over "leftism" was not a purely literary affair.

"Leftism" and Politics in the United States

The Americans' grasp of the issues involved in the post-1931 Soviet attack on "leftism" was partial at best, since *International Literature* was

44. Robin, pp. 10, 202–3.

largely in the hands of the RAPP-era "dialectical materialists" and then the socialist realists. Even though they partook of the "Proletkult" enthusiasm for worker-authored texts, the U.S. literary radicals were for the most part not exposed to the prodocumentarist political arguments advanced by the Soviet "leftists"; the Americans' enthusiasm reflected an economistic workerism as much as an impulse toward revolutionary egalitarianism.[45] The debate over "leftism" in the United States gravitated toward questions of literary form without a clear context in class struggle. To endorse a cognitive aesthetics in the U.S. setting was not a hard-fought political position, but a gesture of common sense, confirmed by the apparent compatibility between the literary theories advanced by I.A. Richards on the one hand and by Marx and Engels on the other. The stakes in the struggle against "leftism" in the United States were not nearly as high as they were in the USSR.

Nonetheless, the equation of tendentiousness with "leftism," along with the stigmatization of both terms by their mutual association, was hardly a maneuver devoid of political consequences. By the mid-1930s, the prominent New Masses Marxists were evincing uneasiness with certain aspects of the attack on "leftism." At the 1935 Writers Congress, Hicks warned that "the attempt to write criticism in terms of experience and sensibility, rather than ideas and attitudes, may, though certainly sound in itself, lead to vagueness, aestheticism, and a kind of ivory tower." In the same year Freeman wrote to Hicks of the antirevolutionary tendencies embedded in what he designated as the "definite trend toward revisionism" in the literary movement. "Under the guise of attacking 'vulgar' Marxism," he remarked, "these people are pushing the cult of 'form' in the direction of art for arts [sic] sake." A year later he reiterated his concern, remarking that "our literary movement is much too full of the most shameless logrolling accompanied by attacks on so-called 'leftism.' "[46]

45. Howard Lee Hertz argues that after 1932 International Literature was run by pronationalist revisionists who favored substituting "socialist construction," and later "socialist realism," for the more left-wing slogan "proletarian realism" to denote the goal of Soviet writing. See "Writer and Revolutionary: The Life and Works of Michael Gold, Father of Proletarian Literature in the United States," 2 vols., Ph.D. Thesis, U of Texas at Austin, 1974, vol. 2, pp. 495–539.

46. Hicks, "The Dialectics of the Development of Marxist Criticism," AWC, p. 97; Freeman to Hicks, April 3, 1935, Box 21, Hicks Papers; Freeman to Hicks, June 15, 1936, Box 21, Hicks Papers.

Hicks and Freeman were justifiably alarmed at the formalism and anti-Communism they saw cropping up in the literary left. But they themselves did not stand on firm ground. Hicks's critical writings had never theorized the role of "ideas" and "attitudes" in literary creation. Freeman's valorization of "experience" as the basis of literature had left him scant grounds from which to combat the "cult of 'form.'" In many of its essentials, the aesthetic doctrine that he and Hicks had been promoting was identical to that urged by Rahv, Phelps, and Calmer—most probably the "these people" to whom he made disparaging reference. When Freeman objected in 1936 to the political "logrolling" being carried out in the name of upholding the integrity of literary form, he was too late. For the *New Masses* group had been complicit in devising and elaborating the aesthetic that would be used as a club with which the self-proclaimed "anti-Stalinist left" would bludgeon the entire project of proletarian literature.

Indeed, by a further irony, the U.S. literary Marxists can be seen as complicit in defining—or at least as wholly inadequate in combating—the aesthetic that would facilitate their eventual banishment from the annals of American literary history. As we will recall from chapter 1, it was the conjunction of the New York Intellectuals with the New Critics that resulted in the promulgation of the formalist critical doctrines that would be used to brand as "propaganda" the entire left-wing literary legacy of the 1930s. The "heresy of the didactic," the New Critics' oft-repeated slogan, would rationalize on apparently formal grounds what was in essence a political witch hunt in the realm of literary and cultural history. But let us review the litany that the literary Marxists themselves devised to describe proletarian literature's sins against itself: "hysterical revolutionism," "lumpy ideology," "schematism," "abstraction," "abstract ideology," "wish-fulfillment," "sloganeering." The anti-Communists did not need to invent a new pejorative vocabulary to label and dismiss—as "propaganda"—the legacy of 1930s literary radicalism. The literary radicals had provided this vocabulary themselves.

   ➤   ➤   ➤   ➤   ➤

I have been demonstrating that the standard account of the Third-Period Communist critics as ultraleft and dogmatically prescriptive is not borne out by a careful analysis of the historical record. Rather than prescribing an aesthetic rigidly in line with Soviet developments, the American Marxists followed their own inclinations and, within the context of general agreement over basic principles of revolutionary literature, entertained quite a broad range of conceptions of what proletarian literature might be and do. Moreover, rather than insisting that radical writers subordinate their work to the immediate agitational demands of the Communist movement, the critics were if anything militant in their rejection of openly "propagandistic" texts. In framing their attack on "leftism," which they largely equated with hortatory and didactic writing, the Americans in part were making use of contemporaneous bourgeois aesthetic theory, against which they never mounted a serious political attack. To a considerable extent, the U.S. radicals took their cue from the USSR, where a cognitive, anti-instrumentalist view of art and literature was developing in conjunction with a recoil from the egalitarian "leftism" of the cultural revolution years. Above all, their theorizing about the relation of art to propaganda was shaped by existing Marxist theory, which assumed an opposition between image and idea, cognition and agitation. Rather than working out a rhetorical theory that would describe—and thereby legitimate—the didactic strategies peculiar to works written with "propagandistic" intent, the 1930s U.S. Marxists subscribed to the bourgeois binary opposition of art to propaganda that invariably denigrated the latter term.

Having criticized the aesthetic theory of U.S. literary radicalism "from the left," as it were, I now hasten to put these comments in perspective. It is currently fashionable—not only among conservatives and establishment liberals but also among various voices on the postmodernist left—to see only disaster in the major twentieth-century attempts to build revolutionary movements, construct egalitarian workers' societies, and develop revolutionary cultures. Whether the left movement is faulted for ignoring the greed embedded in human nature, for failing to appreciate democratic pluralism, for ignoring the linguistic construction of the subject, for clinging to a "scientistic" paradigm based on "class reductionism," or for succumbing to Stalinism, commentators are largely in accord that there is little that we have to learn—except lessons of a negative and cautionary variety—from the experience of past Communist-led movements. A revisionary look at the 1930s literary left requires us to reconsider this ready dismissal. Much of the recent work on the politics of textuality enables present-day academic Marxists to discern signal shortcomings in the assumptions about language, ideology, and representation espoused by the

1930s literary radicals. Yet most of the commentary on the politics of language currently issuing from the pens of academic leftists shares little of the impassioned commitment to revolutionary social change that motivated the 1930s Marxists. When the Depression-era literary radicals called for a proletarian literature that would be a weapon in the struggle to advance and liberate the working class, they were espousing a conception of the politics of discourse quite different from that endorsed by the great majority of post- or neo-Marxists. The 1930s Marxists were constrained in their efforts to work out a revolutionary aesthetic not by some inherent incompatibility between Communist politics and art, or by the constrictions imposed by an authoritarian party, but by the political and epistemological limits of the broader cultural movement of which these commentators were part. Present-day students and practitioners of revolutionary culture have much to learn from the efforts and achievements of the 1930s literary leftists, even as we strive to move beyond their limits.

CHAPTER 5

Race, Class, and the "Negro Question"

Until quite recently studies of the relation of the Depression-era left to American blacks—including black writers—have been strongly influenced by Cold War-era paradigms. Wilson Record's *The American Negro and the Communist Party* (1951), published during the height of the postwar repression, posed the thesis that the "red enchantress" failed to seduce American blacks not only because of its "umbilical attachment to the Kremlin" but also because of its inability to recognize the Negro's fundamentally "democratic" and "patriotic" character. Harold Cruse, in *The Crisis of the Negro Intellectual* (1967), insisted that the integrationist politics espoused by the 1930s left were simply a cover for the white nationalism of Jews who dominated the left movement. "The great brainwashing of Negro radical intellectuals was not achieved . . . by the capitalistic bourgeoisie, but by Jewish intellectuals in the American Communist Party." The major literary histories published in the 1960s and 1970s concur that the Communist left's involvement with black writers was manipulative and hypocritical. Robert Bone concedes that the CP, "by enjoining the Negro author to explore his own tradition, . . . advanced the legitimate development of Negro art." This achievement was, however, "inadvertent." Bone concludes, "It is not the first time in history that the American Communist Party has done the right thing for the wrong reasons." James Young contends that the "artistic impulses" of black writers were "stifled" by the "political formulas prescribed by proletarian fiction." Addison Gayle maintains that the party's pretensions to multiracial equality were specious since, in the political program advocated by the CP, "salvation for [the black man] . . . was possible [only] through the arrival of a white deus ex machina."[1]

1. Wilson Record, *The Negro and the Communist Party* (New 1951; rpt. New York: Atheneum, 1971), pp. 312–13; Harold Cruse, *The Crisis of the Negro Intellectual* (New

Such adverse judgments have been sustained by the predominantly negative portrayal of Communists and Communism in a number of novels and memoirs by black writers who were active with the left in the years between the wars—e.g., Claude McKay's A Long Way from Home (1937), Chester Himes's Lonely Crusade (1947), Ralph Ellison's Invisible Man (1953), and Richard Wright's The Outsider (1953) and American Hunger (1974)—part of which appeared originally in Richard Crossman's 1950 anthology of recantations, The God That Failed (1950). The strongly anti-Communist impact of these texts was for years sufficiently powerful to fore-close analysis of any complexities and contradictions—let alone positive features—in the Communist program for black liberation. A party that re-mained virtually all-white in its top leadership, it is widely claimed, cyni-cally exploited the oppression and anger of American blacks in order to further its own ends—or, more precisely, those of the Moscow-dominated Comintern. The CPUSA may have paid lip service to supporting black im-pulses toward self-determination, but it ruthlessly crushed any deviant ex-pressions of black autonomy and relentlessly subordinated specific issues of race to its agenda of class-based revolutionary change.

Recent scholarship, however, has facilitated more nuanced investiga-tions into the ways in which 1930s leftists, both black and white, formu-lated the relation of race to class and nurtured the development of an antiracist culture in the United States. Arnold Rampersad's two-volume biography of Langston Hughes, while leaving a certain aura of mystery around Hughes's political motivations, thoroughly documents the writer's long-term fellow-traveling relationship to American Communism. Faith Berry's recently reissued Langston Hughes: Before and Beyond Harlem sympathetically details Hughes's radical social beliefs. Martin Duberman's biography of Paul Robeson reveals that black Communists were involved in debating and determining party policy at all levels. Margaret Walker's reminiscences about her relationship with Wright illuminate the little-known activities of the Depression-era black literary fellow-travelers in the Chicago South Side Writers Group. Wayne Cooper's biography of McKay supplements the writer's own highly subjective narrative of the CP's line

---

York: William Morrow, 1967), p. 158; Robert Bone, The Negro Novel in America (New Haven: Yale UP, 1965), p. 116; James O. Young, Black Writers of the Thirties (Baton Rouge: Louisiana State University P, 1973), p. 180; Addison Gayle, Jr., The Way of the New World: The Black Novel in America (Garden City, NY: Doubleday, 1976), p. 189.

and practice with a carefully documented account of the political and psychological complexities surrounding McKay's apostasy from the left. Nell Painter's oral history of the life of Hosea Hudson, a black Communist who organized for several decades in the South, dispels the mythic view of black Communists taking their orders from whites. Gerald Horne's study of the Communist-led Civil Rights Congress, while focusing on the post-war period, gives extensive evidence of the CP's abiding commitment, even amidst the severe repression of the 1950s, to the antiracist activism begun in the 1930s. Mark Naison's *Communists in Harlem during the Depression* takes issue with the portraits of Depression-era American Communism supplied by Record and Cruse and demonstrates the effectiveness of many aspects of urban Communist organizing around the "Negro question" in the 1930s. Robin D. G. Kelley's recent study of the politics and culture of the Depression-era Alabama CP effectively refutes the received view that Communists never managed to garner a significant base among blacks during the Third Period. While some historians of the American left—for example, Harvey Klehr—continue to argue from within anti-Communist paradigms, much recent scholarship suggests that the left's appeal to Depression-era blacks cannot be dismissed as manipulation and bad faith.[2]

2. Arnold Rampersad, *The Life of Langston Hughes*, 2 vols. (New York: Oxford UP, 1986); Faith Berry, *Langston Hughes: Before and Beyond Harlem*, rev. ed. (New York: Citadel P, 1992); Martin Bauml Duberman, *Paul Robeson* (New York: Alfred A. Knopf, 1988); Margaret Walker, *Richard Wright, Daemonic Genius: A Portrait of the Man, A Critical Look at His Work* (New York: Amistad, 1988); Wayne Cooper, *Claude McKay: Rebel Sojourner in the Harlem Renaissance: A Biography* (Baton Rouge and London: Louisiana State UP, 1987); Nell Irvin Painter, *The Narrative of Hosea Hudson: His Life as a Negro Communist in the South* (Cambridge, Mass.: Harvard UP, 1979); Gerald Horne, *Communist Front?: The Civil Right Congress, 1946–1956* (Teaneck, NJ: Fairleigh Dickinson UP, 1988); Mark Naison, *Communists in Harlem during the Depression* (New York: Grove, 1983); Robin D. G. Kelley, *Hammer and Hoe: Alabama Communists during the Depression* (Chapel Hill and London: U of North Carolina P, 1990). For perhaps the crudest McCarthy-era analysis of CP antiracist activity as propaganda designed to entrap blacks, see William Nolan, *Communism Versus the Negro* (Chicago: Regnery, 1951). Klehr, who carries forward the banner of Draper-School historiography on the CPUSA, argues that the Comintern dominated the racial politics of the American Communists, who "allowed foreigners to define and interpret an essential part of their own national history" (Klehr and William Tompson, "Self-Determination in the Black Belt: Origins of a Communist Policy," *Labor History* 30 [Summer 1989]: 366). See also Klehr and John Earl Haynes, *The*

In the present chapter I hope to contribute to this emerging body of revisionary scholarship by reopening discussion of the relation of the CP's analysis of the "Negro question" to proletarian writers, both black and white, who treated the relation of race to class. First, I shall examine the dualities in line and practice resulting from the party's simultaneous espousal of class-based and nationalist politics. Second, I shall describe the implications of this duality for the conceptions of black culture, both folk and proletarian, shaping Communist cultural politics at different points in the 1930s. Third, I shall analyze the propositions about race and class set forth in selected works of proletarian fiction. I shall reserve fuller discussion of representational strategy for Part II of this volume; my primary purpose here is to examine the manifest political discourse articulated in the texts in question.

The "Negro Question": Line and Practice

The line and practice of the 1930s Communist movement in regard to the "Negro question" were more complex than is often granted. Throughout most of the 1920s the party did little to develop beyond the old Socialist party's analysis that racial oppression was essentially identical with class oppression: as Eugene Debs had put it in the prewar years, speaking for the Socialist Party, "We have nothing special to offer the Negro." The loosely formulated character of the dominant position on black liberation was indicated in a 1925 *Daily Worker* article:

> The Negro proletariat holds the key of salvation of the race. The Communist society of the future alone will save the race, and it will be in the new society only that the inherent and native power of the race will be enabled to bloom forth in full fruition, and the Negro to give his true and real worth to human progress.

Position papers endorsed by party commissions called for increased political organizing among black workers, but in practice party formations such as the American Negro Labor Congress (ANLC) and the Trade Union Edu-

---

American Communist Movement: Storming Heaven Itself (New York: Twayne, 1992), p. 73.

cational League (TUEL) accomplished only marginal gains in recruiting blacks to the ranks of the movement. In 1928 there were only fifty blacks in the entire American party.[3]

At the landmark Sixth World Congress of the Communist International in 1928, where the American adherents of both Bukharin and Trotsky were vanquished and the leftward course was set for the Third Period, the role of American blacks in the revolutionary struggle was a main topic of discussion and debate. The majority of the American delegation—black and white alike—initially favored an integrationist position that analyzed American blacks as an oppressed "race" and stressed the community of interests between white and black proletarians. The position that eventually won out, however—promoted by Comintern theorists from the Soviet Union, Finland, Mexico, and Japan, as well as by the black American delegate Harry Haywood—drew upon both Lenin's and Stalin's writings on the "national question." The formulation theorized American blacks as an oppressed "nation," comparable to the national minorities that comprised the different "republics" in the USSR. Setting the struggle for black liberation in the context of anti-imperialism, this position called for both multiracial workers' solidarity *and* self-determination in the so-called Black Belt— that is, those Southern states in which 50 percent or more of the population was black. The position was summarized in the *Daily Worker* as follows:

> National self-determination means the right to establish [the Negro masses'] own Negro State, if they choose to do so. The Communist Party declares that it respects the decision of the Negro masses about the form of realization of this self-determination. At the same time it is the duty of the Negro comrades to emphasize the solidarity of the Negro and white workers and to make clear to the Negro masses that only a victorious proletarian revolution can fully and definitely solve the national question in the Solid South in favor of the oppressed Negro masses.[4]

3. Eugene Debs, cited in Herbert Aptheker, *Negro Slave Revolts in the United States, 1526–1860* (New York: International, 1939), pp. 17–18; Lovett Fort-Whiteman, "The Racial Question in Soviet Russia," *DW* (May 7, 1925), rpt. in Philip S. Foner and James S. Allen, eds., *American Communism and Black Americans: A Documentary History, 1919– 29* (Philadelphia: Temple UP, 1987), p. 97.

4. "The Communists Are for a Black Republic," *DW* (February 26, 1929), rpt. in Foner and Allen, p. 199. Some representative positions in the debate recorded in the *Communist*, the CPUSA's theoretical organ, would include the following: Jos. Prokopec, "Negroes

The logic behind the "oppressed nation" theory was that, while increasing numbers of blacks had migrated to the North and become assimilated to the proletariat, the substantial majority who remained in the South as sharecroppers were participating in a quasi-feudalist economy. After the defeat of Reconstruction, this economy had been only partially incorporated into the modern capitalist economy of the nation as a whole. For rural-based blacks, the most pressing economic need was control of the land, and the most pressing political need was completion of the bourgeois-democratic revolution in the South. Self-determination in those states possessing a black majority was thus a necessary stage in the revolutionary struggle for socialism. Whether the black seizure of state power in the South would substantially predate a proletarian insurrection or—in accordance with Lenin's theory of the "weak links in the imperialist chain"—precipitate one seems never to have been completely agreed upon. What was determined, however, was that to treat blacks *simply* as an extra-exploited segment of the proletariat was insufficient. Whether as sharecroppers or as industrial workers, blacks constituted a "nation within a nation," marked by a distinct culture and subject to distinct forms of discrimination. While their interests were ultimately identical with those of white workers, the black masses could not fully ally themselves with the white proletariat in the struggle for socialism until they had achieved a position of autonomy and equality comparable to that enjoyed by the different national minorities constituting the population of the USSR.[5]

This strategy for black emancipation, its proponents urged, was not opposed to the interests of white workers or to multiracial unity. Poor whites in the Black Belt would not be subjugated under a black republic, but would instead enjoy whatever benefits that republic had achieved. Besides, fighting for black self-determination was a prerequisite to the winning of the

as an Oppressed National Minority," *Communist* 9 (March 1930): 239–45; Harry Haywood, "Against Bourgeois-Liberal Distortions of Leninism on the Negro Question in the United States," *Communist* 9 (August 1930): 694–712; Robert Minor, "The Negro and His Judases," *Communist* 10 (July 1931): 632–39; Earl Browder, "For National Liberation of the Negroes! War Against White Chauvinism!" *Communist* 11 (April 1932): 295–309.

5. For a full statement of the self-determination position, see Haywood, *Black Bolshevik: Autobiography of an Afro-American Communist* (Chicago: Liberator P, 1978), pp. 218–44; Haywood, *Negro Liberation* (New York: International, 1948); and James S. Allen, *The Negro Question in the United States* (New York: International, 1936).

egalitarian society needed by all producers, rural and urban. White and black workers and poor farmers were natural allies, and the development of multiracial proletarian solidarity was not merely the prerequisite to a successful fight for black self-determination, but in fact the only means by which white workers could achieve genuine class-consciousness. As one organizer from Norfolk, Virginia, noted in 1931, "Working conditions are miserable, wages are very small, and the average working day is ten hours" for white workers. But since "the general tendency is to compare their standard of living with that of the poorest class of workers—that is, the masses of Negro workers, [white workers] do not consider themselves in as poor a condition as they really are."[6]

Moreover, self-determination theorists urged, the call for a Black Republic was not a call for all-class black unity, but instead a summons to the black masses to rise up against all their oppressors, including those reformist black leaders who attempted to contain black militancy within the capitalist framework. As Harry Haywood and other theoreticians proclaimed, the "petty-bourgeois nationalism" of the black middle classes was corrupt and retrograde; only a nationalism based solidly in the proletariat and the peasantry could lead to revolutionary change. At times the black middle class was dropped out of the equation altogether, and "nation" was essentially conflated with "class." The left-wing (then Communist) sociologist Scott Nearing put it tersely in his 1929 study *Black America*: "To be black in the United States is to be proletarian."[7]

6. Irving Keith, "Organizing in Virginia," *DW* (May 6, 1929), rpt. in Foner and Allen, p. 211.

7. Haywood, "Against Petty-Bourgeois Liberal Distortions"; Scott Nearing, *Black America* (New York: Vanguard, 1929), p. 130. Haywood remarked that "white chauvinism" was the "main danger" facing the working class but that "petit-bourgeois nationalism" was the main danger facing the revolutionary movement. See his "The Road to Negro Liberation" (New York: Workers Library, 1934). In his biography of Nearing, Stephen J. Whitfield claims that Nearing, while a member of the CP when he was composing *Black America*, "wrote too soon to reflect the new line" on self-determination (*Scott Nearing: Apostle of American Radicalism* [New York and London: Columbia UP, 1974], p. 68). The carefully documented discussion of land ownership—in a chapter tellingly entitled "The Black Belt" (pp. 23–28)—in many ways, however, anticipates Allen's method and argument in *The Negro Question in the United States* (1936). John A. Saltmarsh argues that Nearing's analysis of racism in *Black America* "echo[es] the party line" (*Scott Nearing: An Intellectual Biography* [Philadelphia: Temple UP, 1991] p. 228).

Despite the complications this program entailed, the American party's endorsement of the 1928 Comintern position provided the impetus for unprecedented levels of antiracist activity. It is simply not true that, as Klehr and Tompson argue, party work in the South was "made even more difficult by the [self-determination] line." During the Third Period, the party initiated aggressive campaigns against lynch terror and for black/white workers' unity in the Jim Crow South. The party's vigorous campaign in defense of the Scottsboro boys; the organizing into the Share Croppers Union of thousands of farmers (mostly black, but including a few whites) against the brutal debt peonage of the tenant-farming system; the campaigns for unionization in urban centers such as Birmingham; the principled stand for a platform of multiracial proletarian unity among strikers in the textile mills of the Carolinas and the mines of Kentucky; the protracted defense campaign for Angelo Herndon, a young black Communist sentenced to twenty years on a Georgia chain gang for organizing unemployed blacks and whites in a protest for relief—these and related activities, often undertaken under extremely dangerous circumstances, attested to the Communists' commitment to making the Black Belt a site of sharply contested class struggle. By 1934, Kelley reports, there were 1,000 Communists in Alabama, 95 percent of them black. The Birmingham ILD had 3,000 members, and the Birmingham CP was several times larger than the local NAACP. Indeed, to its detractors the Alabama CP was known as the "nigger party."[8]

Significant struggles against white chauvinism and for black/white working-class solidarity also took place in the North. An event signaling the party's strengthened commitment to eradicating racism among its

8. Klehr and Tompson, "Self-Determination in the Black Belt," 366; Kelley, *Hammer and Hoe*, p. 90 and passim; Painter, passim; and Angelo Herndon, *Let Me Live* (1937; rpt. New York: Arno and the New York Times, 1969), passim. For more on the violence encountered by the SCU, see Theodore Rosengarten's oral history, *All God's Dangers: The Life of Nate Shaw* (New York: Knopf, 1974), esp. pp. 303–16. Rosengarten's "Nate Shaw" was Ned Cobb, a party member and SCU activist. For more on antiracism in the Gastonia strike, see Vera Buch Weisbord, *A Radical Life* (Bloomington and London: Indiana UP, 1977), pp. 258–60. Philip Foner comments of the CP's organizing among miners in Harlan, Kentucky, "Although only about 300 or 400 Negro miners went out on strike, the NMU organizers insisted that blacks be treated as equals and eat in the same soup kitchens and sit at the same tables with the white miners" (*Organized Labor and the Black Worker 1919–1981* [New York: International, 1974], p. 195).

white members was the 1931 party trial of August Yokinen, a Finnish Communist janitor of a Harlem dance hall who had attempted to block the party from using the hall for a multiracial dance. Widely publicized in the black press, the Yokinen trial served to assure blacks attracted to Marxist politics that, with regard to the battle against white chauvinism, the party put its money where its mouth was. The importance that the party placed upon forging an alliance between black and white workers was underlined by many of its Northern urban activities, including multiracial confrontations with police carrying out evictions; agitation against segregation in trade unions, spearheaded by the League for Struggle for Negro Rights (LSNR), successor to the relatively ineffective ANLC of the late 1920s; the injection of a politics of black/white labor unity into "Don't Buy Where You Can't Work" campaigns to hire black clerks in inner-city stores; insistent opposition not only to the NAACP but also to Garveyites and other black nationalists who preached the impossibility of cross-race alliance.[9]

That such activities succeeded in inspiring confidence in white and black workers alike is suggested by the nature and size of crowds at urban Communist-led demonstrations. "In Shreveport, Louisiana," reports Philip Foner, "unemployed blacks and whites demanded 'work or feed' and battled police who tried to arrest them. Of 2,000 hunger marchers in the same city in 1931, 500 were blacks. . . . By the fall of 1931 it was a common sight to see blacks appearing at the heads of unemployed demonstrations at numerous state capitals." A significant number of blacks participated in the March 1930 demonstration in Union Square that put the Communists on the map in New York City. Witnessing the spectacle of black and white workers fighting side by side against the police, Cyril Briggs, a former nationalist turned Communist, celebrated "the successful breaking down of the wall of prejudice between white and Negro workers fostered by the employers and the substitution of working-class solidarity and fraternization." At a 1931 funeral march called out to protest police killings of three

9. On the Yokinen trial, see Naison, pp. 47–49, and "Race Hatred on Trial: The Yokinen Trial," in Philip S. Foner and Herbert Shapiro, eds., *American Communism and Black Americans: A Documentary History 1930–1934* (Philadelphia: Temple UP, 1991), pp. 147–81. Hosea Hudson was impressed by the CP's struggles against internal white chauvinism when he visited his first national training school in the North (Painter, pp. 195–213).

young black workers in an anti-eviction demonstration on Chicago's South Side, according to the John Reed Club organ *Left Front*, 100,000 people turned out, including 40,000 white workers. Even if these figures are scaled down considerably—Michel Fabré, Wright's biographer, claims that only 10,000 attended the march, while Haywood sets the number at 30,000—the fact remains that Third-Period Communists achieved significant success in implementing an antiracist platform that stressed the need for white workers to support their black brothers and sisters.[10]

With the transition to Popular Front politics in 1935, the party's strategy for antiracist organizing changed dramatically. "Petty-bourgeois" nationalists in the NAACP and the Urban League, formerly stigmatized as enemies of the Negro masses, were first approached hesitantly as potential allies, then welcomed as friends and asked to join the CP-led National Negro Congress (NNC), which superseded the LSNR in 1936. In the South, Kelley argues, this strategy was largely ineffective: the party lost its base among militant tenant farmers but failed to build bridges with white liberals. In the Northern urban centers, however, the Popular Front strategy brought the party both prestige and numbers. Less attention was placed upon militant street activities—eviction protests, unemployment and relief demonstrations—but more attention was devoted to building integrationist organizations. CIO organizing, which absorbed more and more of the party's attention in the later years of the decade, was consistently antisegregationist, and hundreds of thousands of black and white workers were affected by the Communists' insistence that black/white unity be a main plank in its platform. The party's antifascist campaigns were undertaken to establish links between multiracial unity in the United States and support of internationalist causes. When Mussolini's armies invaded Ethiopia, according to James Ford, the CP organized a demonstration of 100,000, including

10. Foner, *Organized Labor*, p. 151; Fraser Ottanelli, *The Communist Party of the US: From the Depression to World War II* (New Brunswick and London: Rutgers UP, 1991) p. 37; Edith Margo, "The South Side Sees Red," *Left Front* 1, no. 1 (1933): 2, 3, 10; and 1, no. 3 (1934): 4–6; Michel Fabré, *The Unfinished Quest of Richard Wright*, trans. Isabel Barzun (New York: William Morrow, 1973), p. 88; and Haywood, *Black Bolshevik*, p. 443. Mauritz Hallgren, basing his estimate on data from the mainstream press, put the figures of the Chicago march at 20,000 whites and 40,000 blacks (*Seeds of Revolt: A Study of American Life and the Temper of the American People during the Depression* [New York: A. Knopf, 1933], p. 179).

a large contingent of Italian-Americans, to march in protest through the streets of Harlem.[11]

Throughout the 1930s the CP maintained its theoretical allegiance to the self-determination thesis, although its articulation of the doctrine in the midst of actual campaigns varied from South to North and generally waned in the course of the decade. The Third Period was the heyday of the Black Belt doctrine, especially in the South. In fact, the 1928 Comintern resolution was amended in 1930 to stipulate that the self-determination thesis was to be stressed in the South, where ownership of land remained a key political and economic issue. Angelo Herndon, who was originally attracted to the CP because of its contention that "the same vicious interests that were oppressing Negro workers were doing the same thing to white workers," recalled that he first heard the self-determination position stated by CP leader Robert Minor at a Scottsboro rally in 1931. The Black Belt was frequently discussed in the *Southern Worker* in the early 1930s, however, and was invoked as a long-term strategy of the Share Croppers Union. In certain respects, indeed, according to Kelley, "black Communist rhetoric in the South was hardly distinguishable from the literary expressions of Garveyism." *Daily Worker* articles about Southern campaigns were less likely to mention self-determination, however, since the *Daily Worker* was published—and had its significant readership—in the North. The self-determination thesis was brought up infrequently during Third-Period struggles against discrimination in the North, where the operating assumption was that northern blacks sought integration and assimilation.[12]

During the Popular Front, the call for self-determination in the Black

11. Kelley, *Hammer and Hoe*, pp. 119–94; James W. Ford, *The Negro and the Democratic Front* (New York: International, 1938), p. 162; Naison, pp. 169–286. Alexander Saxton's novel *The Great Midland* (New York: Appleton Century Crofts, 1948) details the often intricate racial politics involved in CIO organizing in the late 1930s.

12. Herndon, pp. 79, 81; Kelley, " 'Comrades, praise Gawd for Lenin and Them!': Ideology and Culture among Black Communists in Alabama, 1930–1935," *Science and Society* 52 (Spring 1988): 69. For an example of *Daily Worker* (*DW*) reporting on Southern activities, see Clara Holden, "The Importance of Unemployed Councils and Agrarian Work in the South": "In the two fields of Unemployed Council work and agrarian work, white and Negro workers can see that their problems are identical" (*DW* [January 5, 1932], p. 4). Holden mentions only the multiracial unity position and does not even refer to the call for self-determination.

Belt was for practical purposes eliminated from the party's mass campaigns, South and North: a politics of class-based multiracial unity was proving to have greater appeal to the party's constituents, black as well as white. Nonetheless, even though during the Popular Front the party reversed its position on many vital issues—its analysis of social fascism, its attitude toward the New Deal, its interpretation of the "main danger" on the international scene—it retained its adherence to the Black Belt thesis, at least in theory. James S. Allen's *The Negro Question in the United States* (1936), which presented a formidable array of statistics about population concentration in the deep South to support the Black Belt analysis adumbrated by Third-Period theoreticians like Haywood, remained a definitive text throughout the decade. James Ford—an integrationist who replaced Haywood as the party chief theorist on the "Negro question" in the mid-1930s—continued to place the antiracist struggle in the context of Black Belt self-determination. Ford insisted that the call for a black republic was not merely a symbolic gesture, even if it was apparent that a war for self-determination was not on the horizon. Earl Browder, who was rapidly backpedaling from the left-wing stance asserted in Foster's 1932 *Toward Soviet America*, insisted in his 1936 *What Is Communism?* that Black Belt self-determination remained a "right" of the Negro people. Given all the changes in the party's line and practice at this time, it would have been simple to bury quietly, if not disavow openly, the theory guiding Third-Period formulations of the "Negro question." That the party chose not to do so indicates that, in spite of the theoretical and practical difficulties it posed, the view of blacks as a "nation within a nation" continued to act as an important guide to the party's strategies for leading the class struggle in the United States.[13]

As we look back upon the Depression-era left's theorization of black liberation, it is important not to dismiss out of hand a doctrine that may strike many today as chimerical at best and segregationist at worst. There were significant flaws in the Black Belt thesis. The analogy between American blacks and Soviet national minorities was obviously incomplete, since

13. Allen, passim; Ford, passim; Browder, *What Is Communism?* (New York: Vanguard, 1936), pp. 186–89. Arthur Zipser, in his biography of William Z. Foster, notes that the Black Belt position was officially abandoned only in 1959 (*Working-Class Giant: The Life of William Z. Foster* [New York: International, 1981], pp. 183–84).

American blacks, despite all the characteristically African survivals in their culture, did not possess a language distinctly their own—a criterion that both Lenin and Stalin held to be crucial to the definition of a "national minority." Furthermore, the formulation that American blacks constituted a "nation"—with the frequent assumption that this "nation" was tantamount to a "class"—confused the categories of class analysis, even if it was continually stipulated that petty-bourgeois nationalism had nothing to do with the nationalism of the oppressed masses. If the goal of self-determination was to establish a Black Republic prior to the socialist revolution, and if this republic might well take its time about deciding to align itself with the United Socialist States of America (USSA), the black bourgeoisie was slated to play a historical role that must be construed as objectively progressive. Most serious of all, however, was the difficulty of dispelling the aura of segregationism surrounding the Black Belt proposal. Protest as they might that there was no contradiction between black self-determination and multiracial workers' unity, American Communists had some difficulty marshaling arguments that would completely allay the charge that the black nationalism they were advocating was not itself racist or discriminatory. The continuing debate in Depression-era theoretical documents over the segregationist overtones of the call for a Black Republic indicates that the CP experienced abiding difficulty with the contradictory implications of its formulation of the relation of racial emancipation to class struggle.[14]

In spite of its various theoretical and practical shortcomings, however, the self-determination thesis offered the American left a means of addressing the special nature of racial oppression while linking it to a class-based revolutionary agenda. By endorsing and acting upon this analysis, the radical working-class movement for the first time in U.S. history moved itself off dead center with regard to the issue of confronting racism. Com-

14. Haywood, whose political career centered on the defense and elaboration of the Black Belt thesis, felt that it was important to fight to establish a Negro republic; he was quite bitter about the party's lessening enthusiasm for self-determination after the Third Period. Allen was also a strong proponent of self-determination as a realizable demand. Both Foster and Browder, by contrast, seem to have felt that the position was abstract and did not commit the party to fighting for a Negro republic in any immediate sense. See Foster, *History of the Communist Party of the United States* (New York: International, 1952), pp. 266–67; and Browder, *What Is Communism?*

munism, previously seen as irrelevant by the overwhelming majority of American blacks, attracted a significant mass base in black communities. William Jones, editor of the *Baltimore Afro-American*, one of the few all-black weeklies in the United States, was cited in *International Literature* in 1932 as stating, "There are fifteen million potential Communists in the United States today. I know this because I know what is on the minds of these people." Junius Scales, a white CP organizer in the South who went to jail in the 1950s for his Communist activities, reflected back with pride upon the CP's record in fighting racism. He might have contributed to organizing workers or fighting fascism without joining the party, he reflected; but "when it came to opposing white supremacy, there was nowhere else to go." The 1930s antiracist movement, as Horne demonstrates, was in important respects not merely a precursor but a progenitor of the Civil Rights movement of the 1950s and 1960s. That this earlier movement should have been inspired by a program carrying segregationist overtones is one of the ironies of history that we may be happier to live with.[15]

Black Culture: Folk or Proletarian?

The various complexities and contradictions in the Depression-era Communist formulation of the political and economic relation of race to class liberation manifested themselves in the left's antiracist cultural program in a number of ways. Of particular interest to our investigation here are the implications of the CP's ambivalent nationalism for the concepts of the "folk" that guided Communist discussions of proletarian and revolutionary art.

During the Third Period, when the Communist party was both more insistent in its call for a Black Republic and more unrelenting in its attack upon the black bourgeoisie, left-wing organizers and cultural critics

15. William Jones, cited in "Intellectuals Go Left," *IL* 1 (1933): 151–52; Junius Irving Scales and Richard Nickson, *Cause at Heart: A Former Communist Remembers* (Athens, Ga., and London: U of Georgia P, 1987), p. 320; Horne, passim. Scales became involved in CP activity primarily in the period 1939–41, when, as Kelley reports, there was to some degree a revival of Third-Period style militancy in party work in the South (*Hammer and Hoe*, pp. 195–219).

sought out black cultural practices that served as indices to the revolutionary spirit of the black masses and that, moreover, might be effectively mobilized in winning black workers and farmers to the Communist movement. The formulation most commonly accompanying this project was drawn from the Bolsheviks' experience with national minorities in the Soviet Union: black cultural practices, which were often carried over from slavery, should be understood as "national in form, but proletarian in content." [16]

Communist cultural commentators made varying claims about the political significance of black folk culture. In keeping with the Third-Period enthusiasm for worker-correspondence and worker-authored literature, some Marxists writing in the early 1930s celebrated black music and folk mythology as intrinsically oppositional. Lawrence Gellert, who spent several years gathering songs for his 1936 collection *Negro Songs of Protest*, noted in 1931 that "Negro culture is perhaps the most genuine workers' culture in America." The songs gathered in his volume, he declared, attested to "the living voice of an otherwise inarticulate resentment against injustice—a part of the unrest that is stirring in the South." Yet Marxist commentators tended to draw the line at spirituals and other expressions of folk consciousness that did not express open resistance. "The political use of the spiritual was sporadic prior to the Popular Front era," notes Serge Denisoff. It was only in the era of the Popular Front that "spirituals which were not overt assertions of protest were placed within an ideological framework and considered true expressions of people's art." [17]

The expressions of black folk culture that aroused the most enthusiastic response among Third-Period commentators—and that appear to have

16. Haywood, *Black Bolshevik*, pp. 157–60. In the USSR, the slogan was slightly different: "National in form and socialist in content" (*IL* 1 [1933]: 107).

17. Lawrence Gellert, "Negro Songs of Protest," *NM* 6 (November 1930): 10–11; Gellert, comp., *Negro Songs of Protest* (New York: American Music League, 1936), p. 7; Serge Denisoff, *Great Day Coming: Folk Music and the American Left* (Urbana, Chicago, and London: U of Illinois P, 1971), pp. 38, 39. See also Robbie Lieberman, "*My Song Is My Weapon*": *People's Songs, American Communism, and the Politics of Culture, 1930–1950* (Urbana and Chicago: U of Illinois P, 1989). Lieberman stresses that during the Third Period the dominant preference in CP cultural circles was for choral singing in the European tradition; even Aunt Molly Jackson, the popular ballad singer from Kentucky, was shunned by the Composers' Collective (pp. 30–39).

served the most useful function in the Communist movement—were songs and tales that grafted explicitly revolutionary lyrics onto preexisting folk idioms. Gold noted in the *Daily Worker* in 1932 that the black Chicago workers who turned "Old Time Religion" into "Gimme that New Communist Spirit" were "transmut[ing] . . . their religious past . . . into a Communist present." In the South this sort of revolutionary rearticulation was central to the discourse through which the Communism of the Alabama Share Croppers Union defined itself. Religious songs were frequently recast as anthems for the antiracist movement. The spiritual "My Mother's Got a Stone That Was Hewn Out of the Mountain" (sometimes called "A Stone Came Rolling Out of Babylon") was rewritten to include the refrain, "Came a-rollin' through Dixie / A tearing down the kingdom of the boss"; the song served as the anthem of the ILD. In Grace Lumpkin's *A Sign for Cain*, the radicalized spiritual "We Shall Not Be Moved," which the Communist organizer Denis attributes to Alabama sharecroppers, serves as a rallying cry to the fledgling Communist movement he is helping to build. Party meetings in Montgomery often opened with a prayer, Kelley notes, and revolutionary consciousness was routinely referred to as the "Lenin spirit." [18]

The political translatability of religious culture was paralleled by the susceptibility of inherited folk mythology to revolutionary reinscription. Communists working among black sharecroppers found it relatively easy to explain their revolutionary program by reference to the popular folk interpretation of history, according to which, in the new Civil War needed to fulfill the aborted promise of the first, Russians were to be the "new Yankees" and Stalin the "new Lincoln." For this reason, Kelley remarks, "Southern propaganda which portrayed the Communists as being Soviet agents often worked to the party's advantage in the black community." The grafting of revolutionary Marxist theory onto popular narratives and songs, both religious and secular, thus displayed the Communists' skillful adaptation of existing folk culture to explicitly revolutionary ends. While the dangers of opportunistic appropriation were evident—revolution could be simply converted into a second coming—so also were the advantages

18. Gold, "Negro Reds of Chicago," *DW* (September 30, 1932), p. 4; "New Defense Song Gains Wide Popularity in the South," *DW* (November 7, 1933), p. 5; Richard Frank, "Negro Revolutionary Music," *NM* 11 (May 15, 1934): 29, 30; Kelley, " 'Praise Gawd,' " 62.

of articulating workers' revolution within the familiar terms of popular apocalyptic discourse. "The Alabama CP was resilient enough to conform to black cultural traditions," Kelley concludes, "but taut enough to remain Marxist at the core."[19]

In their efforts to find in existing *literary* culture an antiracist "usable past," however—or, for that matter, a usable present—Third-Period cultural critics encountered a more problematic situation. For the slogan "national in form, proletarian in content" clearly meant something different in relation to the relatively elite—and usually urban and Northern—sphere of literature than it did in relation to the largely oral folk culture of the Southern masses. The contradictions embedded in the concept of a black nation emerged with considerable sharpness when it was no longer possible to treat race as essentially equivalent to class. Communist cultural critics generally condemned the great majority of past and contemporaneous black writers for their neurotic subjectivism, their defeatism, and their snobbery (or, conversely, their primitivism). Eugene Clay castigated middle-class black writers for their separation from the rebellious traditions of the black masses. Eugene Gordon dismissed the entire modern Afro-American literary tradition extending from Chesnutt and DuBois to McKay, Cullen, Fauset, Fisher, Schuyler, and Thurman. Although American blacks were "a homogeneous people possessing all the characteristics of a nation," with a "national psychology" and a "national culture," Gordon argued, they constituted "an artificially created nation" whose culture and psychology were consequently "unhealthy." "Middle-class nationalism," he concluded, was the basis of the "psychosis" of black culture. Only when there emerged numbers of "Negro writers who have been developed in the blast furnace of the Black Belt class struggle, and in the class struggle outside that zone," he noted, could there emerge "a body of literature, the aim of which is preparation to seize and hold political power."[20]

Indeed, both black and white commentators on the Third-Period literary scene concluded that the only progressive literary expressions of Negro consciousness were those that led toward a multiracial working-

19. Kelley, " 'Praise Gawd,' " 67; Kelley, *Hammer and Hoe*, p. 116.
20. Eugene Clay, "The Negro in Recent American Literature," *American Writers Congress*, ed. Henry Hart (New York: International, 1935), pp. 145–53; Eugene Gordon, *AWC*, pp. 143, 144, 145.

class politics. Gold asserted that McKay's *Banjo*, while praiseworthy for its gritty depiction of Marseilles street life and its repudiation of the culture of the "educated fringe," evinced too much "racial patriotism" and dwelt too little on proletarian themes. Walt Carmon—in the same article where he complained that Smedley's class anger was problematized by "the anger of a woman"—concluded that, even though Hughes's *Not Without Laughter* had, "under its black skin, real proletarian blood running though it," the text was "marred as [a] class nove[l]" because it was "steeled in the hatred of an oppressed race." Gordon observed that *Babouk*, Guy Endore's fictional reenactment of the Haitian revolution, was flawed because it failed to depict the necessity for black/white labor unity. Clay, in his 1935 address to the American Writers Congress, singled out for praise poems that explicitly called for multiracial unity, such as Sterling Brown's "Black Worker and White Worker" and various revolutionary pieces by Hughes and Wright. Clay remarked that it was "racialist" for a black writer to "specialize" in representations of black life that raised no larger class context.[21]

For these and other commentators on Third-Period literary culture, the slogan "national in form, proletarian in content" was ordinarily interpreted to privilege content over form. Indeed, Carmon's troubling anatomical metaphor carried the distinct implication that class and race are not simply equivalent, but that class is essence, and race mere epiphenomenon. The nationalism of Southern black sharecroppers was acceptable because it voiced a pure folk consciousness largely indistinguishable from class consciousness. Literary texts, however—even those representing the life of the black masses—should contain explicit advocacy of black/white class unity if they were to qualify as "proletarian." Despite the clearly nationalist implications of the Black Belt thesis that was being urged in party theory and practice, when it came to literary matters Third-Period commentators unequivocally urged proletarian writers to advocate class-based multiracial unity.

During the years of the Popular Front, Communist and fellow-traveler cultural critics generally evinced greater flexibility in their discussions

21. Gold, "Dark with Sunlight," *NM* 5 (July 1929): 17; Walt Carmon, "Away from Harlem," *NM* 6 (October 1930): 18; Gordon, "Black and White, Unite and Fight!" *NM* 13 (October 23, 1934): 24–25; Clay, p. 152.

of the relation of race to class. With the reduced stress upon the Black Belt thesis and the more tolerant attitude toward the black middle class, as well as the downplaying of revolutionary politics in the party's overall practice and rhetoric, left-wing critics more readily discovered progressive models in already existing folk—and literary—culture. As the party came to advocate a more consistently integrationist politics, it identified itself, somewhat paradoxically, with what Naison calls a "muted cultural nationalism." One manifestation of the altering formulation of the relation of race to class was the discourse about nationalism and Marxism in The New Challenge. A short-lived periodical succeeding Dorothy West's Challenge (1935–37), The New Challenge—edited by West and her friend Marion Minus, with Wright serving as associate editor—embodied the concerns of Popular Front-era black writers interested in articulating a version of Negro nationalism assimilable to Communist politics. In its first and only editorial statement, The New Challenge called for work stressing "the life of the Negro masses" and treating "folk material . . . as a source of creative material." The New Challenge published poems exhibiting a range of political stands, from pure proletarian to cultural nationalist. Frank Marshall Davis's "Snapshots of the Cotton South" depicts a "starving black" and a "starving white" battling over the "dark soil" while the "rich plantation owner" holds his whip over them; Robert Davis's "South Chicago, May 30, 1937" offers a meditation on the Memorial Day massacre. Sterling Brown's "Old Lem," however, makes no mention of multiracial unity in its vivid representation of black resistance to Jim Crow. Owen Dodson's "From Those Shores We have Come" and Margaret Walker's "People of Unrest and Hunger" prophesy black resistance to oppression without specifying any precise political agenda, multiracial or otherwise.[22]

The New Challenge also published theoretical articles treating the con-

22. Naison, p. 207; "Editorial," The New Challenge (hereinafter NC) 2 (Fall 1937): 3; Frank Marshall Davis, "Snapshots of the Cotton South," NC 2 (Fall 1937): 40; Robert Davis, "South Chicago, May 30, 1937," NC 2 (Fall 1937): 49; Sterling Brown, "Old Lem," NC 2 (Fall 1937): 46–48; Owen Dodson, "From Those Shores We Have Come," NC 2 (Fall 1937): 48; Margaret Walker, "People of Unrest and Hunger," NC 2 (Fall 1937): 49. For more on the association of New Challenge with the South Side Writers Group, see Margaret Walker, Richard Wright, pp. 71, 110–11. For an account of Dorothy West's uneasiness with the Chicago-based radicals, see Adelaide M. Cromwell, "Afterword" to Dorothy West, The Living Is Easy (1948; rpt. New York: Feminist P, 1982), pp. 356–57.

nections between nationalism and class-based politics. Allyn Keith, in "A Note on Negro Nationalism," condemned "isolationist nationalism" and argued that even "cooperative nationalism" is productive only insofar as it points toward "common class position" as "the lowest common denominator of group activity toward social improvement." He concluded, "The Negro writer returning to the soil folk and the industrial masses as creative sources must know the true difference between nationalism as a limiting concept and nationalism as a phase which is difficult but rich in the materials for progress into wider channels." Alain Locke, in a largely unsympathetic review of Claude McKay's anti-Communist *A Long Way From Home*, observed that "The program of the Negro Renaissance was to interpret the folk to itself, to vitalize it from within; it was a wholesome, vigorous, assertive racialism, even if not explicitly proletarian in conception and justification." The exploration of this racialism remained the main task of the Negro writer, Locke declared, "even if the added formula of proletarian art be necessary to cure this literary anemia and make our art the nourishing life blood of the people rather than the caviar and cake of the artists themselves." It would appear that black intellectuals aligned with the Communist movement were attempting to reserve considerable space for the expression of nationalist impulses at the same time that they repudiated elitism and affirmed the broader goals of class-based solidarity.[23]

The most important theoretical statement to appear in the pages of *The New Challenge* was Richard Wright's "A Blueprint for Negro Writing." "Negro writers must accept the nationalist implications of their lives," Wright declared, "not in order to encourage them, but in order to change and transcend them. . . . [A] nationalist spirit in Negro writing means a nationalism carrying the highest possible pitch of social consciousness. It means a nationalism that knows its origins, its limitations; that is aware of the dangers of its position; that knows its ultimate aims are unrealizable within the framework of capitalist America." Entry into the domain of the folk, according to Wright, entails neither a conflation of race with class nor an escape from confronting their interrelation, but instead a means of investing the writer with revolutionary consciousness—"a consciousness which draws for its strength upon the fluid lore of a great people,

23. Allyn Keith, "A Note on Negro Nationalism," NC 2 (Fall 1937): 65–69, quoted 69; Alain Locke, "Spiritual Truancy," NC 2 (Fall 1937): 85.

and moulds this lore with the concepts that move and direct the forces of history today." The view of totality afforded by the "Marxist conception of reality and society" will enable the Negro writer to "learn to view the life of a Negro living in New York's Harlem or Chicago's South Side with the consciousness that one-sixth of the earth's surface belongs to the working class." The goal of working-class revolution is thus in no way contradictory to the fostering of a vital Negro nationalism: Negro writers must "weed out [the] choking growths of reactionary nationalism and replace them with hardier and sturdier types." In Wright's dialectical formulation, national- ism would point the way to revolutionary class consciousness, be trans- formed, and eventually be negated by the higher level of consciousness to which it had given rise.[24]

The party's encouragement of various forms of black nationalist cultural expression in literature and music during the Popular Front years was not designed to entail any abandonment of the left's commitment to an integra- tionist, class-based politics. Rather, it was viewed as a way of celebrating the multicultural character of American society and of arguing for the key role played by blacks in many aspects of the national experience. The ac- knowledgment of plurality and "difference" is so familiar—and tame—a feature of contemporary mainstream multiculturalism that it is difficult to recreate the radical impact that such propositions had over half a cen- tury ago. Left-wing commentators frequently argued that blacks were not merely one more element in the American melting pot, but possessed an experience that epitomized American social existence. When Wright re- marked in the *New York Amsterdam News* in 1938 that "I have found in the Negro worker the real symbol of the working class in America," or when Paul Robeson claimed at the culmination of the multicultural "Ballad for Americans," "I Am America," the point was being made that blacks were not simply integral to, but in fact representative of, the body politic.[25]

In one sense, as Naison notes, this proposition that blacks "represented" American society had far-reaching antiracist implications, for it demon- strated the extent to which "the Party's position on the Negro question had transcended its origins as a Comintern imperative and had linked up with

24. Richard Wright, "A Blueprint for Negro Writing," NC 2 (Fall 1937): 58, 59, 62, 64–65.

25. Wright, *New Amsterdam News*, February 27, 1938, cited in Fabré, p. 553.

powerful cultural impulses in American society." It is worthwhile quoting Naison at length.

> By defining Black America's struggle for cultural recognition as a source of creative energy for the entire nation, party spokesmen helped give their white constituency a sense that they had a personal stake in black empowerment and that cultural interchange between the races represented a *defining* feature of the American experience, something to be celebrated and dramatized rather than hidden, or made the butt of jokes. In the Popular Front era, writers close to the Party spoke of the attraction whites historically displayed toward black music, dance, and theatre—or even black language and the black sense of style—as the affirmation of a democratic impulse rather than a journey to the heart of darkness. In doing so, they helped give the struggle for racial equality the aura of a movement of cultural regeneration. The uniqueness of this perspective cannot be emphasized enough. Historically, opponents of civil rights had argued that racial equality meant cultural degeneracy, that black culture embodied a barbarism that would undermine American civilization if blacks were not prohibited from "social intercourse" with whites and excluded from positions of political power. Popular Front critics turned this argument on its head, arguing that the distinctive culture of blacks contributed to much that was vital and original in American life and that their full emancipation would strengthen the entire nation.

By means of its multicultural iconography, the Communist left broadened the basis for its call for class-based solidarity of black and white beyond the relatively economistic arguments offered during the Third Period. Common economic imperatives, as well as the need for political alliance against the capitalist class, might furnish the material ground for multiracial unity. But the Communist advocacy of a multicultural politics in which blacks played a leading role enriched and expanded the concept of class-based unity. Whites were called upon not simply to ally, but actually identify, with their black brothers and sisters.[26]

From a revolutionary standpoint, however, Popular Front multicultural politics entailed a retreat from Third-Period formulations of interracial class solidarity. The party's more tolerant attitude toward black national-

---

26. Naison, pp. 216–17. CP cultural policy entailed an "'Americanism' that exemplified *real* respect for differentness rather than attempting, as did official mainstream liberalism, to disparage and destroy ethnic variations under the guise of championing the superior virtue of the 'melting pot,'" notes Duberman (p. 250).

ism, its new friendliness with black bourgeois forces, no doubt clouded the class issue in various ways. But more crucially—as is indicated by Naison's approving comment that the "entire nation" might be "strengthened" by its acknowledgment of what blacks had "contributed"—a different type of nationalism emerged as assimilable to the program of the left—namely, American patriotism. Originally it was the *distinctiveness* of black folk culture—its intrinsically oppositional position relative to bourgeois cultural hegemony—that was heralded by radical critics seeking a usable black cultural tradition. By the late 1930s, however, this adversarial particularity was being inscribed in a nationalistic discourse that posited a synecdochic relation between black folk experience and that of the nation as a whole. As James Ford noted in 1938, black people were from among the "first families" of the United States and thus enjoyed a position comparable to that of Washington, Jefferson, and Lincoln—the anomalous household gods of a reformist Communism that now proclaimed itself to be the most genuine bearer of "twentieth-century Americanism." [27]

The antiracism undergirding this democratic-populist proposition is, of course, patent: slaves had as much title to citizenship as did their owners. But such arguments also carried the implication that the descendants of both slaveholders and slaves could now be nonantagonistically united in a common democratic program. As Wright put it in his 1941 *Twelve Million Black Voices*, "We black folk, our history and our present being, are a mirror of all the manifold experiences of America. What we want, what we represent, what we endure is what America *is*. If we black folk perish, America will perish." This formulation conveyed an unmistakable note of threat. It also affirmed, however, that black emancipation was part of the progressiveness of the American democratic experience. In a curious political inversion, the distinctive cultural expressions of the black "oppressed nation," originally held to be inherently antagonistic to capitalist and neo-feudalist oppression, were assimilated to a "left" American nationalism that, as the decade progressed, became increasingly difficult to distinguish from garden-variety American patriotism. Indeed, one of

27. Ford, 137–39. Ford exhibits some of the political contortions that Popular Front patriotism entailed for the Party's antiracist platform—as, for example, in his defense of Thomas Jefferson as a progressive antiracist against conservative Southern Senator Bilbo, who was claiming that Jefferson had believed in black inferiority, or in his comparison of George Washington with Stalin (pp. 188–89, 139).

the finer ironies of Popular Front politics was the playing of the "Ballad for Americans"—albeit without Robeson at the microphone—at the 1940 Republican Convention.[28]

The annals of Popular Front cultural politics are filled with such anomalies. But it would be mistaken to conclude that the party's significant Popular Front-era concessions to nationalism—both American and Negro—made its antiracist program either incoherent or ineffective. In both the Popular Front era and the Third Period, integrationism and nationalism existed in contradictory unity in the American Communists' line and practice—as, for that matter, did reformism and revolutionism. As we shall see in chapters 9 through 11, the open tension between integrationism and nationalism had distinct ramifications for the rhetorical strategies adopted in proletarian novels that foregrounded questions of race and class. Troubling as the CP's dualistic line proved in some respects to be, it opened up an important arena of political and cultural discourse in American literature. Rather than stifling black or antiracist white writers, the party's analysis of black liberation inspired writers to address questions of racism with passion and urgency.

White Writers and the Dialectic of Race and Class

By no means all white proletarian writers have an unblemished record regarding the representation of race in their novels. "White chauvinism" was actively combated in the activist ranks, but it manifests itself in several proletarian texts. Racism is articulated through a combination of silence and stereotype. In her documentary Gastonia novel Strike!, Mary Heaton Vorse sloughs over the organizers' attempts to win white workers to antiracism, even though most of the actual CP leaders in Gastonia—whose activities Vorse as a journalist observed at first—struggled to implement this party policy. Indeed, Vorse's only reference to black workers is a character's off-the-cuff remark about their laziness—a comment that the novelist takes no steps to ironize or counter by other means. Similarly, throughout Dos Passos's U.S.A., which purports to represent the totality of American

28. Wright, Twelve Million Black Voices (1941; rpt. New York: Arno and The New York Times, 1969), p. 144.

society through its spectrum of typical fictional characters, not a single black (or other non-white) character is featured as a protagonist. Moreover, Dos Passos's few black and latin characters are portrayed through a mutually reinforcing racist and homophobic discourse that presupposes the reader's assent. Margo Dowling's Cuban husband Tony whines, steals, and turns out to be homosexual; the black male prostitutes who solicit Richard Ellsworth Savage in the Harlem scene in The Big Money flash their yellow teeth and take all his money. Racism also interlocks with sexism in Albert Halper's Union Square, where the voluptuous Comrade Helen is continually shown panting in the animal embrace of her Mexican lover José. These texts make no attempt to raise antiracism as a political issue and reveal an authorial political unconscious in which racist assumptions are deeply embedded.

Even in novels that aspire to address the "Negro question" from a Communist standpoint, race and racism are at times presented in problematic ways. In Jordanstown, Josephine Johnson points out the centrality of black/white unity to the working-class resistance developing among the starving and unemployed denizens of the "Bottom." In particular, she invests the wise and militant Anna with heroic status. But this honorific characterization is contradicted by the narrator's suggestion of Anna's exceptionality: Anna is, we learn, "too articulate and brooding for her own people." Fielding Burke's Call Home the Heart reveals a left-wing author's acquired antiracist doctrine battling with deeply ingrained racist attitudes. In this Gastonia novel, Burke, unlike Vorse, stresses the importance of fighting racism among white workers. Moreover, she treats the protagonist's encounter with her own bigotry as a central moment of political self-knowledge. Yet the incident precipitating Ishma's self-critical awakening—a grateful embrace by black Gaffie, whose husband Butch Ishma has just saved from racist vigilantes—is portrayed in language undermining the manifest intent of the episode:

> [Gaffie's] lips were heavy, and her teeth so large that one needed the sure avouch of eyes to believe in them. It was impossible to associate her with woe, though tears were racing down her cheeks. As her fat body moved she shook off an odor that an unwashed collie would have disowned. . . .
>
> [Gaffie's] rolling arms lay heavy on her neck. The fat bosom shook against her own. The sickening smell of disturbed animal sweat rose and fell with the black body. Gaffie could not see Ishma's blazing eyes, but she felt the white arms stiffen.

In describing Ishma's subsequent flight from Winbury (Gastonia) back to the mountains, Burke clearly wishes to expose the extent to which even the most progressive Southern white workers are fatally flawed by their racist attitudes. As John Reilly notes, "The radical union and party had enabled Ishma to overcome her racial prejudice on an immediate public level and work collectively for political and economic ends. Her personal reflex, however, is still of the past." But the voice depicting Gaffie speaks with an authority transcending Ishma's limitations. The "one" who needs "the sure avouch of eyes" to believe the monstrous size of Gaffie's teeth is not just the text's protagonist. Ishma may be "sickened" at Gaffie's odor, but the comparison of this odor with "disturbed animal sweat" is the narrator's. It would appear that Ishma's feelings of repulsion are ones with which the author identifies, in spite of herself.[29]

The authors cited above cannot all be unproblematically identified with the left or seen as reflective of the left's values. Vorse was a middle-aged left-liberal labor journalist who was well set in her ways by the time she wrote Strike!; she maintained a somewhat critical distance from the CP and felt under no obligation to reflect or publicize its line on racism. Dos Passos was at most a cautious friend of the left, even during his enthusiasm of the early 1930s; by the time he wrote The Big Money—by far the most racially problematic of the three volumes of U.S.A.—he was well along his trajectory away from left-wing commitments. Halper was never especially friendly to the CP and, in Union Square, launched a cruel polemic against the party's efforts to organize the unemployed and create a proletarian culture. Johnson, while clearly sympathetic to an idealistic version of communism, never wrote for the left press or participated in any of the party's united front writers' groups. Burke, a white southerner, was fifty-eight years old and had very recently discovered Communist politics when she published Call Home the Heart in 1932. In their expressions of entrenched assumptions about race, these novelists cannot therefore be taken to exemplify a white chauvinism that can be attributed to the CP. What is noteworthy, however, is that the various CP literary figures who reviewed these texts—including Jerome, Hicks, Rolfe, and Schneider—failed to rebuke the authors for their negative representations of people of color, even

29. Josephine Johnson, Jordanstown (New York: Simon and Schuster, 1937), pp. 39–40; Fielding Burke, Call Home the Heart (1932; rpt. New York: Feminist P, 1983), p. 383; John Reilly, "Images of Gastonia," Georgia Review 28 (1972): 510.

though the critics faulted the novelists on other points of political doctrine. White chauvinism was one of the most serious charges that could be leveled by one party member against another; personal practice on this question met with sharp criticism and self-criticism. But novelistic expressions of subliminal white chauvinism seem not to have been subjected to comparable scrutiny.[30]

It would be wrong, however, to place primary emphasis upon the shortcomings of Communist-influenced white writers' attempts to treat issues of race and racism. The preponderant effect of the 1930s left's line on the "Negro question" was to give a powerful impetus to the production of an antiracist literature. Even when they were assigned relatively minor roles, black characters usually performed important functions in mapping the terms of a text's political discourse. One such function was to demonstrate, by way of negative example, how the protagonist's backwardness on racial matters—usually directed against blacks, but at times against other racial and ethnic minorities—was an index to the false consciousness that more generally kept him/her locked into a state of oppression. In Louis Colman's _Lumber_, a novel detailing a lumber worker's loss of left-wing commitment and eventual death as a scab, Jimmie Logan's prejudice against "Portugee" coworkers leads directly to his demise, insofar as he refuses to acknowledge the workers' common need for safe working conditions. In Robert Cantwell's _The Land of Plenty_, the racist attitudes that the college student Walt displays toward the "half-breed" Winters are an index to the elitism that leads him to scab. In the stirring conclusion to _The Young Manhood of Studs Lonigan_, James T. Farrell shows the drunken Studs stretched out in the streets of his racially changing South Side Chicago neighborhood, viewed with hostility by the blacks toward whom he has expressed only scorn and abuse. In _Tobacco Road_, "Kneel to the Rising Sun," and other accounts of white and black sharecroppers, Erskine Caldwell demonstrates how the whites' endorsement of antiblack attitudes not only makes them complicit in the blacks' violent deaths but also reinforces their own vir-

---

30. For more on Vorse, Dos Passos, Halper, and Burke, respectively, see Dee Garrison, _Mary Heaton Vorse: The Life of an American Insurgent_ (Philadelphia: Temple UP, 1989); Melvin Landsberg, _Dos Passos's Path to U. S. A._ (Boulder: U of Colorado P, 1973), and G. Townsend Ludington, _John Dos Passos: A Twentieth-Century Odyssey_ (New York: E. P. Dutton, 1980); Albert Halper, _Good-bye, Union Square: A Writer's Memoir of the Thirties_ (Chicago: Quadrangle, 1970); and Anna W. Shannon, "Biographical Afterword," _Call Home the Heart_, 433–46.

tual enslavement to the capitalists and plantation owners. In these and other narratives of false consciousness, the characters' inability to grant the humanity of nonwhite fellow workers signals their inability to break free from bourgeois ideology in other ways.

Conversely, a white character's articulation of antiracist ideas and attitudes is frequently treated as an index to his/her possession of working-class consciousness and presages his/her development into a revolutionary leader. In *You Can't Sleep Here*, a novel portraying a young unemployed journalist's experiences in a Manhattan Hooverville, Gene Marsay's willingness to defend Hopkins, the shantytown's one black resident, signals his increasingly revolutionary identification with the wretched of the earth. In Lumpkin's *To Make My Bread*, Bonnie McClure's growing friendship with the black mill worker Mary Allen enables her to combat the Race Domination propagandists who attempt to split and destroy the textile workers' strike. In William Cunningham's *The Green Corn Rebellion*, a novel reconstructing an abortive antiwar rebellion among Oklahoma farmers during World War I, the protagonist Jim Tetley is inspired to greater levels of militancy by the participation of the black farmer Bill Johnson, who has suffered privations far greater than any of the whites but nonetheless declares his commitment to their common cause. In *The Disinherited*, Larry Donovan's growing class consciousness is signaled by his friendship with the black Mose, who prompts Larry to think in more class-conscious terms and is himself saved from death when Larry calls upon the other workers to halt production when Mose has a stroke. In *A World to Win*, Conroy makes the St. Louis Communist organizer "Fatfolks," who carries the "Lenin spirit," the catalytic character winning the Hurley brothers to the revolutionary cause. (Indeed, Conroy's portrayal of "Fatfolks" was sufficiently stirring to lead the radical black journalist and poet Melvin B. Tolson to praise it as "the most heroic picture of a Negro I've seen in a novel.") Other proletarian novels include nonwhite characters who prompt white protagonists toward greater class consciousness and militancy: comparable figures appear in Armstrong's *Parched Earth*, Smedley's *Daughter of Earth*, Page's *Moscow Yankee* and *Daughter of the Hills*, and Weatherwax's *Marching! Marching!* [31]

31. Melvin B. Tolson, *Caviar and Cabbage: Selected Columns by Melvin B. Tolson from the Washington Tribune, 1937–49*, ed. Robert M. Farnsworth (Columbia and London: U of Missouri P, 1982), p. 56. Apparently Larry Donavan's antiracism is based on

Most white proletarian novelists relegated black characters to minor roles. Some, however, assigned major roles to blacks, treating the issue of black/white unity as more than simply one question among many. In *A Stone Came Rolling*, the sequel to *Call Home the Heart*, Burke overcame her earlier difficulties in positively depicting black characters and stressed the recruitment of blacks into the left-led union movement. Where in the earlier novel the rescue of the black activist Butch brings into the open Ishma's—and Burke's—bigotry, in the sequel a parallel episode—the rescue of the union organizer Stomp from a lynch mob—spurs further commitment to multiracial organizing on the part of Ishma and her comrades. Burke's decision to name her novel after the ILD anthem reveals the importance of antiracist themes to the text. Myra Page, in *Gathering Storm: A Story of the Black Belt*, intertwined the stories of two Southern millworker families, white and black. While she interiorized the white characters more fully than she did the black, Page gave black characters key motivating roles in the plot. The rape and murder of Martha precipitate almost her entire family's murder and cause her brother Fred to move to the North. Fred's subsequent courageous act of saving the white Tom from drowning amidst a longshoremen's brawl begins a friendship that eventually lands them both back in the South as Communist organizers. In *A Sign for Cain*, Lumpkin places the politics of building multiracial unity at center stage. Her two major Communist characters, the black Denis and the white Bill, share responsibilities for organizing a multiracial group of sharecroppers to fight for a variety of badly needed reforms. Although Lumpkin initially traces the consciousness of both characters, she soon loses track of Denis; when he is lynched in his jail cell at the end of the novel, we only hear of the event afterward. Nonetheless, Lumpkin manages to construct a complex political discourse that addresses the role of the black church, class divisions among Southern whites, survivals of plantation loyalties among the older generation of blacks, and other issues central to rural Southern Communist organizing. In spite of their hesitancy to probe deeply into the consciousness of black characters, then, Burke, Page, and Lump-

---

Conroy's own experiences. Conroy was repulsed by racism after witnessing a lynching when a child; his parents, both loyal unionists, hosted a black couple over threats by neighborhood racists. See Daniel Neil Morris, "The 'Anvil' Writers: Oral History and Quantification Conjoined," Ph.D. Thesis, U of Missouri, Columbia, 1988, pp. 90–91.

kin—all of them, incidentally, Southern-born white women—produced texts that treated the Communist experience in the South in particularity and depth.[32]

In the texts I have discussed thus far, the authors focused primarily upon the integrationist aspects of the CP's analysis of the "Negro question." Occasionally, however, the self-determination thesis made its way into white-authored proletarian novels. Burke, in *Call Home the Heart*, at one point has the radical doctor Derry Unthank declare that he can sympathize with those blacks who desire a separate state. Page, in her tellingly subtitled *Gathering Storm: A Story of the Black Belt*, on one occasion has a white character explicitly remark that Southern blacks should have the right to live in an independent Negro republic: "A long, bitter scrap's brewin'. Us Communists, white n' colored, gotta organize n' lead it. . . . The first Civil War didn't free them, but this one will." Burke's and Page's invocations of the Black Belt thesis have a somewhat perfunctory ring, since their narratives do not pursue or explore the logic of self-determination. Nonetheless, the references to a Negro republic indicate that some antiracist white writers thought that this aspect of the party line warranted inclusion in their texts.[33]

A few white writers devoted substantial space to exploring the rationale for the nationalist position. In *Free Born: An Unpublishable Novel*—a barely fictionalized re-presentation of the information and argument contained in his 1929 sociological work, *Black America*—the social scientist Scott Nearing creates a protagonist, Jim Rogers, whose life exemplifies in microcosm the experience of American blacks. Nearing frames the text with an assertion of the integrationist position, bluntly announcing to the reader in a "Prefatory Note," "The thesis of the book is important. No more vital issue confronts the American people than the widespread use

32. For more on Lumpkin, Page and Burke as female Southern writers, see Sylvia Jenkins Cook, *From Tobacco Road to Route 66: The Southern Poor White in Fiction* (Chapel Hill: U of North Carolina P, 1976), pp. 98–124.

33. Page, *Gathering Storm: A Story of the Black Belt* (New York: International, 1933), p. 327. Page is noteworthy for antiracism, shown in her portraiture of the black miner Ike in *Daughter of the Hills* and Ned, the black autoworker turned Soviet citizen in *Moscow Yankee*. See also her theoretical and sociological writings on the subject: "Interracial Relations Among Southern Workers," *Communist* 9 (February 1930): 154–65, and *Southern Cotton Mills and Labor*, intro. Bill Dunne (New York: Workers Library, 1929).

of black workers to break the back of the labor movement, and no aspect of the labor movement is more encouraging than the growing consciousness of labor solidarity, irrespective of race or color." This thesis is confirmed by events depicted in the final pages of the novel, where Jim encounters the Communist party, peruses the writings of Lenin, joins the NLC, and organizes black strikebreakers to join in solidarity with white strikers. Yet the substantial bulk of the novel is given over to a catalog of Jim's experiences with Southern and Northern racism that offers no inkling of the relation between these experiences and the framing discourse of multiracial revolutionism. From Jim's early victimization under the system of debt peonage and Jim Crow—the burning of his schoolhouse by envious whites, the rape/murder of his girlfriend—to his encounters with Northern racism—job discrimination, the violence of the 1919 Chicago race riot, the slow death through impoverishment of his sister—the novel confirms the logic of Jim's separatist sentiments. Located within Jim's center of consciousness, the narrative portrays white workers as benefiting from their relatively privileged positions and as accountable for the brutality of the 1919 riot. Throughout most of the novel, nationalism seems a "natural" response to the experience of racist oppression.

When it comes time for Jim to "realize" that all his experiences of white oppression are best understood within the framework of a class analysis, however, and that white workers are victimized by their own racism, Nearing does not show Jim undergoing a struggle with his nationalist consciousness. Instead, near the end of the novel Nearing introduces an anomalous moment of political retrospection: "Often the Negroes got a worse deal than the whites but Jim now remembered vividly a white man who had worked beside him in the machine shop; the man had bad lungs and kept spitting blood." Memory—not plot or argument, but memory—is supposed to supply the political bridge between nationalism and integrationism. Rather than negating the nationalist position through a process of active synthesis, however, the integrationist position mechanically supersedes it. In *Free Born*, experience confirms the logic of nationalism, while theory dictates the correctness of integrationism. Nearing felt committed to presenting both points of view, but clearly he did not deeply feel their logical connection.[34]

34. The conjunction between *Black America* and much of *Free Born* is quite remarkable. From the description of the lynching to the account of Jim's firing from the elevator

Although his chosen subject matter raises a different set of historical issues, a comparable ideological irresolution accompanies Guy Endore's attempt in *Babouk* to depict from a Marxist standpoint the political dynamics of the Haitian revolution. Endore, like Nearing, ends his tale with a ringing endorsement of a class-based, multiracial politics. The final chapter is prefaced by two epigraphs that carry obvious Marxist implications:

> "Divide and rule."
>
>> Policy of the Imperialists
>
> "Black and white, unite and fight!"
>
>> Modern Rallying Cry for World Justice.

Throughout the narrative Endore has stressed the economic basis of slavery, drawing upon his entire rhetorical arsenal to educate the reader about the history of colonialism and genocide and angrily addressing slaveholders who cannot "show yourselves worthy of civilization." Yet up to the novel's closing pages Endore offers no indication that white civilization as such should not be held responsible for the historical crimes against Africans. Indeed, the vast bulk of the novel—detailing the horrors of the midpassage, Babouk's having an ear sliced off in retaliation for an escape attempt, and other brutalities—stresses Babouk's entirely justifiable detestation of all whites. As in *Free Born*, the politics asserted in the movement toward closure contradict the politics that have previously been announced and embedded in the narrative.[35]

Gordon, in his review of *Babouk*, offered the somewhat anachronistic criticism that the novel did not illustrate multiracial unity between slaves and poor whites. But he correctly perceived that the novel failed to illumi-

---

job, the novel reiterates the sociological text's catalogue of racist abuse and injustices. The fact that Nearing was no longer a Party member when *Free Born* was published seems not to have affected his highly favorable estimate of Party line and activity around the "Negro question." Yet in *Black America* the issue of multiracial proletarian unity is also tacked on in the last chapter and does not synthesize with the rest of the book's argument.

35. Guy Endore, *Babouk* (New York: Vanguard, 1934), p. 285. Another white writer who focused a critique of racism around the portraiture of a black protagonist was John L. Spivak, whose *Georgia Nigger* (New York: Brewer, Warren and Putnam, 1932) treated the brutality of debt peonage and the chain gang. Spivak's narrative, while powerful, is not discussed here because it belongs more to the tradition of journalistic exposé than to that of proletarianism.

nate the logic of the integrationist position that in its final pages it formally espoused. Nearing, in *Free Born*, can in part be excused for his failure to anticipate Jim's "conversion" on the grounds that he has chosen to restrict himself without commentary to the limits of his protagonist's consciousness. It cannot be objected, however, that the injection of a class-based politics would be artificial in *Babouk*, since Endore's intrusive narrator indulges in frequent meditation on global historical and economic matters. It would have been possible, for example, for Endore to have raised the effects of the Triangle Trade upon enclosure and industrialization in England, where white workers were victimized by the same drive toward primitive accumulation of capital that resulted in the enslavement and genocide of Africans. Endore's ambivalent embrace of a class analysis of racism is further signaled by the narrative's closing query: "Oh, black man, when your turn comes, will you be so generous to us who do not deserve it?" Even though the narrative voice has elsewhere in the text sharply upbraided the slaveholding class as an antagonistic "you," the "us" in which he finally includes himself suggests a cross-class white consciousness that has little to do with revolutionary Marxist politics.[36]

Babouk and *Free Born* reveal the political and rhetorical difficulties experienced by white writers committed to the correctness of integrationist politics but drawn—whether through guilt or logic—to the nationalist position. White writers who assigned minor roles to their black characters had no difficulty asserting the priority of a class-based, integrationist politics. Those who attempted to foreground the experience of black characters, however, seem to have been sharply divided in their political allegiances. Their moves toward synthesis are problematic: nationalist and integrationist politics coexist in an uneasy tension.

36. Gordon, "Black and White, Unite and Fight!" passim; Endore, *Babouk*, p. 297. For more on Endore's treatment of the economics of slavery, see David Barry Gaspar and Michel-Rolph Trouillot, "Afterword: History, Fiction, and the Slave Experience," *Babouk* (New York: Monthly Review, 1991), pp. 183–99. Alan Wald points out that "Endore defended himself in a letter to Gordon remarking that it was hard to promote a Leninist political line 'in an historical novel antedating Lenin,' and, also, that Haiti was one of those countries where 'there are no whites to unite with,' as in India, China, and the Malay States." Wald rightly observes that Endore saw himself as "a conscious radical artist opposed to the do-gooder, uplift tradition of the liberal." In my view, however, Endore's handling of narratorial voice in *Babouk* suggests his incomplete reconciliation of class and nationalist perspectives. See Wald, "The Subaltern Speaks," *Monthly Review* 43 (April 1, 1992): 17–29, quoted 22, 24.

Nationalism and Integrationism in Attaway and Wright

Left-wing black writers generally produced more successful dialectical syntheses of the contradictory elements in the CP's analysis of the "Negro question." The principal black practitioners of the proletarian novel, William Attaway and Richard Wright, demonstrate that the Communist left's conjunction of nationalist and integrationist politics could be represented in single texts in a nonreductionist yet coherent manner.[37]

37. Since our focus here is specifically on proletarian novels, we cannot examine the full range of texts reflecting black writers' complex reactions to the discourse about race and class generated by the left movement of the 1930s. A partial list of such texts would include Margaret Walker's *For My People* (1942; rpt. New York, Arno, 1968), as well as her *Jubilee* (Boston; Houghton Mifflin, 1966), which was begun in the 1930s; Tolson's *Caviar and Cabbage* and *A Gallery of Harlem Portraits*, ed. Robert Farnsworth (Columbia, MO: U of Missouri P, 1979); Sterling Brown's series of poems *No Hiding Place*, which was, according to Henry Louis Gates, "rejected for publication in the thirties because of its political subjects" (*Figures in Black: Words, Signs, and the 'Racial' Self* [New York and Oxford: Oxford UP, 1987], p. 229); Frank Marshall Davis's *I Am the American Negro* (1937; rpt. Freeport, NY: Books for Libraries P, 1971); and, above all, the revolutionary short fiction and poetry of Langston Hughes, who served for years, as Rampersad notes, as a "brilliant and prolific . . . propagandist for the far left" ("Future Scholarly Projects on Langston Hughes," *Black American Literature Forum* 21 [Fall 1987]: 309). Indeed, a close examination of the entire oeuvre of a number of prominent black writers would suggest that the left possessed a strong attraction to a significant number—perhaps a majority—of the writers who were either actively productive or in apprenticeship during the Depression decade. Countee Cullen joined the party for about a year in 1932; Alain Locke spoke at Communist-affiliated conferences throughout the decade; Robert Hayden in his youth was known as the "people's poet" of Detroit (Fred M. Fetrow, *Robert Hayden* [Boston: Twayne, 1984], p. 7). Ralph Ellison, who was to attack the CPUSA in *Invisible Man*, published stories in the *New Masses* in the early 1940s. Moreover, Ellison criticized Attaway's *Blood on the Forge* for not demonstrating that the folk qualities being destroyed by urbanization were being "re[born] on a higher level"—that is, for not being adequately Marxist ("Transition," *Negro Quarterly* 1 [Spring 1942]: 90–91, quoted in Richard Yarborough, "Afterword," *Blood on the Forge* [1941; rpt. New York: Monthly Review, 1987], p. 308). Arna Bontemps's *Black Thunder* will be discussed below, chapter 10. I do not discuss Wright's *Lawd Today* and Hughes's *Not Without Laughter* here because, despite their proletarian subject matter, these novels do not assume a left-wing perspective. *Lawd Today*, while written during Wright's membership in the South Side Writers Group, was not published until 1963. *Not Without Laughter*, however, appeared in the period when *New Masses* critics were stressing proletarian authorship as the criterion for adjudging a text "proletarian"; it was occasionally referred to as a "proletarian" novel. Portions of *Not Without Laughter* were reprinted in the *New Masses* in 1930—

In *Blood on the Forge*, the relation between nationalist and class consciousness is the central issue at stake. Focusing upon the lives of the three Moss brothers, Big Mat, Chinatown, and Melody, the novel explores the demographic and political ramifications of the great migration of black workers to northern industrial cities around the time of World War I. All three brothers are forced to flee the South when Big Mat violently attacks the riding boss who insults Mat's wife Hattie. When they arrive in the urban environment of a Monongahela Valley steel town, the Moss brothers are equipped with folk qualities and talents that have sustained and enriched their former rural life. Mat, a deeply sensual man, displaces much of his inarticulate passion into the religious realm. Chinatown takes a simple delight in beautiful things, symbolized by the gold tooth he naively parades. Melody has a musical talent enabling him to contend with suffering and deprivation through the ironic consolation of the blues, such as the "Mr. Bossman" song that he sings in the novel's opening chapter. A few white workers whom the Mosses encounter in the Northern town make hesitant gestures of friendship, but both the union and the bosses foment racial antagonisms, and the black brothers are flung onto their own resources for survival. Attaway maintains a narrative point of view insistently located within the consciousness of either Matt or Melody and refrains almost completely from any narratorial commentary indicating his protagonists' limitations. The brothers' nationalism is rendered warranted and plausible.

Yet Attaway points out the fragility of a folk-based nationalism that cannot respond to the social and economic forces operative in the hostile urban industrial environment. Chinatown is blinded in a mill explosion. Melody, unable to draw sustenance from the blues in his new setting, allows his guitar-picking hand to be crushed. Mat, alienated from his religious beliefs as well as his sexuality, becomes a thug for the strike-breaking bosses. The novel's climactic moment comes when Mat, having just assaulted a Ukrainian-born striker is clubbed to death by another white striker and

---

i.e., "Sister Johnson's Story," NM 6 (June 1930): 6–8, and "Party for White Folks," NM 6 (July 1930): 6. In July 1930 Hughes was featured as the *New Masses* author of the month; in August 1930 the *New Masses*'s back cover carried an advertisement for *Not Without Laughter* describing it as the "First Novel of Negro Working-Class Life." Hughes's poetry was where he put his revolutionary energies; his fiction was not explicitly left-wing.

faintly realizes, as his consciousness fades, that he has been duped: "A long time ago in the red hills he had done this thing and run away. Had that riding boss been as he was now? Big Mat went farther away and no longer could distinguish himself from these other figures. They were all one and all the same. In that confusion he sensed something true. Maybe somewhere in these mills a new Mr. Johnston was creating riding bosses, making a difference where none existed."[38]

Most critics of *Blood on the Forge* have commented adversely on the passage describing Mat's glimmering "conversion" to class consciousness. They claim that the passage produces a disruptive intrusion of Marxist politics into the narrative; it is at once privileged and anomalous, signaling a "real" politics that Attaway has been withholding thus far. But this climactic episode, while explicitly articulating the possibility for moving, as Wright urged, "beyond nationalism," does not thereby supplant, cancel out, or redefine all that has come before. Whereas in *Free Born* the reader is asked simply to forget the nationalist attitudes that had characterized Jim's early years, in *Blood on the Forge* Mat's consciousness is presented as a site of contradiction. "Is" is not simply converted by an act of authorial will into "ought." Mat's nationalist consciousness remains as a fact to be contended with—at once an inadequate and a historically inevitable response of the black worker to his experience of oppression. Yet Attaway clearly suggests that a deeper understanding of the relation of racial to class oppression might have saved Mat from his tragic and senseless death. The reader is not left in the position of political cliff-hanging that characterizes the end of *Babouk*. Attaway may not assert that "ought" can be conflated with "is," but his conception of the "ought" facing the black working class is manifest.[39]

38. Attaway, *Blood on the Forge*, p. 288.

39. Young states that the passage "rings a false note . . . submerg[ing] race conflict within the context of class conflict (Young, 229). Bone argues that the passage "damages the aesthetic structure of the novel beyond repair" by "reducing [the] protagonist from a tragic hero to a mere mouthpiece of [Attaway's] own views" (Bone, 139). Bernard Bell, who is on the whole more sympathetic to Attaway's politics than Young or Bone, still objects that in Big Mat's "vision just before his death, the truth belatedly and implausibly comes to him" (*The Afro-American Novel and Its Tradition* [Amherst: U of Massachusetts P, 1987], p. 170). Bell himself makes the somewhat implausible statement that Attaway was "not a Marxist," even though "his analysis in *Blood on the Forge* of

While Attaway explored various implications of the Communist position on race and class in considerable depth, his project was constrained by
the traditional form in which he chose to tell his tale in *Blood on the Forge*.
Having limited his narration to the Moss brothers' point of view, Attaway
encountered problems finding the rhetorical means to make class analysis
as compelling as nationalist analysis. He was, as we shall see in chapter 10,
pressing up against the limits of realism. By contrast, in his Depression-era
fiction Richard Wright developed dialectical narrative strategies that enabled him to explore the full implications of the contradictory admixture
of integrationist and nationalist tendencies in the Communist approach to
the "Negro question."

First published as a book in 1938 (reissued with the inclusion of "The
Ethics of Living Jim Crow" and "Bright and Morning Star" in 1940), the
stories in *Uncle Tom's Children* were written between 1934 and the end
of the decade, thus spanning a period encompassing the end of the Third
Period and the Popular Front. As a number of critics have noted—and as
Wright himself intended—the careful progression set up among the stories
in the volume warrants discussion of the text as a unified work of fiction,
if not precisely a "novel." For the tales represent a range of protagonists
focused upon different concerns and, especially in the first three stories,
manifesting different degrees of false consciousness. Big Boy is preoccupied with individual survival; Brother Mann with family; Silas with self,
property, and race. In the final two stories, multiracial class unity and revolutionary commitment are put on the political agenda. In "Fire and Cloud,"
Reverend Taylor achieves an embryonic class consciousness and becomes
willing to ally with Communists. In "Bright and Morning Star," both Aunt
Sue and her sons are committed to the multiracial class-based unity embodied in the Communist party. The alignment of the tales in this evolving pattern allows full expression to each character's differential level of
consciousness while pointing to the larger political scheme of which all

---

the dynamics of capitalism as it alienates men from the land and themselves is the best
Marxist interpretation of society in the tradition of the Afro-American novel" (p. 171).
Cynthia Hamilton, in a reading of the novel rare for its sympathy with Attaway's politics,
reaches quite a different judgment of the description of Big Mat's awakening, noting that
it is "one of the most moving passages in the book" ("Work and Culture: The Evolution of
Consciousness in Urban Industrial Society in the Fiction of William Attaway and Peter
Abraham," *Black American Literature Forum* 21 [Spring–Summer 1987]: 160).

the characters' efforts at rebellion (first faint, then increasingly coherent and successful) are a part. *Uncle Tom's Children*, particularly in the later edition containing "Bright and Morning Star," is the most explicitly Marxist in its analysis—and pro-Communist in its stance—of Wright's longer fictional works.[40]

The Marxism of *Uncle Tom's Children* is not, however, a Marxism that unproblematically privileges class over race. The developing progression of the stories indicates an ultimate endorsement of integrationism. In the first two stories, "Big Boy Leaves Home" and "Down by the Riverside," the protagonists are confronted with situations in which whites react against blacks in a violently racist manner. Gradations of social class among these whites are irrelevant to the beleaguered protagonists, whose nationalist consciousness appears an appropriate response to the virulent racism they confront. In "Long Black Song," the pivotal tale of the group, a shift occurs. Silas, the central male figure, learning of the rape/seduction of his wife by a white traveling salesman, goes to his death defying a system that has deprived him—and, as he sees it, all black men—of selfhood. Heroic for his militancy, he nonetheless is limited in his capacity to fight back by his adherence to an essentially petty-bourgeois and sexist ethos; as he exclaims in despair, "The white folks ain never gimme a chance! They ain never give no black man a chance! There ain nothin in yo whole life yuh kin keep from em! They take yo lan! They take yo freedom! They take yo women! N then they take yo life!" By contrast, Sarah, his wife, intuits that the "river of blood," the "killing of white men by black men and killing of black men by white men" must end, that blacks and whites are "linked, like the spokes in a spinning wheel," although "she could not say how."[41]

In the final two stories this "how" is clearly associated with a revolutionary multiracialism that proposes class analysis as the negation of nationalism. In "Fire and Cloud," Reverend Taylor learns the fallacy of individualistic passivity and the necessity for multiracial collective action. While Taylor does not achieve anything resembling Marxist consciousness, his willingness to align himself with the Communist organizers who

---

40. Wright noted that he had planned *Uncle Tom's Children* from the outset as a unified collection based on a developmental theme (*Writers' Club Bulletin*, Columbia U, 1 [1938]: 15–16). See also Fabré, pp. 157–64.

41. Wright, *Uncle Tom's Children*, (1940; rpt. New York: Perennial, 1965), p. 125.

have been urging the protest march suggests that he has become a new kind of Moses for his people, as is indicated by the echoes of Exodus in the story's title. Like the Alabama Communists described by Kelley, Taylor is on the way to transforming his insight that "God's with the people" into the "Lenin spirit." In "Bright and Morning Star," which also records events based upon the experiences of the CP in the South, the party has apparently built a movement among sharecroppers, white and black, that threatens the local power structure. Johnny, Aunt Sue's son, has attained a class consciousness unavailable to Big Boy: "Ah cant see white n Ah cant see black," he explains to his mother. "Ah sees rich men n Ah sees po men." Aunt Sue, struggling against the nationalist consciousness instilled by a long life's experience of Jim Crow violence, achieves a Communist apotheosis in the course of the story. Playing to the white sheriff's stereotyped notion that elderly black women are passive, she conceals a pistol beneath the sheet she carries and shoots Booker, thus sacrificing her own life and that of her son to guarantee the survival of the party. Like the Alabama Communists who opened their party meetings with prayers, Aunt Sue has converted her inherited faith in the "bright and morning star" of Christianity to "one more terrible vision to give her the strength to live and act."[42]

Yet Wright's stirring representation of the necessity for blacks' acquiring class consciousness contains suggestions that nationalism is by no means relinquished when blacks enter into solidarity with their white class brothers and sisters. In "Fire and Cloud," Taylor's principal concern remains his black congregation: the white poor with whom they will ally are a vague presence, a faceless stream to be joined with for pragmatic purposes only. Even in "Bright and Morning Star," Johnny's enthusiastic class consciousness apparently blinds him to the harsh realities that Aunt Sue acknowledges. The police agent within the sharecroppers' union is a white man (appropriately named Booker); Sue's skepticism about the

---

42. Wright, Uncle Tom's Children, pp. 192, 206. The multiracial march in "Fire and Cloud" resembles the Georgia march led by Angelo Herndon (Herndon, pp. 187–92). For a discussion of the Alabama CP's use of "trickster" tactics, see Kelley, Hammer and Hoe, p. 102. Possibly Wright's decision to have Aunt Sue hide her pistol in a winding sheet is derived from the practice of Birmingham female CPers of hiding leaflets and stencils in baskets of laundry.

advisability of trusting whites, however leavened by her affection for the young white woman Reva, remains to a degree justified by the tale's tragic turn of events. *Uncle Tom's Children* thus leaves the reader with the sense that Wright is arguing a contradictory political position. The text is unambiguous in its affirmation of the ultimate necessity for a multiracial, class-based politics. Yet it also posits the legitimacy of nationalism—which is portrayed not simply as a barrier to be superseded on the path to integrationist consciousness, but as a reality that cannot be readily dispelled and that must form part of the Communist movement's discourse and program.

The politics conveyed in *Native Son* are more complex still, since they reflect not only the duality characterizing the Depression-era CP's line on black liberation but also Wright's own growing skepticism toward the party as a viable agent for revolutionary change. Wright's cynical reduction of the party to Jan, Max, and the wealthy fellow-traveler Mary Dalton gives a distorted representation of the composition of the Chicago CP, which by the late 1930s was an integrated organization rooted in the working class. (Wright himself admitted as much in his otherwise hostile representation of the party in *American Hunger*.) Yet it is a mistake to conclude that the politics of *Native Son* diverge substantially from those of the CP or that the novel presages Wright's split with the party, which occurred a full four years after the novel's publication.[43]

Had Wright wished simply to assert the irrelevance of the party's analysis and practice to the experience of a Bigger Thomas, he could have done so with considerable ease. After all, his decision to focalize the narrative through his protagonist's consciousness provided him with an opportunity for exploring—and validating—Bigger's intense nationalism. But Wright did not restrict himself to Bigger's point of view. Instead, he overlaid upon the text two important statements about Bigger's experience, statements which insist that the reader contextualize Bigger's life and thoughts in

43. Wright, "I Tried to be a Communist," in Richard Crossman, ed., *The God that Failed: André Gide, Richard Wright, Ignazio Silore, Arthur Koestler, and Louis Fischer Describe their Journeys into Communism and their Disillusioned Return* (1950; rpt. New York: Bantam, 1965), pp. 103–46; Fabré, pp. 169–87. Fabré takes issue with the accuracy of a number of Wright's statements in "I Tried To Be a Communist," noting that Wright's descriptions of "certain confrontations" with party members are "placed in a biased context and out of chronological order" (p. 137).

a broader explanatory framework. The first of these, Max's speech to the court, has—like the description of Mat's embryonic political awareness in *Blood on the Forge*—prompted much adverse commentary. James Baldwin has called it "one of the most desperate performances in American fiction"; other critics have faulted it for injecting a clumsy didacticism redundant with propositions embedded elsewhere in the narrative. Actually, the charge of tautology is inaccurate, for the speech provides both information and analysis not inferrable from the story of Bigger's crime and punishment. The relation between the State's Attorney's fervid prosecution of Bigger and the need of the city and state governments to distract attention from their failure to provide public relief; the theory that the twelve million blacks in the United States "constitute a separate nation, stunted, stripped, and held captive *within* this nation"—these and other conclusions reached by Max do not arise inevitably from the rest of the text's represented events. Instead, they point to the political analysis necessary for fully comprehending the dimensions of Bigger's fate. Furthermore, Max's narration of the world-historical drama of which Bigger's tale is a tiny part (a narration strikingly similar to that which would appear in Wright's *Twelve Million Black Voices* a year later) places the drama of Bigger's alienation within the context of slavery and urban black migration, "a dislocation so vast as to stagger the imagination." Accordingly, Bigger's brief and tragic career assumes typifying status; he becomes, as Max puts it, "a tiny social symbol in relation to our whole sick social organism." "Multiply Bigger Thomas twelve million times," Max declares, "allowing for environmental and temperamental variations, and for those Negroes who are completely under the influence of the church, and you have the psychology of the Negro people." Through this speech, Wright does not simply reinforce a meaning already inherent in Bigger's tale, but takes the opportunity to account for Bigger's fate in terms fundamentally defined by the CP's position around self-determination. Bigger is a member of a nation within a nation; his existential nationalism is a reflection of this sociological fact.[44]

44. Wright, *Native Son* (1940; rpt. New York: Perennial, 1966), p. 357. The quotations below are from pp. 354 and 364. James Baldwin, "Notes of a Native Son," in Houston A. Baker, ed., *Twentieth-Century Interpretations of Native Son: A Collection of Critical Essays* (Englewood Cliffs, NJ: Prentice-Hall, 1972), p. 65. For more negative comments on Max's speech, see Russell Carl Brignano, *Richard Wright: An Introduction to the Man*

Interestingly, however, even the rhetorical occasion offered by Max's speech apparently did not provide Wright with sufficient space for political argument. He therefore appended to the second—and every subsequent—edition of *Native Son* the essay "How Bigger Was Born," in which he detailed the process by which Bigger Thomas came to attain reality in his imagination. Much of this essay recapitulates the political analysis implied through the novel's plot and explicitly rendered in the courtroom address. But a good deal of the essay is given over to analyzing an entirely new feature of Bigger's tale—namely, its synecdochic function in relation to the lives of alienated and disaffected youth of *any* nation or race. Where Max's speech makes only passing reference to the likeness between Bigger and the "millions of others more or less like him, black or white," Wright's introductory essay dwells upon the ways in which "Bigger Thomas was not black all the time; he was white, too, and there were literally millions of him." Wright contemplates the similarities between Bigger's angry alienation and that of German youth attracted to fascism. Moreover, he parallels Bigger's sense of exclusion from the institutions of his society with Lenin's declaration to Gorki that Big Ben and the Houses of Parliament were "*their* Big Ben, *their* Houses of Parliament." Bigger's sense of dislocation, Wright concludes, "transcended national and racial boundaries." Where Max's speech stressed Bigger's typification of the oppressed nation of which he was a part, Wright's authorial commentary emphasizes Bigger's symbolic status as an exemplar of *class*-based disaffection—possessed of "*snarled* and *confused* nationalist feelings" but nonetheless a product of a quintessentially capitalist social process.[45]

"How Bigger Was Born" enabled Wright to explore still another feature of the political landscape of which Bigger Thomas's tale was a part. In one sense the class analysis offered in the essay supersedes the nationalist analysis offered in the narrative, for it encloses Bigger's blind antipathy to whites, as well as the theory of black oppression offered by Max, within

---

and His Work (Pittsburgh: U of Pittsburgh P, 1970), p. 82, and Dan McCall, *The Example of Richard Wright* (New York: Harcourt, Brace, and World, 1969), p. 93. For fuller explication of the formal issues raised by Max's speech, see my own "The Politics of Poetics: Ideology and Narrative Form in Dreiser's *An American Tragedy* and Wright's *Native Son*" (*Narrative Poetics: Innovations, Limits, Challenges*, ed. James Phelan, Papers in Comparative Studies, vol. 5 [Columbus: Ohio State UP, 1988], pp. 55–67).

45. Wright, *Native Son*, pp. 368, xiv, xvii, xxiv.

a broader explanatory context. Yet the essay does not cancel out Bigger's responses or Max's analysis, for in it Wright confesses to his desire to examine Bigger's incoherent nationalist feelings from the standpoint of "*conscious* and *informed* [nationalist feelings] of my own" (p. xxiv). All three perspectives upon Bigger's experience coexist in the novel, vying for the reader's consideration and judgment.

➤   ➤   ➤   ➤   ➤

In *Uncle Tom's Children* and *Native Son*, Wright discovered multileveled discursive forms that enabled him to articulate the complexity of the politics guiding his analysis of American racism. These forms invite—indeed, require—the codification of meaning; they do not result in political open-endedness. But they demonstrate that, in Wright's case at least, the writer's desire to give fictional expression to the left's line on black liberation did not entail reduction and simplification. Indeed, Wright's achievement suggests just the opposite: the pressures of politics—in this case, the felt requirement to do justice to both the class-based and nationalist aspects of the party's antiracist position—impelled the writer to devise rhetorical strategies for exposing the reader to quite divergent and often competing lines of argument. Despite the undoubted power of his portrayal of the Moss brothers' tragedy, Attaway was struggling against the ideological closure of traditional novelistic realism. By contrast, Wright, without relinquishing any of the commonly accepted markers of realism—his radical fiction from the 1930s is not in any obvious sense "experimental"—managed to show that realism need not be repressive or limiting. If writers could devise means for introducing political perspective "from outside," realism could in fact furnish highly dialectical means for representing reality. We will bear Wright's example in mind when we address the politics of realism in the different genres of proletarian fiction.

CHAPTER 6

>

Women and the Left in the 1930s

Given the current interest in gender as a constitutive category of literary production and critical reception, it is important to delineate the relation of women to 1930s literary radicalism. As we noted in chapter 1, there is emerging a significant body of scholarship on leftist women novelists of the Depression era. With the recent reissuing of several important women's proletarian novels, we may anticipate that the names of Josephine Herbst, Agnes Smedley, Mary Heaton Vorse, Fielding Burke (Olive Dilford Targan), Myra Page, Leane Zugsmith, Grace Lumpkin, Meridel Le Sueur, Josephine Johnson, Ruth McKenney, Clara Weatherwax, and Tillie Olsen, now known to a relatively limited coterie of enthusiasts, will gain currency among Americanists and women's studies scholars. Poststructuralism's concern with the suppressed or marginalized "other" and feminism's increasingly self-critical awareness of the necessity for addressing considerations of class (and race) have been largely responsible for the revival of interest in the literature produced by Depression-era women radicals.[1]

1. It may appear that, after mentioning race, I am making it invisible in this chapter by discussing no black women writers. Black women writers did contribute to the discourse of literary proletarianism, but not in the genre of the novel. Margaret Walker's *Jubilee* (1966), begun in the mid-1930s when Walker was a member of the South Side Writers Group in Chicago, is the only full-length work of prose fiction by a black woman writer in any way associated with the proletarian movement. I do not discuss *Jubilee* here because it neither treats the proletariat nor treats its historical theme from an explicitly Marxist perspective—as Endore does in *Babouk*, for example, or Bontemps does in *Black Thunder*. For more on Walker's political outlook when writing *Jubilee*, see Walker, "How I Wrote *Jubilee*" (Chicago: Third World Press, 1972), and Walker, *Richard Wright: Daemonic Genius: A Portrait of the Man/ A Critical Look at His Work* (New York: Warner, 1978), pp. 74–81. For more on Walker in the context of literary proletarianism, see Hazel Carby, "Ideologies of Black Folk: The Historical Novel of Slavery," in *Slavery and the Literary Imagination: Selected Papers from the English Institute, 1987*, n.s., no. 13, ed. Deborah E. McDowell and Arnold Rampersad (Baltimore and London: Johns Hopkins

Yet a close scrutiny of the relation of women to 1930s cultural radical-ism requires us to reconsider various political axioms often unquestioned in poststructuralist and feminist criticism. For it is frequently postulated—though more often assumed than argued—that the model of "intersection" best studies the interrelations of race, gender, and class, which, hetero-geneous and autonomous, are describable by a paradigm stressing their essentially conjunctural relation to one another. The Marxism that has his-torically sought to account for the primacy and determinacy of class is often viewed with suspicion unless it hastily qualifies itself with a prefa-tory "post" or "neo" attesting to its nonhegemonic designs. Class is per-mitted a role in the analytical paradigm, but only if it relinquishes any pretension to providing scientific or totalizing explanations for oppression or models for emancipation. In the spirit of the new textual *perestroika*, Marxism must rewrite, revise, rethink itself so that it acknowledges the ir-reducible alterity of other "subject positions," particularly those of gender and race.

The first section of this chapter will be devoted to assessing the limita-tions and strengths of the American Communist party's line and practice with regards to what was termed the "woman question." Much of the con-temporary feminist distrust of Marxism is based in the perception that the left—whether the old left of the pre-1960s era or the New Left with which present-day feminists are more likely to be directly familiar—has

---

UP, 1989), pp. 125–43. For samples of Depression-era poetry, reportage, and short fiction by black women, see the pieces by Walker, Elizabeth Thomas, Mollie V. Lewis, Edith Manuel Durham, Kathleen Tankersley Young, Ramona Lowe, and Marita Bonner in *Writ-ing Red: An Anthology of American Women Writers 1930–1940*, ed. Paula Rabinowitz and Charlotte Nekola (New York: Feminist Press, 1987). For more on the position of black women in the 1930s, see Jacqueline Jones, *Labor of Love, Labor of Sorrow: Black Women, Work, and the Family from Slavery to the Present* (New York: Random House, Vintage Books, 1986), pp. 196–231. For the relation of black women to the left in Harlem and in Alabama, see Mark Naison, *Communists in Harlem during the Depression* (New York: Grove, 1983), and Robin D. G. Kelley, *Hammer and Hoe: The Alabama Communist Party, 1931–35* (Chapel Hill, NC: U of North Carolina P, 1990). James Ford, the party's vice-presidential candidate in 1932 and 1936, claimed in 1938 that Negro women were "clamouring to join the Communist Party. They are beating at our doors! I think this is a fine thing." In his discussion of important black intellectuals and artists of the 1930s, however, Ford slipped when he referred to one "Zora Neal Thurston" (James Ford, *The Negro and the Democratic Front* [New York: International, 1938], pp. 94–95, 206).

been signally inadequate in formulating a theory and a practice to address women's oppression. The 1930s CP, we shall see, did not, in comparison with other issues, place adequate stress upon the "woman question" and to a degree uncritically reproduced the sexism of the dominant culture. Yet the Communist-led movement of the 1930s deserves more credit than it often receives for its efforts to combat male chauvinism. Despite its shortcomings, the left made the question of male-female equality a live issue; it involved women in the class struggle and addressed a number of issues of urgent concern to working-class women. It is thus simplistic to dismiss weaknesses in the theory and practice of the 1930s left as manifestations of a patriarchal authoritarianism intrinsic to Marxism. Rather than invoking a theoretical incommensurability—or even antipathy—between modes of analysis based in gender and in class, it makes more sense to look to the 1930s left's historical inadequacies in grasping the full implications of revolutionary Communist politics for the entire domain of social relations. What is needed is not less class analysis, but more and sharper class analysis.

The second section of this chapter will examine the representation of gender in proletarian fiction. My primary interest here is in questions of subject matter and theme. While in Part II of this volume I shall examine politics and genre from the standpoint of narrative theory, here I shall focus on ideas and attitudes signaled on the level of manifest political content. I shall emphasize the contribution of female writers to the discourse about gender in the proletarian novel but shall also remark upon the treatment of gender in a number of texts authored by men.

Before I begin, two provisos are in order. The first has to do with issues of tone and judgment. It is difficult not to use terms such as "weaknesses," "shortcomings," "inadequacies," and "sexism" in discussing the 1930s left and the "woman question." Yet the frustration motivating the deployment of such terms is in some ways anachronistic, a product of a 1990s perspective inaccessible to even the most revolutionary Depression-era activists and writers. We inevitably encounter, and react to, the discourse of the 1930s from within our own frames of reference. But our own (presumably) more advanced awareness of the politics of gender is itself a historical phenomenon, produced in part by the very movement we now turn to criticize. We are not obliged to be moral relativists. But if we recognize the actual limits within which the Depression-era radicals were constructing their discourse and practice, we are required in some degree to be historical relativists.

At the same time, historical relativism, if taken too far, can divest any critique of its political force. The notion that nothing more could be expected of the 1930s left—that the conception of the "woman question" inherited from the old socialist movement was too flawed, that the sexism of the mainstream society was too overwhelming, that the other issues confronting the left were too urgent—has the effect of exculpating the 1930s radicals from any errors of politics or will. The principal limits on any process are the product not of an iron necessity imposed from without but of a set of conditions generated by contradictions among and between different elements constituting the process itself. As we study the 1930s left's construction of gender issues, we should be alert to different political tendencies within that left and try to analyze why some tendencies rather than others ended up shaping its theory and practice.

The second proviso has to do with issues of critical emphasis and method. Because of the mixed nature of the 1930s left's achievement with regard to the "woman question," it is tempting to adopt the strategy of the balance sheet: pros over here, cons over there. Deborah Rosenfelt's comments articulate the dualism found in most informed discussions of the subject: "The Left was a profoundly masculinist world in many of its human relationships, in the orientation of its literature, and even in the language used to articulate its cultural criticism; simultaneously, the Left gave serious attention to women's issues, valued women's contributions to public as well as private life, and generated an important body of theory on the Woman Question." Rosenfelt's use of the term "simultaneously" suggests the dichotomous nature of the analytical problem we confront. In evaluating the discourse and activity of the 1930s left, it is simply not possible to separate out advanced and retrograde zones of theory and practice: the same zones "simultaneously" partake of both qualities. As we proceed, then, we inevitably find ourselves keeping score, as though the discovery of more pros than cons, or vice versa, might settle the issue. But the answer to the problem of evaluation is not quantitative. The conceptual challenge is to understand the pros and cons in a way that permits a coherent qualitative judgment to emerge.[2]

2. Deborah Rosenfelt, "From the Thirties: Tillie Olsen and the Radical Tradition," *Feminist Studies* 7 (Fall 1981): 381. See also Alice Kessler-Harris and Paul Lauter, "Intro-

The CP and the "Woman Question"

Some recent scholars of women and the 1930s left argue that masculinism manifested itself not only in matters of political line and practice but also in broader cultural assumptions. Alice Kessler-Harris and Paul Lauter have remarked that "[t]hough leftist ideology in the 1930s recognized the 'special oppression' of women and formally espoused sexual equality, in practice, the Left tended to subordinate problems of gender to the overwhelming tasks of organizing the working class and fighting fascism." Moreover, they note, "The cultural apparatus of the Left in the thirties was, if anything, more firmly masculinist than its political institutions" (p. ix). Paula Rabinowitz agrees with this assessment, remarking that "[t]he equation of literary and political vitality with masculinity created a series of obstacles to any woman who wanted to write revolutionary literature." Constance Coiner, while conceding that "the Party's work among women in the 1930s should be carefully evaluated as part of the struggle for women's liberation in the United States," argues that "fundamental problems within the 1930s Communist party and Marxism itself" required writers like Le Sueur and Olsen to "subvert" the "official" doctrines of the party "orthodoxy."[3]

There is no doubt that the Communist-led movement left a good deal to be desired in its work among women, as well as in its conceptualization of the significance of gender in revolutionary change. A 1928 Comintern resolution stipulated that political organizing among women workers was a priority, but on-the-job work among women was in fact sporadic. William Z. Foster's *Toward Soviet America*—a primer of the party's Third-Period program—rhapsodized over socialism's benefits for women but said virtually nothing about their contribution to the process of making revolution.

---

duction," Fielding Burke, *Call Home the Heart* (Old Westbury, NY: Feminist, 1983), pp. vii–xvi; Robert Schaffer, "Women and the Communist Party, U. S. A., 1930–1940," *Socialist Review* 45 (May–June 1979): 73–118; and Rosalyn Fraad Baxandall, *Words on Fire: The Life and Writing of Elizabeth Gurley Flynn* (New Brunswick and London: Rutgers UP, 1987), pp. 50–52.

3. Kessler-Harris and Lauter, p. xi; Rabinowitz, "Women and U. S. Literary Radicalism," in *Writing Red*, p. 4; Constance Coiner, "Literature of Resistance: The Intersection of Feminism and the Communist Left in Meridel Le Sueur and Tillie Olsen," in *Left Politics and the Literary Profession*, ed. Lennard J. Davis and Bella Mirabella (New York: Columbia UP, 1990): pp. 162–85, quoted pp. 164, 175, 165.

Throughout the Third Period, in fact, party activists routinely complained about the low priority assigned to work among women. One "Comrade Lusovsky," writing in the *Communist* in 1930, remarked that organizing women was still seen almost exclusively as a task for women, not men, to undertake. Trade Union Unity League (TUUL) organizer Anna Cornblath chastised party factions for not drawing more women into their activities. Anna Damon, one of the party's more prominent woman leaders, called upon the Central Committee to give fuller support to Women's Department struggles among factory workers, the unemployed, and black women. Communist organizers among miners noted that the importance of women in the mining fields was consistently underestimated, with the result that the entire party campaign was being seriously held back. An organizer from Texas complained that Southern male party members were biased against women and consistently made the fight against racism a priority over the fight against sexism—even though in the South lynch terror was fomented and justified by the conflation of racist and sexist myths. Even female party organizers were at times accused of exhibiting insensitivity to the particular needs of women in strike situations. In short, there was a significant gulf between theory and practice in the Third-Period CP's approach to women workers. Women were proletarians too, but generally not as important as their brothers, husbands, and fathers.[4]

In the era of the Popular Front, female participation in the CP rose to about 40 percent (from a mere 16 percent in 1933). This change occurred in large part because the party increasingly addressed the concerns

4. William Z. Foster, *Toward Soviet America* (New York: Howard McCann, 1932), pp. 306–9; Comrade Lusovsky, "Plenum of Women Workers' Committee of the RILU," *Communist* 9 (March 1930): 224–30; Anna Cornblath, "International Women's Day," *Labor Unity* 7 (March 1932): 17; Anna Damon, "Tasks of International Women's Day," *Party Organizer* (hereinafter PO) 7 (February 1934): 29–30; Anonymous, "Work Among Women in the Mining Fields," *PO* 7 (April 1934): 23–25; Marie Harrison Pierce, "Some Problems in Our Women's Work," *PO* 9 (October 1936): 10; Anonymous, "Work Among Women: Attitudes Which Hinder the Work," *PO* 4 (September–October 1931): 30. Especially in the early 1930s, the yearly arrival of International Women's Day seems to have prompted self-criticism of the party's inadequacies in organizing women. For a balanced assessment of the CP's strengths and weaknesses in reaching women workers, see Schaffer. For a bibliography of women and the U.S. left, see Jayne Loader, "Women in the Left, 1906–1941: A Bibliography of Primary Sources," *University of Michigan Papers in Women's Studies* 2 (September 1975): 9–82.

of working-class housewives, and not just women workers. But it did so through formations—women's trade union auxiliaries, shoppers' leagues, organizations against war and fascism—stressing women's roles as nurturers and helpmates and reproducing mainstream notions of the domestic sphere. Women who joined trade-union auxiliaries were urged not just to support their husbands on the job but to raise class-conscious children. Shoppers Leagues stressed that women should exercise their power as consumers, calling boycotts to support male workers' demands in shops. One contributor to *Woman Today* (the party's Popular Front-era magazine for women) declared that "woman is by nature and civilization for peace. . . . Therefore the two, fascism and women, must be enemies." For the Popular Front CP, sex roles in the conventional nuclear family furnished a ground on which to base working-class political activism, rather than a target for political critique. Wives were even encouraged not to nag their husbands and to keep disputes with mothers-in-law "strictly between the ladies." In fact, in the late 1930s Communism was held up as a means of preserving the traditional family, rather than of challenging or destroying it. As Earl Browder proclaimed in *The People's Front* (1938), "Abolish poverty, and the problem of divorce will disappear."[5]

Personal relations between and among men and women in the left movement reflected an ambivalent commitment to sexual egalitarianism. Myra Page, in *Daughter of the Hills*, and Fielding Burke, in *Call Home the Heart* and *A Stone Came Rolling*, presented positive portraits of men and women who are both lovers and comrades. Tillie Olsen recalls that party women could bring their husbands up on charges of male chauvinism; one male Communist was removed from leadership for refusing to help with child care. But many novels and reminiscences by women and men who were

5. Erma Lee, "Trade Unions," *Woman Today* (hereinafter WT) (March 1936): 18; Sonya Sanders, "Story of a Woman's Day Unit," PO 11 (March 1938): 39–40; A. Perry, "Building Women's Trade Union Auxiliaries," PO 10 (January 1937): 10–12; Thelma Nurenberg, "Shopping for Justice," WT (March 1936): 9, 14; Sonia Branting, "Breeding for Fascism," WT (March 1936): 6; Jean Lyon, "There's More Than One Way to Nag," WT (April 1937): 19; Lyon, "Have You a Mother-in-Law!?" WT (March 1937): 13; Earl Browder, *The People's Front* (New York: International, 1938), p. 201. The CP was attacked by the right, of course, for advocating "free love" and the "community of women." See Elizabeth Dilling, *The Red Network: A Who's Who and Handbook for Patriots* (Chicago: published by the author, 1939), pp. 27–28.

political activists in the 1930s show another side of the coin. Peggy Dennis, wife of Eugene Dennis (general secretary of the CPUSA in the 1950s), recounts the strong pressure she felt to subordinate her activism to her role as a young wife and parent. Josephine Herbst, in her largely autobiographical *Rope of Gold*, depicts male party organizers naturally assuming that their responsibility is to involve and recruit other males, bypassing women who in fact might emerge as better comrades. Lester Cole, in his reflections upon Hollywood leftism, recalls that "although in the Party we were supposed to have more enlightened views regarding women than 'the bourgeoisie'—and perhaps we did—in practice . . . there was little difference between our male-female relationships and the sharing of duties that existed among those we considered less enlightened." In her interviews with former CP activists in *The Romance of American Communism*, Vivian Gornick records numerous instances of female comrades' resentment of the gulf between theory and practice in their husbands' espoused egalitarianism.[6]

The left press, reproducing the unenlightened personal practice of large numbers of 1930s leftists, often presupposed sexist assumptions in its readership. Particularly in the late 1920s and early 1930s, the *New Masses* routinely published cartoons of big-bosomed leisure class women; while purporting to lampoon these women's wealth and decadence, these drawings were often at least equally as satirical of their anatomy. Petros Pikros, describing one "Comrade Juanita" who was killed by fascist soldiers, concluded in a 1928 *New Masses* piece that, in her revolutionary self-sacrifice,

6. Olsen quoted in Rosenfelt, "From the Thirties," 399; Peggy Dennis, *The Autobiography of an American Communist: A Personal View of a Political Life 1925–1975* (Westport and Berkeley: Lawrence Hill, 1977); Lester Cole, *Hollywood Red: The Autobiography of Lester Cole* (Palo Alto: Ramparts, 1981), p. 173; Vivian Gornick, *The Romance of American Communism* (New York: Basic Books, 1977). See also Dorothy Healey and Maurice Isserman, *Dorothy Healey Remembers: A Life in the American Communist Party* (New York: Oxford UP, 1990), and Howard Fast, *The Naked God: The Writer and the Communist Party* (New York: Praeger, 1957). Fast, commenting on a somewhat later period (the 1940s and 1950s), notes of the typical party leader, "He makes it plain that however much he may be a stern apostle of the future in all other matters, when it comes to women, he is just a plain, solid, down-to-earth, old-fashioned citizen" (p. 94). In reading Fast's account, one should allow for its recantatory posture: Fast, like other ex-radical memoirists of the 1950s, was backpedaling as furiously as possible from his earlier commitments. His later memoir, *Being Red* (Boston: Houghton Mifflin, 1990), is considerably less jaundiced.

"though very much a woman, Juanita died like a brave man, just as all her deeds had been those of a brave, good man." Edward Newhouse, relating his weeks on the bum in the South of 1930, gratuitously included a narcissistic account of his seduction of a five and dime cashier in Durham, North Carolina. "Pretty girl. Nice shape. Some looker," he wrote. "I wipe the make-up off her face with a napkin." Martin Russak, recounting the activities of the militant women in the 1935 Banford textile mill strike, voyeuristically described one union leader as "an attractive woman of thirty-one or thirty-two, full and well-built in stature . . . her shoulders level, back straight, bosom high and firmly rounded . . . still retain[ing] in her throat, arms and ankles the slenderness and agility of girlhood." Apparently the Communist press lacked editorial policies that would discourage its correspondents from adopting a male gaze.[7]

Moreover, the dominant tendency in the iconography and discourse of the left was to construct the category of "worker" as male. Muscular male proletarians routinely appeared on the covers and in the pages of the *New Masses*; if a female member of the working class was featured, she was usually at the side of her husband. Sol Funaroff's poem "American Worker" epitomizes the assumptions about gender and proletarian-ness found in any number of 1930s poems. The proletarian, "stand[ing] solid," is made of

> unbudging newengland rock:
> and his head rears firm, mighty,
> a high mountain in the Rockies,
> into the red fields of sunrise.
> *His heart's the dynamo that runs this country:*
> A land of broad straight plains,—
> a back thousands of tons of buffalo have trod strong
>   with thunder.
> And his tense muscles are steelrails humming
> with the coming of the dynamic 20th Century.
> Arms, hands, fists, bred by machine into the precise
> swift strength of pistons, hit like the 20th Century.

7. Petros Pikros, "Comrade Juanita," *NM* 4 (September 1928): 14–15; Edward Newhouse, "New York to New Orleans," *NM* 6 (January 1931): 13–14; Martin Russak, "The Women's Battalion," *NM* 17 (November 19, 1935): 15. For insights into the visual iconography of the early *New Masses*, I am indebted to Nina Miller-Scheuerlein's 1987 Northwestern University graduate paper, "Women in the *New Masses*."

In unwitting self-caricature, male strength is associated here with both the heritage of the land and the promise of technological advance. Socialist transformation, it is implied, entails the unfettering of productive forces that are intrinsically masculine.[8]

The dominance of a distinctly male literary voice in the official publications and formations of the literary left gave little encouragement to women writers to articulate revolutionary politics in a distinctly female voice. Women were essentially absent from the organized cultural formations of the left. The John Reed Clubs, Cowley reports, were virtually all-male preserves. The mastheads of the *New Masses* and other left literary organs listed very few women, and then routinely in noneditorial positions. One female *New Masses* reader, noting that many issues printed pieces only by male writers, wrote angrily, "Do you feel that women are lacking in ability, or do you admit you have failed to recognize their ability?" Moreover, sometimes leftist critical discourse displayed a marked gender bias. *Jews Without Money* was praised for its "vigorously masculine" style; the militant songs of black sharecroppers were hailed for their "virility." In his 1929 essay "Go Left, Young Writers," we will recall, Gold described the emerging proletarian writer in unmistakably phallic terms as "a wild youth," the "son of working class parents," who works in the industries of lumbering, mining, and steel and "writes in jets." As in the Funaroff poem about the archetypal American worker, Gold's celebration of the proletarian writer envisions revolutionism as an intrinsic (and presumably male) essence, rather than as the ungendered product of political activity and struggle. The "young writer" of working-class origins already possesses all the requisites for revolutionary consciousness. All "he" needs is to conquer new terrain, "go left"—in Gold's anomalous echo of Horace Greeley's "Go West, Young Man."[9]

8. Funaroff, "American Worker," *Left* 1 (Summer–Autumn 1931): 82. Cary Nelson observes that, while in the left press the "revolutionary worker was almost always male," in contemporaneous black magazines (*Crisis, Opportunity*) women were frequently featured on the covers "offer[ing] women a variety of subject positions they might choose to identify with or resist" (*Repression and Recovery: Modern American Poetry and the Politics of Cultural Memory, 1910–1945* [U of Wisconsin P, 1989], p. 201).

9. Cowley, *The Dream of the Golden Mountains* (New York: Viking, 1980), p. 135; Ann Weedon, "Letter," *New Masses* 16 (July 16, 1935): 22. Rebecca Pitts defended the *New Masses* against Weedon's charges, saying that the magazine provided "illumination

Women could be welcomed into this new terrain: Grace Lumpkin and Clara Weatherwax won the two main prizes for proletarian fiction in the 1930s. But women were also cautioned not to sound too much like women —or at least the wrong kinds of women. In 1929, we will recall, *New Masses* editor Walt Carmon praised Smedley's *Daughter of Earth* for having the "broad, healthy stride . . . of a woman, a proletarian to the marrow, . . . a fellow-worker . . . [who] is one of us." A year later, however, he qualified this generous admission to the club by observing that Smedley's autobiographical novel was "marred as [a] class novel" because it derived "its bias from the bitterness of a woman." Alan Calmer, in his critical summary of Weatherwax's prize-winning novel in the *New Masses* 1935 proletarian novel contest, commented that Weatherwax's anonymously submitted *Marching! Marching!*—a novel containing such naturalistic descriptions of bodily functions that it had to be rewritten to avoid censorship—manifested the "soft touch of a woman." V. J. Jerome noted that Ishma Waycaster Hensley, the protagonist of Fielding Burke's *Call Home the Heart*, "is the main character of the drama, but not . . . the protagonist. Greater than Ishma is one who is organically less related to the story, but who hovers in the overtone when the book is laid down. It is the Communist strike leader, the 'comrade from the North.'" Since this "comrade from the

---

of our common predicament" ("Women in the New Masses," *NM* 21 [December 1, 1936]: 15). The editors of *Working Woman* clearly felt that Weedon's letter raised an important issue, for they reprinted it in *Working Woman* (6 [September 1935]: 13) and invited responses. For uses of "masculine" as a term of praise in the criticism of proletarian literature, see J. Q. Neets, review of *Jews Without Money*, *NM* 5 (March 1930): 15, and Richard Frank, "Negro Revolutionary Music," *NM* 11 (May 15, 1934): 29. The quotation from Gold is from "Go Left, Young Writers," *NM* 4 (January 1929): 3–4. The West metaphor was one of Gold's favorites. At the close of the 1930s, he wrote of the project of proletarian literature as an expansion of the frontier: "[A] few hardy settlers fought off the Indians, cleared the virgin forest, built their shanties, and tilled the earth" (*The Hollow Men* [New York: International, 1941], pp. 34–35). I would not conclude from this, as Paula Rabinowitz does, that the party's outlook for proletarian literature can be conflated with "invasion, exploration, and rape" ("Response" to Barbara Foley, "Marxist Critics and Bourgeois Aesthetic Theory," MMLA Convention, November 1987.) But the metaphor is obviously highly problematic, both sexually and racially. The locus classicus for analysis of sexual conquest in the American iconography of the frontier is Annette Kolodny's *The Lay of the Land: Metaphor as Expression and History in American Life and Letters* (Chapel Hill: U of North Carolina P, 1975).

North" simply enters the novel for a few pages to give a stirring speech about Communism from the back of a train, Jerome's remarks suggest that Ishma's protracted struggle to free herself from the restrictions of child-bearing, nuclear-family parenting, and economic dependence has little to do with class struggle, or, for that matter, Communism.[10]

In sum, received sexist notions about gender and gender relations were often quite uncritically reproduced in the discourse and practice of the left. But the 1930s radicals also took conscious steps toward sexual egalitarian-ism: their legacy with regard to gender is contradictory. There is another side to the balance sheet.

In spite of its lack of any well-formulated line about the relation of women's oppression to the exploitation of the proletariat, the CP offered, as Kessler-Harris and Lauter note, "a forum and more serious attention to women's questions than any other group of the decade." Women's struggles may have been marginalized in comparison with men's, but the party spearheaded a number of important strikes of women workers and developed proletarian women's leadership abilities. The party press hailed the militancy of female strikers. The St. Louis nutpickers' strike, involving black and white women, received laudatory coverage in the New Masses. Reporting on a 1934 female cannery workers' strike, Vivian Dahl exclaimed, "Those Women Sure Are Scrappers!" Moreover, party-led community organizing away from the point of production enabled home-makers to take a leading role in struggles for relief and unemployment benefits. Robin Kelley notes that the Third-Period CP branch in Birming-ham, Alabama, was built largely among black women who, in mobilizing anti-eviction demonstrations, "often proved more militant than their male comrades." Women's trade union auxiliaries played a key role in winning various strikes—of which the 1937 Flint sit-down strike is only the most famous—and drew many working-class women away from the domestic

10. Carmon, review of *Daughter of Earth*, NM 5 (August 1929): 17; Carmon, "Away From Harlem," NM 6 (October 1930): 18; Calmer, "Reader's Report," NM 16 (September 16, 1935): 15; V. J. Jerome, "Toward a Proletarian Novel," NM 8 (August 1932): 15. In the original draft of *Marching! Marching!*, the organizer protagonist Mario is sodomized with a hammer handle. For more on the John Day Publishing Company's concern about possible obscenity charges, see Christian Suggs, "Introduction," *Marching! Marching!* (1935; rpt. Detroit: Omnigraphics, 1990). See also the letter from Richard Walsh of John Day to Hicks (Hicks Papers, Box 16, Arents Library, Syracuse University).

sphere. Ann Barton noted that the wives of striking anthracite miners "are questioning the precept of meekness. . . . The 'backward' women of the anthracite now, as before, polish their stoves to a stage where they shine like glass. But their talk is of other things . . . of class struggle, of meetings, of demands." Suda Gates of the Women's Branch of the National Miners Union praised the Communist-led union for the role it assigned to miners' wives in Straight Creek, Kentucky:

> Now is the time that the woman has some right to fight with her husband and by both fighting we can win in time to come. The good thing about the National Miners Union is that they don't leave the women out and so, not like in the other times, many times the wives make the husbands go back to work. The wives must meet with their husbands and together plan because it is as much to the wives as to the miners. . . . We never had nothing to do before but cook some beans. Now we have something to do.

The party press stressed the image of wives fighting shoulder to shoulder with their husbands but also represented wives prodding their husbands to greater militancy. One article by a *Daily Worker* worker-correspondent carried the headline, "Women Play Leading Role in Spreading Strike in Kentucky: Wife Demands Husband Come Out on Strike or Get a Divorce." While one might argue that threats of divorce to alter a husband's behavior affirm as much as they subvert traditional notions of a woman's sphere, the trade union auxiliaries addressed the reality that many working-class women, while homemakers, were participants in class struggle.[11]

Furthermore, the CP supported demands for a number of publicly

11. Kessler-Harris and Lauter, p. ix; Vivienne Dahl, " 'Them Women Sure Are Scrappers,' " *WW* 5 (August 1934): 7; Kelley, "A New War in Dixie: Communists and the Unemployed in Birmingham, Alabama, 1930–33," *Labor History* 30 (Summer 1989): 383; Anonymous, "Special Approach to Women Results in Victorious Strike," *PO* 6 (February 1933): 68–70; Anonymous, "Concentration in the Chicago Stockyards," *PO* 7 (May–June 1934): 55–57; Communist Party of the United States, *American Working Women and the Class Struggle* (New York: Workers Library, 1930); Joseph North, "Militant Women in Strikes," *WW* 5 (September 1934): 2; Ann Barton, "Women of Maltby," *NM* 8 (July 1933): 12; Suda Gates, Speech, Samuel Ornitz Papers, Box 7 (Harlan County), Wisconsin State Historical Society; *DW* (January 12, 1932), 3; *DW* (January 12, 1933), 3. The activities of the Women's Emergency Brigade in the Flint strike are chronicled in the description of Genora Johnson Dollinger, the brigade's head, in Jeane Westin, *Making Do: How Women Survived the '30s* (Chicago: Follett, 1976), pp. 308–18.

funded services especially beneficial to women—day care, maternity leave, birth control—and, at least during the Third Period, often linked these to a critique of the capitalist nuclear family. The most common arguments in favor of such demands hinged on a comparison of women's situations in the United States and the Soviet Union. Indeed, the praise of the presumed revolution in Soviet gender relations was at times embarrassingly uncritical. As one pair of *Daily Worker* headlines announced, "Legend of the 'Weaker Sex' Effectively Smashed by the Position of Women in the Soviet Union" / "All Inequality Abolished by the October Revolution." The abolition of prostitution, the institution of unregistered marriage, the establishment of workplace day care, the entry of large numbers of women into previously sex-segregated jobs—all these dramatic Soviet reforms were greeted with marked enthusiasm by male and female radicals alike. Joshua Kunitz wrote a *New Masses* series on the Soviet Union stressing the emergence of the "new Soviet woman." The *New Masses* published highly favorable reviews of translations of Gladkov's *Cement* and Kollontai's *Red Love*, feminist Bolshevik novels that fundamentally challenged monogamy and the nuclear family. Joseph Freeman's long chapter on Soviet fiction in *Voices of October* stressed the centrality of altered male/female relations in literary representations of the revolution and socialist construction. Austrian Communist Fannina Halle's studies of women's status in the Soviet Union—both Russia and the East—were translated and published in the United States. In *Red Virtue: Human Relations in the New Russia*, Ella Winter rhapsodized over the changed conceptions of love enabled by socialist egalitarianism. Some enthusiasts for the "new Soviet woman" looked askance at "free love," maintaining that monogamous marriage was strengthened by the socialization of child care and various types of domestic labor. But commentators on the USSR pointed out that marriage was no longer linked to religious or legal compulsion or, above all, economic necessity. The left press's publication of such positive representations of the relations between the sexes in the Soviet Union sent a loud and clear message to U.S. women: only socialism could meet their material and psychological needs.[12]

12. DW (September 2, 1935), 5, cited in Coiner, pp. 176, 185; Joshua Kunitz, "New Women in Old Asia," NM 13 (October 2, 1934): 23–27, and NM 13 (October 9, 1934): 15–19; Helen Black, review of Gladkov, Cement, NM 5 (September 1929): 20; Black, "Love and Revolution," NM 5 (September 1929): 18–19; Freeman, "Men and Women in Soviet

Moreover, even though proletarian unity was emphasized and bour-geois feminism derided, the theoretical status of working-class women was not simply conflated with that of male proletarians. A number of party theorists attempted to situate women's oppression in relation to capital-ism. Grace Hutchins's *Women Who Work*, an empirical study of women's employment, emphasized that working-class women suffered under the "double burden" of wage-slavery and unpaid service to family and home. Rebecca Pitts, arguing from Engels's historical ascription of women's op-pression to the development of private property, noted that the basis of women's continuing oppression consisted in their status as a "reserve labor army maintained in the interests of employers." Pitts conjoined economics with a cultural analysis of women's "sexual servility," however, conclud-ing that, as long as capitalism existed, women would be torn apart in the "tragic battle between the demands of personal life and the capacity for impersonal creative living."[13]

Mary Inman, a party theorist from the West Coast active in the late 1930s, proposed the political relation of gender to class in the Popular Front language of alliance. "Women must be activized in the interests of the people," she argued, "and the people must be activized in the interests of women." But Inman relied primarily on class analysis, locating women's special oppression not in "the exploitation of women wage workers," but in "the relation of housewives' work to social production." Because they pro-vided services indispensable to the continuation of capitalist exploitation, Inman argued, housewives' labor should be counted part of the surplus labor appropriated at the point of production. Moreover, Inman argued, "It is . . . fallacious to assume, as some socialists do, that nothing can be done under capitalism to improve housewives' outmoded method of labor, and that we must first have socialism before women put their minds to this problem and tackle its solution." Inman's work prompted a sharp debate. Her position, supported by Harrison George and other West Coast com-

---

Literature," in Freeman, with Kunitz and Louis Lozowick, *Voices of October: Art and Lit-erature in Soviet Russia* (New York: Vanguard, 1930), pp. 66–173; Fannina Halle, *Women in Soviet Russia,* trans. Margaret M. Green (London: Routledge, 1933), and *Women in the Soviet East,* trans. Margaret M. Green (New York: E. P. Dutton, 1938); Ella Winter, *Red Virtue: Human Relations in the New Russia* (New York: Harcourt, Brace, 1933).

13. Hutchins, *Women Who Work* (New York: International, 1934), esp. pp. 43–56; Pitts, "Women and Communism," NM 14 (February 19, 1934): 14–16, 20.

rades, was attacked by Al Landy and Ruth McKenney, who argued that women's domestic labor, while undoubtedly an arena of oppression, could not be considered exploitation, since it took place away from the point of production. Inman ended up leaving the party over the dispute. Clearly the debate over the economic status of housework that many contemporary feminists trace to the 1960s actually took place some thirty years before in the CPUSA. Although rarely cited today, 1930s Communist theorists such as Hutchins, Pitts, and Inman addressed important aspects of the material basis of women's oppression. They encouraged women to link their emancipation primarily with the fight for socialism but insisted that significant reforms on behalf of women should be fought for in the prerevolutionary period.[14]

The party's program on the "woman question" was distilled in Working Woman, a magazine indispensable to any study of women and the left in the 1930s. Published with the official blessing of the party—an advertisement on the back cover of a 1934 issue carried the laudatory greetings of Foster, then party chairman—Working Woman gave extensive coverage to women's participation in class struggle and framed women's oppression in a revolutionary anticapitalist analysis. It reported on the militant activities of the wives of striking Southern Illinois miners—detailing one meeting of a thousand women—and chronicled the support given to striking Philadelphia milk-deliverers by housewives who overturned scab milk trucks. Working Woman repeatedly stressed the extra oppression faced by black women, reporting on their strikes, featuring them in its graphics, publicizing the views of the Scottsboro mothers, and calling for women's multiracial unity. It educated its readership about women's history, highlighting women's roles in the Paris Commune and the Bolshevik Revolution. In addition, Working Woman described the various forms of sexual exploitation practiced in countries around the world and analyzed the dependence of the rising Nazi regime upon the relegation of women to the status of breeders. Contrasting Soviet women's access to day care, birth control, and abortion with the situation confronting U.S. women, Working Woman outlined the CP-sponsored "Mother's Bill of Rights," which

14. Inman, In Woman's Defense (Los Angeles: Committee to Organize the Advancement of Women, 1940), pp. 8, 135, 155; Ruth McKenney, "Women Are Human Beings," NM 37 (December 10, 1940): 6–7, and NM 37 (December 17, 1940): 9–10; Harrison George, "22,000,000 Housewives, Take Notice," NM 38 (February 11, 1941): 10–11.

made comprehensive demands of the government. One article described the great-granddaughter of Betsy Ross attending a party rally in Cleveland and waving the red flag in rhythm with the Internationale.[15]

Although primarily a news journal, *Working Woman* also promoted proletarian literature written by women. It reprinted substantial portions of female-authored novels such as Page's *Gathering Storm* and Lumpkin's *To Make My Bread*, selecting passages that stressed issues such as sexual assault and women's leadership in class struggle. The male editors of the anthology *Proletarian Literature in the United States* chose to excerpt from Lumpkin's novel the passage where John Stevens instructs John McClure about "the message" [Communism]—one of very few scenes in which a female is not present. *Working Woman*, by contrast, opted for the passage describing Bonnie McClure's death and funeral in the midst of the Gastonia strike. Moreover, *Working Woman* published some of the few experiments with collective authorship undertaken by the American left, including a poem composed by a dozen women in a *Working Woman* reading circle in Utah and the serialized story "Stockyard Stella," written by a group of female meat packers.[16]

15. Back cover, *Working Woman* (hereinafter *WW*) 5 (January 30, 1934); F. Burich, "Miners' Wives Will Fight," *WW* 5 (February 28, 1934): 7; Bella Previn, "Women's Leagues Help Philadelphia Milk Drivers Strike," *WW* 5 (January 10, 1934): 6; Anna Damon, "March 8th: A Day of Struggle," *WW* 5 (January 30, 1934): 2; Sadie Van Deen, "Unemployed Women Raise Voices," *WW* 5 (March 31, 1934): 5; cover to *WW* 5 (July 31, 1934), showing black female cannery strikers battling the police in Seabrook, NJ; Eugene Gordon, "Unconquered Spirit: The Negro Woman in Action," *WW* 6 (March 1935): 7, 14; Sasha Small, "Louise Michel," *WW* 5 (February 28, 1934): 12–13; Grace Hutchins, "Women Heroes on the Barricades," *WW* 5 (February 28, 1934): 3; Wang Yiu, "Slavery in Chinese Textile Mills," *WW* 5 (April 30, 1934): 14; Erna Straus, "Hitler 'Cranks-Up' Marriages," *WW* 5 (February 28, 1934): 14; Vera Smith, "Women of the New Order," *WW* 5 (April 30, 1934): 9; "How We Live—By Soviet Women Workers," *WW* 5 (April 30, 1934): 8–9; Irene Rhinehart, "Another Baby?" *WW* 6 (May 1935): 13; "A Mother's Bill of Rights," *WW* 5 (December 1934): 2; "Two Flags," *WW* 6 (July 1935): 4. In relation to the Scottsboro case, *Working Woman* also published interviews with Ruby Bates, the white woman who originally accused the Scottsboro defendants of rape but later recanted her testimony, which she claimed had been extracted from her by the police under pressure. Bates became a strong CP supporter, describing the NAACP—an antagonist of the party in the early phases of the Scottsboro defense—as a "tool of the capitalists" (*WW* 5 [April 1934]: 10).

16. Myra Page, "Lynch Terror," *WW* 5 (March 31, 1934): 8–9; Lumpkin, *To Make My Bread* (excerpt), *WW* 5 (January 30, 1934): 8–9; Lumpkin, "John Stevens," in *Proletarian*

Working Woman can be charged with conceding to various conventional conceptions of women's concerns. In 1934 it began publishing Frances Oliver's "Household Corner," a column featuring recipes and tips on hair and skin care, and Gwen Bard's "Fashion Letter," which carried dress patterns and advice on inexpensive ways to update a wardrobe. But—bypassing the feminist debate over the politics of fashion and beauty—we should note that Oliver and Bard usually attempted to combine left-wing analysis with their domestic and cosmetic advice. As Bard noted in one column, "You know of course that these ideas are not offered as little dabs of cheer to try to make us content with our lot; experience has taught us that such individual solutions are really not solutions at all." Moreover, Oliver's and Bard's columns occupied only a limited space in the pages of *Working Woman*. While it has been suggested that *Working Woman* was strongly colored by these columns, in fact they ordinarily occupied one or two pages in a sizable magazine otherwise completely devoted to news and commentary on women's roles in class struggle.[17]

The Popular Front successor to *Working Woman*, *Woman Today*, did indeed play down women's militancy; its fiction, graphics, and news analysis held up a considerably more middle-class image of exemplary womanhood. In the first issue of *Woman Today*, the narrative of woman's rebellion took the form of a story about a middle-class teenager who gets a permanent wave in opposition to her father. Subsequent issues accompa-

---

Literature in the United States, ed. Hicks (New York: International, 1935), pp. 110–15; "A Poem—Written by a Group of Twelve Women in the Working Woman Readers Circle, Utah City, Utah," WW 6 (May 1935): 8; "Stockyard Stella—Serial Love Story—By a Group of Workers and Jane Benton," WW 6 (January 1935): 4–5; 6 (February 1935): 4–5; 6 (March 1935): 5–6; and 6 (April 1935): 4–5.

17. Gwen Bard, "Fashion Letter," WW 5 (November 1934): 15; Elsa Jane Dixler, "The Woman Question: Women and the American Communist Party, 1929–1941," Ph.D. Thesis, Yale University, 1974. Alun Howkins has argued that there was in virtually all trade union and leftist magazines of the 1920s and 1930s a "wives' page" that dealt with "recipes and . . . perhaps occasional remarks on politics and union affairs." By contrast, the *Daily Worker* (Great Britain) addressed the political organization of women—as both workers and wives—and the different positions of women in capitalist nations and the USSR. See "Class Against Class: The Political Culture of the Communist Party of Great Britain, 1930–35," in Frank Gloversmith, ed., *Class, Culture and Social Change: A New View of the 1930s* (Sussex: Harvester P and Atlantic Highlands, NJ: Humanities P, 1980), p. 246.

nied excerpts from Fielding Burke's *A Stone Came Rolling* with drawings that portrayed Burke's hero Ishma—a mountain woman turned millworker turned Communist organizer—as a well-coifed housewife who could have appeared in the pages of the *Ladies Home Journal*. But the tone of *Working Woman*—which ceased publication in December 1935—was preponderantly proletarian and militant. At least during the Third Period, the party's principal women's magazine addressed a broad range of women's issues and was openly revolutionary in outlook.[18]

Representations of Gender in Proletarian Fiction

The representations of gender in proletarian fiction both reflect and reproduce the left's contradictory theory and practice with regard to the "woman question." As we might expect, male-authored texts were more likely to articulate traditionally sexist attitudes. A number of novels by men depict female characters as threats to the autonomy of revolutionary (or would-be revolutionary) males. In Newhouse's *You Can't Sleep Here*, Gene Marsay confides to the reader about his girlfriend Eileen, who "chatters adorably," that "[i]f you stayed with her long enough at a time she became a terrific responsibility and her presence came to dominate you and it took time to recover your independence." In Halper's *Union Square*, the voluptuous "Comrade Helen" teases and manipulates the puny Leon into a frenzy of frustrated lust; it is only when he frees himself from the toils of desire for her that he can develop as a man and a political being. In Conroy's *The Disinherited*, Larry Donovan, finding his identity as a leftist organizer, decides that he must release himself from any obligations to Bonny Fern. "I thought she looked prettier every year," he muses, "even if she was tanned and freckled and her hands were red. But I had to be free." Even when they wished to project honorific portraits of class-conscious women, male-authored proletarian novels at times encoded denigrating assumptions about women's roles and capacities. In *Jews Without Money*, Gold elevates his mother as an embodiment of proletarian virtue but declares

18. Margaret Weymouth Jackson, "The Permanent Wave," *WT* (March 1936), 4–5, 22, 24, 27–28; illustration accompanying Fielding Burke, *A Stone Came Rolling* (excerpt), *WT* (May 1936), 5.

that his "old maid teacher"—whose anti-Semitism he rightfully rejects—is as pitiable as "a cow with no milk or calf or bull." The novel's critique of retrograde social attitudes presupposes a denigration of female spinsterhood. In *The Land of Plenty*, Ellen, an office worker, ends up supporting the lumber workers' strike. But her main function in the plot is not to explore the issues involved in building male/female labor unity, but instead to provide Johnny Hagen with a sexual initiation that parallels his political initiation into manhood.[19]

It might be objected that some of the authors of the texts cited here were not party members and were not voicing official left-wing doctrine when they marginalized or stereotyped women. To be sure, every manifestation of male chauvinism in these novels cannot be laid at the door of the party, just as every expression of racism in proletarian novels cannot be read as an articulation of Communist bigotry. But the reviews these texts received in the left press made no mention of their problematic treatments of gender. Demeaning representations of women could exist side by side with otherwise revolutionary social insights precisely because they were embedded in a tissue of attitudes simply assumed on the part of the reader. So long as sexist ideas and attitudes were not asserted in the explicit argument of a text—and they rarely were—they generally escaped notice.[20]

But the inadequacies in the left's construction of gender issues were by no means restricted to men: some female writers also glossed over issues

19. Newhouse, *You Can't Sleep Here* (New York: Macaulay, 1934), p. 184; Conroy, *The Disinherited* (1933; rpt. New York: Hill and Wang, 1963), pp. 308–9; Gold, *Jews Without Money* (New York: Liveright: 1930), pp. 36–37. Rabinowitz suggests that Gold's representation of his mother as an ideal proletarian here contrasts sharply with the masculinist coding of the working class in his criticism: "In Gold's novel, proletarian realism is clearly tied to femininity—both his mother and his aunt organize strikes—but his criticism implies that it is through masculine workers that Marxist intellectuals can find their proper literary stance. Gold's regendering of (masculine) workers and (feminine) artists in his criticism was perhaps a refusal of the novel's gender implications" (*Labor and Desire: Women's Revolutionary Fiction in Depression America* [Chapel Hill and London: University of North Carolina P, 1992], p. 187).

20. See the commentaries on these novels in the *New Masses*: Joseph Freeman, "You Can Fight Here," *NM* 13 (December 11, 1934): 25–26; Mike Gold, "A Letter to the Author of a First Book," *NM* 10 (January 9, 1934): 25–26; Norman MacLeod, "With Malice Toward None," *NM* 11 (April 24, 1934): 24–25; Neets, 15; Granville Hicks, "Proletarian Mastery," *NM* 16 (July 16, 1935): 23.

that might prove troublesome, evinced difficulty with the representation of female heroism, and even adopted a male gaze. Herbst, in *Rope of Gold*, suppresses mention of her sister's death from an abortion or her own lesbian affair with a sculptor, replacing such disturbing autobiographical materials with tamer fictional analogues. Page, in *Daughter of the Hills*, uncritically depicts her female hero, Dolly Cooper, sacrificing her own growth as a political leader to remain by the side of her injured miner husband. Lumpkin, who structures her Gastonia novel *To Make My Bread* as the bildungsroman of Bonnie McClure, passes the baton of political leadership after Bonnie's death to Bonnie's brother John, who acquires a fuller understanding of revolutionary politics than Bonnie ever has. Even though Bonnie is modeled on the Gastonia strike leader Ella May Wiggins and John McClure is wholly fictive, Lumpkin did not see fit to make Bonnie the recipient of the "message" delivered by the Communist organizer John Stevens.[21]

To a significant extent, however, proletarian novels by both men and women queried traditional gender relations and linked women's oppression with the exploitation of the working class. Not all leftist male writers considered testosterone a necessary component of proletarian selfhood. In *Conveyer*, James Steele (Robert Cruden) offers a critique of Jim Brogan, an unemployed Detroit auto worker who, after a few short years of enjoying the American dream—his homebound wife Marie is happy behind her white picket fence—abuses Marie and neglects his child, sliding into a self-destructive depression. When Marie, again pregnant, abandons Jim to live with her mother, Jim's plight elicits little sympathy from the

---

21. Lumpkin, *A Sign for Cain* (New York: Lee Furman, 1935), p. 264. Rosenfelt provides a critique of Page's treatment of Dolly Cooper in *Daughter of the Hills* in her Afterword to the Feminist Press edition of the text (New York, 1986), p. 364. Herbst's affair with Marion Greenwood is detailed in Elinor Langer, *Josephine Herbst* (Boston and Toronto; Little, Brown, 1983). For further evidence of the party's uneasiness with the issue of lesbianism, see Irene Thirer's comments on the movie version of Lillian Hellman's *The Children's Hour*, which Thirer applauds for successfully "get[ting] around the point which bothered the censors: unnatural love for one woman by another" (*WT* [April 1936], 3). Interestingly, the dust jacket for *To Make My Bread* represents a strong male sheltering his wife in his arm, with two children by their sides. In the novel, Bonnie's husband deserts her, and she—like the historical Wiggins—is left to raise her numerous children.

reader; his personal suffering is the price he pays for his false consciousness. In *All Brides Are Beautiful*, by contrast, Thomas Bell portrays Peter
Cummings, an unemployed male radical, quite contentedly doing domestic labor while his wife Susan works. One critic has commented that Bell's
novel is "unique among proletarian novels in that the sound of silverware
is used as a weapon in the class struggle." In their second proletarian
novels, Newhouse and Conroy made attempts to correct some of the male
chauvinist errors of their first novels. Newhouse's Gene Marsay, having
relinquished the Yardley-scented Eileen for the left-wing Alma, finds that
political activism cannot excuse him from marital responsibility. Conroy,
in *A World to Win*, depicts Leo Hurley coming to class consciousness
largely through witnessing his wife's childbirth death in a roadside ditch.
In these novels, male/female relations in the working class are the object of
directed scrutiny. Ideologies of male dominance are linked with false consciousness of other kinds; supportive and caring relations between men
and women are linked with political egalitarianism.[22]

Sometimes gender relations figure as a means of representing in microcosm the distortions and brutalities of the capitalist social order. In
Rollins's *The Shadow Before*, bourgeois rule is clearly associated with male
dominance through the sexual opportunism of the scab Ramon Viera and
the pathological sexual repression of Dorothy and Marjorie Thayer, wife
and daughter of the factory manager. In Armstrong's *Parched Earth*, Everett
Caldwell's destructive hegemony in the California town bearing his name
is emblematized by the syphilis that he spreads through the town through

---

22. Robin William Day, "The Politics of Art: A Reading of Selected Proletarian
Novels," Ph.D. Thesis, Drew University, 1983, p. 138. Further glimpses of Bell's own af-
finity for the domestic sphere are afforded in his poignant memoir, *In the Midst of Life*,
which was undertaken while Bell was slowly dying of stomach cancer in the late 1950s
(New York: Atheneum, 1961). Interestingly, Bell's CIO-era novel, *Out of This Furnace*
(discussed below in chapter 10), presents the nuclear family quite uncritically as a haven
in a heartless world. The difference between *All Brides Are Beautiful* (1936) and *Out of
This Furnace* (1941) indicates something about the changing discourse regarding gender
on the left in the latter part of the 1930s. In relation to Anna's continually pregnant state
in *A World to Win*, Conroy wrote to Hicks, "One editor objected that contraceptives are
available to everybody now, so the main thesis of the story was absurd. I know a damned
sight better than this" (n.d., Hicks Papers, Box 14). Le Sueur, in her review of *A World
to Win*, applauded Conroy for his more accurate specification of the relation of gender to
class in his second novel (*New Masses* 16 [July 9, 1935]: 25).

Belle Vazquez, the town prostitute and the mother of Wally Vazquez, his unacknowledged idiot son. In *Blood on the Forge*, the alienation of the newly proletarianized Moss brothers is epitomized in their commodified sexual exchanges. The frustrations that lead Big Mat to seek a sense of power as a thug for the mill bosses are existentially experienced as sexual. While Rabinowitz complains that male-authored proletarian novels privilege labor over desire, production over subjectivity, these novels suggest that distortions in sexuality are not merely treated as "symptomatic" of capitalist dysfunctionality but also *mediate* that dysfunctionality. Sexual misery *is* oppression even as it both reflects and reproduces structures of capitalist exploitation.[23]

To be sure, some of these texts limit or dilute their critique of traditional assumptions about gender. *Conveyer* and *A World to Win* close with valorized portraits of their heroes, freed from female encumbrances, bonding with other male organizers. Even as he conscientiously addresses Alma's needs, Newhouse's hero complacently wonders whether "he would ever be enough of a Communist to regulate his sexual behavior exclusively or primarily with the interests of the Party at heart, wondering if anyone ever had."[24] Rollins's syphilitic metaphor, while intended to target the capitalist class as the source of disease, simultaneously reinforces a certain repugnance at female sexuality. In these texts, however, manifestations of sexism operate on the level of presupposition: on the level of manifest political argument, the novels contest male dominance and expose its consequences for both men and women.

The principal contribution to the development of a Marxist analysis of gender and class appears, however—as we might expect—in the writings of women. Most female proletarian novelists insistently link women's liberation with class emancipation. These writers accomplish this task in part by focusing upon the specifically gendered plight of the working-class woman. Page's *The Gathering Storm*, Lumpkin's *To Make My Bread*, and Smedley's *Daughter of Earth* portray the physical and psychological deterioration of overworked women burdened with child-rearing and continual

23. For another reading of the treatment of sexuality in *The Shadow Before*, see Joseph R. Urgo, "Proletarian Literature and Feminism: The Gastonia Novels and Feminist Protest," *minnesota review*, n.s. 24 (Spring 1985): 79–83.

24. Newhouse, *This Is Your Day* (New York: Lee Furman, 1937), p. 171.

pregnancy. Olsen's *Yonnondio: From the Thirties* and Le Sueur's *The Girl* represent marital violence as a grotesque accompaniment to class oppression. Burke's *Call Home the Heart* demonstrates that a working woman's freedom from the restrictive nuclear-family definitions of wifehood and motherhood is a precondition for her full political participation in class struggle. While none of these texts excuses men for reproducing the dynamics of class hierarchy in the home—Smedley and Olsen are particularly harsh in their indictments of male domestic violence—all clearly suggest that men and women alike suffer from the degradations of class society and would alike benefit from the abolition of the wage relation. As Rabinowitz points out in relation to Jim Holbrook's battering of his wife Anna in *Yonnondio*, "When the family is most troubled, Jim can least afford his masculine position of authority; out of this fluidity, the family becomes a potential site for resistance." In these texts, the working-class family emerges as a primary locus for reproducing hierarchical and violent behaviors that hurt women, dehumanize men, and reinforce capitalist hegemony.[25]

Women writers' insistence upon the continuity of the personal with the political at times enables them to criticize rightist tendencies within the Communist movement. In *The Unpossessed*, Tess Slesinger's satiric treatment of the petty bourgeois political isolation of a group of male literary radicals is conjoined with her representation of these men's perfidious and oppressive behavior as husbands and lovers. In *Rope of Gold*, Herbst portrays the degeneration of Victoria and Jonathan Chance's personal relationship as causally linked to the opportunistic role he plays as a party "front" among liberal supporters. Just as in the Bolshevik Alexandra Kollontai's earlier *Love Among Worker Bees*, which conjoins a critique of the NEP with a portrayal of a male Communist's oppression of his wife, in Herbst's novel criticism of the class-collaborationist features of the Popular Front is associated with criticism of sexist social relations. Antisexism provides a means of spotting other departures from revolutionary practice.

25. Rabinowitz, *Labor and Desire*, p. 134. Sylvia Jenkins Cook, commenting on the frequent treatment of abortion and birth control in the Gastonia novels, remarks, "the repeated guarded attempts to discuss birth control, the open portrayal of the anguish of each pregnancy, the grisly tales of amateur abortion efforts, sometimes suggest that Margaret Sanger rather than Marx might have been the hero the authors sought" (*From Tobacco Road to Route 66: The Southern Poor White in Fiction* [Chapel Hill: U of North Carolina P, 1976], p. 99).

Women writers' most important contribution to a discourse about revolutionary social transformation, however, consists in their representations of identity and selfhood. A distinctive feature of 1930s women's fiction is its conception of the class struggle as occurring not simply "out there," in the mill or on the picket line, but as dialectically embedded in, and mediated through, everyday experience. Class consciousness thus consists in the development of a new, more collective self, one that acquires identity through acknowledging rather than denying its multiple extensions into others. These texts powerfully assert the roots of Communist egalitarianism in the present, suggesting that revolution entails not just the seizure and collectivization of the means of production but the establishment of dramatically altered social relations. Funaroff's and Gold's masculinist formulations of proletarian heroism carry distinctly nationalist and workerist overtones and fetishize developing productive forces as the site of revolutionary change. By contrast, many women's texts demonstrate the centrality of cultural change to the process of revolutionary transformation.

In many women's novels the depiction of parenting moves beyond a celebration of authentic proletarian traditions and folkways to assert the social essence of selfhood. In *Yonnondio* the one epiphanic moment in young Mazie's otherwise grim childhood occurs when, ensconced in her mother's embrace, she intuits that the feeling of "boundlessness" she experiences is integral to the "boundedness" of the social relations that define them both. In *Gathering Storm*, *To Make My Bread*, and *Call Home the Heart*, the female protagonist's close childhood relationship with a class-conscious grandmother develops her later capacities for political activism. In *The Girl* the stress upon nurturing as the origin of individual consciousness is extended beyond the family to the community of women with whom the unnamed protagonist lives; it is no accident that the novel's principal mentor character, the Workers Alliance organizer Amelia, is also a midwife. By exploring the painful contradictions involved in the reproduction of the next generation of labor power, as well as the processes by which knowledge is transmitted through nurturing, these texts combat individualistic illusions of self-generation and autonomy.

Moreover, women's proletarian novels frequently foreground the relation of sexuality to political conviction, thus developing the notion that class emancipation is both a premise to and an outgrowth of personal liberation. In Page's *Moscow Yankee*, the male hero, an unemployed Detroit auto worker who goes to work in the USSR during the first Five-Year Plan, grasps the true meaning of socialist construction only when he comes to terms with the egalitarian gender relations that it entails. In *Daughter of Earth*, Marie Rogers's ability to feel sexual passion after a lifetime of defensive distrust is profoundly linked to her confidence in her Indian lover as a political comrade—just as her subsequent withdrawal from the relationship is linked to her realization of his inability to disavow the sexism of his political cohorts. In *Daughter of the Hills*, Dolly overcomes her deep-rooted suspicion of men by coming to terms with the fact that her father, despite his betrayal of his wife, also led a heroic multiracial effort to free the miners from the scourge of prison labor, which divided black and white workers and destroyed the miners' livelihood. Dolly's physical and emotional acceptance of John Cooper thus takes shape as an acceptance of her class heritage; her commitment to build with John a better marriage than her parents had is integral to her commitment to the class struggle. In novels such as these, desire is not a respite from the class struggle but embedded in it, and the fight for sexual equality and fulfillment is integrally related to the fight for a better world.

All in all, women's texts construct a notion of proletarian heroism that is often simply more Communist than that appearing in men's proletarian novels. Works such as Cantwell's *The Land of Plenty* and Tippett's *Horse Shoe Bottoms* emphasize the mass nature of workers' movements and the necessarily collective nature of leadership. But they end up featuring protagonists whose broad individual shoulders are metonymic of proletarian strength. Women's novels, by contrast, are more likely to emphasize mutual dependence among male and female working-class activists. In Vorse's *Strike!*, the principal male organizer, Fer Deane, is portrayed as frequently petty, vain, and cowardly. His right-hand woman, Irma Rankin, is given little public credit for leadership but reliably steps into his shoes during his periodic crises. In Zugsmith's *A Time to Remember*, a novel set among striking department store workers, the reader's attention continually shifts between the stories of the text's male and female protagonists. Zugsmith juxtaposes her account of Aline Weinman's growing political commitment and independence from her domineering father with the narrative of Matt's struggle to free himself from a mutually destructive relationship with his wife: leadership emerges from the ranks of men and women alike as workers make the personal choices enabling them to be more effective politically. This baton-passing has its problematic aspects. When the female protagonists of *Gathering Storm* and *To Make My Bread* are supplanted by their organizer brothers, or when Steve Carson rather than Victoria Chance occupies the reader's attention at the end of *Rope of Gold*, Page, Lumpkin, and Herbst falter in their creation of fully realized revolutionary female heroes. But showing male characters taking up where females leave off does not wholly negate the women's achievements, for it stresses that both men's and women's participation is necessary in the class struggle. Where novels by male radicals frequently establish male heroism at the expense of female political growth, novels by women radicals are more consistently egalitarian, eschewing binary oppositions measuring one character's strength by another's weakness.

As we shall see in future chapters, this tendency of proletarian women's fiction to stress the collective dimensions of selfhood has important consequences for the interplay of generic and doctrinal politics in different types of proletarian fiction. Inherited models of novelistic realism carry the ideological baggage of bourgeois individualism, embodied in the premise that character, constituted by intrinsic "traits," needs to be revealed more than formed. The predisposition to treat character as autonomous and self-generating is especially encoded in the classically realistic modes of the bildungsroman and the social novel, the two most popular genres of proletarian fiction. While the commitments of left-wing writers led them to reject this proposition on a conceptual level, they at times succumbed to the ideological pressures of conventions—particularly when their doctrinal politics left them vulnerable to such pressures. Time and again, we shall see, hierarchical assumptions about gender were centrally implicated in proletarian novels' projection of individualistic conceptions of selfhood.

Women writers were of course not exempt from the pressures exerted by the generic politics of inherited novelistic forms or by the doctrinal politics of gender inequality. In *Call Home the Heart*, Burke's portrayal of Ishma as a folk/unionist superwoman, endowed with remarkable qualities of body and mind, reinforces the idealist conception of character as given that undergirds the bildungsroman. In *A Sign for Cain*, Lumpkin's stereotypical representation of upper-class Caroline Gault as frigid and shrill contributes to the simplistic heroization of the Communist organizer Bill. Indeed, as Rabinowitz points out, even Le Sueur's *The Girl*, with its utopian portrait of a left-wing feminist collective, can be charged with "maintain[ing] the gender polarities of proletarianism even as it inverts them to feminize class consciousness." Le Sueur's implied equation of motherhood with revolutionism "verges on essentialism because it invokes women's biological capacity to bear children without interrogating the cultural platitudes surrounding motherhood." Even the categories that proletarian women writers developed to combat women's marginalization, in short, could reproduce gendered binary oppositions. Generic politics thus to a degree rein in these writers' attempts to construct oppositional female subjectivities; "the conventions of domestic fiction . . . contain the unruly textual/sexual politics" striving for expression.[26] Nonetheless, as we shall see, women writers as a group are less likely than their male peers to reproduce individualistic conceptions of selfhood. Perhaps Calmer was right (if for the wrong reasons) when he observed that Clara Weatherwax's *Marching! Marching!*—the decade's most ambitious novelistic effort to dissolve bourgeois individuality and project a collective proletarian protagonist— manifested the "touch of a woman."

Balancing the Balance Sheet

What can we conclude about the relationship between women and the left in the 1930s? What is the principal legacy of this relationship? What lessons does it teach?

One could argue that the Communist movement's mixed record in addressing gender issues points to the necessity for a feminist discourse to supplement and correct Marxist discourse. The crowded balance sheet recording the cons and pros of Communist theory and practice regarding the "woman question" reveals no coherent set of principles guiding party policy. Sometimes this policy appears to have been motivated by a serious attention to women's oppression; at other times it virtually ignored the issue. The vastly different treatment accorded women in the *New Masses* and *Working Woman* demonstrates even within the revolutionary movement an urgent need for a separate forum where women could voice their distinctive needs and concerns. As Coiner puts it, "The experience of CP women demonstrates . . . that autonomous organizations of women are central to the development of a revolutionary socialist movement."[27] The left was essentially male and essentially sexist; to the extent that women con-

26. Rabinowitz, ibid., pp. 124, 123, 15.

27. Constance Coiner " 'Pessimism of the Mind, Optimism of the Will': Literature of Resistance," Ph.D. Thesis, UCLA, 1987, pp. 78–79.

tributed anything distinctive to the oppositional discourse of the decade, they did so largely because of their isolation from the principal organs and formations of the left.

Indeed, the argument continues, the differential approaches to questions of oppression and liberation in women's and men's proletarian fiction suggest that women literary radicals framed their own political line on the question of gender and class, a line that in various essentials contradicted the line of the party. As Rabinowitz puts it, "Women occluded in the central discourses and institutions of the CPUSA negotiated continuous revisions of line, whether as organizers of needle-trade workers or as authors of novels about those same workers." By focusing, moreover, on the question of reproduction—not just of the next generation of laborers, but of ideology and consciousness—women radicals revealed the limitations of Marxism's productivist bias. Coiner remarks that Le Sueur and Olsen "implicitly questioned Marxism's primacy-of-production theory, which defines production as *the* distinguishing human activity. . . . [T]heir texts subvert the Party's productivism and sexism." By emphasizing the politics of personal relationships, furthermore, left-wing women writers demonstrated the fallacy of the reductionist view that all social contradictions are mediations of one central contradiction, that is, the class struggle. When women writers explored new conceptions of collectivity and selfhood, they were not expanding upon Marxist principles but demonstrating Marxism's need for supplementation by a distinctively feminist discourse. To the extent that class-based and feminist perspectives coexist in these women leftists' work, then, such coexistence is necessarily uneasy and provisional.[28]

The above line of argument reflects an understandable frustration with the 1930s left's inconsistent attention to gender questions, its marginalization of women in major cultural organs, and its weakness in theorizing the relation of reproduction to production. But the position contains two difficulties. First, it minimizes the conscious commitment of women leftists to the Communist-led movement. Whether theorists—Rebecca Pitts, Grace Hutchins, Mary Inman—or writers—Grace Lumpkin, Leane Zugsmith,

---

28. Rabinowitz, ibid., p. 62; Coiner, "Literature of Resistance," p. 181. Coiner's work on Le Sueur and Olsen is ground-breaking, but I disagree with her characterization of the Communist party as endorsing a "separation of public and private spheres" and the "teleological notion that revolutionary struggles will achieve an ideal, static 'state'"— and, especially, as "minimizing consciousness as a site of ideological struggle" ("Literature of Resistance," p. 179).

Tillie Olsen, Meridel Le Sueur, Clara Weatherwax, Myra Page, Fielding Burke—the women contributing to the discourse of the left were by no means politically naive. They may have felt that they had something distinctive to add to the Communist movement's line and practice, but they considered themselves leftists and knew what this meant as well as did their male colleagues. The female novelists were at least as fervent in their espousal of party politics as were many of the men; indeed, *Gathering Storm* and *Marching! Marching!* offer more encyclopedic summaries of the party program than do any other novels of the decade. Theorists and novelists alike were intelligent and bold women. There is no reason to suppose that they were suppressing or redirecting feminist leanings that they felt incompatible with their commitment to Marxism.[29]

Second, these women's writings reveal that the female literary radicals did not—covertly, unconsciously, or otherwise—espouse a different political line. Their subject position as females enabled them to speak with particular knowledge and concern about the status of women. But—with the possible exception of Le Sueur in *The Girl*—they were not articulating a proto-Chodorowian conception of women as the bearers of a superior ethics when they delineated their visions of collective selfhood. Nor were they, in a proto-Baudrillarian maneuver, repudiating the basic Marxist principle that production explains exploitation and alienation when they stressed the centrality of reproduction to the material and political survival of the working class. To the extent that women writers constitute a distinctive voice within the 1930s left, this occurs not because they offered a

29. Grace Lumpkin testified before the Senate Permanent Investigating Sub-Committee in 1953 that she had been coerced by the CP into including pro-Communist propaganda in her *A Sign for Cain* (1934). As Rideout notes, however, this "confession" needs to be taken with a grain of salt: "One would find her charge of coercion more compelling if she had not already, apparently on her own initiative, 'written Communist propaganda' into *To Make My Bread*, published in 1932" (Walter B. Rideout, *The Radical Novel in the United States 1900–1954: Some Interrelations of Literature and Society* [New York: Hill and Wang, 1956], p. 311n.). While writing *To Make My Bread*, Lumpkin noted many years later, she used to discuss "the perfect world we were going to make" with "brilliant young Communists" of her acquaintance (letter to Kenneth Toombs, June 22, 1971, Lumpkin Papers, So. Caroliniana Library, U of South Carolina, Columbia, cited in Sandra Adickes, English Department, Winona State U, "Three Visions of Gastonia: Mary Heaton Vorse's *Strike!*, Grace Lumpkin's *To Make My Bread*, and Myra Page's *Gathering Storm*," unpublished essay).

discourse counter to Marxism, but because they developed Marxism along important lines and indicated further directions in which it required—arguably, still requires—expansion. The best framework for assessing the disparities between these women's discourse and that of the movement as a whole is not one that counterposes Marxism with women's emancipation but one that theorizes the historical weaknesses and strengths of the Marxism of the 1930s left.

As I have pointed out in my discussion of the party's changing positions on the "woman question," this Marxism was by no means a constant throughout the decade. The line of the left regarding women's oppression and emancipation changed significantly between the beginning of the Third Period and the end of the Popular Front. Up to 1936, women were generally featured as fighters in the class struggle—most commonly at the point of production, but also in their capacity as homemakers. Moreover, in line with the Third Period's more revolutionary character, the notion of a "woman's sphere" was in various ways contested, and the gains made by women in the USSR were routinely contrasted with women's lot in the United States. By contrast, during the Popular Front the organizing of women workers became less of a priority. In line with the period's affirmation of Communism as "twentieth-century Americanism," moreover, gender relations in the traditional nuclear family were generally viewed as unproblematic. With the supersession of the fight for socialism by the struggle against fascism and for New Deal reforms, Popular Front organizing initiatives among women less frequently targeted the political economy of capitalism as the source of women's oppression.

On the basis of this narrative, it is tempting to conclude that, if we seek the impediments to the 1930s left's formulating a revolutionary discourse about gender and class, we should look to the Popular Front as the source of all evil. As Working Woman indicates, toward the end of the Third Period the party was shedding its earlier insistence on focusing on women only in their capacity as workers. The CP had developed a program that spoke to a range of women's concerns and had found ways to acknowledge the domestic sphere as a primary locus of many working-class women's identities. Yet it had not abandoned its commitment to revolution as the means of achieving social equality, and it still queried a number of the premises—or at least the functions—of the capitalist nuclear family. As with other issues we have been examining—the line on the "Negro question," the evolving definition of proletarian literature—the years 1934 and 1935 pose the query, "What if . . . ?" In the context of the "woman question," the query is: What if the Communist-led movement had persisted in its leftward trajectory while developing increasingly effective ways of enlarging its constituency among women?

The left's adoption of Popular Frontism closed off the possibility of more fully articulating a revolutionary discourse—and constructing a revolutionary practice—in relation to women's emancipation. But we should not oversimplify the trajectory of the decade. After all, it was when the party's line was boldest in its challenge to the traditional family and most emphatic in its insistence that women were proletarians that there appeared the greatest number of complaints in the *Communist* and *Party Organizer* that work among women was being ignored. When the left was most uncompromising in its call for socialist egalitarianism, it was often using a masculinist iconography of the proletariat that effectively excluded half the working class. Yet if in the period of "twentieth-century Americanism" the CP adopted an increasingly class-collaborationist political strategy, at this time some of the more powerfully feminist proletarian novels—*The Girl, Rope of Gold, Daughter of the Hills*—were written. While Earl Browder was praising the nuclear family as a fount of proletarian values, Mary Inman was penning the decade's most searching critique of women's exploitation in the home. Even though it is crucial to link the changing constructions of the "woman question" with the larger drift toward revisionism and liberalism, it is important to note that there was uneven development over the decade and to avoid what Alan Wald calls the "closed classificatory systems" imposed by a rigid separation of the Third Period from the Popular Front.[30] Some political tendencies engendered in the early 1930s did not bear full fruit until the late 1930s. We exclude any part of the decade from our purview at the risk of losing sight of the whole.

If we wish fully to understand the principal barrier to the 1930s left's formulating a more consistently revolutionary approach to the issue of women's emancipation, we must turn to the doctrine of productive forces determinism that heavily influenced the Communist movement—both in the United States and internationally—throughout the decade. By "pro-

---

30. Alan Wald, review of Rabinowitz, *Labor and Desire*, in *These Times* (March 25–31, 1992), 19.

ductive forces determinism" I do not mean "productivist bias," a term commonly used by neo-Marxists to denote Marxism's presumably undue stress upon production as the basis of social analysis. Rather, "productive forces determinism" denotes the doctrine that the development of productive forces is the principal determinant of social change and that the class struggle is a reflex of the "fettering" of productive forces by outmoded productive relations.

One important consequence of the doctrine of productive forces determinism was the theory of gradualism, or stages—that is, the notion that people should engage in the struggle to overthrow an inhumane social order but not anticipate significant changes in personal relationships—the "superstructure"—so long as capitalism remains entrenched. This doctrine—embraced by all 1930s leftist formations, not just the Stalinists—had consequences for Communist positions on a wide range of issues, from the relation of mental to manual labor in socialist construction to the relation of insurgent to inherited forms in revolutionary cultural movements. As applied specifically to the question of gender relations, this widely accepted doctrine meant that socialism, but only socialism, would provide an answer to the "woman question." Until there occurred a successful insurrection for state power, the "woman question" remained just that—a question. Unless we cynically refuse to take their testimonies at face value, we should acknowledge most Depression-era leftists' fervent belief that altered relations between men and women would be one of the most valued benefits of the "better world" for which they were fighting. But the unevenness of the leftists' record in addressing gender issues indicates their equally strong belief that these fruits were largely unavailable in the present and that changing gender relations now could play no significant role in bringing the "better world" into being any sooner. Cultural revolution, in other words, would occur after the political and economic revolution.[31]

31. For more on the Marxist-feminist debate, see Lise Vogel, *Marxism and the Oppression of Women: Toward a Unitary Theory* (New Brunswick: Rutgers UP, 1983); Joan B. Landes, "Marxism and the 'Woman Question,'" in *Promissory Notes: Women in the Transition to Socialism*, ed. Sonia Kruks, et al. (New York: Monthly Review, 1989), pp. 15–28; Elizabeth Waters, "In the Shadow of the Comintern: The Communist Women's Movement, 1920–43," in Kruks, pp. 29–56; and Lydia Sargent, ed., *Women and Revolution: A Discussion of the Unhappy Marriage of Marxism and Feminism* (Boston: South End P,

Women writers stand out in the discourse of the 1930s left not because they had a different "line"—unformulated or not—on the relation of gender to class or because they "subverted" Marxist orthodoxy, but because they contemplated questions of cultural revolution more fully as a group than did their male colleagues. The female literary radicals raised a series of considerations about consciousness and selfhood that invited their readers to move beyond familiar bourgeois ideological paradigms. By emphasizing the question of reproduction, they directed attention to the conditions under which the working class reproduces itself to serve capitalism and suggested how it should reproduce itself to fight for an egalitarian society. By delineating individual identity as a social phenomenon, they urged their readers not only to rethink their assumptions about fixed male and female potentialities but also to reconsider the very notion of individuality itself, contradistinguishing it from individualism. As Le Sueur remarked in her riposte to Horace Gregory's expressions of reluctance about aligning himself with the party,

> I do not feel any subtle equivocation between the individual and the new disciplined groups of the Communist Party. I do not care for the bourgeois "individual" that I am. . . .
>
> Belief is an action for the writer. The writer's action is full belief, from which follows a complete birth, not a fascistic abortion, but a creation of a new nucleus of a communal society in which at last the writer can act fully and not react equivocally. In a new and mature integrity.[32]

Women writers were not burrowers from within against the "official" doctrines of the 1930s left, but its visionary conscience.

1981). Vogel's analysis of the Marxist notion of the "living wage" in relation to women's oppression under capitalism offers productive insights needing further development in Marxist-feminist theory.

32. Le Sueur, "The Fetish of Being Outside," rpt. in Rabinowitz and Nekola, p. 303.

PART TWO

➤

CHAPTER 7

Realism and Didacticism in Proletarian Fiction

It is time to redirect our attention to the subtitle of *Radical Representations*—namely, *Politics and Form in Proletarian Fiction*. Up to this point I have held the term "novel" as a constant in my discussions of 1930s politics, as these relate both to the line and practice of the Communist left in general and to debates over literary proletarianism in particular. I have wanted to indicate that this politics (these politics) is (are) both singular and plural and that a range of positions on a number of questions was accessible to any critic or writer participating in the discourse of the Depression-era left. I have mentioned a number of literary texts, but my methodology has been self-consciously naive, insofar as I have treated these texts as embodiments of, or receptacles for, various themes, ideas, and subject matters.

In future chapters I shall retain the plural signification of "politics" as I consider the relationship between genre and didacticism in a range of proletarian novels. Throughout most of the present chapter, however, I shall for purposes of argument hold the term "politics" constant as I explore various theoretical aspects of novelistic rhetoric. First, I shall examine the current debate over whether or not, as a form historically linked to bourgeois individualism, the novel—in particular, the realistic novel—can be effectively deployed as a vehicle for contesting bourgeois consciousness and articulating class or collective consciousness. In the context of this discussion of the politics *of* the novel, I shall set forth my reasons for using a typology based on genre to analyze the proletarian novels discussed in chapters 8 through 11. Second, I shall explain here the key narratological concepts that I shall use in investigating how politics can be expressed *in* the novel form. I shall theorize the principal strategies by which didacticism can be embedded or declared in the form of the novel and speculate about the specific benefits and impediments that these strategies may present to the writer of proletarian fiction.

Throughout this discussion I shall be arguing that the proletarian novel is a propagandistic form—not in the general sense that all literature is "propaganda" for one worldview or another (an important point in its own right and one generally conceded by the 1930s literary left), but in the specific sense that the proletarian novel is motivated by didactic aims. The 1930s Marxists for the most part denied that proletarian novels were propaganda; subsequent critics have dismissed these texts as propaganda. In my view, it is no insult to state that proletarian writers were writing propaganda; indeed, if one embraces a conception of *critique engagée* and shares some of the goals and commitments of the 1930s literary left, the term can be complimentary. But to call a body of literature propaganda entails an obligation to analyze it as such. In this chapter I shall develop and explain the main theoretical premises and analytical categories that will be used throughout my discussion of the relation of politics to form in the different genres of proletarian fiction.

Macroanalysis: Politics, Realism, and the Novel Form

The 1930s literary radicals frequently remarked that literary proletarianism entailed a challenge not only to bourgeois thought but to bourgeois aesthetic conventions as well. The editors of John Reed Club-sponsored magazines, we will recall, spoke of the necessity for cultivating new forms to reflect the "rhythms of the new order." Mike Gold wrote of "proletarian realism" as a "new form." Hicks proclaimed that Dos Passos's kaleidoscopic technique in *U.S.A.* had "shown the way" for other proletarian writers. Mary Heaton Vorse compared her own and Grace Lumpkin's conventionally realistic representations of the Gastonia strike with Rollins's treatment in *The Shadow Before* and proclaimed the superiority of Rollins's experimental method. "Everyone who is interested in the new forms of writing and the labor movement should read this exciting book," she declared, "and see how much closer to the truth the author has gone than have any of his predecessors."[1]

Various Soviet theorists participating in the debates of the 1928–31 "cultural revolution," as well as some European commentators writing during

1. Mary Heaton Vorse, review of *The Shadow Before*, NM 11 (April 17, 1934): 6.

the 1930s, took the position that relinquishing inherited narrative forms was not just a future option, but a present necessity, for writers interested in promoting revolutionary change. Soviet critics of the doctrine that fiction should represent the "living man" held that "psychologism" reintroduced bourgeois ideology through the back door. Inherited forms such as the novel, LEF critics asserted, were " 'microbes of a social influence which is alien and harmful.' " The alternative, urged Tretiakov and other members of the left within RAPP, was to create documentary forms in which "[n]othing was to be made up out of the writer's head." The British Communist novelist Edward Upward noted that "speculation about future literary forms is idle unless it is accompanied by the realisation that already now the old forms can no longer adequately reflect the fundamental forces of the modern world. The writer's job is to create new forms now, to arrive by hard work at the emotional truth about present-day reality." Ernst Ottwalt, an opponent of Georg Lukács in the important *Linkskurve* debates of 1931–32 over proletarian literature, criticized inherited literary forms for "striving after a closed-in work of art that is content and complete in itself, and before which the reader is automatically transformed into a hedonist consumer, drawing no conclusions and being satisfied with what is given to him." The goal of proletarian literature, Ottwalt insisted, was "not [to] stabiliz[e] the consciousness of the readers: it seeks to alter it." Brecht, who more than any other figure is associated with the advocacy of forms defamiliarizing old ideological paradigms, argued that "[m]ethods become exhausted; stimuli no longer work. New problems appear and demand new methods. Reality changes; in order to represent it, modes of representation must also change. Nothing comes from nothing; the new comes from the old, but that is why it is new." These theorists and commentators may have differed about what new forms—documentary, collectivist, or otherwise experimental—would most successfully replace the genres dominant in capitalist society. But they were agreed that the production of social revolution enabled, and was enabled by, the production of revolutionary forms of representation—and that continuing to use inherited forms would in fact impede the promotion of revolutionary consciousness.[2]

2. Herman Ermolaev, *Soviet Literary Theories 1917–1934: The Genesis of Socialist Realism*, U of California Publications in Modern Philology, vol. 69 (Berkeley and Los Angeles: U of California P, 1963), p. 75; Matthew Josephson, "The Role of the Writer in

By contrast, the Americans' enthusiasm for experimental forms did not generally lead them to the conclusion that new forms were in any way necessary to the project of the proletarian literary artist. Most U.S. literary radicals operated from the assumption that the novel form, despite its historical association with bourgeois individualism, carried with it little political baggage. Writers should be congratulated for achieving breakthroughs in style or structure, but their failure to do so was no demerit: the old forms would do perfectly well. Eva Goldbeck, in her review of *Somebody in Boots*, noted that in Algren's text the "technique and emotional attitude" were "those of the biographical novel, which is considered a typically bourgeois product; but of course the account of an individual's reaction to the world is classless." Moishe Nadir argued that there was no necessity for cultivating new forms in the present, since changes in form would inevitably accompany a revolutionized society: "In a time of social upheaval and revolution there is really no time to be concerned with revolutionary art forms," he declared. "Far more important is it to employ all current art forms, as a means to a revolutionary end, which forms themselves are subject to undergo a complete revolution, as soon as our final aim is achieved." Hicks, in his influential "Revolution and the Novel" series in the *New Masses*, argued forthrightly that the novel form is "flexibl[e]" and "lends itself to many purposes and all points of view." Even though the novel "has closely corresponded to the rise of the bourgeoisie and has fully expressed . . . the mind of the bourgeoisie, it cannot be limited to any

the Soviet Union," *American Writers Congress*, ed. Henry Hart (New York: International, 1935), hereinafter *AWC*, p. 41; Edward Upward, "Sketch for a Marxist Interpretation of Literature," in C. Day Lewis, ed., *The Mind in Chains: Socialism and the Cultural Revolution* (London: Frederick Muller, 1937), p. 54; Ernst Ottwalt quoted in Georg Lukács, *Essays in Realism*, ed. Rodney Livingstone, trans. David Fernbach (Cambridge, Mass.: MIT P, 1980), pp. 66, 65; Bertolt Brecht, "Against Georg Lukács," trans. Stuart Hood, in Ernst Bloch, et al., eds., *Aesthetics and Politics* (London: NLB, 1977), p. 82. Stanley Mitchell, commenting on the importance of experimental aesthetics to the European cultural left, notes, "Throughout the left-wing avant-garde art of the twenties and thirties, the belief predominated that to attack and repudiate 'illusionism' or 'representation' itself constituted a progressive political act, constituted *the* way in which politics could enter directly into art. This belief continues to affect all radical and left thinking on aesthetics today" (Introduction, Walter Benjamin, *Understanding Brecht*, ed. Mitchell, trans. Anna Bostock [London: Verso, 1983], p. xvi).

one class." In fact, according to Hicks, the novel "is not a form at all," but instead "a term . . . describing a great variety of literary forms." For Hicks and other U.S. commentators on proletarian literature, the association of the novel with bourgeois ideology was historical, but merely historical: the form's past usage did not significantly determine its present or future capacities.[3]

Hicks, Gold, and their colleagues on the *New Masses* (and those on the *Partisan Review!*) would no doubt be shocked if they were to step out of the grave for a day, visit an MLA Convention, and listen in on the attacks on the novel form—or at least on its dominant mode, realism—that have become a staple of literary-critical discourse in the past decade. While different postmodernist theorists claim different intellectual and political lineages, three figures exercise predominant influence in what can be called the postmodernist critique of novelistic realism. The first is Roland Barthes, whose early polemics against the "readerly" text—premised to a significant degree upon a critique of the "closed character of Stalinist language"—have called into question the covert authoritarianism presumably embedded in an aesthetic of transparency. The second is Louis Althusser, whose Lacanian theorization of the illusory "subjectivity" supplied by Ideology has furnished the basis for querying both the positioning of the reader as well as the notion of "character" undergirding realistic representation. The third of these is Brecht, who—albeit through one-sided readings that often turn him into a protodeconstructionist and efface his Communist political commitments—is frequently invoked as a champion of open-ended and disjunctive literary forms that require constant intellection and probing on the part of a text's audience. "The continuity of the ego is a myth. Man is an atom that continually breaks up and forms anew": Brecht's radical apprehension of the contradictions inherent in selfhood is taken as the epistemological ground for an exclusive validation of representation as rupture or interrogation. The premise of the postmodernist position is that there is no "reality" beyond textuality against which to

3. Moishe Nadir, "The Writer in a Minority Language," in *American Writers Congress*, p. 156; Hicks, "Revolution and the Novel" (1934; rpt. in Jack Allan Robbins, ed., *Granville Hicks in the New Masses* [Port Washington, NY: Kennikat, 1974], p. 19). The review by Goldbeck was written for the *Nation* but apparently never published; it can be found among the papers of Goldbeck's husband, the composer Marc Blitzstein (Box 10, Blitzstein Papers, Wisconsin State Historical Society).

measure a text's truth-value. Thus the text conducts its battles against authoritarianism and repression not primarily in its partisan representation of social conflict in its "real-world" referent, but through its adoption of strategies of subversion in the zone of textuality itself. Ideological class struggle is displaced onto the text's conflicting rhetorical maneuvers of resistance and control, subversion and recuperation.[4]

Because it has exercised considerable influence upon recent commentary on politics and the novel in general and of proletarian (or working-class or socialist) fiction in particular, the postmodernist critique of realism should be subjected to careful scrutiny. The main line of argument goes something like this. (1) Realism sets up a pseudo-debate in texts by erecting a *hierarchy of discourses*: one position is established in advance as preferable to others. The narrative may give the impression of open-endedness, but the ideological dice are loaded. The text may pretend to dialogism but in reality is monologic. (2) Realism contains and forecloses contradiction specifically through its movement toward *closure*, which enlists the momentum of the narrative to "prove" the irrefutable superiority of the discourse occupying the peak of the hierarchy of discourses. What looks like a natural product of narrative causality is an ideological product of presupposition. (3) Realism promotes asocial and ahistorical conceptions of personal development by fetishizing *character* as a function of intrinsic "traits." Selfhood is presented not as a product of social relations, but as an emanation of a priori identity. The social environment provides either a mere backdrop to personal dilemmas—"setting"—or else a context *in opposition to which* individuals are defined. (4) Realism conflates the spheres of personal morality and political value. Individual moral change, the principal "development" outlined in most novels, is offered as the key to—or, really, the substitute for—larger social change. (5) Realism implicates the reader in a specious sense of freedom. Not only are characters

<hr>

4. Roland Barthes, *Writing Degree Zero*, trans. Annette Lavers and Colin Smith (London: Cape, 1967), and *S/Z*, trans. Richard Miller (New York: Hill and Wang, 1974); Louis Althusser, "Ideology and Ideological State Apparatuses," in *Lenin and Philosophy and Other Essays*, trans. Ben Brewster (New York and London: Monthly Review, 1971), pp. 127–80; Brecht cited in Catherine Belsey, *Critical Practice* (New York and London: Methuen, 1980). Fredric Jameson notes that participants in the "Brecht-Industrie" frequently forget Brecht's open hostility to "purely formal experimentation" (Jameson, *The Ideologies of Theory: Essays 1971–1986*, 2 vols. [Minneapolis: U of Minnesota P, 1988], 1:142).

falsely constructed as autonomous individuals, but readers are also flattered into thinking of themselves as coconspirators of the author. Readers of realistic texts are led to feel that they are making up their own minds as they read, while actually their minds are being made up for them.[5]

According to a number of its contemporary critics, then, realism turns out to be just the opposite of what it pretends to be. Rather than offering a pluralistic discourse that objectively analyzes social and moral complexities, it implicates the reader in a hegemonic discourse that discourages critical or skeptical thinking. It is coercive and authoritarian. It is, in fact, not a means of contesting dominant ideology, but itself quintessentially ideological discourse.

The implications of this argument for proletarian fiction should be apparent. The logic of the postmodernist critique of realism is that, hard as they might have tried to make realism serve the ends of an oppositional—even a revolutionary—politics, the proletarian novelists were doomed in advance by their adherence to an intrinsically conservative and repressive mode of writing. The political line explicitly urged in a text—the necessity for militant participation in class struggle, the falsity of petty bourgeois aspirations, even the desirability of Communism as an alternative to capitalism—cannot move the reader leftward if it is embedded in a discursive mode premised upon a bourgeois epistemology and bourgeois assumptions about selfhood. Indeed, the very posture of political certainty encouraged by realistic form produces an effect of ideological closure: if a text wishes to query the existing order of things in a thoroughgoing way, it must itself adopt what Catherine Belsey calls an "interrogative" form, that is, one that decenters all putatively authoritative expressions of politics. Despite its posture of confronting and unmasking reactionary idealisms with an unflinching portraiture of "what is," the argument goes, realism turns out to be not an ally but an antagonist to the project of literary radicalism. However left-wing their intentions, proletarian writers who work in the form of the realistic novel end up confirming the very world order that they originally set out to oppose.[6]

5. This critique of realism is a composite of positions taken by Belsey, pp. 56–84, and Lennard J. Davis, *Resisting Novels: Ideology and Fiction* (New York and London: Methuen, 1987).

6. Not all contemporary theorists of the novel dismiss realism as monologic and authoritarian. In particular, apostles of M. M. Bakhtin propose that the novel form—

Some commentators argue that the proletarian novel never managed to break out of the mold of the realistic novel and that formal conservatism doomed the genre to political and literary inefficacy. Stanley Aronowitz traces the "formulaic" nature of the "execrable" proletarian novel to the genre's commitment to "social realism." Because "from 1930 onwards the spirit of revolutionary experimentation, in form as well as in content, was extirpated from Communist literature," Aronowitz claims, the proletarian novel was consigned to imitating the nineteenth-century historical novel, of which it was merely a "pulp fiction" caricature. Valentine Cunningham, discussing the "failure" of the British proletarian novel, argues that the formal traditionalism of Soviet socialist realism "helped to slow down literary experimentation and to smash up modernism especially in the novel, thus pushing the novel back beyond Henry James into the arms of nineteenth-century bourgeois naturalism." Roy Johnson contends that worker-writers were defeated by the overwhelming influence of bourgeois realism. The proletarian writer, he opines, is placed in a "fragile, almost unbearable position," insofar as "he feels that he must try to register his human experience in all its distinctive difference but is drawn irresistibly towards the models of middle-class literary expression that are constantly before him." For these critics, the pressure to write in traditional realistic style doomed proletarian novelists, who were too timid and inexperienced

---

including realism in all its modes—is intrinsically dialogic, allowing for the interplay and struggle of contending voices. For example, feminist critic Diane Price Herndl, citing Bakhtin's concept of novelistic heteroglossia, argues that the novel is historically a "feminine genre" and that "[n]ovelistic discourse achieves a state of non-definability, of otherness, of freedom from hierarchy" ("The Dilemmas of a Feminine Dialogic," in *Feminism, Bakhtin, and the Dialogic*, ed. Dale M. Bauer and Susan Janet Mckinstry [Albany: State UP of New York, 1991], pp. 7–24, quoted p. 13). But Herndl, like some other self-professed Bakhtinians, oversimplifies Bakhtin. At times he spoke of the novel as "a genre that is both critical and self-critical . . . in all its openendedness" ("Epic and Novel," in *The Dialogic Imagination: Four Essays*, ed. Michael Holquist, trans. Caryl Emerson and Holquist [Austin: U of Texas P, 1981], pp. 10, 11). But Bakhtin also polemically distinguished what he viewed as Dostoievsky's attainment of a "plural-voiced" novel form from the "monologism" that he saw characterizing all modes of the novel before—and most after— the novelist's time. For Bakhtin, "heteroglossia" did not signify protopoststructuralist subversion and free play, but the contradictory coexistence of different social discourses within a single text (M. M. Bakhtin, *Problems in Dostoievsky's Poetics*, ed. and trans. Caryl Emerson [Minneapolis: U of Minnesota P, 1984], pp. 5–46).

to break out on their own. Lennard J. Davis extends the point even further, arguing that all novels, *qua* novels, "fundamentally resis[t] change." It is quite possible, Davis remarks, "to think, as an author, that you are making a progressive statement with a novel and, at the same time, to have the form of the novel defeat that statement. . . . [A]s soon as an author creates characters, puts them in a place, has them engage in dialogue, and gets embroiled in a plot . . . the novelist is stuck with the baggage of ideology, and no porter in the world is going to be able to help alleviate that problem." For Davis, it is not even realism, but fictional narrative itself, that co-opts and recuperates any gestures of would-be resistance.[7]

Not all contemporary commentators on proletarian fiction have been so quick to conclude that it is impossible to write proletarian fiction. But all carefully circumscribe the zone within which proletarian writers can be said to articulate an emancipatory discourse. Some theorists contend that, even though the form of the classically realistic novel has proven unusable by proletarian writers, other modes of novelistic representation have enabled the effective expression of an oppositional working-class politics. In his introduction to the recent reissue of the collective novel *Marching! Marching!*, for instance, Jon Christian Suggs argues that Weatherwax and other experimental proletarian novelists countered the novel's traditional tendency to "isolat[e] private sensibility from public identity" by adopting anti-individualistic modes of representation. By abandoning focused narrative point of view, a stress on individual fortunes, love plots, and, above all, "settlement of [the] central issue," collective novelists negated "the privileged position that individual destiny occupies in capitalist culture." N. W. Visser, along similar lines, asserts that "formal properties undermine political stance" in texts aspiring to "appropriate the form [of critical realism] for radical purposes." Texts like Wright's *Native Son* and Malraux's *Man's Fate* thus remain—despite their obviously radical intentions—constricted by their "intense focusing on individuals." But novels like Ignazio Silone's *Fontamara* and Victor Serge's *Birth of Our Power* demonstrate the rhetorical resources available to texts departing from standard novelistic formats. These collective texts, Visser notes—in a swipe against the "anti-

7. Stanley Aronowitz, *The Crisis in Historical Materialism: Class, Politics and Culture in Marxist Theory* (New York: Praeger, 1981), p. 234; Valentine Cunningham, *British Writers of the Thirties* (Oxford and New York: Oxford UP, 1988), p. 99; Roy Johnson, "The Proletarian Novel," *Literature and History* 2, no. 2 (1975): 91; Davis, p. 228.

humanism of Althusser"—do not "decente[r] the subject, effectively precluding any possibility of individual human agency, and hence of praxis."
They "neither den[y] individual agency nor eliminat[e] interiority in [their]
characters." But by adopting a collectivist mode that stresses at all times
the group-nature of individual consciousness, these novels "situat[e] the
subject and the subject's interiority fully within the horizons of their social
determinations," thereby "socializing . . . the self." According to Suggs and
Visser, the novel form is protean enough to allow for the effective articulation of radical attitudes and ideas. It is only outmoded and ideologically
saturated genres such as the bildungsroman and the novel of social realism
that entrap writers in a bourgeois epistemological—and political—web.[8]

   Other critics have argued that novelistic realism—even of the most classical type—has been and can still be deployed for left-wing political purposes. Typically, however, these critics make their case in qualified and
apologetic terms; realism is on the defensive. Peter Hitchcock, for example,
expresses strong agreement with Belsey's argument about the conservative implications of novelistic realism before he demurs, "What is important in theorizing working-class fiction is not form for form's sake, but the
struggles over form. . . . The interrogative text of which Belsey writes may
be antirealist in the classic sense, but nevertheless we should entertain
the possibility that such a text may still be realist." H. Gustav Klaus notes
that it is mechanical and ahistorical to insist that the politics motivating a
text cannot counter whatever ideological pressures may be intrinsic to its
inherited genre:

> Form, whether as narrative mode or technical device, is doubtless a carrier
> of ideology. However, form is not the only [ideological] constituent of a text,
> and it is, above all, not some kind of cosmic, transhistorical category im-
> mune to change. Hence to accord an ultimate determinant effect, or even
> priority, to inherited forms is an abstract and constricting conception leading
> to formalism in the denigratory sense of the term.

Nonetheless, Klaus concedes that representing individuality has always
posed a real and serious problem to writers of what he calls "socialist fiction." The "positive hero" of socialist fiction can be substituted for the

   8. Christian Suggs, "Introduction" to *Marching! Marching!* (Detroit: Omnigraphics,
Proletarian Literature Series, 1990), p. xxiii; N. W. Visser, "The Novel as Liberal Narrative: The Possibilities of Radical Fiction," *Works and Days* 3 (1985): 7–28.

"problematic hero" of the bildungsroman, Klaus concludes, only at the risk of effacing "the central fact of the class struggle to the lives of individuals." Hitchcock and Klaus hedge their support for left-wing realistic fiction by postulating a tension between form and idea: even if inherited novelistic conventions pull a text to the right, its doctrinal content may pull it back to the left. There is, however, no way of knowing in advance which side in the dialectic will prevail.[9]

Occasionally among contemporary commentators on proletarian fiction one even encounters the argument that idea is determining and form subordinate. Peter Widdowson remarks that the liberal humanism which had previously generated and sustained the individualism of the novel entered into a period of "ideological crisis" in the 1930s. As a consequence, he asserts, the novel, without relinquishing its formal commitment to representing individual experience, was "forced . . . to expand in an attempt to find a strategy for engaging directly with the large processes of society which form and control the individuals within it." Carole Snee takes issue with the "dominant critical practice [which] argues that because the realist novel has been concerned historically with the individual, and its narrative structures operate through one—or a series of—individual consciousnesses, its philosophy is always essentially 'liberal.'" Indeed, she points out, "the working class may have a different perception of the individual, and what constitutes individuality." Accordingly, the realistic novel "does not simply at best reveal and interrogate the dominant, unstated ideology, or exist uncritically within it, but can also incorporate a *conscious* ideological or class perspective, which in itself undercuts the ideological parameters of the genre, without necessarily transforming its structural boundaries." Widdowson and Snee recapitulate some of the formal agnosticism of a Hicks: form is secondary, politics primary. But they do not recapitulate the *New Masses* critic's sense that form is *neutral*. If a realistic text is successfully to articulate left-wing politics, it must subvert or

9. Peter Hitchcock, *Working-Class Fiction in Theory and Practice: A Reading of Alan Sillitoe* (Ann Arbor, London: UMI, 1989), p. 97; Klaus, Introduction, *The Socialist Novel in Britain: Towards the Recovery of a Tradition*, ed. Klaus (New York: St. Martin's P, 1982), p. 2; Klaus, *The Literature of Labor, Two Hundred Years of Working-Class Writing* (New York: St. Martin's P, 1985), p. 127. See also George Goodin, *The Poetics of Protest: Literary Form and Political Implication in the Victim-of-Society Novel*, esp. "Conclusion: Literary Form and Political Implication," pp. 191–96.

otherwise counter the "ideological parameters of the genre," which are ir-remediably bourgeois. If a text conveys left-wing politics, this happens in spite of, rather than because of, its realistic form.[10]

Having outlined the current debate over the politics of realism, I owe it to my readers to indicate the hypothesis that shapes my own inquiry. As a programmatic stance, the postmodernist attack on realism is, as Klaus points out, formalistic and ahistorical. One must ask: Can the inherited conventions accompanying any genre so decisively shape the political effect of a text that the ideas and subject matters embedded in its narrative are cancelled out? Can any form, however rooted in a historically determinate epistemology and politics, be seen to undergo no change at all when it is deployed by different sorts of people under different circumstances for different purposes? Moreover, postmodernism's antipathy to centered subjects—whether characters or readers—is politically regressive. Even if traditional novelistic realism does promote bourgeois conceptions of self-hood, the desired alternative is not, one may object, the dissolution of subjectivity as such, but the construction and articulation of oppositional subjectivities. It is difficult to imagine how proletarian fiction could address the issue of revolution without positing the proletariat as a centered subject, constituted by coherent individual subjectivities. If the proletariat is to make a bid for power, and if narratives are to represent it as the agent of this bid, it must in some sense be centered. Pace the critics of class reductionism, centeredness does not, as a feature of epistemological and political subject position, a priori entail a bourgeois conception of individuality. Finally, the postmodernist disdain for narrative resolution can carry the problematic implication that resolution of any kind is a bad thing. But openendedness is, one might note, as openendedness does: its automatic privileging can involve a reintroduction of New Critical canons of ambiguity and irony, with the concomitant thesis (and not-so-covert anti-

10. Peter Widdowson, "Between the Acts? English Fiction in the Thirties," in Jon Clark et al., eds., *Culture and Crisis in Britain in the Thirties* (London: Lawrence and Wishart, 1979), p. 135; Carole Snee, "Working-Class Literature or Proletarian Writing?" in Clark, pp. 168–69. A number of the British critics writing about proletarian fiction make a distinction between "working-class" writing (authored by workers) and "proletarian" writing (having a left-wing perspective). See Raymond Williams, "Working-Class, Proletarian, Socialist: Problems in Some Welsh Novels," in Klaus, ed., *The Socialist Novel in Britain*, pp. 110–21.

Communist message) that political certainty of any kind is antipathetic to genuine literary richness or depth.

Clearly I do not agree with an across-the-board postmodernist assault upon novelistic realism, for this can only result in an abrupt dismissal of the great majority of proletarian novels. Indeed, there would be no point in writing *Radical Representations* if I felt that the novel form as such is so irretrievably bourgeois as to make "proletarian fiction" a contradiction in terms. Nor would there be much point if I were to reserve my admiration only for texts that can be termed "experimental," since the great majority of proletarian novels are realistic in the traditional sense of the word. Nonetheless, each of the separate points in the postmodernist critique of realism warrants careful consideration in any critical reevaluation of the proletarian novel. The only possible move is not a Lukácsian reassertion of realism's privileged capacity to interpret and represent social reality. The tendency of realistic narrative to dissolve contradiction in the movement toward closure; its characteristic opposition of the social to the personal, and its displacement of social critique onto personal ethical choice; its insistence upon the uniqueness, and often the superiority, of its protagonist(s); its co-optation of the reader into agreement with the discourse occupying the apex of the text's implied hierarchy of discourses— these defining features of novelistic realism can indeed undermine, if not cancel out, the proletarian novel's espoused political commitments. The postmodernist critique of realism requires theoretical acknowledgment and response.

I find myself more in sympathy with various forms of the "tendency" position voiced by critics who grant the limitations of conventional realism in articulating an oppositional politics but who still argue that many proletarian texts do manage to give fictional embodiment to such a politics. What I stipulate, however, is that politics in the plural sense must here enter the theoretical discussion. There is no way of knowing in advance the degree to which a text deploying traditionally realistic narrative conventions will succumb to the pressure exerted by these conventions. In terms of political effect, where any given text ends up is a function of both its form and its "line," as well as of the class struggle that fights itself out between them. I am hypothesizing here that texts will more readily resist generic pressures toward bourgeois ideology—containment of contradiction, for example, or fetishization of personality—if they are anchored in a "left" as opposed to a reformist or economist doctrine. To use Snee's formulation: conventionally realistic texts will "undercut the ideological parameters of the[ir] genre[s]" and contest the "liberal" paradigm insofar as they propose "a *conscious* ideological or class perspective." Clearly it will be easier for a text to articulate a revolutionary politics if it is relatively unburdened by the ideological baggage of bourgeois literary practice. But texts making use of formally "revolutionary" narrative modes are by no means guaranteed to produce "left" effects. An author who has shrugged off various bourgeois preconceptions about representation may still adhere to any number of bourgeois ideas about capitalism, class struggle, and communism.

If we endorse the "tendency" thesis—and I think this is the only reasonable position to take—we must therefore insist that discussions of the ideologies embedded in genres always be linked to discussions of the specific politics encoded in specific proletarian novels. In particular, in determining the pressure points in proletarian novels, we should look to pressure points in the doctrinal politics of the 1930s left. Ambiguities in the relation between race and class with regard to the "Negro question"; vacillating or uneven commitment to women's emancipation, especially with regard to the definition of the "domestic sphere"; general ambivalence between revolutionary goals on the one hand, workerism and spontaneism on the other—these key areas of irresolution in the line and practice of the CP enter texts, we may speculate, not just as "content," but as premises influencing various "formal" options. "Tendency" is best understood, in other words, as the intersection of *generic politics* and *doctrinal politics*. And both these terms are plural as well as singular, signifying a range of ideological tendencies within different genres and a range of possible political positions.

The need to get at the interplay between generic politics and doctrinal politics structures my mode of inquiry in Part II of *Radical Representations*. This inquiry will proceed as an investigation of four generically defined novelistic subspecies: fictional autobiography, bildungsroman, social novel, and collective novel. These groupings focus attention on novelistic genre as both a formal and a historical phenomenon. The two middle categories—bildungsroman and social novel—belong squarely within the bourgeois tradition of critical realism. The first and last categories—fictional autobiography and collective novel—represent novelistic modes that, to different degrees, encourage the writer to experiment with non-traditional ways of representing proletarian experience and articulating left-wing politics. Each chapter will, first, analyze the ways that texts of a given genre articulate left-wing politics. The discussion will then examine how embedded ideological tendencies of each genre impede the articulation of a revolutionary stance. Each chapter will close with a discussion of generic politics in relation to doctrinal politics and an assessment of the particular resources and impediments accompanying each genre.

I am aware that my decision to organize this discussion by generic taxonomy leaves me open to the charge of formalism. I acknowledge that my groupings by no means furnish the only valid categories for approaching proletarian novels. If I chose to address other aspects of the political discourse in proletarian novels, other analytical categories might well be more appropriate. A conceptual framework structured around categories such as male/female, black/white, rural/urban, or middle-class/working-class would doubtless prove more useful in getting at issues centering on authorial subject position. A taxonomy (such as Rideout's) that is based on key themes—strike novels, tales of conversion, accounts of the proletarianized petty bourgeoisie—would get at crucial considerations of subject matter. A paradigm based on categories such as reformist/revolutionary, fellow traveler/party, and Third Period/Popular Front would help to focus more directly on questions of political doctrine. My decision to approach proletarian novels through the analytical paradigm of genre reflects my concern with the politics of form. But it does not signal formalism in the pejorative sense. Recognizing that ideology is to one degree or another embedded in all modes of discourse, my conceptual schema asks: how determining is this influence? In asking this question, I am attempting not to establish the *priority* of form, but simply to query its relation to doctrine.

Readers familiar with the 1930s literary left will note the correspondence of my categories with those proposed by Hicks in his influential "Revolution and the Novel" *New Masses* series. His "biographical" novel overlaps with my two genres of single-protagonist fiction, the fictional autobiography and the bildungsroman. His "complex" novel closely approximates my "social" novel. The term "collective novel" is common to us both. In consciously drawing part of my analytical paradigm from Hicks, I am not claiming a particular historical privilege for his terms; that is, I am not claiming that writers had his categories in mind when they wrote their novels. Nor am I endorsing Hicks's agnosticism on the issue of generic politics. Hicks was attempting to write a "how to" manual for aspiring novelists: any novelistic genre, in his view, could be readily turned to revolutionary political ends. I am querying this premise. Nonetheless, Hicks's categories remain useful because of their link to practice, past and present. In his open letter to writers whom he was inviting to do reviews for the *New Masses*, we will recall, Hicks declared that "[e]very one of us believes that the capitalist system must be destroyed by the power of the proletariat, in alliance with the exploited farmers, the ruined middle class and the aroused intellectual and professional class. . . . Every one is resolved to support the workers and poor farmers of America wherever they are struggling against injustice, starvation, and oppression. And these convictions and this determination are fundamental, the very basis of [our] attitudes and judgments." Hicks was asking: given a writer's revolutionary commitment, what formal options are available to him/her for representing and articulating that commitment?

It is difficult in the 1990s to share Hicks's optimism. Skepticism—about doctrines, about discourses—is the order of the day. But the social crisis to which Hicks and his colleagues were responding abides; his political commitment remains relevant. Moreover, writers continue to compose novels expressing the desire for revolutionary change. Despite Hicks's naïveté with regard to what we now call textual politics, his categories still offer a useful starting point for an investigation of politics and form in the novel and, passed through the grid of 1990's skepticism, may offer useful guideposts to aspiring left-wing writers.

Microanalysis: Narratology and Didacticism

If we wish to determine how politics gain articulation in narrative texts, generalizations about politics and the novel form—even about particular genres of novelistic form and particular political doctrines—will take us only so far. At best categories based on genre provide macroanalytical insight into novelistic strategy. If we wish to speak with any tactical precision about how specific proletarian novels produce specific political effects, it is necessary to use a terminology that permits us to examine issues of fictional rhetoric—characterization, action, voice, point of view—in greater detail.

It may come as a surprise to some readers that I find such a terminology in the discipline of narratology. Narratology might seem to epitomize the formalist and ahistoricist approach to literary texts. Plots are ripped from historically determinate contexts, dismembered, and reassembled on archetypal screens; sentences are dissected for their presentation of duration, summary, or focalization, but rarely treated as articulations of larger ideological discourses. In spite of their frequent deployment in narrowly technical exercises, however, certain terms and concepts from narratology can provide the critic with precise instruments for determining exactly how readers are being positioned to respond to an author's assertions and assumptions. As Susan Suleiman has demonstrated in her narratological study of didactic fiction, there is only a small distance to travel from determining formally how readers are positioned to analyzing the political consequences of this positioning.[11]

A fundamental distinction between "story" and "discourse" provides the basis for all narratological investigations. Seymour Chatman summarizes the distinction succinctly: "The what of narrative I call its 'story'; the way I call its 'discourse.'" First formulated by the Russian Formalists as the relation of "fabula" to "sujet," the "story"/"discourse" distinction signifies the difference between the basic *elements* of character and event that constitute the building blocks of the narrative and the *treatment* of these elements. In its "widest sense," Émil Benveniste declares, "'discourse'" signifies "every utterance assuming a speaker and a hearer, and in the speaker, the intention of influencing the other in some way." Whereas "'story,'" is, Gérard Genette notes, in "purely linguistic terms . . . objective," "'discourse'" is "subjective," in that it denotes language expressing the opinions and attitudes of some subject. Perhaps it goes without

---

11. Susan Rubin Suleiman, *Authoritarian Fictions: The Ideological Novel as a Literary Genre* (New York: Columbia UP, 1983). Readers familiar with Suleiman's work will note its influence upon my analytical scheme for approaching proletarian fiction. I disagree with Suleiman's thesis that "authoritarian" novels of the right and the left pursue didactic strategies that can be considered formally equivalent. Nonetheless, I am indebted to her insights into the formal procedures of self-consciously "ideological" fiction. Throughout this discussion of premise and declaration in proletarian literature, I have also been influenced by Peter J. Rabinowitz's work on fictional audiences ("Truth in Fiction: A Reexamination of Audiences," *Critical Inquiry* 4 [Autumn 1973]: 121–41, and "Assertion and Assumption: Fictional Patterns and the External World," *PMLA* 96 [May 1981]: 408–19).

saying that "story" and "discourse" are separable only for analytical purposes: "In practice," as Benveniste remarks, "one passes from one to the other instantaneously."[12]

"Story" and "discourse" comprise separate functions. The domain of "story," according to Chatman's distillation of Genette's schema, is constituted by "existents" and "events." The term "existents" signifies "characters" or "settings" (including "contexts" in the general sense). "Events" signifies "actions" (performances by characters) and "happenings" (occurrences without agents). In terms of their centrality to a narrative, "events" can also be divided into "kernels" (crucial elements) and "satellites" (non-crucial, though aesthetically useful, elements). Even though, in a narrative of any complexity, "story" rarely manifests itself in "pure" form, it is useful as an analytical category insofar as it enables the theorist to point out paradigmatic—the unsympathetic term is "formulaic"—plot types underlying apparently diverse and unique instances of narrative. "Story" thus signifies building blocks of narrative that are in a sense prelinguistic. Even though they are known only through language, these fundamental elements exist apart from their particular linguistic encoding and can imaginably be represented by means of alternate encodings.[13]

The domain of "discourse" takes in "narration," "focalization," and "temporal organization." "Narration" comprises a number of functions, including addressing the reader, interpreting characters and events, and testifying to the narrator's own authority. Whether a narrator enters into wise and witty collusion with the reader or maintains a posture of neutrality; whether a narrator conveys the thoughts of characters in a way suggesting approbation or skepticism—the study of such aspects of a text's rhetoric takes us into the domain of "narration." The term "focalization" refers to the vantage point from which the narrative is being told—pri-

12. Seymour Chatman, *Story and Discourse: Narrative Structure in Fiction and Film* (Ithaca: Cornell UP, 1978), p. 9; Emil Benveniste, *Problems in General Linguistics*, trans. Mary Elizabeth Meek (Coral Gables, Fla.: U of Miami P, 1971), p. 209; Gérard Genette, *Figures of Literary Discourse*, trans. Alan Shencken (New York: Columbia UP, 1982), p. 138. When I place the terms "story" and "discourse" between quotation marks, I signify the specialized narratological meanings of the terms; otherwise I intend their routine usage.

13. Chatman, pp. 43–145. For more on "prelinguistic" elements in fiction, see James Phelan, *Worlds from Words: A Theory of Language in Fiction* (Chicago: U of Chicago P, 1981).

marily whether that of one character or many. "Focalization" comprises not only narrative point of view (first-person, third-person broad or limited omniscient, etc.) but also "perspective" in a more general sense. If a text unfolds in such a way that one character's interests predominate over those of other characters—regardless of narrative point of view—this is an aspect of the text's focalization. "Temporal organization" refers to matters such as the order in which events are told (whether or not flashbacks are used, for instance) and the duration of these events (whether, for instance, they are summarized or rendered in completely dramatized scenes). "Temporal organization" may seem inseparable from the sequence of events constituting "story," but it warrants analytical differentiation. A novelist's decision to narrate one event in detail but to summarize another concisely, for instance, may have a significant effect upon the reader's partisan identification with certain characters or issues.[14]

As I have outlined them here, the analytical categories of "story" and "discourse" do not in themselves tell us much about how an author is attempting to influence a reader's social attitudes and political views. In the hands of a Propp or a Todorov, the designation of paradigmatic plot types is a fairly abstract and ahistorical proposition. And discourse analysis, as any student of linguistics knows, is routinely quite far removed from matters of politics. Indeed, in response to the criticism lodged by Wayne Booth and other ethical critics that discourse analysis lacks a moral perspective, Genette has unabashedly asserted that he considers himself a "formalist" and an "aesthete." But narratological analysis can be mobilized in penetrating explorations of textual ideology when, as Suleiman demonstrates, it is conjoined with an examination of "redundancy." Stripping the term of the largely negative associations given to it in Barthes' critical analysis of the "readerly" text, Suleiman argues that redundancy signifies patterns of repetition and stress that enable a writer to convey meaning in an unambiguous way. It does not entail tautology but is instead "an essential means of conserving information and an equally essential means of creating syntactic and semantic *coherence*." According to Suleiman, redundancy is

14. Chatman, pp. 146–260; Genette, *Narrative Discourse*, pp. 189–94. "Focalization" should not be collapsed into "point of view," although the two may be closely related. As Chatman notes, "*The perspective and the expression need not be lodged in the same person*" (p. 153).

crucial to the process of narrative persuasion. It operates in all texts, realistic and experimental. But since realism presents itself as transparently reflecting a given reality, analysis of redundancy is particularly crucial to uncovering how a realistic text purveys ideology.[15]

According to Suleiman, there are three principal ways in which redundancy operates to clarify and reinforce narrative meaning in the didactic novel, or *roman à thèse*—on the level of "story" alone, on the level of "discourse" alone, and between the levels of "story" and "discourse." When "kernel" events constitute patterns of thematic repetition, or when characters—as heroes, helpers, mentors, or opponents—are aligned as positive or negative foils to one another, redundancies on the level of "story" display a highly encoded ideological message. In the didactic novel, Suleiman argues, "story"-level redundancies routinely result in two types of paradigmatic plots. The single-protagonist plot is developed around a theme of apprenticeship, which sometimes is successful (the character achieves the desired level of awareness) and sometimes not (the character fails to change in the correct direction, for reasons that are made clear to the reader). The multiple-protagonist plot, by contrast, focuses around a large social confrontation. Here the principal characters' political positions are usually (though not always) established in advance, and the reader's interest derives more from suspense (will the insurgent forces win?) than from vicarious identification with a protagonist's acquisition of knowledge. While the two types of plots develop suspense and depth along different axes, they can overlap to a degree. In *The Land of Plenty*, for example, the confrontation plot built around the strike is largely displaced onto, and resolved by, the story of Johnny Hagen's growth in class consciousness.[16]

Most redundancies on the level of "story" are deeply embedded and convey didacticism implicitly. For example, if two characters with whom the reader identifies face separate dilemmas but arrive at similar solutions, the sheer momentum of the plot attaches value and significance to whatever this answer happens to be. At the end of Conroy's *A World to Win*, the two Hurley brothers, who occupy different class sectors and have been alienated from one another for years, find themselves fighting the police side by side in a Communist-led demonstration for relief. Commentary

15. Genette, *Narrative Discourse Revisited*, trans. Jane E. Lewin (Ithaca: Cornell UP, 1988), pp. 153–54; Suleiman, p. 152.

16. Suleiman, pp. 63–148.

issuing from a point external to "story" is largely unnecessary to make the point that revolutionary organizing provides the only viable solution for worker and petty-bourgeois alike. When "story"-level machinations of plot and character sufficiently articulate and underline the text's doctrine, there is less need for overt declarations from the narrator.

The second type of redundancy—that is, redundancy on the level of "discourse" alone—articulates a text's values by creating (and then fulfilling) certain expectations about how the tale will be told. For example, when the narrator habitually chats with the reader and establishes a bond based upon presumably common values and beliefs, this generally predisposes the reader to have confidence in the narrator's substantive judgments upon characters and events. In Endore's *Babouk*, the narrator's consistent address to the reader as a "you" who inherits the guilt of centuries of slavery operates powerfully to induce the reader to place confidence in the narrator as an authority on the history of the entire slave trade. "Discourse"-level redundancy need not always center on narratorial voice, however. If a narrative consistently adopts the viewpoint of a particular character, the reader's experience of the text is necessarily shaped by identification with the interests of that character. In proletarian bildungsromans that feature the political growth of individual heroes, or in strike novels where certain key characters' vacillating political allegiances furnish ongoing narrative interest, the text's consistent reference to the thoughts and feelings of familiar characters becomes a crucial carrier of the political propositions the author is trying to reinforce. In Myra Page's *Moscow Yankee*, the reader is led to sympathize with Andy, an unemployed Detroit auto worker settling in the USSR, largely through immersion in Andy's confused thoughts. In Walter Havinghurst's *Pier 17*, a novel that moves rapidly among the different viewpoints of different sailors involved in a strike, the reader comes to anticipate that each successive passage conveying the thoughts of Noonan, the seasoned radical, will clarify and deepen the meaning of the developing labor struggle.

In practice, however, redundancies *within* the level of "discourse" are generally hard to separate from the third and principal form that the reinforcement of meaning takes in narratives—namely, redundancies *between* the levels of "story" and "discourse." Since "discourse" comprises a broad range of features of narrative, redundancies between "story" and "discourse" take a variety of forms. The most obvious of these is commentary issuing from a narratorial voice. Any narrator who delivers a running commentary—laconic or polemical, satiric or sentimental—is in a strong position to influence the reader's response to characters and events. As we shall see, such narrators frequently play a major didactic role in proletarian novels. Sometimes narratorial commentary simply underlines or extends points that are implicit in "story"; at other times it reinforces opinions explicitly stated by characters. In *Daughter of Earth*, for example, the narrator-protagonist Marie Rogers, looking back on the lessons she learned from her mentor Sardarji, regrets her inability to absorb and pass on all that he taught her. "Had I been otherwise I might have spoken in words so deep, so true, so convincing, that even people of my country . . . might have listened," she remarks, "and seen that difference of race, color and creed are [sic] as shadows on the face of a stream . . . that subjection of any kind and in any place is beneath the dignity of man." Whether narrators reinforce doctrine embedded in character and event or explicitly signaled in dialogue or monologue, rhetorical overdetermination is the frequent result.[17]

There are other equally important—if more embedded and less obvious—means by which the "way" of a narrative can underline its "what." The use of free indirect discourse to render a character's thoughts provides a crucial means of positioning the reader as an automatic accomplice to the narrator's values. Whether or not the free indirect statement is tagged ("She was depressed: she saw that the strike was losing momentum") or untagged ("She was depressed: the strike was losing momentum"), the effect is much the same: the reader is assumed to hold the belief that it is a bad thing for strikes to weaken. When tagged free indirect discourse is used to indicate a character's adoption of the values of the narrator—usually through the use of expressions such as "realized" or "saw"—the reader is mobilized as a partisan to the doctrine informing the text: "She realized that the victory of the working class was inevitable, regardless of the outcome of the strike." As narratologist Oswald Ducrot notes, "When one places the expression *X knows that* in front of a proposition *p*, it is often simply in order to reinforce the truth of *p*. *X knows that* . . . can, in such cases, almost be considered as a model phrase, analogous to *it is true that*."[18]

"Discourse" also takes in textual maneuvers of selection, compression,

17. Suleiman, pp. 153–71; Agnes Smedley, *Daughter of Earth* (1934; rpt. Old Westbury, NY: Feminist P., 1974), p. 269.

18. Ducrot, cited in Suleiman, p. 75.

and judgment. Adjustments of a text's spatial and temporal dimensions can covertly reinforce central values and ideas. A narrator's decision to give a full scenic portrayal to an episode (describing, say, the blow-by-blow beating of strikers by police) as opposed to a brief summary ("The strikers were beaten back") molds and directs the reader's sympathies. Similarly, the strategic juxtaposition of incidents from the lives of characters who may not even know one another suggests larger interpretive points about the totality into which these characters are inserted. The fact that the auto worker Steve Carson and the radical journalist Victoria Chance never meet in *Rope of Gold,* even in the novel's interspliced climactic scenes, means that the reader is invited to formulate the thematic principle that would make them both "belong" in the same novel. As the prelinguistic raw material constituting the core elements of narrative, "existents" and "events"—workers and bosses locked in struggle, individuals moving toward class consciousness—are clearly saturated in political meaning. But the rhetorical presentation of character and action—through selection, extension, telescoping, juxtaposition—also carries political significance. A text's "how" is as implicated in ideology as its "what."

To summarize: "story" and "discourse" signify different components of narrative, and redundancies within each level or between the two operate in different ways to secure the reader's political allegiance. Patterns of repetition or stress among characters and events tend to produce didacticism on what could be described as an internal or implicit level. Genette asserts that the prelinguistic materials constituting "story" furnish the text's rhetorical essence:

> I do not believe that the techniques of narrative discourse are especially instrumental in producing . . . affective impulses. Sympathy or antipathy for a character depends essentially on the psychological or moral (or physical!) characteristics the author gives [a character], the behavior and speeches he attributes to him, and very little on the techniques of the narrative in which he appears. . . .
>
> The strengths and weaknesses, the graces or disgraces of heroes basically depend on neither the narrative nor the narrator but on the story—that is, the content or . . . the *diegesis.*

To state that elements of "story" function through implicitness is not to assert that they are covert. Readers are more likely to be aware of whether or not they like characters, and why, than of other ideological processes that are going on in novels. But "story"-level didactic elements operate largely through co-optation. If readers wish to read the text at all, they are strongly urged to accede to interlocked sets of values and judgments that need not be explicitly set forth by the narrator.[19]

Redundancies on the level of "discourse," by contrast, or between the levels of "discourse" and "story," tend to display the author's beliefs in quite a different fashion. These more "external," or "explicit," rhetorical elements are not all necessarily more direct or more visible. Free indirect discourse—especially of the "she realized that" variety—can operate as a carrier of propaganda in a relatively covert way, as can the option to juxtapose characters' situations in order to suggest larger principles of unity or irony. But in its most common mode of redundancy—that is, as interpretive commentary by the narrator—"discourse" calls attention to itself as a forum in which authorial opinion can be clearly articulated. *Pace* Genette, choices among techniques for telling a tale *are* frequently saturated in ideological presupposition and *are* "instrumental . . . in producing affective impulses." As I shall show in future chapters, studying the "way" of a text can to a significant degree illuminate its "why."[20]

This fairly straightforward differentiation between "story" and "discourse" is, however, complicated by two types of "story"-level redundancies that quite explicitly point to the doctrine underlying the text and blur any simple distinction between the two levels of narrative—namely, speeches and dialogues. Utterances by "mouthpiece" characters and mentors, coupled with debates and dialogues between these characters and the protagonist(s), furnish one of the principal means by which characters and readers alike are exposed to left-wing political ideas. Since we will be devoting considerable attention to these didactic elements in the chapters that follow, their theoretical status in narrative needs to be clarified.

The status of didactic speeches and dialogues is the subject of some dispute among narratologists. According to Benveniste's definition of "dis-

19. Genette, *Narrative Discourse Revisited*, p. 154; Suleiman, pp. 39–42.

20. Genette's position on this issue shifted between *Narrative Discourse* (1980) and *Narrative Discourse Revisited* (1988). In the first study he wryly noted that the terms "showing" and "telling" "speedily became the Ormazd and the Ahriman of novelistic aesthetics in the Anglo-American normative vulgate." The terms should not be counterposed, he argued. " 'Showing' can only be a way of 'telling' " (*Narrative Discourse*, pp. 163, 166).

course"—"an utterance assuming . . . in the speaker the intention of influencing the [hearer] in some way"—such rhetorical features are logically components of "discourse." For Genette, too, speeches and dialogues belong more properly under the rubric of "discourse" than under that of "story." The "ideological function" is, Genette maintains, the only narratorial function that "does not of necessity revert to the narrator"; it is possible to "transfer onto some of [the] characters the task of commentary and didactic discourse." Chatman, by contrast, argues that "[e]ven when a character is telling a story within the main story [or, we might add, espousing a view], his speech acts always inhabit the story, rather than the primary discourse." For Chatman, speeches and dialogues are not the object of narratorial commentary; they reach the reader in a direct and unmediated fashion. The speech acts of characters are ontologically contained within the text's fictive domain and must remain logically distinct from the text's "primary discourse," which unambiguously signals authorial values.[21]

To dwell upon this debate may seem to be splitting narratological hairs. But the basic issue involved is not trivial. On the one hand, Benveniste and Genette are right to point out that speeches and dialogues provide a conduit for authorial declarations. When a left-wing character in a proletarian novel gives a speech about the necessity for waging class struggle, or when a seasoned organizer engages naive workers in argument, there is little likelihood that these articulations are subjected to ironic distancing. Barring the exceptional text like Steinbeck's In Dubious Battle, which signals highly ambiguous attitudes toward its Communist-organizer protagonists, proletarian novels are usually fairly clear about where the reader's approval should be directed. Yet Chatman correctly insists that such rhetorical elements are nonetheless part of "story." For implicit in the representation of left-wing speeches and dialogues as part of the novel's ontological domain—and in their being shown to have dramatic impact upon the lives of individuals—is the notion that such "discourses" are in fact a plausible and typical feature of the U.S. political landscape of the 1930s. Even if "preaching" narrators and "preaching" characters make the same points, they do so in crucially different ways. When a text relies on the narrator rather than on a character or characters to perform this task, talk about revolution is not necessarily part of the novel's ontological domain.

21. Genette, *Narrative Discourse*, p. 57; Chatman, p. 165.

But when characters are shown debating left-wing politics, the very *fact* that this "discourse" occurs constitutes a declaration on the author's part not simply of "ought," but of "is": "discourse" becomes "event."

If we can work around the dryness and technicality of its vocabulary, narratological theory proves helpful to the study of didacticism in proletarian fiction because it enables us to examine on a microanalytical level the formal maneuvers by which narratives induce readers to subscribe to their guiding values. That is, narratological categories assist us in examining the rhetoric of didacticism. When the novelist Robert Cantwell declared that he had written *The Land of Plenty* as "propaganda," Hicks, we will recall, responded that he did not know what Cantwell meant and doubted whether Cantwell did either. Narratological analysis provides an opening for investigating the issue that Hicks—and most other literary leftists, except for Kenneth Burke—generally shunned. Because of their defensiveness against the charge that proletarian literature was "propaganda," as well as because of their intellectual commitment to a cognitivist aesthetic, the 1930s Marxists tended to lump together all modes of didacticism and castigate them as "leftist." There were two serious consequences to this gesture. First, they underestimated the extent to which politics exist not simply "in" a text, but in the contract a text holds out to its readers. In the writings of the literary leftists, "preaching" and "sloganeering"—effects generally traceable to the text's manipulations of "discourse"—were treated as compositionally equivalent to "wish-fulfillment," "conversion" endings, and "Cinderella formulas"—effects derived largely from the prelinguistic building-blocks of plot constituting "story." Because they did not distinguish among these rhetorical maneuvers, the 1930s critics failed to note that these maneuvers can position readers in very different ways. Some maneuvers co-opt possible readerly disagreement through assuming ideological unity; others exhort and engage in direct address. The critics' reluctance to view the texts as "propaganda" blunted their ability to analyze and assess them as works of rhetoric—that is, as literary discourse. Second, the critics' dismissal of didacticism as "leftist" prevented them from analyzing and assessing proletarian texts as political discourse. For the unfortunate label "leftist" implied that all overt expressions of doctrine in proletarian novels entailed a too-insistent articulation of revolutionary doctrine. The persistently denigrating use of this term made it virtually impossible to distinguish between ideas implying workerism or economism and ideas enabling a deeper level of specifically revolutionary understanding.

Narratology and Proletarian Didacticism

Lenin's comments on the role of the revolutionary party bear a suggestive relation to the problems of consciousness-raising in proletarian fiction that we have been considering up to now in general narratological terms. For proletarian fiction, while sharing many features with other kinds of didactic fiction, is not simply one among several formally identical modes. Its distinctive political goal of persuading readers to support—indeed, make—working-class revolution entails distinctive rhetorical strategies.

In *What Is To Be Done?*, Lenin discusses the dangers of reinforcing what he calls "economism"—that is, a political strategy limited to militant trade union goals and demands. He warns,

> The consciousness of the working masses cannot be genuine class-consciousness, unless the workers learn, from concrete, and above all topical, political facts and events to observe *every* other social class in *all* the manifestations of its intellectual, ethical, and political life, unless they learn to apply in practice the materialist analysis and the materialist estimate of *all* aspects of the life and activity of *all* classes, strata, and groups of the population.

Furthermore, he argues, such totalizing awareness cannot be a function of experience itself, even though experience of class oppression and class struggle is an essential precondition to the masses' revolutionary consciousness. "Class political consciousness can be brought to the workers *only from without*, that is, only from outside the economic struggle, from outside the sphere of relations between workers and employers. The sphere from which alone it is possible to obtain this knowledge of the sphere of relationships of *all* classes and strata to the state and the government, the sphere of the interrelations between *all* classes." To posit that the working class can obtain revolutionary consciousness simply from participating in economic struggle is to endorse "spontaneism"—that is, the doctrine that organizing by professional revolutionaries is unnecessary to bring the working class to the stage of insurrection.[22]

Lenin's polemic was specifically directed against the position, associated with the reformists grouped around *Rabocheye Dyelo*, that the role of the revolutionary party is restricted to trade-union level agitation. But

22. V. I. Lenin, *What Is To Be Done?*, *Collected Works*, 45 vols., 5: 374–75.

his comments have broader bearing on issues of representation and rhetoric in proletarian fiction. Lenin insists, first, that the workers' grounding in "concrete and . . . topical facts and events" must be linked to a grasp of totality if they are to gain revolutionary understanding. Their own engagement in class struggle, however authentic, can in and of itself produce only fragmentary, and thus necessarily economist, consciousness; the goal of revolutionary political activity is thus above all else to endow workers with the ability to "apply . . . the materialist analysis and the materialist estimate of *all* aspects of the life and activity of *all* classes, strata, and groups of the population." Second, Lenin posits that such awareness of totality can come "*only from without.*" The revolutionary party, while immersed in the day-to-day struggles of the working class, is politically positioned, by virtue of its grasp of Marxist doctrine, *external* to the limitations imposed by any particular class perspective. The party's grasp of totality has meaning only if this understanding is embodied in the practice of class struggle; but revolutionary theory is not thereby simply reflexive of, or coterminous with, this practice. Lenin's view of the role of the party is thus founded on a contradiction: the goal of revolutionary organizers is to lead workers to recognize society as a totality and to view their own oppression and exploitation as determined by their position in this totality. In order to view the social formation steadily and whole, however, the revolutionary must occupy a position politically and epistemologically "outside" that formation so as to dislodge fixed ideological assumptions about the naturalness and unchangeability of existing social relationships. Immersion in totality and externality to totality are thus implicated in a complex political dialectic.

Clearly there is no direct or simple correlation between fictional expressions of didacticism that come from a position "external" to a novel's line of action and the revolutionary function of a party purporting to address the working class from a position "outside" of the limitations imposed by that class's experience. Nor can one argue that an antipathy to overt expression of "line" in fiction—by either novelists or critics—in itself indicates a rejection of Communist politics. Nonetheless, the literary radicals' advocacy of transparent, nonhortatory representation implies a certain spontaneism. For by endorsing an aesthetic that a priori repudiates overt didacticism as "abstract" and "schematic"—indeed, "leftist"—the literary proletarians were stipulating, in the literary domain, that readers (workers) had little need for interpretive strategies that would explicitly draw revolutionary lessons from the text's portrayal of class antagonism. The text (the class struggle) would yield up its representation of totality spontaneously, as it were; there was little necessity for the voice of an author or a valorized character (the party) to illuminate the revolutionary implications of events from a position exterior to the characters' immediate experience of those events. Indeed, any text that too insistently pointed toward the future revolutionary overthrow of bourgeois power—that was too "leftist"—ran the risk of diminished authenticity.

No doubt the 1930s Marxists cautioned against overt didacticism because they wanted to discourage "bad writing." Moreover, the cognitivist bent of inherited Marxist (as well as bourgeois) aesthetic theory assured them that classical realism could encompass social totality and reveal its essential dialectics. Nonetheless, the literary left's failure to theorize the range of rhetorical strategies available to the proletarian novelist—and to theorize "propaganda" as a legitimate mode of "writing" that might be either "good" or "bad"—can be seen as a failure to apply Leninist doctrine to literary criticism. Even though in practice some writers insistently educated their readers about leftist ideas, and even though the critics at times admired novels that were openly didactic, the literary radicals' overall uneasiness with literary strategies coming from outside the level of "story" indicated that a certain spontaneism guided their assumptions about what proletarian literature ought to be and do. The literary radicals were not necessarily literary Leninists.

In chapters 8 through 11 we shall examine the different genres of proletarian fiction as didactic modes. Politics in the plural sense will reenter our inquiry as we examine the interplay between doctrinal and generic politics. We may close this discussion of realism and didacticism in proletarian fiction with a brief consideration of reader positioning. How might readers be affected by the intersection of different doctrinal politics on the one hand and different didactic maneuvers on the other?

Marxist critics of the 1930s, as we have seen, tended to favor novels pursuing strategies of implicit didactic commentary, in which expressions of political doctrine would be woven, blended, or otherwise embedded in the narrative. This preference can be translated, in narratological terms, into an approval of texts relying primarily upon "story" as opposed to "discourse," that is, of texts engaged in "showing" rather than "telling." The rhetorical and political benefits of this approach are apparent. The narrator's abstention from a stance of preaching or hectoring has the possible advantage of not putting readers on the defensive. Particularly for readers skeptical about left-wing politics, the text's posture—even if it is only a posture—of allowing its readers to make up their own minds can encourage readers to absorb the text's implied political doctrine without feeling immediately challenged to apply this doctrine to their own lives. Moreover, this strategy of withholding direct commentary need not entail a reformist politics. On the contrary: the text's reliance upon thematic patterning of characters and events can convince readers that the text's representation of an emergent social reality is in fact "typical." That is, by constructing an entire narrative around a strike in which workers learn their power or a "conversion" in which a worker gains class-consciousness, the text can effectively persuade its readers that "ought" is equivalent to "is." Even if the novel's insurgent proletarians do not constitute a statistical majority in the world of the reader, they point to nascent social forces that will shape the future. The novel's strategy of embedding larger meanings in specific elements of character and event thus enacts in literary terms the dialectical principle of concreteness: the movement toward revolution is not an abstract construct willed by the writer, but a process immanent to the reality being described. Through its Hegelian "return to the concrete," the text implies that the social forces shaping characters and events correspond with the forces producing change in the world of its readers. Analogy thus provides the basis for a didactic commentary entirely confined to the level of the implicit. When he noted that B. Traven's *The Treasure of the Sierra Madre* "is so thoroughly revolutionary in all the implications that slogans are unnecessary," Hicks was approving didacticism based on this kind of "story"-level redundancy.

We may speculate, however, that a heavy reliance upon "story" as the carrier of political meaning could simply reinforce the known-ness of a "familiar" reality and thus bolster familiar (and nonrevolutionary) ideas and attitudes. In its effort to create an "authentic" proletarian hero not characterized by an implausibly high level of class consciousness, for example, the text might fail to engage the reader in a political struggle to move beyond the ideological limitations of the protagonist. Through the very force of mimetic identification, the reader might be placed at the level of a non-class-conscious "bottom dogs" hero—and, in the absence of any cautionary interventions from the level of "discourse," remain there. The reader would lose sight of any larger revolutionary drift; the "ought" of revolutionary change bears little intrinsic relation to the "is" in the text. In texts that focalize entirely through the consciousness of less-than-exemplary heroes, the protagonist's authenticity can signal not a dialectical conception of concreteness, but an empiricist one: typicality is supplanted by immediacy. A text abstaining from "discourse"-level commentary can underestimate its readers and fail to move them to a significantly higher level of consciousness.

That at least some 1930s literary radicals were aware of the risks entailed in the close adherence to the consciousness of a proletarian antihero is indicated in Robert Cantwell's comments on James T. Farrell's *Studs Lonigan*. Writing to his friend in 1934, Cantwell voiced a rigorous critique that is worth quoting at length:

> You evidently feel that you must write of Lonigan in his own terms. . . . You write about Lonigan and his friends. You submerge yourself in that environment; you write of it as it seems to one submerged in it. You refuse to lug in outside meanings, standards and judgments brought from another world, from another environment. You write as if Lonigan's environment existed by itself, bounded on the north by one somewhat similar, on the south by one not much different, because that is the way it seems to Lonigan. But my observation is that these units, groups, are not self-contained, that they respond to other pressures, propulsions, besides those of the group itself. Lonigan, for instance, may be relatively uninfluenced by someone with whom he is in daily contact, and yet respond very sharply and dramatically to the decision of someone he has never seen, some banker, say, whose decision critically affects Lonigan's father, which in turn is of influence in Lonigan's career. The banker's decision in turn may be the result of a complex of pressures over which he has no or little control. I feel that the isolation of these powerful and invisible connectives is one of the tasks of modern fiction. I also feel that you are violating reality in not attempting to trace them.[23]

While Cantwell uses the language of neither Genette nor Lenin, what he is noting here is how Farrell's focalization exclusively within Studs's point of view precludes any perspective "from outside" that would explain the social totality that constitutes the protagonist's false consciousness.

23. Robert Cantwell to James T. Farrell, June 12, 1934, Cantwell Papers, U of Oregon.

But didactic strategies based heavily upon "story"-level redundancies could reinforce leftist utopianism as readily as they could fail significantly to move the reader to the left. In a bildungsroman portraying an unproblematically positive proletarian hero—such as Tom Tippett's *Horse Shoe Bottoms*—or in one depicting too few barriers and complications to the protagonist's attainment of revolutionary class consciousness—such as Scott Nearing's *Free Born*—patterns of stress and repetition among characters and events can produce an effect of implausibility. Rather than being asked to believe *too little* in the existence of an insurgent revolutionary proletariat, the reader is asked to take *too much* on faith. And since the text engages the reader in insufficient explicit argument on behalf of revolutionary politics, the protagonist takes an excessive didactic burden on his/her shoulders (which, while often physically broad, may be politically too narrow for the rhetorical freight they are asked to carry). "Ought" crowds out "is," and the ideal type supplants dialectical typicality. When 1930s Marxist critics castigated writers for turning out "conversion narratives"—as Calmer did, we will recall, in his reader's report for the *New Masses* novel contest—what they were reacting against may not always have been a text's inadequately dialectical representation of internal change, but its excessive dependence on character and event as carriers of political argument. Calmer, along with the great majority of his colleagues, disdained as "leftist" any rhetorical maneuvers that would openly declare the text's revolutionary intentions, thereby relieving the protagonist of the responsibility to articulate doctrine as realization. But in texts that smack of "conversion" and "wish-fulfillment," the problem is not primarily one of "leftist" doctrinal politics, but one of reader positioning. In faulting texts for their "conversion" endings, 1930s Marxist critics routinely failed to see that more "discourse"-level commentary—"preaching" that, if you will, comes "from outside" the characters' experience—might have offset the utopianism produced by plots seamlessly converting "is" to "ought."

To be sure, a number of the texts that the Marxist critics accused of "sloganeering" and editorializing" can justly be criticized for relying too heavily on "discourse"-level redundancies to reinforce political meaning. Writers who filled their novels with talk and neglected narrative dynamics did not necessarily position their readers more effectively for didactic purposes. In a novel where the narrator is constantly intruding him/herself, or mentor characters are continually talking to the reader over other characters' shoulders, or the narration makes heavy-handed use of free indirect discourse ("He finally saw that . . ."), readers can indeed experience re-luctance about entering into a seemingly authoritarian author/reader con-tract. Rather than feeling a common bond with the narrator, readers might feel patronized: doesn't the author know that I know *that* much? they might be tempted to ask. Moreover, in texts extensively using "discourse"-level commentary, the articulation of the relation of "is" to "ought" can be proclaimed rather than concretely rendered, and the relation of the text's emergent revolutionary proletariat to their real-life equivalents can become blurred. In the process, abstract and hortatory calls for a "better world" can supplant an engagement with the concreteness of the here and now. "Subjective tendentiousness," as Lukács warned, substitutes for the dialectical representation of typicality.

Moreover, texts abounding in "discourse"-level redundancies are not by virtue of this fact necessarily any more left-wing. After all, writers as diverse as Henry Fielding, Harriet Beecher Stowe, and Kurt Vonnegut have hectored and cajoled their readers without intending their narratorial inter-ventions to produce revolutionary class consciousness. If a proletarian writer feels free to inject narratorial commentary—as, for example, Tillie Olsen does in *Yonnondio*—this may facilitate the expression of revolu-tionary insights and conclusions not flowing naturally from the plot and needing to be drawn in "from outside." But, as we shall see in novels such as Thomas Bell's *Out of This Furnace* and Ruth McKenney's *Industrial Valley*, texts voicing the politics of Popular Front reformism can engage in rhetorical overkill as readily as can texts articulating a revolutionary or highly class-conscious agenda. "Redundancy" in the narratological sense can simply produce redundancy in the everyday sense—that is, tautol-ogy—and the text, instead of offering a Leninist view of totality, can end up vigorously polemicizing on behalf of ideological positions not particularly to the left of the mainstream.

In spite of the potential drawbacks involved in an extensive reliance upon explicit argument—drawbacks to which the 1930s Marxists were clearly well attuned—certain important didactic possibilities are opened up in novels shaped by hortatory rather than cognitivist notions of literary discourse. To begin with, readers can enter such texts in their own right, as narratees to whom political doctrine is directly imparted. Characters and events, the core elements in narrative, may receive short shrift in the pro-cess. But the potential advantage is that readers are neither abandoned at the level of economism nor co-opted into voluntarist utopianism, but instead invited directly to contemplate and weigh the political ideas shaping the narrative. In conventionally realistic works like Endore's *Babouk*, this direct impartation of doctrine occurs most frequently through narratorial commentary. But much of what passed under the rubric of "experimentation" in the proletarian project entailed a search for innovative means of injecting political commentary into fictional narrative. *Pace* Rahv, experimentation was often not a way of escaping from "leftism"—at least in the doctrinal sense—but a way of being more effectively "leftist." When William Rollins interrupted his strike novel *The Shadow Before* with block capitals stating "*WORKERS OF THE WORLD UNITE*" in several languages, he was not evading revolutionary ideas.

Besides positioning the reader as a participant in formulating political doctrine, the use of "discourse"-level commentary can outline the larger political and historical totality of which the characters' lives are part. For instance, in a novel depicting a protagonist who never achieves class-consciousness or even retreats into scabbing or bourgeois apologism, the hero's defeat need not entail the demoralization of the reader. By commenting on the meaning of the character's development (or lack thereof), the narrator offers reassurance that, despite present-day false consciousness, proletarian revolution is still on the agenda. Conversely, in texts about the development of exemplary working-class heroes, "discourse"-level commentary can release the protagonists from the responsibility of bearing the entire weight of their own "conversions." Fictional characters need not be portrayed as more articulate or noble than their analogues in real life. The "ought" at which the text is pointing is not conflated with the "is" of the protagonist's development (or, for that matter, with the victory of any larger group of sympathetic protagonists, as in a strike novel). Patently "subjectivist" intrusions by the narrator may help the reader to gain a more "objective" grasp of social forces than would be possible if the text avoided interpretive commentary. Narratorial interventions "from outside" the level of "story" may enable the articulation of a revolutionary perspective coming "from outside" the characters' experience.

➤   ➤   ➤   ➤   ➤

As we apply the theoretical model developed in this chapter, a few guide-post comments are in order. Chapters 8 through 11 will test out the hypotheses about realism and didacticism set forth here. Considering the four main genres of proletarian fiction, we shall attempt to determine how a writer's choice of genre affected the text's articulation of radical politics. But we shall also be investigating how different doctrinal politics reinforce or contest the ideological tendencies embedded in each genre. Our broad concern will be with the relation between left-wing politics on the one hand and the novel on the other. But since each of these categories comprises a range of possibilities, our project will examine the intersection of plural categories—several types of generic politics, several types of doctrinal politics.

Cutting across questions of genre and political "line" will be narratological analyses of didactic technique. The concepts of "story" and "discourse" will provide the organizing rubrics for these discussions, since these terms help us to distinguish between texts that depend upon implicit and cognitive representational strategies and those that make use of explicit or hortatory strategies. Considerations of the politics of realism will guide the argument, both through the chapters on different novelistic genres and within each chapter's assessment of generic tendency. Microanalysis of didactic strategy will indicate the range of rhetorical effects possible in each genre, thus helping us evaluate each genre's political efficacy.

We may now examine the relationship of politics to form in each of the modes of U.S. proletarian fiction.

CHAPTER 8

➤

The Proletarian Fictional Autobiography

American proletarian fictional autobiographies constitute a hybrid form, poised between bourgeois and revolutionary discursive traditions. Texts such as Agnes Smedley's *Daughter of Earth*, Mike Gold's *Jews Without Money*, Jack Conroy's *The Disinherited*, and Isidor Schneider's *From the Kingdom of Necessity* draw to a significant degree upon the model of the bildungsroman, or novel of education. Yet the education the protagonist gains in the proletarian fictional autobiography obviously differs in political content from the knowledge gained by the hero of the classic bildungsroman. As their titles indicate, these texts propose that recognition of one's place in social relations entails the seizure of what is rightfully one's own: cognition produces action. Readers who identify with the text's hero are thus positioned to undergo an education of their own, thereby experiencing an ideological effect very different from that accompanying the classic bildungsroman. The text is expressly didactic, teaching not the fixity of the bourgeois world, but its ripeness for revolution. Proletarian fictional autobiographies, like bildungsromans, posit the synecdochic relation of their protagonists to their social groups. But they speak for a collective, not an individual self. As Mike Gold put it at the beginning of his career as a proletarian writer, "The tenement is in my blood. When I think it is the tenement thinking. When I hope it is the tenement hoping. I am not an individual; I am all that the tenement group poured into me during those early years of my spiritual travail."[1]

On the level of manifest content, the proletarian fictional autobiography rejects the bourgeois conceptions of selfhood, personal development, and social accommodation accompanying a classical bildungsroman such as Dickens's *David Copperfield*. Yet, in its exclusive focus on an individual consciousness and its identification of the reader with a single hero, the

---

1. Mike Gold, "Toward Proletarian Art," in Michael Folsom, ed., *Mike Gold: A Literary Anthology* (New York: International, 1972), p. 65.

bildungsroman—as well as its modernist variant, the fictional autobiography of the artist-hero—the genre carries a bourgeois inheritance. The
bourgeois bildungsroman, writes J. M. Bernstein, "regiment[s] . . . novel
writing . . . to the end of self-recognition [and] . . . relativizes the world to
the self and meaning to identity." The proletarian fictional autobiographer,
by taking up the form of realistic first-person narrative, inevitably takes up
the baggage of bourgeois tradition. A tension is set up between, on the one
hand, an espoused politics of class struggle and collective consciousness
and, on the other, a narrative vehicle designed to meet different—indeed,
opposed—political ends.[2]

But the proletarian fictional autobiography also has a literary kinship
with testimonial modes of first-person narrative that have traditionally expressed the experience and consciousness of the marginalized. Raymond
Williams, discussing nineteenth-century working-class autobiographies,
remarks that "the form coming down through the religious tradition was of
the witness confessing the story of his life, or there was the defence speech
at the trial when a man tells the judge who he is and what he has done."
These oral genres, Williams argues, provided much more useful models
to the working-class writer than did the novel. William Andrews, in his
study of U.S. slave narratives, notes that the preoccupation of the self in
these texts is not to discover identity but to find the means to assert it. John
Beverly, analyzing the rhetoric of contemporary Latin American *testimo-
nios*, argues that "[t]he narrator in *testimonio* . . . speaks for, or in the name
of, a community or group, approximating in this way the symbolic function of the epic hero, without at the same time assuming his hierarchical
and patriarchal status." *Testimonio*, Beverly asserts, "is a fundamentally
democratic and egalitarian form of narrative in the sense that it implies
that *any* life so narrated can have a kind of representational value."[3]

2. J. M. Bernstein, *The Philosophy of the Novel: Georg Lukács, Marxism and the Dialectics of Form* (U of Minnesota P, 1984), p. 150. For further discussion of the reality
effects accompanying the modernist fictional autobiography as a genre, see my *Telling
the Truth: The Theory and Practice of Documentary Fiction* (Ithaca: Cornell UP, 1986),
pp. 185–232.

3. Raymond Williams, "The Writer: Commitment and Alignment," *Marxism Today*
(June 1980), 25; William Andrews, *To Tell a Free Story: The First Century of Afro-
American Autobiography* (Urbana: U of Illinois P, 1986); John Beverly, "The Margin at
the Center: On *Testimonio* (Testimonial Narrative)," *Modern Fiction Studies* 35 (Spring
1989): 16.

The traditions of subaltern documentary writing clearly vary with time and place. The type of testimonial narrative most influential on the proletarian fictional autobiography was, I would argue, one produced within the ranks of literary proletarianism itself—namely, the "sketch." A product of 1920s Proletkult radicalism, the autobiographical "sketch," which was characteristically brief and unembellished, depicted one or several stages in the worker-author's growth toward revolutionary class consciousness. In the "sketch," the individual speaker projects little interiority and unabashedly serves as a vehicle for exploring larger political questions. This literary form rapidly acquired practitioners internationally among left-wing writers of proletarian origins. The *New Masses* from 1926 onward published "sketches" by a range of then-unknown writers; *International Literature* for several years brought out "sketches" in great numbers, juxtaposing vignettes by Ed Falkowski, Martin Russak, Agnes Smedley, and Robert Cruden with texts by German, Hungarian, Japanese, and Soviet worker-writers. Conroy, we will recall, testified in his address to the 1935 Writers Congress to the inspiration he had gained from the Soviet collection of testimonials, *Those Who Built Stalingrad*, remarking that "the men and women who built Stalingrad are the stuff we proletarian writers of America must be looking for." The paper mill worker Joseph Kalar wrote in 1932 that "the greatest art of the future, as far as the written word is concerned, will not be the short story or the novel or poetry, but the proletarian sketch, combining not only the basic elements of action but permitting a greater latitude to self. The best stuff written in the United States today are sketches." The "sketch" was a popular form with proletarian fictional autobiographers, some of whom were quite conscious that, in composing their longer narratives, they were extending and developing "sketch" material.[4]

In this chapter we shall examine some of the consequences of this mixed discursive ancestry for the rhetoric of the proletarian fictional autobiography. What was the impact of the text's characteristic admixture of fact and fiction? Did the proletarian fictional autobiography tend to rely more on implicit ("story"-level) modes of didacticism or on explicit ("discourse"-level) articulations of political doctrine? If the bourgeois model seems to be dominant in some texts, and the revolutionary

4. Joseph Kalar to Warren Huddlestone, November 6, 1932, in *Joseph A. Kalar: Poet of Protest*, ed. Richard G. Kalar (Minneapolis: RGK Publications, 1985), p. 155. Both Gold and Conroy had previously published large segments of their "novels" as separate pieces in the *New Masses*, the *American Mercury*, and other literary magazines.

model in others, to what can this difference be attributed? What is the role that doctrinal politics play in determining the extent to which a text will be *formally* pulled in one direction or another?

In addressing these questions, we shall examine the four texts mentioned at the outset of this chapter: Gold's *Jews Without Money*, Conroy's *The Disinherited*, Schneider's *From the Kingdom of Necessity*, and Smedley's *Daughter of Earth*. Since in future chapters my generalizations about genre and form will be based on significantly larger numbers of examples, a comment on the relatively small number of texts I am examining here is in order. To begin with, I am using the analytical categories of "story" and "discourse" for the first time in this chapter. It is my hope that the procedure of treating fewer texts in somewhat greater detail will clarify various narratological terms and concepts that may be unfamiliar to some readers, thus facilitating a more compressed method of formal analysis later one. But there are also simply fewer texts to talk about here than there are in subsequent chapters. Not as many writers were attracted to the proletarian autobiography as to other genres of proletarian fiction. The sizable number of working-class writers who composed narrative prose fiction, and who might be supposed to take naturally to the genre of fictional autobiography, either preferred the brevity of the "sketch" (Ed Falkowski), never found the time to complete a book-length manuscript (Martin Russak, Norman MacLeod), or simply preferred to work in other fictional genres (Tom Tippett, Robert Cruden, Mike Pell, Thomas Bell, Tillie Olsen).

My selection of texts is limited, moreover, because I have defined the genre of the proletarian autobiography in a way that excludes certain autobiographically based proletarian novels. Such accounts of life on the bum as Tom Kromer's *Waiting for Nothing*, Nelson Algren's *Somebody in Boots*, Edward Dahlberg's *Bottom Dogs*, and Edward Newhouse's *You Can't Sleep Here* are autobiographical in origin; they resonate with veracity. But none treats the entire life span of its hero and focuses its didacticism around the dialectical issue of simultaneously retaining and negating working-class origins. Since I am interested in testing out a hypothesis about "tendency" that pits the proletarian testimonial narrative of self-discovery against the traditional bildungsroman, I exclude texts that do not centrally depict the development of a revolutionary working-class identity.[5]

---

5. For more on the worker-writer wing of U.S. literary proletarianism, see Douglas Wixson's forthcoming book. Some readers may be puzzled by the exclusion of B. Traven's

Fact and Fiction in the Proletarian Fictional Autobiography

The proletarian fictional autobiography routinely projects a protagonist who is constituted by a peculiar mixture of fictionality and actuality. To some degree, the protagonist is "characterized" for the reader as an identity separable from the author. Schneider dubs his protagonist "Isaac Hyman" and narrates in the third person. Smedley and Conroy tell their stories from the point of view of "I"-narrators, but they name these characters Marie Rogers and Larry Donovan, respectively. Gold, who comes closest to projecting a straightforwardly autobiographical persona—his hero is named "Mikey Gold" and speaks in the first person—nonetheless composes dramatic scenes and dialogue suggestive of fictional representation.[6]

But proletarian fictional autobiographies efface the boundaries demarcating any firm distinctions between author, narrator, and protagonist. Isaac Hyman blurs into the teller of the tale even in the opening passage of *From the Kingdom of Necessity:*

> A village in Eastern Europe. The memory labors back thirty years to a dark room in a mud hovel where a bedridden boy, five years old, yearns for the sunlight, unaware that here it shines upon one of the most forgotten corners of "the nether part of Europe." It is as golden to him as the sunlight over America, which is a country all in gilt, besides; and it is nothing to him that

---

The Death Ship from this chapter (and of novels such as those in his "Jungle" series from later chapters). I regret the exclusion, since Traven's work would reinforce and expand my argument: the Gerard Gales who speaks in *The Death Ship* and *The Cotton-Pickers,* for example, is a fine exemplar of class-conscious proletarian narration (see John M. Reilly, "The Voice of *The Death Ship,*" *minnesota review* 9 [1977]: 112–15). Without taking a position in the controversy over Traven's nationality (scholars argue passionately about the identity of this elusive author), I exclude Traven because most of his novels were translated from German or Spanish. For the debate over who Traven was, see Ernst Schuner and Philip Jenkins, eds., *B. Traven: Life and Work* (University Park and London: Pennsylvania State UP, 1987).

6. Gold, who was born Irwin Granich, in the early 1920s took the name of a Civil War veteran whom he admired. See Marcus Klein, "Itzok Granich and Mike Gold," in *Foreigners: The Making of American Literature 1900–1940* (Chicago and London: U of Chicago P, 1981), p. 34. See also Michael B. Folsom, "The Education of Mike Gold," in David Madden, ed., *Proletarian Writers of the Thirties* (Carbondale and Edwardsville: Southern Illinois UP, 1969), pp. 222–51.

the streets are almost fluid, that the adjacent field is a public latrine, that chickens and men inhabit the same houses.

Schneider is attempting to establish a critical distance between the young Isaac and the narrator. The unpublished manuscript of *From the Kingdom of Necessity* opens with Isaac's first-person declaration, "Listen, I've had a story to tell for a long time but I've been too self-conscious about it"— and situates the reader in medias res with Isaac's struggle to find employment as a young man; only gradually does this manuscript version reflect back to moments in his childhood. By contrast, the narrator in the third-person published version immediately refers to the many harsh realities of which the child Isaac is "unaware." Moreover, the narrator goes on to comment ironically on the inapplicability of the American Dream to Isaac's family, remarking that Morris Hyman, having failed to make his fortune in the United States, is returning in defeat. In spite of these clear markers of fictionality in the third-person published text, however, Schneider problematizes the fictional status of the text with the comment that "memory goes back thirty years" in order to recover this episode. The didactic voice that subsequently analyzes the predicament of the Hyman family—and that will continue to share its wisdom in interspersed passages of political commentary throughout the novel—is signaled to be the product of the character's experience; narrator and character are conflated with one another and, the reader intuits, with the author as well. Despite his evident desire to achieve greater objectivity and distance through the third-person narrator, Schneider leaves multiple traces of heavily autobiographical first-person narration in his novel. In large part the text demands to be read as "true."[7]

---

7. Isidor Schneider, *From the Kingdom of Necessity* (New York: G. P. Putnam's Sons, 1935), p. 3; manuscript of *From the Kingdom of Necessity*, Schneider Papers, Butler Library, Columbia U. The manuscript edition went through several changes: Schneider's projected narration started, it seems, in the third person, switched to the first person, and then changed back to the third person. It is interesting that Schneider's narrator in *From the Kingdom of Necessity* speaks of "the memory labor[ing] back thirty years," since Schneider once declared in an interview that "I remember nothing of my birthplace, Horodenko, a small town in Western Ukraine. . . . I arrived in this country at the age of five." (The village in the novel is called Horodemal.) "The one thing I wanted most during my growing years," Schneider continued, "was to escape the sort of life I was living. . . . For a long time I looked away from my past, which I would have had to

Conroy begins *The Disinherited* in a somewhat more conventionally novelistic manner.

> The Monkey Nest coal mine tipple stood twenty years; its dirt dump grew from a diminutive hillock among the scrub oaks to the height of a young mountain. . . . Cold and white like the belly of some deep-sea monster incongruously cast out of the depths, the dump dominated Monkey Nest camp like an Old World cathedral, towering over peasants' huts. . . .
>
> I first saw the Monkey Nest shaft when it was only head high to Old Man Vaughan. Father led me to the brink and I peered over fearsomely, clinging to his legs.[8]

The narratorial voice here is endowed with both a writer's grasp of the mythic dimension of everyday experience and a political radical's insight into the cultural and economic means by which ruling classes have historically maintained their control over the laboring masses. Readers have no reason to separate narrator from author, but neither are they immediately invited to conflate the two.

In the subsequent narration, however, the "I" who tells the story gives the reader ample occasion to project that "Larry Donovan" and Jack Conroy are indeed equivalent persons. In describing the confining Detroit slums inhabited by "Kentucky hill billies," for example, the narrator remarks, "Cribbed, cabined and confined in a diminutive 'living room' and a microscopic kitchenette, the walls press on their minds. Decaying relics of a pristine gentility, the rooming houses are unsanitary, dark, and fetid. When you stumble up the sudden stairs and snap on an unshaded bulb, a million cockroaches scamper for the shelter of a dank and rusty sink" (p. 208). Since there is encoded in the text no narratee—that is, a character whose function it is to listen to the discourse of the narrator—the "you" alluded to here might possibly be the reader. But the narrator of *The Disinherited* does not, like the jovial narrator in *Tom Jones*, characteristically lecture or cajole the reader. The more probable referent of "you" is therefore "I"— not the narratorial "I," but the "I" of the author in propria persona. In this passage—and several others similar to it—Conroy suggests that postulating a "Larry Donovan" different from Conroy himself is merely a rhetorical

---

re-enter if I wanted to write realistically" (Stanley J. Kunitz and Howard Haycroft, eds., *Twentieth-Century Authors: A Biographical Dictionary of Modern Literature* [New York: H. W. Wilson, 1942], p. 1243).

8. Jack Conroy, *The Disinherited* (1933; rpt. New York: Hill and Wang, 1963), p. 9.

convenience. Even though his treatment of Larry as a novelistic character permits the author to judge Larry's petty-bourgeois illusions from a critical standpoint, at strategic moments such as this it becomes clear that Conroy also *is* the character he describes.[9]

In Agnes Smedley's *Daughter of Earth*, the separation of author from narrator/character is more tenuous still. The text's different editions signal its strongly autobiographical nature. In the 1929 edition, Smedley narrates the life of her hero Marie Rogers up to the outbreak of World War I; the novel's final scene portrays Marie's anguish as her brother Dan marches off to war. The 1934 edition, which goes on to give an account of Marie's subsequent incarceration for antiwar activity and her later experiences with radicals in the Indian nationalist movement, begins right where the 1929 edition left off. The later edition in no ways poses itself as a sequel to the earlier one, as might be plausible in a novel following a character through various stages of her life. The 1934 *Daughter of Earth* is simply a later version of the "same" book. The principle of coherence shaping the text thus derives from the narrative's close correspondence to the events of Smedley's own life; the text is not patterned on Marie's development as a novelistic "character."

In addition, Smedley's narrator addresses the reader with a directness and intimacy that make it virtually impossible to separate her from the authorial intelligence shaping the text as a whole. Take, for example, Marie's opening declaration of her reasons for writing about her life:

> For months I have been here, watching the sea—and writing this story of a human life. What I have written is not a work of beauty, created that someone may spend an hour pleasantly; not a symphony to lift up the spirit, to release it from the dreariness of reality. It is the story of a life, written in desperation, in unhappiness.
>
> I write of the earth, on which we all, by some strange circumstance, happen to be living. I write of the joys and sorrows of the lowly. Of loneliness. Of pain. And of love.
>
> To die would have been beautiful. But I belong to those who do not die for the sake of beauty. I belong to those who die from other causes—exhausted

9. For the autobiographical basis of *The Disinherited*, see Douglas Wixson's introduction to the recent reissue of the novel (Columbia: U of Missouri P, 1991). Conroy noted that the character of Ed in *The Disinherited* was based on his own nephew (Conroy and Curt Johnson, eds., *Writers in Revolt: The Anvil Anthology* [New York and Westport: Lawrence Hill, 1973], p. xii).

by poverty, victims of wealth and power, fighters in a great cause. A few of us die, desperate from the pain or disillusionment of love, but for most of us "the earthquake but discloseth new fountains." For we are of the earth and our struggle is the struggle of the earth.

Acceptance of the narrator who addresses us with such painful directness is premised upon the reader's viewing her with a complete lack of irony. Certain assertions here verge on bathos—for example, "To die would have been beautiful. But I belong to those who do not die for the sake of beauty." It is impossible, however, to distance and ironize Marie as one might an ordinary fictional character; the narrator-character must be accepted unequivocally as honest and wise if the book is to be read at all. The very act of becoming the implied reader of *Daughter of Earth* involves granting the text its autobiographical premise. Even though in fact some parts of Marie's life substantially rework the corresponding phases of Smedley's own life—such as the account of Marie's short-lived but intense marriage with the Indian revolutionary Anand—the reader is continually reminded that Marie Rogers *is* her author.[10]

Gold more forthrightly asserts the basis of his narrative in personal experience than do most proletarian fictional autobiographers. He insistently reminds the reader that the highly colorful descriptions of life on Manhattan's lower East Side are the product of an authorial consciousness that continually confronts and analyzes images from its past. The opening chapter begins, "I can never forget the East Side street where I lived as a boy." The text then goes on to deliver a pungent description

10. Agnes Smedley, *Daughter of Earth* (Old Westbury, NY: Feminist P, 1976), pp. 3–4. For a full account of those aspects of Smedley's life that parallel and diverge from the events of *Daughter of Earth*, see Janice R. MacKinnon and Stephen R. MacKinnon, *Agnes Smedley: The Life and Times of an American Radical* (Berkeley and Los Angeles: U of California P, 1988). The MacKinnons note that Smedley, when active in the Indian nationalist movement, used to sign letters "M. A. Rogers, Secretary to P. B. Bose" (p. 41). (Pulin Behari Bose was the Indian National party's representative in the United States.) Smedley's statement of intent in her novel was blunt: "It [*Daughter of Earth*] will be based on my life and I plan to make it a document that will be direct and true." The first titles she contemplated for *Daughter of Earth* were *The Outcast* and *An Outcast* (p. 104). For a discussion of the lack of irony characteristically accompanying fictional autobiographies as a genre, see Ralph W. Rader, "Defoe, Richardson, Joyce and the Concept of Form in the Novel," in William Matthews and Rader, eds., *Autobiography, Biography and the Novel* (Los Angeles: William Andrews Clark Memorial Library, 1973), pp. 31–72.

of a cross-section of Jewish ghetto life, ending with the framing assertion, "Excitement, dirt, fighting, chaos! The sound of my street lifted like the blast of a great carnival or catastrophe. The noise was always in my ears. Even in sleep I could hear it; I can hear it now." Gold's text aims at the immediacy of direct personal statement. Scholars who have investigated Gold's life have remarked that in fact the text departs from Gold's life on several important points. Despite his slum beginnings, Gold saved up and went on to attend Harvard, if only for one semester; his father's attempts to become petty bourgeois were more sustained and somewhat more successful than the text portrays; the relations between Gold's parents were a good deal more strained than are the relations between father and mother in *Jews Without Money*. Gold himself once stated that the text was about 85 percent autobiography. The reader is given no indication of where fact leaves off and fiction begins, however. In terms of the generic contract held out to the reader by the author-narrator, *Jews Without Money* might as well be 100 percent factual.[11]

The true-to-life quality noted in these texts is not, of course, unique to proletarian variants on the form of the fictional autobiography. As I have argued elsewhere, the modernist fictional autobiography of the artist-hero—for example, Gertrude Stein's *The Autobiography of Alice B. Toklas*, Christopher Isherwood's *Goodbye to Berlin*, Thomas Wolfe's *Look Homeward, Angel*, and of course Joyce's *A Portrait of the Artist as a Young Man*—is also infused with a strong sense of actuality. But the impression of veracity accompanying the two types of novels produces quite different

11. Michael Gold, *Jews Without Money* (1930; rpt., New York: Carroll and Graf, 1984), pp. 13–14; Michael Brewer Folsom, "The Book of Poverty," *Nation* 102 (February 28, 1966): 243. Folsom notes, "It's a bit archly literary-critical to speak of a 'narrator' in Gold's book; every word of it is spoken in his own voice, as in his own adopted name." Folsom reveals that *Jews Without Money* was not conceived precisely as a "novel" by Gold, who earlier in the 1920s had drafted a third-person novel about East Side life with which he was dissatisfied. The manuscript of this novel is lost, but apparently Gold lifted a few chapters, put them into first-person form, and made them part of *Jews Without Money* (242). For more on the differences between the lives of Mike Gold and "Mikey" Gold, see Klein, "Itzok Granich and Mike Gold," in *Foreigners, The Making of American Literature 1900–1940* (Chicago and London: U of Chicago P, 1981), pp. 29–48; and Howard Lee Hertz, *Writer and Revolutionary: The Life and Works of Michael Gold, Father of Proletarian Literature in the United States*, 2 vols., Ph.D. Thesis, U of Texas at Austin, 1974.

effects. In the modernist fictional autobiography, the artist-hero reduces the world to the self; egoism becomes a means of controlling an alienated and mystifying social reality, and the text's aura of actuality functions to mark and privilege the protagonist's sensibility. In the proletarian fictional autobiography, authenticity serves primarily to reinforce the point that the represented world is *independent* of the text's maker. Whatever wisdom the narrator/author/character acquires is a consequence not of his/her capacity imaginatively to assimilate world to self, but of his/her ability to grasp the world in its objectivity as a precondition to revolutionary activity. As Conroy remarked to Hicks of his own bystander status in *The Disinherited*, "It somehow seems egotistical to me for the relater of a first person narrative to occupy the center of the stage." Conroy was referring specifically to his decision to move from first-person to third-person narration, but the remark has wider applicability. The last thing that he wanted— or that any proletarian fictional autobiographer wanted—was to dominate the narrative with self.[12]

Events, Characters, and the Developing Self

Since the character's process of becoming the narrator/author who writes the book provides the main focus of the narrative, the issue of development is central in the proletarian fictional autobiography. Most texts place considerable stress on the events and characters that contribute to the protagonist's growth. Didacticism is encoded into the building blocks of narrative, which convey an implicit argument about the lessons in class-consciousness that can and should be drawn from proletarian experience.

The "kernel" events constituting the narrative backbone of the proletarian fictional autobiography are arranged in patterns characterized by a high degree of redundancy: incidents pile up in such a way that their implication becomes overwhelming for character and reader alike. In *Daughter of Earth*, the reader is exposed to instance after instance of the effects of poverty upon Marie's family: the father beats the mother repeatedly, the family fortunes bump along from town to town, ill-paying job to ill-paying job. Moreover, the psychically and physically brutalizing effects of exploitation are not idiosyncratic to Marie's family: after Marie leaves

12. Foley, *Telling the Truth*; Conroy to Hicks, n.d., Box 14, Hicks Papers.

home, the text gives an unrelenting account of warped and destructive relations between men and women, ranging from the Colorado newlyweds whose billing and cooing turns into marital rape to the New York Socialist party radicals who carry their political maneuverings into the bedroom. In *Daughter of Earth*, the effect of this accumulated representation of oppression is not only to reinforce the necessity for Marie's rebellion but also to provide a larger causal framework for the protagonist's intense unhappiness. Even without any commentary from the narratorial/authorial voice, the repeated thematic pattern internal to the plot invites the reader to seek the roots of sexual alienation and violence in poverty and exploitation.

Similarly, redundancies among events in *The Disinherited* endow Larry Donovan's transformation into a fighter for his class with an aura of inevitability. The maiming and eventual deaths of Larry's father and brother in mine accidents; the death of Larry's uncle Rollie Weems at the hands of strikebreakers; Larry's own subjection to speedup in the Detroit auto industry; his desperate attempts to find even the most marginal employment at the onset of the Depression—these and other experiences create a narrative trajectory that attaches both plausibility and urgency to Larry's eventual decision to help lead the disruption of a farm foreclosure and to dedicate himself to organizing his class. Larry's final "conversion" (he decides to join his mentor Hans as a traveling organizer) takes shape as the only logical answer to the message encoded in the events of his life. Hicks and other critics complained that the novel was too episodic. Conroy himself acknowledged that the text was pasted together from a series of "sketches"; on different occasions he either called it a "picaresque novel" or denied it the title of "novel" at all. But the very disjointedness of the narrative reflects, as John Reilly notes, the "rootless" status of the proletarian who is "interchangeable with any other person willing to work for wages." A clear implication emerges from the relentless succession of incidents in *The Disinherited*: capitalism offers no recourse or relief for the working class.[13]

Sometimes, however, the accumulated episodes function not so much

13. John M. Reilly, "Two Novels of Working-Class Consciousness," *Midwest Quarterly* 14 (Winter 1973): 189. Conroy said of the genre of *The Disinherited*, "I should prefer not to call the book a novel, but I suppose the term fits as well as any. It's really a collection of autobiographical sketches with a cumulative effect" (Conroy to Hicks, May 28, 1932, Box 14, Hicks Papers). Conroy referred to the novel as a "picaresque" in Robert Thompson, "An Interview with Jack Conroy," *Missouri Review* 10 (Fall 1983): 152.

to explain the protagonist's development as to provide as wide-ranging a portrait of oppression as possible. In *Jews Without Money*, there are relatively few "actions" moving the plot ahead. From the first page to the last, where he hears the revolutionary orator who proclaims a "great Beginning" (p. 309), Mikey Gold is a relatively passive character, resigned to the fact that he is "bound for nowhere" (p. 308). What it lacks in "actions," however, the text compensates for in its comprehensive survey of states of affairs, or its "existents" and "happenings." Most chapters in Gold's text are given over to describing events—Louis One-Eye's criminal activities, the fortunes of local prostitutes, the survival techniques adopted by different members of Mikey's "little band of Yids," the hypocrisy and meaninglessness of the older generation's religious rituals—that underscore the oppressiveness of ghetto life. Virtually interchangeable in their ordering— in fact Gold did rearrange them to a considerable extent in his editing of the text—these chapters contain an unambiguous, if implied, political argument. If, as so many commentators have remarked, there are problems with the text's "conversion" ending, they do not stem from the narrative's failure to treat revolutionary consciousness as a logical response to oppression. The message continually stressed by the text's many episodes is that the great mass of East Siders are indeed "bound for nowhere" as long as the current system remains in place.[14]

The heroes of proletarian fictional autobiographies do not experience the fate of their class alone; they continually interact with other characters, most of whom opt for less laudable courses of action. Redundancies among these multiple implied comparisons frequently make the point that the protagonist is in some sense extraordinary: his/her development toward revolutionary class consciousness is the product of choice, and not simply of destiny. In *The Disinherited*, Larry is juxtaposed on the one hand with the non-class-conscious Detroit auto worker Jasper Collins, who regales his friends with dirty jokes, and, on the other, with the German socialist Hans, who struggles with Larry to "find something to take hold of besides the

14. For an analysis of the reordering of events in *Jews Without Money*, see Hertz, 1: 402–53. In the version of the ending of the novel published in the *New Masses*, the closing scene with the orator does not appear. Folsom states that "[p]art of the passage [Gold] simply lifted from the foreword to an earlier collection of his short works, *120 Million*" ("The Education of Mike Gold," p. 238). Folsom also notes that the ending was omitted in two post-1930 editions of the novel before it was restored in the 1966 Avon printing (p. 238).

ambition to rise about this factory." In *Daughter of Earth* Marie is shown to draw sustenance from the exemplary models of her grandmother and her Aunt Helen—both strong, defiant women—at the same time that she repudiates the passivity of her mother and of most of the other women she knows. In *From the Kingdom of Necessity*, Schneider juxtaposes Isaac's uneven but steady progress toward a Communist understanding with the false consciousness of many of his relations and friends. Isaac's father Morris, who in spite of his failure to attain the American Dream insists upon naming his second son after Theodore Roosevelt; Isaac's friend Mendel, who lacks the courage to follow through on his radical convictions; Isaac's brother Sol, who settles into an unhappy marriage out of cynicism and passivity—these and other characters highlight by contrast Isaac's integrity in becoming a revolutionist and delaying marriage until he finds a like-minded spouse. The thematic pattern emerging from the representation of these and other characters strongly suggests that Isaac is empowered to enter the "kingdom of Freedom" precisely because he has developed the capacity to become an agent of change. Unlike those family members and friends who persist in seeking a freedom defined in capitalist terms, Isaac can depart from the realm of necessity because he recognizes it as such.[15]

In some proletarian fictional autobiographies, the protagonist is, in line with the bildungsroman tradition, set apart from the rest of the class that he/she represents. As in the Lukácsian dialectic: the typical is not the mediocre but the exceptional. In positing this exceptionality, however, the writer makes an oppositional argument about the nature of individuality. When the protagonists in these texts achieve revolutionary insight into the necessary destiny of their class, they do so not because they possess intrinsic traits that make them remarkable, but because they have made a series of conscious choices. Certainly these heroes possess "traits": Marie is "character"-ized as combative and morose, Isaac as sensitive and self-conscious. But even more pronounced than the proposition of the individual's uniqueness is the proposition that "traits" are products of experi-

---

15. Schneider takes his title from Engels's famous statement about the revolutionary transition to a classless society: "Only from that time will man himself, more and more consciously, make his own history—only from that time will the social causes set in movement by him have, in the main and in a constantly growing measure, the results intended by him. It is the ascent of man from the kingdom of necessity to the kingdom of freedom"(*Socialism: Utopian and Scientific*, trans. Edward Aveling [New York, International, 1935], p. 73).

ence, signaling still-to-be-defined potentialities, rather than emanations of a priori essences. Proletarian fictional autobiographers make use of the form of the bourgeois novel of quest and education, but they do so to suggest the collective destiny registered in the protagonist's struggle against the limitations imposed by membership in the working class. The subjectivity celebrated in classic realism usually posits difference as superiority or inferiority; it defines the protagonist in *opposition to* others. The subjectivity heralded in the proletarian fictional autobiography emerges as distinctive to the degree that it perceives its own agency in the revolutionary process. The function of the many redundancies encoded in character and plot is to establish a specifically *proletarian* typicality. Marie is a daughter of earth, Larry one of the disinherited, Mikey a Jew without money, Isaac an entrant into the kingdom of Freedom.

Retrospective Narrators

Events and characters—the building blocks of "story"—do much to delineate the protagonist's achievement of class consciousness in the proletarian fictional autobiography. But narratorial voice also plays a crucial role in articulating political doctrine and guiding the reader toward identification with the protagonist. As we shall see in future chapters, the narratorial voice heard in most types of realistic proletarian fiction speaks for the author, but usually as an absent presence that slips in opinions and judgments through a narration purporting to be transparent and unmediated. In the fictional autobiography, by contrast, authorial voice is directly present. Rather than being an object of representation seen through the proscenium arch of the text, the worker-protagonist of the fictional autobiography *is* the subject, the creator, of his/her own text. "Authenticity"— the quality of worker-writing so highly valued by 1930s literary leftists— inheres not simply in the writer's intimate knowledge of the text's subject matter (Gold truly "knows" the lower East Side, Conroy the interior of an auto plant) but also in the persuasive actuality of the voice that interprets the meaning of its own destiny.

The degree and nature of this narratorial presence vary from text to text. Some author-narrators continually offer interpretive remarks about what is going on in the narrative. In *Jews Without Money*, Gold compensates for the relative naïveté of the experiencing Mikey by presenting a running narratorial commentary by the older and wiser Mike Gold. This intervening narrator comments on his own reliability as a register to truth. "Bedbugs are what people mean when they say: Poverty," the narrator declares. "There are enough pleasant superficial liars writing in America. I will write a truthful book of Poverty; I will mention bedbugs" (p. 71). Here "discourse" is redundant with itself, remarking on its own veracity. The narrator also asserts values with which the reader is forced to acquiesce in order to accept a characterization as "given": for example, "My mother had that dark proletarian instinct which distrusts all that is connected with money-making" (p. 44). In this passage, "discourse" is redundant with characterization through event: Gold's mother, whose "proletarian" virtues have already been displayed through various episodes illustrating her instinctive generosity and egalitarianism, is now interpreted in a political context by the articulated judgment of the narrator.

The authorial voice in *Jews Without Money* assumes, moreover, a prophetic stance. "O golden dyspeptic God of America," he intones, "you were in a bad mood that winter. We were poor, and you punished us harshly for this worst of our sins" (p. 244). The ironic invocation here directly assaults the conventional religious notion that humanity's misfortunes are caused by its transgressions. But it also underlines by satiric inversion a point that has just been made by an episode in the narrative: Mikey's younger sister Esther, who was run over by a milk truck in the crowded, icy streets, was hardly guilty of any "sin" warranting such "harsh punishment." When at the novel's conclusion the authorial/narratorial voice apostrophizes the "workers' Revolution" that "brought hope to me, a lonely suicidal boy" (p. 309), the reader, who has become accustomed to relying upon this voice for commentary and guidance of various kinds, is positioned to agree that a "great Beginning" is indeed at hand. In a conventionally realistic novel, such a direct invocation of social processes beyond the pages of the text would be outside the rules. In *Jews Without Money*, however, the reader has been exposed to the author's judgments throughout the narration. Mikey's final epiphany may be jarring—but not, as some critics have proposed, because the author is guilty of suddenly talking too much and violating the text's integrity as narrative. The older Mike Gold has been hectoring, lecturing, and cajoling his readers all along.[16]

16. Hertz, analyzing the minor stylistic as well as major structural changes Gold made between earlier published fragments and the novel, observes that the changes resulted

In texts featuring protagonists who undergo a more gradual political development than does Gold's Mikey, the narratorial voice usually serves not so much to offer general social analysis as to comment on the protagonist's maturation. Political insights emerge as the object of the hero's knowledge and become incorporated into the quest for identity that has been central to the trajectory of "story." In *The Disinherited*, Conroy notes of an incident when his compassionate mother gave food to a black strikebreaker, "I had never before regarded a scab as a puppet manipulated by those who stood to gain the most, but who never braved the wrath of the strikers. I could not hate the Negro" (pp. 61–62). Here the narrator does not address the reader directly with the proposition that bosses deliberately bring in black scabs to divide the working class. But the idea is presented through free indirect discourse, with the implied tag, "I understood that . . . ." When Conroy describes the state of relatively advanced political awareness at which Larry has arrived just prior to Hans's second appearance, he again offers argument—workers should relinquish their petty-bourgeois aspirations—by describing what his insights were at the time: "The fat on my bones melted away under the glare of the burnished sun, and the fat in my mind dissolved, too. It dripped in sweat off the end of my nose onto the bricks, dampened the sand. I felt weak as from the loss of blood, but also resigned. I felt like a man whose feet have been splashing about in ooze and at last have come to rest on a solid rock, even though it lay far below his former level" (p. 286). The Larry Donovan who tells his own tale from a grounding on "solid rock" is less obviously intrusive than Gold's narrator, who directly intervenes. But Larry by no means refrains from political commentary. Events alone do not illustrate the protagonist's internal transformation. In his discursive posture the narrator insists that this transformation become an explicit object of the reader's recognition; free indirect discourse converts experience into didactic argument.

---

in more understatement and a "reduction of 'explicit commentary'" (Hertz, 1: 327–93, Gold quoted p. 346). Critics who comment negatively on the end of the novel include Klein, *Foreigners*, pp. 184–92; Amy Godine, "Notes Toward a Reappraisal of Depression Literature," in Jack Salzman, ed., *Prospects: An Annual of American Cultural Studies*, vol. 5 (New York: Burt Franklin, 1980), pp. 205–7; Walter B. Rideout, *The Radical Novel in the United States 1900–1954: Some Interrelations of Literature and Society* (New York: Hill and Wang, 1956), pp. 187–88; and James D. Bloom, *Left Letters: The Culture Wars of Mike Gold and Joseph Freeman* (New York: Columbia UP, 1992), p. 135.

Daughter of Earth and *From the Kingdom of Necessity* combine both types of narratorial functions, offering direct interpretive commentary as well as argument conveyed through the character's thoughts. In the opening passage of *Daughter of Earth* cited above, the narrator immediately comments on the frankly utilitarian tenor of her own writing, noting that "what I have written is not a work of beauty, created that someone may spend an hour pleasantly." Marie validates her own text by creating redundancy *within* the level of "discourse." But she also remarks upon the larger significance of characters and events at various points in the text, thus setting up patterns of mutual reinforcement between the levels of "story" and "discourse." When she has just described her Aunt Helen's decision to work as a prostitute, Marie/Smedley asks the reader to understand Helen's actions in terms of analysis drawn from dialectics. "Why," she queries, "must the oppositions walk hand in hand? Why should the things that gave distinction to Helen lead to her destruction?" Moreover, the author/ narrator embeds argument in free indirect discourse, assigning crucial insights to the experiencing character. When the police agent Juan Diaz, who is trying to intimidate Marie into exposing her comrades, takes off his multicolored belt before raping her, she hazily associates the belt with a similar one worn by her father, who is also linked in her consciousness with male brutality. "Where had I sat just like this before and seen that belt buckle? . . . Some memory was haunting me" (281–82). Here the character's semi-conscious thoughts convey a political proposition, namely, that sexist violence is both an unreflective practice pervasive in the working class and a tactic of intimidation and demoralization used by ruling-class agents.[17]

In *From the Kingdom of Necessity,* Schneider makes frequent use of

17. For more on the contradictions within the autobiographical voice in *Daughter of Earth,* see Peter Hitchcock, "The Other Agnes," in *The Dialogism of the Oppressed* (Minneapolis: U of Minnesota P, 1992, forthcoming). Hitchcock remarks of the novel's opening passage, "The identification of author/narrator is so strong as to suggest that semantic authority is here indivisible and inviolate; for there can be no greater monologism than the centered subjectivity of such an 'I', even when the story is of 'a life, written in desperation and unhappiness.' . . . This semantic authority, however, quickly breaks down into self-questioning. The novel will be autobiographical only to the extent that it is polemical: that is, it begins to reflect the discourse of others in forms of solidarity and antagonism."

both narratorial interventions and free indirect discourse. But the text maintains a critical distinction between the types of insight these devices afford: the characters are shown to know something, but the narrator knows more. For example, after a description of the Hymans' departure from the lower East Side for a presumably better neighborhood in Harlem, the narrator notes, "But through all this movement and expansion and hope men felt themselves to be wanderers in social range as well as in space; unfixed, not members of determinate classes. The differences between the rich and poor were known, were realities too great to evade; but as yet, they spurred the poor only to hope for riches—to deny, with hysterical revulsion, their own class, and their class destiny" (p. 25). Here the narrator's authority analyzes the Hymans' illusions of upward mobility as a reflection of bourgeois ideology. Their unwillingness to grant their own typicality—their denial of "their own class, and their class identity"—indicates their typical entrapment within the dominant American mythos of classlessness.

By the end of Schneider's novel, many of the observations previously entrusted to the narrator are transferred to Isaac, who has been metamorphosing toward the wisdom of his creator. But, unlike Smedley's Marie, who becomes the voice narrating her own destiny, Schneider's protagonist is kept at a certain distance from the narrator. In the closing passage of the novel, the narrator remarks,

It was Passover of the spring of 1926. Coolidge was President. There would be years more of the fitful 'boom'. . . . These years with their blare and glare were to keep Isaac from understanding the unease he felt that night when, with a wife beautiful and beloved beside him, money in his pocket and his installation as a writer begun, he visited and departed from his family. He had set out from the kingdom of necessity; he had found a way out, the escape from his class, only to find that, outside, he was homeless. He was to learn that no one enters the kingdom of freedom alone. He would return to his class. With it, he would march, taking his place in the advancing lines in the irresistible movement of the masses of mankind from the kingdom of necessity to the kingdom of Freedom. (p. 450)

The narrator is willing to assign a significant degree of political insight to the protagonist, who "[finds] out" that "escape from his class" has only left him "homeless." But relating the thoughts of the character (tagged free indirect discourse) will not suffice to present all the author's views. The Isaac/Schneider of 1926—who has not yet experienced the ravages of the

Depression and, more crucially, has not yet cast in his lot with the Communist party—cannot yet "speak for" the authorial self of 1934. Toward the conclusion of *From the Kingdom of Necessity,* narratorial interventions *tend toward* redundancy with the character's perceptions, but never become conflated with them; the political argument made available through "discourse" remains distinct from that rendered through the "story" of the protagonist's growth. Both arguments afford views of the totality that the text is designed to illuminate, but they do not completely overlap with one another.

No doubt the intrusive narratorial commentary characteristic of the proletarian fictional autobiography can be faulted for rhetorical overkill. The 1930s Marxists, we will recall, came down hard on texts that "editorialized"; subsequent commentators have chided proletarian writing for its finger-pointing at political doctrine. It would be foolish to argue that proletarian fictional autobiographies never belabor the obvious. Throughout *Daughter of Earth,* Marie/Smedley could get away with fewer reminders that she is "of the earth." These assertions provide no real illumination of the meaning of the protagonist's life and imply, if anything, that revolutionary politics flow from the soil rather than from the proletariat's conscious articulations of its own class needs. Besides, Marie/Smedley exudes nary a glimmer of humor. Where Gold's narrator in *Jews Without Money* wittily boasts of the advantages afforded by his own commentary ("I will speak of bedbugs"), Smedley's is often painfully unself-conscious. Even if there is to be no ontological distance between narrator and author, a little rhetorical distance now and then could do no harm.

Similarly, the narrator in *From the Kingdom of Necessity* can be irksome, particularly when he offers commentary that does not provide a new dimension to the argument embedded in "story" but simply renders explicit propositions that the reader has already gleaned from the text. The novel amply enough illustrates the alienation of the artist under capitalism, for instance, to render superfluous the narrator's retrospective remark accompanying the description of Morris Hyman's demand that young Isaac tell his stories for money:

> Long afterwards he was to remember how he felt then, and that this feeling was a clew to the dissatisfaction that artists and writers felt in their relation with the public. The payment of money, and the hope of such payment, breaks the bond between them. The only natural payment for art is

response. When money becomes the payment the artist and the audience become strangers. They even become contemptuous and suspicious of one another, like any merchant and his customer. (p. 70)

Here "discourse"-level commentary is not merely redundant in the narratological sense of reinforcing and clarifying a message encoded in "story." It is also redundant in the everyday sense of the word—that is, tautological. The effect of this unnecessary multiplication of identical messages is somewhat patronizing, for readers sense the author's lack of confidence in their ability to infer the relationship between the implicit and explicit levels of argument in the text. There is excessive rhetorical overdetermination.

Hovering author/narrators can produce claustrophobic effects when they position readers as recipients of lectures that provide no new knowledge or insight. But many narratorial interventions in proletarian fictional autobiographies could be eliminated only at the cost of dramatically reducing the texts' capacity to convey revolutionary insight. Smedley's retrospective commentary from her outpost by the "grey Danish Sea" continually reminds the reader of the tremendous personal alienation that is, for the author/narrator, the price she has paid for her independence and political wisdom. Conroy enters into Larry's thoughts to make explicit his hero's discovery of the "solid rock" of class partisanship, after his feet have been "splashing around in the ooze" of false consciousness; this intervention is critical in persuading the reader to accept the leftward turn completing the protagonist's lengthy apprenticeship. In *From the Kingdom of Necessity,* which Obed Brooks faulted for its "lumpy ideology," most of the narratorial interventions do not simply repeat the propositions implied through story but provide added insights into the workings of bourgeois ideology. Without these remarks, indeed, the text's implied argument on the level of "story"—poor Jewish boys like Isaac *can* by dint of hard effort and talent break away from the ghetto and become self-supporting writers—would in fact subvert the text's manifest intention to argue against the fallacy of the American dream of classlessness. The various meditations of the politically seasoned narrator in *Jews Without Money* are the only elements in the narrative that inject an anticapitalist analysis into what would otherwise be just one more nostalgic account of a childhood of harsh but colorful poverty. Regarding Louis One-Eye's cruelties, for example, the narrator asserts, "Every one went on hating Louis One-Eye, and I did too. Now I hate more those who took an East Side boy and turned him into a monster useful to bosses in strikes, and to politicians on election day" (p. 140). Since the story of Gold's youth is so insistently *nonteleological*, the political commentary offered by the older and wiser narrator is crucial in demonstrating to the reader that the cruelties Mikey experiences are directly traceable not simply to the hard lot of the urban immigrant but to capital's structural compulsion to exploit and oppress. Although James Bloom argues that "not simple partisan animus and ideological assertion but dialogic contestation" constitute the novel's political discourse, the narrator's observations provide the text with a clear moral and political center. "Partisan animus and ideological assertion" are fundamental to the text's political rhetoric.[18]

In all four works, "editorializing" commentary interrupts the flow of the narrative and requires the reader to draw larger lessons from the protagonist's represented experience. No doubt this intrusive presence compromises the text's realistic transparency. But the device performs a crucial rhetorical—and political—function. Experience itself, as rendered through "story," will not spontaneously yield up its revolutionary meaning. If the reader is not to be kept at the level of the relatively naive experiencing protagonist, but brought into alignment with the perceptions of the politically seasoned writer/narrator, it is indeed helpful for the text to include "discursive" interventions "from outside."

Mentor Characters

In the preceding chapter I noted that mentor characters occupy a special rhetorical space in didactic fiction. To the extent that they articulate the doctrine informing the text, they engage in dialogues and speeches that function as part of "discourse" rather than "story." Yet mentor characters are also *characters*, not narrators. Everything they say is framed within the text's represented world and is therefore part of "story." The mentor character's function is therefore somewhat different from that of the intervening narrator. The political debate introduced by the mentor character is itself an event at the same time that it is privileged to illuminate and

18. Bloom, p. 29. Here I differ with Bloom, who reads the text as a Bakhtinian "critical counterpointing of ideological stances," especially "modern secular socialism" versus "traditional religious messianism" (p. 30). Gold may allow a multiplicity of voices to speak, but, in my view, there is no ambiguity about where he himself stands.

explain the text's other events. While the general truth the mentor purveys is, *qua* generalization, abstract, it is on an ontological par with the concrete elements of lived experience embodied in character and event. This situation poses both opportunities and challenges to the proletarian writer.

Proletarian fictional autobiographies routinely assign significant roles to leftist mentor characters, for the protagonist learns to rebel not simply by experiencing oppression but also by receiving an education in the theory of rebellion. But mentors often are actual persons with whom the author/narrator entered into debate and not simply novelistic constructs. All the mentors or would-be mentors appearing in the novel do not therefore function as mouthpieces for unambiguous authorial doctrine. Proletarian fictional autobiographies vary considerably in the relations they establish between protagonist and mentor. In *From the Kingdom of Necessity*, Schneider exposes Isaac to not one but many possible mentors: from the harangues about the Great War delivered by Mendel and Ziegler to Isaac's heated debates over socialism and Bolshevism with Miller, the text is full of contestation over left-wing ideas. Marxist politics are part of the air that the young Isaac breathes. Yet none of the older leftists is shown to exercise any particularly strong or lasting influence upon the hero. The protagonist's discovery of political identity entails repudiating the half-baked leftism of the Socialist party and embracing a genuinely revolutionary theory and practice in the fledgling Communist (then Workers) party. But because the novel's narrative terminates in 1926, several years before Isaac/Schneider actually joined the CP, the text's mentors perform a complex rhetorical function. They display the limitations of the pre-CP left at the same time that they educate Isaac—and the reader—in fundamental principles of Marxist analysis endorsed by Socialists and Communists alike.

Throughout most of *Jews Without Money*, by contrast, Gold minimizes the impact of radical ideas upon his somewhat naive and passive hero. According to one commentator, in "real life" Gold's own brother Manny actually became deeply involved in revolutionary politics and played a key role in radicalizing his sibling. In the text, however, Manny does not appear at all. Mikey's Aunt Lena, who participates in a strike and then becomes romantically involved with a left-wing doctor, is assigned a marginal role in *Jews Without Money*. On one occasion, Gold narrates, Mikey's non-class-conscious father "defended the rights of millionaires against the enthusiastic Doctor. . . . [E]ven I joined in the orgy of talk that lasted until three in the morning" (pp. 239–40). Nothing of the actual substance of this "orgy of talk" is, however, relayed to the reader. We can infer that from his early years Gold's Mikey, like Schneider's Isaac, must have been exposed to the Marxist political culture common among New York's working-class Jewish immigrants. Gold reserves the catalytic consciousness-raising role for the soapbox orator who appears on the novel's last page. But even here the actual *content* of the orator's speech is omitted: all we learn is that the apostrophized "Revolution" forced the narrator "to think, to struggle and to live" (p. 309). In *Jews Without Money*, the roles of diverse mentor characters are so deeply embedded in "story" that political debates among characters cannot even be overheard by the reader. Moral value is unambiguously associated with Mikey's mother, whose unflagging concern for others is, the narrator tells us, the source of his deep loyalty to his class: "The world must be made gracious for the poor! Momma, you taught me that!" (p. 158). But instinctive collective ethics are never translated into revolutionary theory, by Momma or any other fictional character; the narrator's acquired wisdom clearly derives from another—extratextual—source. "Discourse" functions in *Jews Without Money* are thus almost wholly the province of the narrator; within the text's range of represented characters, virtually no fictional voice intervenes "from outside" to pose the revolutionary alternative.[19]

Not all proletarian fictional autobiographies treat protagonists from environments as saturated with radical ideas as was Schneider's and Gold's East Side. When political debate is not taken for granted, however, but must be sought out by the apprentice-protagonist, mentor figures are assigned a more dramatic role. In *Daughter of Earth*, it is the Indian nationalist Sardarji who gives Marie her first systematic exposure to a Marxist analysis of imperialism. Marie does not come to his tutelage altogether naive. Cowboys and pioneer women have shaped her youthful rebelliousness; in young adulthood she has been introduced to socialist politics by her first husband Knut and his sister Karin; in her short-lived university experience she has tested her political mettle by contesting her racist and patriotic professors. Sardarji, however, renders Marie a political being and

19. Commentators have noted that the revolutionary orator featured on the closing page of *Jews Without Money* was, in Gold's own life, a female. Folsom identifies her as Elizabeth Gurley Flynn, the "Rebel Girl" of the IWW and later a CP leader ("The Education of Mike Gold," p. 223); Hertz identifies the orator as Emma Goldman (1: 147n.).

helps her to develop the internationalist commitments that shape her subsequent career (and, beyond the world of the text, the career of Smedley herself, who was to promote and defend not only the Indian left but also the revolutionary movement in China).

The discussions with Sardarji serve both to introduce the reader to contemporaneous Marxist analysis of the "national question" and to delineate the impact of this analysis upon the protagonist. The text renders in some detail Marie's reactions to her mentor—including important disagreements with tendencies in his position that she finds bourgeois nationalist rather than proletarian internationalist. The protagonist's intense interactions with the mentor reveal what revolutionary theory actually means to Marie, as both a body of doctrine and a motivation for her growing personal commitments. The role of the mentor in *Daughter of Earth* thus reflects the seriousness of political ideas to character and author alike: to appreciate the importance of a Marxist understanding of class struggle in Marie's life, we must know not only *that* Marie learned, but also *what* she learned. Sardarji does not, however, assume the status of an authorial mouthpiece; he never persuades Marie of his interpretation of the "national question." His views are not delivered ex cathedra but subjected to scrutiny on the level of "story." The debate over nationalist theory is to a degree abstract— a component of pure "discourse"—but it is rendered concrete by being incorporated into the text's tissue of character and event.

In *The Disinherited*, the young Larry Donovan is shown to be strongly influenced by the radical German worker Hans. Larry appears to have inherited a gut-level class consciousness from both his parents—especially from his union militant father. It is, however, Hans—a former follower of Karl Liebknecht in the German revolutionary movement—who urges Larry to abandon his fantasy of escaping from the working class. At the Detroit auto plant, Hans counsels Larry and upbraids the hedonistic and politically backward Jasper for his refusal to read Marx, who, he says, "charted the course of civilization." "Your brains will never tell you what Marx taught," Hans chides Jasper, "but in the course of time your belly will tell you. It may all work out the same in the end" (p. 178).

Hans appears at three important junctures in the plot of *The Disinherited*: when Larry, still relatively non-class-conscious, is working in Detroit; when Larry has been laboring at a series of backbreaking construction jobs that barely afford him a living; and at the end, when Larry participates in leading the eviction protest and then decides to dedicate himself to the emancipation of his class. It is important to stipulate that Hans "appears" because, despite his obviously important role in guiding Larry to militant class consciousness, his function is that of a catalyst rather than a cause: crucially, he is not shown to be "organizing" Larry until Larry has already organized himself. After Hans advises Larry and Jasper to read Marx, he disappears for over a hundred pages, only to reappear mysteriously *after* Larry, on his own (and apparently without having read Marx), has shed his petty-bourgeois illusions. Hans seems to be putting his own theory into practice, for his body bears the visible marks of the class war: "He had changed. His hair, which had always stood stubbornly erect, was iron grey, his face lean and scarred. His right cheek was concave, as though the teeth might be gone. He threw up his mutilated hand in greeting" (p. 286). Hans and Larry go off and have some sort of meeting—of which the substance is not revealed to the reader—and Hans then disappears for several months, only to reappear on the day before the farm eviction. Larry, apparently spontaneously, has organized a group of workers from the town to support the farmers at the eviction protest. Here Larry makes a speech— of which, again, the substance is not revealed to the reader, even though Larry notes that "I was soon at ease and enkindled by the response of the crowd [and] thought happily that I must have inherited some of my father's gift" (p. 307). Larry's "inheritance" consists in discovering a capacity to articulate class consciousness that has been, it would seem, latent in him all his life. Hans's function, as he himself puts it, is simply to "throw the spark" (p. 309). In *The Disinherited*, the mentor's role in the narrative is confined almost completely to the level of "story," with virtually no over-the-shoulder commentary directed at the reader. Indeed, even within the "story" this figure plays a catalytic rather than a causal role; his appearances are "happenings" rather than "actions."[20]

20. Klein argues that the plot of *The Disinherited* is arranged as "a series of adventures in folk identity" and remarks that Larry's discovery of himself as a militant organizer entails a "recognition of what he has known from the beginning" (p. 151). Conroy identified his own story closely with that of his father. Initially discouraged by the negative reception his book was getting from publishers (including Macmillan, where Hicks, as reader, had not recommended acceptance), Conroy wrote to Hicks wondering whether, should he wish to "recast" the book, he might "possibly write a novel about the coal camp motif, using my father as the protagonist" (n.d., Box 14, Hicks Papers).

By virtue of their dual positioning as components of both "story" and "discourse," mentor characters perform important functions in clarifying and articulating left-wing political doctrine in the proletarian fictional autobiography. Characters like Mendel, Aunt Lena, Sardarji, and Hans do not simply cue the reader to opinions that the authors wish to be heard. They also validate the political judgments that can be inferred from thematic patterns of comparison, contrast, and repetition among events and characters, furnishing an explicit analysis that reinforces implicit themes. Sardarji "proves" that Marie has all along been right to reject passivity and resist oppression; Hans "proves" that Larry will regain his inheritance by finding his voice in the class struggle. Despite their key role in rendering explicit the text's embedded political argument, however, these mentor characters do not furnish the only—or, in some cases, even the principal—means by which political commentary is given novelistic expression. Indeed, it could be argued that some proletarian fictional autobiographers use mentor characters too sparingly. Conroy and Gold no doubt were wary of overloading their books with long political discussions that would divest the narrative of concreteness and immediacy; they preferred to let the sheer weight of descriptive detail, in combination with occasional narratorial intrusions, carry the burden of political argument. But, ironically, the consequence of this concrete didactic strategy is a certain abstractness, since the sources of the narrator's revolutionary outlook are only asserted, but never shown, to be rooted in the text's represented world. Schneider and Smedley load down their narratives with more discussions and debates, assigning more functions of "discourse" to fictional characters. Perhaps this strategy renders their narratives, as narratives, more abstract. But the source of narratorial consciousness is more evident in these texts than in those by Gold and Conroy. There is no gap between experience and theory precisely because theory is shown to be a component of experience; it is concrete.

Larry Donovan's life diverged from that of his author in at least one important respect. Whereas Larry remains footloose and goes West, Conroy married. "While Jack was working on The Disinherited," noted a critic who knew the Conroys, "Gladys kept him eating by working in a shoe factory: so she deserves much credit for this good book" (L. Barnes, "The Proletarian Novel," Mainstream 16 [July 1963]: 57).

Sexism, Spontaneism, and the Problem of Closure

I have been suggesting that proletarian fictional autobiographers were largely successful in their efforts to fashion narrative forms that would convey a protagonist's quest for genuine class consciousness. In response to the 1930s Marxists' charge that infusing the texts with narratorial commentary and political debates resulted in abstract sloganeering, I have argued that such didactic devices could supply—though did not necessarily guarantee—greater concreteness. In response to the postmodernist charge that fictions centering on the individual fetishize individuality, I have demonstrated that these texts conceive and construct selfhood as the product of social forces. By providing a forum in which the worker-writer—or writer of working-class origin—articulates a revolutionary subjectivity, the proletarian fictional autobiography combats the bourgeois ideological tendency of the bildungsroman. The kinship of the proletarian fictional autobiography with Proletkult documentarism helps this mode of single-protagonist narrative express a collectivist notion of selfhood.

Various features of the proletarian fictional autobiography remain problematic, however, both rhetorically and politically. The 1930s Marxists' charge that stories about political "conversion" smack of "wish-fulfillment" remains to be addressed, as does the postmodernists' contention that realistic narratives foreclose contradiction and co-opt the reader into agreement. Since both complaints focus around narrative closure, we will scrutinize the intersection of generic and doctrinal politics in the endings of our texts.

The *locus classicus* of troublesome closure in the proletarian novel is *Jews Without Money,* which from 1930 to the present has repeatedly been criticized for its epiphanic ending. On the second-to-last page of the novel, the narrator, describing Mikey's "shame and humiliation" in job-hunting, remarks that "[t]here can be no freedom in the world while men must beg for jobs." The experiencing hero, however, has as of yet learned little about the necessity for revolution: "I was one of the many. . . . I was nothing, bound for nowhere" (p. 308). But when we turn the page—accompanied, in the text's first edition, by a woodcut of an orator, hand upraised, in a sea of workers—we suddenly witness the catalytic event that has apparently turned Mikey into a revolutionary, converting the experiencing into the narrating hero:

A man on an East Side soap-box, one night, proclaimed that out of the despair, melancholy and helpless rage of millions, a world movement had been born to abolish poverty.

I listened to him.

O workers' Revolution, you brought hope to me, a lonely, suicidal boy. You are the true Messiah. You will destroy the East Side when you come, and build there a garden for the human spirit.

O Revolution, that forced me to think, to struggle and to live.

O great Beginning! (p. 309)

The finale to *Jews Without Money* is indeed vulnerable to the charge of being "tacked on." Up to this point there has been little description of any quantitative process internal to Mikey that leads to this qualitative realization of the necessity for revolution. The change in the protagonist/ narrator seems a "conversion" enacted by some force external to the text at least as much as a logical working out of a process embedded in the narrative. Moreover, the metaphorical language used to describe the revolution carries heavily idealist overtones. Gold purports to be using his terms dialectically, arguing that Communism is the truth (the "true Messiah") that counters the mystification of religion and enables oppressed people to realize in materiality their aspirations for a better world ("build a garden for the human spirit"). Arguably, however, Gold's thesis is countered by his chosen trope, which implies transcendence rather than conscious agency as the engine of change. The text has amply illustrated the barriers to "true" class consciousness among the East Siders—habits of religious ritual, belief in the American Dream, racial and ethnic divisions. Indeed, throughout the text the witty and sardonic commentary of the narrator has been in constant counterpoint with the varying degrees of false consciousness attributed to the Jews without money whom he describes. But at the moment of closure the struggle between opposing paradigms disappears— without having been moving to a higher level through a dialectical process of negation. Narrative closure substitutes for conceptual closure. The revolutionary doctrine to which the author adheres simply assumes a position of rhetorical primacy; any objections the reader might wish to register are swept away in the apocalyptic "sense of an ending." While 1930s Marxists and postmodernist critics would find little to agree upon, they would probably concur about the ideological opportunism of the conclusion to *Jews Without Money*: "wish-fulfillment" converges with the containment of contradiction.

The problems accompanying closure in *The Disinherited* are somewhat different, for Conroy has delineated the quantitative process leading to the protagonist's qualitative transformation in much more materialist terms than has Gold. Larry's experiences with speedup and unemployment and his growing recognition of the need for multiracial workers' unity have done much to ready him for his leftward turn. But since Conroy has taken such care to restrict Hans's role to that of mere catalyst, the reader is still largely unprepared for Larry's sudden decision to accompany Hans West as an organizer—presumably a revolutionary organizer, though we never know for sure. Indeed, for all the didactic force of Larry's status as a type of his class, the novel seems to turn less on the Communist theme of constructing an identity than on the essentially bourgeois motif of finding one. Larry's discovery of his father's latent powers within himself, as well as his decision to forge this identity in the West—that traditional "frontier" for white male self-discovery in U.S. cultural myth—suggests that the novel has projected onto left-wing materials a conventionally individualistic conception of character development.[21]

Larry's leave-taking of Bonnie Fern reflects the admixture of revolutionary and traditional values in the course that he has mapped for himself as a proletarian pioneer:

> "You must be careful," [said Bonny Fern].
>
> "I can't promise to be careful," I replied. "In the kind of work I want to do, that would mean to be cowardly."
>
> "Well, be as careful as you can," she amended tearfully. Her eyes appealed almost frantically, but I turned my head. I didn't want her to take anything for granted. I thought she looked prettier every year, even if she was tanned and freckled and her hands rough and red. But I had to be free. (pp. 308–9)

Bonnie Fern used to be the girl of Larry's dreams, middle-class and unattainable. Because her family has been proletarianized by the Depression,

21. Critics of Conroy, fond of quoting his remark that "looking at Marx on the shelf always gives me a headache," stress his apparent naïveté about things Marxist and often conclude that he was not explicitly pro-Communist (Thompson, "Interview," 165). But Conroy wrote to Hicks in 1932, "As a Communist, I am also interested in what seems to be an awakening of social consciousness in your work. This requires courage in a man of your position; as for me if I think at all I must be a Communist, for I think my work will reveal that all my life has been spent among the lower strata of society and my book will be a cry *de profundis* to horrify the bourgeois who can afford to buy novels" (Conroy to Hicks, May 28, 1932, Box 14, Hicks Papers).

Bonnie Fern is now "of" Larry's class, and the two are strongly attracted to one another. Larry's repudiation of marriage with Bonnie Fern—clearly his lot if he remains at home any longer—is on one level an index to his dedication to the proletariat: he will have to travel light if he is to be an organizer. Yet what the text argues on the level of assertion it negates on the level of assumption. For the paradigmatic plot invoked here is gendered in a consummately individualistic and masculinist way: girl wants to marry boy, marriage is a trap, boy must get out if he is to be "free" to do what he has to do. At the moment of narrative closure, traditional male-coded notions of selfhood come to the fore. What is in some ways a tale of awakening to revolutionary class consciousness is, in other respects, a familiar narrative of male self-discovery.

Although Schneider is careful throughout *From the Kingdom of Necessity* to maintain a critical distance on his protagonist, his conclusion, like Conroy's, is premised upon quite unrevolutionary ideas about individual development. In the novel's final chapter—entitled, we will recall, "Return and Departure"—Isaac is shown going back to his parents' home bearing all the markers of "success": "a wife beautiful and beloved beside him, money in his pocket and his installation as a writer begun." On the level of manifest content, Schneider's point in ending his novel this way is to demonstrate that the end is a new beginning: Isaac feels increasingly ill at ease with his parents' values and, the narrator reminds us, will find real freedom only when he finally repudiates the temptation to "escape from his class" by becoming a Communist. But the novelist's decision to treat the moment of "return" as the impetus for "departure" in some ways subverts his dialectical intentions. For the text's ending at the moment of the protagonist's marriage—the most traditional of closures in the tradition of classical realism—conveys, on the level of "story," a sense of finality and achieved selfhood contradicting the revolutionary critique that the narrative is posing of the hero's still limited state of political consciousness.

The treatment of gender, once again, emerges as a crucial element in signaling the text's larger limitations in narrating a tale of an individual's revolutionary transformation. Take the triadic description of the markers of Isaac's "success": "a wife beautiful and beloved beside him, money in his pocket and his installation as a writer begun." The latter two markers of bourgeois achievement have been insistently queried in the text. But the first item in the series, the "wife beautiful and beloved"—who is, significantly, treated as grammatically equivalent to the latter two—occupies an ambiguous status. She is testimony to Isaac's achievement, something he has acquired, but also—unlike the last two items—presumably something that he will *not* grow beyond or repudiate. The wife is an indicator of a "real" success, one eminently compatible with the protagonist's development toward being a revolutionary. Even though the text has been urging a break with familiar bourgeois criteria for measuring personal value, at its moment of closure it invokes the zone of the familiar: selfhood is manhood, and manhood is indicated by the possession of a "beautiful and beloved" wife. As a commentary on gender relations, the formulation of marriage as possession obviously signals a regressive politics. But this formulation also calls into question the text's larger critique of bourgeois consciousness. If the "wife beautiful and beloved" is not to be repudiated, perhaps the other items in the triad—money, professional status—also retain their appeal. Isaac may be "departing" from the more obvious forms of false consciousness in which he was raised, but he may have "returned" to other, less obvious aspects of a bourgeois paradigm. While *From the Kingdom of Necessity* poses a revolutionary critique of many aspects of bourgeois aestheticism, it also offers a left-wing variant on the portrait of the artist as a young man.[22]

The problems accompanying closure in *Daughter of Earth* are quite different. Because the novel has continually emphasized Marie's political development, at its ending it avoids the aura of epiphany surrounding Mikey's discovery of revolutionary politics. And because it has unflaggingly exposed the destructiveness of conventional conceptions of gender—in both the society at large and the revolutionary movement—at its finale the text hardly portrays Marie "finding" an identity coded in the sorts of traditionally gendered terms invoked in the novels by Gold and Schneider. Self-

22. Halper, in his review of the novel, noted the centrality of the issue of male self-identity. He expressed discomfort at all the "neat little lecture[s]" the author had inserted. He noted, however, that "Young Isaac's fumbling affairs with the fair sex are presented with impact and telling effect. To this reviewer they are the meat of the book" ("Coming of Age on New York's East Side," *NYHTB* [October 27, 1935], 4). Herbst, for one, appreciated the novel's writerly theme. "I am . . . perfectly aware how hard an autobiographical book is to do, how difficult to make objective in the way it should be and yet be self-revealing and passionately one-sided, as it also should be," she wrote to Schneider in praise. "It's the first real book about writers and writing in this era" (Herbst to Schneider, n.d., Schneider Papers).

hood is, for Marie, something to be not discovered but created. In spite of its insistently political discourse about the social forces constructing—or destroying—identities, however, *Daughter of Earth* ends with an affirmation of the solitary individual. Describing the silence that descends after Anand leaves, Marie states: "Emptiness. Hours passed. The coffee beside my bed was long since cold. I was cold and numb. Slowly, with difficulty, I arose and began to pack. Out of this house—out of this country" (p. 391). "Out of this house—out of this country"—Marie refuses to comply with both the individuals and the social order that have made her "cold and numb." Yet she is also bound "out" of the society she knows—she is now an "outsider," an "outcast." Marie asserts her selfhood not just in defiance, but in opposition, to her social world; at least in the novel's closing segment, she takes on features of the alienated "problematic hero" of the bildungsroman. The novel's narrative trajectory affirms the integrity of an individual who, though bruised and battered, has survived the test of experience. As Beverly notes, "[E]ven when its subject is a person 'of the left,' as for example in Agnes Smedley's *Daughter of Earth*, . . . the autobiographical novel is [an] essentially conservative mod[e] in the sense that [it] impl[ies] that individual triumph over circumstances is possible in spite of 'obstacles.' " On the level of manifest content, however, *Daughter of Earth* profoundly queries the notions of unitary selfhood and individual transcendence. Smedley's text thus reveals a revolutionary conception of identity warring with a narrative vehicle that hypostatizes individualism.[23]

We can now take up the theoretical hypothesis set forth in the preceding chapter. How should we understand these manifestations of bourgeois ideological "tendency" in the proletarian fictional autobiography? A "strong" version of the "tendency" thesis would conclude that even though texts may set forth revolutionary ideas, these are essentially undermined by form, which exacts its tribute from the writer. The ghost of the bildungsroman—of bourgeois individualism—cannot be readily dispelled. The felt

23. Beverly, 23. We should note that *Daughter of Earth* was written when Smedley was emerging from psychoanalysis. Smedley was aware of the potential individualist pitfulls associated with this experience. As she wrote to a friend in 1926, "I was born in misery and my roots are in misery. If I thought that my analysis would take me away from the class struggle, then I would never be analyzed. If I thought love would blind my eyes to it, would make me think that me and mine were the only things worth while, or the chief things, then I would stop the analysis" (MacKinnons, p. 109).

need to end the narrative with the achievement of a satisfactory and stable identity, the drive to "relativiz[e] world to the self and meaning to identity"—such preoccupations intrinsic to realistic single-protagonist narrative mean that assertions of revolutionary political doctrine can go only so far in determining political effect in the proletarian fictional autobiography. There is also a generic politics—masculinist, conservative, individualistic—at work, continually sabotaging the writer's left-wing intention. Indeed, a committed proponent of the "strong tendency" thesis might argue that this textual politics, because rooted in unexamined assumptions presumably shared by author and reader alike, is more genuine, more essential, than any politics articulated on the level of assertion. A text may argue for a break with the old bourgeois ways of seeing and knowing. But if, in its bedrock assumptions about selfhood, it recapitulates the doctrines it is consciously attempting to refute, its subliminal affirmation of these doctrines is a more truthful indicator of where the novel "really" stands. Textual politics are the return of the repressed, exposing, under scrutiny, the stranglehold that old epistemologies and values have even on those attempting to inject new ideas into inherited modes of representation.

The "strong tendency" position has the virtue of pointing out the devious stratagems of genre. But it runs the risk of reducing ideas to reflexes and, moreover, of unproblematically privileging the political "unconscious" over the political "conscious." It provides no calculus for determining whether, or to what extent, an argument on the level of manifest content might either compound or contest an assumption on the level of form. In the "strong tendency" argument, form always wins the ideological battle. Furthermore, the "strong tendency" thesis leaves no space for the intersection of generic politics and doctrinal politics. What is needed is a version of the "tendency" thesis that acknowledges the baggage of inherited convention but theorizes this burden as lightened or increased by specific doctrinal politics.

The conception of individuality accompanying the bildungsroman form is without doubt preponderantly masculinist. But the inadequacies of the 1930s left in confronting the "woman question" are also reflected in the sexist premises shaping the heroes' sense of achieved selfhood in the closing sections of *From the Kingdom of Necessity* and *The Disinherited*. Both texts have made a conscious attempt to address women's oppression. Conroy portrays the prostitute Wilma and the housewife Lena as victims of male abuse; Hans demonstrates his egalitarian values by refusing to join Jasper and his friends in gazing at pornographic postcards. Isaac's alienation from his job as an advertising copywriter stems largely from his unwillingness to collude in the commodification of the female body. Yet—though one takes a wife and the other leaves a potential wife behind—both Isaac and Larry end up confirming women's marginality: the heroes find their politics as they find their manhood, and women are adjunctive to both processes.

What Conroy's and Schneider's novels reflect is not simply the bildungsroman's conventional equation of selfhood with manhood, but also the Communist-led left's failure to contest the separation of men's and women's spheres. In both texts, women remain associated with the domestic, the emotional, the "merely" personal. The attainment of "true" proletarian selfhood occurs in the world of men, the world of Funaroff's "American Worker." Conroy's and Schneider's representations of protagonists seeking and attaining distinctly male revolutionary working-class identities recapitulate the 1930s left's inadequate theory and practice with regard to the role that female members of the working class can and should play in the revolutionary process. The male-centered and individualistic premises of the genre converge with regressive doctrinal politics. We may recall Kempton's parodic description of the plot of the "conversion" novel: "[B]oy sees vision of exploitation, boy goes on strike, boy finds vision of freedom." While this account is patronizing, distorting, and reductive, it suggests a link between formulaism and genderedness. "Boy meets girl" is paradigmatically congruent with "boy finds vision of freedom," even if "freedom is construed in radically oppositional terms."[24]

The effect of idealistic "conversion" accompanying the endings to *Jews Without Money* and *The Disinherited* can also be traced to spontaneist aspects of the left's program. In both novels the protagonist's decision to dedicate himself to the revolution is sudden, even apocalyptic, putting pressure on readers to endorse a point of view to which they have not necessarily been won. But this co-optation of readerly agreement occurs not just because the writers' chosen novelistic form tends toward foreclos-

24. A poem published by Schneider in the *New Masses* attests to the genderedness of his revolutionary fervor: "I espouse the revolution, I put to it,/put to its courage, its wisdom, its will,/all that is left fertile in me, to father/new Bolshevik being." ("Ancestors," *NM* 20 [September 15, 1936]: 6)

ing contradiction, but also because both writers adhere to an empiricist conception of the nature of revolutionary process. Gold, we will recall, repeatedly spoke of "concrete facts" as "the final answer we can give to the intellectual abstractions of the bourgeoisie." Conroy's Hans proclaims to Jasper that if reading Marx does not bring Jasper to revolution, his belly will: "It may work out the same in the end." Experience, in other words, furnishes virtually the entire basis of revolutionary consciousness. Revolutionary theory simply supplies the catalyst—and is itself so much an outgrowth of experience that it need not even be repeated for the reader's benefit. The narrative's tendency to eliminate complications and co-opt the reader into agreement is reinforced by an implied political doctrine that minimizes the guiding role of theory in the relationship between politics and practice in the revolutionary movement.

➤   ➤   ➤   ➤   ➤

Having duly noted both generic conservatism and doctrinal shortcomings at work in the proletarian fictional autobiography, I now take a step backward. It is easy enough to call attention to the ways in which would-be revolutionary novelists, writing in a prerevolutionary situation, failed to be fully revolutionary. It is crucial, however, to view these writers' works dialectically. Are the flaws—generic, doctrinal, or in combination—primary and essence-determining? Or are they secondary to the texts' capacity for arousing revolutionary insight and instilling revolutionary will?

Adjudicating the "primary" and "secondary" aspects of contradictions is not a neutral enterprise; it entails a judgment call that invariably reveals the politics of the judge. Nor is this adjudication a simple task when the interlocked but conflicting tendencies operate on different levels—generic politics and doctrinal politics, the political unconscious and the political conscious. Some feminist critics may find that the masculinist aspects of some of the texts studied here outweigh whatever strengths the texts have as anticapitalist commentary. Critics placing high value on a text's capacity for rupturing fixed paradigms about selfhood and subjectivity might conclude that these works' epistemological conservatism compromises their efforts to convey a truly oppositional politics. My own view is that we should fully acknowledge the limitations posed by the political unconscious but pay due attention to the political conscious—that we should take these texts, in a sense, at their word. Despite their entrapment in bourgeois narrative conventions, these novels offer stirring portraits of individuals working to attain class-conscious identities so that they may speak for others—the tenement, the earth, the disinherited. The texts represent selves who articulate a world that is struggling to come into being. In various places these novels' generic politics contradict their doctrinal politics—but do not thereby negate those doctrinal politics. Even though at times the texts voice a less than revolutionary view of human essence and potentiality, these moments are, in my view, neither frequent enough nor powerful enough to cancel out the texts' revolutionary message and didactic force. In the main, these proletarian autobiographies possess the quality that Gold, for all his fetishism of facts, pronounced as indispensable in proletarian literature—"revolutionary élan."

In its projection of an authentic and highly articulate proletarian self, however, the fictional autobiography is in some respects a nontraditional form, drawing sustenance not only from conventional modes of novelistic realism but also from testimonial discourses of the marginalized and oppressed. It remains to be seen whether fully fictionalized forms more completely marked by their bourgeois origins—the bildungsroman, the social novel—could perform their tasks as well.

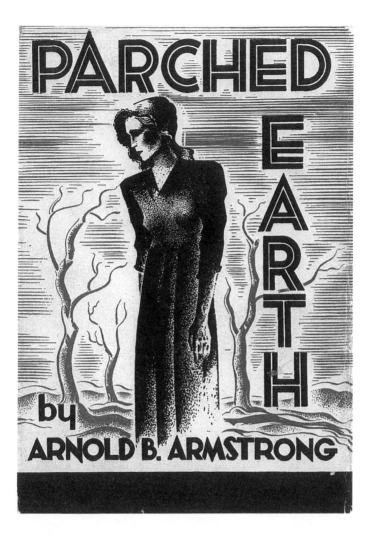

1934

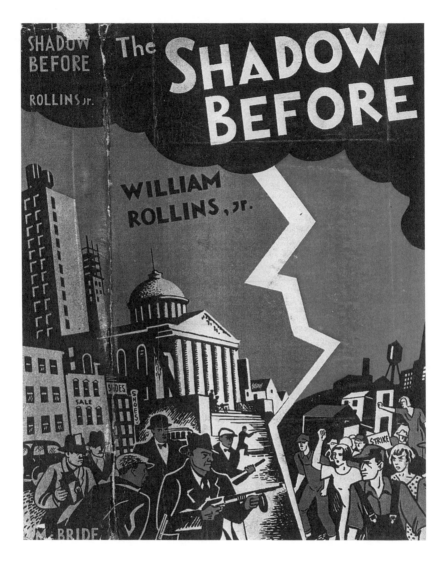

1934

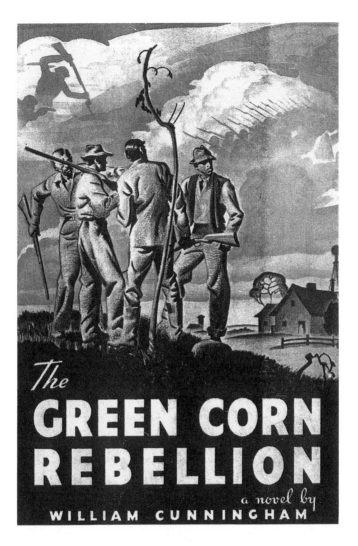

The
GREEN CORN
REBELLION
a novel by
WILLIAM CUNNINGHAM

1935

1935

CHAPTER 9

The Proletarian Bildungsroman

The bildungsroman is the classic form of the bourgeois novel. In texts of this genre, naive protagonists, usually young, encounter various trials that enable them to test their mettle. They undergo apprenticeships in the lessons of life and emerge older and wiser. Their careers serve the functions of synecdochic commentary, for they are "types" representing the broader lineaments of their time and place. Yet bildungsroman heroes are usually set apart from their peers by a number of distinctive traits—looks, intelligence, ambition. They are at once ordinary and extraordinary.

In the bourgeois bildungsroman, many of the features for which postmodern critics fault realistic narration are routinely prominent. Environment may be described in extensive detail, but it furnishes a stage on which heroes display inherent "traits" of character as much as a formative context that makes the heroes what they are. Furthermore, readers generally come to identify with the perspectives, or at least the interests, of bildungsroman protagonists and are therefore positioned to want what has been established to be "good" for these protagonists. Alternative potentialities for personal development are explored through a complex hierarchy of discourses, but narrative closure, which guarantees the fulfillment of readerly expectations, establishes the ideological supremacy of authorial doctrines and ethical standards over possibly competing doctrines and moral positions. Readers are drawn willy-nilly into political alliance with authors, who, screening themselves behind omniscient narrators, position readers as coconspirators presumably cognizant of the values toward which the more or less naive protagonists are fumbling. Both in establishing the "subject-ivity" of characters and in confirming the "Subject-ivity" of readers, bildungsromans represent, in the Althusserian paradigm, a quintessentially ideological form of discourse.[1]

1. See Louis Althusser, "Ideology and Ideological State Apparatuses," in *Lenin and Philosophy and Other Essays*, trans. Ben Brewster (New York and London: Monthly

Theorists of the bildungsroman generally concur that this genre is privileged to articulate bourgeois individuality. Hegel, describing the conventions of the emergent novelistic form epitomized in Goethe's *Wilhelm Meister*, noted that texts of this type depict "the education of the individual at the hands of the given reality. . . . For the conclusion of such an apprenticeship usually amounts to the hero getting the rough spots knocked off him. . . . In the last analysis he usually gets his girl and some kind of job, marries, and becomes a philistine just like all the others." Dilthey, without Hegel's irony, coined the term *bildungsroman* to describe a novel featuring a hero who "enters into life in a blissful state of ignorance, seeks related souls, experiences friendship and love, struggles with the hard realities of the world and thus armed with a variety of experiences, matures, finds himself and his mission in the world." James Hardin, outlining the classical paradigm of the bildungsroman, argues that most texts in the genre feature accommodation through their depiction of "the intellectual and social development of a central figure who, after going out into the world and experiencing both defeats and triumphs, comes to a better understanding of self and to a generally affirmative view of the world."[2]

Subsequent theorists of the bildungsroman have sought to broaden the genre's ideological scope, noting that it can stress conflict over accommodation. Georg Lukács and Lucien Goldmann argue that bildungsromans in the critical realist tradition generally pit their "problematic heroes" against the social order. Martin Swales and Jeffrey Sammons remark that, especially in its modernist variants, the genre allows ample room for irony and open-endedness. But even texts that portray alienation or rebellion, Hartmut Steinecke remarks, presuppose a division between self and world, a "confrontation with society." The bildungsroman projects, according to Swales, "a tension between a concern for the sheer complexity of individual potentiality on the one hand and, on the other, a recognition that practical reality—marriage, family, a career—is a necessary dimension of

---

Review, 1971), pp. 127–80; Catherine Belsey, *Critical Practice* (New York and London: Methuen, 1980), pp. 56–84.

2. Hegel quoted in Georg Lukács, "Critical Realism and Socialist Realism," *The Meaning of Contemporary Realism*, trans. John and Necke Mander (London: Merlin, 1963), p. 112; Dilthey quoted in James Hardin, "An Introduction," *Reflection and Action: Essays on the Bildungsroman*, ed. Hardin (Columbia: U of South Carolina P, 1991), p. xiv; Hardin, p. xiii.

the hero's self-realization, albeit one that implies a limitation, indeed a constriction, of the self." Moreover, the genre is based upon a largely a priori conception of individual identity. As Sammons puts it, "The concept of *Bildung* is intensely bourgeois: it carries with it many assumptions about the autonomy and relative integrity of the self, its potential self-creative energies, its relative range of options within material, social, even psychological determinants." Even when the bildungsroman focuses on society as well as subjectivity, it presupposes a "character" possessing intrinsic potentialities who enters an "environment" that either fulfills or restricts his/her individuality. The bildungsroman, which purports transparently to convey the essential qualities of both self and world, thus furnishes the textual epitome of "programmatic individualism." [3]

It might seem that writers motivated by left-wing politics would work in the genre of the bildungsroman only at considerable peril. But radical writers of the 1930s seem not to have been deterred by skepticism about the capacity of the bildungsroman to convey a revolutionary perspective; in fact, they used this form more than any other. Our investigation in this chapter will therefore lead to a frontal confrontation with the question of revolutionary politics and traditional form. Could the new wine of literary proletarianism be successfully put into the old bottles of bourgeois convention? Do the individualistic premises of the genre subvert the proletarian bildungsroman's attempt to portray protagonists struggling to move from individualistic to collective consciousness? Does the modulation of the "apprenticeship" plot into the "conversion" plot lead to the production of "formulaic" narratives of "wish-fulfillment," as has so often been charged? In exploring these issues, I shall refer to a broad and representative range of texts. The rationale for this method is that I wish to examine the variety of subject matters, themes, and political questions raised in the genre of the proletarian bildungsroman. If I were interested simply in the question

3. Georg Lukács, *The Theory of the Novel,* trans. Anna Bostock (Cambridge, Mass.: MIT P, 1971); Lucien Goldmann, *Towards a Sociology of the Novel,* trans. Alan Sheridan (London: Tavistock, 1975); Hartmut Steinecke, "The Novel and the Individual: The Significance of Goethe's *Wilhelm Meister* in the Debate about the Bildungsroman," in Hardin, p. 95; Martin Swales, "Irony and the Novel: Reflections on the German Bildungsroman," in Hardin, p. 51; Jeffrey L. Sammons, "The Bildungsroman for Nonspecialists: An Attempt at Clarification," in Hardin, p. 42; N. W. Visser, "The Novel as Liberal Narrative: The Possibilities of Radical Fiction," *Works and Days* 3 (1985): 7–28.

of representational strategy, I would analyze in greater detail a smaller number of paradigmatic novels. But bildungsroman writers addressed diverse issues and adopted a range of ideological perspectives: even though the politics of the bildungsroman can be analyzed as a unitary entity, the politics encoded in bildungsromans are plural, not singular. Since we wish eventually to address the relation of generic to doctrinal politics, it is necessary to examine the proletarian bildungsroman in both its singularity and its plurality.[4]

Varieties of Conversion (and Nonconversion)

The bildungsroman form offered proletarian writers a broader range of subject matters than did the fictional autobiography. Where authors of fictional autobiographies are obviously limited to their personal experience, authors of bildungsromans, as writers of texts that are patently fictional, can treat protagonists whose experience and course of political develop-

---

4. Readers familiar with 1930s fiction may note the omission of Henry Roth's *Call It Sleep* from the following discussion, since in some ways this is a classic "coming of age" novel. Moreover, Roth was "on the left" when he wrote it, for he joined the CP right after the novel was completed. Roth noted, however, that he did not want the novel to "illustrate or reflect the massive class struggle that was going on at that time [1910]" (cited in Diane Levenberg, "Three Jewish Writers and the Spirit of the Thirties: Michael Gold, Anzia Yezierska, and Henry Roth," *Book Forum* 6 [1982]: 241). "My own feeling was that what I had written was far too private for me to have given much thought to specific social problems," Roth remarked. "My personal involvement had absorbed my entire consciousness, leaving no room to focus on anything else" (cited in Cheryl Sue Davis, "A Rhetorical Study of Selected Proletarian Novels of the 1930s: Vehicles for Protest and Engines for Change," Ph.D. Thesis, U of Utah, 1976, p. 1960). The novel mentions left-wing politics once, and then only obliquely. It therefore does not constitute a "proletarian" novel as we have been treating the genre here. *Call It Sleep* originally received a hostile review in the *New Masses;* it was subsequently defended by, among others, Kenneth Burke and Edwin Seaver. For the controversy over *Call It Sleep* in the *New Masses,* see NM 14 (February 12, 1935): 7; NM 14 (February 19, 1935): 20; NM 14 (February 26, 1935): 21; NM 14 (March 5, 1935): 21. Seaver, in the closing salvo of the exchange, defended the novel for depicting "a 'prepolitical' period of our history"; it showed, he declared, the potentiality for the hero's childhood to "mature into a revolutionary manhood." Seaver chided the original anonymous reviewer for manifesting the "infantile disorder of 'Leftism.' "

ment (or nondevelopment) vary substantially from their own. Sometimes writers choose to feature past moments in the class struggle. In *Horse Shoe Bottoms*, Tom Tippett—himself primarily a labor organizer and historian of the labor movement, and only secondarily a novelist—uses the life of John Stafford as a vehicle for exploring the origins of militant unionism among turn-of-the-century Welsh immigrant coal miners in southern Illinois. John's saga of growing class consciousness, militant resistance, and premature death embody in miniature the struggle for survival and advancement of a key segment of the U.S. working class; the dedication of the new union hall on the day of the hero's funeral exemplifies a triumph for both the individual and his class.[5] In *Daughter of the Hills*, Myra Page uses a series of flashbacks to place the growth of her protagonist Dolly Hawkins Cooper in the context of her father's earlier struggles to abolish the use of convict labor in the Kentucky mines. The text moves back and forth between two levels of historical narration, comparing and contrasting Dolly's sexual and political maturation with her father's successes as a class fighter and failures as a husband.

In *The Green Corn Rebellion*, William Cunningham treats a little-known effort on the part of Oklahoma farmers to halt U.S. entry into World War I. The political capitulation of the protagonist Jim Tetley—who, after the rebellion's defeat, allows himself to be drafted into the army—is offset by the inclusion of newspaper headlines announcing the Bolshevik Revolution and the prophetic words of Jim's radical father-in-law Mack, who declares that "in twenty years, or maybe fifty years, there'll be thousands of fellers who are real leaders and revolutionists, and millions of farmers and working men like us ready to follow these leaders. Then it'll happen. It's got to happen." In *Babouk*, Guy Endore goes back to the eighteenth century to portray the experiences of an enslaved African who emerges as a leader in the Haitian revolution. The class struggles of the past prefigure those

5. For an instance of Tippett's writings on the labor movement, see his account of the textile strikes in Gastonia, Marion, and other North Carolina towns in *When Southern Labor Stirs* (New York: Jonathan Cape and Harrison Smith, 1931). Myra Page notes that Tippett was active in the Brookwood Labor College as a non-CP-affiliated labor activist and historian (Myra Page, Oral History of the American Left, Tape 1, Tamiment Library, New York U). For more on Tippett's militant trade unionist politics, see Richard J. Altenbaugh, *Education for Struggle: The American Labor Colleges of the 1920s and 1930s* (Philadelphia: Temple UP, 1990), pp. 118–19.

of the present: as the narrator declares to his hero, "Your voice is lost in the past. . . . And yet it cannot be lost altogether, Babouk. . . . The wavering voices of the complaining Negro, be they of the dead or the living, of Africa, or America, yet they will some day be woven into a great net and they will pull that deaf master out of his flowery garden and down into the muddy, stinking field." In bildungsromans of this kind, the author establishes a "red line in history," entering into the minds and lives of imagined actors in the "muddy stinking field" of oppression to create a usable past for revolutionaries in the present.[6]

Most often, however, the proletarian bildungsroman treats the experience of a modern-day protagonist. Whatever political insight and commitment the character has gained, it is implied, the reader can gain as well. In *Free Born*, Scott Nearing, after taking his hero Jim Rogers through a series of brutalizing experiences with U.S. racism, South and North, lands him in the political tutelage of his Communist lover Jane, whence Jim departs to organize black strikebreakers in support of white strikers in the Eastern Ohio mines. In *Call Home the Heart*, Fielding Burke focuses concerns with both class and gender emancipation in her depiction of Ishma Waycaster Hensley, who, abandoning a life of rural privation with her beloved husband, lives for several years out of wedlock with another man and enters into the class struggle in Gastonia (Winbury). In *To Make My Bread*, another Gastonia novel, Grace Lumpkin depicts the proletarianization of North Carolina "hill people" through her protagonist Bonnie McClure, who emerges as a fictional analogue to Ella May Wiggins, the strike's ballad-singing martyr. In *The Girl*, Meridel Le Sueur portrays the process by which her nameless first-person protagonist asserts herself against both sexual and economic abuse, moving from girlhood to womanhood through her discovery of the sustaining power of friendship with other working-class women. In *Moscow Yankee*, Myra Page details the gradual espousal of Soviet socialism by Frank Andrews (Andy), a transplanted Detroit auto worker; the novel stresses the role played in his political transformation by the altered relations between men and women in the USSR. *Conveyor*, a novel by the worker-writer Robert Cruden, also takes a Detroit auto worker as its hero—although Cruden's Jimmy, stubbornly adhering to the Ameri-

6. William Cunningham, *The Green Corn Rebellion* (New York: Vanguard, 1935), p. 253; Guy Endore, *Babouk* (New York: Vanguard, 1934), p. 160.

can Dream, falls into alcoholism and watches his marriage fall apart before he rediscovers a sense of self as a militant unionist. Tillie Olsen, in her unfinished novel *Yonnondio: From the Thirties*, describes the early stages in a young girl's harsh awakening to the effects of capitalist exploitation on relations within the proletarian family. In these texts the protagonist's espousal of—or at least growth toward—revolutionary class consciousness embodies in microcosm the change that is occurring, and must continue to occur on a larger scale, in the working class. The mimetic encloses the didactic: positioned to identify with the protagonist's "conversion," readers presumably carry the text's implied lessons over into their own lives.

Most proletarian bildungsromans treat working-class protagonists in the process of acquiring militant or revolutionary class consciousness. Some, however, treat the further struggles that protagonists undergo on the basis of an *already achieved*—that is, Communist—consciousness. In *This Is Your Day*, Edward Newhouse takes Gene Marsay, the sophomoric hero of *You Can't Sleep Here*, to a higher political level. Recently married and now a member of the Communist party, Gene is torn between his commitment to do whatever work the party needs—in this case, leaving New York to organize in a remote rural area—and his desire to remain with his wife, Alma. In *All Brides Are Beautiful*, Thomas Bell also treats the intersection of sexuality, domesticity, and revolution. The novel's hero, Peter Cummings, takes an earthy delight in cooking, eating, and making love with his wife Susan; he is unemployed or marginally employed throughout most of the narrative, and—a rarity in proletarian fiction—seems to do most of the cooking. For most of the novel, Peter's membership in the Communist party occupies a relatively small part of his consciousness. As the crisis of the Depression affects more members of his and Susan's families, however, he shakes off his lassitude and activates himself in union work. Joining the party does not change the character of one's quotidian existence, Bell implies; Communists enter into history only when they put their beliefs into practice. These novels by Newhouse and Bell, presupposing an acquaintance with the dynamics of the Communist movement, position the reader quite differently than do most other proletarian bildungsromans, for they do not establish sympathy with naive heroes first coming into contact with left-wing politics. Rather, the novels ask, what does it mean to have made a revolutionary commitment?

Some proletarian bildungsromans, however, portray heroes who to one degree or another fail to mature in a leftward direction; these are tales of nonconversion, or antibildungsromans. Where most radical novels of apprenticeship show their protagonists gradually approaching the authorial values that shape the texts, in these narratives about non-class-conscious members of the proletariat, there exists a decisive gap between the character's level of awareness and that of his creator. In the *Studs Lonigan* trilogy, James T. Farrell depicts a lower-middle-class Chicago Irish-American who becomes the victim of his own false consciousness. Repudiating the nonconformist stance that enables his double, Danny O'Neill, to break away from the intellectual sterility and political impoverishment of their South Side neighborhood, Studs vents his alienation in racist, antisocial, and self-destructive practices; he eventually dies an alcoholic. In *Lumber*, Louis Colman sketches the portrait of a lumber-mill worker, Jimmie Logan, who, having flirted briefly with the Wobblies in his young manhood, degenerates into a strikebreaker; after a fight with a foreign-born fellow worker, he is killed in a grotesque accident with a band saw. In what is undoubtedly the most famous proletarian antibildungsroman, *Native Son*, Richard Wright explores the irony that Bigger's extreme alienation and political ignorance lead him to admire Hitler and Mussolini and to gain a sense of self through murdering first Mary Dalton and then Bessie Mears. Some youths on the fringes of the black working class, Wright warns, have been so abused by capitalism that they attack not only the bourgeoisie but the working class as well. In such tales of proletarian protagonists who align themselves with ideas and practices that contradict their class (and personal) interests, the authors demonstrate the necessity for revolutionary class consciousness— as well as the threat of developing fascism among those who reject this necessity.

Paradigmatic Plots

In the proletarian bildungsroman, the trajectory of the plot must render inevitable the protagonist's development of class consciousness (or, in the antibildungsroman, must demonstrate the full tragic consequences of his/ her failure to become class-conscious). Process, in other words, is of primary importance. Events and characters should exhibit patterns of redundancy embodying the dynamics of historical necessity.

As in the fictional autobiography, many redundancies in the proletarian bildungsroman derive from thematic repetition: the protagonist is exposed to multiple instances of exploitation and abuse that reveal to him or her—or at least to the reader—the devastating physical and psychological effects of capitalism on the mass of producers. In *Free Born*, Jim endures an encyclopedic catalog of racist horrors, from the rape/murder of his girlfriend and the lynching of his parents in the South to job discrimination and urban race rioting in the North. The hero's adoption of a politics of multiracial workers' unity emerges as the only solution for the black working class. Reality, in *Yonnondio*, becomes a blur of marital abuse to young Mazie, so often does Jim Holbrook vent his frustrations against his exhausted wife, Anna. Although the novel is unfinished, Olsen's comments on her original plan for *Yonnondio* indicate that she intended to have Mazie eventually become a left-wing organizer: presumably alienation would be converted into rebellion.[7] *Babouk* details atrocity after atrocity perpetrated on Babouk and other enslaved Africans, from the graphically described midpassage to Babouk's mutilation as punishment for attempted escape. Through vicarious identification with the protagonist, readers are positioned to endorse the bondspeople's resort to emancipatory acts of violence. As in the fictional autobiography, in the proletarian bildungsroman the protagonist's decision to rebel is endowed with inevitability through the sheer pressure of accumulated representations of oppression. The reader, positioned to sympathize with the hero's building frustration, is moved to endorse rebellion—or revolution—as the "way out."

But where plot in the fictional autobiography is episodic and linear, relying heavily upon thematic repetition to reinforce its political message, events and actions in the bildungsroman often are patterned in more complex arrangements that diffuse the locus of causality. In *Moscow Yankee*, various subplots—involving the American engineers Crampton and Boardman and their families; Ned and Mac, two American radical expatriates, one black, one white; the White Russian Katia Boudnikova and the saboteur Alex Turin—expand the canvas of the novel beyond the relatively simple story of Andy's apprenticeship in the mores of socialist society. Moreover, while they provide reinforcement to the main issue of the Andy-

7. Deborah Rosenfelt, "From the Thirties: Tillie Olsen and the Radical Tradition," *Feminist Studies* 7 (Fall 1981): 370–406.

plot—will he or will he not remain in the USSR?—these "satellite" sub-plots possess narrative impetus and suspense of their own. Indeed, the novel's climactic event—Ned's successful rescue of the tractor plant from a bomb planted by Alex—has little direct relation to the account of Andy's growing political awareness. Similarly, the "kernel" events in *Horse Shoe Bottoms* are causally unaffected by the subplot concerning the miner Ralph Smith who, after saving several of his fellow miners, was trapped in a flooded mine fifteen years before. When Smith's body is eventually dis-covered in a posture suggesting his calmness and courage at the moment of death, the episode further exemplifies the proletarian collectivity and steadfastness illustrated through the account of John Stafford's political odyssey. In these texts, redundancies on the level of "story" underpin political doctrine not only by revealing the social forces impelling the protagonist to develop and change but also by depicting other charac-ters whose lives intersect with and parallel that of the protagonist. The hero's "conversion" presumably fulfills the needs of both the individual and the class.

Proletarian bildungsromans featuring the political development of an exemplary character pattern other characters to highlight the hero's dis-tinctive class consciousness. In *The Green Corn Rebellion*, the affable, sen-sual Jim, who not only allies himself with the farmer rebels but also has a passionate affair with his wife's sister, Happy, is contrasted favorably throughout the narration with his grasping, upwardly mobile brother Ted, who tells anti-Semitic jokes and lusts in vain after Happy. In *Call Home the Heart*, Ishma's bold and generous temperament—which leads her to risk losing the love of her husband, undergo a political apprenticeship in Winbury, and dedicate her energies to the cause of her class—is contrasted with the whining personality of her slovenly sister Bainie, who thrusts off responsibilities onto others and manipulates Ishma into giving over her small life's savings. In *To Make My Bread*, Bonnie's steady growth toward antiracist and collective values is both paralleled with her younger brother John's development into a revolutionary organizer and contrasted with her older brother Basil's pursuit of a white-collar job and a loveless marriage with his boss's daughter. In *This Is Your Day*, Gene's forthright attempt to meet the conflicting demands of political activity and marriage is implicitly contrasted with the craven behavior of his opportunistic brother-in-law Harold Darvis, a university instructor who attempts to evade his responsibility for impregnating Dolly, an undergraduate student. Such patterns of comparison and contrast with other characters from similar environments suggest that experiences of oppression and alienation alone do not produce class consciousness. Proletarian heroes are those members of the working class who make the conscious decision to dedicate themselves to the class struggle.

Proletarian bildungsromans do not always feature exemplary heroes, however: redundancies among characters can also work to comment negatively upon protagonists' inadequacies in grasping the nature of the historical necessity guiding their lives. In some texts this negative commentary is fairly gentle. In the early sections of *All Brides Are Beautiful,* the politically inactive Peter is ironically paralleled with non-class-conscious characters whom he disdains, like his brother-in-law Hank. But Hank—largely because of Peter's influence—decides not to scab in a strike at his workplace. In the novel's final pages, both characters signal the emergence of a new spirit of resistance and revolt in the proletariat. In *The Girl,* the nameless protagonist is initially immobilized by her attraction to the macho Butch; at this stage, she invites comparison with her mother, who passively submitted to her father's brutality. Eventually, however, the girl gains courage from her friends Belle and Clara and above all from the Workers Alliance organizer Amelia. The protagonist emerges as a woman who will nurture and guide her own girl-baby in accordance with collectivist values. At the beginning of *Moscow Yankee,* the patriotic and bigoted Andy is grouped with Tim and Morse, two American workers who express contempt for the changed social relations in socialist Moscow. Andy is receptive to the new society where they are not, however, and gradually splits apart from them, joining with the cluster of left-wing characters—his *tovarisch* Sasha, the American Communists Ned and Mac, and above all his mentor and love-interest Natasha—all of whom the reader has come to view as spokespersons for authorial politics. In these texts, the protagonist's juxtaposition with other characters reveals the gradual expansion of his/her consciousness. "Conversion" is mapped not as the revelation of embedded traits, but as actual change; growth is a function of the working out of internal contradictions, rather than the discovery of internal essences.

When they appear in narratives of nonconversion, however, ironic comparisons among characters can be relentless in emphasizing traits of character—as well as conscious decisions—that lock the protagonists into their alienated situations. In Farrell's trilogy, Studs initially has affinities with somewhat sympathetic characters like Davy Cohen, who is marginalized because of his Jewishness. Increasingly, however, Studs groups himself with the more retrograde elements in his conformist peer group, such as Three Star Hennessey and Weary Reilley. While Danny O'Neill moves to the left, Studs grows into a reactionary who rejects out of hand the speeches of the radical soapbox orators in the South Side's Washington Park. In *Lumber*, Jimmie repudiates the Wobblies, breaks a strike, and adopts increasingly racist attitudes toward his Portuguese fellow workers. His wife Pearl, who initially opposes Jimmie's radical leanings, gauges his political degeneration when even she berates him as a traitor for deserting his iww friends. In these narratives of nonconversion, ironic redundancies on the level of "story" help to highlight and comment on the tragic trajectory of the protagonist's decline; political argument is embedded in the patterns of comparison and contrast that the reader is invited to formulate among the novel's characters. The cautionary lesson to the reader is clear.

Mentor Characters

As in the fictional autobiography, mentor characters in the novel of apprenticeship articulate, and often win the protagonist to endorse, left-wing political doctrine. In the fictional autobiography, however, the felt conjunction of narrator, character, and author produces strong rhetorical overdetermination: it is virtually impossible not to know what the author thinks. Mentor characters may help to explain how the protagonist moved to the left, but they are not the text's only source of political commentary. In the bildungsroman, by contrast, mentor characters routinely elucidate arguments and ideas that cannot necessarily be inferred from "story." In some works, these characters constitute the text's only means of bringing in revolutionary theory "from the outside."

Sometimes mentors occupy cameo roles and have little direct impact upon the plot. In *Yonnondio*, Anna and Jim Holbrook, Mazie's parents, are immersed in day-to-day struggles, both against one another and against the poverty enveloping their family. It is through Old Man Caldwell, an alienated petty-bourgeois radical who cast off his class moorings years before, that Mazie is introduced to science as a method of understanding both nature and society. He reminds her, moreover, of the value of her working-class heritage: "Whatever happens, remember, everything, the nourishment, the roots you need, are where you are now." Old Man Caldwell dies soon after delivering this speech, however, and is never mentioned in the subsequent narration; Olsen does not rely on him as a primary source of political argument. The organizer John Stevens who appears toward the end of *To Make My Bread* plays a more explicitly Communist role, for he informs Bonnie's brother John McClure of the "message" that has liberated millions in "another country" overseas. Although John Stevens patently advocates Soviet socialism, he avoids using the C-word or mentioning the USSR by name. His satellite role is adjunctive to the kernel events in the main plot, which depicts Bonnie's development of a militant unionist consciousness and subsequent martyrdom. In *Call Home the Heart*, the Northern organizer who addresses the Gastonia strikers from the back of a train performs a still more explicitly didactic role. In a lengthy speech (nine pages in the text), the organizer outlines the differences between Communism and capitalism as world systems and unambiguously advocates the former. Then, however, he rides off on his train. In these texts, mentor characters play a Leninist role, raising ideas that do not automatically emerge from the events themselves. Old Man Caldwell indicates that experience produces revolutionary knowledge only in combination with the systematic analysis of totality; Lumpkin's and Burke's organizers assert that nothing less than socialism should be the goal of workers engaged in reform struggle. But these mentors do not profoundly affect narrative causality; they remain within the orbits of their satellite plots.[8]

More common in proletarian bildungsromans are mentor characters

8. Tillie Olsen, *Yonnondio: From the Thirties* (New York: Dell, 1974), p. 50; Grace Lumpkin, *To Make My Bread* (New York: Macaulay, 1932), pp. 324–28; Fielding Burke, *Call Home the Heart* (1932; rpt. Old Westbury, NY: Feminist P, 1983), pp. 283–91. A *Nation* reporter present at the actual Northern organizer's speech in Gastonia gave a different impression of its impact on the mill-worker crowd: "On the red clay banks of the railroad track they sit in their overalls listening to the Communist strike leader. . . . They hear with blank faces about international solidarity and class power. But when one of their own number stands up and shouts: 'Every striker git a scab and the strike will soon be over,' they howl with delight" (Paul Blanshard, "Communism in Southern Cotton Mills," *Nation* 128 [April 24, 1929]: 556).

who struggle over left-wing ideas with the protagonist (and, in the process, with the reader as well). In *Moscow Yankee*, Andy continually turns to Mac for insight into Soviet mores, as well as to Natasha, who fascinates him both politically and sexually. Friendship and romance alike are full of talk.[9] In *Call Home the Heart*, the nameless Northern organizer plays a far less influential role in Ishma's life than does the radical doctor Derry Unthank, who chides Ishma for her backward ideas and steadily pushes her leftward. Yet Derry (who appears to be falling in love with Ishma) is attracted not just to her physical beauty but also to her quickness in absorbing and reinterpreting what he tells her; the proletarian pupil ends up teaching the middle-class mentor. In *Free Born*, the mentor/mentee relation involves close personal bonding: the character from whom the desperate and alienated Jim learns about revolutionary politics is the Communist Jane, who is equally forthcoming with love and Lenin. In *The Girl*, there is nothing specifically erotic in the bond between the protagonist and Amelia or her other female friends. But Le Sueur's highly sympathetic treatment of the women's communal household establishes a close link between class struggle and personal friendship and interdependency. In depicting intimate relationships between mentors and mentees, these texts envision political radicalization as a process involving a fundamental transformation of human relations—especially along lines of gender.

Mentor characters in proletarian bildungsromans do not, however, always succeed in reaching, let alone transforming, the protagonist. In *Lumber*, the reader learns about working-class solidarity from the Wobbly organizers whom Jimmie encounters. Jimmie, however, proves impervious to their messages; he stands by passively during the brutal lynchings of his former comrades in the aftermath of World War I. Bigger Thomas, in *Native Son*, struggles to comprehend the meaning of Max's speech about him; he ultimately fails, however, asserting instead an identity defined by the tragic limitations on his consciousness: "What I killed for, I am."[10] In

9. Page reveals that the character of Natasha was based on a young Russian woman by whom she was impressed during her sojourn in the USSR. Andy was based on a mechanic from Detroit, and Boardman was based on a Detroit engineer whom she liked for his "pioneer spirit" (Oral History of the American Left, Tape 1). For more on American expatriates in the USSR, see Paula Garb, *They Came to Stay: North Americans in the USSR* (Moscow: Progress, 1987).

10. Richard Wright, *Native Son* (1940; rpt. New York: Harper and Row, 1966), pp. 91–92.

Judgement Day, Studs Lonigan is not even aware of the May Day march that passes by while he lies on his deathbed: the mentee is oblivious to the message of a potential mentor. In novels of nonconversion, characters representing the discourse of radical politics articulate their truths to deaf ears. But the reader hears. By positioning the reader as judge and ally, the texts depict failure in the protagonist but energize their readers to think about the questions the protagonist ignores.

Transparent Narrative and Conspiring Narrators

In the fictional autobiography, the narratorial voice addressing the reader is intuited to be roughly equivalent with both the protagonist and the author. The text cannot be charged with covert manipulation, for it wears its politics on its narratorial sleeve. In the bildungsroman, by contrast, the author characteristically operates from behind an illusionist screen. The values of the narratorial voice are not explicitly associated with those of the man or woman who writes the novel; authorial judgments are embedded, but rarely directly declared. How does this narrative transparency affect the political positioning of the reader? Does it set up situations in which the reader is co-opted rather than persuaded into agreeing with political doctrine?

Narrators in proletarian bildungsromans employ a variety of tones. Some bring to mind the omniscient narratorial voice heard in nineteenth-century fiction—calm, beneficent, apparently nonjudgmental. Take, for example, the bird's-eye view with which Lumpkin begins *To Make My Bread*:

> Beginning this side of South Range and thirty miles as the crow flies to North Range, the life of the mountain people centers around Swain's Crossing. At one place the road to the outside crosses the trail from South Range and Thunderhead. Here is Swain's store and post office. . . .
>
> On April the nineteenth, 1900, two men left their steers, hitched to sledges, in front of the store and joined another man around the stove inside. A light snow had begun to fall and the warmth of the stove was very welcome. Presently another man came in. He was Sam Wesley, whose cabin was in Possum Hollow, on the South Range trail. (p. 1)

Although the narrator offers no explicit judgments of the persons and actions she describes, she secures the reader's trust in a number of ways.

She has "inside" knowledge of the locale and its inhabitants: geographical markers are familiar to her, as are the mores of the mountain people. Moreover, the nostalgic image of the simple country life here resembles a Norman Rockwell poster, celebrating the pleasures of neighborly conversation, steer-drawn sledges, and cozy stoves. But the narrator's postulation of the centrality of Swain's store to the life of the community named after him suggests that power in this otherwise idyllic setting is not equally shared—a hint soon borne out by Swain's determining role in buying up the farmers' land for lumber and precipitating their proletarianization. Despite her pretension to objectivity and transparency, the narrator draws the reader into collusion with a set of "universalistic" values invoked on behalf of a partisan political argument. To side with the workers in the class struggle is to affirm simple folkways and the harmonious relation between humanity and nature before the capitalist fall.

Frequently, however, the narratorial voice in the proletarian bildungsroman more directly asserts political values. The opening of *All Brides Are Beautiful* projects an unabashedly left-wing inflection:

> The Bronx may be identified as that one of New York City's five boroughs which is on the mainland of the North American continent, the others being distributed over three islands off its coast. It has a population of one and a half millions, it is cold in winter, tropically hot in summer, and on a Jewish holiday indistinguishable from a city stricken with a completely successful general strike. A zoo, a cocktail, and a derisory cheer have been named after it. Most of its employed residents earn—receive—twenty-five dollars or less per week and pay an average monthly rental of ten dollars per room. The customary price of a glass of beer is ten cents, of admission to a picture twenty-five cents, of a woman two dollars.
>
> Susan, Peter, and the Beasleys lived in the Bronx.

As in the opening to *To Make My Bread*, the narrator establishes his authority as a reliable insider to the environment described. But Bell's narrator articulates distinctly Marxist attitudes and convictions. A strike that paralyzes a city is "completely successful"; landlords engage in rent-gouging; pleasures are commodified and escapist, with prostitution on a par with any other purchase; workers—as producers of surplus value—"receive" far less than they "earn." This narrator may not announce his politics, but his partisanship is evident.[11]

---

11. Thomas Bell, *All Brides Are Beautiful* (Boston: Little, Brown, 1936), p. 3.

A few proletarian bildungsromans are entirely focalized through the protagonist's consciousness; there is no independent narratorial voice that comments or sets the scene. Authorial judgments emerge either through validation of the character's perspective by events in the narrative or through ironic disjunction between what the character thinks and what the reader is led to believe. The opening to *The Girl* illustrates this rhetorical strategy:

> Saturday was the big day at the German Village where I was lucky to get a job in those bad times, and Clara and I were the only waitresses and had to be going up and down from the bar to the bootleg rooms upstairs. My mama had told me that the cities were Sodom and Gomorrah, and terrible things could be happening to you, which made me scared most of the time.
>
> I was lucky to get the job after all the walking and hunting Clara and I had been doing. I was lucky to have Clara showing me how to wander on the street and not be picked up by plainclothesmen and police matrons. They will pick you up, Clara told me, and give you tests and sterilize you or send you to the woman's prison.

The protagonist tells her own story, but it is implicitly framed by a series of authorial judgments. The girl's categories for understanding her situation are immature and idealist. Her mother's mythic categorization of the evils of the big city produces in the protagonist fear but no understanding: the specifically sexist forms of oppression faced by young working-class women like herself are dissolved into ahistorical notions of sin and divine punishment. Moreover, the girl evinces no awareness that the police, presumably her protectors, are in fact the greatest threat to her welfare. The nameless protagonist, who typifies many proletarianized young farm women thrust into the urban environment, fails to see the big picture. She attributes her survival to fortune: she is "lucky" to have been told the right way for an unemployed female to "wander the street," and she is "lucky" to have landed a low-paying, exhausting job.[12]

Although narrative in *The Girl* purports to be objectivist, the reader is positioned to understand the girl's situation in accordance with a fairly un-

---

12. Meridel Le Sueur, *The Girl* (Albuquerque: West End P, 1978, rev. ed., 1990), p. 1. For a discussion of women's employment conditions in the Twin Cities during the Depression, as well as of the activities of the Workers Alliance, see Elizabeth Victoria Faue, "Women, Work and Community, Minneapolis 1929–1946," Ph.D. Thesis, U of Minnesota, 1987.

ambiguous framework of political judgment. As the narrative proceeds, Le Sueur measures her protagonist's growth by the girl's assimilation of this framework as her own. In the novel's final chapter, the girl makes no distinction between her own ideas and those of the other women who jointly write a leaflet condemning the relief agency for Clara's death:

> Was she a criminal? Was she a danger? Clara never got any wealth. She died a pauper. She never stole timber or wheat or made poor flour. She never stole anyone's land or took it for high interest on the mortgage. She never got rich on the labor of others. She never fattened off a war. She never made ammunition or guns. She never hurt any one. Who killed Clara? Who will kill us?
>
> O it was something to hear and see their anger. And their power. (p. 130)

The protagonist no longer looks to "luck" to explain the events in her world. Le Sueur engages in no narratorial intrusions throughout the novel. It is virtually impossible to read the text at all, however, without implicitly endorsing the authorial values that invite the reader to construct the girl's growth toward collectivism as a growth toward true selfhood.

Some texts combine omniscient narratorial commentary with focalization through the protagonist. The opening pages of *Moscow Yankee*, which depict Andy on his way to Moscow, simultaneously assert narratorial judgments and permit evaluations to emerge spontaneously through the representation of the character's own thoughts:

> Rollicking, headstrong, the express was charging with its unwilling passenger Frank Anderson between two worlds.
>
> . . . . Christ, what a train! Jumbled images, spotted red, green and purple, jazzed crazily past his weighted eyelids. His head, slipping free from his body, wobbled foolishly from side to side, keeping time with the click-click of the narrow-gauge tracks. . . .
>
> The Detroiter felt for a light. What big feet that bum [across the aisle] had. He'd enjoy planting a cool one on those broad slats. He had never liked square-heads anyway. His straw-boss Mike Feldman had been a square-head. Swear you blue in the face, yelling "Step On it! Get 'Em Out!" And when he'd got the can, had Mike so much as said . . . He could've been an old wrench they were tossing on the scrap heap. Him not yet thirty, going strong, when they . . . Can it, no use griping. Each fellow for himself, and devil take the hindmost. He'd had the bad break, and Jeez didn't he have company. Half of Detroit.

The narrator's opening description of Andy asserts the protagonist's position in history: he is on the train of historical transition, "between two worlds," between capitalism and socialism. But he cannot make sense of the images flashing before him; while the train is "headstrong," Andy's own head (consciousness), only precariously linked to his body (material necessity), wobbles "foolishly." [13]

The subsequent passage of free indirect discourse, introducing the reader to Andy's thought processes, invites ironic interpretation, but also a sympathetic understanding of the basis of Andy's false consciousness in his experience under capitalism. Andy denigrates "squareheads," espouses the precept of "each fellow for himself," and concludes, like Le Sueur's girl, that his situation is a function of luck, a "bad break." Yet his bigotry is linked with his hatred of his straw boss, and he hazily realizes that the "bad break" which has thrown him onto his own resources has also affected half of the Detroit working class. Through both narratorial commentary and the ironic revelation of character, Page poses the thesis that her protagonist—and, by extension, much of the American proletariat—is in a state of political confusion, but not as intrinsically reactionary as it might first appear. While presently aligned with the ideology of the dominant class, Andy, like other workers, is positioned by historical circumstance to be receptive to the message of socialism. Where he or they (or the reader) will end up is a matter of experience and education. By focalizing through Andy, Page requires the reader to identify, if not with his consciousness, at least with his interests. *Tout comprendre, c'est tout pardonner.* [14]

Narrators who provide entry into the protagonist's consciousness rely largely upon free indirect discourse to examine politics as lived and breathed. In *Lumber,* Colman's representation of Jimmie's thoughts about his two sons—Hubert, whom he has just buried, and Tommy, the lone survivor—reveals that Jimmie is entrapped in, and probably will be destroyed by, his own stubborn illusions;

> Hell, he still had Tommy. After all, what would Hubert have amounted to, anyhow? A fine man, most likely. And what was that? Something for the

---

13. Myra Page, *Moscow Yankee* (New York: G. P. Putnam's Sons, 1935), pp. 3, 5–6.

14. Page prided herself on having done a much better job of "psychological development" in *Moscow Yankee* than in *Gathering Storm* (Page to Hicks, April 7, 1934, Box 48, Hicks Papers, Arents Library, Syracuse U).

mill-owners, the lumber operators, the bosses, to work and starve and feed at their pleasure. A plaything for men like the man Tommy would grow up to be. . . .

[Tommy]'d get the best out of life there was. He'd have men such as Hubert would have been to kill, if he needed them.

The unrelenting succession of tragedies in Jimmie's life apprises the reader that it is highly unlikely that Tommy will escape the fate of the rest of his class. Yet Jimmie, a victim of capitalist oppression, takes on the brutality of the exploiters, hoping that his remaining son will "get the best out of life" by using, even killing, other workers. By being party to the text's situational irony—that is, by recognizing false consciousness as false consciousness—the reader is presumed to know what is true.[15]

In texts depicting a proletarian hero's growth toward class consciousness, free indirect discourse can convey quite the opposite effect: revolutionary understanding is asserted to be the possession of the disinherited. In *The Green Corn Rebellion*, readers are exposed to a direct statement of authorial politics when they encounter Jim's meditations about whether or not to lie to his wife, Jeanie, about his intended participation in the antiwar rebellion:

It wasn't always your own fault if you told a lie. Sometimes it was the fault of the person you lied to, or sometimes it was the fault of conditions. The big capitalists were the worst liars and thieves in the world. That's the way they got ahead. If people tried to get ahead and stay honest, like Jeanie, they didn't get ahead, but they turned into drudges, and other people lied to them and stole from them. Any way you looked at it, it was this damned competitive system that made people liars and thieves. (pp. 154–55)

Jim's meditation is entirely untagged—that is, unprefaced by a narratorial phrase such as "Jim understood that ———." Yet there is no doubt that the character's thoughts coincide with those of his creator. The ideas Jim articulates are corroborated by the portraiture of class antagonisms presented throughout the narration: "discourse" is redundant with "story." No lesson is explicitly drawn, however: the text *assumes* that the reader, having grasped the doctrinal argument being made through the novel's action, acquiesces in the implied judgment that Jim is drawing legitimate conclusions.

In most proletarian bildungsromans, authors do their rhetorical work

---

15. Louis Colman, *Lumber* (Boston: Little, Brown, 1931), p. 259.

by showing rather than telling. Authorial views are expressed, but usually implicitly. The reader enters into collusion with the author—as an appreciator of irony, an approver of growth, a judge of limitations. If doctrinal politics is overtly articulated, this almost always occurs through a character rather than a narrator. A few novelists, however, engage in commentary that sounds as though it is coming from the author in propria persona. In *Yonnondio,* Olsen intersperses a number of italicized passages in which she explicitly brings revolutionary politics to the fore. One such passage is addressed to a worker named Jim Tracy, who refused to commit himself to marrying and having children, engaged in a self-destructive rebellion against his boss, and died on a chain gang in Florida:

> And there's nothing to say, Jim Tracy. I'm sorry, Jim Tracy, sorry as hell we weren't stronger and could get to you in time and show you that kind of individual revolt was no good, kid, no good at all, you had to bide your time and take it till there were enough of you to fight it all together on the job, and bide your time, and take it till the day millions of fists clamped in yours, and you could wipe out the whole thing, the whole goddam thing, and a human could be a human for the first time on earth. (p. 79)

The narratorial voice in this passage has little in common with the voice who tells most of the story, alternately focalizing through the childishly acute awareness of the young Mazie and the harsh, alienated thoughts of her parents. There is, moreover, no "I-narrator" elsewhere in the text. The "I" who here expresses sorrow at Tracy's wasted militancy, and who regrets that "we" didn't get to him in time, can therefore be inferred to articulate the standpoint of the author herself. Jim Holbrook, Tracy's friend, is far from realizing that it is necessary to "wipe out . . . the whole goddam thing." Nor do events in the narrative make this larger truth self-evident. In order to bring in the revolutionary doctrine that is "outside" the purview of "story," Olsen creates a narrator who addresses the reader "from outside" the bounds of the text. As Olsen revealed to Constance Coiner, "I was writing the reason why we have to have a revolution." Coiner notes, "[Olsen] did not trust the novel, if stripped of these didactic passages, fully to affect her readers, to make them 'feel the impact,' and to indicate the causes and remedies for the Holbrooks' misery, which they themselves perceive and articulate only in a limited way." [16]

16. Olsen quoted in Constance Coiner, "Literature of Resistance: The Intersection of Feminism and the Communist Left in Meridel Le Sueur and Tillie Olsen," in *Left Poli-*

In *Babouk*, Endore's narrator even more frequently disrupts the narrative to inject commentary. At times the narratorial voice addresses the hero; at others, he turns to the slaveholders, whom he ironically advises that "it would be a mistake to be kind to [the Africans], for they were only looking to take advantage of your kindness" (pp. 147–48). The narrator's most common addressee, however, is the reader, who is positioned to squirm under his accusatory finger. Recalling Twain's grotesque anticolonialist iconography in "King Leopold's Soliloquy," the authorial voice at one point describes a huge chain binding together Africans on a slaveship, declaring, "Could you conceive of a strength able to lift up this great chain with all these Negroes suspended to it, you would have a gigantic necklace of blacks" (p. 363). Readers are implicated in the slave trade simply by virtue of being addressed: they "would have" the macabre jewelry. But readers are prevented from escaping responsibility by assuming that their own age is superior to that of Babouk. Inadvertently "slipping" into the "error" of contemplating more broadly the "whole subject of whether it's right or wrong to punish a Negro for a crime he did not commit, for example to lynch a nigger who did or did not rape a certain girl," the narrator issues a fulsome apology: "I beg the reader's pardon. That was an anachronistic

---

tics and the Literary Profession, ed. Lennard J. Davis and M. Bella Mirabella (New York: Columbia UP, 1990), p. 177. While remarking that "it is unlikely that Olsen knew she was employing a Brechtian device," Coiner points out the parallels between Olsen's method and Brecht's Verfremdung: "Such intrusions counter traditional realism, in which the present social order appears as natural, static, and immutable rather than contradictory, discontinuous, and, potentially, the object of revolutionary change" (p. 177). I question, however, Coiner's conclusion that Yonnondio "constrain[s]" the reader by imposing a "closure of meaning" (p. 178): arguably, the narrator's prophetic rhetoric liberates the reader by showing—to borrow the "leftist" but perhaps still useful term—the "way out." For negative criticisms of Olsen's narratorial voice, see Rosenfelt, 391–94, and Amy Godine, "Notes Toward a Reappraisal of Depression Literature," Prospects: An Annual of American Cultural Studies, vol. 5, ed. Jack Salzman (New York: Burt Franklin, 1980), pp. 216–18. In her journals accompanying the writing of Yonnondio, Olsen warned herself not to be "so rhetorical or figurative or whatever it is." But she also proclaimed her revolutionary conviction in rhapsodic terms: "O communism—how you come to those of whom I write is more incredibly beautiful than manna" (cited in Rosenfelt, 491). According to Conroy, Olsen (then Tillie Lerner) showed up at the first Writers Congress in a Young Communist League uniform (Robert Thompson, "Interview with Jack Conroy," Missouri Review 7 [Fall 1983]: 153).

slip. This is a novel about an eighteenth-century Negro. Today the black man is everywhere free and equal to the white" (p. 188). Endore's angry, judgmental narrator provides a running commentary redundant with the brutalities described in the narrative of the protagonist's captivity. He also ironically mimics the presumed neutrality of the genre of the historical novel: "This is a novel about an eighteenth-century Negro." The narratorial voice produces redundancy within "discourse" as well as between "story" and "discourse." Babouk's rebellion does not explain its own relation to the economics of colonialism, let alone its bearing upon the struggle for black liberation or for proletarian revolution in the twentieth century. In order for these matters to be explored, the text resorts to a knowledge—and a prophetic voice—coming from a sphere external to the narrative.[17]

Ideological Baggage

I have been examining the rhetorical strategies by which proletarian writers harnessed the conventions of a quintessentially bourgeois genre, the bildungsroman, to serve left-wing political ends. But the question of "tendency" must now be addressed. To what extent did the ideological presuppositions embedded in the genre of the bildungsroman contradict or subvert the manifest intent of these texts to instill class-conscious and collectivist values and attitudes? Could the "centered" hero of the classical bildungsroman be transposed to the proletarian bildungsroman without the baggage of bourgeois conceptions of selfhood? How compatible was the didactic plot of "conversion" with the genre's premise of seamless transparency?

In some proletarian bildungsromans, we have seen, writers successfully portray protagonists who become heroes because they actually change: they grasp the dialectic of historical necessity and transform themselves into its agents. Other novels, however, fetishize individuality and posit character as largely "given." The competitive hierarchies set up among

17. The character of Babouk was based on the historical Boukman Dutty, a Saint-Domingue slave who was "the most famous rebel leader before the rise of Toussaint L'Ouverture" (David Barry Gaspar and Michel-Rolph Trouillot, "Afterword: History, Fiction, and the Slave Experience," *Babouk* [New York: Monthly Review, 1991], p. 191).

characters highlight the uniqueness—even the inherent uniqueness—of the protagonist. Heroes in some novels are endowed with a valorized proletarian essence, emblematized by physical strength or sexual magnetism. In *The Green Corn Rebellion*, Jim's desire to roll in the hay with the equally sensual Happy takes shape as a spontaneous expression of an untrammeled proletarian gusto, thematically linked to his "natural" class consciousness. In a sexual loading of the dice of class, Jim's love of life is contrasted with the commodified lust of his businessman brother Tim—who visits prostitutes—and the asexual dreariness of his upwardly mobile wife Jeanie. In *Daughter of the Hills*, Dolly Hawkins is drawn to the banjo-playing John Cooper because of his musicality—suggestive of proletarian creativity—and dancing black eyes, thick mane of hair, and chest thick as a tree trunk—suggestive of proletarian strength. Even when he loses a leg in a mining accident, John never stops playing his banjo, nor does Dolly flag in her devotion, emotional and physical. John Stafford in *Horse Shoe Bottoms* is another miner whose proletarian virtues are signaled by physical vitality and sexual appeal. Contrasted with the boss's son, Don Simpson, whose "high boots, tightly laced up the leg, shortened his appearance," John "belongs to the pits." How else, the narrator asks, "could he have developed those broad shoulders, bulging with strength, the arms overlapped with thick muscles, a waist so thin and yet able to hold together such a frame?" In *Call Home the Heart*, Burke's Ishma exudes a similarly magnetic aura, although her appeal invokes an odd combination of elitist and proletarian values. While Ishma's "straight figure" is "built for strength," Burke cannot resist the narratorial aside that her protagonist has a "correct" nose, with "thin" nostrils (p. 13). Ishma's boldness and perseverance in the political realm are reinforced by her extraordinary physical qualities. When she is hospitalized after a car accident, her fractured thigh "heal[s] with a swiftness that amaze[s] the nurses" (p. 243). Eroticism produces co-optation: the reader of these novels is tempted to endorse their advocacy of working-class militancy out of romantic and sexual attraction to—or identification with—the protagonists.[18]

Accompanying the symbolic treatment of strength and sexuality in the

18. Tippett, *Horse Shoe Bottoms* (New York and London: Harper and Bros. 1935), p. 153. For an astute analysis of how the eroticization of protagonists reinforces ideology in novels, see Lennard J. Davis, *Resisting Novels: Ideology and Fiction* (New York and London: Methuen, 1987), pp. 123–30.

protagonist is, in some texts, a corollary type of mimetic opportunism—namely, the characterization of antagonist characters—villains, non-class-conscious workers—by traits that are largely irrelevant to the specifically doctrinal qualities for which these characters are being criticized. Suleiman uses the term "amalgam" to describe the technique whereby "a character is constructed in such a way that his or her culturally negative qualities are redundant with qualities whose pertinence is specifically ideological." "Culturally negative qualities," according to Suleiman, are traits that are perceived as undesirable by the culture as a whole, assume a common fund of values and attitudes, and furnish the basis for a priori judgments.[19] Characterization in some proletarian bildungsromans entails a certain amount of argument by amalgam. In *Moscow Yankee*, Crampton, the "bad" American engineer who has no concern about involving workers in decisions about production, is short and fat, continually stuffing himself with caviar. In *To Make My Bread*, Basil, the McClure brother who opts for the life of an upwardly mobile white-collar worker, ends up marrying his boss's daughter, who, glimpsed behind her veil, is, naturally, "ugly as homemade sin" (p. 263). In *Call Home the Heart*, Ishma's selfish and "wearily incompetent" (p. 2) sister Bainie has "cunning, greedy eyes" (p. 61) and is missing all her back molars (Ishma, of course, has all hers). Alma's brother Harold in *This Is Your Day* is academically unsuccessful and sexually repulsive as well as politically right wing. In *The Green Corn Rebellion*, Jim's venal and perfidious brother Tim has, emblematically, "a crippled back and funny legs" (p. 30); he never takes a bath. Any possible debate over the values encoded in the hierarchy of discourses that counterposes Tim with Jim—is it in fact so unproblematically positive that Jim, the lusty man of the soil, likes to have sex with his wife's sister?—is precluded by the reader's prior "re-cognition" of Tim's undesirable qualities.

In these texts, physical details—the concrete, in the crudest sense—are invested with the rhetorical power to generalize about class-defined essences—which, while "material," are hardly signaled by bodily features. Bourgeois values are treated as coterminous with Communist values: a discourse proposing a radical transformation of human potentialities and relations is embedded in narrative conventions premised upon the notion

---

19. Susan Rubin Suleiman, *Authoritarian Fictions: The Ideological Novel as a Literary Genre* (New York: Columbia UP, 1983), p. 190.

that character is fixed and intrinsic, recognizable by pseudoconcrete conventional indicators of "character."

Conventions of plot inherited from the classic bildungsroman can compound the depoliticizing effect of conventions of characterization. Some proletarian bildungsromans attempt to adapt to radical ends plot structures that foreclose rather than facilitate questioning of the fixity of inherited social relations. In particular, the movement toward a closure affirming the protagonist's discovery of meaningful selfhood can purport to "resolve" issues that in fact defy encapsulation within the narrative of an individual's odyssey. Intersecting and overlapping lines of action in a text's plot, we have seen, can suggest important parallels between the "private" zone of the individual character's development and the more obviously "public" arena of the class struggle. But mutually reinforcing plot lines can displace the narrative momentum associated with satellite events onto kernel events, thus evading political complications and producing a false sense of seamless completeness.

Romantic narrative conventions centering on the protagonist's achievement of sexual maturity and discovery of the right partner—perhaps the single most important impetus toward closure in the bourgeois bildungsroman—can lead to a blurring of political issues in the proletarian bildungsroman. In *Moscow Yankee*, Andy is never forced to confront the implications of his growing attraction to the Russian Natasha and his responsibility to his American fiancée Elsie, who, immersed in consumerism and status-seeking, has never had the benefit of the Moscow experience. Elsie at one point declares that she is planning to join Andy in the USSR, thus precipitating a dilemma of choice and conscience. Fortunately for Andy, however, the novel's action next focuses on the sabotage plot, which climaxes in Ned's chasing down the nefarious Alex and saving the Red Star tractor plant. This suspenseful episode rhetorically dwarfs the Elsie question: after the stakes in socialist construction have been shown to be so high, it feels only right that Andy should forget about Elsie, marry Natasha, and remain in the Soviet Union to contribute to the building of the workers' state. The momentum toward closure produced by mutually complicating plot lines thus effaces—or at least reduces—moral choice and sexual responsibility. The reader gets the impression that Andy has struggled through the Elsie/Natasha issue; actually, Page has simply let her hero off the hook. Asserted in the novel's climax and denouement, the overwhelming importance of the class struggle in its larger manifestations papers over important, if less global, questions about the politics of personal relationships.

Narrative closure can work in the opposite direction as well, falsely settling issues in the "public" sphere through the vicarious emotional satisfactions gained by resolving problems in the "private" sphere. The early and middle sections of *Moscow Yankee* broach the question of the division of mental and manual labor under socialism: what should be the relationship between the engineers who plan and oversee production and the workers who carry it out? The characterization of Boardman as a "good" engineer and Crampton as a "bad" one, as well as the various subplots dealing with workers' control of the assembly line, indicate that Page considered the nature of production relations an urgent issue that had not been satisfactorily resolved in the Soviet factory system. The sabotage subplot, however, poses that the impediment to building socialism consists not in the retention of wage-based relations of production, but in an external enemy—the White Russians and their henchmen. When the climax provided by this subplot is reinforced by the romantic resolution of the Andy-plot, the narrative loses its ability to interrogate any possible flaws in socialist construction itself. All that is needed to build the workers' state, it appears, is the zealous commitment of individual workers—Andy, Sasha, Ned, Natasha—plus tractors. The logic of the bildungsroman plot displaces the "public" onto the "personal": the latter functions not as a synecdoche for the former, but as a surrogate. The aura of "wish-fulfillment" surrounding the ending to *Moscow Yankee*—the "pink sunset" of which the *New Masses* reviewer complained—is not a function of the text's overly tendentious portrayal of Andy's "conversion" to socialism, but of its implied proposition that this "conversion" signals all that is necessary to effect successful socialist construction. Obscured in the bildungsroman's characteristic concentration on individual moral development is the fact that changes within individuals contribute crucially to the construction of socialism but do not necessarily typify larger social developments.[20]

20. This is not to say that the issue of industrial sabotage by the enemies of socialism was an opportunistic invention on the author's part. According to one Walter Rukeyser, who worked as a consultant mining engineer in the USSR during the first Five-Year Plan, sabotage was a key factor in preventing industrial enterprises for attaining their production goals. Apparently some 1,000 U.S. engineers worked in the USSR in 1931–

Romantic resolution to the bildungsroman plot also prematurely syn-
thesizes larger political contradictions in *Call Home the Heart*. In its final
pages the novel degenerates into a silly comic denouement about mistaken pairings: Ishma thinks that Britt has fallen in love with his neighbor
Julie during Ishma's absence, but Julie, it eventually turns out, has become attached to Ishma's brother Steve. (Julie's ambiguous references to
an unnamed "he" have led Ishma to think that Julie intends to marry Britt.)
Burke's reliance upon time-worn conventions of the comedy of errors trivi-
alizes the novel's feminist plot, which has constructed a hero who chooses
knowledge of the industrial world and the class struggle over life with
the man, and among the mountains, that she loves. But these melodramatic shenanigans—which bring Ishma to the verge of suicide one night
on the mountainside—also enable Burke to bypass the troublesome questions posed by the event that precipitated Ishma's hasty departure from
Winbury—namely, her revulsion at the embrace of the black Gaffie Wells.
Ishma chastises herself bitterly during the few pages that describe her train
ride back to the hills that are calling home her heart. But Ishma's bigotry is
entirely forgotten amidst the romantic plot's strong pressures toward closure. Although as readers we judge Ishma negatively for her flight from
Winbury, it is difficult not to shift into sympathetic gear as, privy to the dramatic irony surrounding her confusions in the final chapters, we root for
her to learn the truth about Britt and Julie before she kills herself in despair.
The erotic explosiveness of the reconciled lovers' embrace on the mountainside may be vicariously satisfying; however, it resolves none of the
crucial "public sphere" issues that have provided the dynamis of the plot
during the preceding three hundred pages. Indeed, Ishma's compromise
decision—she will keep a hand in the struggle by bringing mill children
out to the farm in the summers for a couple of weeks' vacation—deflects
the text from revolutionary class struggle to Fresh Air Fund liberalism.[21]

---

32 alone. See Peter J. Kuznick, *Beyond the Laboratory: Scientists as Political Activists in
1930s America* (Chicago and London: U of Chicago P, 1987), esp. "The Soviet Model: An
Alternative Vision of Science and Society," pp. 106–43.

21. In fairness to Burke, it should be pointed out that she did not consider the romantic mountainside epiphany the final word on her hero: the sequel to *Call Home the Heart*
was already in her mind. In response to some of Hicks's criticisms of the ending of *Call
Home the Heart*—including "the use of the Negro incident as the turning point"—Burke

Even in novels that do not produce closure through the reconciliation of lovers, the gendered conventions of the bildungsroman work against the articulation of a revolutionary critique of capitalist social relations. For embedded in the classic narrative of apprenticeship is the presumed separation of the worlds of domesticity and work: the former may obliquely reflect the latter, but it remains largely autonomous. Cruden's *Conveyor* offers an interesting commentary on the pervasive genderedness of bildungsroman conventions, for in its manifest content the novel contests and criticizes the view of the home as a haven in a heartless world. Jim is portrayed as an average proletarian, hating his boss in the auto plant but paying scant attention to the union organizers who urge collective action and rebellion. His false consciousness is registered primarily through his attitude toward Marie, his wife. When times are good, his being is wholly focused around his family, his bungalow with the white picket fence, and the things he plans to buy. After he loses his job and the bank forecloses on the house, he expresses his alienation by beating his wife, neglecting his child, and abandoning hearth and home for the tavern. Cruden focuses, moreover, on the contradictory character of the Depression's effects on women. While Jim feels emasculated and threatened by Marie's forced entry into the work force, Marie gains a new measure of independence and self-confidence, even though her factory job is exhausting, low-paying, and dangerous.

In the movement toward closure, however, Cruden closes off the text's discourse about the impact of sexism on class consciousness. For once Marie, again pregnant, abandons Jim, the narrative drops her story and follows Jim's increasing interest in what the organizers have to say. The novel ends with Jim leading a sit-down action in the Rivers plant, discovering a renewed sense of self-worth in the male peer group of auto workers and organizers, and receiving congratulations from the mentor character Bill Seaman: "I really admire you, Jim, for puttin' up the fight you did. Only I'm sayin' that your fightin' should be directed so it'll mean something, 'at's all I'm sayin.' . . . Now what we gotta do, Jim, is get you guys t'gether an' put up an organized front against Rivers an' the only way to do it's through the

---

remarked in 1932, "The incident of Ishma's retreat would have been handled differently had I not believed at the time that I would be able to write a second book continuing the story from that closing night on the mountain" (Burke to Hicks, January 2, 1932, Box 10, Hicks Papers).

Auto Workers Union." The text advocates class consciousness, but it has become the tale of an individual triumphing over adversity and discovering his identity. Even though Jim's relations with Marie have constituted the primary locus of his false consciousness, at the moment of closure the domestic sphere simply disappears. The plot of discovering class consciousness becomes the plot of a solitary male finding selfhood at the point of production.[22]

Character and plot, the fundamental building blocks of "story," can carry considerable ideological baggage in the proletarian bildungsroman. But narrative transparency can also inhibit the articulation of revolutionary perspectives. Not only the tale the novel tells, but the *way* it tells that tale, can reinforce the mechanisms of dominant ideology. The convention of focalizing through the protagonist's consciousness, for instance, can restrict the narrative to the hero's level of awareness, thereby placing con-

---

22. Cruden's subject matter certainly gave him the opportunity to treat Communist politics much more directly than he did in *Conveyor*. His description of the massacre of unemployed workers outside the Ford River Rouge plant in 1932 depicts the violence, but not the politics, of what transpired. Fraser Ottanelli gives this account:

> On a cold Monday morning, between 3,000 and 5,000 men and women marched from Detroit to the River Rouge Ford plant in Dearborn to present a list of demands to the company's management. At the gates of the factory marchers were confronted by police, firemen, and Ford's thugs who prevented them from entering the plant. A fight broke out, and suddenly policemen began firing into the crowd. By the time the shooting was over, twenty-three workers had been wounded and four were killed, including a sixteen-year-old boy and Joe York, the Young Communist League district organizer. The bodies of the four men lay in state for several days at the Workers Hall under a huge red flag with a picture of Lenin, and over 30,000 people marched in the funeral procession down Dearborn's Woodward Avenue. (*The Communist Party in the United States: From the Depression to World War II* [New Brunswick and London: Rutgers UP, 1991], pp. 33–34)

Cruden, honored as Writer of the Month in the *New Masses* in 1933, was quoted as saying that he was "planning to get to the Soviet Union, to work in auto plants there" (NM 6 [April 1933]: 23). In 1933 Cruden was working on the staff of the Locomotive Engineers Journal in Detroit. He wrote to Hicks, "I help edit the shop paper which the CP nucleus in Fisher Body gets out, although I am not a member of the Party" (Cruden to Hicks, March 9, 1933, Box 15, Hicks Papers). See also David Anderson, "Michigan Proletarian Writers and the Great Depression," *Midamerica* 9 (1982): 76–97. For more on the genderedness of bildungsroman conventions, see Elizabeth Abel, Marianne Hirsch, and Elizabeth Langland, eds., *The Voyage In: Fictions of Female Development* (Hanover: UP of New England, 1983), and Susan Fraiman, "*The Mill on the Floss*, the Critics, and the Bildungsroman," *PMLA* 108 (January 1993): 136–50.

siderable strain on the text's didactic resources. In Nearing's *Free Born*, Jim Rogers's embrace of a politics of multiracial workers' unity is posited as the ideological breakthrough necessary for the black proletariat, which will otherwise remain mired in the destructive nationalism that is a comprehensible but nonetheless incorrect response to these workers' victimization. But, as was noted previously (see chapter 5), Jim's awakening occurs through not represented experience, but memory. Having been introduced to a Marxist analysis of racism by Jane, Jim, we will recall, "realizes" that white workers are also oppressed by suddenly recalling a white fellow worker who continually spat blood as he labored. Jim's interaction with this character was never represented in the narrative, which has been given over to depicting the multiple experiences with white racism that have fostered Jim's hatred and distrust of whites. If Nearing had drawn a broader social canvas, including a range of characters, black and white, characterized by differing levels and types of political awareness, he might, we may speculate, have encountered less difficulty in depicting Jim's "conversion" to the notion of black/white labor unity as a "natural" outgrowth of his experience. Because the text is locked into the synecdochic presumption that Jim himself embodies the entire black proletariat, it cannot successfully locate a standpoint from which to introduce a solution that is in fact largely external to the hero's personal experience. The effect of "wish-fulfillment" accompanying the description of Jim's "conversion" results not from an overly aggressive articulation of "red" ideas, but, if anything, from their restricted representation. The text's insistence that its hero stands for the totality restricts access to that totality.

While focalization on the protagonist can confine readers to his/her limitations, the bildungsroman's characteristic reliance on free indirect discourse to articulate political doctrine can have the opposite effect—namely, of co-opting readers into agreement with ideas of which they may not have been persuaded and of which they may not wish to be persuaded. Most left-leaning readers will have little difficulty identifying with the values of the narratorial voice in *All Brides Are Beautiful* or *Moscow Yankee*. But some readers may squirm when positioned to share Ishma's repugnance at Gaffie's embrace. Others may feel reluctant to be included in Gene Marsay's complacent thoughts in *This Is Your Day* about the dilemma of male party organizers tempted to go to bed with women in the party's political base: "[He wondered whether] he would ever be enough of a Communist to regulate his sexual behavior exclusively or primarily with the interests of the Party at heart, wondering if anyone ever had."[23] The voice that in Newhouse's *New Masses* journalism boasts of seducing a five-and-dime clerk here reasserts itself as Gene's, implicating the reader in an approval of reds as red-blooded guys who are as roosterish as anyone else.

When the reader might be inclined to endorse the values guiding a text, however, free indirect discourse can short-circuit the procedure of actually winning the reader to these values. Rather than being required to query the legitimacy of revolutionary ideas, or directly confront the applicability of these ideas to their own lives, readers can be positioned as complicit with the author, occupying an Archimedean vantage point above the text. Take, for example, the following passage from near the end of *All Brides Are Beautiful*. The text has up to this point made it clear that Peter considers himself a Communist, but virtually nothing has been said about what this means in doctrinal terms. At the moment of closure, however, we are privy to Peter's thoughts as he contemplates the future that awaits himself, Susan, and the rest of the U.S. working class:

> And men and women everywhere were, it seemed to Peter, stirring to the promise of that new world. They were as yet puzzled, baffled, hardly aware of their power, but bitter with suffering and sure only that there must be a change. In a hundred thousand places they went on about their living, talking and acting much as they always had, one day like another. Yet things were stirring, changing, and perhaps even long afterward when you looked back you could find no place to put your finger and say, This is the boundary between the old and the new. That was how a child became a man, how a man grew old, how revolutions were made, how worlds changed; little by little, day by day.
>
> America was stirring, the ordinary men and women of its houses and streets and farms and shops, in a hundred thousand places the hundred million people who were America, massed from ocean to ocean under night that was a low ceiling, themselves like another sea, cast, in the darkness a presence, a restless surge, as if the invisible stars were goading it, higher and higher. (pp. 355–56)

Bell here delivers a little lesson in historical dialectics: the working class is stirring to self-awareness; slow quantitative changes in outlook will

23. Edward Newhouse, *This Is Your Day* (New York: Lee Furman, 1937), p. 171.

produce qualitative revolutionary change; the new is emerging out of the womb of the old. This knowledge is presented as the possession of the protagonist: "it seemed to Peter" that the ideas posed here are true. But while the use of tagged free indirect discourse proposes that workers like Peter are awakening to a sense of their historic task, the task itself is offered as something to be re-cognized, rather than cognized. Out of liking for Peter, readers may be glad that he has come to terms with his Communist responsibility. But this does not mean that they themselves have necessarily come to grasp that responsibility any more deeply. The text's presentation of doctrine in the form of internal meditation conflates truth with conviction. The closing metaphor, which conveys Peter's associative mental process, effectively reveals political doctrine as something felt, and not simply endorsed. But the metaphor's subjective impressionism further blurs the question of revolutionary agency, for it articulates the "people," or "America," as a natural force that will arise on its own—a "restless surge" guided by "invisible stars." A contemporaneous reviewer of *All Brides Are Beautiful* complained that Peter's Communism "seems at once undefined and yet too largely taken for granted by the author."[24] The conventions of the bildungsroman, which posit truth as an attribute of the hero's consciousness, are implicated in this narrative opportunism.

From the 1930s to the present, various critics have responded unsympathetically to the proletarian novel of "conversion," charging it with utopianism and formulaism. There is some validity to this charge. In their desire to project a "way out," writers of proletarian bildungsromans do frequently place the burden of confirming and articulating the text's doctrine on the protagonist. Through his/her experience, sometimes with the help of a left-wing mentor, the protagonist comes to "see" the truth of the doctrine molding and directing the narrative. But the at times strained effect accompanying these portrayals of developing class consciousness does not derive, as has been usually stated, from an excess of revolutionary zeal that forces "literature" into the mold of "propaganda." These texts are not, in my view, "leftist"—either in the sense of espousing ultrarevolutionary doctrine or in the sense of being excessively didactic. Rather, the difficulty encountered by writers of "conversion" tales stems in part from the authors' choice of a medium for telling these tales. The form of the bildungsroman,

24. F. Cudworth Flint, "Recent Fiction," *Southern Review* 2 (1937): 849.

with its tendency to focus on the individual and to foreclose contradiction in the movement toward closure, significantly inhibits the expression of a politics advocating collective consciousness and revolutionary change. Indeed, the genre loses some of the very qualities that make it an effective (if politically loaded) medium for exploring bourgeois consciousness and destiny. Transposed to the task of articulating an antibourgeois politics, the genre's cognitivist premise conflicts with its hortatory function.

Granville Hicks, defending himself in 1937 against the accusation of the *Partisan Review* group that he had encouraged the production of stereotyped and mediocre tales of "conversion," maintained that he had been right in encouraging writers to project revolutionary optimism. "The essential hopefulness of Communism is a fact, no mere theory," he declared. He was self-critical for "not hav[ing] borne down so heavily as I might have on writing that, in one way or another, I recognized as bad." If he had "tolerated" formulaic narratives, Hicks remarked, this was because "there is a dramatic reality in conversion. . . . and I have hoped that some day the formulas would be transcended." In my view, Hicks was justified in urging novelists to compose narratives displaying class-conscious change in the proletariat and its middle-class allies. But his later self-criticism was somewhat misplaced. For in contending that the "biographical" novel carried no ideological baggage and was as useful a medium as any other for telling the story of change, he had counseled an uncritical appropriation of the bildungsroman form. It was difficult for writers to transcend formulas when the genre in which they were working was, in many of its premises, antagonistically opposed to the very doctrine the writers were trying to articulate and embody.[25]

Doctrinal Politics and Generic Politics

The "tendency" argument poses that writers of proletarian bildungsromans were hamstrung by their choice of form. But, as we saw in the previous chapter, the "tendency" argument, in its "strong" form, runs the risk of formalistic determinism. We should recall Klaus's warning: "[T]o accord an

25. Hicks, review of Horace Gregory, *New Letters in America,* in Robbins, pp. 382, 383.

ultimate determinant effect, or even priority, to inherited forms is an abstract and constricting conception leading to formalism in the denigrating sense of the term." What can we say about the conjunction of generic and doctrinal politics in the texts we have been treating? When do generic and doctrinal politics provide mutual reinforcement? When do they conflict with one another?

Traditional conceptions of gender and gender roles, we have noted, are centrally implicated in both characterization and closure in the proletarian bildungsroman. The felt necessity to eroticize protagonists, to treat antagonists as sexually repulsive amalgams, and to simplify political issues through romantic plot resolution reveals that substantial numbers of proletarian writers relied upon the gendered conventions of classic single-protagonist realism. Even when a text sets forth a revolutionary critique of capitalist gender relations, it can reproduce deeply embedded—"familiar"—notions of male and female. But this susceptibility is not just a matter of form and convention. It reflects not just generic politics, but doctrinal politics. The CP-led left's various and sundry inadequacies in framing an answer to the "woman question" (see above, chapter 6) inevitably influenced the uncritical invocation of gendered literary conventions. John Stafford's torso recapitulates the barrel-chested iconography of the male proletarian in the *New Masses*. Ishma's gorgeous limbs implicate the reader in the male gaze frequently assumed in left-wing journalism. Moreover, the use of romantic plot conventions—or, conversely, the relegation of "domestic" plots to the sidelines—inscribes the widespread acceptance on the left of differential male and female spheres. Andy's settling in with the "right girl" reflects the left's largely uncritical valorization of the proletarian nuclear family; Jim Brogan's ready acceptance of Marie's departure and discovery of himself as a union militant articulates the sexual division of labor common, Vivian Gornick reports, in Depression-era left-wing families. These texts can reproduce familiar gendered literary conventions because they reproduce familiar discourses and practices.

Contradictions in the left's analysis of the issue of racism also influence the shaping of narrative in some of the texts we have examined here. In *Free Born*, the anomalous insertion of Jim Rogers's memory of the oppressed white worker is enabled by the text's insistent focalization through the protagonist and representation of political knowledge as the outgrowth of his experience. But the bildungsroman form does not *cause* the truncation of the argument for multiracial unity that results from this narrative treatment. This anomalous and strained moment, which produces an effect of "wish-fulfillment," also reflects Nearing's own hesitation about the relation of national to class oppression—a hesitation that in turn reflects the lack of clarity on this issue in the CP of the late 1920s, as manifested in the lengthy and impassioned debates on the subject throughout the theoretical literature of the left. (It is noteworthy that Nearing's sociological treatise *Black America* [1929], an important contribution to this literature, also ends with a wholly unanticipated argument for multiracial class-based unity. Certainly this text cannot be charged with conforming to the dictates of the bildungsroman form!) Similarly, in *Call Home the Heart*, Burke's abandonment of the question of Ishma's racism is facilitated, but not determined, by the strong impetus toward closure produced by the romantic plot. For the novel's political discourse, as articulated by Derry, opens up a conflicted doctrinal space with regards to race and racism. Derry chides Ishma for her "Neanderthal" racial attitudes and maintains that "workers, of whatever race or color, in these southern United States, . . . must take hands industrially and stand together." Yet he also opines, "I hope we'll not assimilate the black folk. I'd like to see a black race keeping to its own lines of life, intuitive, rhythmic with nature, building its own shelters for burgeoning" (p. 355). The Black Belt demand for Negro autonomy shades over, in Derry's statement, into an advocacy of black separatism; the political discourse of the text provides a rationale for keeping Gaffie out of Ishma's life. Literary segregation occurs in *Call Home the Heart* not just because the impetus of the love plot precludes deeper attention to "public" issues at the moment of closure, but also because the political doctrine informing the text does not make Gaffie's integration a compelling necessity.

Furthermore, workerist and economistic tendencies in the line and practice of the 1930s left are implicated in the proletarian bildungsroman's tendency to essentialize character and efface contradiction. John Stafford's Mr. Universe torso, John Cooper's magnetic musicality, and Ishma's Wonderwoman thigh are products of the assumption that workers are, *qua* workers, a revolutionary force. In *Conveyor*, the effect of ideological reduction accompanying Jim's salvation through discovery of a new identity as a militant unionist stems not just from the narrative's impetus toward closure but also from the economistic/doctrinal politics guiding the text. It is easy for Cruden to shut off the questions he has been posing about the viability of the proletarian nuclear family because his novel does not even raise the possibility that there might be an alternative social order. Bill Seaman may be a Communist (we never know for sure); in *Conveyor*, however, revolutionary politics are not on the agenda. The novel's final chapter represents Jim "finding" himself as a fighter for higher wages and better working conditions because these goals represent the limits within which the text has from the outset defined its political doctrine.

Productive forces determinism and spontaneism also contribute to foreclosed narrative contradiction. In *Moscow Yankee*, the emotional impact accompanying the satellite events in the sabotage plot can be deflected without difficulty onto the kernel events in the Andy plot not just because the bildungsroman form is intrinsically biased toward the hero's story, but also because the sabotage plot articulates key tenets in the Third-Period Communist view of socialist construction. The development of the productive forces—through proletarian muscle, enthusiasm, and commitment—is the overwhelmingly important task; changes in productive relations are important, but they can wait. The "pink sunset" at the novel's end is thus a function not just of sentimental romantic conventions but also of a technological-determinist-plus-voluntarist projection of how socialism will be safeguarded and built. Protect and expand the machinery, and everything else will take care of itself. The novel's genuinely revolutionary discourse about the "new Soviet man" and the "new Soviet woman" is juxtaposed with a counterdiscourse sanctioning the retention of wages and the continuing division of mental and manual labor.[26]

26. For a critique of productive forces determinism in Soviet socialist construction, see Charles Bettelheim, *Class Struggles in the USSR*, trans. Brian Pearce, 2 vols. (London: Monthly Review P, 1976–78), and Ira Gollobin, *Dialectical Materialism: Its Laws, Categories and Practice* (New York: Petras, 1986), pp. 457–72. Bettelheim remarks on the universal receptance of this outlook among 1920s and 1930s Marxists. Trotsky, for example, "accepts the thesis of the primacy of the development forces in its uttermost implications." Trotsky's statement that " 'Marxism sets out from the development of technique as the fundamental spring of progress and constructs the communist programme upon the dynamic of the productive forces' " is, Bettelheim asserts, a "caricature of Stalin's formula according to which the communist program must 'proceed primarily from the laws of development of production.' " Bettelheim notes that "despite the different conclusions drawn, [Stalin's and Trotsky's] theses (on the disappearance of antagonistic classes in the USSR and on the primacy of the development of the productive forces) were a sort of 'commonplace' in 'European Marxism' in the 1930s (remaining so until a comparatively recent date), which tended to obstruct analysis of the transformation of society in terms of the class struggle" (pp. 28–29).

Even in *All Brides Are Beautiful,* a novel presumably about a Communist worker, revolutionary politics are largely bypassed. In the closing passage previously cited, the movement toward socialism is presented as occurring without human agency, or at least without plan. The revolution will be made bit by bit, day by day. Its dialectics of process are entirely quantitative: qualitative change will be discerned only retrospectively, after the process has been completed. Peter can comfortably reflect on the truth he has recognized because it is not, in fact, a particularly incendiary truth. Even though the text has valorized his odyssey toward becoming a more involved party member, it has been notably silent on precisely what that means, other than becoming active and militant in on-the-job struggles. Narrative co-optation—"realizing" the truth of the character's insight—accompanies without strain an essentially reformist and meliorist view of change. Readers can be expected to agree because, in fact, they are not being asked to agree with anything startlingly new.

In sum, the relation of generic to doctrinal politics cannot simply be reduced to a relation of "form" to "content," of literary convention to political line. The conservative aspects of the bildungsroman form assert themselves most decisively when they coincide with, and reinforce, sexist, racist, economistic, or spontaneist attitudes or doctrine. Insofar as proletarian novels of "conversion" at times smack of formulaism, then, this occurs not because they are too revolutionary, but because they are not revolutionary enough.

There still remains, however, the issue of evaluating the efficacy of the bildungsroman as a means of conveying revolutionary politics. Was the ideological baggage of individualism and foreclosed contradiction the genre's only legacy to the proletarian writer? Or did it prove a usable form? John Reilly argues that, in novels written from a Marxist perspective,

> the representation of consciousness in realism assumes a new significance. The subject matter of the novel is not only individuals, but specific groups, represented by individuals acting in opposition to other groups, and, within the conflict, constituting history. The drama of character consciousness becomes a rising awareness of the interaction of individuals and the groups within which they find identity. In this rational apprehension lies the promise of liberation.[27]

27. John M. Reilly, "Images of Gastonia: A Revolutionary Chapter in American Social Fiction," *Georgia Review* 28 (1972): 516.

"Conversion," according to this argument, is the individual's "rational apprehension" of his/her class identity. The proletarian bildungsroman is therefore a paradox. The story of an individual's growth into mature selfhood involves a growth away from false consciousness—an abandonment of the illusion of uniqueness, a recognition of the necessity constraining and shaping personal experience. Taking a form historically designed to represent the individual's particularity, the proletarian bildungsroman tells the story of an individual learning to correlate his/her particularity with the destiny of his/her class.

I am less sanguine than Reilly that the conventions of realism can display the origins and dynamics of consciousness without shaping the terms in which consciousness is conceived. But it is important to acknowledge the extent to which doctrinal politics are plural and contradictory, not singular and monologic: they can counter, if not subvert, the narrative vehicle by which they are conveyed. Although closure in *Call Home the Heart* shows Ishma's heart being called home to husband and domesticity, the text has demonstrated that relations between men and women must be transformed—before the revolution—if revolution is to occur at all. In *Moscow Yankee*, the opportunistic intermingling of the love interest plot with the production plot does not entirely negate Andy's growth into a "new Soviet man" whose head no longer "wobbles" on his shoulders. *Free Born*, for all the problems accompanying its representation of Jim's "realization" of the common oppression of black and white workers, sharply poses the question of proletarian unity as the negation of nationalist false consciousness. *Native Son* masterfully uses the bildungsroman form to illustrate the tragedy of failed black awareness, from the standpoint of both nation *and* class: Bigger's non-"conversion" is marked by his failure to imagine beyond the bounds of self. Le Sueur's *The Girl* represents a young woman's personal maturation as inseparable from her maturation into a fighter for her class: she learns to think not in terms of an "I" ruled by "luck," but in terms of a "we" taking pride in the "anger" and "power" of her class. Even if in *All Brides Are Beautiful* the hero's Communist convictions are assumed rather than asserted, Peter has been shown to emerge from the cocoon of newlywedded bliss into a recognition of his place among the "hundred million people" who are "bitter with suffering" and "stirring to the promise of a new world." In these novels, "conversion" entails the characters' conceptual negation of individualistic false consciousness by class-conscious individuality.

In some proletarian bildungsromans, moreover, the synecdochic presumption of the genre is called into question: the text's single-protagonist format serves largely as a rhetorical convenience, one readily altered as the text develops new rhetorical imperatives. In *To Make My Bread*, the supersession of Bonnie McClure by her brother John signals that the proletariat is constituted by individuals who are interdependent, not autonomous. The novel starts out as Bonnie's story but ends focused on the political development of the strikers as a group; as Cantwell noted, "The points of reference in *To Make My Bread* are not what is fixed and rigid in society, but what is in the process of change." In *Babouk*, Endore continually halts the account of his hero's growing rebelliousness with extensive commentaries on racism and imperialism, past and present. The reader sympathizes with Babouk, but the constant interventions preclude cathartic identification. Endore, aware of the implications of his method, noted to Hicks that a fuller emphasis on the experience and feelings of his hero would have "ma[de] the story an individual one, . . . thereby leaving the enslaved mass behind." In *Yonnondio*, Mazie is the hero, but much of the narrative is focalized through her parents or the highly opinionated narrator, who emerges as a character in her own right. The text makes its revolutionary address to Jim Tracy without either the "conversion" of his friend Jim Holbrook or the intervention of a mentor. In Olsen's novel, the intrusive narrator guarantees that the reader understands the necessity for revolution, even if Mazie and her parents do not. As Olsen once commented, literary techniques directed toward revealing an individual's "core of self" were irrelevant to her enterprise, for she wished to delineate precisely those social forces that "tampered with" and "harmed" the presumed inviolability of the individual. As Coiner observes, in *Yonnondio* the voices of Mazie and her parents, in conjunction with the narrative's editorial voice, "compose a collective protagonist" and prefigure a "postindividual form" for novelistic discourse."[28]

In novels like *To Make My Bread*, *Babouk*, and *Yonnondio*, "conversion" is taken out of the realm of individual experience. The texts effect their

28. Robert Cantwell, "No Landmarks," in Morton Dauwen Zabel, ed., *Literary Opinion in America* (New York: Harper, 1951), p. 540; Endore to Hicks, June 4, 1934, Box 19, Hicks Papers; Olsen cited in Erika Duncan, "Coming of Age in the Thirties: A Portrait of Tillie Olsen," *Book Forum* 6 (1982): 211; Coiner, "Literature of Resistance," p. 178.

"return to the concrete" by reaching "outside" the boundaries of single-protagonist realistic narrative to bring in a knowledge of totality gained "outside" the limits of individual experience. These narratives explore the outer limits of the bildungsroman genre and bring us to the category of the social novel.

CHAPTER 10

➤

The Proletarian Social Novel

The term "proletarian social novel" denotes a multiple-protagonist work of fiction using traditionally realistic techniques of representation. The characters are generally drawn from a range of social classes; through their juxtaposition and interaction they delineate significant patterns and forces in the class struggle. There may be relatively few important characters, or a dozen or more; all, however, are correlated with one another through a plot indicating their interconnectedness, and all are subjected to a controlling narratorial point of view. Although it contains a bildungsroman component—characters learn and change—the social novel routinely focuses upon a strike or some other event in the class struggle and stresses confrontation over apprenticeship. Readers of social novels are moved toward revolutionary sympathies not so much from being educated along with the protagonist as from identifying with characters who have already chosen sides. Politics are frequently asserted in the proletarian social novel, but partisanship is largely assumed.

All generic classifications are arbitrary to some extent; some texts always are central to the defined category, others more marginal. The social novel is perhaps the hardest to define of the four types of proletarian fiction I am treating in this study. The term "social novel" does not denote a qualitatively defined species of writing, but rather an area along the narrative spectrum that blurs into the categories abutting it on either side. As a genre, it is heuristically defined. At one edge of the category are texts like Jack Conroy's A World to Win and William Attaway's Blood on the Forge, which diffuse their focus over siblings in the same family. Such texts have clear affinities with novels of education like To Make My Bread and Yonnondio, which, while initially featuring individuals, extend their focus over whole proletarian families undergoing crisis and development. At the other end of the category we have texts like The Foundry and The Land of Plenty, which, in their treatment of a range of characters involved in the clash between bosses and workers, have a good deal in common with "collective" strike novels such as Mary Heaton Vorse's *Strike!* and William Rollins's *The Shadow Before*. Several of the novels I treat in this chapter have in fact been considered collective novels by other critics and commentators.

Despite the occasional taxonomic difficulties it poses, the term "social novel" is essential to a generic analysis of proletarian fiction because it denotes a substantial body of realistic novels that cannot be successfully encompassed by the categories of the bildungsroman and the collective novel. Hicks devised the term "complex novel" to denote works occupying the space between the "biographical" novel and the "collective" novel. "The complex novel," he asserted, "has no individual hero, no one central character; but at the same time the various characters do not compose a collective entity; they may or may not have a factual relationship, but they do not have the psychological relationship that would entitle them to be called a group." Where the bildungsroman focuses primarily upon the education (or lack thereof) of an exemplary protagonist, the social novel characteristically subordinates the theme of the individual's development to the text's larger representation of social conflict. But where the collective novel treats the group as more than the sum of its individuals and often signals this interest in the group-phenomenon through various non-realistic narrative devices, the social novel preserves careful individuation among its characters, unifies them in a single narrative discourse, and presents their interactions by means of conventionally realistic narrative techniques.

The multiple-protagonist premise of the proletarian social novel clearly differentiates this genre from the single-protagonist modes of proletarian fiction. Is it then a more appropriate vehicle for conveying left-wing politics? Left-wing novelist Meyer Levin, discussing the theory of the "group-novel," noted in 1940 that "the group method, which eliminates the central character, and uses the interwoven experiences of many characters of equal value for the building of a story, is particularly à propos for the social novel. By its very lack of central-character emphasis it declares democracy. Moreover, its multiple viewpoint makes possible a more complete analysis of social forces than can usually be shown in central-character stories."[1] By virtue of its ability to undertake "a more complete analysis of social forces," we may speculate, the social novel gives the writer greater

---

1. Meyer Levin, "Novels of Another War," *The Clipper* 1 (August 1940): 5.

access to totality. Lenin, we will recall, stipulated that revolutionary activity aimed to supersede the fragmented and one-sided politics of reformism by "apply[ing] . . . the materialist analysis and the materialist estimate of *all* aspects of the life and activity of *all* classes, strata, and groups of the population." To the extent that the social novel represents the dialectical interconnections between classes, as well as within classes, it may be especially suited to position the reader "outside" the framework of bourgeois ideology. The "loose, baggy monsters" of literary proletarianism may turn out to offer privileged access to Leninist doctrine.

Yet the social novel is, *qua* genre, hardly a revolutionary form; it has roots deep in the liberal critical realist tradition represented by texts such as *Bleak House, Middlemarch,* and *A Hazard of New Fortunes.* As Christian Suggs has argued, even multiple-protagonist realistic novels are routinely premised upon the primacy of the individual:

> The novel gives the writer space to trace the processes through which the autonomous personality must find its identity, acquire its mate, define its best interests, identify the conflicts which surround that definition and resolve them, establish a family, and secure its fortune. A truly complex novel can do this for more than one character and chart decline as well as ascension, never losing sight of the privileged position that individual destiny occupies in capitalist culture.

We may speculate that certain conventions of novelistic realism will remain in force in the proletarian social novel. The genre's highly partisan— at times Manichaean—dichotomization of bosses and workers may rely upon essentialized conceptions of character. The drive toward a victorious—or at least optimistic—closure may mean that multiple strands of plot get woven into a single narrative thread simplifying complex social contradictions. Moreover, the text's strategy of what Susan Suleiman calls "persuasion by co-optation" may end up opportunistically positioning the reader. Contrasting the novel of confrontation with the novel of apprenticeship, Suleiman notes that, in the former, "the reader's evolution is placed between parentheses: the reader, like the hero himself, is presumed to be *already* on the 'right' side when the story begins." Such presumption can result in a subtle type of ideological pressure. If the reader is open to being co-opted into agreement, well and good. But if the reader resists co-optation, problems may arise. Whether or not proletarian social novels fall prey to realism's tendency toward covert control—and, if so, how and why—will occupy our attention in this chapter.[2]

Before we begin our examination of textual politics, a note on the place of the social novel in the brief life span of proletarian fiction is in order. As a group, social novels tended to appear later rather than earlier in the short life span of literary proletarianism: with the exception of *Gathering Storm: A Story of the Black Belt* (1932), all the texts discussed here were published in 1934 or after. As we will recall from Part I of this volume, discussions about proletarian literature in the years 1934–35 contained alternative potentialities. On the one hand, workerism was being subjected to critical scrutiny, and revolutionary perspective was being advanced over proletarian authorship as the decisive criterion for considering a text "proletarian." On the other hand, at this time the attack against "leftism"—that is, "schematism" and "tendentiousness"—was being waged and won. Proletarian social novels, we may anticipate, will both reflect and articulate the debates over politics and form occurring in the historical context out of which they were written.

Multiple Characters, Multiple Events

As in other forms of realistic proletarian fiction, patterns of comparison and contrast among characters in the social novel serve to outline the political values and beliefs of the author. If anything, such patterns perform an even more important rhetorical function in this genre than they do in the fictional autobiography or the bildungsroman. For the text's complex array of fictional characters invites the reader to translate comparative judgments of personality and morality into explicit political judgments about class and class consciousness.

In some texts, a distinct hierarchy of discourses is set up among working-class characters who make different sorts of political choices. In *A Time to Remember*, a novel set amidst a strike among New York City de-

2. Christian Suggs, Introduction, *Marching! Marching!* (Detroit: Omnigraphics, Proletarian Literature Series, 1990), pp. xxii–xxiii; Susan Rubin Suleiman, *Authoritarian Fictions: The Ideological Novel as a Literary Genre* (New York: Columbia UP, 1983), p. 143.

partment store workers (and closely resembling the 1934 Ohrbach's strike in which Leane Zugsmith herself was an activist supporter in the League of Women Shoppers), it is demonstrated that not all workers will conceive of their interests in the same way. Aline Weinman, a former student forced to drop out of college because of her family's worsening financial situation, wrests her personal independence from her patriarchal father through the process of joining with, and eventually helping to lead, the strikers. Doni Roberts discovers that selfhood means putting down the year-old torch she has carried for a young doctor who loved her and left her. By contrast, the shoe salesman Ralph Leamy becomes a spy for management in exchange for a paltry wage increase, even though doing so means losing the allegiance of his pro-union wife Stell.[3]

In *The Land of Plenty*, a novel about a strike in a Northwest coast lumber mill, Robert Cantwell erects a comparable structure for evaluating different political tendencies within the proletariat. All the bona fide workers—from the intrepid Hagen to his callow son Johnny to the honest Waino to the dour Winters—prove open to leftist politics; some, like both Hagens, emerge as leaders of their class. It is the summer laborer Walt Connor, a college student bent upon getting the attention of the mill owner's daughter, who attempts to rape his fellow-worker Marie, aligns himself with management, and finks on the strike organizers. Where Zugsmith, through Aline, suggests that some of the strongest fighters for the working class can be disenfranchised members of the petty bourgeoisie, Cantwell concludes that only a movement solidly based among those born and bred in the working class can escape sell-out and betrayal. Both authors, however, disperse their commentary on class origins and class partisanship over a broad range of characters. No single individual serves as a synecdoche for the working class or its cause.

The multiple-protagonist structure of the proletarian social novel also enables the writer to explore relations among and between classes. In novels of confrontation, the author frequently seizes the option to enter the

3. For more on Zugsmith's activities with the League of Women Shoppers, see Matthew Josephson, "Leane Zugsmith: The Social Novel of the Thirties," *Southern Review* 1 (July 1975): 530–52. For more on the role of the League of Women Shoppers in supporting striking workers, see Thelma Nurenberg, "Shopping for Justice," *Woman Today* (March 1936), 9, 14. Zugsmith may have named her protagonist Aline Weinman after Mrs. Aline Hays, the honorary national president of the League of Women Shoppers. Hays addressed the League of American Writers Congress in 1941.

consciousness of bosses and workers alike. In *The Foundry*, Albert Halper delves into the thoughts not only of various workers—August Kafka, the aspiring composer; Pinky, the wit; Buckley, the braggart—but also of the partners in the front office—Ezekiel Cranly, who is beset less by production worries than by his hemorrhoids; Max'l Steuben, who ends up incapacitated by a stroke caused by his gross bulk; and Jack Duffy, who enters into a narcissistic love affair, loses all his assets in the crash, and commits suicide in the plant bathroom. Halper is driving home the point that only the workers, who gain in power and cohesion in the course of the narrative, have the strength to confront the impending capitalist crisis. In *A Sign for Cain*, a novel treating the beginnings of multiracial Communist organizing in the South, Grace Lumpkin also juxtaposes workers and bosses. Various rank-and-file characters—the black Denis and the white Bill, both radicals recently returned from the North; the white farmer Lee Foster; the black house-servants Selah and Nancy—are implicitly contrasted with various members of the wealthy Gault family—Colonel Gault, the patriarch who cannot accept the decline of the plantation system and its accompanying chivalric ideology; Caroline, the bourgeois feminist daughter who manifests a voyeuristic sympathy with poor Southern women but under stress aligns herself with her reactionary family; Jim, the good-for-nothing son who murders his aunt Evelyn Gardner for money, pins the crime on Denis, and then murders him in his prison cell. As in *The Foundry*, this redundant thematic patterning invites the reader to draw the inevitable conclusion that right—if not justice—is on the side of the workers and sharecroppers. But in both texts this patterning of multiple protagonists permits the author to explore social reality from the vantage point of the exploiters as well as of the exploited. Capitalism, the novels demonstrate, produces alienation and misery among members of the bourgeoisie: even if they fight to defend their class position, as human beings the ruling elite are warped and confined by the roles they are scripted to play.[4]

Intertwined plot lines represent the pressures producing the confronta-

4. Halper noted that the character of Pinky was autobiographical (*Good-Bye, Union Square: A Writer's Memoir of the Thirties* [Chicago: Quadrangle, 1970], p. 151). One scholar suggests that, in spite of *A Sign for Cain*'s strong allegiance to its working-class characters, the portrait of Colonel Gault evinces a "nostaligia" on Lumpkin's part for her own roots in the Southern elite (Calvin Everett Harris, "Twentieth-Century American Political Fiction: An Analysis of Proletarian Fiction," Ph.D. Thesis, U of Oregon, 1979, p. 92).

tions of class warfare. In most proletarian social novels, there is no longer a distinction between kernel and satellite events: all are equally important. In *Pier 17*, Walter Havinghurst's novel about a violent Seattle mariners' strike, the plot line detailing the incidents that lead to the death of young Adrian Scarf, a would-be writer who envisions the strike as a clash of cosmic forces, is counterpointed by accounts of Tim Conners, the company stool who "sold out for four bucks a day"; of Lars Holderby, an experienced class fighter who dreads not the strike's violence but the "poison[ing] [effects] . . . of hate and fear"; of Taffy, a staunch but slow-witted striker who can never finish the letters home that he begins to write; and of Ann Bagley, an ambitious young reporter who will not hesitate to exploit her sexual attractiveness to get interviews with various participants in the strike. The truth of the meditations of the revolutionary Noonan—who reflects that the strike reveals "the great struggle, the classes warring with each other for the future of the world"—is borne out by the text's representation of the complex ideological warfare going on within the working class itself.[5]

In *Out of This Furnace*, Thomas Bell's CIO-era saga about the roots of union organizing among Slovak immigrant steelworkers in Braddock, Pennsylvania, the different plot lines are not concurrent but continuous. The narrative takes a single family through three generations and culminates in the participation of Joe Dobrejcak (Dobie) in the successful unionization drive of the late 1930s. Repeated parallels between and among the experiences of Djuro Kracha, his daughter Mary and his son-in-law Mike, and then his grandson Dobie make the unmistakable point that whatever progress has occurred in the Monongahela Valley mills has been the result of sharp class struggle. Mike's death in a pre-World War I mill explosion is avenged in his son's wresting a landmark contract from the company. In *Pier 17* and *Out of This Furnace*, the accretion of multiple instances of privation and oppression positions the reader to side with the workers when confrontation erupts. Didacticism hinges largely on "story"-level redundancies among the various plot lines constituting the narrative.

But the social novel's interconnections among different elements of plot can denote patterns of complex causality as well as simple repetition. In some texts, the braiding together of different story lines enables the author to explore the left's specific program for uniting various class sectors in

5. Walter Havinghurst, *Pier 17* (New York: Macaulay, 1935), pp. 61, 234, 85.

revolutionary class struggle. In Myra Page's *Gathering Storm*, the rape/ murder of Martha Morgan by the son of the local planter, followed by the lynching of Martha's parents and younger siblings, demonstrates the relation of Jim Crow terrorism to class rule. The development of Fred Morgan and Tom Crenshaw as organizers among Chicago packinghouse and Southern textile workers illustrates the necessity for multiracial unity among the oppressed. Marge's exhausting experiences with childbearing and child-rearing delineate the necessity for a socialist society that will free women from the burden of reproducing labor power in the context of the nuclear family. Eventually, conjoined in the Gastonia strike, the lives of Tom, Fred, and Marge suggest that workers' revolution is the only possible recourse for oppressed workers, black and white, female and male.[6]

In *A Stone Came Rolling*, Fielding Burke moves from the bildungs-roman format of *Call Home the Heart* to the genre of the social novel to explore the cross-currents of class struggle in the North Carolina textile mills. The plot devoted to Bly Emberson—an industrialist who hungers for the nonalienated social relations of a classless society and hands over his factory to worker management, but nonetheless ends up committing suicide—demonstrates the limits of liberal paternalism: not syndicalism but revolution will result in workers' power. The key roles played by various white and black characters—including Ishma's and Britt's son Ned, who seems to have inherited none of the bigotry plaguing his mother in *Call Home the Heart*, and Stomp Nelson, a less problematic successor to Butch and Gaffie of the earlier novel—illustrate the centrality of multiracial politics to the struggle for unionization. The story of Ishma's initial rejection of organized religion as a reactionary force, followed by her acceptance of Christianity as a potential site of oppositional politics, raises the issue of the church's function in grass-roots popular movements and suggests the possibility of coalition between Communist and non-Communist forces. The tying together of these different strands of narrative into the master

6. Paula Rabinowitz observes that Page's feminism emerges through the determining role the rape plays in the novel's plot: "More than merely a symbolic reenactment of bour-geois male degeneracy, rape functions politically as a form of oppression of the working-class (female) body as surely as do low wages (for the male) and, as such, produces its own historical effect, thereby motivating narrative" (*Labor and Desire: Women's Revolutionary Fiction in Depression America* [Chapel Hill and London: U of North Carolina P, 1992], p. 91).

plot of the unionization movement suggests that the struggle against the owning class cannot be won without sharp ideological struggle within the proletariat. The doctrinal politics encoded in *Gathering Storm* and *A Stone Came Rolling* differ significantly: Burke's novel, appearing three years later than Page's, is obviously influenced by the CP's Popular Front-era advocacy of alliance politics with progressive churches. The narrative strategy used in both works, however, is quite similar: intersecting patterns of structural causality within the pages of the text imply corresponding patterns of causality in the historical world inhabited by the reader.[7]

In *Gathering Storm* and *A Stone Came Rolling*, mutually reinforcing plot lines are mobilized in arguments explicitly demonstrating the correctness of the Communist analysis of contemporaneous social issues. In *Black Thunder*, Arna Bontemps uses the multiple-protagonist form to set forth a Marxist reenactment of the abortive slave revolt led by Gabriel Prosser in 1800. The main plot line, centering on Gabriel, his lover Juba, and other slaves who either abet or impede the planned insurrection, is spliced with the stories of M. Creuzot, a cynical Enlightenment liberal, and Alexander Biddenhurst, a radical proponent of the Rights of Man movement. (Biddenhurst declares prophetically, "We have the merchants, the poor whites, the free blacks, the slaves—classes, classes, classes. . . . I tell you . . . the whole world must know that these are not natural distinctions but artificial ones.") Gabriel, overhearing Biddenhurst in conversation with Creuzot, is strengthened in his resolve to storm the Richmond arsenal, for Biddenhurst's words signal "things that had been in his mind, things that he didn't know had names." The didactic connection between the two lines of narrative in *Black Thunder* establishes the relevance of Gabriel's rebellion for the world of the present—where, presumably, black rebels need no longer hesitate to reach out to their white allies, and white radicals need no longer feel powerless to act in solidarity with their black compeers.[8]

---

7. Sylvia Jenkins Cook comments on the thematic and structural difference between *Call Home the Heart* and *A Stone Came Rolling*: "This second novel is again ostensibly about the tension between contrary principles. [But it is] no longer a private war between head and heart for Ishma but a collective battle for the entire community between the rational Utopia promised by Communism and the supernatural heaven promised by Christianity" (*From Tobacco Road to Route 66: The Southern Poor White in Fiction* [Chapel Hill: U of North Carolina P, 1976], p. 108).

8. Arna Bontemps, *Black Thunder* (1936; rpt. Boston: Beacon, 1968), p. 21. Arnold Rampersad comments that "Bontemps discovered a link between the slave narrative and

In *The Land of Plenty*, Cantwell also sets up reverberations among the different elements in his plot and implies a prophetic drift in the events his tale recounts. As in *A Sign for Cain* and *The Foundry*, Cantwell delves into the lives of both bosses and workers. But his goal is not simply to indicate moral juxtaposition but to suggest the very different futures that class rule by each group will entail. In the first section of the novel—appropriately entitled "Power and Light"—Carl, the "efficiency expert," is both power-less and benighted when the lumber mill stops running because of an electrical failure. "In the blindness of no light he could only wait helplessly and believe that the miracle that had robbed him of his sight would soon give it back to him." MacMahon, the owner of the mill, is still less competent to find his way: in a fine comic scene, Carl and MacMahon are shown slogging blindly through the muddy flats beneath the mill, searching for a way out. By contrast, the workers, headed by the electrician Hagen, are not deterred by the darkness, for their intimate knowledge of the plant enables them to get it running again. Indeed, it is in the darkness that the workers discover their power and press toward the ensuing strike. The movement of the narrative implies not simply that the workers need to wrest reform concessions from these bosses, but that the entire working class needs to seize control of the means of production from the capitalists and their "experts." This will be the workers' "way out."[9]

Individual political development thus performs a different didactic function in the proletarian social novel than in single-protagonist proletarian fiction. Social novels by no means ignore the growth and education of particular characters. In *A World to Win*, Leo, the more proletarian of the two Hurley half-brothers, changes from a stool pigeon and strikebreaker to a militant organizer.[10] The final section of *The Land of Plenty* is en-

---

the revolutionary social and political goals that in the 1930s were associated almost exclusively with communism. That link was the crucial role played by the most radical egalitarian philosophy and activism of the French Revolution—the Jacobin tradition—in stimulating blacks to rise against their masters in Haiti, defeat the vaunted French army, and win their freedom" ("Introduction to the 1992 Edition," *Black Thunder* [Boston: Beacon, 1992], p. xii).

9. Robert Cantwell, *The Land of Plenty* (New York: Farrar and Rinehart, 1934), p. 4. According to Matthew Josephson, in the early 1930s Cantwell "used to talk as if he expected the Revolution to break forth almost any hour" (*Infidel in the Temple: A Memoir of the Nineteen-Thirties* [New York: Knopf, 1967], p. 178).

10. Interestingly, the novel had its origin in a short story featuring a single hero simi-

titled "The Education of a Worker" because of its strong stress upon Johnny Hagen's maturation. A Time to Remember features the growth of Aline and Doni as well as of Matt Matthews, a fellow worker who shrugs off personal and political passivity by discovering a unionist identity and considering leaving his loveless and mutually destructive marriage. Blood on the Forge, with its portraiture of fatal false consciousness, resembles a novel of non-conversion. Big Mat never finds the appropriate target for his alienation, taking out his pent-up rage and frustration on the closest available target: the mule that dragged his dying mother over the fields; his wife, Hattie; Anna, a fifteen-year-old prostitute; a nameless Ukrainian striker. When, after Mat's death, the blinded Chinatown sits across from a blinded World War I veteran on a train, Attaway pessimistically posits the failure of the black working class to see what is being done to it and by whom.

In these and other novels of confrontation, however, narratives of individual conversion—or nonconversion—are significant primarily for their relevance to the text's larger representation of class warfare. In bildungs-romans like The Girl and Moscow Yankee, didacticism is accomplished largely through the reader's vicarious identification with the naive hero who receives a political education. In Gathering Storm, by contrast, the burden of political education that first rests upon Marge soon shifts to the shoulders of Fred and Tom. The reader's initial impulse to identify with Marge and envision her as a synecdochic protagonist is supplanted by a drive to understand the meaning of the interlocked fates of Marge, Tom, and Fred. In Blood on the Forge, the full significance of the black migra-tion to the North is embodied neither in Big Mat's ironic failure to shrug off his nationalism, nor even in the fates of the three Moss brothers, but in the relations among all the workers—black and white, class-conscious and non-class-conscious—who have appeared in the novel. Meaning must be inferred from represented totality. In Call Home the Heart, the reader

lar to Leo. As Conroy wrote to Hicks, "I am plotting a novel about the theme of a short story which may see the light in Mr. Calverton's Modern Monthly after being rejected by every other magazine in existence. It will be the story of a scissors-bill worker who keeps begetting kids in spite of all efforts to dam the flood. 'Little Stranger,' the title of the story, would also serve as a title for the novel" (Conroy to Hicks, n.d., Box 14, Hicks Papers, Arents Library, Syracuse U). Apparently it was Covici-Friede, the novel's publisher, that wanted the title "A World to Win" (The Jack Conroy Reader, ed. Jack Salzman and David Ray [New York: Burt Franklin, 1979], p. 140).

is invited to participate imaginatively in Ishma's political education at the hands of Derry. In *A Stone Came Rolling*, by contrast, the focus of the narrative continually turns to other characters—Bly Emberson, Stomp Nelson, Derry himself. Ishma is still eroticized by her creator—both Derry and Bly appear to be hopelessly in love with her, as is, of course, Britt— but she emerges in the sequel text as one among several protagonists. The text's dissemination of narrative interest over a series of characters and plot lines requires the reader to analyze the social forces giving coherence to the novel's different elements. In the proletarian social novel, typicality derives from the range of represented characters and actions rather than from the synecdochic status of any single character's political odyssey. The "ought" of the text's larger political argument rarely hinges on an assertion that the protagonist's development "is" exemplary of the proletariat.

Mentor Characters: Views from Inside and Outside

A further consequence of the expansion of the narrative canvas in proletarian social novels is that mentor characters, both as actors in the plot and as educators of the reader, end up playing somewhat different roles than they do in single-protagonist novels. Because there is less emphasis on individual protagonists' internal development, in multiple-protagonist texts mentor characters are often less visible and audible than they are in single-protagonist texts. In *The Foundry*, the radical Karl Heitman drops some class-conscious remarks now and then about the drift of the precrash economy; but the text's prophecy of impending class warfare emerges primarily from the implicit contrast between parasitic bosses and resourceful workers. In *The Land of Plenty*, the former Wobbly Vin Garl is hinted to have "red" politics, but he keeps these under his hat. When at the novel's end Vin Garl tells Johnny Hagen that his father has been killed, we learn that Johnny and another nameless striker "sat there listening to [Vin], their faces dark with misery and anger, listening and waiting for the darkness to come like a friend and set them free" (p. 369). The reader may speculate that Vin is teaching Johnny and the wounded striker about the need for workers' power: the word "listen" is stressed, and it is suggested that the coming emancipatory darkness (the class war?) will negate the darkness on their faces, bringing, eventually, genuine "power and light." But the text only hints at such an interpretation. The mentor himself is, to the reader—who "listens" over Johnny's shoulder—notably silent.[11]

In fact, mentor characters in proletarian social novels infrequently play a crucial role in shaping the consciousness of other characters. Zugsmith —who through her own participation in the activities of the League of Women Shoppers was aware of the leading role played by Communists in the Ohrbach's strike—keeps the role of the party under wraps in *A Time to Remember*. Indeed, the organizer Bert has only one opportunity—and then at the novel's end—to speculate to Aline, "Suppose human beings had to forego love and ties of affection for a space of years so that millions of human beings could come out of their cellars and enjoy love because, for once, they'll have enough to eat and time to rest." While contributing to the novel's discourse about the relationship between love and class struggle, Bert's comment only adds a pinkish gloss to an already completed portrait of social relations. In *A World to Win*, the black Communist organizer Fatfolks makes three brief appearances in the novel—once near the beginning when he refers to the "Lenin speerit," once near the middle when he tells Robert to "clear them capitalis' cobwebs outen yo' brain," and once at the end as the martyr whose death at the hands of the police prompts Leo's decision to join the "comrades." But Leo's political radicalization results not from anything Fatfolks has said to him (whether overheard by the reader or not) but from what he himself has gone through—in particular, he tells Robert, from the brutal childbed death of his wife Anna in a roadside ditch. The mentor enters not to cause, but to validate, the protagonist's decision to join the movement to overthrow capitalism. The proletarian social novel's reduced concentration upon individual "conversion" generally results in a significant reduction in the rhetorical function of mentor characters, both as "story"-level helpers influencing the development of central characters and as "discourse"-level agents educating the reader.[12]

But if left-wing characters appear less frequently as mentors to naive protagonists in some texts, in others they move beyond ancillary "helper"

11. Cantwell apparently knew Wobblies like Vin Garl from personal experience. Josephson remarks that Cantwell was "of working-class origin with Western radicals of the IWW in his family" (*Infidel*, p. 144).

12. Leane Zugsmith, *A Time to Remember* (New York: Random House, 1936), p. 339; Jack Conroy, *A World to Win* (New York: Covici-Friede, 1935), pp. 59, 160.

functions and emerge as characters in their own right. They are not simply listened to, but focalized. In *A Sign for Cain*, Lumpkin assigns interiority to a number of her characters, giving the reader direct access to the thoughts not only of the sharecroppers and their wealthy antagonists but also of the Communists like Denis and Bill who are trying to weld the rank-and-file into a fighting force. In *Pier 17*, the cynicism of Lars Holderby, who "had been through . . . [the] hunger and waiting and emptiness," (p. 34) and the spontaneism of Taffy, who beats up scabs but is incapable of weighing the larger meaning of his acts, are counterposed with the patient wisdom of Noonan, who realizes the need for both militancy and caution and reflects that "there is nothing real but human need and human right and human welfare" (p. 85). The inclusion of Noonan among the text's several protagonists demonstrates that the strike is not simply a contest between bosses and workers over working conditions, but a struggle over which ideas will lead the proletariat in the longer run. The presence of politically radical characters among the social novel's dramatis personae asserts the existence of articulate revolutionary forces right within the working-class movement. The organized left is portrayed not as "converting" future leaders from the ranks of the proletariat but as organizing Communist activity in the present. Readers are assumed not to need catechism, but instead to "recognize" such types out of their own experience in class struggle.

In proletarian social novels, long monologues about class struggle and the merits of Communism are generally superseded by dialogue. At the beginning of *Gathering Storm*, Granny Crenshaw has a chat with young Marge in which she sets her granddaughter straight about the proletarianization of the mountain people, the inherent antagonism of workers and bosses, and the causes of imperialist war. Later in the novel, the necessity for black self-determination comes out in a discussion between Tom Crenshaw and one of his coworkers. In *A Stone Came Rolling*, Burke—certainly one of the windier proletarian novelists—guarantees the reader's political education through plenty of talk about politics: Dr. Schermerhorn fulminates against the status quo as "the dictatorship of capital"; Ishma and Bly discuss the role of the machine in creating leisure time under Communism; an anonymous "Negro radical" addresses an Independence Day crowd about the devastating "crisis of overproduction" that is "keepin' twenty million of us hungry and half naked." Nonetheless, *A Stone Came Rolling* contains no didactic moment equivalent to the long speech about Communism by the "Northern organizer" in *Call Home the Heart*. Presumably the Northern organizer's audience now talk about left-wing ideas without his inspiration. In *Black Thunder*, the debates among Gabriel, Juba, Mingo, and other slaves about the tactics of their revolt furnish, Rampersad notes, "a broad spectrum of political sophistication" and reinforce the thesis that it is the masses, and not great leaders, who make history. Even though Gabriel leads the planning to seize the arsenal, he utters no lengthy speeches that establish his unique qualities. It is dialogue among the rebels—including Mingo's prophetic remark that "You ain' free for true till all yo' kin peoples is free with you" (p. 115)—that provides the attempted insurgency's rationale. In these texts, talk about rebellion and revolution is part of the text's referent. It is not incumbent on the narrator—or a stand-in for the narrator—to raise left-wing ideas; the oppressed are already discussing them.[13]

Transparent Narrative and Views of Totality

Because of their tendency to embed rather than proclaim political doctrine, proletarian social novels usually adopt a fairly transparent method for telling their stories. Narrators are generally subdued rather than noisy, with free indirect discourse performing many of the functions of narratorial intrusion. As Suleiman notes, when "the characters themselves . . . interpret their story, . . . the narrator's interpretation is [rendered] superfluous" (p. 39).

Page's *Gathering Storm* is the exception that proves the rule: the rhetorical difficulties Page encounters in combining narratorial commentary with multiple-character focalization demonstrate how unnecessary a talky narrator is in a proletarian social novel that has other available means for getting the point across. The text abounds with instances of tautologi-

13. Fielding Burke, *A Stone Came Rolling* (New York: Longman, Green, 1935), pp. 94, 160; Rampersad, p. xv. Hazel Carby, arguing that *Black Thunder* challenges the "ideolog[y] of a romantic rural folk tradition," notes that the novel represents "the collective accoun[t] of a black community as [a] sign for [a] future collective accoun[t] of rebellion and liberation" ("Ideologies of Black Folk: The Historical Novel of Slavery," in Deborah McDowell and Arnold Rampersad, eds., *Slavery and the Literary Imagination: Selected Papers from the English Institute* [Baltimore and London: Johns Hopkins UP, 1989], p. 140).

cal political commentary. When young Charlie and Myrtle Morgan are re-
buffed by the racist parents of their white playmates, Billy and Sam, the
narrator remarks, "Charlie and Myrtle, like Billy and Sam, had been taught
their first lesson in race prejudice. Never again was the shaded lane of
over-hanging trees to be a care-free place in which to play. Part of the glow
of the creek was gone forever. Something ugly and mean, dimly compre-
hended but deeply emotional, entered their souls and tainted their breath"
(p. 71). When Tom Crenshaw later reads in the newspaper of the victory
of the Bolsheviks, the narrator conveys Tom's thoughts; " 'This is the first
break in capitalism's chain. *And it won't stop here.*' " The narrator then
adds, "Everywhere in the city working people were celebrating. The first
break in the chain." The narrator next abandons Tom and, interrupting the
narrative for four pages, goes on to provide additional political analysis
of the World War I period, including a critique of U.S. government propaganda, the suppression of the left, and the AFL's treachery. But even
such narratorial intervention is apparently inadequate to the job. Then
Page introduces a letter written to Marge by her husband Bob, recounting
a story about one Will Hendricks, a draftee from the Kentucky hills who
rebels against military discipline, flees from the authorities, and ends up
mangled under the wheels of a freight train. This incident is supposedly
being reported in Bob's letter. But Page forgets about her epistolary vehicle
and dramatizes parts of the Will Hendricks tale in full, including dialogue.
(When challenged by a "snappy second lieutenant" about his open collar,
an unspecified narrator reports, " 'I can't stand the damn thing,' Will stut-
tered. The men snickered.") Meanwhile Tom has been left sitting with his
newspaper.[14]

Page was a fledgling writer of fiction when she composed *Gathering Storm;* it is easy to view such instances of cliché-ridden style and
poorly oiled plot simply as evidence of inept workmanship. Even left-
wing reviewers who applauded Page's forthrightly revolutionary political
stance disliked the text's heavy-handed maneuvers. Page herself noted
self-critically many years later that she had tried to "put everything but
the kitchen stove" into this first novel. But Page's difficulties in *Gathering
Storm* stem not just from a tyro's desire to say everything but also from the

14. Myra Page, *Gathering Storm: A Story of the Black Belt* (New York: International,
1932), pp. 71, 154, 165.

tautological redundancies she sets up between "story" and "discourse." The incident in which Myrtle and Charlie are spurned by their playmates' parents quite transparently reveals its own meaning, particularly when juxtaposed with other incidents documenting the Morgan family's racial victimization. Bob's interactions with other draftees, Will Hendricks's story, and Tom's meditations on the revolutionary possibilities opened up by the Great War render superfluous the narrator's extended comments on the war. The intersecting lives and juxtaposed thoughts of the novel's multiple characters tell us a great deal about the dynamics of oppression and resistance; the narrator need only minimally guide the reader's responses. In *Gathering Storm*, most redundancies between "story" and "discourse" provide little new knowledge; the author's desire to explain every episode works against the text's generic premise of seamless transparency.[15]

Most proletarian social novels, however, make quite sparing use of narratorial commentary. For when a many-stranded plot sets forth an implicit analysis of social phenomena, there is relatively little need for a narrator to explain the surrounding totality. In *Black Thunder*, Bontemps relies entirely upon intersecting plot lines and parallel characters to argue his thesis about the necessity for class-conscious multiracial unity. He reserves free indirect discourse for glossing the text's larger political lessons—as when, in comparing Creuzot and Biddenhurst, the narrator notes that the former "did not think, as did the young man with the bushy hair, the thick-lensed spectacles and the copy of the *Dictionnarie Philosophique* under his arm, that there was hope for the masses in Virginia, that white and black workers, given a torch, could be united in a quest" (p. 24). Similarly, Attaway's narrator in *Blood on the Forge* only rarely engages in interpretive commentary—as when he describes the efforts of the Moss brothers to grasp their relation to the black scabs who, like themselves, have fled from Southern lynch violence and been transported North in boxcars: "They

15. Page, Tape 1, Oral History of the American Left, Tamiment Library, NYU. Page, like Tippett, was a social scientist turned novelist: she had a Ph.D. in sociology and taught at the university level for a decade. *Gathering Storm* was published by the CP's International Publishers: it was too far left for any of the mainstream publishers, one of which wanted her to take out all the material about antiracism. The *New Masses* reviewer, while congratulating Page on writing from the perspective of "one who has studied Marxism and Leninism," didn't think much of *Gathering Storm* as a novel, noting that it was like a too-rapid movie reel (Esther Lowell, "*Gathering Storm*," *NM* 8 [May 1933]: 29).

sensed the relationship of themselves to the trouble in the mills. They knew all of those men herded in the black cars. . . . For a minute they were those men—bewildered and afraid in the dark, coming from hate into a new kind of hate." But the limitations on the Moss brothers' consciousness are mostly conveyed by situational irony: the reader sees what they do not.[16] In *The Land of Plenty* Cantwell's narrator refrains almost completely from offering interpretations and generalizations about the meaning of the collision between workers and management during the plant blackout. A rare commentary occurs at the end of "Power and Light," which has described the workers' growing awareness of their ability to carry forward and strike: "They had their first sure knowledge of their strength" (p. 204). In these texts, didacticism is mainly conveyed not through narratorial voice, but through the juxtaposed actions and personalities of oppressors and oppressed.

When narrators in social novels do comment on the larger meaning of the narrative, they often reserve this option for the moment of closure. At times the narratorial comment is oblique. In the last sentence of *The Foundry*, Halper's narrator, who has been notably noninterpretive throughout the narrative, observes that the printing plates produced by the workers "lay [upon Jack Duffy's table] long and cruel and gleaming, waiting to be checked off and clamped upon the presses." He implies that the foundry workers, who have just demonstrated their strength in a showdown with the bosses, are gaining an awareness of their power that will make them a dangerous adversary in the future. On the last page of *A Sign for Cain*, the narrator, having described the multiracial group of sharecroppers that has been consolidated into a core of organized fighters out of Denis's murder, remarks that "[t]he light from the lantern spread over the men as they passed through the back door. It made them appear larger, of heroic proportions, and their shadows thrown against the white-washed wall of the cabin made it seem that others were walking with them, so that their number was multiplied." The narrator is present as an observer of some kind: to whom else did the size and number of the organizers "seem" and "appear" so significant? But her voice has no distinctive quality. Readers are simply assumed to agree that the radicals are "heroic." As in Halper's novel, the

16. William Attaway, *Blood on the Forge* (1941; rpt. New York: Monthly Review, 1987), p. 224.

narrator presages without actually predicting the revolutionary upsurge—and without explicitly taking sides.[17]

Other proletarian social novels close with overt authorial directives about how characters are to be viewed. We will recall that Attaway, who has held his didactic punches throughout most of *Blood on the Forge*, attributes to Big Mat at his death a glimmering of class consciousness: "Maybe somewhere in these mills a new Mr. Johnson was creating riding bosses, making a difference where none existed" (p. 288). Free indirect discourse carries the burden of political argument: Big Mat is shown to "realize" the argument that Attaway has to this point conveyed almost completely by implication. The narratorial intervention at the end of *A World to Win*, which describes Robert and Leo finally united in the context of the Communist movement, espouses revolutionary politics:

> They sat enclosed warmly in the comradeship of sorrow and weariness and anger, fellows of the men and women—fighting, laboring, seeing—who cry out relentlessly and passionately at factory gates, who mass in thousands on the steps of city halls and in the streets to reiterate endlessly and inexorably their harsh questioning of those who batten on the flesh and blood of the inarticulate and the submerged. Their breath a whisper that will not die—the prelude to storm. (pp. 347–48)

The voice that decries those who "batten on the flesh and blood of the inarticulate and the submerged" unambiguously expresses authorial values. Until now, however, Conroy has quite rigorously confined himself to the perspective of either Leo or Robert. What is striking about this passage is its rhetorical exteriority to preceding events: the narrator is engaged not in informing or persuading, but in summing up. As in *The Foundry*, *A Sign for Cain*, and *Blood on the Forge*, closing narratorial commentary simply places a seal upon arguments that have already been didactically conveyed through "story"-level elements of characterization and plot.

The doctrinal politics articulated at the moment of closure in the pro-

---

17. Albert Halper, *The Foundry* (New York: Viking, 1934), p. 499; Grace Lumpkin, *A Sign for Cain* (New York: Lee Furman, 1935), p. 374. Marcus Klein notes that Halper moved substantially to the left after *Union Square*, which offers a cynical view of workers and Communists alike. "The revolutionary program you are projecting is the only way out of the mess and wreckage which our statesmen still insist on calling civilization," Halper wrote to the *New Masses* in 1934 (cited in Klein, "Introduction," *Union Square* [1933; rpt. Detroit: Omnigraphics, 1990], p. ix).

letarian social novel do not, of course, have to be revolutionary. At the end of Bell's *Out of This Furnace*, Dobie's thoughts about the usability of democratic institutions by insurgent workers articulate the Popular Front reformism that the author wishes to impress upon the reader:

> "I hope it's all in the Declaration of Independence and the Bill of Rights," Dobie reflected, "though that never kept the company from pushing us around whenever it happened to feel like it. And they'd still be pushing us around and the Declaration of Independence and the Bill of Rights would still be nothing but a couple papers in a glass case down in Washington if a lot of us hadn't got together and started fighting for what we believed in. And maybe it'll always be like that. I don't know. . . .
>
> "Patrick Henry, Junior—that's me. Give me liberty or give me death. But he meant every word of it and by God I think I do too."
>
> *Out of this furnace, this metal.*

The narrator's final italicized comment stresses what Dobie "realizes" is the truth: "America" can be made to work for the workers. While free indirect discourse furnishes the principal means of argument, the narratorial intrusion guarantees that the point will not be missed.[18]

In the proletarian social novel, characters may converse, but narrators do not engage in a lot of talking. "Discourse"-level didacticism generally works at levels of which the reader is only hazily aware. The strategic juxtaposition of different plot lines—a feature of "discourse," we will recall, and not, strictly speaking, of "story"—reinforces important points of political doctrine without requiring the narrator to offer an interpretive gloss. In *A Time to Remember*, Zugsmith immediately follows her account of Ralph Leamy's attempt to seduce Aline Weinman with a description of the circumstances leading to the present pathetic state of Matt's wife Myrtle, who, we learn, some time ago destroyed her eyelashes with dangerous cosmetics and now despairs of ever attracting her husband again. By paralleling the two plot lines, the text links the politics of personal relationships with those of the class struggle. Narcissism emerges as a distinctively capitalist distortion of sexuality. In *Black Thunder*, Bontemps connects the Rights of Man movement with the Prosser rebellion by juxtaposing Gabriel's hanging with the death by stoning of M. Creuzot's servant Laurent, who is branded a "Jacobin" by a mob of reactionary whites. In

18. Thomas Bell, *Out of This Furnace* (1941: U of Pittsburgh P, 1976), pp. 411–12.

both texts, an argument about totality is embedded in a form structurally reproducing that totality.

It would appear that many proletarian social novelists accorded with the literary left's aesthetic program and steered clear of those overt didactic strategies that drew down the wrath of the Marxist critics. "Editorializing" and "sloganeering" are obviated by a representational strategy that effaces partisan narratorial voices and refracts political argument through a variety of figures who discuss and debate. Readers not in agreement with these texts' view of where history is heading may view them as utopian. But utopianism on the level of "story"—consisting in "conversion plots" and "wish-fulfillment" endings—is to a significant degree avoided by the removal of the burden of political argument from single protagonists and the diffusion of character development over a range of characters, none of whom is required to signal an exemplary path. Furthermore, the social novel's characteristic reliance upon implicitness means that argument proceeds through concreteness: guiding abstractions, as the Marxist critics counseled, tend to be "woven" into and "blended" through particulars of character, plot, and point of view. Totality emerges through the dialectical synthesis of these particulars, and the interconnections among real historical classes are laid bare by the interrelations among their fictional analogues. Didacticism emerges primarily from cognition, not exhortation. In short, the social novel would seem to have fulfilled many 1930s literary radicals' stipulations regarding the relation of politics to form in proletarian fiction. Its practitioners can lay claim to being left-wing without being "leftist."

Co-optation

As we have seen in Part I of this study, however, the criticism of "leftism" had various "rightist" aspects. Even though the proletarian social novel as a genre repudiates a number of the individualistic premises of single-protagonist fiction, it makes wide use of representational strategies derived from classical novelistic realism. Do these strategies in any way undermine the text's doctrinal politics? Does the social novel's counterposition of groups engaged in sharp class conflict encourage essentialist characterization? Does the genre's plot of confrontation bypass the task of reader education by assuming in advance the reader's political allegiance?

Does the very embeddedness of the general in the particular—the implicit-ness and "woven"-ness of the narrative—in any way hamper the text's expression of revolutionary politics?

Some writers of proletarian bildungsromans, we have seen, posit inher-ent conceptions of character that opportunistically invoke cultural biases unrelated to the doctrinal points at issue. In social novels comprising mul-tiple fictional actors sketched by very few brushstrokes, the temptation to reduce character to caricature—particularly in the case of villains—can be greater still. In proletarian novels of confrontation, capitalists are often incompetent and physically repulsive. In *The Foundry*, Max'l is despicable as much for his vast bulk as for his abusive treatment of the workers; more satiric barbs are directed at Cranly's hemorrhoids than at his inadequacy as a financial manager. In *A Time to Remember*, Sigmund Diamond, the department store owner, is predictably endowed with a large belly and a cigar. In *The Land of Plenty*, Carl's inability to make a single correct decision about production verges on idiocy.

No doubt it could be argued that such stereotypes are based in reality: because they are not engaged in productive labor, bosses are likely to be fat and incompetent. Cantwell took this line of argument when, responding to Farrell's objection that Carl and MacMahon were "created out of a theory," he remarked,

> Several people have accused me of having credited the ruling classes with too little, but when I pressed them for their own experiences they have invari-ably been reminded of individuals no more astute than Carl or MacMahon. I don't know whether the picture is true in a broad sense or not. I only know that my own experience has been that extremely stupid individuals seem to be selected for the task of overseeing labor.

Nonetheless, such characterization presupposes the reader's agreement that "the picture is true in the broad sense." As Farrell complained of multiple-protagonist strike novels like Cantwell's, "The author depends on the reader to adopt the same attitude which he has in back of the book he is writing. . . and an agreement with a couple of Marxian abstractions about class war and the division of groups into two opposing classes. The book is then written with this theory in mind."[19]

19. Cantwell to Farrell, April 30, 1934; Cantwell to Farrell, June 12, 1934, Cantwell Papers, U of Oregon Library.

Some proletarian social novels, moreover, uncritically incorporate traditional gender stereotypes. In *Pier 17*, the reporter Ann Bagley is classically bitchy as she exploits her sexual attractiveness to the second mate Ralph MacCharl and the seaman-poet Adrian Scarf. The text's critique of careerist reporters who will do anything to get a story is conflated with an assumed repugnance at Circe-like females who send up a "warm and subtle fragrance" (p. 221). In *A World to Win*, the reactionary politics of Robert's girlfriend Nell, who supports him for a long time when he is out of work, are inseparable from her sexual greed. Robert's rediscovery of his allegiance with Leo—his recuperation of self in an all-male sphere—is coupled with his recognition that he has been Nell's "gigolo" (p. 344). In *A Sign for Cain*, Caroline Gault not only exploits the working-class women she purports to be befriending but also has a shrill voice and is sexually frigid. In her final encounter with Bill, where she reveals the shallowness of her bourgeois feminist politics, he suddenly notices the ugly age lines appearing on her forehead. The woman he had once thought of marrying is now, in his eyes, "like an earth worm that writhes when it is dug out of the ground and feels the disturbance from the spade and the unwelcome light" (p. 371). In these texts, women associated with the exploiting class are routinely amalgams combining doctrinally reprehensible class-traits with negative features of gender that have nothing to do with the text's anticapitalist political stance.

Not only villains but also protagonists in the proletarian social novel can suffer from the essentialist assumptions about personality guiding inherited novelistic conventions of heroic characterization. Because no single character needs to typify the emergent working class, "positive heroes" tend to be free of the more blatantly workerist features of the protagonists in bildungsromans such as *Horse Shoe Bottoms*, *Call Home the Heart*, and *Daughter of the Hills*. But this very diffusion of argument over a range of characters, as well as the narrative's stress upon confrontation over development, can pose character as static and given rather than as the product of social experience—even when the text is explicitly arguing that class struggle is the crucible in which consciousness is formed. In *A Sign for Cain*, Lumpkin gives short shrift to the process of radicalization that brings her range of white and black minor characters to active participation in Communist-led activity. The white Nate Foster seems always to have been aware of the role poor whites have historically played in serving as a buffer between oppressed blacks and the white planter class; he does not need to be won over to a class line on racism. Similarly, the black share-croppers and domestic workers to whom Denis teaches "We Shall Not Be Moved" take up the radical lyrics as if they had known them all their lives.

But even the central characters in proletarian social novels are at times static. Their "conversion" to left-wing politics is tucked away as part of their past; all that matters is their present allegiance. In *A Stone Came Rolling*, how Ishma and Britt came to their qualitatively heightened levels of political commitment is bracketed as something "always already" re-solved. Readers of this novel and its precursor, *Call Home the Heart*, may be puzzled by a number of developments presumably occurring in the hia-tus between the two. Why and how did Britt, who in the first novel was purely a man of the mountains and the banjo, become enlisted as a reliable sympathizer with the Communist movement? How did Ishma manage to overcome her racist reactions to blacks? How and when did she join the party? The narrator's decision to begin *A Stone Came Rolling* in medias res, and only gradually to reveal the sequence of events that has brought Britt and Ishma back from the mountains to a farm on the outskirts of Dunmow (Marion), requires that the reader accept Ishma's Communist activity— and Britt's firm support—as faits accomplis.

Even in *A World to Win*, which centers on the political development of the Hurley brothers, the protagonists' actual movement to the left is rapidly passed over. The account of Leo's acquisition of class consciousness sub-sequent to Anna's death is given not through narrative, but through Leo's brief retrospective report to Robert at the novel's end: "I laid awake fer two weeks ever' night, thinkin', thinkin'" (pp. 330–31). In spite of the text's proclamation that Leo has changed, the Leo who invites Robert for coffee with the comrades at the end of the novel seems to have reverted to an old self as much as to have constructed a new one. For when Leo draws Robert into a hiding place where they can escape from the police, he exclaims, "You remember how we used t' play outlaw down in Happy Hollow, Bob? . . . We're real outlaws now. We'll have t' remember how we used t' dodge old King Brady and Old Sleuth when they come gunnin' fer us. I was allers Jesse James and you was the whole Quantrell gang at on-cet" (p. 347). In this peculiar invocation of American frontier mythology, Conroy posits at once that his protagonists have learned something new— they are "real outlaws now"—and that they are returning to earlier selves that their proletarian politics have simply released into full articulateness. Even though *A World to Win*—as its title indicates—confronts revolutionary politics more squarely than does *The Disinherited*, both texts graft the "Lenin speerit" onto a nostalgic view of the Wild West as a symbolic terrain for the discovery—or perhaps the recovery—of manhood. In *The Disinherited*, this theme is at least woven into the plot of the hero's self-discovery. In Conroy's second novel, by contrast, the Wild West motif is slipped in at the emotional and rhetorical climax of the plot of confrontation. Essences are revealed rather than shaped: Leo simply *is* a rebel at heart, while Robert simply *is* his faithful sidekick. As in *A Stone Came Rolling*, the supersession of "conversion" by confrontation means that characters do not really change. A plot aimed at capturing the dialectics of totality largely effaces the dialectics of process.

Not simply the events depicted, but the text's way of *telling* these events, can foreclose attention to development. Critics commenting adversely on Attaway's attribution of class consciousness to Big Mat at the end of *Blood on the Forge* wrongly object to the incident as a sudden infusion of Marxist politics (see chapter 6), for the entire novel illustrates alienation and false consciousness. But the critics are right in noting the anomalousness of the *way* Attaway makes explicit his thesis. By positing the necessity for multiracial proletarian unity as the object of Mat's "realization," the novel simply positions the reader as complicit with this belief. In *A Sign for Cain*, too, free indirect discourse bypasses any confrontation with possible doctrinal disagreements. Lumpkin never directly presents the reader with the experiences that have prompted Denis and Bill to risk their lives as Communist organizers in the deep South. In the following portrait of Denis's sense of frustration with the difficulties confronting the movement, his commitment is a premise:

> He was thinking again of the problem of carrying on the work. From the experience he had accumulated and from his reading and beliefs he had acquired some skill, and he knew he would acquire more. . . . He knew this skill did not come in a burst of inspiration, . . . but must be learned, like a tree planted by the water learns to direct its roots between the hard surface rocks deep into the ground so that it will become so firmly rooted the rushing waters of the spring flood will not move it. (p. 224)

Tagged free indirect discourse ("He was thinking . . .") asserts Denis's commitment. But the experiential basis of Denis's understanding is taken as given. Indeed, the metaphor of the tree planted by the water—echoing, for the initiated reader, the sharecroppers' song "We Shall Not Be Moved"—takes the place of reflection upon experience in Denis's thoughts. Denis's dedication to the cause is powerfully rendered but remains curiously abstract. "Experience," "reading," "beliefs," and "skill," it would appear, are presumed to have prior referents in the consciousness the reader brings to the text.

The passage cited above in fact represents a rare moment of interiority for Denis, from whose consciousness Lumpkin routinely maintains a certain distance. But even the white organizer Bill, whose thoughts are frequently relayed to the reader, is strangely devoid of internal process. During a meeting the laughter of the sharecroppers suddenly reminds Bill of "the laughter of strikers he had marched with as they went along the street toward the men with guns who were waiting at the mill gates around the corner" (pp. 120–21). Merely mentioning this memory presumably provides the reader with a sufficient explanatory context. Later in the novel, when Lee Foster tells Bill of Denis's murder, Lumpkin conveys Bill's reactions through a peculiar conjunction of temporal perspectives:

> [Bill] remained at the desk a long time without speaking and Lee did not disturb him. Though Lee did not notice it until long afterward, at that time, while Bill sat before his desk, a change began to take place in him. The change was not apparent at once, but even then it began to show on his face. The soft contours of adolescence sloughed off and the more determined and manly planes sharpened at his cheekbones and jaw. Four horizontal lines on his forehead deepened and became permanent. (p. 364)

Jumping ahead to a distant future moment when the maturation process begun in the narrative present has reached its fruition (Lee will notice the deep change in Bill only "long afterward"), the narrator underlines the importance of Denis's martyrdom by positing its future consequences for Bill, who becomes a more steeled revolutionary as a result of his friend's murder. (We may note in passing that a lined face, which simply renders Caroline ugly, suggests a "more determined . . . and manly" commitment in Bill.) Free indirect discourse is tagged at an additional remove: rather than being told Lee's thoughts directly, the reader is informed of what they will be at some future time. But, as in the earlier reference to Bill's memories of the Northern class struggles where he received his political education, the bracketing of Bill's political development into another temporal moment brackets the question of the reader's political development as well. Rather than being directly confronted with arguments that win us to understand the world in the same terms as Bill—as occurs in the passage at the end of Lumpkin's earlier novel, where John McClure is directly confronted with revolutionary politics by John Stevens—we are co-opted into acknowledging the correctness of the Communists' line and practice. Bill's dedication, like Denis's, is simply a self-evident fact. The protagonists of proletarian social novels do not, as a rule, experience internal contradiction; their commitment is "given."

Because plots of confrontation need to enlist readers as unequivocal partisans, closure in proletarian social novels can entail the suppression rather than the dialectical negation of contradictions that have surfaced in the narrative. Love plots exert less pull in multiple-protagonist novels than in bildungsromans, but they can still create a specious sense of completeness and narrative fulfillment. *Out of This Furnace*, which contrasts the happy marriage of Dobie and his wife Julie with the embattled and tragic marriages of the two earlier generations, ends with the couple's impending parenthood. We are gratified that Dobie has a happier family life than his forebears. But the cozy domestic finale has precious little bearing on the plot of CIO unionization, let alone on the strong anticapitalist critique embedded in the account of the first two generations of the Dobreczak clan. Indeed, Dobie's final meditation—that "the world my kid grows up in ought to be a little better than the one I was born into, and . . . I had something to do with making it better" (p. 412)—effaces the text's earlier implication that capitalism intrinsically entails exploitation and injustice. Love is enlisted on the side of Roosevelt-era reformism.

Even in confrontation plots foregrounding the relation of sexuality to class struggle, inherited conventions of romantic closure at times foreclose rather than resolve ideological debate. In *A Time to Remember*, Zugsmith examines the impact of sharpening class struggle upon a number of male-female relationships: Doni and her mythologized doctor-lover Will and, later, Matt; Matt and his wife Myrtle; Ralph Leamy and his wife Stell; Ralph and Aline; Aline and her father. These relationships all link the battle of the sexes to the class struggle; each appears to be heading toward its own distinctive resolution. Nonetheless, the very fact that two of these plots become merged into one—Matt is freed by Myrtle's suicide and ends up with Doni, who has come to realize Matt's unglamorous superiority to the man of her dreams—means that, at the moment of closure, the romantic plot takes rhetorical precedence over other plots that in fact raise the text's more explicitly feminist concerns. Moreover, Myrtle's suicide releases Matt—and the author—from facing squarely the dilemma of whether Matt should in fact leave Myrtle, who is hardly to blame for the social forces that have produced her abysmally low self-esteem. The emotional impact of the ending to A Time to Remember was registered by Lumpkin, who, in a fatuous but revealing review for Woman Today, remarked that "one of the especially fine things about the novel" was "that there are love stories, real love stories in it. And another thing is that though there are tragedies, the ending is a happy one." [20] There is, of course, nothing intrinsically nonrevolutionary about a love plot, as is demonstrated by the powerful romance between Marie and Anand in Daughter of Earth. But in A Time to Remember the love plot, rather than increasing understanding of the politics of personal love, leaves the reader with a fuzzy good feeling. Larger questions about revolutionary change in the social order as a whole—not least among which is the very legitimacy of the capitalist nuclear family—go unanswered amidst the vicarious pleasures readers derive from sharing Matt's and Doni's good luck in having found one another.

Even in A Stone Came Rolling, one of the more overtly didactic social novels, the movement toward closure glosses over some of the contradictions that have given the text its political complexity. An urgent political issue throughout the novel has been the destructive role of the church on insurgent workers' movements. From the Right Reverend Jenson Baird, who preaches otherworldliness to angry strikers, to the interdenominational committee of church leaders who attempt to sway the workers toward Kik, the company unionist, religious forces are portrayed as unremittingly hostile to the Communist-led union movement. Nonetheless, the debate is lively, for a number of positively portrayed characters—the mill worker Tom Jeff, his daughter Fairinda, and Ishma's husband Britt—are shown to be sympathetic to Christianity. The issue reaches its emotional climax when Britt, dying in Ishma's arms after being shot for defending his wife's name at a revivalist meeting, requests that the crowd sing his favorite hymn, "Fling Wide the Gates." After this episode the text stays closely

---

20. Grace Lumpkin, review of A Time to Remember, Woman Today (December 1936), 18.

with Ishma as she retreats to the mountains to work through her grief at Britt's death; there are no indications that the bosses and the revivalists have in any way let up their ideological assault on the strikers. When Ishma returns to Dunmow in the novel's final pages, however, we learn suddenly of a group of workers from the Tom Ray mill who have come under the influence of a radical young Presbyterian minister named Emory, whose preaching that all men are "masters and users of the physical world" gives the workers "warrant to go after what was rightly theirs" (p. 392). Even though no development internal to the politics of the strike makes this resolution especially plausible, the opposition of left politics to religion has been dissolved by the discovery that there is such a thing as a progressive people's church after all. Communism emerges as the fulfillment on earth of the urge for moral retribution, a stone that will come rolling not into Babylon, but, as the anthem of the Southern ILD proclaimed, "into the kingdom of the boss."

No doubt this change in the text's political position can be attributed in part to the increasingly tolerant attitude that the CP was taking toward organized religion in the mid-1930s.[21] The Burke who wrote the closing chapters of *A Stone Came Rolling* (which was published in the latter part of 1935) may have simply changed her mind about how to depict the role of churches but not bothered to revise earlier parts of the text. Even if inconsistencies among textual elements can be traced to extratextual causes, however, the text's movement toward closure enables the Tom Ray workers and the Reverend Emory to be smuggled in. For the debate over politics and religion is settled not by any logic internal to the dynamics of the

21. For more on changes in the CP's relation to churches in the South between the Third Period and the Popular Front, see Robin D. G. Kelley, *Hammer and Hoe: The Alabama Communist Party during the Depression* (Chapel Hill: U of North Carolina P, 1991), and Liston Pope, *Millhands and Preachers: A Study of Gastonia* (New Haven: Yale UP and London: Oxford UP, 1942). Pope, a liberal churchman, was shocked at the collusion between organized religion and the mill bosses in Gaston County. He concluded that "in the cultural crisis of 1929 Gastonia ministers . . . were products of the economic system in which they lived, with no serious modification by any transcendent economic or religious standard. They were willing to allow the power of religious institutions to be used against those who challenged this economic system, and themselves assisted in such use" (p. 330). Pope concludes that the Communists' atheism got them expelled from the mill towns. His study does not reflect the growing coalition between Communists and progressive churches that Burke suggests at the end of *A Stone Came Rolling*.

union situation, but by a displacement of the emotional sweep of the love plot. Identifying with Ishma in her grief, the reader is moved to associate the powerful charge of the strikers' singing "Fling Wide the Gates" with a negation of the reactionary forces that have led to Britt's death. As in *A Time to Remember*, the strong pull toward closure, coupled with the reader's romantic vicarious involvement, blurs issues that have been sharply drawn earlier in the text. The good guys are no longer divided among themselves; they have achieved seamless unity against the class enemy. But what feels like synthesis proves, upon examination, to be a pseudo-synthesis in which "evidence" has been brought in a posteriori to validate an ending that simplifies rather than resolves what has come before.

In sum, even as it deploys critical realism to offer a totalizing and dialectical representation of class struggle, the proletarian social novel is frequently implicated in the ideological assumptions and maneuvers embedded in its genre. The convention that social being is reducible to "character" and that "character" is signaled by a bundle of "traits" reliably indicating essence can lead to opportunistic shortcuts in characterization. Rather than confronting the difficult task of basing readers' negative reactions to characters wholly on political grounds, novelists can arouse strong responses by invoking widespread "bourgeois" beliefs—for example, fat people are repulsive, careerist women emasculating—and then give these a political coloration a posteriori by associating them with characters marked as bad in the text's hierarchy of specifically political discourses. Conversely, rather than directing attention to contradictions internal to the proletariat, writers can describe the "good guys" as unequivocally "good," beset by doubts and disunities that are at most temporary. If some of these texts stereotype, however, this occurs not because their authors' "propagandistic" aims necessarily produce reductive and banal characterization, but because the didactic enterprise of the proletarian social novel is largely dependent on inherited conventions of novelistic discourse. Complex political judgments of social processes are conveyed through relatively simply moral judgments of individuals.

Moreover, the movement toward closure can impel writers to close off debate over issues requiring further conceptual exploration. Important questions facing the movement—the changes possible in male-female relationships through class struggle, the relation of reform struggles to the fight for state power, the role of religion in insurgent mass movements—can be "resolved" through narrative ploys having little to do with the political contradictions posed. Above all, readers, positioned as peers who share the narrator's knowledge and values, can be co-opted into agreement—rather than persuaded to agree—with the politics guiding the text. The social novel's partisan enlistment of its readers can rescue them from possibly unwelcome preachment. But it can end up reducing the text's didactic force by embedding its most crucial propositions in the realm of assumption, not assertion. The very trait for which the social novel was most widely praised by 1930s critics—its seamlessness and transparency—can thus depoliticize the text. The repudiation of "leftist" strategies of representation at times entails the downplaying of "leftist" politics.

Generic Politics and Doctrinal Politics

As in the other modes of realistic fiction we have been examining, however, generic politics do not operate independently of doctrinal politics. Inherited conventions of classic realist form exert their strongest influence in proletarian social novels at the texts' points of greatest political vulnerability. These points of vulnerability should by now be familiar. Once again, the uncritical incorporation of received conceptions of gender identity figures prominently in opportunistic characterization. Havinghurst's portrait of Ann Bagley, Conroy's of Nell, and Lumpkin's of Caroline invoke unexamined assumptions about domineering women; the critique of these characters' petty-bourgeois values is blurred by the authors' insistence that they are manipulative and castrating. Moreover, traditionally gendered notions of self, love, and family inform many of the social novel's plot motifs. Cantwell's Johnny Hagen cannot achieve real manhood as a union militant unless he "has" his first woman in the heat of the strike. The lovers Doni and Matt occupy center stage in the closing sections of A Time to Remember precisely because Zugsmith backs away from answering some of the touchier questions she has earlier raised about the capitalist family. Proletarian social novels appear to be especially reliant upon repressive plot mechanisms and stereotyped modes of characterization when they do not scrutinize the assumptions built into inherited conceptions of womanhood, manhood, and romantic love.

Furthermore, tendencies toward simplification and containment of contradiction assert themselves most strongly at moments where narrative teleology is directed toward economistic goals. At the end of Bell's Dobreczak saga, the narrator's ringing pronouncement that Dobie is the "metal" that has been forged "out of this furnace" carries more fire than heat. Is the furnace the class struggle or the forces of production over which class struggle is fought? The novel's tamely unionist ending, which poses Dobie as a modern-day Patrick Henry, suggests the latter. Similarly, the multiple strands of the plot of *The Foundry* can be so readily tucked away because Halper addresses only trade-union politics. The novel's closing image of the glistening printing plates piled on Duffy's table may prophesy proletarian resistance, but their signification remains abstractly symbolic. Nothing in the novel's implied argument to this point has suggested that any of the workers—other than perhaps Heitman—has any interest in fundamentally transforming the social relations of labor. *A Time to Remember* falls back upon the Doni-Matt plot as its principal agent for closure in part because the novel only hesitantly inquires into the relation of party and revolution to the department store strike. After all, it is the judgment of Al, the novel's closest approach to a Communist mentor-figure, that "what the strike means" is that "[f]ive hundred middle-class white-collar workers tore off their phony white collars and declared themselves workers!" (p. 341). The text's reformist politics and conventionally romantic narrative closure are closely interrelated. Even *A Sign for Cain*, which raises more explicitly Communist politics than do the novels of Bell, Halper, and Zugsmith, rushes toward a melodramatic resolution largely because Lumpkin has never invested the novel's key *political* issue—how to build a multiracial Communist-led movement in the lynch-terror South— with real dramatic tension. The novel gains its narrative momentum from suspenseful but largely apolitical issues: Will Jim Gault be exposed as the true killer? Will the Northern lawyers arrive in time to take Denis's case? Even though the novel closes with the murder of Denis and the powerful description of elongated and multiplied shadows presaging intensified class struggle, closure results more from the novel's reliance upon conventional sources of narrative suspense than from its resolution of any conflict within the ranks of the movement. To the extent that proletarian social novels construe the arena of confrontation as the immediate class battle and make only oblique reference to the larger class war or to the internal transformation of individuals caught up in it, they fall prey to realism's tendency to foreclose contradiction.[22]

Like the proletarian bildungsroman, the proletarian social novel most blatantly exhibits the regressive ideological tendencies of realism at points where generic and doctrinal politics coincide. While both genres are marked by their bourgeois origins, however, there is an important difference. Where the bildungsroman remains primarily focused upon an individual, the social novel spreads its narrative interest over a range of people and situations. This dispersal has various political consequences. First, it affects the representation of gender. Even if A World to Win and The Land of Plenty convey traditionally gendered notions of plot and character, their reliance upon culturally loaded motifs is less complete than in texts like The Disinherited and This Is Your Day, which depend more fully upon the convention that plot development entails a young man's growth into sexual and social maturity. In A World to Win, Nell's function as a figure threatening Robert's manhood is set off by Anna's function as a catalyst of Leo's political transformation. In The Land of Plenty, Johnny's entry into sexual experience with Ellen during the strike is preceded by the account of Walt's attempt to rape Marie, as well as by the grueling description of Marie's postabortion trauma. The gendered bias of realistic single-protagonist fiction toward tales of male self-discovery is reduced in proletarian social novels that treat multiple characters and situations. Even in texts featuring male protagonists, the search for selfhood need not revolve around a traditional quest for manhood.

Similarly, the social novel seems to have opened up possibilities for treating the relation of class to race oppression less reductionistically than was the case in some bildungsromans. Although Gathering Storm introduces the Black Belt thesis somewhat perfunctorily, it manages to indicate various complexities in the relation of black self-determination to proletarian revolution. Where Nearing, in Free Born, distorts and oversimplifies the relation of nationalistic to working-class consciousness by attempting to keep political argument confined to the thoughts of one character,

22. Cook associates the sacrifice of politics to melodrama in A Sign for Cain with Lumpkin's opportunistic use of Gothic conventions in depicting the Old South: "[T]here is a distortion, a ripping out of context in this kind of selective portrayal of Southern horror—a disorientation that refuses to admit the aesthetic rules of the Gothic but nevertheless wishes to capitalize on its terrifying effects" (pp. 117–18).

Page allows space for alternative positions to define themselves. In *Blood on the Forge*, the creation of a tripartite protagonist—Melody/Chinatown/ Big Mat—means that no single Moss brother is obliged to typify the consciousness of the black industrial working class. Big Mat may experience a glimmering awareness of how he has come to resemble his former riding boss, but this experience—even if it points at a class-based analysis beyond all the brothers' consciousness—does not constitute a "conversion" on which the text's political doctrine hinges. Similarly, *Black Thunder*, by creating a thread of argument for multiracial unity through the different strands of its plot, takes the load for "realizing" the full dimensions of its political perspective from the shoulders of Gabriel. The multiple-protagonist format of the social novel thus permits writers analyzing the relation of race to class from a Marxist standpoint to explore this relation through the motivations and actions of a range of characters. Form does not mechanically determine political possibility: Wright, as we have seen, used the single-protagonist form to powerful effect in *Native Son*. But the structure of the social novel enabled antiracist novelists quite successfully to depict the dialectical relation between class- and race-consciousness that was espoused by the 1930s left.

Most writers of proletarian social fiction manage to avoid the workerist outlook often accompanying single-protagonist texts. In novels like *Horse Shoe Bottoms*, *Call Home the Heart*, and *Daughter of the Hills*, the author's desire to present an exemplary working-class protagonist results in a fetishization of working-class origins and an erotic idealization of the working-class hero. By contrast, proletarian social novels usually avoid the temptation of holding up one character as a carrier of proletarian virtue. The bosses in *The Foundry* may be stereotypes. The worker-composer Augustus Kafka is not, however, a sexy and magnetic proletarian artist-hero—like the banjo-strumming John Cooper of *Daughter of the Hills*—but just a quirky young man whose music remarkably reflects the rhythms and tensions of the plant. Aline Weinman in *A Time to Remember* undergoes no dramatic transformations, as does the Ishma of Burke's first novel, nor does she fall in love. The sentimentality of the Doni-Matt plot is thus offset by this parallel plot of a young woman's growth into a class-conscious leader. Moreover, even if some proletarian social novels reflect the drift toward Popular Front politics, they tend not to pose working-class experience as an intrinsic ground for radical consciousness. Social novels like

Out of This Furnace may be economistic, but they are less likely to be workerist than are single-protagonist works of proletarian fiction.

Perhaps the most serious charge that can be leveled against the proletarian social novel is that its characteristic use of a confrontation plot co-opts the reader into agreement. As I have demonstrated, the articulation of politics by assumption rather than assertion is a problematic—at times highly problematic—feature of a number of proletarian social novels. But we should keep in mind the political position of the contemporaneous reader to whom and for whom these novels were written. Denis's and Bill's memories of their past involvement in strikes; Biddenhurst's off-the-cuff reference to "classes" as "artificial distinctions"; Noonan's private meditations about "classes . . . warring for the future of the world"; Fatfolks's invocation of the "Lenin speerit"; Ishma's and Bly's chatting about control of the forces of production under socialism—such passages, while encoding a high degree of reader assent, also reflect the existence of a contemporaneous historical readership whose sympathetic understanding on such points *could* in fact be assumed. When defining the project of proletarian literature, we will recall, most literary radicals described their audience as the class-conscious segment of the proletariat and/or the proletarianized petty bourgeoisie: rarely did they claim that they were writing for the "average" proletarian. Proletarian social novelists presumably felt that brief references, throwaway comments, and overheard conversations would adequately resonate in their readers' experience.

Indeed, these writers may have assumed that, at least for a significant portion of their readership, the key issue to be addressed was not the knowledge or theory of class struggle, but practice: would the reader take sides and get out into the streets? In this case, positioning the reader as "always already" in agreement with the text's doctrinal politics can be seen as an act not of co-optation but of engagement. Perhaps the author/reader compact does not have to entail continually reinventing the political wheel with stories of "conversion." For readers already to some degree possessing a left-wing consciousness, narratives of confrontation may not close off debate but move debate ahead by posing the logic of partisanship: if one agrees, what does one do on the basis of this agreement?

It is difficult for many readers in the 1990s to recreate the context of 1930s literary proletarianism—not so much the breadlines and plant closings and relief protests as the political discourse in which millions were engaged. This discourse is, however, as much a part of proletarian fiction as is the "subject matter" that this literature explicitly treats. The implied contract between author and reader in many proletarian social novels tells us a good deal about this discourse. The uneasiness that some 1990s readers may feel in becoming the implied reader of some proletarian social novels should not be automatically translated into a judgment that the texts are engaged in unfair rhetorical or political practices. It is important to examine how the use of inherited conventions of fiction implicated radical writers in inherited conventions of thought and, at times, precluded a more revolutionary exploration of social contradictions. But it is also crucial to be aware of the historicity of literary response. The novelistic discourse that may strike some present-day readers as closed and coercive may have struck left-leaning readers of the 1930s as both dynamic and emancipatory. Even as novelistic realism came trailing the mists of bourgeois ideology into the proletarian social novel, it enabled writers and readers to address the implications of the positions they were taking in the class confrontations of the day.

CHAPTER 11

>

The Collective Novel

Of the four modes of proletarian fiction, the collective novel is the only one that is primarily the product of 1930s literary radicalism. The term "proletarian collective novel" would therefore be tautological. Left-wing critics from both the United States and other countries heralded the collective novel as a narrative form distinctly empowered to represent what Henri Barbusse called "a new protagonist, the most imposing of all: the masses." *Linkskurve* editor Otto Biha noted in 1931 that the emerging genre of the collective novel might eventually render the term "novel" obsolete: "The bourgeois novel is declining. The wholesome proletarian and revolutionary contents are still presented to-day mostly in old, borrowed garb which certainly misfits them; nevertheless, the new contents are quite in evidence. It is essential to harmonize the form with the contents, and it doesn't matter whether or not the final product will be in the shape of a novel." In 1934 Granville Hicks wrote with excitement about recently translated collective novels from Germany and the USSR—Kataev's *Time, Forward!*, Newkrantz's *Barricades in Berlin*, and Fadayev's *The Nineteen*. The numbers of texts written in this mode, Hicks prophesied, "would undoubtedly increase with great rapidity in the course of building socialism." Remarking upon the genre's increasing popularity among American writers, he concluded, "This may or may not mean that the critics are right in predicting that the collective novel will be the novel of the future, but in any case it is even now a legitimate form." [1]

Biha and Hicks insisted that more traditional novelistic forms continued to serve crucial mimetic functions. Biha, an ally of Georg Lukács in

1. Henri Barbusse, "Writing and War," in Joseph North, ed., *New Masses: An Anthology of the Rebel Thirties* (New York: International, 1969), p. 14; Otto Biha, "On the Question of Proletarian Revolutionary Literature in Germany," *IL* 1, no. 4 (1931): 91; Granville Hicks, "Revolution and the Novel," in *Granville Hicks in the New Masses*, ed. Jack Alan Robbins (Port Washington, NY: Kennikat, 1974), p. 28.

debates with the "ultraleft" documentarists, observed that experimentation with collectivist narrative forms was in its infancy; he warned against "ignor[ing] the realities of today for the sake of abstract speculation as regards a distant future." Hicks, who strongly argued that writers continue to work in the modes of the "biographical" and "complex" novels, maintained that, especially in nonrevolutionary settings such as the United States, "there are many important and representative situations that could not possibly be treated in the collective novel." Nonetheless, both critics spoke for a wide segment of international Marxist critical opinion in their enthusiastic endorsement of the mimetic possibilities embodied in the form of the collective novel.[2]

Depression-era critics proved better at heralding the collective novel, however, than at defining it. Hicks offered a definition based primarily upon subject matter:

> The collective novel not only has no individual hero; some group of persons occupies in it a position analogous to that of the hero in conventional fiction. Without lapsing into the mysticism of those pseudo-psychologists who talk about the group-mind, we can see that, under certain circumstances, a group may come into existence that is independent of and more important than any of the individuals who compose it. Such a group could be portrayed through the eyes of a single individual—in other words, in terms of the traditional novel. But it might be more effective to portray the group as a group, to show forth objectively and unmistakably its independent reality. To do this requires a new technique, the technique of the collective novel.

Hicks's definition was useful as far as it went, but it did not discuss with any specificity what was meant by "the technique of the collective novel." Accordingly, Hicks was compelled to concede that it was frequently difficult to distinguish between the collective novel and what he was calling the "complex novel." Noting that "the problem of creating credible individuals without destroying the sense of group unity" was "the great problem of the collective novel," he remarked, "Obviously there is a certain area within which the collective novel and the complex novel are very much alike; e.g., whenever the author of the collective novel is treating his characters as separate individuals. Apart from their group relationship, he follows the techniques of the complex novel" (pp. 28–29). On the basis of this defi-

2. Biha, ibid.; Hicks, ibid.

nition it would be difficult to determine whether a given text qualified as a "collective novel" or not. Commentators used the term frequently but did not always agree about its applicability. Hicks, for example, considered the different volumes of John Dos Passos's *U.S.A.* trilogy complex novels, while Isidor Schneider and Malcolm Cowley considered them instances of "collective" fiction. Proclaiming that the collective novel existed did not in itself make taxonomic analysis any easier.[3]

Collective novels clearly overlap with other modes of proletarian fiction in subject matter and theme. William Rollins's *The Shadow Before*, which focuses on the group dynamics of a strike, bears a close resemblance to *The Land of Plenty* or *A Time to Remember*. John Steinbeck's treatment of the Joads as exemplars of their class in *The Grapes of Wrath* recalls Lumpkin's synecdochic treatment of the McClure family in *To Make My Bread*. The ironic juxtaposition of members of the bourgeoisie and the proletariat performs much the same didactic function in Arnold Armstrong's *Parched Earth* as it does in Halper's *The Foundry*. The young writer-heroes in Josephine Johnson's *Jordanstown* and Mary Heaton Vorse's *Strike!* undergo "conversions" comparable to Isaac Hyman's odyssey in *From the Kingdom of Necessity*.

Despite the many shared concerns linking it to other modes of proletarian fiction, the collective novel is a distinct novelistic mode characterized by a distinct set of novelistic devices. It is generally marked by at least one of three defining (if frequently overlapping) features. First, the collective novel's treatment of the group as a phenomenon greater than—and different from—the sum of the individuals who constitute it means that it tends to foreground interconnection as such. Sometimes this is accomplished through direct assertions of the group's cohesiveness: narratorial interventions unambiguously remind readers that they should conceive of the characters as a unified group. At times, however, this sense of oneness is achieved through the author's *refusal* to fulfill conventional mimetic expectations or to provide commentary through a narrator. Characters do *not* interact; their interconnections are *not* made explicit on the level of "story" or through "discourse"-level intervention. Readers who wish to

3. Hicks, ibid., pp. 27, 28–29; Isidor Schneider, "Greatness," NM 20 (August 11, 1936): 40–41; Malcolm Cowley, review of *Nineteen Nineteen*, New Republic (April 27, 1932), 304; review of *The Big Money*, New Republic (September 9, 1936), 134.

understand the rationale for various characters' presence within a single narrative are thus compelled to look beyond the "text itself"—and usually to Marxist class analysis—in order to grasp the text's principle of coherence. Even when it uses otherwise conventionally realistic techniques, the collective novel often creates tensions between the totality of the text's fictional world and the totality of the "real world." The two may overlap, but they do not unproblematically correspond; into the epistemological gap between them the reader must intervene as an articulator of larger meanings.

A second distinguishing feature of collective novels is their frequent use of experimental devices that break up the narrative and rupture the illusion of seamless transparency. Collectivism entails an exercise in formal modernism; indeed, many collective novels give the impression of having been cinematically conceived. These devices direct attention to the process of textual construction and invite the reader consciously to consider the paradigm the author has chosen for describing and explaining the social totality. As the British writer and critic Storm Jameson noted in 1937, the key difficulty confronting writers of collective fiction was "expressing, in such a way that they are at once seen to be intimately connected, the relations between things (men, acts) widely separated in space or in the social complex." Where writers of conventionally realistic proletarian fiction attempt to construct a simulacrum of the "social complex" through mimesis, collective novelists position their readers to think about "relations" and "intimate connect[ions]." This does not mean that collective novels are doctrinally more "open-ended" than traditionally realistic texts; collective novels do not hold up indeterminacy as a political value or polyphony as a rhetorical strategy. Nonetheless, most collective novels insist that their readers not simply empathize with, but understand, the process that has led the novelists to generalize and judge as they have done. Rupture of illusionism serves the end not of querying totality, but of encouraging critical totalization.[4]

4. Storm Jameson, cited in Stuart Laing, "Presenting 'Things As They Are': John Sommerfield's May Day and Mass Observation," in Frank Gloversmith, ed., Class, Culture and Social Change: A New View of the 1930s (Sussex: Harvester, and Atlantic Highlands, NJ: Humanities P, 1980), p. 148. For more on the relation of the collective novel to the cinema, see Laing; also Valentine Cunningham, British Writers of the Thirties (Oxford and New York: Oxford UP, 1988), pp. 322–27.

Third, collective novels frequently assert direct documentary links with the world of the reader. Many proletarian novels can of course be considered "documentary" in one sense or another. Some texts, by virtue of their detailed evocation of work processes and their verisimilitudinous descriptions of environment, could be said to "document" contemporaneous reality. Others—for example, the Gastonia bildungsromans *Call Home the Heart* and *To Make My Bread*—make unambiguous reference to verifiable episodes in the class struggle. Bonnie McClure, as a fictional re-creation of Ella May Wiggins, sings Wiggins's actual ballads; Wiggins herself appears as a character in *Gathering Storm*. Fictional autobiographies, pursuing a different documentary strategy, aim at establishing veracity in their felt equation of character, narrator, and author.[5] In the collective novel, however, "factual" references—newspaper headlines and news stories, fragments of popular culture, brief vignettes introducing "real" people, both ordinary and famous—signal larger historical processes and forces and suggest a context beyond the immediate environment of the characters. These documentary devices frequently direct attention to the problem of ideology, insofar as they represent not merely historical processes and forces but also the discursive practices through which these are known. The documentary aura pervading the fictional autobiography produces a strong sense of *intensive* totality; the nonfictional presence in the collective novel generally produces an effect of *extensive* totality. The multiple "factual" threads connecting the text to the world of the reader connect unifying causes and existing realities with the paradigms through which these are understood.

Characters, Plots, and Totalities

In collective novels strongly tied to conventional multiprotagonist realism, texts, characters, and plot lines perform many of the same didactic functions as in the social novel. Yet collective texts ordinarily fix more attention on the "big picture" as a political construct; they produce cognition

---

5. For more on different markers and genres of documentary fiction—including verisimilitude, verifiability, and veracity—see my *Telling the Truth: The Theory and Practice of Documentary Fiction* (Ithaca: Cornell UP, 1986).

of totality through the diminution—and at times subversion—of narrative transparency.

As in the social novel, the wide array of characters in the collective novel permits the author to devise patterns of repetition and contrast that provide implicit commentary upon relations both within and among classes. In *The Shadow Before*, Rollins focuses on the sexual repression and emotional psychopathology of bourgeois life. Paralleling the lascivious Dorothy Thayer, the sex-starved wife of a textile plant manager, with both her repressed and paranoid daughter Marjorie and the anarchistically violent Harry Baumann, scion of a mill-owning family, Rollins depicts the bourgeoisie's decadence as an index to its parasitic class position. In *S.S. Utah*, a novel treating the growth of class consciousness among sailors on an American ship that visits the Soviet Union in the early 1930s, Mike Pell stresses uneven political development within the proletariat. In order to unite the crew as an effective entity, the Communist organizer Slim must not only win the class-conscious Pitts to join the party but also teach self-control to the angry Gunnar and prop up the timid Lag and Finn. In *U.S.A.*, Dos Passos presents through Mac, Joe Williams, and Charley Anderson a commentary on various options available to white male working-class characters at different junctures in early twentieth-century U.S. society. Mac, an itinerant printer, repudiates conventional married life, flirts with the Wobblies, and ends up a marginalized expatriate in Mexico. Joe, a merchant marine sailor, is driven from port to port and dies in a racist barroom brawl on Armistice Night. Charley rises from mechanic to engineer, pursues the lure of the big money among social strata where he never finds a place, and dies an emotional and financial wreck. In these and other collective novels, comparisons among characters from comparable social origins illustrate the authors' varying estimates of the role of dominant—or, conversely, revolutionary—ideology in determining consciousness within different classes.

As in the social novel, thematic patterning of characters from different classes permits the authors of collective novels to query the relation between class origins and class consciousness. In *The Company*, Edwin Seaver's account of alienation in a New York advertising firm, the text stresses the workers' shared political limitations. With the exception of Aarons, the lone Jewish "troublemaker" who reminds the copywriters of the absurdity of their work, all the employees—from the rule-conscious secretary Miss Butler to the status-obsessed manager Mr. Reynolds—suppress their personal grievances and bow to the company's regimen. By contrast, in *Rope of Gold*, the final novel of Josephine Herbst's largely autobiographical trilogy about the falling fortunes of the Trexler-Wendel family, the stories of Victoria and Jonathan Chance, two radical writers involved in Communist politics, are juxtaposed not only with those of other members of their families but also with that of the militant leftist auto worker Steve Carson. Despite differences in class background, Jonathan and especially Vicky have far more in common with Steve than with the petty-bourgeois and bourgeois families to whom they are linked by blood. In *Jordanstown*, a novel about the development of left-wing resistance in a small Ohio town, Josephine Johnson continually counterposes the solidarity experienced by the increasingly militant rank-and-file characters who live in the "Bottom" with the complacency and isolation of the middle-class Jean Phillips and the wealthy John Chapman. The decision of Allen Craig and his friend Dave Woolf to relinquish their tattered petty-bourgeois patrimony and throw in their lot with the proletariat signals an exemplary course for others like them. In *Rope of Gold* and *Jordanstown*, patterns of redundancy among characters from different social classes reinforce the message that people are bound by their class origins only to the extent that they themselves permit: the role one plays in history is a function not of where one comes from but of what one does.

Some collective novels use "story"-level redundancies in conventionally realistic ways. But characters are not obliged to interact. Sometimes they touch upon one another's lives very little, if at all: ironic juxtaposition supplants interaction. In *U.S.A.*, the fates of Mac, Joe, and Charley are never interwoven in a plot that makes their common destiny transparent or self-evident. If readers wish to discern the points of thematic tangency in these characters' wasted lives, they are compelled to construct the relevant principles of textual coherence—that is, to contemplate the relation between the American Dream and the actual conditions of working-class existence in the United States. In *Rope of Gold*, Steve Carson and Victoria Chance never meet, even though their different paths to radicalism commonly embody the sorts of changes that will have to occur on a massive scale if revolution is to take place in the Depression-era United States. Steve's and Victoria's very lack of interaction suggests that affiliation with the Communist movement involves the individual in a historical process not encompassable within familiar categories of personal experience. As Paula Rabinowitz notes, "Reading *Rope of Gold* is like unraveling a thick cord in which the entwined strands produce a knot of historical complexity." In *The Company*, where common place of employment furnishes the text's unifying principle, many characters are never shown in relation to their coworkers. For example, in the chapter entitled "The Jew," which recounts Aarons's decision to quit, the narrator slips into using "we" to define narrative perspective: "After Aarons left the office we all felt much better. Not that Aarons was a bad sort. On the contrary we all liked him quite a lot even though he was a Jew." But the "I" who constitutes part of this anti-Semitic "we" is never given a distinct identity or shown in dialogue with any other character. As a result, the reader is invited to conceptualize an essence, the "company," that is more than the sum of the relationships of discrete individuals. Alienation and herd mentality are generated not just by competition for status, but by larger social structures and ideological practices never understood by the "I's" enmeshed in them.[6]

In some collective novels, the opposite phenomenon occurs: the group is stressed to the point where individual identities become absorbed into it. In *Industrial Valley*, Ruth McKenney's factually based account of unionization among rubber workers in Akron, Ohio, the narrative's two "fictional" characters, Job Hendricks and Tom Gettling, enter the text only twice. Even though they change markedly between their two appearances—at the start they are cowed and timid, at the end rebellious and assertive—their metamorphosis is an indicator but not a carrier of political significance. McKenney's preoccupation is with the tens of thousands of Akron's actual citizens, not with any fictional individuals who might serve as synecdochic surrogates. In *S.S. Utah*, attention is gradually displaced from the individual to the group. Slim, the Communist organizer, occupies center stage in the first half of the text. But as they gain class consciousness, other members of the crew come to the fore as narrative agents. By the novel's end, the strike carried on by the entire group—and supported by anony-

---

6. Paula Rabinowitz, *Labor and Desire: Women's Revolutionary Fiction in Depression America* (Chapel Hill and London: U of North Carolina P, 1992), p. 160; Edwin Seaver, *The Company* (New York: Macmillan, 1930), p. 145. While I am not discussing it here as a collective novel, Richard Wright's thematically unified series of short stories, *Uncle Tom's Children*, obviously accomplishes many of the political and rhetorical functions I am discussing in this chapter. See above, chapter 5.

mous longshoremen on the wharf—is the sole relevant activity of the text's characters. In these novels, individuals clearly matter: without the purposive activity of the Jobs and Slims, there would be no class struggle. But what matters most of all is the activity of the class; the text's design forces the reader to abandon conceptions of individual heroism and to focus upon the social effects of individual deeds.

Plot lines in collective novels frequently use traditional realistic methods for reinforcing meaning. In *Industrial Valley*, accumulated references to bank failures and layoffs contribute to the sense of inevitability accompanying the text's account of developing proletarian resistance. In *Jordanstown*, the successive woes that befall the characters of the "Bottom"—the burning down of the people's hall, the deaths of Jessie Schmidt from malnutrition and of Dave from police violence—pose the key dilemma confronting the "Bottom" as an entity: will it or will it not be able to muster the resources to overcome its oppressors? In *The Grapes of Wrath*, Steinbeck's desire to demonstrate exhaustively the Okies' predicament dictates much of the text's narrative structure. Even though no dynamic internal to the plot requires that the Joads, after their experience with the Hooverville, the government camp, and the strike, endure the additional hardship of the Visalia flood, Steinbeck was bent on including in his novel a comprehensive catalog of the sufferings he himself had witnessed in his research into life among the migrants.[7] Because of their strong interest in the conditions and causes of group formation, collective novelists often construct narratives with a high degree of redundancy on the level of "story."

7. Steinbeck wrote in February 1939,

I must go over to the interior valleys. There are about five thousand families starving to death over there, not just hungry but actually starving. The government is trying to feed them and get medical attention to them with the fascist group of utilities and banks and huge growers sabotaging the thing all along the line. . . . In one tent there are twenty people quarantined for smallpox and two of the women are to have babies in that tent this week. . . . The states and the counties will give them nothing because they are outsiders. But the crops of any part of this state could not be harvested without these outsiders. I'm pretty mad about it.

(*Working Days: The Journals of the Grapes of Wrath, 1938–1941*, ed. Robert De Mott [New York: Viking, 1989], p. xxxvii). Regarding the documentary aspects of *The Grapes of Wrath*, see Anonymous, "Speaking of Pictures . . . These by *Life* Prove Facts in *The Grapes of Wrath*," *Life* 8 (February 19, 1940): 10–11.

Some collective novelists—especially those painting apocalyptic portraits of social conflict—create quite conventional plot complications to produce a sense of suspense and closure. In *Strike!*, a novel closely based on the Gastonia events Vorse herself had witnessed at first hand, the author builds on the melodrama of the "real life" strike by adding her own embellishments. The text finds love partners among the strikers for her heroes Fer Deane (the historical CP strike leader Fred Beal) and Mamie Lewes (Ella May Wiggins). Furthermore, the text parallels Fer and Mamie as martyrs, since, in Vorse's version of events, both are shot in the course of strike activity. (The historical Wiggins was indeed shot by vigilantes while on the way to a rally. Beal, hardly a martyr, jumped bail and ran off to the USSR— something that occurred after Vorse completed her narrative, which was composed in medias res.)[8] In *The Shadow Before*, both Mrs. Thatcher and Harry Baumann commit suicide—the former realizing that she cannot simultaneously slake her boundless sexual hunger and retain her respectable class status, the latter frustrated with his failed attempt to burn down his father's textile mill. Even though Marvin, the union organizer (Rollins's version of Beal), ends up serving a fifteen-year prison sentence, the field is clear, it is implied, for the insurgent forces to win the day. The bourgeoisie barely needs proletarian gravediggers to put it six feet under. In Armstrong's *Parched Earth*, a novel set in the California fruit-picking town of Caldwell, the plot is structured by a motif of disease and revenge. Belle

8. Vorse's own experiences in Gastonia are given in her journal of the Gastonia strike ("Gastonia: Typescript 'Strike' Journal 1929," Vorse Papers, Box 155, Archives of Labor History and Urban Affairs, Wayne State U). See also Dee Garrison, *Mary Heaton Vorse: The Life of an American Insurgent* (Philadelphia: Temple UP, 1989), pp. 213–41, and Fred Beal, *Proletarian Journey: New England, Gastonia, Moscow* (New York: Hillman-Carl, 1937). Sandra Adickes comments on the close relation between Vorse and her character Ed Hoskins, a seasoned labor reporter: "Perhaps Vorse changed the gender of her representative because her identity was so special, so well-known, that she did not want to make herself recognizable in the novel" ("Three Visions of Gastonia: Mary Heaton Vorse's *Strike!*, Grace Lumpkin's *To Make My Bread*, Myra Page's *Gathering Storm*," unpublished essay). Regarding the traditional form of *Strike!*, Sylvia Jenkins Cook remarks, "As one of the earliest proletarian novels in America, *Strike!* holds little promise of radical innovations in technique to match the ideology; the novel is heroless, or rather it has as multiple hero the entire body of strikers, but otherwise it is quite conventional in form and style" (*From Tobacco Road to Route 66: The Southern Poor White in Fiction* [Chapel Hill: U of North Carolina P, 1966], p. 94).

Vazquez, the town whore whose family was dispossessed of vast tracts of land by the Caldwell family years before, contracts syphilis from Everett Caldwell and spreads it to virtually every middle-class man in town. In somewhat bizarre narrative overdetermination, Armstrong preempts the slow process of internal decay by having Wally Vazquez, the idiot bastard son of Belle and Everett Caldwell, inadvertently blow up the dam above the town, causing an inundation from which only a few select radical proletarian characters escape by climbing a windmill. In *Parched Earth*, conventions of melodrama and suspense operate quite literally with a vengeance. As in *The Shadow Before*, the tragic course of personal fates prophesies the imminence of the "final conflict."

Many collective novels enlist traditional plot mechanisms of repetition and complication. But they often end in ways that are not entirely predictable. The additive accumulation of episodes frequently implies that the group has experienced a growth greater than has any of the individuals constituting it. Steinbeck's finale to *The Grapes of Wrath*—the querulous Rose of Sharon's selfless gesture of giving her breast to an unknown starving man—makes little sense in terms of individual character development. But it works well as an indicator that Ma Joad's collective outlook has won out—that the Joads have *become* the generalized people moving "from 'I' to 'we'" depicted in the interchapters.[9] The ending to *Jordanstown*, which finds Allen and his comrades bound by an even firmer resolve as their year of tactical defeats comes full circle, intimates that the higher degree of proletarian solidarity resulting from the struggle for change is more important than any reform victory. In *S.S. Utah*, the closing scene, which pictures longshoremen rallying to the support of the striking crewmen, by no means ties up the threads of the preceding narrative, since the reader never learns whether Slim (or any of the other militant sailors) is the target of the two shots that ring out on the novel's penultimate page. But this ambiguity poses difficulties only if Slim is the locus of reader identification. If the group is primary, Pell's withholding of the identity of the gunfire victim(s) is appropriate, even if it disrupts conventional expectations. In these texts, there is a disjunction between the episodes building toward closure and the finale itself. Only when the text's protagonist is construed as a transindividual entity does the trajectory of the narrative gain coherence.

Even when plot lines in the collective novel are motivated by famil-

9. John Steinbeck, *The Grapes of Wrath* (1939; rpt. Penguin, 1976), p. 194.

iar kinds of narrative suspense or romantic interest, the implied locus of causality is quite different from what one finds in conventionally realistic texts. Where love affairs in bildungsromans such as *Moscow Yankee* and social novels such as *A Time to Remember* figure centrally in narrative resolution, in *Strike!* the love affairs end up playing no causative role in the course of events. In most collective novels, purely personal emotions are irrelevant to the larger course of history. In *The Shadow Before*, the suicides of Mrs. Thatcher and Harry Baumann are incidental to the strike, which proceeds according to a logic of its own. In *Parched Earth*, the cataclysm wiping out almost the entire town of Everett is too overwhelming to be linked to the personal sins of Everett Caldwell, nefarious as he is depicted to be. Moreover, it sweeps up not only large numbers of characters with whom the reader has been made acquainted but several others—for example, the moonshiner Josh Barnes, the undertaker Eddie Owens, the newspaper editor Bascom Root—who appear for the first time in the closing pages of the text only to be engulfed by the flood. The impending revolutionary struggle symbolized by the breaking dam, readers conclude, will implicate not only known agents but also bystanders—nonagents, perhaps, like ourselves. Even as they depict individuals in interaction, these collective novels query the conventional realistic premise that personal destinies embody in microcosm the dynamics of historical change. Fictional mimesis may reflect certain aspects of these dynamics, but it cannot pretend to encompass their totality. There is a limit to the synecdochic presumption of realistic narrative.

Furthermore, collective novels treat mentor characters quite differently than do other types of proletarian fiction. In single-protagonist works, the mentor often develops a lasting friendship with the protagonist: in *The Disinherited*, Hans is Larry's companion on his organizing mission to points West; in *Moscow Yankee*, Natasha marries Andy; in *To Make My Bread*, John Stevens reminds John McClure that the strike they have been through is just the beginning. In social novels, pedagogues in radical politics either remain in place for future political activity (Noonan in *Pier 17*, Bert in *A Time to Remember*) or, if they die, pass on their legacy to a clearly defined inheritor (as Denis does in *A Sign for Cain* and Fatfolks does in *A World to Win*). In collective novels mentors sometimes continue as part of the class-conscious group they have helped to define. In *Parched Earth*, the Communist organizer, Dave Washburne, who has proclaimed that "we're building for a new day," ends up with Hattie and Hop in the windmill above the flood.[10] But more frequently mentors slip away into the mass, and the reader never hears of them again. Tom Joad, promising his mother to be "ever'where—wherever you look" (p. 537), becomes a participant in unknown future strikes. Mario, after his beating by vigilantes, drops out of the plot of Clara Weatherwax's *Marching! Marching!* Marvin goes off to jail in *The Shadow Before*. Slim in *S.S. Utah* may or may not have survived the police attack. In these novels, plot often short-circuits the expectation that the ending will let us know how our friends are doing—much less reward them for their virtue. Mentors help to explain the historical process; they then disappear into it.

In sum, the collective novel's use of "story"-level redundancies in both characterization and plot entails a departure from the didactic strategies embedded in more traditional forms of multiprotagonist fiction. Hicks was correct to spot vital continuities between complex and collective novels. But he was not accurate in his assertion that the two fictional modes follow essentially identical strategies for representing "characters as separate individuals . . . apart from their group relationship." Even though the collective novel ordinarily depicts individuated protagonists, the threads of the characters' lives are not woven together according to familiar novelistic formulas. As a political proposition, the notion that the class struggle transcends any group of people participating in it is, as we have seen, a common theme—almost a cliché—in much proletarian fiction. It underlies Matt's contention in *A Time to Remember* that the class struggle is "bigger than you and me" (p. 351), as well as Peter's closing realization in *All Brides Are Beautiful* that "[i]n a hundred thousand places . . . things were stirring, changing" (p. 355). In their projection of group-heroes and group-actions, however, collective novels both assert and demonstrate the proletariat to be more than the sum of its constituent parts. These texts represent Barbusse's "new protagonist, the most imposing of all: the masses."

Voices, Fragments, Facts, and Commentary

Some more nonexperimental collective novels make use of various "discourse"-level devices inherited from the realistic tradition. For example, a

10. Arnold Armstrong, *Parched Earth* (New York: Macmillan, 1934), p. 191.

highly opinionated and controlling narratorial voice can play an important role in emphasizing group-identity. In *Strike!*, Vorse's narrator frankly asserts her view that "[the strike] was like a living thing which had a life of its own. It was strong and lusty, it almost bled to death, it grew feeble, and again it became stronger." In *Jordanstown*, there periodically appear italicized passages in which the narrator muses upon the "great four winds of life"—the "fierce west wind of passion, of hate and anger," the "foul east wind of the desire for power," the "bitter and arctic wind of necessity," and the "strong south wind of love"—that drive the characters forward. But the narrator also remarks in less metaphysical terms upon the need for collective consciousness. As Allen and Dave begin their organizing, we are told, "*Jordanstown in those days was a cluster of parallel, isolated lives. Separate, but drawing nearer and nearer to each other.*" In *Industrial Valley*, the narrator occasionally halts the montagelike presentation of sharpening class conflict to comment directly upon its meaning. Describing the desperation of rubber workers wrenched from their old systems for understanding reality, she remarks, "In the fall of 1934 proletarian Akron watched the shadow of permanent unemployment fall over the city. Now, too, men who had held out so far against the union, men who still cherished some vestiges of the old "American Dream," realized that even when what the newspapers called the 'Depression' was over, even when prosperity came back for sure, even then, thousands of rubberworkers would never again have a job." At this point in the crisis, the narrator informs us, "proletarian Akron" is becoming a unified agent; the false consciousness that would constitute "thousands of rubberworkers" as separate individuals is waning under the "shadow of permanent unemployment." In these novels, an authoritative narrator intervenes to stress the collective identities being welded in the heat of class struggle. Patterns of repetition and emphasis emerging from represented characters and events—the ebb and flow of solidarity among the Gastonia strikers, the politicization of the "Bottom," the unionization drive in Akron—are reinforced by the narrator's guiding observations.[11]

Some collective novels avoid authoritative narrators and instead use

11. Mary Heaton Vorse, *Strike!* (New York: Horace Liveright, 1930), p. 187; Josephine Johnson, *Jordanstown* (New York: Simon and Schuster, 1937), pp. 3, 90; Ruth McKenney, *Industrial Valley* (New York: Harcourt, Brace, 1939), p. 181.

free indirect discourse and focalization to convey the phenomenon of group-consciousness. In *Rope of Gold*, Herbst routinely surrenders her narrative to the thoughts of whatever character she is describing. Ed Thompson, the Detroit businessman who is Jonathan Chance's brother-in-law, sees the growing labor unrest through the lenses of his profascist politics: "Loyalty was the finest thing in the world and when he thought of how disloyal those guys were to the plant that was feeding them, he could cry." To the Robb family threatened with dispossession of their farm, reigning social institutions look quite different: "The Bank became a maw to be filled. It was like a bull critter. . . . The Bank got snacks and it growled. It got a full meal and it purred." Since the text moves rapidly from one viewpoint to another, different characters' values are continually set in opposition, unmediated by a controlling narrator. Even though Jonathan, Victoria, and Steve remain the main characters of the novel, these frequent forays into the minds of other characters reveal a world constituted by multiple class sectors, all viewing reality in distinctive—and often mutually antagonistic—ways.[12]

Some collective novels are fairly conventional in their use of narratorial voice and focalization; others are boldly experimental. *Marching! Marching!* contains perhaps the most dramatic attempt at collective focalization in all U.S. proletarian fiction. For the novel not merely juxtaposes multiple perspectives but intermittently welds these perspectives into one. Describing the reactions of loggers carrying the body of Tim, a fellow worker just killed in an accident caused by a faulty cable, the narrator notes,

> So talking went slow, but when a guy looked at anybody he could see they were all thinking around pretty much the same things. One, stopping to scrape a lot of leaves and truck off the bottoms of his boots, probably thinking *I got to get me them new calks* or first thing I'll slip and it'll be like Tim and another guy likely as not jumping his mind ahead to Joe who didn't know about this yet, or thinking *Christ it'll be tough on Annie* Maybe some *It's like Mario says. We got to get organized, real rank-and-file organized and demand a few things . . . .* or maybe they were wondering *What chance have we got? You tell them the cable's busted or rotten and they say splice her up and use her again. Cable's expensive they say.*[13]

12. Josephine Herbst, *Rope of Gold* (1939; rpt. Old Westbury, NY: Feminist P, 1984), pp. 290, 52.

13. Clara Weatherwax, *Marching! Marching!* (New York: John Day, 1935), p. 20.

Collective focalization here telescopes narrative background and functions as exposition: Annie is Tim's wife, Joe his brother, Mario a respected organizer. But the text also establishes the group-identity that will be its protagonist. Even though the narrator appears uncertain whether any specific character is actually thinking the thoughts she postulates—each idea is "probably" or "likely" entertained by one or more of the loggers—she is confident that such considerations characterize the consciousness of the group as a whole. Not any given character's feelings about the tragedy, but the politics of the work team's mixed response are what matter most.

Even when relating the thoughts of a single character, Weatherwax attempts to convey the notion that consciousness is a collective phenomenon. Thus Pete, a former student turned worker, recalls:

> His mind again returning, like a flashback in a film: the narrowback administration, student strikes, hired thugs and campus vigilantes rotten-egging the demonstrators; discrimination against and limitation of Jewish students, as if they were bastards like him only worse; R. O. T. C.; the police attacking the protest meeting against the *Karlsruhe*. . . Remembering the meetings and the earnest friendly people all marked by labor. The literature selling for one to five cents and the workers buying hungrily as if it were bread. He remembered he remembered. Understanding growing luminous and bright like a searchlight to examine everything. (pp. 32–33)

Weatherwax offers a whirlwind summary of the experiences that have presumably brought Pete to his present level of "understanding"; exposition is accomplished through flashback. But she also treats Pete's consciousness as a "searchlight to examine everything." Free indirect discourse registers not individual subjectivity but the experience of the group. Weatherwax places a strain upon inherited narrative conventions: it is difficult to imagine that any character's spontaneous reflections would faithfully render so comprehensive a summary of the CP's Third-Period campus campaigns.[14] But this somewhat implausible maneuver at least precludes readerly co-

14. For more on the CP's program and activities among college students, see *Student Review*, published by the CP-led National Student League, especially "Program of the National Student League," *SR* (December 1933), 11–13. A detailed portrait of campus CP work is available in the papers of Oakley Johnson, John Reed Clubs president, who was fired from his teaching position in the English Department at CCNY in the early 1930s (Box 2, Oakley Johnson Papers, Labadie Collection, U of Michigan Library). See also James Wechsler, *Revolt on the Campus* (New York: Covici Friede, 1935).

optation. In *A Sign for Cain*, Bill's and Denis's memories of past experiences in class struggle are referred to, not described; it is simply assumed that the reader can and will fill in the blanks. In *Marching! Marching!*, by contrast, Pete's memories are the domain of the group. They are, "like a flashback in a film," simply inserted into one mind for narrative convenience. The reader is informed of this public legacy; prior knowledge and agreement—are not taken for granted.

Some collective novels experiment with narrative technique by introducing unmediated bits of environmental buzz—slogans, songs, newsbroadcasts, noise. Such materials at times appear in bildungsromans and social novels, but there they tend to be directly subsumed within "story." In *The Land of Plenty*, Hagen hears patriotic antiunion speeches over the radio on July Fourth; in *Moscow Yankee*, Andy reads a poem called "Look Here, Stalingrad" and hears a Soviet labor song that is transcribed in the text. In *Parched Earth*, by contrast, a radio commentator frequently interrupts the narrative to remark on local and national affairs. Even though some of the characters may hear this commentator, he has no specified audience in the text; the reader is obliged to fill in as listener. In *The Shadow Before*, Rollins introduces a series of devices that similarly rupture the illusion of narrative transparency. The "*THUMP—THROB; thump throb*" of the textile mill is injected at random moments, reminding the reader of the industrial process over which bosses and workers are warring. The narrative is interrupted by fragments of the "Internationale" and other labor songs, as well as by gigantic boldface political slogans: four versions of "Workers of the World Unite! You have nothing to lose but your—"—in English, French, Portuguese, and Polish—appear in a description of a picket line.[15] In *Parched Earth* and *The Shadow Before*, such linguistic fragments have no specified fictional agent or recipient. While didactic intent is clear, no connection between particular events and general principles is spelled out. It is incumbent upon the reader to formulate—"from outside"—imaginative connections between these discursive flurries and the characters whose environment they constitute.

Some collective novels do not simply intersperse background noise but set apart whole sections of narrative introducing people and events un-

15. William Rollins, *The Shadow Before* (New York: Robert M. McBride, 1934), pp. 212–15.

related to the main action of the plot. Mentors generally exercise limited functions in collective novels because there are so many other opportunities for voicing political ideas. Throughout her *Rope of Gold* trilogy, Herbst juxtaposes accounts of the stories of her various fictional characters with prose poems featuring anonymous voices and persons. These passages, of one or two pages in length, represent experiences of people far removed from the fictional characters—shoe bargainers in Havana, migrant laborers in New Jersey, members of the Abraham Lincoln Brigade in Spain. In the earlier novels of the trilogy—*Pity Is Not Enough* (1933) and *The Executioner Waits* (1934)—these interpolations refer to events more or less contemporaneous with the writing of the novel, even though the surrounding fictional account dates back into the early years of the twentieth century. For example, all the short passages in the second half of *The Executioner Waits* are dated from 1934, even though the accompanying narrative, detailing Jonathan's and Vicky's courtship and marriage, is situated in the 1920s. In *Rope of Gold* (1939), most events referred to in the interspersed passages are closely aligned with the fiction's chronology, which covers the Depression decade. Interestingly, however, the final prose poem jumps ahead of the fictional narrative—which features Steve Carson at the outset of the Flint Sit-Down Strike of early 1937—to feature an anonymous voice speaking from "Tortosa, Barcelona Road, 1938":

> Yes, they can shuffle the cards and stuff the deck and draw every ace but one. They can buy guns and bombs and bring in a crew from Germany, from Italy to rub us off. England will snuffle in a corner, France can hide her head. . . . Satisfy the gluttons, spread the butter of peace. The smell of death. The sellout.
>
> But they haven't got one little card.
>
> We got the living, they got the dead. There's some guys won't sell out for a crust of bread. (p. 407)

Herbst projects movement into the future even as she portrays fictional events reaching their dramatic finale; the battle against a repressive American industrial oligarchy has its international climax in the antifascist struggle in Spain. Throughout the *Rope of Gold* trilogy, the historical interchapters query the synecdochic status of the Trexler-Wendel-Chance family and suggest the larger arena in which its fortunes are played out. The voices heard in the prose poems are not simply historical "background."

They are articulations from other lives—"real" lives—presumably as rich and meaningful—and potentially as typical—as the fictional ones Herbst has chosen to feature.[16]

In *The Grapes of Wrath*, Steinbeck makes still bolder didactic use of interspersed passages. As he noted in the journals accompanying the writing of the novel, the two narratives, while parallel, treat their subjects from quite different vantage points and need to be contradistinguished. After finishing the interchapter treating the tractors that remove the farmers from the land, Steinbeck remarked, "Yesterday the general and now back to the particular. I find I am not very satisfied with the numbering of these chapters. It may be that they will simply be numbered with large numerals for the general and small for the particular. The reason is that I want the reader to be able to keep them separate in his mind." Apparently Steinbeck— or his publisher—decided against the use of different-sized numerals in the novel's final version. But the author's comments on this typographical demarcation indicate his intention: the general illuminates, but is merged into, the particular.[17]

Critics have commented extensively upon Steinbeck's thematic counterpoint in *The Grapes of Wrath*. Most Steinbeck scholarship posits that the two narrative modes provide mutual rhetorical reinforcement.[18] But the

16. Herbst, whose marriage with CP organizer and writer John Herrmann was falling apart during the mid-1930s, drew personal sustenance from her involvement in the left-wing movement. As she wrote to Hicks, "I am convinced that the only way to bear up in this present period is by getting closer to actual worker struggles. For myself, doubts become just ordinary stones in a clear path when I am in any real struggle. And more, and most important, I am really only happy then. This is what I am trying to say in my novel. With all the reasons and the background leading to it. If it had not been for Cuba, and Flint, and Spain, I would be dead, other things having been that bad for me often in the last few years" (n.d., Box 27, Hicks Papers).

17. Steinbeck, *Working Days*, pp. 23–24.

18. For the argument that the interchapters and the Joad story are mutually reinforcing, see Peter Lisca, "The Dynamics of Community in *The Grapes of Wrath*," in John Ditsky, ed., *Critical Essays on the Grapes of Wrath* (Boston: G. K. Hall, 1989), pp. 87–97; Howard Levant, "The Fully Matured Art: *The Grapes of Wrath*," in Harold Bloom, ed., *John Steinbeck's The Grapes of Wrath: Modern Critical Interpretations* (New York: Chelsea House, 1988), pp. 17–44; Louis Owens, *The Grapes of Wrath: Trouble in the Promised Land* (Boston: Twayne, 1989), pp. 27–38; and Stephen Railton, "Pilgrim's Politics: Steinbeck's Art of Conversion," in David Wyatt, ed., *New Essays on the Grapes of Wrath* (Cambridge: Cambridge UP, 1990), pp. 27–46. Railton makes an interesting rhe-

politics articulated in the interchapters and the fictional narrative do *not* precisely mesh with one another. The prophetic voice remarking upon the larger context and meaning of the Joads' experience formulates insights about politics and history considerably more revolutionary than those achieved by even the most left-leaning of the fictional characters. Casy's intuition that "all men got one big soul ever'body's a part of" (p. 31) and Tom's promise that "wherever they's a fight so hungry people can eat, I'll be there" (p. 537) remain within the discourse of a militant humanism. But the voice who hectors the growers—"you who hate change and fear revolution"—and warns them of their imminent downfall has undertaken a more searching analysis of the economic crisis: "If you who own the things people must have could understand this, you might preserve yourself. If you could separate causes from results; if you could know that Paine, Marx, Jefferson, Lenin, were results, not causes, you might survive. But that you cannot know. For the quality of owning freezes you forever into 'I,' and cuts you off forever from the 'we.' " The threat here is barely veiled: the growers will *not* "survive." Tom's and Casy's actions demonstrate the openness of the disenfranchised masses to revolutionary practice; the prophetic voice articulates revolutionary theory.

To note that Steinbeck's narrative method gives him useful opportunities for setting forth political doctrine is not to argue that his chosen doctrine is an especially revolutionary one. Steinbeck was a Popular Frontist when he wrote *The Grapes of Wrath*: he railed against the "fascist utilities and banks" running California and was loosely affiliated with the CP through the League of American Writers (of which he remained a member after the 1939 Hitler-Stalin pact). As the coupling of Paine and Jefferson with Marx and Lenin suggests, however, what this democratic antifascism entailed was an etiolation of the text's class warfare theme, even in the interchapters where the prophet fulminates most angrily. But the interchapters do not always articulate a doctrine to the left of that embedded on the level of "story." Toward the end of the novel, the depiction of dramatically altered relations between men and women in the Joad family

---

torical argument: Because the interchapters indicate what will happen to the Joads before it happens, "what will happen next is made narratively inescapable. . . . The narrative enacts its own kind of oppression, and, by arousing in its readers a desire to fight this sense of inevitability, it works to arouse us toward action to change the status quo" (p. 32).

is undermined by the patriarchal claims of the interchapter voice. The novel opens with a description of the ravages of the Dust Bowl in which the women watch the men and wonder whether they will break. The final interchapter reiterates this motif, adding the motif of fermenting grapes that has developed in intervening interchapters: "The women watched the men, watched to see whether the break had come at last. . . . And where a number of men gathered together, the fear went from their faces, and anger took its place. And the women sighed with relief, for they knew it was all right—the break had not come; and the break would never come as long as fear could turn to wrath" (p. 556). This passage offsets the sentimentalism of the novel's fictional finale—Rose of Sharon's nursing the starving man— by reminding the reader that the "wrath" of proletarian class conscious- ness and resistance will continue to mount. But this militant message is yoked with a proposition about the relation of female to male—the women still watch the men for leadership—that the intervening fictional chap- ters have refuted. Pap has just finished conceding to Ma, "Funny! Woman takin' over the fambly. Woman sayin' we'll do this here, an' we'll go there. An' I don't even care" (p. 540). The more revolutionary gender politics emerging from the developmental pattern of "story" contradict the image of social conflict rendered on the level of "discourse." By virtue of their positioning external to "story," the interchapters do not produce a politi- cal doctrine that is necessarily more revolutionary than that embedded in character and event. On the question of class conflict, the interchapters are generally to the left of the Joad story; on the question of gender rela- tions, they are to the right. What this very disparity reveals, however, is that the interchapters engage in political interpretation and analysis not necessarily subordinated to the thematic demands of the narrative. They derive from and account for experience, but they are not simple reflexes of it.[19]

19. For more on Steinbeck's politics in the 1930s, see Sylvia Jenkins Cook, "Stein- beck, the People, and the Party," in Ralph Bogardus and Fred Hobson, eds., *Literature at the Barricades: The American Writer in the 1930s* (University: U of Alabama P, 1982), pp. 82–95, Steinbeck quoted p. 92. Steinbeck had a divided assessment of the CP members whom he knew: "Except for the field organizers of strikes, who were pretty tough mon- keys and devoted, most of the so-called Communists I met were middle-class, middle- aged people playing a game of dreams" ("A Primer on the 30's," *Esquire* 53 [June 1960]: 91). Steinbeck explained his novelistic method as follows: "Superficially [the planned

In *Rope of Gold* and *The Grapes of Wrath*, the interchapters evoke Depression-era locales—the Spanish Civil War, the Dust Bowl—but do not situate the novel's happenings in specific historical events. Some collective novels, however, refer directly to real persons and occasions. In *Strike!*, the names of key characters and places bear a loosely anagrammatic relation to their historical originals: Fred Beal becomes Fer Deane, Gastonia becomes Stonerton, the Manville-Jenckes mill becomes the Basil-Schenk mill, and Ella May Wiggins becomes Mamie Lewes. Moreover, the key phases and occurrences represented in Vorse's narrative—the tactical use of female-staffed roving picket lines, the burning down of the union hall, the eviction of strikers from their homes, the erection of the tent city, the shooting death of Gastonia Sheriff Aderholt in a police attack on the tent city, the subsequent murder trial of Dean and other strike leaders, the murder of Wiggins by vigilantes—all codify the version of the strike given in the left-wing press and contest the version offered by the journalistic mouthpieces for the mill owners. Bildungsromans loosely based upon Gastonia routinely refer to these events. *Call Home the Heart* depicts the burning of the union hall; *To Make My Bread* features the death of Wiggins; *Gathering Storm* includes the killing of Aderholt. But no other Gastonia novel relies so fully upon the actual historical record as does *Strike!* or so directly refutes alternative narratives. In the other Gastonia novels, references to a known historical background enhance the text's *credibility* as a register to typicality; in Vorse's, factual detail augments the text's historical

---

design of all my work] begins with the very simple reactions of a given individual to an unique incident and it goes through all states until, so far, it ends up with the group (symbolic) and the generalized individual (also symbolic) subjected to all incidents." Interestingly, he predicted that after *The Grapes of Wrath* he would abandon fiction altogether: "[T]hat's why the novel—prose form as we know it—is finished for me. The picture as nearly as I can present it, is done. The field must now broaden. The new work must jump to include other species beside the human. That is why my interest in biology and ecology have [sic] become so sharpened" ("Dear Joe," n.d., Correspondence, Floyd Dell Papers, Newberry Library). For more on the novel's feminism, see Mimi Reisel Gladstein, "The Indestructible Women: Ma Joad and Rose of Sharon," in Bloom, pp. 115–27; and John Ditsky, "The Ending of *The Grapes of Wrath*: A Further Commentary," in Ditsky, pp. 116–23. Steinbeck's wife Carol—who, according to the novel's dedication, "willed this book"—was a committed feminist and had a decisive impact on the book's representation of women.

authority. Clearly not all documentary proletarian fictions are collective novels, or vice versa. Documentarism nonetheless is central to the peculiar "collectivity" of *Strike!* because it links the text's collective protagonist to historical actuality by multiple threads of reference. The novel has no hero because reality has no hero.[20]

More frequently, however, documentarism in the collective novel is not seamlessly interwoven but instead calls attention to its own discursive status. At the outset of *Industrial Valley,* McKenney announces the hybrid nature of her narrative: "This is a true story of Akron, Ohio. It is also a true story of America's industrial valleys the country over" (p. xviii). The novel will lay simultaneous claim to general and particular truth. McKenney's prefatory acknowledgments note her indebtedness to the Akron *Beacon Journal,* the Akron *Times-Press,* the archives of the Akron Chamber of Commerce and the publicity department of the Goodyear Tire and Rubber Company (p. vii). The ensuing chronicle of Akron's deepening economic crisis is rendered, however, through "press" circulars and "newspaper" headlines and articles that obviously issue from the writer's own pen. A passage dated February 23, 1933, for example, is entitled "Dark Sunday" and reads, "Horrible rumors spread through West Hill. Bank officials didn't show up at church services and weren't home at one o'clock to eat the usual big Sunday dinner with their families" (p. 66). There are, it would seem, no "facts" independent of partisan articulation: McKenney's unabashedly colored account foregrounds not just the author's pro-union politics but also the pro-boss politics routinely shaping reports on labor strife. *Industrial Valley* is a "true story" of both Akron and "America's industrial valleys the country over" because it portrays typical processes

---

20. Vorse never publicly disputed the CP's version of events at Gastonia, but her critical account of Deane's vacillation and narcissism targets Fred Beal. Off the record Vorse was quite negative in her assessment of the party's activities and accomplishments in Gastonia. Declining an invitation from Hicks to review Grace Hutchins's *Women Who Work,* Vorse voiced strong criticisms of CP factional infighting and inefficiency at Gastonia: "[O]ne of the greatest opportunities ever open to the party was lost through mismanagement." Hutchins's book, Vorse claimed, rendered an inaccurate account of what happened in Gastonia. "I do not want to attack her," Vorse concluded. "I do not and cannot wish to expose the failures in the South for obvious reasons. I will send the book back. . . . [L]et someone do it who does not know so much as I" (Vorse to Hicks, n.d., Box 64, Hicks Papers). In *Gathering Storm,* Page produces her own interpretation on the Gastonia events by suggesting that Aderholt was shot by his own policemen.

at the same time that it comments on the process by which typicality itself is ideologically constructed.

In novels less unremittingly documentary than *Industrial Valley*, inserted segments of presumably verifiable factual material help to articulate political doctrine. In *The Shadow Before*, Rollins accompanies his fictional account of the strikers' courtroom experience with a direct transcription of portions of the historical Gastonia trial, in which Vera Buch Weisbord (here Bogusloff Weinberg) and other Communist leaders, when cornered by the prosecution, openly asserted their revolutionary convictions:

> Q: *Mrs. Weinberg, . . . [D]o you believe in violence, in revolution, as a means to overthrow our present government?*
>
> (Objection—overruled. Exception.)
>
> A: *If conditions warrant it and there are not other means of changing the present system.*
>
> Q: *In other words, you believe the time may come when our present government ought to be overthrown by force? Will you answer that question yes or no, Mrs. Weinberg?*
>
> (Objection—overruled. Exception.)
>
> A: *Yes.* (p. 350)

The inclusion of testimony from the historical Gastonia trial injects a harsh note of actuality into Rollins's satiric representation of bourgeois justice. Even though the novel is set among a multinational group of immigrant laborers in a New England town (presumably New Bedford), rather than among native-born Southern mill workers, the documentary echoes of Gastonia position the text on the borderline between fact and fiction and reinforce its representation of labor strife and capitalist justice. Even the fictional strike activist Micky acquires a mixed ontological status. For at the novel's end Micky is incorporated into the "real" factory's "thump— throb" as she attaches spindles to the looms: "THE GIRL WITH AUBURN HAIR MOVES FINGERS SNAPPING ONE OFF AND BRUSHING IT BACK AND CLAMP ONE ON 'YOU DON'T GET TIME TO BREATHE!' SHE SHOUTS AND CLAMPS ONE ON" (p. 389). Identified as "THE GIRL WITH THE AUBURN HAIR," Micky is absorbed into the documentary apparatus that has throughout the text functioned to remind the reader of the text's tangency with actuality. In the course of the narrative, Micky has undergone a "conversion" of sorts; previously a flirt who measured her value according to her attractiveness to men, she is now a strong and determined strike leader. But didacticism results less from any cathartic identification with Micky than from the realization that, as a representative of the proletariat that will outlive the Harry Baumanns and Mrs. Thayers, Micky is in some sense a real historical agent. Her endurance is not merely a novelistic but also a documentary fact.[21]

In *Marching! Marching!*, Weatherwax similarly deploys a documentary apparatus that roots the text's representation of a collective proletarian protagonist in a verifiable actuality. All of chapter 12, which describes the tense labor confrontation in Aberdeen, is given over to a double-columned comparison of journalistic responses to the strike. On the left appear excerpts from the boss-controlled press, on the right strike leaflets and clippings from left-wing newspapers. For example:

POLICE NOTIFIED TO BE READY TO QUELL VIOLENCE	HARBOR STRIKE IS SPREADING
Plea for Delay by Mediating Board is Refused	Mediation Board Prepares to Betray Workers
The Harbor Lumbermen's Association today notified S. J. Steinbeck, Chief of Police, of the complete collapse of efforts toward a peaceful settlement of the strikes now gripping various harbor mills. The Association further demanded adequate police protection in their attempt to run the closed mills with new crews.	Labor Fakers Try Splitting Tactics Following the lead of the militant workers in the Bayliss Mill, workers of the Dent Cedar Mill Company and the Tide City Veneer Works have voted to go out on strike in sympathy with the Bayliss workers and for demands of their own.

21. For more on the Gastonia trial, see Beal; also Vera Buch Weisbord, *A Radical Life* (Bloomington and London: Indiana UP, 1977). The model for Rollins's Bogusloff Weinberg, Weisbord also provides the prototype for Irma Rankin in Vorse's *Strike!* Rollins collaborated on a report on the Gastonia trial published in the *New Masses* (William Rollins and Jessie Lloyd, "The Gastonia Trial," *NM* 5 [October 1929]: 3–6). The report dramatically proclaimed, "Liberals who continue to deplore the use of the term 'class warfare' should go down to Gastonia and reality" (5). Edmund Wilson commented that observers of the Gastonia trial, reminded of Sacco and Vanzetti, feared "another judicial lynching" ("The Literary Consequences of the Crash," in *The Shores of Light: A Literary Chronicle of the Twenties and Thirties* [New York: Strauss and Young, 1952], p. 497).

> Picket lines are being tight-
> ened, discipline among the
> workers is good, and a strong
> determination to win is mani-
> fest everywhere. (p. 213)

The didactic function of this device is fairly obvious: bosses and workers construct reality in accordance with different paradigms. What the left press calls a "sympathy strike" the bourgeois press depicts as a threat of "violence"; what the proletarian press sees as attempts of "labor fakers" to "betray workers" the pro-company press portrays as "efforts toward a peaceful settlement."

Beyond demonstrating the political bias of all journalism, however, Weatherwax's documentary strategy recasts the text's fictionality. Even though Granny Whittle, Mario, Joe, Annie, and other novelistic charac-ters remain fictional constructs, the world in which they move is invested with an aura of actuality. Indeed, the characters' world eventually merges with that of the narrator, who herself becomes a participant in the strike. Describing the final confrontation of the strikers with armed police, the narrator—who has until this point been entirely invisible—declares, "For a few seconds we hear only the sound of our own feet, the steady pound of ourselves marching forward. Then suddenly Annie turns and waves a sig-nal to our marshals. Each lifts a hand for a moment while a word is spoken from rank to rank. The signalling hands go down in unison and we're all singing: 'Hold the fort for we are coming; Workingmen be strong!' " (p. 256). Annie no longer exists simply as a creature framed by fiction, just as the anonymous voices of the Aberdeen working class are no longer the object of narratorial conjecture. Rather, all are here conjoined in a "we" that, speaking in the present tense, asserts its reality in the reader's world. Nar-rative momentum gathers rapidly at the end of Marching! Marching!, and closure is apocalyptic. By collapsing its distinctions between fiction and reality, however, the narrative shows the continuity of contradiction. The text has represented militant Communist-led organizing as the negation of the proletariat's fragmentation and intimidation: in a doctrinal sense the novel's dialectics are anything but open-ended. The text does not, however, show the triumph of the workers, who are last seen marching toward the bayonets of the National Guardsmen. Presumably we have to learn what eventually "happens" to the workers by becoming part of the "we" ourselves. While as fervently partisan as many social novels—for example, *A Sign for Cain* or *A Time to Remember*—*Marching! Marching!* does not take the reader's agreement for granted. There is no catharsis in watching the massing of the proletariat in a world sealed off by the "pastness" of fictionality. Didacticism in large part results from the text's challenge that the reader join in the struggle represented in the text.[22]

Collective novels depart in various ways from the conventions of realistic storytelling. *S.S. Utah* and *The Company* rely almost entirely upon familiar modes of novelistic representation, even though they postulate an unfamiliar collective subject. *Jordanstown* and *Parched Earth* introduce experimental devices that invite the reader to reflect consciously on the relation between the novel's fictional microcosm and the larger totality to which it corresponds. *Rope of Gold* and *The Grapes of Wrath* set up a discursive counterpoint between clearly demarcated zones of fiction and rhetorical commentary. *Strike!*, *Industrial Valley*, *The Shadow Before*, and *Marching! Marching!* deploy documentary apparatuses that assert multiple points of tangency between novel and history and, in the process, query the ideological construction of factuality. Committed not simply to representing and advocating class solidarity but to demonstrating the development of classes as historical subjects, many collective novelists developed

---

22. Robert Cantwell in 1936 commented on the historical error of Weatherwax's closing portrayal of the workers marching into the guns of the National Guardsmen. "In actuality," he noted, "the great strike that took place last year [in Aberdeen] was won by the strikers hands down. . . . The lumber strike itself, although it received little publicity, was one of the biggest in American labor history, and the conflict in Aberdeen was decisive in determining the immediate future of the organized labor movement of a whole area and a major industry" ("A Town and Its Novels," *NR* 86 [February 19, 1936]: 51). See also Paul Garon, "American Labor Fiction in the 20th Century," *AP Bookman's Weekly* (February 19, 1990), 744. Rabinowitz, praising the experimental form of *Marching! Marching!*, points out that "the narrative loses sight of the individual characters who have participated in the strike because the mass movement replaces the characters as the narrative focus. The narrative never reaches closure; instead of ending, it links its reader to the future struggle" (p. 70). But I disagree with her conclusion that Communist didacticism undermines feminist modernism: "[T]he narrative is deterritorialized away from realism, only to be reterritorialized through the incessant party doctrine that infuses the novel's form. . . . [F]eminist desire interrupts the discourse of masculine labor, deflecting the narrative away from the strike, just as history resists closure and demands another ending" (pp. 70, 107, 114).

narrative devices that produce cognition "from outside" the realm of character and plot. Redundancies between levels of "discourse" and "story" do not simply reinforce the political points embedded in "story"; they pose the political as a zone of conscious scrutiny. There is indeed—as Hicks remarked but did not elaborate—a distinctive "technique"—or, set of techniques—to the collective novel.

Dos Passos and Literary Collectivism

The figure who hovers in the background of the preceding discussion of technique is John Dos Passos. Certainly in the United States, and possibly in the entire international sphere of literary proletarianism outside the USSR, Dos Passos is the single most important pioneer in the form of the collective novel. Absent the influence of Dos Passos, Weatherwax, Rollins, and Steinbeck would not have written their novels as they did. Dos Passos's experiments with style and narrative structure are thus important enough to warrant separate analysis. Since, like *The Grapes of Wrath, U.S.A.* has been subjected to extensive thematic and formal exegesis, I shall make no attempt to offer a comprehensive discussion of Dos Passos's complex project in his trilogy. Rather, I shall focus upon those aspects of his method constituting his main contribution to the genre of the collective novel.[23]

Dos Passos's choice of a title for his trilogy—initially published as *The Forty-Second Parallel* (1930), *Nineteen Nineteen* (1932), and *The Big Money* (1936)—suggests, as many critics have noted, that the text's collective protagonist is the nation itself. What is less frequently acknowledged, however—at least in critical commentaries composed since the 1930s—is the extent to which Dos Passos's conception of historical contradiction is shaped by a Marxist notion of class struggle. To be sure, Dos Passos never fully committed himself to revolution or, in particular, to the program of the CPUSA. Many other nonparty proletarian novelists—Conroy, Page, Cunningham, Wright, Burke, Bell, McKenney, to name just a few—aligned

23. See Allen Belkind, ed., *Dos Passos, the Critics, and the Artist's Intention* (Carbondale and Edwardsville: Southern Illinois UP, 1969); Melvin J. Landsberg, *Dos Passos' Path to U.S.A.* (Boulder: University of Colorado P, 1974); and Donald Pizer, *Dos Passos' U.S.A.: A Critical Study* (Charlottesville: U of Virginia P, 1988).

themselves more decisively with 1930s Communism than did Dos Passos. Nor did Dos Passos habitually use the language of class analysis. Even in the trilogy's climactic statement of social and political polarization, the author/narrator declares, "all right we are two nations"—not "all right we are two classes." Nor is it to claim that U.S.A. holds up proletarian heroes or groups its characters in clearly opposed camps of bosses and workers. With the exception of Mac, the Wobbly, Mary French, the doggedly faithful fellow-traveler, and Ben Compton, the party member (and later Trotskyist apostate), Dos Passos's main characters are largely non-class-conscious. Indeed, most of them (interior decorators, advertising copywriters, engineers) inhabit ambiguous class sectors. Even though he was never a "pure proletarian," however, Dos Passos subscribed to a class-based analysis of social conflict in U.S.A. and developed a narrative method that was profoundly dialectical and materialist. As many contemporaneous critics—Soviet as well as American—realized, Dos Passos's narrative strategy was a rich mine of collectivist technique and deserved close scrutiny, even if his cynical (and, in The Big Money, overtly anti-Communist) political doctrine was, from a Marxist standpoint, open to critique.[24]

Dos Passos signals his class approach to the question of national identity by framing the trilogy with the portraits "U.S.A." and "Vag." The opening "U.S.A." sketch depicts a Whitmanesque young man walking the streets in search of "answering flicker of eyes" (p. v); it closes with the statement,

> U.S.A. is the slice of a continent. U.S.A. is a group of holding companies, some aggregations of trade unions, a set of laws bound in calf, a radio

24. John Dos Passos, The Big Money (New York; Modern Library, 1937), p. 467. The different novels of the U.S.A. trilogy are all contained in the Modern Library single-volume edition, but each is separately paginated. For instances of 1930s critics' reactions to Dos Passos's politics, see the reviews of Schneider, Cowley, and Hicks (n. 1). See also the New Masses review of Nineteen Nineteen: "This sympathetic understanding of individuals—of an amazing variety of individuals, too—is what, when taken along with his command over mass movements, gives Dos Passos's fiction a quality we might call diaectical. . . . He is a good enough Marxist also to do justice to destiny and will" (NM 7 [June 1932]: 26). For more on Dos Passos's reception in the Soviet Union, see Deming Brown's chapter on Dos Passos in Soviet Attitudes Toward American Writing (Princeton: Princeton UP, 1962), pp. 83–108. For the influence of Dos Passos on proletarian writers in Great Britain, see Ramon Lopez Ortega, "The Language of the Working-Class Novel in the 1930s," in H. Gustav Klaus, ed., The Socialist Novel in Britain: Towards the Recovery of a Tradition (Brighton, Sussex: Harvester, 1982), pp. 122–44.

network, a chain of moving picture theatres, a column of stock-quotations rubbed out and written in by a Western Union boy on a blackboard, a publiclibrary full of old newspapers and dogeared historybooks with protests scrawled on the margins in pencil. U.S.A. is the world's greatest rivervalley fringed with mountains and hills, U.S.A. is a set of bigmouthed officials with too many bankaccounts. U.S.A. is a lot of men buried in their uniforms in Arlington Cemetery. U.S.A. is the letters at the end of an address when you are away from home. But mostly U.S.A. is the speech of the people. (p. vii)

Critics of the trilogy, fastening upon this final sentence, have frequently concluded that Dos Passos's overriding interest is in the ethics, politics, and psychology of language. Dos Passos is indeed preoccupied with language as a site of both control and resistance. But language is here unambiguously linked to power, and power is defined in class terms. The initial opposition of capital and labor (holding companies and unions) is succeeded by references to the law, the media, mass culture, commodity fetishism, and written documents—that last of which furnish both ruling-class ideology and the possibility for resistance (albeit a literally marginalized one). The "speech of the people" is hardly a populist slogan. The discursive collectivity constituting the nation is anything but classless or seamless.[25]

In "Vag," the partner sketch to "U.S.A." that closes *The Big Money*, the anonymous Whitmanesque hero reappears, much the worse for wear, as a Depression-era vagrant hitchhiker. As cars speed past and a businessman in an airplane above "vomits into the carton container the steak and mushrooms he ate in New York," the vagrant "waits with swimming head, needs knot the belly, idle hands numb." His past desires float before him: "went to school, books said opportunity, ads promised speed, own your home, shine bigger than your neighbor, the radiocrooner whispered girls, ghosts of platinum girls coaxed from the screen, millions in winnings were chalked up on the boards in the offices, paychecks were for hands willing to work, the cleared desk of an executive with three telephones on it" (*TBM*, p. 561). Echoing various motifs presented in the

25. See Pizer for the fullest discussion of the theme of language betrayed in *U.S.A.* See also Dos Passos's "The Writer as Technician," in Henry Hart, ed., *American Writers Congress* (New York: International, 1935), pp. 78–82.

"U.S.A." sketch—bosses, workers, mass media, mass culture, stock market charts—this closing image reveals the victory of capital over labor and targets the key role played by false consciousness in the proletariat's defeat. Moreover, the sketch's status as a "biography"—it is presented in the prose poem style of the other biographical sketches, not the transparent naturalistic prose of the fictional narratives—suggests that Vag is the anonymous face of the historical present. He is both representative and real.

The "U.S.A." and "Vag" sketches furnish "discourse"-level commentary inviting the reader to view the United States as an embattled site. The fictional narratives that make up the trilogy's narrative backbone also engage the reader in conscious analytical activity. In some ways U.S.A. operates as a conventionally realistic multiprotagonist text delineating numerous "story"-level connections among its various characters. Eleanor Stoddard, Janey Williams, Eveline Hutchins, and Richard Ellsworth Savage are drawn into the orbit of J. Ward Moorehouse's word-mongering empire. Eveline has a brief affair with Charley Anderson and is friends with Ada Cohn, herself a friend of Mary French; Mary in turn has a short-lived romance with Ben Compton. Joe Williams is Janey's brother, Daughter is Savage's girl friend, Charley is Margo Dowling's "sugar daddy"; Mac once sits across the table from a blowhard oil publicity man who turns out to be Moorehouse. Moreover, there appear various minor characters—the con man turned health-food evangelist E. R. Bingham, the journalist Jerry Burnham, the party careerist Don Stevens, the "labor-faker" G. H. Barrow—who establish further links among the main characters. But, with the exception of the cluster grouped around Moorehouse, the trilogy's fictional characters are more noteworthy for their isolation from one another than for their interaction. The cocktail party at the end of The Big Money brings into a single room Mary, Eveline, Margo, and Moorehouse. But it is if anything a parody of narrative endings that tie up all the loose threads, since it is neither the product of narrative momentum nor a means to narrative resolution. The reader who wishes to understand the connections between Mary and Moorehouse—let alone between Ben Compton and Janey Williams, who, like most of the trilogy's characters, never meet—must look to the larger pattern of class relations.

Readers are not left to their own resources in framing this larger pattern, however; Dos Passos's documentary and rhetorical apparatus provides many "discourse"-level guidelines. The Newsreels involve the reader as a participant in the process of forming interpretive paradigms. Consisting of newspaper headlines, fragments of newsstories, advertising slogans, and snatches of popular (and occasionally political) songs, the Newsreels present a collage of events, at once real and linguistically constructed, that form the characters' discursive and historical context. At times the Newsreels bear directly upon the fiction. A catalog of want ads precedes the narrative of Mary French's search for a job. Several Newsreels featuring advertising from the mid-1920s Florida land boom, as well as news stories detailing the disastrous 1926 hurricane, surround Charley's final frenzied days in Miami Beach.

As a rule, however, the Newsreels' relation to the fictional narrative is oblique and mediated, requiring synthesizing activity on the part of the reader. This activity has two main components. First, by presenting diverse and at times conflicting views, the Newsreels draw attention to voice as a register and carrier of politics. Usually the Newsreel voice articulates triumphal bourgeois self-congratulation. The opening Newsreel of *The Forty-Second Parallel*, for example, begins with a song celebrating the charge up San Juan Hill ("*It was that emancipated race/That was chargin up the hill*") and then blares forth the apocalyptic jingoism of the "American Century": "NOISE GREETS NEW CENTURY / LABOR GREETS NEW CENTURY / CHURCHES GREET NEW CENTURY" (*42P*, pp. 3–4). As the trilogy reveals growing opposition to ruling-class hegemony, however, other voices intermingle. In a Newsreel from *The Big Money* dating from the postwar recession, two juxtaposed headlines cover the same event: "EX-SERVICEMEN DEMAND JOBS / JOBLESS RIOT AT AGENCY" (*TBM*, p. 26). In the second headline, presumably drawn from the bourgeois press, the unemployed are identified by their lack—they are "jobless"—and their protest is irrational and violent (a "riot"). In the first, however, presumably drawn from the left-wing press, it is suggested that the unemployed are unemployed for a reason—they just got out of the armed services—and that they are rational agents pursuing a legitimate end. The Newsreel furnishes historical background to events occurring on the level of "story": Charley, while not rioting, is one of the ex-servicemen desperate for employment. But the Newsreel also directs attention to history-as-discourse—as both events and their ideological construction.

Second, the Newsreels challenge the reader to devise explanatory schemes that would draw apparently unrelated fragments together in a coherent totality. A Newsreel directly preceding the "House of Morgan" sketch in *Nineteen Nineteen* juxtaposes headlines and songs bearing an overt relation to politics, war, and profit with elements having little or no clear relevance to such issues:

WHOLE WORLD IS SHORT OF PLATINUM

.   .   .

the quotation of United Cigar Stores made this month of $167 per share means $501 per share for the old stock upon which present stockholders are receiving 27% per share as formerly held. Through peace and war it has maintained and increased its dividends

6 TRAPPED ON UPPER FLOOR

How are you goin' to keep 'em down on the farm
After they've seen Paree

.   .   .

11 WOMEN MISSING IN BLUEBEARD MYSTERY

.   .   .

I. W. W. IN PLOT TO KILL WILSON

Find 10,000 Bags of Decayed Onions

FALL ON STAIRS KILLS WEALTHY CITIZEN

.   .   .

OVERTHROW OF SOVIET RULE SURE.

(1919, pp. 334–35)

The apparently anomalous elements here are the references to the people trapped on an upper floor, the missing women, the bags of onions, and the wealthy citizen's accidental death. What have these to do with the supply of natural resources, corporate profits, alienated returning GI's, and anti-Bolshevik propaganda? Perhaps Dos Passos is teasing those who would insist on making everything a political issue; he is having fun with the onions. But even the hard-to-account-for elements here are assimilable to class analysis. The "6 trapped on upper floor" may have died in a firetrap building where profits took precedence over safety; the "wealthy citizen's" fall on the stairs is news precisely because this *was* a wealthy citizen; the Bluebeard mystery murders are suggestively related to the exploitative, commodified, and violent gender relations depicted throughout the trilogy.

The onions may be miscommandeered military rations or hijacked goods. It does not matter whether any of these interpretive speculations is "true." What matters is that Dos Passos's method invites—indeed, requires—the reader to incorporate apparently random fragments into a dialectical paradigm. To read this Newsreel and relate it to surrounding narrative elements is to engage in conscious totalization.

The biographies of *U.S.A.* leave a good deal less to the interpretive imagination than do the Newsreels; the narrator's judgments upon his biographical subjects are frequently complex but never ambiguous. Big Bill Haywood, for all the pathos of his final years, is a hero of the working class; Minor Keith, who murdered thousands in setting up the United Fruit Company, has earned the "uneasy look under the eyes" haunting his portrait (*42P*, p. 244); Rudolph Valentino's death by peritonitis mirrors the rot of his existence; Thorstein Veblen's refusal to "get his mouth round the essential yes" (*TBM*, p. 98) testifies to his lonely integrity. "Meester Veelson" (Woodrow Wilson), the Puritan as imperialist, is the villain of the piece; his act of "[bringing] a bouquet of poppies" (*1919*, p. 472) to the grave of the Unknown Soldier is the trilogy's consummate act of hypocrisy. Through the mordant irony of the biographies' narratorial voice, Dos Passos directly presents a sophisticated analysis of class relations beyond the reach of even his most politically conscious fictional characters. Like the interchapters in *The Grapes of Wrath*, the biographical sketches in *U.S.A.* function as political mentors for the reader, obviating any necessity for characters who teach or preach.

Juxtaposed with stories of fictional characters clearly influenced by historical forces that the biographical figures help to set in motion, the biographical sketches raise the complex issue of causality in history. Is history made by the "great"? Or is it the outcome of the fumbling, self-centered activities of the Daughters and Charley Andersons? Are the two types of historical agents dialectically related, and, if so, how? What precisely is the nature of "forces" in history? On these questions, the narratorial voice, for all his sardonic wisdom, offers no explicit guidance, leaving only hints and clues for the reader to piece together into a theory of historical determination. Henry Ford, who institutionalized the large-scale assembly line production that has revolutionized the American landscape, is swept along by the industrial process he has helped to create; he cannot bring back the "horse and buggy days" (*TBM*, p. 53) upon which he sentimentally fixates.

Charley, a "dumb mechanic" mystified by high finance, blindly contributes to the massive 1929 banking disaster chronicled in the trilogy's final Newsreel. But Dos Passos relates Ford to Charley only obliquely: Ford's 1920 decision to make his dealers pay in full for their inventory causes a financial crisis in Charley's family; Charley eventually loses his heart and soul to the "big money" in Ford's Detroit. Without active participation from the reader, history in U.S.A. is indeed nothing more than the chaotic fragments that impinge upon the characters. But through readerly analysis— aided by authorial coaching—history emerges as a process possessing both determinacy and knowable causality.

Throughout U.S.A., as some scholars have noted, Dos Passos's paradigms for understanding the relation of individuals to larger historical processes undergo change. The Forty-Second Parallel evinces a residual confidence in American democratic institutions, as personified in "Fighting Bob" La Follette, the Wisconsin senator who, in Dos Passos's honorific portrait, valiantly filibusters to keep the nation out of World War I. Nineteen Nineteen, written at the peak of Dos Passos' commitment to left-wing politics, suggests strong sympathy with proletarian fighters and a virulent antipathy to capitalism and its apologists—as is suggested by the opposition of the martyred Wobblies Wesley Everest and Joe Hill with Meester Veelson and the House of Morgan. The Big Money takes the technocratic Veblen as its prophetic hero, despairs of working-class resistance, and reveals open hostility to the CP. Regardless of the particular emphases in the different volumes' political perspectives, however, the biographical sketches in all three novels urge the reader to go beyond an empiricist grasping after mere facts. If the totality that constitutes the U.S.A. is to be understood, totalizing analytical paradigms are necessary.[26]

The Camera Eye passages, which document the author's experience from early childhood (1900, when Dos Passos was four) to politically engaged adulthood (1931, when Dos Passos was thirty-five), appear to have little significance to Dos Passos's collectivist project. The memories they feature are largely subjective, often to the point of obscurantism. Most of

---

26. For more on Dos Passos's shifting politics during the composition of U.S.A., see Landsberg; Robert C. Rosen, John Dos Passos: Politics and the Writer (Lincoln and London: U of Nebraska P, 1981), pp. 69–72, 78–91; and Townsend Ludington, John Dos Passos: A Twentieth-Century Odyssey (New York: E. P. Dutton, 1980), pp. 284–359.

the Camera Eye passages of *The Forty-Second Parallel*—ranging from episodes illustrating the author's Oedipal resentment of his overbearing father to accounts of battles with prep school classmates—focus on the highly personal sources of the author's alienation. Even those passages in *The Big Money* treating Dos Passos's struggle to formulate a radical political commitment during the 1920s emphasize the existential dimension of his attempt to "hock the old raincoat of incertitude" (*TBM*, p. 196). But the text's focus on aspects of experience that seem wholly apolitical underlines the author's point: he can self-critically represent the standpoint from which he conceives and narrates the entire trilogy only if he exposes all the forces that have shaped him—not just those generating his public anger but also those establishing his private zones of indecision and ambivalence.[27]

The Camera Eye's odyssey from petty-bourgeois isolation to proletarian partisanship is a familiar theme in proletarian fiction; in reaching the realization that there are "two nations," the Camera Eye undergoes a kind of "conversion." Dos Passos does not refrain from using the Camera Eye as a conventional ethical foil to other characters. In *Nineteen Nineteen*, two very different political paths are taken by Richard Ellsworth Savage and the Camera Eye. The former enters the ambulance service, sees the war's hypocrisies, but eventually betrays his values by lining up with Moorehouse. The latter also joins the ambulance service and is expelled for insubordination, but then—like John Andrews in *Three Soldiers*—joins the army as an enlisted man and entertains fervent revolutionary hopes for May Day, 1919. The Camera Eye presents the author's emerging class consciousness as not simply a theme, but an epistemological vantage point. Rather than positing the political perspective informing the trilogy as given, Dos Passos invites the reader to follow the formation of his own interpretive paradigm. Deeply felt personal struggles result in the perception of two nations. The "I" who finally identifies himself as "we" does not allow the reader to take for granted the radical class-consciousness shaping the trilogy; collective awareness is not a priori, but the product of a long and anguished battle with ideological conditioning.

Throughout *U.S.A.*, the fictional narratives are kept separate from the Newsreels, biographies, and Camera Eye passages interspersed among

27. Ludington has undertaken a careful tracing of the relation of the Camera Eye passages to Dos Passos's life in his Dos Passos biography.

them. As with Steinbeck's demarcation of "general" and "particular" chapters in *The Grapes of Wrath*, Dos Passos maintains ontological distinctions among the various components of his narrative. But at the trilogy's climactic moment—the 1927 execution of Sacco and Vanzetti—the different narrative components undergo rhetorical fusion. A fictional segment showing Mary French protesting the executions ends with Mary and other arrested picketers singing the *Internationale* in a paddy wagon: "Arise, ye prisoners of starvation" are the final words of her narrative. The subsequent words of the *Internationale* continue over into the following Newsreel, which is devoted to the Sacco and Vanzetti affair:

HOLMES DENIES STAY
A better world's in birth

. . .

CHICAGO BARS MEETINGS
For justice thunders condemnation

WASHINGTON KEEPS EYE ON RADICALS
Arise rejected of the earth

. . .

SACCO AND VANZETTI MUST DIE
Shall be the human race

Much I thought of you when I was lying in the death house. . . . I wish I could see you every moment, but I feel better that you will not come to the death house so that you could not see the horrible picture of three living in agony waiting to be electrocuted. (TBM, pp. 460–61)

Closing with a quotation from one of Vanzetti's letters to his wife, the Newsreel is followed by the climactic Camera Eye (50). Heretofore reserved for private meditations, the Camera Eye is interrupted by a further quotation from Vanzetti:

the men in the deathhouse made the old words new before they died.

If it had not been for these things, I might have lived out my life talking at streetcorners to scorning men. I might have died unknown, unmarked, a failure. This is our career and our triumph. Never in our full life can we hope to do such work for tolerance, for justice, for man's understanding of man as now we do by an accident

now their work is over. (TBM, pp. 460–63)

This formal confluence is a unique structural event because the execution of Sacco and Vanzetti occupies a privileged political place in *U.S.A.* Not only does the execution reveal that American society has moved toward irreparable polarization. It also furnishes an account of the text's moment of inspiration: Dos Passos began writing *The Forty-Second Parallel* almost immediately after he emerged from jail, where he had spent a night after being arrested, like Mary French, in protest activity. The trilogy's movement toward closure is decisive. But narrative momentum derives more from the teleology of public events than from patterning internal to the fictional stories. Rather than being positioned as a coconspirator assumed to endorse the values informing the text, the reader is confronted with a narrative of how and why the author came to endorse those values.[28]

While Dos Passos devised a narrative form peculiarly suited to depicting class struggle and exploring Marxist politics, he was by no means a left-winger in many of his specific propositions about people and politics, particularly in *The Big Money*. Dos Passos's denigrating representation of nonwhite characters—such as Margo's Cuban husband Tony and the black male prostitutes who rough up Savage—reveals his uncritical acceptance of a range of racist stereotypes. Moreover, his portraiture of gender relations as uniformly unfulfilled and unfulfilling places more blame on women than on men. Margo is a tease, Eveline a vamp, Eleanor a frigid bitch; Charley, Joe, and Mac, if irresponsible and exploitative, are pitiable victims of false consciousness. Furthermore, Dos Passos's politics are, to say the least, hardly pro-Communist. The first two volumes of *U.S.A.* evince considerable sympathy with Wobblies and socialists; the story of CP-member Ben Compton is laced with quotations from *The Communist Manifesto*. But the party comes out of the trilogy's last novel in tat-

28. The Sacco and Vanzetti executions provided the inspiration for the composition of *U.S.A.*, which was begun soon after Dos Passos emerged from his night in jail. "I had seceded privately the night Sacco and Vanzetti were executed," he later stated. "I had seceded into my private conscience like Thoreau in Concord Jail" (cited in Townsend Ludington, *The Fourteenth Chronicle: Letters and Diaries of John Dos Passos* [Boston; Gambit, 1973], p. 383). For more on Dos Passos's manipulation of time sequences, see my "From *U.S.A.* to *Ragtime*: Notes on the Forms of Historical Consciousness in Modern Fiction," *American Literature* 50 (March 1978): 85–105; "History, Fiction, and Satirical Form," *Genre* 12 (Fall 1979): 357–78; and "The Treatment of Time in *The Big Money*: An Examination of Ideology and Literary Form," *Modern Fiction Studies* 26 (Autumn 1980): 447–67.

ters. Dos Passos's scathing portraiture of the opportunistic party hack Don Stevens, counterposed by no more favorable depiction of Communists, implies Stevens's typicality. The fellow traveler Mary French, who seems to be motivated as much by sexual hunger and ego insecurity as by political commitment, hardly offers a role model to any potential left-wing activist. Ben Compton, initially likable for his revolutionary zeal, degenerates into a sectarian Trotskyist victimized by Stalinist bureaucrats.

Generic politics do not produce doctrinal politics: Dos Passos's experiments with collective form did not make him a revolutionary. Nonetheless, he broke new ground for writers committed to representing social relations and class struggle from a class-conscious point of view. In 1933, we will recall, Matthew Josephson wrote to Joshua Kunitz from the Soviet Union that "the two most discussed foreign writers are Shakespeare and Dos Passos." Hicks in 1934 concluded that, as manifested in *The Forty-Second Parallel* and *Nineteen Nineteen*, Dos Passos's "deep realization" of "the concept of class struggle and the trend towards revolution" had led him to invent a form that would "sho[w] . . . the relations between apparently isolated events and . . . see the fundamental unity beneath the seemingly chaotic complexity of American life." Even when Hicks later reacted in disappointment at Dos Passos's attacks on Communism in *The Big Money* and *In All Countries*, he still insisted that Dos Passos was "the most talented of American novelists." The abiding attraction that Dos Passos held out to writers otherwise disturbed by his doctrinal politics suggests that, as the inventor of a revolutionary new form for the proletarian novel, Dos Passos had indeed, as Hicks put it, "show[n] the way." [29]

The Collective Novel: A Privileged Form for Proletarian Fiction?

What can we conclude about the relation between generic and doctrinal politics in the genre of the collective novel? Do the formal means devised

---

29. Hicks, *The Great Tradition: An Interpretation of American Literature since the Civil War* (New York: Macmillan, 1933), pp. 290, 292; "The Moods and Tenses of John Dos Passos," in Robbins, 137. Cowley wrote to Dos Passos in 1935 of the excitement in the movement and remarked, "I'm sorry you're missing it" (Cowley to Dos Passos, June 3, 1935, Cowley Papers, Newberry Library).

for representing group-processes run any risks of reincorporating bour-geois conceptions of historical process? Or do collective novels generally overcome the different rhetorical and political problems encountered by writers using conventionally realistic genres?

Dos Passos's example shows that experimentation with collectivist forms does not necessarily push the writer toward a more revolutionary political doctrine. Weatherwax articulates her approval of many facets of the Third-Period CP's program; Armstrong ringingly advocates revolution-ary insurgency; Rollins quotes *The Communist Manifesto* in four languages to stress its universal relevance. But Vorse's novel, despite its evocation of felt reality, essentially ignores the CP's militantly antiracist stance at Gastonia and overlooks the party's attempts to infuse revolutionary poli-tics into the struggle for unionization. *Strike!*'s politics, while militant, are fundamentally economistic.[30] *The Grapes of Wrath* does not confront the class warfare for which it has issued a call and features the New Deal gov-ernment camp as a more viable alternative for the migrant laborers than the "red" activity that Tom presumably joins. Writers who experimented with new ways of representing group-consciousness were not for that rea-son more likely to be aligned with the Communist movement or inclined to endorse revolution.

Indeed, one could argue that certain aspects of the form of the collec-tive novel reify and depoliticize social forces. In novels dating from the Third Period, apocalyptic representations of groups in conflict can blur human agency, associating causality with productive forces determinism. In *The Shadow Before*, Rollins's forecast of impending crisis is weakened by his portrayal of the bourgeoisie, embodied in the Thayers and Harry Baumann, as decadent to the point of self-obliteration. Moreover, his unre-mitting association of the proletarian characters with the machines domi-nating their lives results in a conflation of forces and agents of production.

---

30. Vorse's depiction of Mamie Lewes omits mention of Wiggins's strong antiracism. Dee Garrison, Vorse's biographer, remarks, "Wiggins had attempted the unthinkable. She had approached a few black workers in the mills and passed union cards to them" (p. 223). Weisbord too stresses this quality in Wiggins, noting, "I am certain it was as an organizer of Negroes that Mrs. Wiggins was killed" (p. 260). The *New Masses* review of *Strike!*, while generally favorable, observed, "In *Strike!*, . . . [the mill owners] do not fear the few who are leading the strike alone, but it's 'what's behind them they're scared of.' . . . 'What's behind them' does not appear in the story" (*NM* 6 [November 1930]: 18).

The bourgeois characters' graves will be dug, it is implied, as much by the "thump— THROB" of the textile mill—into which Micky is mechanically inserted at the novel's end—as by conscious activity on the workers' part. In *Parched Earth*, the catalyst of the flood signaling the workers' revenge is not any of the text's proletarian agents, but Wally, the crazed, non-class-conscious product of capitalism's rape of the dispossessed. The force pulling the waters down upon the town is natural, not social; moreover, it is luck, not a superior political practice, that enables Hattie, Hop, and their friends to ascend the windmill. Revolution is explicitly on the novel's agenda: Dave Washburne advocates Communism as "the only chance of possessing the machines that grind you down, and which should lift you up" (p. 191). Hicks praised the ending of the novel for "giv[ing] a kind of emotional satisfaction that few revolutionary novels have achieved."[31] But the text's naturalistic portrayal of historical forces obscures the revolutionary process by which the workers themselves will take possession—not just of the machines, but of the state and its legitimating cultural apparatus as well.

Even in *Marching! Marching!*, a novel that can hardly be charged with giving short shrift to Third-Period politics, the closing portraiture of the "we" marching into machine guns and bayonets conveys a utopian—indeed, suicidal—voluntarism. Yet the scene's militancy has an economistic core, insofar as the group-entity of a working class united around reform demands is conflated with the group-entity of an insurgent revolutionary proletariat. Even though the text has not traced the "conversion" of an individual hero, its finale reflects a degree of "wish-fulfillment." The angry workers of today are the revolutionaries of tomorrow; revolution is simply a strike plus guns. *Parched Earth*, *The Shadow Before*, *Marching! Marching!*, and other Third-Period texts are undeniably left-wing in their attempts to forecast the larger class war of which present-day strikes are preparatory skirmishes. But these novels' representations of collectivity articulate either a productive forces determinism or a romantic workerism that obscures various facets of the political process by which militant workers will constitute not simply a collective, but a *revolutionary* agent. Texts that feature Barbusse's "new protagonist, the most imposing of all: the masses" can fetishize the "massness" of their subject and elevate spontaneism.

31. Hicks, "Symbol of Revolution," in Robbins, p. 77.

Conversely, collective novels written during the Popular Front are more likely to mystify group-identity along the lines of nationalist and populist reformism. In *The Grapes of Wrath*, Casy's vision of human solidarity has affinities, as various critics have noted, with the Emersonian doctrine of the "Oversoul"; the Joads' oneness with the land invokes Jeffersonian agrarianism. The text's portraiture of the expropriated and the exploited as the sole bearers of historical progress thus coexists uneasily with a nationalism equating the disinherited with the essentially classless category of "the people." In *Industrial Valley*, the Communist CIO organizer Jim Keller equates the Goodyear workers' success in winning their union with national destiny: "[I]f you fellows take the picket line back to the tire machines and the mill room, the Goodyear strike will be America's new declaration of freedom. . . . You are the new pioneers" (p. 369). Even though the novel has portrayed in Akron a community deeply divided by class antagonism, its closure suggests that the successfully unionized workers *are* "America." Assertion of synecdoche supersedes dialectical resolution.[32]

In *Jordanstown*, Johnson's informing metaphor of the four winds driving oppressors and oppressed alike to a degree dehistoricizes the very process of group-formation that the metaphor describes. Hate, necessity, power, love: these terms signify human motivations but not their specific class encoding. The novel's final call for unity—Allen's closing promise to "go on planning and protesting and building until we see the earth again a great altar where the fruit and grain wait as communion for all men" (pp. 258–59)—obscures the text's earlier claim that the interests of those in the "Bottom" and on the "Hill" are antagonistically opposed. Grounding its appeal for socialism in a universalizing discourse, the novel's closing

---

32. For a discussion of Emersonianism and Jeffersonianism in *The Grapes of Wrath*, see Frederick I. Carpenter, "The Philosophical Joads," in Bloom, ed., pp. 7–15; John J. Condor, "Steinbeck and Nature's Self," in Bloom, ed., pp. 99–114; and Cook, *From Tobacco Road*, pp. 168–83. Cook's assessment of the consequences of these philosophies for the politics of the novel is quite negative: "Real economic conditions are not distorted, but instead of challenging them with real economic or political solutions, Steinbeck alters the people to make them more competent to deal with the situation by returning to their traditions of courage and generosity and philosophies of optimism and endurance" (p. 183). McKenney apparently received a rave review of *Industrial Valley* from anti-Communist CIO leader John L. Lewis, who, she reported, "really went to town" over the book (Marian Hart to Hicks, Book Union folder, Box 8, Hicks Papers).

prophecy is absorbed into the abstract religious metaphor that it intends to concretize and transcend: Communism dissolves into communion. In Popular Front-era collective novels, the representation of collectivity can facilitate non-class-specific definition of social groups, denying the intrinsic and unremitting opposition of labor and capital.

➤   ➤   ➤   ➤   ➤

The decision to use and develop the form of the collective novel does not, in short, free the proletarian writer from the snares of bourgeois ideology. Insofar as it can attract the writer to reified or mystical conceptions of the group and apocalyptic views of historical process, the genre even poses its own set of rhetorical and political problems, distinct from those posed by novelistic realism. In general, however, the collective novel's generic politics reinforce rather than undermine the possibility of articulating a revolutionary doctrinal politics. For one thing, the collective novel facilitates, indeed requires, focus on the group as a group; it proposes social consciousness as its starting point rather than its terminus. Single-protagonist modes of realistic fiction—the bildungsroman but to a lesser extent the fictional autobiography as well—are premised on the notion that the individual is of paramount importance: class consciousness is the object of the hero's quest, it is what he/she must come to know to be true. Hence experience—as lived by the protagonist, and occasionally as illuminated by a mentor character or a commenting narrator—is what conveys the proposition that the essence of the individual is social. But, in these genres, experience generally delimits the reader's knowledge to what can be known by the hero. Other types of knowledge, while raised by other components in the narrative, are subordinated to, and controlled by, the hero's tale. In the collective novel, by contrast, what the reader learns does not significantly hinge upon what the separate protagonists may learn. Individual patterns of growth are just moments in the larger process by which the group—that is, the class—attains knowledge of itself, *as a group, as a class*. Characters need not be attributed essences making them by nature more or less open to revolutionary doctrine. Contradictions peripheral to the lives of particular characters can be played out and resolved—or, for that matter, left unresolved—in other narrative arenas. Moreover, these texts can assert collectivity as a positive good—and an emergent reality—even in the prerevolutionary present. While this proposition can be made in a workerist or spontaneist way, the collective novel's portraiture of the proletariat-as-hero can also transcend reformism and effectively prefigure aspects of Communist discourse and social relations.

Furthermore, the collective novel opens up possibilities for voicing revolutionary politics because it engages the reader in a procedure of critical totalization. Social novels, as we have seen, bypass a number of the problems generated by the individualistic premises of the bildungsroman. By dispersing narrative interest over multiple characters, they generally avoid the bildungsroman's fetishization of heroes and villains; like collective novels, they produce a knowledge of social relations that does not depend solely on what individual characters "learn." But social novels are often limited in their capacity to educate and move their readers because they assume in advance these readers' agreement and partisanship. Moreover, as a genre they tie didacticism primarily to plot. Readers learn that the totality of the interactions of the characters in the text corresponds to the totality of social relations in their own world: the unit of cognition is the "image." In most collective novels, by contrast, readers acquire political insight only in part from reflecting on textual patterning; to a significant degree, knowledge comes "from outside." By disappointing conventional expectations of narrative resolution; by problematizing the ontological relation between text and actuality; by foregrounding interpretation as an ideological enterprise—through these defamiliarizing strategies collective novels open up a space for revolutionary political doctrine not readily available in proletarian novels based upon more conventionally transparent techniques of narrative. Defamiliarization does mean that readers are led to embrace open-endedness or reject revolutionary doctrine as monologic. Rather, situated as conscious participants in the process of making "intimate connect[ions] . . . between things (men, acts) widely separated in space or in the social complex," readers see through and beyond the existing social totality. They become not dialogists, but dialecticians.

AFTERWORD

> ➤

In *Radical Representations* I have offered a revisionary reading of U.S. literary proletarianism and the fiction it generated and inspired. I have refuted key tenets of the arguments—historical, political, literary—routinely invoked to denigrate and dismiss this body of writing. The 1930s Marxist critics, I have shown, did not march in lockstep with Soviet directives, nor did they attempt to force literature into the vise of a narrow utilitarianism that would sacrifice literature to propaganda. Indeed, the aesthetic theory embraced by the Depression-era cultural left was on important points in fundamental alignment with the bourgeois tradition. Moreover, I have argued, 1930s literary leftism did not, as it is sometimes charged, mechanically conflate issues of race and gender with issues of class. Some African-American writers working in the ambience of the left produced compelling dialectical syntheses of nationalist and class perspectives; various female writers expanded the discourse of both women's and workers' emancipation through their representations of gender relations in the proletariat.

Furthermore, I have demonstrated that the postmodernist analysis of novelistic realism does not provide an adequate framework for criticizing form and politics in the proletarian novel. Even though the fictional genres most closely associated with traditional realism—the bildungsroman, the social novel—bear multiple traces of their bourgeois origins, many proletarian writers to a significant degree transcend these genres' limitations. There is, I argue, a complex interplay between generic and doctrinal politics. Finally, novelistic modes shaped in the crucible of literary proletarianism itself—the fictional autobiography and, especially, the collective novel—move beyond many of the constraints of familiar fictional forms. In their explorations of both inherited and experimental forms, U.S. proletarian writers were not hamstrung by an authoritarian party, nor did they practice a dull, confining "Stalinist" realism.

But if *Radical Representations* is revisionary, it is not celebratory. I aim to rescue proletarian literature from undeserved neglect, but I also wish to subject it to a politically rigorous and historically informed critique. The 1930s Marxists were justified in attacking mechanical and dogmatic writing, but they committed a grave error in conflating inferior artistry with didacticism with "leftism." This maneuver reflects not simply the strong influence of a cognitivist aesthetic on Marxist theory but also economistic tendencies in the political analysis and program of the Communist-led left. Reflecting these tendencies, many proletarian novels, despite their projection of what Gold called "revolutionary élan," uncritically reproduce a range of received assumptions about selfhood. These assumptions are to a degree reinforced by the generic politics encoded in different novelistic modes. But generic politics are in turn buttressed by doctrinal politics—regarding the "Negro question," the "woman question," the relation of revolutionary agency to spontaneism—that display the left's shortcomings in breaking with inherited ways of thinking and doing. To call for a serious reconsideration and positive reassessment of 1930s literary radicalism is not to proclaim its legacy unambiguous.

Perhaps this "on the one hand/on the other hand" stance will send out confusing signals to those readers whom I am trying to interest in reading and/or teaching proletarian novels. By no means am I discouraging such curiosity or implying that it will not be amply rewarded. Many of the books I have discussed in *Radical Representations* have considerable merit; quite a few are well crafted, moving, thought-provoking. Students— especially "naive" students who have not yet absorbed the prejudice that literature and left-wing political doctrine are somehow incompatible— often read these novels with pleasure and interest, and in so doing gain valuable insight into the life and political discourse of the Depression era. Left-oriented readers who share some of the values and assumptions of the proletarian writers will, I predict, be pleasantly surprised as they work their way through the substantial body of proletarian fiction now available in paperback, as well as through various dusty texts presently accessible only through interlibrary loan.

My "on the one hand/on the other hand" analytical standpoint in this study is, however, justified—indeed, necessitated—by the political imperatives of the present moment. As I bring this study to a close in the early months of 1993, U.S. politicians and pundits are united in their ebullient proclamations of the failure of socialism and the death of Communism. Even if one is not inclined to agree with the usual grounds for these claims—the intrinsic greed of the human species, the "naturalness" of the market—the fact remains that the twentieth-century socialist experiment first derailed and then self-destructed. Literary proletarianism testifies to the egalitarian impulse and collective consciousness that animated the participants in the movement for "a better world" some sixty years ago. But this literary movement also reveals, in intricate and telling ways, the left's inadequacies in finding new paradigms to supersede the modes of perception and explanation inherited from the bourgeois era. Depression-era literary radicalism thus exhibits both revolutionary energies and the limitations on these energies produced by contradictions internal to the left-wing movement itself. Some readers—and I hope they are many—will find themselves aroused, perhaps inspired, by the vision of human possibility encoded in proletarian novels. To confront these texts' shortcomings is not to betray that vision, but to affirm it.

INDEX

➤

BARBARA FOLEY

is Associate Professor in the Department
of English at Rutgers University. She is the author
of *Telling the Truth: The Theory and Practice
of Documentary Fiction*.

Library of Congress
Cataloging-in-Publication Data

Foley, Barbara, 1948-
Radical representations : politics and form in
U.S. proletarian fiction, 1929–1941 / by Barbara Foley.
p.   cm.—(Post-contemporary interventions) Includes index.
ISBN 0-8223-1361-8 (cl.).—ISBN 0-8223-1394-4 (pbk.)
1. American fiction—20th century—History and criticism.
2. Politics and literature—United States—History—20th
century.   3. Working class writings, American—History
and criticism.   4. Political fiction, American—History and
criticism.   5. Social problems in literature. 6. Proletariat
in literature.   7. Radicalism in literature.
I. Title.   II. Series. PS374.P6F65   1993
813'.5209358—dc20   93-18687
CIP

ACP5869

12/8/93
56

PS
374
P6
F65
1993

973-353-8037
973-353-5279
BFOLEY@ANDROMEDA.RUTGERS.EDU